Cuba

Conner Gorry

Contents

CITY OF HAVANA P58
HAVANA P139
MATANZAS P185
VILLA CLARA P236
PINAR DEL RÍO P161
CIENFUEGOS P223
SANCTI SPÍRITUS P251
CIEGO DE ÁVILA P274
ISLA DE LA JUVENTUD (SPECIAL MUNICIPALITY) P147
CAMAGÜEY P286
LAS TUNAS P302
HOLGUÍN P311
GRANMA P332
SANTIAGO DE CUBA P351
GUANTÁNAMO P388

Lonely Planet books provide independent advice. Lonely Planet does not accept advertising in guidebooks, nor do we accept payment in exchange for listing or endorsing any place or business. Lonely Planet writers do not accept discounts or payments in exchange for positive coverage of any sort.

Los libros de Lonely Planet ofrecen información independiente. La editorial no acepta ningún tipo de propaganda en las guías, así como tampoco endorsa ninguna entidad comercial o destino. Los escritores de Lonely Planet no aceptan descuentos o pagos de ningún tipo a cambio de comentarios favorables.

Destination: Cuba

You've heard about the socialism and salsa. You know that the cigars are world class, the cars are classic and the White House has had its panties in a twist since Fidel and friends triumphed in 1959. You know all this, maybe more, but what no travelogue or movie can convey are the all-night rumbas (now that's dirty dancing!), the drum-induced trance of a Santería ceremony, the reggae jams on the banks of the Río Almendares, the deserted beaches, the secret waterfalls or the teeming coral reefs. Above all, nothing can prepare you for the Cuban people themselves: educated, cultured, generous, disciplined, friendly, proud, forgiving and, like us all, contradictory. Make some Cuban friends and you'll understand why many travelers can't stay away.

Wholly original, Cuba feels like bottled lightning in its volatile electricity. Almost completely cut off from the maw of McDonald's, Madonna and other global corporate-cultural influences, Cuba retains a refreshing preserved quality. It's a space and place that serves as a beacon for the future – universal education, health care and housing are rights people the world over want, need and deserve – while grappling with problems from the past including machismo, paranoia, inefficiency and confounding bureaucracy.

For everyone except Americans (more on that later), visiting Cuba is straightforward. Independent travel, all-inclusive resorts, studying at university or art school, volunteering, theme trips, activist travel, family reunions and professional conferences are just some of the options here. Whether you're into history, dance, music, art, religion, sports, politics, the beach, antique cars/railroads/furniture, architecture, scuba diving, cycling or solidarity, Cuba delivers.

Welcome to a country so special, a concept so rare, that it has to be experienced firsthand to be believed, let alone understood.

RICHARD I'ANSON

UNITED STATES
OF AMERICA
(Florida)

Florida Keys

Straits of Florida

HAVANA (p58)
Colonial churches, palaces,
museums and fortresses

VARADERO (p197)
Twenty kilometers of unbroken
white sand luring golfers,
skydivers, sailors and scuba divers

SANTA CLARA (p239)
Monuments to
Che Guevara

GULF OF MEXICO

Tropic of Cancer

VIÑALES (p173)
Picturesque region honey-combed
with caves and cliffs

Archipiélago de Sabana

HAVANA

Playas del Este

Varadero

Archipiélago de los Colorados

Las Terrazas
Soroa

Matanzas
Cárdenas

Viñales

Autopista Habana-Pinar del Río

Surgidero
de Batabanó

Autopista Nacional

Carretera Central

Pinar del Río

Santa Clara

Cienfuegos

Ciénaga de Zapata

Nueva
Gerona

Archipiélago de los Canarreos

Topes de
Collantes

PLAYA MARÍA LA GORDA (p171)
A paradise for scuba diving,
snorkeling, yachting and
beachcombing

Isla de la
Juventud

Cayo Largo
del Sur

Trinidad

BAHÍA DE COCHINOS (p220)
Invasion site now better
known as a scuba diving center

PRESIDIO MODELO (p156)
Prison where young revolutionary
Fidel Castro was held

TRINIDAD (p259)
Best-preserved
Spanish colonial town

**CAYO LARGO DEL
SUR (p158)**
Site of Cuba's top
Caribbean resorts

Little
Cayman

ELEVATION

Cayman
Brac

Grand
Cayman

**CAYMAN
ISLANDS
(UK)**

GEORGE TOWN

	1800m
	1500m
	1200m
	900m
	600m
	300m
	150m
	75m
	0

CARIBBEAN SEA

0 ——— 100 km
0 ——— 60 mi

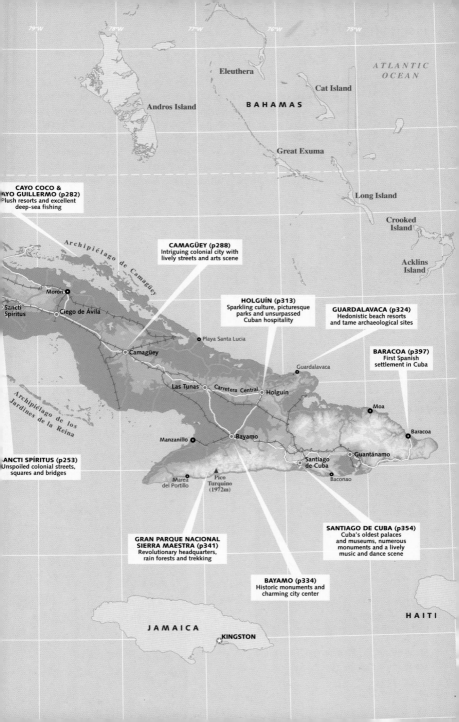

**CAYO COCO &
CAYO GUILLERMO (p282)**
Plush resorts and excellent
deep-sea fishing

CAMAGÜEY (p288)
Intriguing colonial city with
lively streets and arts scene

HOLGUÍN (p313)
Sparkling culture, picturesque
parks and unsurpassed
Cuban hospitality

GUARDALAVACA (p324)
Hedonistic beach resorts
and tame archaeological sites

BARACOA (p397)
First Spanish
settlement in Cuba

SANCTI SPÍRITUS (p253)
Unspoiled colonial streets,
squares and bridges

**GRAN PARQUE NACIONAL
SIERRA MAESTRA (p341)**
Revolutionary headquarters,
rain forests and trekking

SANTIAGO DE CUBA (p354)
Cuba's oldest palaces
and museums, numerous
monuments and a lively
music and dance scene

BAYAMO (p334)
Historic monuments and
charming city center

*ATLANTIC
OCEAN*

Eleuthera

Cat Island

BAHAMAS

Great Exuma

Long Island

Crooked
Island

Acklins
Island

Archipiélago de Camagüey

Morón

Sancti
Spiritus

Ciego de Ávila

Playa Santa Lucia

Camagüey

Guardalavaca

Moa

*Archipiélago de los
Jardines de la Reina*

Las Tunas

Carretera Central

Holguín

Baracoa

Manzanillo

Bayamo

Santiago
de Cuba

Guantánamo

Marea
del Portillo

Pico
Turquino
(1972m)

Baconao

JAMAICA

KINGSTON

HAITI

Andros Island

'Cosmopolitan' might not spring to mind before Castro or coral reef when someone mentions Cuba, but the cities are hopping with spectacular art and architecture, plus jamming music, charming accommodation and secret pockets. With its amazing colonial buildings and happening music scene, **Trinidad** (p259) is a Unesco World Heritage site not to be missed. Known as the 'city of parks,' **Holguín** (p313) is like a Latin lover: it'll charm your pants off. **Camagüey** (p288) is famous for its wildly crooked streets, flanked by pretty pastel facades, while dancing and singing are everywhere in Oriente cities like **Bayamo** (p334).

RICK GERHARTER

Chill out in the streets of **Santiago de Cuba** (p354)

Enjoy a mojito or three at **Hotel Inglaterra** (p74), Havana

DOUG Mc

RICHARD I'ANSON

Stroll along the **Malecón** (p81) at sunset for views of the Havana skyline

ALFREDO MAIQUEZ

Sample the Cuban cuisine at Havana's most celebrated bar, **La Bodeguita del Medio** (p99)

JERRY ALEXANDER

Cruise around **Havana** (p58) in a 1955 Chevrolet taxi

Move to the rhythms of Cuban **music** (p40)

DOUG McKINLAY

Hide out in sleepy **Cienfuegos** (p225) for a spell

RICHARD I'ANSON

With close to 300 natural beaches, one of the world's largest coral reefs and anything from superstar resorts to romantic, secluded campsites, there's a patch of Cuban sand to suit you. The country has no shortage of picture-perfect beaches and you'll be hard pressed to decide what's prettiest: **Cayo Coco** (p282), **Cayo Levisa** (p180) and **Playa Ensenachos** (p249) are all equally beautiful spots for some fun in the sun. **Playa Girón** (p221), site of the first defeat of the US in the Americas, has terrific snorkeling and scuba diving, plus loads of history.

MARTIN LLADO

Discover the delights of **Playa Ancón** (p268), just a hop, skip or peddle from colonial Trinidad

Make time for rest and relaxation at **Guardalavaca** (p324)

RICK GERHARTER

Skip out of Havana's chaos with a day trip to the **Playas del Este** (p132)

BRENDA TURN

SIMON FOALE

Comb the beach at gorgeous **María la Gorda** (p171)

ALFREDO MAIQUEZ

luminous waters at **Cayo Largo del Sur** (p158)

Stroll along **Varadero's** (p197) 20km of white sand and unbelievably crystal-clear waters

RICHARD I'ANSON

Two independence wars and over 40 years of successful revolution at the foot of a powerful, control-freaky neighbor? Yup, there are some stellar historic sights to take in. Fidel Castro had his guerilla headquarters in the great, green Sierra Maestra: today you can visit **La Comandancia de La Plata** (p342) high in the mountains. Che's Havana headquaters were across Havana Harbor at the picturesque **Fortaleza de San Carlos de la Cabaña** (p129). Fidel Castro and rebel friends were held in the **Presidio Modelo** (p156) on mellow Isla de la Juventud.

RICHARD I'ANSON

Tip your hat to José Martí in Havana's **Plaza de la Revolución** (p80)

Pay your respects at the **Che memorial** (p240) in Santa Clara

RICHARD I'ANSON

HIGHLIGHTS **Landscapes**

Cuba boasts seven Unesco World Heritage sites, from the cobblestones of **Habana Vieja** (p67) and ramparts of **Santiago de Cuba** (p354) to crumbling sugar mills in the lush **Valle de los Ingenios** (p270). Sprinkle liberally with tobacco hanging out to dry, the sparkling Carribbean sea and the rugged Sierra Maestra mountains, and don't forget your camera. While you're at it, take a long hike through **Topes de Collantes** (p271) and cool off in a gushing waterfall. Or for a glorious sunset, head to the tip of **Punta Gorda** (p230) in Cienfuegos.

Right:
Get a room with a view of the pincushion hills of the **Valle de Viñales** (p173)
PHOTO BY JERRY ALEXANDER

Swinging salsa, super cinema, sculpture gardens, open studios and museums everywhere will leave culture vultures wanting more. See the work of Cuba's greatest artists in the fabulous Colección de Arte Cubano building of the **Museo Nacional de Bellas Artes** (p74). Inside and out, stunning **Teatro Sauto** (p189) in Matanzas is worth a peek; better yet, catch a performance. Visit the **Plaza de la Marqueta** (p317) in Holguín, where whimsical sculptures share space with a mural by Nelson Dominguez. And don't miss the opportunity to see the electric **Conjunto Folklórico Nacional de Cuba** (p102).

ALFREDO MAIQUEZ

Be dazzled by the cabaret at **Tropicana Nightclub** (p120) in Havana

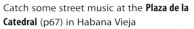

Catch some street music at the **Plaza de la Catedral** (p67) in Habana Vieja

RHONDA GUTENBERG

Take in the public art whichever way you turn in **Havana** (p58)

RICK GE

Getting Started

Cuba has all the eye-popping sun, surf and sand portrayed in slick tourist brochures, and it's surprisingly easy to insert yourself into that idyllic picture. Throw a little flexibility, creativity and good humor into the mix, however, and you'll be embarking on a true adventure. Your visit will be infinitely richer if you (try to) speak Spanish.

WHEN TO GO

If there's a bad time to come to Cuba (there isn't), it would be July and August, when it's unbelievably hot, and most of the world – including Cubans – take their vacation. Beaches, hotels and normally quiet towns are jammed packed and room prices are jacked up by 20% in many cases. Christmas and Easter are also peak travel times when resorts, flights and hotels are full to bursting, prices soar and overbooking can be a problem. Hurricane season (June to November, with the fiercest storms typically blowing through in September and October) can dampen even the liveliest spirits and evacuations of coastal towns and resorts have occurred in years past. In addition, the rainy season runs from May to October, when quick afternoon thundershowers are common.

See Climate Charts (p410) for more information.

The emphasis on everything cultural here means there are phenomenal festivals (film, ballet, jazz etc) year-round; see p414 and p16. Baseball fans won't want to miss the postseason, which runs from April to May. Political junkies may want to catch important days in the socialist calendar, particularly May 1 and July 26.

COSTS & MONEY

Cuba is all over the map as far as costs are concerned but cannot be described as cheap. Solo travelers will feel the bite especially, as room discounts are hard-won in accommodation that is reasonably priced for the Caribbean, expensive for Latin America. In Havana, a double with bath in a colonial mansion costs US$25, while a room for two at a painstakingly restored hotel like the Ambos Mundos in Habana Vieja costs US$110/130 low/high season (for more on accommodation costs, see p405).

DON'T LEAVE HOME WITHOUT...

With US dollars, toothpaste, toilet paper and soap are widely available in Cuba. However, supplies that are unavailable, nauseatingly expensive and/or substandard include: tampons, condoms, aspirin, dental floss, sunscreen, insect repellant, contact-lens solution, reading material in any language besides Spanish, hot sauce and moisturizing lotion. From cough drops to birth-control pills, medicine is scarce.

Some clothing is available (eg smutty disco garb), but is overpriced and low quality. If you're anticipating heavy beach time, you might bring snorkel gear. A flashlight is handy during blackouts, as is an alarm clock for predawn bus departures. A universal plug for sinks and tubs is great when there are water problems. People staying in campismos will want a sheet as linen isn't always provided.

Then there's the food question. Aside from cookies, peanuts and pastries sold in dollar stores and street stalls, munchies are hard to find. Beef jerky, granola and protein bars, nuts, fruit leather, peanut butter and trail mix provide energy, protein and a break from the vicious pizza-ice cream-fried chicken circle. See Staying Fed (p50) for more food advice.

Resorts run the gamut too, from US$50 per person at Varadero's cheapest all-inclusive to US$200 per person at a swanky Playa Esmeralda resort. If you're interested in getting away to the beach, prearranged air and hotel packages from Canada and Europe can be absurdly affordable (like US$465 for seven days in Varadero from Toronto!) and seasoned Cuba travelers often take these deals because it works out cheaper than just the air fare alone. Most resorts and hotels offer deep discounts for children under 12; it's worth asking. Children also travel half-price on Víazul buses, and many museums and attractions offer a 50% discount for kids.

As with most islands, Cuba struggles with food supply and prices reflect that – especially if you crave something imported like canned corn or nuts. Paladares usually offer good value, with monstrous meals, including a pork chop, rice and beans, salad and french fries, costing around US$7. Add a couple of beers, dessert and a tip and you're looking at US$11 (or more). Drinking is considerably more affordable than eating, as a strong mojito costs US$2 and a fresh juice or fruit shake US$1.

For tourists, there are many transport options and prices to go with them. From Havana to Santiago de Cuba for example, a trip of 861km, you'll pay US$108 to fly one way with Cubana, from US$50 to US$62 to take the train and from US$41 to US$52 on the bus. Rental cars start at US$35 a day for the crappiest Fiat to US$220 a day for a convertible Audi (most folks, however, spend around US$50 to US$60 per day for their rental).

HOW MUCH?

Room in private house
US$15–25

Ticket to ballet US$10

Museum entrance
US$1–5

Highball of rum US$2

Malecón serenade US$1

Taxi US$2–4

Bike rental US$3 per day

Internet use US$6 per hour

Print film US$6

CUBA ON THE CHEAP

Accommodation and transport are two areas where foreigners almost always have to pay in dollars and the bill can add up, fast. Food is another budget parasite. Here are some budget-friendly ideas:

- When renting a private room, mention that you're a student and watch the price drop; it's better still if you have some student ID.
- Families traveling together are pulling from the same financial pool; owners of private rooms recognize this and will often offer a discount to travelers with children. This can occur in hotels too.
- In private rooms, try negotiating a discount for multiple nights or by agreeing not to use the air-con.
- Never arrive anywhere with a *jinetero* (male hustler) in tow.
- The cheapest accommodation is in campismo cabins, which are often payable by the person, not the unit: good for solo travelers.
- Astro buses are cheaper than Víazul coaches, and trucks are cheaper than both. Mix and match your transport options by arranging a *botella* (free or cheap lift) with the *amarillas* (yellow jackets; workers charged with matching potential passengers with empty cars) when you can and you'll save bundles.
- Learn the public transport mechanism if you'll be chilling in a city awhile, or rent a bicycle.
- Food sold in pesos – bread at the Empresa Cubana del Pan, fruits and vegetables at *agropecuarios* (agricultural markets) or full meals from someone's living-room window such as pizza or *cajitas* (take-out meals in small boxes) – is very kind on the wallet.
- Cooking at 'home' is cheap and fun. Hit the '*agro*' market and host a dinner or pot-luck party.
- Brush up on some Spanish: nothing jacks up a price or keeps it inflated more effectively than an inability to communicate.

There is, of course, the double economy, whereby US dollars and Cuban pesos circulate simultaneously. In theory, tourists are only supposed to use dollars and in practise, this is largely true (particularly for non-Spanish speakers). However, with an exchange rate of 26 pesos to the dollar, there are fantastic saving opportunities with pesos if you're willing to sacrifice a little (or a lot!) in quality, service and/or comfort. For example, a pizza in a fast-food joint costs US$1, but street pizzas cost seven pesos, less than US$0.25. Pesos are useful for street food, urban transport and some cultural activities (like movies), but almost everything else is sold to foreigners only in dollars: the symphony or theater, interprovincial transport and taxis are but a few examples where Cubans will pay in pesos, but you won't.

Before you become indignant, remember that the double economy cuts both ways: you'll pay US$5 to get into a club while Cubans pay five pesos, but you can also hop a long-distance bus without waiting a week in line, smoke filtered cigarettes or surf the Net – goods and services not available in pesos. Furthermore, Cubans (who earn between 190 and 325 pesos, or US$8 and US$13, a month) are contributing labor to the mix, while you only contribute cash. As a visitor, be grateful if you get something in pesos, but don't be annoyed when you have to pay in dollars. Look at the product or service in terms of price and value: if it's worth it, pay, if not, walk away.

TRAVEL LITERATURE

The title of Zoë Bran's travelogue says it all: *Enduring Cuba* (2002) conveys the daily shortages, slowdowns and *lucha* (struggle) of the Cuban reality with a keen eye for the details that make you feel like you're already there, wondering where all the toilet seats have gone.

Trading with the Enemy: A Yankee Travels Through Castro's Cuba (1992), by Tom Miller, is a rich feast of Cuban lore gleaned during eight months of perceptive travel. It may just be the best travel book about Cuba ever written. Miller also collected the 38 pieces in *Travelers' Tales Cuba: True Stories* (2001), a good medley of views, experiences and takes on the island.

In *The Reader's Companion to Cuba* (1997), Alan Ryan has gathered together some of the finest writing about Cuba by 23 famous travelers, including John Muir, Graham Greene, Mark Kurlansky and Carlo Gébler.

Anthologizing the work of some of Cuba's most famous writers, exiles and diaspora, *Cuba: A Traveler's Literary Companion* (2002), edited by Ann Louise Bardach, is one of the best collections available in English.

If you like it nasty, try Pedro Juan Gutierrez's *Dirty Havana Trilogy*, a filthy but fascinating look at Havana in the '90s. It's repulsive in parts, but somehow hard to turn away from, like a car wreck or equine erection. You can't get this one in Cuba, folks.

No Cuban travel lit list is complete without Hemingway's classic *Old Man and the Sea* (1952), about a Cuban fisherman's fight with a great fish.

INTERNET RESOURCES

AfroCuba Web (www.afrocubaweb.com) Everything imaginable on Cuban culture, with world-wide concert listings, dance and drum workshops, seminars and encounters in Cuba.

Cubatravel.cu (www.cubatravel.cu) Official Ministry of Tourism site; packed with the latest weather, tour packages, events and logistics in several languages.

Granma Internacional (www.granma.cu) Official newspaper of the Communist Party of Cuba, news from Cuba in five languages.

Lonely Planet (www.lonelyplanet.com) Summaries on travelling to Cuba, the Thorn Tree bulletin board, travel news and links to useful travel resources elsewhere on the Web.

University of Texas (http://lanic.utexas.edu/la/ca/cuba) Links supersite with everything from the national archives to a Castro speech database.

THE LP INDEX

Liter of gas
US$0.75–0.90

Bottle of water (1.05L)
US$0.60–1

Bottle of beer US$1

Street snack (pizza)
US$0.20–0.40

Souvenir T-shirt
US$7–10

TOP TENS
OUR FAVORITE FESTIVALS & EVENTS

Dive deep into Cuban culture by checking out any of the myriad special events around the country; from heavy-metal rock festivals to Afro-Cuban religious powwows, there's almost always something on. Below are our 10 favorites, but for a comprehensive listing, see p414.

- Carnaval (Carnival; Santiago de Cuba) July (p368)
- Baseball playoffs (location varies) April-May (p38)
- Romerías de Mayo (May Festival; Holguín) May (p317)
- Festival de Caribe, Fiesta del Fuego (Fire Celebration Festival of Caribbean Culture; Santiago de Cuba) July (p368)
- Festival de Rap Cubano Habana Hip Hop (Havana Hip Hop Cuban Rap Festival; Havana) August (p85)

- Festival Internacional de Ballet (International Ballet Festival; Havana) October 2004 & 2006 (p86)
- Bienal de la Habana (Havana Biennial; Havana) November 2005 & 2007 (p86)
- Festival Internacional del Nuevo Cine Latinoamericano (International Festival of New Latin American Film; Havana) December (p86)
- Festival Internacional de Jazz (Jazz Plaza International Jazz Festival; Havana) December 2004 & 2006 (p86)
- Las Parrandas (Remedios) December 24 (p247)

MUST-SEE MOVIES

Along with its own vibrant film industry, Cuba has inspired many foreign filmmakers. These Cuban classics, plus some foreign-made gems, make a great introduction to Cuban art, humor, politics and esthetics. Most of the following should be available (with English subtitles) at your video store; harder-to-find films can be purchased at www.latinamericanvideo.org or more affordably in Cuba.

- *Strawberry and Chocolate* (1993) Directors: Tomás Gutiérrez Alea & Juan Carlos Tabío
- *Death of a Bureaucrat* (1966) Director: Tomás Gutiérrez Alea
- *Suite Habana* (2003) Director: Fernando Pérez
- *Vampires of Havana* (1987) Director: Juan Padrón
- *Lucia* (1968) Director: Humberto Solás

- *I Am Cuba* (1964) Director: Mikhail Kalatozov
- *Fidel* (1999) Director: Estela Bravo
- *Portrait of Teresa* (1979) Director: Pastor Vega
- *Memories of Underdevelopment* (1968) Director: Tomás Gutiérrez Alea
- *Buena Vista Social Club* (1999) Director: Wim Wenders

DESERT ISLAND DISCS

From lullabies in the cradle to hymns at the grave, music infects every facet of Cuban life. In between life's two extremes, there's *nueva trova* (poetic songs that examine Cuban society), *son* (traditional Cuban music from African and Spanish origins that is extremely popular), salsa, rap, jazz, *timba* (jazz/rap/salsa fusion), rock, classical and more. The recent Cuban music craze means that a greater variety of recordings are available abroad than ever before. Here are 10 listening recommendations. For more on Cuban music, see p40.

- *Al Final de Este Viaje* Silvio Rodríguez
- *NG La Banda en La Calle* NG La Banda
- *Guajiro Natural* Polo Montañez
- *Cuban Hip Hop All Stars, Volume 1* Pablo Herrera (producer)
- *A Lo Cubano* Orishas

- *Afrocubanismo Live* Irakere
- *Dundunbanza 1946–1951* Arsenio Rodríguez (Tumbao)
- *El Bárbaro del Ritmo: 1948–1950* Benny Moré (Tumbao)
- *Lo Último en Vivo* Los Van Van
- *Querido Pablo* Pablo Milanés

Itineraries

CLASSIC ROUTES

HAVANA
1 week–1 month

It's not indulgent to spend an entire month exploring Havana. Indeed, with so much museum-hopping, sightseeing, dancing and feasting a month will fly. Those with only a week will want more.

Mandatory museums include the Cuban collection of the **Museo Nacional de Bellas Artes** (p74); the self-explanatory **Museo de la Revolución** (p74); the **Museo Fortificaciones y Armas** (p130) across the bay; the inspiring (despite so much taxidermy) **Museo Hemingway** (p129); and the fascinating **Museo de Fundación de Naturaleza y El Hombre** (p116).

After museum fatigue sets in, head to the azure waters and white sands of **Playas del Este** (p132), or trot around verdant **Parque Lenin** (p123) on horseback. You can also re-energize with some flower power at the **Jardín Botánico Nacional** (p124).

When the moon goes up, Havana gets down. Music lovers will enjoy **Jazz Club La Zorra y El Cuervo** (p102); the **Teatro Amadeo Roldán** (p104), seat of the national symphony; the **Casa de la Trova** (p101); or just hanging on the **Malecón** (p81). Feel like shaking that thang? For salsa, it's the **Casa de la Música** in Centro Habana (p103) or Miramar (p120); there are **discos** for all types; or check out the legendary rumbas hosted by **Conjunto Folklórico Nacional de Cuba** (p102). Of course, fabulousness happens nightly at the world famous **Tropicana Nightclub** (p120).

Havana has all manner of transport options; see the Getting Around section of that chapter (p109).

Straits of Florida

Playas del Este

Habana Vieja

Vedado

Miramar

Marianao

Centro Habana

Bahía de La Habana

Museo Hemingway

Parque Lenin

Take a week or a month to dive into Havana with gusto. All of these sites are accessible with public transport, so you can find a cool casa particular (negotiate a better long-stay price) and do day trips. The furthest point of interest on this itinerary is Parque Lenin – just 20km from the city center. Rent a moped or get on a bike and ride!

THE WHISTLE STOP

2 weeks–2 months

Each Cuban city has its attractions and jumping around experiencing as many as possible is irresistible. With two weeks and a car you can see a lot of Cuba, but using public transport can give you a good (sometimes better!) taste too. With two months, you can travel the breadth in depth.

Whether you start in Havana, Holguín or Santiago de Cuba, this itinerary snares Cuba's top spots. Good roads mean you can cover the 861km between Havana and Santiago de Cuba in 15 hours or so. If you're on the bus-train combo, add a lot more time (and local color!), but you might have to lop off the Topes de Collantes, as it's hard to reach with public transport.

After ogling **Havana's** (p58) incredible architecture, head to **Santa Clara** (p239) and the venerable **Monumento Ernesto Che Guevara** (p240), with its superb mausoleum. Overnight in a seaside home in charming **Cienfuegos** (p223) before continuing to **Trinidad** (p259). A Unesco World Heritage site, you can easily spend a week in this colonial town hiking in **Topes de Collantes** (p271) and horseback riding in **Valle de los Ingenios** (p270) or lazing at **Playa Ancón** (p268). Smiling is infectious in the labyrinthine streets of **Camagüey** (p288), where you'll get lost and love it. **Guardalavaca** (p324) is one of the finest resort areas (with terrific diving) and a good beach break. Welcome to **Holguín Province** (p311), with its friendly capital and Fidel's childhood home in **Birán** (p330). Leave time for **Santiago de Cuba** (p354) and its many attractions including **El Cobre** (p383), **La Gran Piedra** (p379), the **Castillo de San Pedro del Morro** (p365), the **Cuartel Moncada** (p363) and of course, the kicking nighttime **music scene** (p372).

Most international flights take you into Havana or Santiago de Cuba, but you can easily start this adventure in **Varadero** (p197) or **Holguín** (p311), other popular entry points.

ROADS LESS TRAVELED

THE ORIENTE
2 weeks–1 month

The Oriente offers some of Cuba's most adventurous traveling. Take your time here, getting to know folks and downshifting to the Cuban pace, perhaps camping en route.

Start in **Holguín** (p311), the 'city of parks,' arriving the first week of May for the rocking **Romerías de Mayo** (p317) if possible. Just north is the sweet port town of **Gibara** (p322) with amazing architecture. Stop over in the sleepy town of **Banes** (p329) before connecting with the rough roads south and east of here to arrive in **Parque Nacional Alejandro de Humboldt** (p404). A natural treasure, this park overlooks Bahía de Taco where manatees romp and boat trips can be combined with decent hiking. Summiting **El Yunque** (p400) and splashing in the rejuvenating waters of **Boca de Yumurí** (p400) or **Playa Maguana** (p400) will have you sticking around **Baracoa** (p397). The southern coast between **Cajobabo** (p396) and **Playa Yacabo** (p396) is dotted with beaches beckoning you to picnic and snorkel. Continue through **Santiago de Cuba** (p354), moving west to the long ribbon of coast kissing the feet of the Sierra Maestra mountains; from here start your **Pico Turquino** (p386) ascent. You can do a three-day hike to the other side, coming out near **Bayamo** (p334) or summit and descend, continuing around Cuba's coastal foot through a string of typical towns like **Cabo Cruz** (p348) and **Niquero** (p347).

Many eastern pockets are out of reach of Víazul buses: a great opportunity to ride the rails or local buses, hop on a truck or catch lifts with locals. You can rent a car too.

Back roads and country hospitality require patience and a slower pace – hence the minimum two-week time frame for this itinerary covering 825km. Reaching the summit of Turquino takes at least a day, plus recovery time. Luckily there are good hotels on the route to rest your weary bones after the summit.

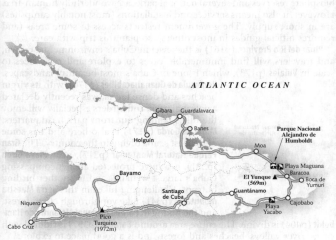

TAILORED TRIPS

PILGRIMAGE
2 weeks–1 month

No one can fill the shoes of Che, Camilo or Fidel, but you *can* follow in their footsteps, visiting pivotal sites in the Cuban Revolution. This itinerary follows a loose chronological order (see map pp28–9).

Start in **Santiago de Cuba** (p354), visiting the **Granjita Siboney** (p378) and **Cuartel Moncada** (p363) before heading to **Playa Las Coloradas** (p348), where the rebels alit from the yacht *Granma*. Diehards might head east along the coast to **El Uvero** (p30), site of the first major rebel victory. Summiting **Pico Turquino** (p386) and coming out the other side at **Comandancia de la Plata** (p342) is memorable. Head west to **Yaguajay** (p273) in Sancti Spíritus, where Camilo Cienfuegos led one of the last battles. From here you might visit the virgin sands of **Cayo Santa María** (p248) – even wannabe rebels need a vacation! – before finally pushing on to **Santa Clara** (p239), where Che led the decisive victory. Finally it's into **Havana** (p58), where that victory was declared. Finish in **Playa Girón** (p221) and the **Bahía de Cochinos (Bay of Pigs)** (p219), which have terrific beaches and snorkeling. If you have extra time, skip over to the **Isla de la Juventud** (p147), where Fidel and others were incarcerated after Moncada.

Rebels with a cause should note that public transport on Santiago de Cuba's coast is tricky and there are no buses out to Cayo Santa María. Access to Isla de la Juventud is by boat or plane. See Transport (p425) for more.

GREEN CUBA
2 weeks–2 months

Ecotourism is still in the developmental stages here, so the six Unesco biosphere reserves and several national parks are wonderfully human-free. However, it also means services and installations (most notably campsites) are in short supply. The government restricts access to some areas (and requires official guides in most others), so plan this trip with care.

Pinar del Río Province (p161) is the jewel in Cuba's environmental crown, and travelers will find innumerable caves to explore and rock faces to scale in **Viñales** (p173), which is one of Cuba's most beautiful landscapes. **Península de Guanahacabibes** (p170), with its virgin beaches and dense fauna, was recently declared a national park, and birders especially will enjoy the hikes fanning out from park headquarters. **María La Gorda** (p171) is also here and has some of the best scuba diving in the country. The **Gran Parque Natural Montemar** (p217), near **Playa Girón** (p221), is a huge protected area encompassing Cuba's largest wetland, and is another birding hotspot. Challenging hikes in the **Sierra Maestra mountains** (p341) take you through cloud forest, and the hiking in **Parque Nacional Alejandro de Humboldt** (p404) is divine. The entire area around **Baracoa** (p397) is riddled with caves, river valleys, beaches and forest, and is a good place to explore.

Getting to some of these areas without your own wheels is challenging, but possible. See Transport (p425) for more information.

The Authors

CONNER GORRY

Conner's first foreign adventure was to Vieques, Puerto Rico at the age of eight, partly explaining her attraction to islands that subvert the dominant paradigm. She got a BA in Latin American Studies and an MA in International Policy (both with Cuba specialization). She first volunteered in Cuba in 1993 and has been finding her way back ever since, as tourist, TV talent scout, Festival Internacional del Nuevo Cine Latinoamericano juror, writer, guide and food critic. She is a hardcore Coppelia junkie and a veteran of the Cuban health system.

My Favorite Trip

We threw the tent, WhisperLite stove, some plantains and pasta in the back of the car and hit the road. Though the WhisperLite choked to death on Cuban gas the first night, camping through Cuba turned out to be a phenomenal adventure.

The curl of coastline between **Playas Larga** (p219) and **Girón** (p221) is sublime camping turf: pocked with little beaches great for snorkeling, fishing and wishing on shooting stars. There's an ace seaside site near the lighthouse in **Rancho Luna** (p233); so nice we stayed awhile. **Topes de**

Collantes (p271) has a campground and good waterfall hiking, though I prefer the chilly falls of **Río Cayajaná** (p257) near Planta Cantú outside Sancti Spíritus. We made memories summiting **Pico Turquino** (p386) and love on the shores of the **Bahía de Taco** (p404), still one of my all-time favorite campsites.

CONTRIBUTING AUTHOR

Dr David Goldberg MD wrote the Health chapter. He completed his training in internal medicine and infectious diseases at Columbia-Presbyterian Medical Center in New York City, where he has also served as voluntary faculty. At present, he is an infectious diseases specialist in Scarsdale, New York State, and the editor-in-chief of the website MDTravelHealth.com.

Snapshot

'*No es fácil.*' You'll hear it in the streets, the stores, the ballpark and the bedroom. From Havana to Baracoa, 'it's not easy' is the refrain, whether you're talking politics, blackouts, the August heat or transport shortages. Cubans are not shy about sharing their views and some of your most rewarding traveling experiences will be in friendly exchanges waiting (and waiting and waiting) for a bus or having coffee in someone's home.

The bellicose posturing of the United States is always on everyone's agenda. George W Bush, Cubans agree, is worse than his father and recent tweaking of the embargo (p30) and Cold War–type tit-for-tat hasn't helped. Among other changes, the US refused to renew the lion's share of licenses allowing Americans to 'legally' travel to Cuba, installed a hard-line fellow as head of the US Interests Section (the closest thing to a US embassy here) and in May 2003 ejected 14 Cuban diplomats from the US.

Immigration is a perennial issue, as complicated as it is provocative. 'Let them go,' is the prevailing attitude among Cubans, who don't begrudge others for leaving (the millions of dollars in family remittances don't hurt either!). It's another story, however, when it endangers innocent people, which is what happened in April 2003 during several hijackings. Two planes and a ferry – all carrying scores of passengers – were commandeered by armed men demanding passage to Florida, where, if they made it, they would be granted immunity and residency. This immediate-residency policy (a magic wand waved *only* for Cubans) shares responsibility for every Cuban immigration crisis since Mariel, including the *balseros* in 1994 and the Elián saga in 1999–2000 (p34). Billboards dotting the countryside reading *Abajo de La Ley Ajuste Cubana* (Down with the Cuban Adjustment Act) decry this preferential treatment, even though tens of thousands of Cubans have taken advantage of it.

Also falling into the 'weird treatment of Cubans by the US' category are the five Cubans being held in US jails. The *cinco prisineros del imperio* (five prisoners of the empire), as they're known in Cuba, immigrated to Florida to infiltrate anti-Castro exile groups, hoping to derail terrorist plots against the island. The US arrested the five on conspiracy to commit espionage charges. Once they were in custody, gross mistreatment of the prisoners – more than 17 months in solitary confinement, denial of counsel, plus trials in hostile Miami – started to attract major international attention. Now the dog fight is in full swing, with some of the best US lawyers defending the five and the Cuban government using the cause to its full advantage. Definitely an issue to watch.

Like the ancient Chevys coughing through the Havana streets, the Cuban economy is sputtering along after the extraordinarily harsh years of the *período especial* (special period; p33). The economy grew by 1.1% in 2002, which is good news, and there are hopes that tourism revenue will buoy the country through hard times to come. The double economy, where dollars are king, is proving as hard to manage as a handful of mercury, and the Cubans are fully aware that they may have made a Faustian bargain. Still, the commitment to Cuban socialism and Fidel Castro remains strong, if proclaimed through a stifled yawn, and the devotion to *patria* (homeland) unshakeable.

FAST FACTS

Population: 11.2 million

Area: 110,860 sq km

GNP: US$25.9 billion

Life expectancy: 74 (men); 78 (women)

Adult literacy rate: 96.7%

Fidel's entry in the *Guinness Book of World Records*: longest UN speech (four hours, 29 minutes)

Student:teacher ratio, kindergarten through twelfth grade: 15:1

Number of Cuban musical acts nominated for Latin Grammys in 2002 & 2003: 34

Number of Cuban musical acts granted visas by the US government to attend the Latin Grammys in 2002 & 2003: 0

History

Cuba has been beleaguered by meddling foreigners since time immemorial. The original inhabitants were decimated by Arawaks escaping their own problems to the east, then Columbus turned up, followed by Teddy Roosevelt and the Rough Riders. Since that battle on San Juan Hill, the US has refused to loosen its grip.

According to carbon dating, Cuba has been inhabited since 2000 BC, although the first humans probably arrived from South America some 1500 years prior. The Siboney and Guanahatabey tribes were happily fishing, hunting and gathering until AD 1250 when a bunch of agriculturalists known as the Taino turned up on their shores. A branch of the Arawak tribe who inhabited most of the Caribbean and northern South America, the Taino were fleeing the fierce Carib tribe in Hispaniola and Puerto Rico. As the Taino arrived in Cuba they pushed the Siboney westward, and by the time the Spanish arrived, three-quarters of Cuba's 100,000 native population were Taino-speaking Arawaks.

DID YOU KNOW?

The Carib tribe was so bad-ass their name was corrupted into the English word 'cannibal.'

FROM COLONY TO REPUBLIC

When Columbus neared Cuba on October 27, 1492, he described it as 'the most beautiful land human eyes have ever seen,' naming it Juana in honor of a Spanish heiress. But beauty is in the eye of the beholder and Columbus, finding little gold, abandoned the island in favor of Hispaniola.

In 1512 Diego Velázquez de Cuéllar led an exhibition from Hispaniola destined to conquer Cuba for the Spanish Crown. By the end of 1514, the conquistadors had seven settlements: Baracoa, Santiago de Cuba, Bayamo, Puerto Príncipe (Camagüey), Sancti Spíritus, Trinidad and the original Havana. Along with death and disease, the Spaniards brought sugarcane to Cuba.

Velázquez made attempts to protect the Indians from Spanish excesses, but the invaders still slaughtered thousands. Hatuey, Taino chief and archetype of Cuban resistance, mounted a rebellion, but was eventually captured and burned at the stake. Before the fire was lit a Franciscan monk tried to baptize Hatuey to save his soul, but the rebel refused, declaring that if there were Spaniards in heaven he preferred the alternative. A hero for the ages, sturdy statues of Hatuey are dotted all around Baracoa (see the boxed text p397) and Cuba's tastiest beer was named after him.

Once Hatuey and Guamá (another resistance leader killed by the Spanish) were out of the way, the Spaniards went to work: gold was extracted from local mines, and large estates were set up under an *encomienda* system, requiring massive amounts of forced indigenous labor. In return these 'heathens' received lessons in Christianity. Fray Bartolomé de Las Casas, the 'Apostle of the Indians,' appealed to the Spanish Crown for more humane treatment, and in 1542 the brutal *encomienda* system was abolished. During this callous exploitation, diseases such as smallpox decimated the native population, and by 1550 only about 5000 scattered survivors remained.

Around 1522, with local labor perishing fast, the Spanish started importing African slaves. Unlike slavery in North America, Cuba's African

Biography of a Runaway Slave, the story of 103-year-old Esteban Montejo as told to Miguel Barnet, is one of the most widely translated books from Cuba. It details the trials, traditions and fight for freedom by this *cimarrón* (runaway slave).

TIMELINE

1508	1512
Sebastián de Ocampo circumnavigates Cuba, proving it's an island and not part of Asia as Columbus thought	Diego Velázquez de Cuéllar lands at Baracoa; Cuba's first rebel Hatuey is burned at the stake

slaves were kept together in tribal groups, enabling them to retain certain elements of their cultures. During this time, cattle ranching, tobacco and finally sugar became Cuba's important cash crops.

From the mid-16th century to the mid-18th century, Cuba was the center of a power struggle between wealthy Spanish traders, pirates and monarchs. Havana was plundered in 1555, leading to the construction of impressive fortifications in the harbors of both Havana (p129) and Santiago de Cuba (p365). More ransacking pirates revealed Spain's weak naval capacity and other European powers began jockeying for regional superiority. The British took Jamaica in 1655, and by 1665 Cuba's towns were under almost continuous threat of attack. Haiti fell to the French in 1697, and some feared Cuba might be next.

In 1762 Spain became involved in the Seven Years' War between Britain and France. With Spanish attentions thus occupied, British troops landed at Cojímar near Havana on June 6 and captured the castle of El Morro from behind on July 30; the Spanish surrendered on August 13. The British occupied Havana for 11 months, profiting by importing a massive 4000 African slaves and throwing open trade with their North American colonies. Tens of thousands of more slaves were imported beginning in 1790, following a slave uprising in Haiti, solidifying Cuba's primacy in sugar production. The 1763 Peace of Paris treaty returned Cuba to Spain in exchange for Florida, and as compensation Spain was given the Louisiana Territory by France.

By the 1820s, Cuba was the world's largest sugar producer and the US was sweet on it. So important was Cuban sugar to their market, the US dissuaded Simón Bolívar from liberating Cuba as he had much of South America, and in 1848 and 1854 they offered Spain US$100 million and US$130 million, respectively, in bids to buy Cuba; Spain refused. More slaves were imported to keep the industry going strong and by the 1840s there were some 400,000 Africans in Cuba. Chinese and Mexican Indian laborers replaced Africans once their importation was effectively stopped in 1865.

Fed up with Spain's reactionary policies and control accorded the *peninsulares* (Spaniards born in Spain), *criollo* landowners (Spaniards born in the New World) around Bayamo began plotting rebellion. On October 10, 1868, sugar plantation owner Carlos Manuel de Céspedes launched the uprising at La Demajagua (see p334) and called for the abolition of slavery, freeing his own by example. But a tactical decision not to invade western Cuba and an alliance between *peninsulares* and the Spanish proved fatal; this First War of Independence extended into a Ten Years' War, with some 200,000 dead. Finally in February 1878 a pact was signed at El Zanjón, but General Antonio Maceo and others rejected this in the 'Protest of Baraguá.' You'll see many sites in Cuba named after the war's heroes including General Calixto García, Céspedes, Antonio Maceo and Máximo Gómez.

During the 1880s there was a boom in railway construction as sugar mills and plantations grew larger, then too large, and US investors snapped up bankrupt plantations for a song. In 1890 tariffs on most trade between the US and Cuba were dropped. While fostering prosperity, this made Cuba totally dependent on sugar and the US. By the end of the 19th century US trade with Cuba was larger than US trade with the rest

If you're sweet on white crystals, the all-time classic *The Sugarmill: The Socioeconomic Complex of Sugar in Cuba (Ingenio)* by Manuel Moreno Fraginals is required reading.

1607	1728
Havana declared capital of Cuba	University of Havana founded

of Latin America combined and Cuba was third-largest trading partner with the US after Britain and Germany. Cuba's monocrop economy was translating into a US monopoly and some wealthy Cuban landowners were advocating annexation to protect the relationship.

Enter José Martí. Poet, patriot and independence leader, Martí spent 14 years in exile in Mexico and the US. He was impressed by American industriousness, but repelled by its materialism and hegemony, and wrote extensively on these themes (see p26).

Dedicating himself to the cause, Martí wrote, spoke, and organized for independence and by 1892 had enough momentum to coax Antonio Maceo out of exile and Máximo Gómez from the Dominican Republic to head the revolution. Martí and the others landed in eastern Cuba in April 1895, and on May 19, Martí, conspicuous on his white horse, was shot and killed. Had he lived he would certainly have become Cuba's first president; instead, he became a hero and a martyr whose life and legacy have inspired generations of Cubans. Martí busts are *everywhere* in Cuba, including atop Pico Turquino (p386).

Conscious of mistakes made during the First War of Independence, Gómez and Maceo stormed west in a scorched earth policy that left every-thing from the Oriente to Matanzas burning. By January 1896 Maceo reached Pinar del Río, while Gómez was fighting near Havana. The Spaniards responded with an equally ruthless character Valeriano Weyler, who built countrywide north–south lines to restrict the rebels' movements. The *guajiros* (country people) were forced into camps in a process called *reconcentración*, and anyone supporting the rebellion was liable for execu-tion. In December 1896 Antonio Maceo was killed south of Havana trying to break out to the east.

By this time Cuba was a mess: thousands were dead, the country was in flames and William Randolph Hearst and the US tabloid press stoked war fever with sensationalized, often inaccurate articles about Spanish atrocities. Secretary of the navy Theodore Roosevelt was right there cheering them on and the US prepared to pounce.

In January 1898 the US battleship *Maine* was sent to Havana to 'protect US citizens.' On February 15, 1898, the *Maine* exploded unexpectedly in Havana Harbor, killing 266 US sailors; a monument to the *Maine* graces Havana's Malecón (p81). The Spanish claimed it was an accident; the Americans blamed the Spanish; and some Cubans accused the US, saying it provided a convenient pretext for intervention (sound familiar?). The real cause may remain one of history's great mysteries, as the hulk was scuttled in deep waters in 1911.

After the *Maine* debacle, the US scrambled to take control. They offered Spain US$300 million for Cuba and when that was rejected, demanded a full withdrawal. This request too embarrassing to entertain, Spain was simply hoping for a quick defeat. The Cubans, you'll note, were not con-sulted. The only important land battle of the war was on July 1, when the US Army attacked Spanish positions on San Juan Hill (p353) just east of Santiago de Cuba. The 700 Spanish defenders held up 6000 US troops all day, killing 223 and wounding 1243 (compared to Spanish casualties of 102 dead and 552 wounded). Despite these losses, future US president Theo-dore Roosevelt personally led the celebrated charge of the 'Rough Riders'

In *The Cuban Way: Capitalism, Communism and Confrontation* (Kumarian Press), Ana Julia Jatar-Hausman distills the confusing theories and realities of the double economy into a readable analysis of the challenges facing Cubans and their system.

DID YOU KNOW?

The term 'yellow journal-ism' sprang from the newspaper circulation battle between William Randolph Hearst's *New York Journal* and Joseph Pulitzer's *New York World*. The two went at it, enflaming the Spanish-American War situation with headlines that shouted 'War? Sure!'

1790	1850
Mass importation of African slaves	The Cuban flag is raised for the first time, by Narciso López in Cárdenas

JOSÉ MARTÍ

Cuba's national hero José Martí was born to Spanish immigrant parents in Havana on January 28, 1853. While still in high school, Martí became involved in anticolonial activities, and in 1869 he published a political tract and the first issue of a newspaper called *La Patria Libre*. A war of independence had broken out in Oriente the previous year, and the Spanish colonial authorities were in no mood to be criticized. In October 1869 Martí was arrested on treason charges, and in April 1870 he was sentenced to six years hard labor.

After several months at a Havana stone quarry, the young prisoner was exiled to the Isla de Pinos (now Isla de la Juventud) in October 1870. There he spent nine weeks before his deportation to Spain, where he was allowed to enroll in university. In 1874 Martí graduated from law school, but both the war and his critical writings had continued, and official permission to return to Cuba was denied. Martí went to Mexico City and started work with a newspaper in 1875. In 1877 he married a Cuban woman and obtained a teaching post in Guatemala.

The First War of Independence ended in 1878 and Martí was able to return to Cuba under a general amnesty. In Havana the authorities prevented Martí from practicing law, and in 1879 his conspiratorial activities and anticolonial statements at public debates led to his arrest and a second sentence of exile to Spain. After traveling to France, the US and Venezuela, Martí finally settled in New York City, where he was to remain until just three and a half months prior to his death.

In New York Martí served as a correspondent for the Buenos Aires newspaper *La Nación* and the Caracas paper *La Opinión Nacional*. His columns describing the North American scene made him well known throughout Latin America, and he was appointed consul of Uruguay in New York. In 1892 Martí's relentless advocacy of Cuban independence and his organizational work in New York and Florida led to his election as chief delegate of the newly formed Partido Revolucionario Cubano.

up San Juan Hill, claiming victory. It was the beginning of the end, and the Spaniards surrendered on July 17, 1898.

On December 12, 1898, a peace treaty ending the 'Spanish-American' War was signed in Paris by the Spanish and the Americans. The Cubans were not invited. The Teller Resolution (after Senator Henry M Teller of Colorado), passed simultaneously with the declaration of war on Spain, committed the US to respect Cuban self-determination. Only this prevented the US from annexing Cuba along with Puerto Rico, Guam and the Philippines. Instead, Cuba was placed under US military occupation.

In November 1900 US governor of Cuba General Leonard Wood convened elected Cuban delegates who drew up a constitution similar to that of the US. Then-Connecticut senator Orville Platt attached a rider to the US Army Appropriations Bill of 1901 giving the US the right, among other things, to intervene militarily in Cuba whenever they saw fit. This was approved by President McKinley, and the Cubans were given the choice of accepting the Platt Amendment or remaining under US military occupation indefinitely. They begrudgingly accepted the amendment as the lesser of two evils, and in 1903 the US used it to obtain a naval base at Guantánamo Bay (see p395).

BETWEEN REPUBLIC & REVOLUTION

On May 20, 1902, Cuba became an independent republic, but US interference endowed Cuba with a series of weak, corrupt and dependent governments, starting with the first president, Tomás Estrada Palma,

1886	1898–1902
Slavery officially abolished	US military government controls Cuba

On April 11, 1895, Martí, the Dominican general Máximo Gómez, and four others landed near Baracoa in eastern Cuba to launch the Second War of Independence. They soon made contact with rebels led by Antonio Maceo, but on May 19, 1895, Martí was killed during a brief skirmish with the Spanish at Dos Ríos on the Cauto River in today's Granma Province. Deprived of their political leader, the Cubans fought on under the military leadership of Maceo and Gómez, only to have imminent victory snatched from them by US intervention three years later.

In his own time, Martí was best known for essays that set out his vision of a secular republic and warned of the threat to Cuba from sporadic US imperialism (the US had annexed half of Mexico less than four decades earlier). Although history was to confirm his worst fears in this regard, it's Martí's poetry that is most appreciated today. In literary circles Martí is regarded as one of the initiators of the school of modernism in Latin American poetry. Decades after his death, lines from Martí's *Versos Sencillos* (Simple Verses; 1891) were incorporated into the best-known Cuban song of all time, *Guajira Guantanamera*:

Yo soy un hombre sincero	I'm a sincere man
de donde crece la palma,	from the land of the palm tree,
y antes de morirme	And before I die
quiero echar mis versos del alma.	I wish to sing these heartfelt verses.
Con los pobres de la tierra	With the poor of the land
quiero yo mi suerte echar,	I want to share a fate,
y el arroyo de la sierra me complace	And the mountain stream pleases me
más que el mar.	more than the sea.

right up to dictator Fulgencio Batista. Additionally, the US intervened militarily in Cuba in 1906, 1912 and 1917, wielding the Platt Amendment like a big stick.

By the 1920s US companies owned two-thirds of Cuba's farmland and most of its mines. The sugar industry was booming and with US Prohibition from 1919 to 1933, tourism based on drinking, gambling and prostitution flourished. When commodity prices collapsed following the Great Depression, Cuba was plunged into chaos and president-turned-dictator Gerardo Machado y Morales (1925–33) went on a terror campaign to root out detractors. In August 1933 Machado was toppled during a spontaneous general strike. An army sergeant named Fulgencio Batista (who took no part in Machado's overthrow) stepped into the power vacuum on September 4.

On Becoming Cuban: Identity, Nationality and Culture by Louis A Perez is the definitive study of the US–Cuban connection from 1850 to 1959. With 991 endnotes (like 19th-century university graduate lists), it's a detailed, erudite tome in classic Perez style.

Batista served as the army's chief of staff from 1934 to 1940, and was duly elected president in 1940, when he drafted a democratic constitution guaranteeing many rights. The next two governments, led by Presidents Ramón Grau San Martín and Carlos Prío Socarrás, were corrupt and inefficient. Batista positioned himself for a comeback, and on March 10, 1952, three months before scheduled elections he was sure to lose, Batista staged a second military coup, which the US government recognized two weeks later. Opposition politicians were unable to unite against the dictator, who later sought legitimacy through rigged elections in 1955 and 1958. By this time over half of Cuba's land, industry and essential services were in foreign hands, and Batista's cronies had enriched themselves with bribes.

1903	1925
US takes Guantánamo naval base	Cuban Communist Party founded by Julio Antonio Mella

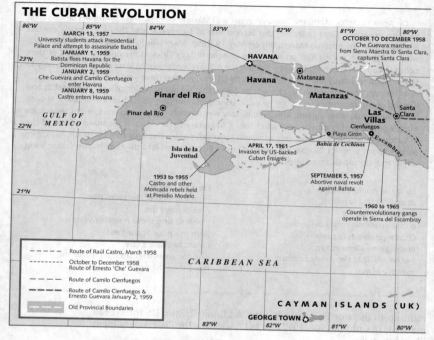

THE CUBAN REVOLUTION

After Batista's second coup, a revolutionary circle formed in Havana, including Abel Santamaría (later tortured to death by Batista's thugs), his sister Haydée Santamaría, Melba Hernández, Fidel Castro and others. On July 26, 1953, Castro led 119 rebels in an attack on the strategically important Moncada army barracks in Santiago de Cuba (see p363). The assault failed when a patrol vehicle encountered Castro's motorcade by chance, costing the attackers the essential element of surprise.

After the abortive assault, 55 of the men caught by the army were cruelly tortured and executed. Castro and a handful of others managed to escape into the nearby mountains, where they planned to initiate their guerrilla campaign. It was only through extraordinary luck (or *ache* as they say in Cuba) that Castro was captured by an army lieutenant named Sarría, who took him to jail instead of immediately shooting him as he was ordered. (One of Fidel's first acts after the revolution triumphed was to release Sarría from the prison where Batista had incarcerated him and give him a commission in the revolutionary army.) Castro's capture soon became known, and he was put on trial. Castro, a lawyer by profession, defended himself with the famous speech that was released as the political manifesto *History Will Absolve Me*. In the end Castro was sentenced to 15 years imprisonment on Isla de Pinos (now Isla de la Juventud; p156).

1934	1952
Platt Amendment abrogated, but Guantánamo US naval base lease extended for 99 years	Batista military coup

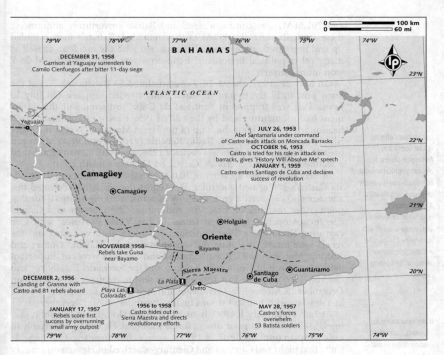

In February 1955 Batista won the presidency in fraudulent elections and freed all political prisoners, including Castro who went to Mexico some months later. Castro left Baptist schoolteacher Frank País in charge of organizing the underground resistance of the 26th of July Movement, or 'M-26-7' as it was called. In December 1955, students at Havana University formed the Directorio Revolucionario (DR), which was led by José Antonio Echeverría.

In Mexico the M-26-7 trained and equipped a revolutionary force, and on December 2, 1956, Castro and 81 companions alit from the *Granma* at Playa Las Coloradas near Niquero in Oriente (p334). The group was routed by Batista's army at Alegría de Pío three days later, but Castro and 11 others (including an Argentine doctor named Ernesto 'Che' Guevara, Fidel's brother Raúl, and future *comandantes* Camilo Cienfuegos and Juan Almeida) escaped into the Sierra Maestra, where the M-26-7 underground leader in Manzanillo, Celia Sánchez, managed to send them supplies.

On January 17, 1957, the guerrillas scored their first success by sacking an army outpost on the south coast and they started gaining followers both in Cuba and abroad. On March 13, 1957, university students attacked the Presidential Palace in Havana (now the Museo de la Revolución; see p74) in an unsuccessful attempt to assassinate Batista – 32 of the 35 attackers were shot as they fled. Radio Reloj (which is still transmitting at 950AM

'Cuban Rebel is Visited in Hideout' by Herbert L Matthews (*New York Times*, February 24, 1957) was the first interview granted by Fidel Castro in his Sierra Maestra headquarters.

Cuba joins Comecon (Council for Mutual Economic Assistance) trading bloc

Terrorist group bombs Cuban jet, killing all 73 aboard

and 101.5FM) was commandeered and Batista's overthrow announced; these students were also killed as they retreated. Batista's men rounded up and murdered anyone vaguely connected with the incident, as well as many other political opponents. Echeverría was killed, and the M-26-7 won more converts.

On May 28, 1957, the M-26-7 overwhelmed 53 Batista soldiers at the army post in El Uvero and captured badly needed supplies. On July 30 Frank País was trapped in Santiago de Cuba and shot. But the movement had momentum and by the end of 1957 Castro established a fixed headquarters at La Plata, high up in the Sierra Maestra. To visit the guerrilla HQ, see p341 or p338. Radio Rebelde (710AM and 96.7FM) began broadcasting from La Plata in February 1958, and Raúl Castro established a second front in the Sierra de Cristal on Oriente's north coast.

In May Batista sent an army of 10,000 into the Sierra Maestra to liquidate Castro's 300 armed guerrillas. By August the rebels had defeated this advance and captured a great quantity of arms, marking a crucial turning point. After marches of incredible endurance, Che Guevara and Camilo Cienfuegos opened additional fronts in Las Villas Province, with Che capturing Santa Clara. Ever conscious of Cuban history, Castro and the rebels were merely repeating the westward drive by Máximo Gómez and Antonio Maceo in 1895. It worked: road and rail links were cut, important battles were won in Guisa near Bayamo and the Sierra del Escambray and Guevara's troops sacked an armored train sent to reinforce Santa Clara on December 28. Meanwhile, Cienfuegos and men were locked in a fierce battle in Yaguajay, with Batista's troops finally surrendering on December 31.

At 2am on January 1, 1959, Batista fled to the Dominican Republic, taking US$40 million in government funds with him. He lived comfortably in exile in Spain until his death in 1973. Castro's column entered Santiago de Cuba that night and Guevara and Cienfuegos arrived in Havana on January 2. Workers across the country responded to the call for a general strike and the rest, as they say, is history.

CONSOLIDATING POWER

On January 5, 1959, the Cuban presidency was assumed by Manuel Urrutia, a judge who had defended the M-26-7 prisoners during the 1953 Moncada trials. Castro was named prime minister on January 16. Among the first acts of the revolutionary government were rent and electricity cost reductions, and the abolition of racial discrimination. These measures were followed by the First Agrarian Reform, which nationalized all holdings over 400 hectares, infuriating Cuba's largest landholders, primarily US companies. President Urrutia turned out to be a panderer to US interests and resigned in July when Castro made a 'him or me' public announcement. Things started heating up.

Entities with vested interests in Cuba grew increasingly bellicose: in October 1959 there was a failed counterrevolutionary coup; Cuban émigrés from Miami buzzed a B-25 bomber over Havana; and Castro formed a popular militia to defend the revolution (still active). Soon after there was a purge of the judicial system, when many judges and lawyers left for Miami. They were followed by professionals, managers and technicians who didn't share Castro's vision. Between 1959 and 1970, 500,000 Cubans left the country.

Get an inside glimpse of Che Guevara in *The Motorcycle Diaries,* his autobiographical account of his two-wheel odyssey through South America. A great companion read is Patrick Symmes' well-written, laugh-out-loud funny *Chasing Che: A Motorcycle Journey in Search of the Guevara Legend.*

If you're yearning for profound, insightful reading material that will broaden your traveling experience and put progressive politics in context, then Peter McLaren's *Che Guevara, Paulo Freire and the Pedagogy of Revolution* is your ticket. No fluff this one.

1977	1990
US establishes Interests Section in Havana; Cuba opens one in Washington DC	*Período especial* (special period) declared

Meanwhile, Cuba's economy went into a tailspin, the US grew more aggressive and the Soviets more friendly. In February 1960 Soviet Vice Premier Anastas Mikoyan visited Cuba to sign important trade contracts and arrange for Russian technicians to replace some of those who had left.

Crisis begot crisis, and in June 1960 Texaco, Standard Oil and Shell refineries in Cuba buckled under US pressure and refused to refine Soviet petroleum. The companies were nationalized two weeks later and President Eisenhower responded by cutting 700,000 tons from the Cuban sugar quota. The USSR stepped in, promising to buy it. In August Cuba nationalized US-owned telephone and electricity companies and 36 sugar mills, including US$800 million in US assets. Outraged, the American government forced through an Organization of American States (OAS) resolution condemning 'extracontinental' (Soviet) intervention in the Western hemisphere, and Cuba responded by establishing diplomatic relations with communist China. In September, Soviet Premier Nikita Khrushchev agreed to supply arms to Cuba and the Cubans established grass roots neighborhood bodies called Committees for the Defense of the Revolution (CDR).

On October 13, 1960, most banks and 382 major Cuban-owned firms were nationalized, and the next day an Urban Reform Law nationalized rental housing. On October 19, 1960, a partial trade embargo was imposed by Washington, to which Cuba responded by nationalizing all remaining US businesses. Quid pro quo Cold War posturing was in full swing, with Cuba maneuvering in the middle.

COLD WAR DEEP FREEZE

In January 1961 the US broke off diplomatic relations with Cuba and banned US citizens from traveling to Cuba in response to US embassy reductions ordered by Castro. In March 1961 President Kennedy abolished the remaining Cuban sugar quota. CIA schemes to kill Castro and/or overthrow his government were receiving millions of dollars, and on April 14, 1961, some 1400 CIA-trained émigrés sailed from Puerto Cabeza, Nicaragua, arriving on April 17 to launch a naval attack against Cuba. Planes bombed Cuban airfields the following day, but failed to eliminate the Cuban Air Force. On April 16, during a speech honoring the seven Cuban airmen killed in the raids, Castro proclaimed the socialist nature of the Cuban revolution for the first time.

The next day US invaders landed at Playa Girón and Playa Larga in the Bahía de Cochinos (Bay of Pigs; see p221). The US took a drubbing, in part because President Kennedy canceled US air cover during the landings, a decision which has been the subject of much revisionist analysis. Ditto Castro's declaration on December 1, 1961, that he had been a Marxist-Leninist since his university days.

After this stinging defeat the Americans declared a full trade embargo in June 1961, and in January 1962 wrangled Cuba's expulsion from the OAS, followed by OAS economic sanctions. America's closest neighbors, Mexico and Canada, refused to bow to American pressure to sever diplomatic relations with Cuba. In April 1962 Khrushchev upped the ante by installing missiles in Cuba. Castro only wanted short-range missiles capable of hitting Miami, but Khrushchev sent medium-range missiles capable of striking anywhere in the US. Even though the US

You gotta love the Freedom of Information Act, the legislation promoting transparency in US government affairs and giving the world books like Peter Kornbluh's *Bay of Pigs Declassified: The Secret CIA Report on the Invasion of Cuba*. Get a load of all the intrigue, mishaps and malfeasance.

CIA Targets Fidel, published by Ocean Press, is a detailed account of CIA plots to assassinate Castro, including the infamous exploding cigar debacle. Pulled from declassified documents, it shows just how ruthless and ridiculous the agency can be.

1991	1993
Soviet Union collapses; future of Cuba enters uncertain waters	US dollars legalized

had surrounded the Soviet Union with far more powerful missiles after WWII, Washington didn't appreciate this reciprocity.

On October 22, 1962, President Kennedy ordered the US Navy to detain Cuba-bound Soviet ships and search for missiles, provoking the Cuban Missile Crisis, which brought the world closer to the nuclear brink than it has ever been. Six days later, only after receiving a secret assurance from Kennedy that Cuba would not be invaded, Khrushchev ordered the missiles dismantled. Castro was not consulted, nor was he informed of the decision until it was already a done deal.

DID YOU KNOW?

In Cuba the Spanish-American War is called the Spanish-Cuban-North American War and the Cuban Missile Crisis is called the October Crisis.

BUILDING SOCIALISM WORLDWIDE

The learning curve was steep in the revolution's first decade. The economy languished despite massive injections of Soviet aid and was marked by inconsistency, production falls, declining quality and bloated bureaucracy. As National Bank president and later minister of industries, Guevara advocated centralization and moral, rather than material, incentives for workers. These attempts to create the 'New Man,' however, proved unsustainable. Adversely, educational advances were rapidfire, particularly the 1961 literacy campaign that sent thousands of teachers fanning out into the country to teach every Cuban to read and write.

In his book *Castro*, American biographer Peter Bourne argues that rather than being a dyed-in-the-wool communist, Castro was forced into his Marxist-Leninist position by the pressure of Cold War events and posturing between the super powers.

The effort to produce a 10-million-ton sugar harvest in 1970 (they cut a *lot* of cane, but only hauled 8.5 million tons) almost led to economic catastrophe, as Cuba obsessed with sugar at the expense of other economic sectors. After this failure more attention was placed on careful economic planning and the sugar harvest was increasingly mechanized. Conditions improved slowly during the 1970s as a new generation of technicians and managers dedicated to the revolution graduated from school to replace those who had left. Cubans began to live more comfortably, due in no small part to burgeoning trade with the Soviet bloc, which increased from 65% of the total in the early 1970s to 87% in 1988. This dependence, however, was to cost the country dearly.

Not satisfied with being stuck between the two superpowers, Cuba started supporting revolutionary efforts in Latin America and Africa. Guevara trained guerrilla forces in the former Zaire, and some 1000 Cuban troops were sent to the Congolese Republic to support a socialist regime. In November 1966 Guevara launched a guerrilla campaign in Bolivia, hoping to spark continental revolution. Unfortunately the Cuban model didn't translate well to the Bolivian reality and Bolivian troops, with heavy US support, captured Guevara on October 8, 1967, and killed him the following day. By this time, Cuba was assisting struggles in Guinea and Mozambique as well.

The Latin American Working Group is a coalition of US politicians and grassroots organizations working to foster fair policies in Latin America. One of its biggest campaigns is Cuba. Learn more at www.lawg.org.

Cuba's involvement in Angola ran deep: in the fall of 1975, Cuba sent 18,000 troops to Angola to help the Marxist MPLA fight against US-backed South African troops. Together they delivered the first military defeat ever to that apartheid regime. By the end of the war in 1988 there were 50,000 Cubans in Angola. Success there led to Cuba's admittance to the Non-Aligned Movement and Castro was elected as its president for a three-year term in 1979.

In 1976 a third Cuban constitution was drawn up and approved by referendum; Fidel Castro replaced Osvaldo Dorticós as president.

1995	1996
Direct foreign investment approved – tourism becomes main money earner	Hostile Brothers to the Rescue planes shot down by Cuban jets

CRISIS AS THE WALL FALLS

After almost 25 years of a top-down Soviet-style economy, it was obvious quality was suffering and quotas were unrealistic. In 1986 the 'rectification of errors' began, a process that aimed to reduce bureaucracy and allow more local level decision making. Midway through this process the Eastern bloc collapsed. As trade and credits amounting to US$5 billion annually vanished, President Castro declared a five-year *período especial* (special period) austerity programme in August 1990. Rationing and rolling blackouts were instituted, shortages became chronic and finding food was a daily struggle. Meals of fried grapefruit skins and microjet rice (cooked with double the water so the grains poofed to twice their size) were common. Cubans share their survivor stories willingly, punctuated by *'no es fácil m'hijita'* ('it's not easy my child').

The US tightened the noose with the 1992 Torricelli Act (still going strong), which forbids foreign subsidiaries of US companies from trading with Cuba and bans ships that have called at Cuban ports from docking at US ports for six months. Ninety percent of the trade banned by this law consists of food, medicine and medical equipment, which led the American Association for World Health to conclude in its 1997 report *Denial of Food and Medicine: The Impact of the US Embargo on Health and Nutrition in Cuba* that in their 'expert opinion...the US embargo has caused a significant rise in suffering – even deaths – in Cuba'. This exhaustive, heartbreaking report belies the human-rights moral high ground the US persists on occupying.

In August 1993, with the country desperate for a fast cash injection, the US dollar was legalized, allowing Cubans to hold and spend foreign currency and open US dollar bank accounts. In September 1993 self-employment in more than 100 trades was legalized, and in October 1994 farmers markets were opened. Class differences reemerged as people with US dollars gained access to goods and services not available in pesos, and touts and prostitutes known as *jineteros/as* (jockeys) reappeared in tourist areas. Although some of the worst shortages have been alleviated thanks to tourism and the legalization of the dollar, it still isn't easy and Cuba does not consider itself yet out of the *período especial* woods.

Though it deprives US businesses of as much as US$2 billion a year in export sales to Cuba and has failed for over 40 years to topple the Cuban government, the embargo policy continues. After the collapse of the Soviet Union, the US presumed that Castro couldn't survive without Soviet aid, so the economic screws were tightened with the 1996 Helms-Burton Bill. The bill allows US investors to take legal action in the American courts against foreign companies utilizing their confiscated property in Cuba. It also prevents any US president from lifting the embargo until a transitional government is in place in Havana and requires US representatives to international financial organizations to oppose loans to Cuba. These attempts by the US to legislate the world have been widely denounced, and every year since 1992 the United Nations General Assembly has voted by an overwhelming margin to condemn the US economic embargo against Cuba. During his visit to Cuba in 1998, Pope John Paul II called for an end to the 'unjust and ethically unacceptable' embargo. Of course, the embargo also allows Fidel Castro to deflect attention from, and responsibility for,

DID YOU KNOW?

In 2000 Cuba ranked #228 (dead last) among countries to which the US sold food; in 2001 Cuba ranked #144; and in 2002 it ranked #46. In 2002 the first US Food & Agribusiness Exhibition in Havana was held. Now a biannual event, it ensures US growers have as much exposure as possible to this fresh market.

The Cuba Solidarity web page at www.cubasolidarity.net has links and information for people who want to get active before, during and after they travel.

See www.ciponline.org/cuba for the latest news on US-Cuban affairs, including pending Congressional legislation.

domestic problems to the hostile northern neighbor, whose aggressions only strengthen an already healthy Cuban nationalism.

INTO THE NEW MILLENNIUM

US immigration policy runs a close second to the embargo in sore subjects. In 1966 the US enacted the Cuban Adjustment Act, which grants residency to any Cuban arriving on US shores. Anyone who has ever tried to obtain residency in the US knows what an incredible windfall this is and people have risked their lives in its pursuit. In 1980, 125,000 people left Cuba from the port of Mariel in search of greener pastures and a green card in the Mariel boat-lift. Another immigration crisis erupted in 1994 when some 35,000 *balseros* (people on balsa or makeshift rafts and inner tubes) struggled across the Florida Straits in traumatic conditions. Once the US determined that the overall majority were economic refugees (allowing them to remain nevertheless), the open door immigration policy was amended so that Cubans intercepted at sea were returned, but those that made it to US soil could stay. The US also promised to issue a minimum of 20,000 visas a year to Cubans wishing to immigrate, which it has faithfully done until 2003: by April of that year, the Bush Administration had only issued 500, likely in an effort to increase immigration pressures and spark another crisis. Such a crisis might prove a handy pretext if the US wanted to step in militarily.

In 1999, US-Cuban immigration issues hit international prime time with the Elián González drama. Crossing the Straits with his mother and 12 others, their vessel capsized; she died, he didn't. Elián was taken to a distant relative's house in Miami, where the histrionic politicking began. The press conferences and coverage, court process, protests and anguish lasted seven months before Elián was returned to his father. The two continue to live in Cárdenas (p213).

Following the important role the Miami exile community played in the 2000 election recount, George W Bush promised to crack down on Cuba. The rhetoric turned venomous after September 11, with Bush officials mentioning Cuba in the same breath as North Korea and Iraq. Subsequently, US policy was rolled back to resemble the worst of the Cold War years: licenses permitting US citizens to travel to Cuba were not renewed, eliminating 70% of 'legal' travel by students, athletes, scientists etc; 14 Cuban diplomats were expelled from the US for unspecified 'activities deemed harmful to the United States'; and the new chief of the US Interests Section in Havana, James Cason, began organizing and supplying dissident groups throughout Cuba in order to bring about a regime change. The Cuban government arrested more than 70 dissidents connected to Cason on charges of 'conspiring with enemies of the state,' held trials and sentenced them to varying jail terms. The arrests were criticized by Human Rights Watch and former US President Jimmy Carter, who visited Cuba in 2002, the first president, in office or not, to do so since Calvin Coolidge in 1928.

Things turned uglier in April 2003 when three hijackings by Cubans seeking transport to the US presaged a possible migratory crisis (Cuban officials uncovered more than 20 other hijacking plans in the works). Armed with guns, knives and, in one case, grenades, two planes and

Cuban-American novelist Christina García has proven she has a masterful talent for writing evocative, melodic prose that captures Cuba. Both her debut novel *Dreaming in Cuban* and her recent *Monkey Hunting* revolve around the immigrant experience.

DID YOU KNOW?

It's estimated the US loses US$1.18 billion annually and some 17,000 new jobs are not created because of the Cuban embargo.

Get informed, get involved or just get a load of what they're up to on Capitol Hill at www.cubacentral.com, brought to you by politicians trying to right Washington's Cuban policy and lift the travel ban on Americans.

1998	2002
Five Cubans are arrested by US authorities on questionable spy charges; they remain in prison	First US Food & Agribusiness Exhibition held in Havana

HUMAN RIGHTS IN CUBA

The Cuban government is often criticized over its human-rights record, and it's a fact that many individuals who would be considered 'prisoners of conscience' in the Western context are presently being held in Cuban jails for voicing opinions critical of Cuba's present leadership or for attempting to organize political opposition. Stiff prison sentences are handed down at summary trials and domestic human-rights groups are not recognized by the government. While this situation has to be condemned, it must also be viewed in the context of a small country perpetually and increasingly threatened with destabilization by a powerful neighbor.

Unlike many other Latin American countries, there are no 'death squads' in Cuba carrying out extrajudicial murders, and lethal 'disappearances' off the streets are unknown. Police violence and official corruption are minimal compared with countries like Colombia, Brazil, Guatemala and Venezuela. In comparison, the constraints Cubans face are usually more subtle, such as limitations on the right to accumulate wealth, buy and sell property, form associations or travel abroad.

The arrest of more than 70 individuals in 2003, journalists and antigovernment activists among them, was vilified outside Cuba, while domestically it was considered a national security issue; there's evidence that the US Interests Section in Havana was facilitating opposition groups within Cuba. Also considered a threat to national security were the armed hijackers who were tried, found guilty and sentenced to death that same year – a decision that sparked international, as well as homegrown, criticism.

When questioned about human rights, Cuban officials usually point to the many social rights (which are often overlooked by human-rights activists) enjoyed by Cubans – Cuba's health and educational facilities are more accessible to the average citizen than those of many rich countries, including the US – and question the sincerity of agencies, such as the International Monetary Fund, which impoverish millions through crippling austerity programs while firing human-rights bullets at selected developing countries' governments they do not control.

a ferry were taken in separate dramatic events that had news, gossip and speculation flying. One plane made it to the US, but the ferry and second plane didn't. Three of the hijackers apprehended in Cuba were tried, sentenced to death and executed, triggering an avalanche of international criticism from intellectuals, human rights advocates, politicians and religious leaders.

In April 2003 Cuba was elected, uncontested, to the UN Human Rights Commission.

2002	2003
Half of Cuba's sugar refineries are closed, signaling the end of an era	George W Bush tightens travel noose for US citizens traveling to Cuba

The Culture

THE NATIONAL PSYCHE

Many visitors are surprised by how critical and good humored Cubans are about their government (privately) and daily reality (publicly). Cubans are, by nature and necessity, survivors. In a small nation bucking the modern socio-political system, where monthly salaries top out around US$13, survival means finding ways to supplement personal income. Oftentimes this is by providing goods and services more efficiently than the government, like the barber giving straight razor shaves on his patio or the lady selling fresh eggs door to door. Other supplemental income, however, may be ill-gotten or garnered through trickery, like the *compañera* (female revolutionary) who filches cooking oil from her job to sell on the side. Old Cuba hands know one of the most popular ways to make extra cash is working with (or over) tourists.

In Cuba, cash dollars rule, primarily because there are places you can go and things you can buy with dollars but not pesos. This double economy has reinvigorated the class system the revolution worked so hard to neutralize and it's no longer rare to see Cubans tooling around in sports utility vehicles or tuning out with a Discman. This stark reemergence of haves and have nots is among the most ticklish issues facing Cuba today. A young intellectual framed it this way: 'The problem is not that one schoolgirl is eating a plain roll, while another eats a ham and cheese sandwich. The problem starts when the girl with the ham and cheese doesn't share it.'

Cuba, which embodies an unparalleled culture of sharing, is far from that point, but once desire converts to need and accumulation turns to greed, things could get stickier still. Government initiatives most visible to tourists (eg heavy taxation of private business owners) are designed precisely to address this polarity. This double economy is one of the most confounding issues travelers are likely to face (romance is the other!).

Then there's the 40 years of undivided attention from the bully to the north. Cubans would like the US off their backs and you'll hear, read and see it everywhere you go. All politics aside, one of the saddest effects of the US-Cuban deep freeze is the broken families. Precipitated by prejudicial immigration policies on Washington's part and economic hardship in Cuba, many Cubans left home in search of brighter horizons and almost everyone has a long-lost sister, cousin, twin or aunt.

Despite all these challenges, Cubans remain the funniest, most gracious and generous people you're likely to find anywhere. Laughter is a great tonic and Cubans apply it liberally with their legendary style of topical and poignant humor.

LIFESTYLE

Cuban socialism dances to its own drummer. Though housing is free, shortages mean three or even four generations might live under the same roof, which gets tight in a two-bedroom apartment. This also cramps budding love lives and Cubans will tell you it's the reason the country has one of the world's highest divorce rates. Gays and lesbians, who do not have the option of getting married and living with the *familia*, are in a particularly difficult spot vis-à-vis their private affairs. On the flip side, a full house means there's almost always someone to babysit, take care of you when you're sick or do the shopping while you're at work.

DID YOU KNOW?

According to the UN Development Programme's Human Development Index for 2002, only one in 1000 Cubans are cellular telephone subscribers, but 100% of births are attended by skilled health staff.

Part documentary, part music clip depicting the daily hustle of a young *jinetera*, *Who the Hell Is Juliette?* is a good primer on Cuban lasses of a type.

C Peter Ripley's *Conversations with Cuba*, in which the author talks to locals about regular topics of daily import, is like an overheard conversation – entertainment, enlightenment and education all rolled into one.

Cuban women have been liberated in the sense that they have access to education and training of whatever sort they desire. In fact, women make up 66.4% of the professional and technical workforce. But, like everywhere, a glass ceiling still exists in some fields (eg politics) and the home is still largely the woman's responsibility, which translates to a 'double work day' – women go to work and then come home, to work. Thanks to specific governmental policies, such as one year guaranteed maternity leave and free day care, it's easier being a mom *and* a career woman in Cuba. Children are an integral part of life and kids are everywhere – the theater, church, restaurants and rock concerts. It's refreshing that Cubans don't drastically alter their lives once they become parents.

That women are turning to the hustle to make some extra cash or attain baubles is disturbing. While some *jineteras* are straight-up hookers, others are just getting friendly with foreigners for the perks they provide: a ride in a car, a night out in a fancy disco or a new pair of jeans. Some are after more, others nothing at all. It's a complicated state of affairs and can be especially confusing for male travelers who get swept up in it. As one American traveler put it: 'Although I've had many relationships with latinas, I'm reluctant to get involved with a Cuban because of the socioeconomic dynamic involved.'

Most homes don't have a phone or computer, infinitesimally few have Internet access and disposable income is an oxymoron. All of this has a huge effect on lifestyle. What makes Cuba different from somewhere like Bolivia or Appalachia though, is the government's heavy subsidies of every facet of life, especially culture. Consider the fact that in Havana there are some 200 movie theaters and a ticket costs two pesos (US$0.08), or that a front row seat at the Gran Teatro de la Habana costs 10 pesos (US$0.40), rap concerts cost two pesos and a patch of cement bench at the ballpark is one peso (US$0.04). Now if only there were transport to get there. Still, with a set of dominoes or a guitar, a bottle of rum and a group of friends, who needs baseball or the ballet?

DID YOU KNOW?

In the summer of 2001, a festive double wedding was held in a Havana neighborhood recreation center. Totally normal, except the two couples tying the knot were the first publicly (but not legally) wed homosexuals in Cuba.

THE RATION CARD

The ration card, or *libreta*, was created in 1962 to provide a basic social safety net for the population and to limit price gouging on basic goods via the black market. During the relatively affluent '70s and '80s, with Soviet subsidized products pouring into Cuba, it seemed that the card might be on the way out, but the economic crisis of the '90s has ensured its survival.

The basic 30-product monthly food basket allotted to every Cuban includes 2.7kg of rice, 1.5kg of refined sugar and 1kg of brown sugar, 0.25kg of beans, a measly amount of coffee, 2kg of salt, 0.25kg of cooking oil and 1.5kg of pasta. Everyone receives one toilet roll a day, plus soap and toothpaste. Chicken, hot dogs, fish and vegetables are distributed pending availability. Another 29 products are distributed irregularly on a per family basis, including cornmeal, food paste, crackers and tinned tomatoes. Children up to the age of one get two bottles of fresh or condensed milk monthly, plus soy yogurt every other day. Children to the age of seven get an allotment of powdered milk. Pensioners, pregnant women, and those with certain chronic diseases or special diets (eg for high cholesterol) also receive special rations.

Rationed goods are sold at bodegas (government stores), at subsidized peso prices that haven't changed for years. The same items sold freely without ration cards at farmers markets cost 20 times more. Bodegas often sell items *libre* (outside the ration card), meaning anyone, including foreigners, can buy those products. Maintaining the ration system is a serious drain on state finances, but without it many Cubans would suffer real hardship in a society where the circulation of two unequal currencies has created tangible class differences. As it is, the monthly ration is only a supplement that must somehow be topped up elsewhere.

POPULATION

The slave trade and triumph of the revolution are two of the most important factors in Cuba's population mix. From Santería traditions to popular slang (you'll hear '¿Qué bolá asere?' daily, which loosely translates as 'What's happening brother?'), Afro-Cuban culture is an integral part of the national identity. At the time of writing, official census figures gathered in 2002 still hadn't been released, but outside estimates say Cuba is 51% mulatto, 37% white and 11% black. Regardless, numbers say nothing about how amazingly integrated Cuban society is.

DID YOU KNOW?

More than 400 million women worldwide are illiterate, but not one of them is Cuban.

A series of post-revolutionary initiatives seriously affected population distribution. Most notably, the invitation to free education, including technical schools and university, had Cubans pouring into the cities from the countryside, so that today the urban population is a whopping 75%. In efforts to stem or reverse this trend the government offered land incentives to urbanites during the special period (see p33) to encourage resettling in rural areas, and since May 1998 Cubans have needed official permission to relocate to Havana.

SPORT

Considered a right of the masses, professional sports were abolished after the revolution and about three million Cubans now participate in organized sports. Amateur athletes traveling abroad are constantly enticed to defect with promises of gold and glory, and scarce resources mean stadium bathrooms or scoreboards don't always work. Given the economic hardship, it's amazing that Cuba hosted the Pan-American Games in 1991, winning 140 gold medals (the first time a Latin American country beat the US), and was placed 10th among competing countries in the 2000 Sydney Olympic Games, bringing home 11 gold medals, 11 silver and seven bronze. In its continued commitment to athletics and its fanatics, the government inaugurated the biannual National Olympics in 2002.

Cuban baseball (pelota) is legendary and the country is riveted during the October to March regular season, turning rabid for the play-offs in April. You can see passions running high in the main square of any provincial capital, where fans debate minute details of the game with lots of finger-wagging hilarity in what is known as a peña deportiva (fan club) or esquina caliente (hot corner). These are among the most opinionated venues in Cuba and the esquina in Havana's Parque Central (p74) is highly entertaining, especially in the postseason when funereal wreaths and offerings to orishas (Santería deities) appear for eliminated teams and those still contending. Every few years a Cuban player is lured to the US, like José Ariel Contreras, who pitched for Pinar and was recently signed to a four-year US$32 million contract with the Yankees. Most players, however, shun the big money bait and the opportunity to play in baseball's greatest stadiums, opting instead to return to their US$13 monthly salary and making their athletic achievements all the more admirable.

Want to know about El Duque's torn rotator cuff or how many Cubans are in the National Baseball Hall of Fame in Cooperstown? You'll get all this and much more (including phenomenal historic photos) at www.cubanball.com.

Cuba is also a giant in amateur boxing, as indicated by champions Teófilo Stevenson, who brought home Olympic gold in 1972, 1976 and 1980, and Félix Savón, another triple medal winner, most recently in 2000. Every sizable town has an arena called a sala polivalente, where big boxing events take place, while training and smaller matches happen at gyms, many of which train Olympic athletes. Travelers interested in sparring lessons or seeing a match should drop in at a gym (see individual regional chapters for information).

Basketball, volleyball (the national women's team won gold in the 2000 Sydney Olympic Games) and, to a lesser extent, soccer are all popular in Cuba, but *dominó* (always referred to in the singular) and chess, both considered sports, are national passions. Self-taught José Raúl Capablanca, touted as the greatest natural chess player that ever lived, became World Chess Champion in 1921 and you'll see chess matches on the street and read about the masters in the sports pages. *Dominó* is everywhere and you'll see quartets of old men and young bucks slugging back shots of rum and slamming down their tiles in every Cuban neighborhood. In March 2003 Havana hosted the first annual Campeonato Mundial de Dominó (World Domino Championship), with 10 countries and thousands of players participating. The finals were held in Ciudad Deportiva, where Cuba won it all.

RELIGION

Religion is among the most misunderstood, misrepresented (by Castro's critics) and complex aspects of Cuban culture. Before the revolution 85% of Cubans were nominal Roman Catholics, though only 10% attended church regularly. Protestants made up most of the rest of the church-going public, though a smattering of Jews and Muslims have always practiced in Cuba and still do. When the revolution triumphed, 140 Catholic priests were expelled for reactionary political activities and another 400 left voluntarily, while the majority of Protestants, who represented society's poorer sector, had less to lose and stayed.

When the government declared itself Marxist-Leninist and therefore atheist, life for *creyentes* (literally 'believers') took on new difficulties. Though church services were never banned and freedom of religion never revoked, Christians were sent to Unidades Militares de Ayuda a la Producción (UMAPs; Military Production Aid Units), where it was hoped hard labor might reform their religious ways; homosexuals and vagrants were also sent to the fields to work. This was a short-lived experiment, however. More trying for believers were the hardline Soviet days of the '70s and '80s when they were prohibited from joining the Communist Party and few, if any, believers held political posts. Certain university careers, notably in the humanities, were off-limits as well.

Things have changed dramatically since then, particularly in 1992 when the constitution was revised, removing all references to the Cuban state as Marxist-Leninist and recapturing the laical nature of the Cuban government. This led to an aperture in civil and political society for religious adherents and leaders and other reforms; for example, believers are now eligible for party membership. Since Cuban Catholicism gained the papal seal of approval with Pope John Paul II's visit in 1998, church attendance has surged and posters welcoming him are still displayed with pride. It's worth noting that churches have a strong youth presence. There are currently 400,000 Catholics regularly attending mass and 300,000 Protestants from 54 denominations. More evangelical denominations such as the Seventh Day Adventists and Pentecostals are rapidly growing in popularity.

The religious beliefs of Africans brought to Cuba as slaves were originally layered over Catholic iconography and doctrines, eventually forming new belief systems; see the boxed text (p40). Santería is the most widespread of these and is an integrated daily part of life here; you'll see initiates dressed in white everywhere you go and many homes have altars tucked into the corners. Santería has served as a cultural ambassador of sorts, with new museums and dance and drum performances becoming standard itinerary fare. Some take exception to this 'folkloricization' of the sacred – dressing all in white has now become fashionable whether you're initiated or not, for example – and curious tourists may be taken to consultations with *babalaos* (priests) more interested in your dollars than your dilemmas.

Dive right into the heart of race and heritage in Cuba with the fine anthology *Afro-Cuban Voices: On Race and Identity in Contemporary Cuba* by Pedro Pérez Sarduy and Jean Stubbs (eds).

Fidel and Religion, by Brazilian priest, educator and activist Frei Betto (now Special Advisor to President Lula of Brazil), is based on 23 hours of conversation with Fidel Castro in 1985. The book took Cuba by storm (readers lined up at the printing factory to get their copy), selling over one million copies in a few months and creating a national dialogue on a then touchy subject.

CUBAN RELIGIONS OF AFRICAN ORIGIN

Slaves brought from West Africa between the 16th and 19th centuries carried with them a system of animistic beliefs that they hid beneath a Catholic veneer. The slave owners were poor missionaries, and they kept tribes together in order to pit one group against another. Tribes such as Arará, Lucumí and Congo are organized in *cabildos* (associations). Abakuá is a secret society made up of male members known as *ñáñigos*. Initiates address each other as *ambia, asere, boncó* and *monina*, and say *'¿qué bolá?'* instead of the usual *'¿qué tal?'* ('what's up?') or *'¿como está?'* ('how are you?'). Such phrases are common in everyday slang.

It's likely there are more followers of the Afro-Cuban religions than practicing Roman Catholics in contemporary Cuba. The largest Afro-Cuban religion is an amalgam of Catholic and Yoruba beliefs known as Santería or Regla de Ocha. In Santería, Catholic saints and apparitions of the Virgin are associated with Yoruba deities, or *orishas*. Unlike Catholic saints, however, the *orishas* do not represent perfection and they have many human frailties. The concepts of original sin and a final judgment are unknown. Instead, ancestral spirits are worshipped.

Among the most important *orishas* is the androgynous creator god Obatalá, who is always dressed in white and associated with Christ or Nuestra Señora de la Merced. Obatalá's wife, Odudúa, goddess of the underworld, is also associated with the Virgin. Obatalá's son, Elegguá (St Anthony), is the god of destiny. Yemayá, the goddess of the ocean and mother of all *orishas*, is identified by the color blue and associated with Nuestra Señora de Regla. Changó, the Yoruba god of fire and war, lives in the tops of the royal palm trees and controls the lightning. His color is red and he's associated with Santa Bárbara. His son Aggayú Solá, god of land and protector of travelers, is associated with San Cristóbal (St Christopher). Ochún, wife of Changó and companion of Yemayá, is the goddess of love and the rivers. As might be expected, she's a very powerful *orisha* and is associated with Cuba's patron saint, the Virgin de la Caridad del Cobre (whose color is yellow). Ogún is associated with John the Baptist. Babalú Ayé (St Lazarus) is the *orisha* of disease.

The rites of Santería are controlled by a male priest called a *babalawo* or *babalao*, of whom there are estimated to be 4000 in Cuba. The *babalawos* are often consulted for advice, to cure sicknesses or to grant protection, and offerings are placed before a small shrine in his home. Although the figures of Catholic saints mounted on the shrines represent a variety of *orishas*, the real power resides in stones draped with colored bead necklaces. The stones are believed to harbor the spirits of the *orishas*, and they must be fed with food, herbs and blood. Animals such as chickens, doves and goats are sacrificed during rituals, and the *babalawo* sprays rum onto the altar from his mouth.

Cubans are surprisingly open about Santería, and travelers are welcome to inspect household shrines and attend ceremonies. It's unlikely anyone will be offended if you ask them about Santería; in fact, they'll probably be pleased that you're interested in Cuban culture. Many hotels stage special Santería shows for visitors, and cult objects are often sold in hotel shops. If you attend a Santería ceremony at a private residence you'll be expected to leave a few dollars for the saint (and *babalawo*) on the altar. Ask about special Santería services on December 4 (the day of Santa Bárbara) or December 17 (the day of San Lázaro), which begin the night before.

ARTS

When the Cuban government prioritizes an issue they mean business and this is supremely evident in the arts. After the revolution, museums opened, theater and dance groups were created, art schools were established and a national film industry was founded. In addition, more than 250 *casas de la cultura* were created around the country, bringing cultural events and opportunities to farflung corners. Some of the most innovative art in Cuba today (especially theater and dance) is happening at these culture houses and events are usually free.

Several governmental organizations oversee the work of writers and artists, extending privileges, support and tacit seals of approval including the revered Casa de las Américas, Unión de Escritores y Artistas de Cuba (UNEAC) and its junior counterpart, Asociacíon Hermanos Saíz.

Music

Ethnomusicologist Fernando Ortíz described Cuban music as 'a love affair between the African drum and the Spanish guitar.' Nowhere is this coupling more passionate than in *son*, music fusing African percussive traditions with Spanish lyrical forms that originated in the Oriente mountains. These days, the global vernacular infuses Cuban music, from thrash metal in Pinar del Río to the hip-hop beats of Alamar.

In its pure form, *son* was played by a sextet: guitar, *tres* (guitar with three sets of double strings), double bass, bongo and two singers who played maracas and *claves* (sticks that tap out the beat, sometimes replaced by a singer imitating the knock-knock sound perfectly). Most of the world became familiar with *son* through Ry Cooder's *Buena Vista Social Club*, the world-famous offspring of generations of rich musical heritage. Respected *son* elders include Ñico Saquito (who wrote over 500 classics such as *Compay Gallo*); Los Compadres, which features different lineups including Compay Segundo from BVSC fame; Trios Matamoros, who wrote the standards *Lagrimas Negras* and *Son de la Loma*; and Arsenio Rodríguez, the blind *tres* player and songwriter whom Harry Belafonte called the 'father of salsa.'

In the '40s and '50s the *son* bands grew from six pieces to eight and beyond until they became big bands boasting full horn and percussion sections playing rumba, *chachachá* (cha-cha) and mambo. The reigning mambo king was Benny Moré (1919–63), who with his velvety voice and rocking 21-piece all-black band was known as 'El Bárbaro del Ritmo' ('The Barbarian of Rhythm'). You'll still hear the master's voice floating from taxi windows; Havana's Salón Rosado Benny Moré (aka La Tropical; p121) is a rocking outdoor venue; Bar Benny is Varadero's (p209) hippest hideout; and every other year Cienfuegos hosts the Benny Moré International Festival of Music.

Salsa emerged from the fertile Latin New York scene of the '60s and '70s when jazz, *son* and rumba blended to create a new style. Cuba's most famous salsa band is Los Van Van, formed by Juan Formell in 1969; they took home a Grammy in 2000 for *Llego Van Van*.

Jazz, considered music of the enemy in the revolution's most dogmatic days, has always seeped into Cuban sounds. Jesus 'Chucho' Valdes' band Irakere, formed in 1973, broke the Cuban music scene wide open with its heavy Afro-Cuban drumming laced with jazz and *son*. Jazz also mixed with rap and deep salsa grooves in a new style called *timba*, championed by NG La Banda, which formed in 1988. Other musicians associated with the Cuban jazz set include pianist Gonzalo Rubalcaba, Isaac Delgado and Adalberto Álvarez y Su Son. All of these cats can be seen live in Cuba.

The whole hemisphere simmered with social protest and politics in the 1960s, sparking creative juices everywhere, including Cuba. This was the *trova* heyday, with *trovadores* (singers) crooning ballads of rhyming eight-syllable verses called *décimas*. The most famous *décima* is from José Martí's *Versos Sencillos*, set to the music of Joseíto Fernández' (1908–79) *Guajira Guantanamera* and popularized by American folk singer Pete Seeger in a 1963 Cuban solidarity concert.

On the heels of this came *nueva trova*, an enduring movement of singer-songwriters who wrote poetic lyrics examining, critiquing and exalting Cuban society. Spearheaded by Silvio Rodríguez, Pablo Milanés, Noel Nicola, Vicente Feliú and Sara González, *nueva trova* is alive and well. Though Silvio and Pablo have virtually stopped appearing in public,

Learn just how dynamic and hopping the contemporary Cuban art scene is with Gerardo Mosquera's *Art Cuba: The New Generation*. All the hottest, most innovative artists are represented here, replete with 100 beautiful color plates.

If you want to browse online for the latest and greatest (and classics too) discs from Cuba, head to www.discuba.com, where you can shop till you drop and the goods are only US$11 or so.

TOP 10 MUSICIANS TO CATCH LIVE

No visit to Cuba is complete without seeing some live music. Whether you drop in at a *casa de la trova* in Camagüey, attend a New Year's concert on the Malecón or a rap *peña* in Santa Clara, everyone should get out and get down. Keep an eye out for concerts by these musicians:

- Interactivo
- Sinfónica Nacional
- Síntesis
- Chucho Valdés
- Zeus

- Los Van Van
- Ars Longa
- Los Muñequitos de Matanzas
- Anónimo Consejo
- Los Kents

For Top Ten listening recommendations see the boxed text (p16).

you might catch concerts by other accomplished *trovadores* like Santiago Feliú (whose insightful lyrics are carried by ripping guitar riffs), the ever-popular Carlos Varela, the humorous Frank Delgado, or the young *santiagüero* William Vivanco. For more suggestions see the boxed text (above). Every big city has a *casa de la trova* and/or *casa de la música*, which are good places to poke around for music events.

The contemporary Cuban music scene is an interesting mix of enduring traditions, modern sounds, old hands and new blood. With low production costs, urban themes and lots of US-inspired styles, hip hop and rap are taking the younger generation by storm. Groups like Obsession, 100% Original, Freehole Negro (cofronted by a woman) and Anónimo Consejo perform regularly and everyone comes out for the Havana Hip Hop Cuban Rap Festival in August (see p85).

It's hard to categorize Interactivo, a collaboration of young, talented musicians led by pianist Robertico Carcassés. Part funk, jazz and rock, and very in the groove, this band jams to the rafters; a guaranteed good time. Interactivo's bassist is Yusa, a young black woman whose eponymous debut album made it clear she's one of the most innovative musicians on the Cuban scene today.

Classical music has its modern practitioners like pianists Frank Fernández, Ramón Valle and Aldo López-Gavilán. If you're lucky, you can hear them interpreting compositions by Ernesto Lecuona (1895–1963), perhaps Cuba's greatest composer.

Thrash metal dominates the rock world; head-bang with energetic groups like Zeus and Trauma at Patio de María in Havana (p102).

For the straight dope on the best of classic Cuban *son*, mambo and more, see the Slipcue guide to Cuban classics at www.slipcue.com.

Literature

In a country strewn with icons like rice at a wedding, José Martí (1853–95) is tops. Visionary, patriot and rebel, he was also a literary giant whose collected plays, essays and poetry fill 30 volumes. Exiled for his writings before he was 20, Martí lived most of his life outside Cuba, primarily in the US. His last book of poetry, *Versos Sencillos* (Simple Verses), is, as the title proclaims, full of simple verses and is arguably one of his best. Though written over a century ago, the essays collected in *Nuestra America* (Our America) and *Los Estados Unidos* are remarkably forward thinking, providing a basis for Latin American self-determination in the face of US hegemony. For more on Martís' role as Cuban independence leader, see the History chapter (p26).

Like Martí, mulatto Nicolás Guillén (1902–89) is considered one of Cuba's world-class poets. Ahead of his time, he was one of the first mainstream champions of Afro-Cuban culture, writing rhythmic poems like *Sóngoro Cosongo* (1931). A communist who believed in social and racial equality, Guillén lived in exile during Batista's regime, writing *Elegía a Jesús Menéndez* (1951) and *La Paloma de Vuelo Popular* (*Elegías*; 1958). Some of his most famous poems are available in the English collection entitled *New Love Poetry: Elegy* (University of Toronto). He returned after the revolution and co-founded the Unión Nacional de Escritores y Artistas Cubanas (UNEAC). Guillén was Cuba's national poet until his death.

Cubans are crazy for poetry, so don't be surprised when someone starts reeling off verses by Dulce María Loynaz (1902–97), recipient of Spain's coveted Miguel de Cervantes award; Eliseo Diego (1920–94), the poet's poet, whose words give wings to the human spirit; or singer-songwriter Silvio Rodríguez, who is a good guitar player, but a great poet (see p40).

In literature, as in poetry, the Cuban bibliography is awe inspiring. Novelist Alejo Carpentier (1904–80) was another exiled writer, returning after the revolution to write *El Recurso del Método* (Resource of Method) and *Concierto Barroco*, both published in 1974. The latter is considered his masterpiece. Havana fans will want to check out his *Ciudad de las Columnas* (The City of Columns; 1970), which juxtaposes B&W photographs of the city's architectural details with insightful prose.

Paradiso by José Lezama Lima (1910–76) was a 'scandalous novel' when it appeared in 1966 because of its erotic (homosexual) scenes. Now it's considered a classic. Lezama was a poet and essayist who cofounded the influential magazine *Orígenes* in 1944.

Notable writers who left Cuba after the revolution include queer playwright Reinaldo Arenas, whose autobiography *Before Night Falls* (1943–90) was made into a critically acclaimed drama for the silver screen, and Guillermo Cabrera Infante (1929–), whose *Tres Tristes Tigres* (Three Trapped Tigers; 1967) describes cultural decadence during the Batista era. Of course, Cuba's most famous foreign writer-in-residence was Ernest Hemingway, who wrote *For Whom the Bell Tolls* in the Ambos Mundos Hotel in Havana (p83).

Cinema & Television

The film industry is run by the Instituto Cubano del Arte e Industria Cinematográficos, better known as ICAIC, and it has been creating quality films since its founding in 1959. You can't talk about ICAIC and not Alfredo Guevara, the institute's longtime director. Guevara is recognized, along with several influential filmmakers including Tomás Gutiérrez Alea (aka Titón, 1928–96), as the spinal column of Cuban cinema. Themes that aren't generally explored in other parts of Cuban society (bureaucratic paranoia, homosexuality and misogyny for starters) are given full airtime in Cuban movies and this quasi-autonomous, critical space carved out by ICAIC is almost one-of-a-kind; *nueva trova* commentary comes close, but few songs are as explicit as *Fresa y Chocolate* for example.

Cuba's macro-cultural approach has fueled other mediums, including animation and video, that cinema snobs might sniff at but which are full-blown industries here. Movies, shorts, videos and animation from all over the hemisphere can be seen at the annual Festival Internacional del Nuevo Cine Latinoamericano in Havana, which is like Cannes without the ass kissing (p105). To say that Cubans are cinema buffs is an understatement: the crush of a crowd shattered the glass doors of a movie theater during the 2001 Festival and an adoring mob nearly rioted trying to get into Steven Spielberg's *Minority Report* premier in 2002. If you're headed for a flick, queue early.

Whatever your reason for discovering Cuba, every traveler should bone up on some José Martí before or after touchdown. Ocean Press's 1999 anthology *José Martí Reader: Writings on the Americas* is split into political essays, letters and poetry and makes a wonderful, thoughtful introduction.

In *Hemingway Adventure*, fellow traveler Michael Palin is on another of his international romps, this time traipsing in the wake of Hemingway from Valencia to Havana – lots of luscious visuals.

Cuban television is special (not least of all because the most unattractive people you're likely to see in Cuba are on it). There are only three national channels, no commercials and charming touches (eg the nightly programming announcement closes with the advisory: 'consume only what is necessary'). Educational programming dominates, with Universidad Para Todos offering full university-level courses in everything from astronomy to film editing and Canal Educativo broadcasting primary and secondary classes. The news is a predictable litany of good things Cuba has done (eg big tobacco harvest, sending doctors to Africa) and bad things the US is up to (eg mucking around in the Middle East, big corporations buying influence). *Mesa Redonda* (Round Table) is a nightly program where several people sharing the same opinion sit around discussing a topic of national or global import. Soap operas are a national obsession and things often grind to a halt when the *telenovela* starts.

Dance

Cuban ballet is synonymous with prima ballerina Alicia Alonso. Well past her *pointe* days, she cofounded the Ballet Nacional de Cuba and her choreography is still in heavy rotation – classic stuff like *Don Quixote* and *Giselle*, with few surprises save the powerful dancers themselves. The International Ballet Festival (p86) takes Havana by storm every other year, when you can see a *Swan Lake* matinee and an evening performance of *Carmen* – a ballet junkie's dream. The Ballet de Camagüey also features talented dancers, with a riskier, less formal, repertory.

Modern dance mixing ballet, folklore and sensualized choreography is the purview of DanzAbierta, Así Somos (founded by US-born Lorna Burdsall in 1981) and Danza Teatro Retazos. The latter is directed by Ecuadorian spitfire Isabel Bustos, who also organizes the Encuentro Internacional de Danza en Paisajes Urbanos, when national and international dance companies take over the streets of Habana Vieja. Danza Contemporánea de Cuba (also cofounded by Burdsall) blends ballet with Cuban rhythms and themes that some purists find too commercial. Still, the dancing is exceptional and the company has fresh choreography, costuming and storytelling ideas. The flexible Lizt Alfonso company has been turning heads lately with their unique blend of Cuban, African and Spanish rhythms and moves. Look for their work called *Elementos*.

The repertory of the Conjunto Folklórico Nacional de Cuba (founded in 1962) is a veritable history of Cuban popular dance, and the palpitating rainbow of traditional Afro-Cuban dances they perform often has Teatro Mella audiences on their feet. You can rumba along with them every Saturday at Havana's El Gran Palenque (p102). La Colmenita is Cuba's respected National Children's Theater Company whose cast of seven- to 15-year-olds interprets classics like Shakespeare's *A Midsummer Night's Dream*.

Of course, Cuba also means salsa. Kids here pair off as soon as they can walk and once the basic steps and turns are rote they move on to *la rueda* (the wheel), where two concentric circles move in opposite directions – boys on the outside, girls on the inside – with each pair taking a twirl together before the wheel turns and they're dancing with someone new. It's as hard as it looks, and you might want to look into some classes when you arrive (p411).

The Environment

THE LAND

With Isla de Juventud, 4195 little low-lying islets and the crocodile-shaped main island, Cuba covers about 110,860 sq km all told. The main island is the world's 15th largest and you can drive from western to eastern tip (1250km) in about 30 hours on mostly good roads. Cuba measures 31km at its skinniest point in western Havana Province, and 191km wide at the 'head' of the crocodile in Camagüey.

Cuba's history and destiny is written by its geography. Cuba's economy flourished in the early colonial period when excellent harbors in Havana, Gibara, Santiago de Cuba and elsewhere hosted Spanish fleets carrying riches between the Old World and New. These days, Cuba's 5746km of coastline, 289 natural beaches and vibrant coral reef (one of the largest in the world and home to over 900 reported fish species and 410 sponge and coral species) is a marine wonderland enticing tourists from all over the globe. Cuba is banking upon these natural attractions for its financial future as it aims to triple tourism revenue by 2010. See National Parks (p48).

The country boasts thousands of islands and cays (most uninhabited) in four major offshore groups: the Archipiélago de los Colorados, off northern Pinar del Río; the Archipiélago de Sabana-Camagüey (or Jardines del Rey), off northern Villa Clara and Ciego de Ávila; the Archipiélago de los Jardines de la Reina, off southern Ciego de Ávila; and the Archipiélago de los Canarreos, around Isla de la Juventud. Most visitors will experience one or more of these island idylls, as the majority of resorts, scuba diving and virgin beaches are found here.

The foamy, white chop of the Atlantic Ocean hugs Cuba's north shore, while the calmer, more brackish Caribbean Sea is to the south. Though more prone to winter cold fronts, the north shore is where you'll find the powdery sands and turquoise and emerald swirls that make Caribbean islands famous. The southern coast is more aggressive, bedeviled by *diente de perro* (jagged rocks that line the shore), but has good fishing and unexplored pockets. Cuba is separated from Haiti by the 77km-wide Windward Passage to the east and is 210km northeast from Mexico across the Yucatán Strait. Jamaica is 270km southwest of Santiago de Cuba and Florida's Key West is 170km northeast of Havana across the treacherous Florida Straits.

The 7200m-deep Cayman Trench between Cuba and Jamaica forms the boundary of the North American and Caribbean plates. Tectonic movements have tilted the island over time, creating uplifted limestone cliffs along parts of the north coast and low mangrove swamps on the south. Over millions of years, Cuba's limestone bedrock has been eroded by underground rivers, creating interesting geological features including the 'haystack' hills of Viñales and more than 20,000 caves countrywide.

Between 25% and 30% of Cuba's mountain ranges are forested, in no small part thanks to reforestation programs in the past 30 years. In Pinar del Río the 175km-long Cordillera de Guaniguanico includes the Sierra de los Órganos and the Sierra del Rosario, neither higher than 699m. Through Cuba's center is the Sierra del Escambray (also known as Sierra de Guamuhaya), which reaches 1140m. To the southeast the rolling countryside of Camagüey climbs into the rugged Sierra Maestra of the Oriente, with the highest peak in the country, Pico Turquino (1972m). The Sierra Maestra stretches 250km from Guantánamo Bay to Cabo Cruz.

DID YOU KNOW?

The respected culture magazine *Caimán Barbudo* takes its name from Cuba's crocodile shape (a caiman is a tropical reptile like a crocodile) and the bearded guerillas (*barbudos*) who fought in the revolution.

Each year hurricanes rip through Cuba blowing over houses, cattle and trees. Hurricane Michelle in 2001 was the worst storm to hit Cuba in 50 years. Get the latest big storm statistics and photos from www.fema.gov.

The one thing Cuba lacks is large lakes and rivers (preventing hydroelectricity). Cuba's longest river is the 343km-long Cauto, north of Bayamo, but it's only navigable by small boats. To compensate, 632 *embalses* or *presas* (reservoirs), larger than 5km altogether, have been created for irrigation and water supply, supplementing the almost unlimited groundwater held in Cuba's limestone bedrock.

WILDLIFE

As isolated landmasses, islands allow unique species to develop, but the fixed amount of resources and competition means predators overrun their prey like hungry tourists at an all-you-can-eat buffet. Construction, waste disposal and population movements also affect wildlife.

Animals

Though Cuba is not known for its wildlife, it hosts 350 varieties of birds and enthusiasts will not be disappointed. Head to the mangroves of Ciénaga de Zapata near the Bay of Pigs or the Península de Guanahacabibes in Pinar del Río and you'll see the incredible *zunzuncito* (bee hummingbird), the world's smallest bird; it's smaller than a toothpick. These areas are also home to the *tocororo* (Cuban trogon), Cuba's national bird, which has red, white and blue plumes. According to ornithologists, the *carpintero real* (royal carpenter woodpecker), last seen in the area of Parque Nacional Alejandro de Humboldt near Baracoa in the late 1980s and believed extinct, may still exist in Cuba. See those regional chapters for more information.

Land mammals have been hunted almost to extinction and it's telling that the largest indigenous one remaining is the *jutía* (tree rat), a 4kg edible rodent that survives on isolated cays. Other odd species include the *mariposa de cristal* (Cuban clearwing butterfly), one of only two clearwinged butterflies in the world; the rare *manjuarí* (Cuban alligator gar), an odd, ancient fish considered a living fossil; and the *polimita*, a unique land snail distinguished by its festive yellow, red and brown bands. Many of these species are so rare that you may not see them outside of reserves or museums. *Polimitas* are used to make necklaces and are peddled all over the Baracoa area.

Reptiles are well represented in Cuba. There are crocodiles, iguanas, lizards, and 15 species of snakes, none of which are poisonous. Cuba's largest snake is the *majá*, a constrictor related to the anaconda that grows up to 4m long; it's nocturnal and doesn't usually mess with humans.

Cuba's marine life makes up for what it lacks in land fauna. The manatee is found in the Bahía de Taco and the Península de Zapata, and whale sharks frequent the María la Gorda area at Cuba's eastern tip from August to November. Four turtle species (leatherback, loggerhead, green and hawksbill) call Cuban seas home and the green moray eel, at 2m or more, is the largest moray found in this part of the world.

Plants

Think Cuba and you think palm trees, and the two are inextricably linked. The national tree is the *palma real* (royal palm), and it's central to the country's coat of arms and Cristal beer logo (you'll see plenty of those!). It's believed there are 20 million royal palms in Cuba. Marching single file by the roadside or clumped on a hill, these majestic trees reach up to 40m tall and are easily identified by their lithesome trunk and green stalk at the top. There are also *cocotero* (coconut palms); *palma barrigona* (big belly palms), with their characteristic bulge; and the extremely rare *palma corcho* (cork palm). This link with the Cretaceous period (between 65 and 135 million years ago) is cherished as a living fossil. You can see examples of it on the grounds of the Museo de Ciencias Naturales Sandalio de Noda or La Ermita, both in Pinar del Río Province (see p48). All told, there are 90 palm tree types in Cuba.

Other important trees among the more than 6000 superior plant species in Cuba include mangroves and pines. Spiderlike mangroves protect the shoreline from erosion and provide an important habitat for small fish and birds. Accounting for 26% of Cuban forests and covering almost 5% of the island's coast, Cuba ranks ninth in global mangrove density; the most extensive swamps are in the Ciénaga de Zapata. The largest pine forests grow on Isla de la Juventud, in western Pinar del Río, in eastern Holguín Province and in central Guantánamo. These forests are especially susceptible to fire damage, and much pine reforestation has been necessary.

Rain forests exist at higher altitudes, between 500m and 1500m, in the Escambray, Sierra Maestra and Macizo de Sagua-Baracoa. Original rain forest species include ebony and mahogany, but today most reforestation is in eucalyptus, which is graceful and fragrant, but invasive.

Ferns, cacti and orchids contribute hundreds of species, many endemic, to Cuba's total tally. There are botanical gardens dedicated to ferns and cacti in Santiago de Cuba (p381), and orchids in Pinar del Río (p181). Although most orchids bloom from November to January, which is when you're likely to see them in the wild, many types bloom year-round at botanical gardens. The national flower is the *mariposa* (butterfly jasmine); you'll know it by its white floppy petals and strong perfume.

Due to a chronic shortage of prescription medicines (largely thanks to the US embargo), Cubans have expanded their use of medicinal plants. Pharmacies are well stocked with effective tinctures like aloe (for cough and congestion) and a bee by-product called *propólio*, used for everything from stomach amoebas to respiratory infections. On the home front, every Cuban patio usually has a pot of *orégano de la tierra* growing and if you start getting a cold you'll be whipped up a wonder elixir made from the fat, flat leaves mixed with lime juice, honey and hot water.

DID YOU KNOW?

Propólio is a wonder remedy containing all the vitamins the body needs except K, and 13 of the 14 necessary minerals (it lacks sulfur). Research studies are investigating its effectiveness in fighting *E. coli* and salmonella.

UNESCO WORLD HERITAGE & BIOSPHERE RESERVE SITES

There are currently six Unesco Biosphere Reserves in Cuba and seven World Heritage sites. A few more sites, such as the coastal area from Guantánamo to Maísi in Guantánamo Province, are under consideration.

The Biosphere Reserves are: the Reserva Sierra del Rosario (25,000 hectares) and the Reserva Península de Guanahacabibes (101,500 hectares), both in Pinar del Río; Ciénega de Zapata (628,171 hectares, declared in 2001) in Matanzas; Buenavista (313,500 hectares, declared in 2000) in parts of Villa Clara, Sancti Spíritus and Ciego de Ávila; Parque Baconao (84,600 hectares) in Santiago de Cuba; and the Reserva Cuchillas de Toa (127,500 hectares) in Guantánamo. The Reserva Sierra del Rosario was declared in 1985, the rest in 1987. Standards, services and administration of these reserves vary greatly. For example, the Península de Guanahacabibes is carefully protected, while Parque Baconao has small communities and many tourist installations within its boundaries.

Cuba boasts seven World Heritage sites: Habana Vieja, the historical core of Havana (declared in 1982); Trinidad and adjacent Valle de los Ingenios (1988) in Sancti Spíritus; Castillo de San Pedro del Morro (1997) and the First Coffee Plantations in the Southeast of Cuba (2000), both in Santiago de Cuba; Desembarco del Granma (1999) in Granma; Viñales Valley (1999) in Pinar del Río; and Alejandro de Humboldt (2001) in Guantánamo.

NATIONAL PARKS

When it comes to any type of protected area – reserve, national park or coastal zone – things are changing fast in Cuba. Since the government recognizes the amazing tourist potential offered by pristine landscapes, new parks are being proposed in rapid succession. In existing parks, visitors centers are being built, trails are being developed and guides are being trained. At present, more than 14% of the country is protected in some way. Still, scarce funds and a steep learning curve mean installations and services in Cuban parks may not be what you're used to in Europe or the US.

At the time of writing, there were six national parks: Parque Nacional Península de Guanahacabibes and Parque Nacional Viñales, both in Pinar del Río; the Gran Parque Natural Montemar (commonly called Parque Nacional Ciénaga de Zapata) in Matanzas; Parque Nacional Desembarco del Granma in Granma and Gran Parque Nacional Sierra Maestra (split between Granma and Santiago de Cuba Provinces); and Parque Nacional Alejandro de Humboldt in Guantánamo. For information on areas with those distinctions, see the boxed text below.

Marine parks under consideration include Punta Francés at Isla de la Juventud; Cayo Piedras del Norte, Cayo Mono and the Península de Hicacos, all in Varadero; and parts of Península de Guanahacabibes, including María la Gorda.

DID YOU KNOW?

It's estimated the Caribbean Sea will rise an incredible 20cm by the year 2030 due to climactic changes like the greenhouse effect.

Park	Features	Activities	Best Time to Visit	Page
Península de Guanahacabibes	mangrove/beach: whale sharks, marine turtles, rare birds	scuba diving, remote hiking, birding	Jun–Oct for nesting turtles, few visitors	170
Viñales	verdant valley: caves, pincushion hills, tobacco fields, visitors center	spelunking, hiking, horseback riding, rock climbing	year-round	173
Ciénaga de Zapata	wetland: mangroves, 190 bird species, manatees, crocodile breeding, Taino village replica	birding, boat tours, fishing	Nov–Apr	217
Sierra Maestra	mountain: Cuban Revolution HQ, cloud forest, high peaks, views, museum	trekking, camping	Oct–May dry season	341 & 386
Desembarco del Granma	forest/beach: rain forest, reef, trails, *Granma* replica, cacti, lighthouse, caves, petroglyphs	hiking, spelunking, swimming, fishing	Sep–Jun	348
Alejandro de Humboldt	mangrove/forest: well-protected bayside setting, on-site specialists, visitors center, manatees, trails	boat tours, birding, hiking	year-round	404

ENVIRONMENTAL ISSUES

Cuba's greatest environmental problems are aggravated by an economy struggling to survive. As the country pins its hopes on tourism to save the financial day, a schizophrenic environmental policy has evolved, cutting right to the heart of the dilemma: how can a developing nation provide for its people *and* maintain high (or at least minimal) ecological standards?

One disaster in this struggle, most experts agree, was the 2km-long stone causeway *(pedraplén)* constructed to link offshore Cayo Sabinal with mainland Camagüey. This massive project involved piling boulders in the sea and laying a road on top, which interrupted water currents and caused irreparable damage to bird and marine life habitats. Other longer causeways were built connecting Los Jardines del Rey to Ciego de Ávila (27km long; p282) and Cayo Santa María to Villa Clara (a 48km-long monster; p248). The full extent of the ecological damage wreaked by these causeways won't be known for another decade at least.

Building new roads and airports, package tourism that shuttles large groups of people into sensitive habitats and the frenzied construction of giant resorts on virgin beaches exacerbates the clash between human activity and environmental protection. The grossly shrunken extents of the Reserva Ecológica Varahicacos in Varadero due to encroaching resorts is just one example. Dolphins rounded up as entertainers has rankled activists as well. Overfishing (including turtles and lobster for tourist consumption), agricultural runoff, industrial pollution and inadequate sewage treatment have contributed to the decay of coral reefs, and diseases like yellow band, black band and nuisance algae have begun to appear.

As soon as you arrive in Havana or Santiago de Cuba you'll realize that air pollution is a problem. Airborne particles, old cars belching black smoke and by-products from burning garbage are some of the culprits. Cement factories, sugar refineries and other heavy industry take their toll. The nickel mines engulfing Moa serve as stark examples of industrial concerns taking precedence: this is some of the prettiest landscape in Cuba, made a barren wasteland of lunar proportions.

On the bright side is the enthusiasm the government has shown for reforestation and protecting natural areas – there are several on the drawing board – and its willingness to confront mistakes from the past. Havana Harbor, once Latin America's most polluted, has been undergoing a massive clean-up project, as has the Río Almendares, which cuts through the heart of the city. Both programs are beginning to show positive results. Sulfur emissions from oil wells near Varadero have been reduced and environmental regulations for developments are now enforced by the Ministry of Science, Technology and the Environment. Fishing regulations, as local fisherman will tell you, have become increasingly strict. Striking the balance between Cuba's immediate needs and the future of its environment is one of the revolution's increasingly pressing challenges.

DID YOU KNOW?

The Cuban government planted over three billion trees in a reforestation program known as Plan Manatí. Though half of those trees perished, another reforestation program aims to recover a million hectares with new trees by 2015.

Food & Drink

DID YOU KNOW?

During the worst of the Special Period (1990–95), every adult Cuban lost between 5lb and 20lb due to food shortages (see p33).

Let's face it, you don't come to Cuba for the food. But while Cuban cuisine is often portrayed as bad, boring or both, the truth is Cuban cooks are extraordinarily creative, and home cooking, whether in someone's home or paladar, is plentiful and delicious – and grease-laden: anyone with high cholesterol might consider vacationing elsewhere.

Resort food is a different story. If you're headed to a good all-inclusive resort, there will be tomatoes in August and cheese year-round. Eating options shrink astronomically as soon as you venture outside the home, paladar or resort and you'll probably find yourself going hungry at least once during your travels. To avoid this fate, see the boxed text below.

STAPLES & SPECIALTIES

Known as *comida criolla* (Creole food), Cuban meals always feature *congrí*, fried plantains (green bananas) and salad. *Congrí* is rice flecked with black beans. In the Oriente it's called *moros y cristianos* (literally 'Moors and Christians') or *congrí oriental* if the beans are red. 'Salad' is a euphemism for 'whatever raw thing is available,' mostly tomato or cucumber slices and/or shredded cabbage.

Protein means pork and you'll become well acquainted with *lomo ahumado* (aromatic smoked loin), *chuletas* (thin juicy filet) and fricassee with peppers and onions. *Filete Uruguayo* is a breaded, deep-fried cutlet stuffed with ham and cheese.

It will seem like Cuban chickens are born already fried and any *pescado* (fish) has made for distant waters. Though you'll come across *pargo* (red snapper) occasionally, you're more likely to see lobster or shrimp *ajillo* (sautéed in oil and garlic) or *enchilado* (in tomato sauce). *Ostiones*, small oysters served with tomato sauce and lime juice, are also popular. Cows

STAYING FED

In Cuba, someone who is always eating, grazing through the streets like a goat on a grassy knoll, is a *jamaliche* or *camelón* (*camelona* in the case of the author). Even if you're on a packaged tour with meals prearranged or at an all-inclusive resort, there's bound to be a moment when you think, 'Gee, I'm hungry.' Here's some advice to keep fellow *jamaliches* fed:

- Always carry some pesos: ice cream, peanuts, pizza, egg sandwiches, fruitshakes, bread, fruits and vegetables are all sold in pesos.
- Always carry a spare plastic bag; you never know when you'll see a bakery or fruit market and have to tote some goodies.
- 24-hour peso stalls (usually with great variety) congregate near hospitals; there are always food stalls in vegetable markets.
- Bring a stash of dried apricots, almonds or other lightweight, high-protein treats from home.
- Be willing to eat fried food, including unidentifiable tidbits sold on the street.
- Carry a spare package of cookies at all times.
- Look for good yogurt in dollar stores and cafeterias.
- Harvest fruit from trees on roads and in parks (guava, mango, avocado etc).
- Rent a room with kitchen privileges, hit the *agropecuario* (vegetable market) and have a dinner party.

are government controlled, so beef products such as steak are sold only in state-run restaurants. Fast-food places sell tasty hamburgers, though there's probably more ham than burger in there.

Yuca (cassava) and *calabaza* (pumpkin-like squash) are served with an insanely addictive sauce called *mojo* made from oil, garlic and bitter orange. Green beans, beets and avocados (June to August) are likely to cross your lips too. However, you're likely to see more vegetables at the market than on your plate.

Very few restaurants do breakfast (though pastries are sold at chains like Pain de Paris and Doña Nely), so if this is an important meal for you, graze at a hotel buffet or arrange for your casas particulares to provide it. Most casas do huge, wonderful breakfasts of eggs, toast, fresh juice, coffee and piles of fruit for US$2 to US$3.

Cuba is famous for its *mojitos* and, if you can't stand another mound of rice and beans, we suggest a liquid supper of these smooth cocktails made from rum, mint, sugar, seltzer and fresh lime juice.

Desserts

At last count there were 14 brands of *helado* (ice cream) and Cubans are aficionados (eg Alondra's strawberry tastes fake, while Nevada's hazelnut is creamy). Coppelia's ice cream is legendary with reason: the ice cream and the outlet's atmosphere are unrivaled and the peso experience is a must. See the boxed text 'Making Cents of Coppelia' (p98).

Flan is baked custard with a caramel glaze served in individual portions. Cubans also make pumpkin and coconut flan of Spanish origin. *Pudin* (bread pudding) is not only charmingly Spanglish, it tastes divine.

DRINKS
Alcoholic Drinks

In Cuba it's all about the rum *(ron)*. Minty mojitos, Cuba libres (rum and Coke), daiquirís, Cubanitos (rum and tomato juice), straight up or on the rocks, it's served all ways. Havana Club is Cuba's most famous brand, with Silver Dry (the cheapest) and three-year-old Carta Blanca used for mixed drinks, while five-year-old Carta de Oro and seven-year-old Añejo are best enjoyed in a highball. Cuba's finest rum is Matusalem Añejo Superior, brewed in Santiago de Cuba since 1872. Other top brands include Varadero, Caribbean Club and Caney (made at the old Bacardí factory in Santiago de Cuba, though the name Bacardí is anathema as the exiled family decided to sue the Cuban government under US embargo laws). Sharing your bottle is all you need to know about Cuban party etiquette.

Fermented cane is called *aguardiente* (fire water) and a few shots will knock you on your ass. In bodegas it's sold as *ron a granel* for 20 pesos ($0.77 per 1500ml) – bring an empty bottle. Local nicknames for this hooch include 'drop her drawers' and 'train spark.' Popular bottled brands are Santero and El Niño. Cubans also make fruit wines from mango, pineapple or raisins. Big city stores usually carry a limited selection of Spanish, Chilean and Cuban wines. Top beer brands include Mayabe (3.8% alcohol) and Hatuey (5.4%). These are like microbreweries though, and you'll spend most of your time drinking super light Cristal (4.9%) or Bucanero (5.4%). Imported beers include Lagarto, Bavaria and Heineken.

Nonalcoholic Drinks

Cuban coffee *(cafecito* or *café cubano)* is strong, black and super sweet. Coffee sold in pesos usually has the sugar already added. A morning treat is a big cup of *café con leche* (a mixture of strong coffee and hot milk) or

DID YOU KNOW?

Killing cows is illegal; the government uses them to produce beef for peso and dollar restaurants and milk for the guaranteed rations offered to babies, pregnant women, pensioners and the sick (see the boxed text, p37).

To discover which Havana Club rums have accents of vanilla and tobacco, while boning up on the Bacardí case or learning how to mix a Cuba Bella, visit www.havanaclub foundation.com.

There is nothing more satisfying than a hearty *comida criolla* followed by an aromatic cigar. Visit www.habanos.net for all the tobacco facts.

leche con chocolate (sickly sweet hot chocolate). *Café americano* is diluted Cuban coffee and only worth mentioning so you can avoid it. There isn't much of a tea *(té)* culture in Cuba, but you can always get a pot of hot water at hotels or restaurants. Tea bags are sold in dollar stores.

Any place serving mojitos can whip up a refreshing *limonada* (limeade). Pure fruit juice *(jugo)*, instant powdered drink *(refresco)* and fruit milkshakes *(batidos)* are sold in street stalls for a few pesos. Note that they are made with water and/or ice, so if you have a sensitive stomach you might take a pass.

Guarapo is sugarcane juice freshly pressed from whole stalks and cooled with ice. Look for stands called *guaraperas*, where they sell glasses of it for one peso (US$0.03). Tourist stalls peddle the same stuff for US$1. *Prú* is a special nonalcoholic brew from the Oriente made from spices, fermented *yuca* (cassava) and secret ingredients *prú*-meisters won't divulge.

Tap water quality is variable and many Cubans have gory amoebic tales, including giardia. To be safe you can drink bottled water *(agua natural)*, but that gets expensive over longer trips. You can also boil it (the local method) or buy bottled chlorine drops called Gotica. Available in most dollar stores for US$1.25, one drop makes three liters of drinkable water; this works well in the provinces, but in Havana it's better to boil or buy bottled water

CELEBRATIONS

New Year's Eve, birthdays, family reunions: whatever the reason, big events are celebrated with *lechón asado* (roast pork). As much about the process and camaraderie as the food, a pig roast is a communal effort where the jokes fly, the rum flows and dancing or *dominó* somehow figures in. Once the pig is killed, cleaned and seasoned, it's slowly pit-roasted over a charcoal fire. Traditional sides include *yuca con mojo*, *congrí* and salad. Stall after stall peddles freshly carved *lechón asado*, sliced down the middle and splayed on platters, during Holguín's Carnival (see p319), and many families celebrate Christmas Eve *(Noche Buena)* with this local favorite.

WHERE TO EAT & DRINK
State-Run Restaurants

Restaurant opening hours are generally 11am to 11pm daily. Don't take it as fact if a restaurant says it's open 24 hours. Government or state-run restaurants are either in pesos or dollars. Peso restaurants are notorious for handing you a nine-page menu (in Spanish), when the only thing available is fried chicken. You might sit around for half an hour before learning this while the waitress gossips, picks at her nails or disappears. Some peso restaurants, however, are quite good; all are absurdly cheap and they're often your only option off the tourist circuit, so don't discount them altogether (Doña Yulla is a nationwide chain to look out for). Sometimes workers in peso restaurants either won't show you the menu in an effort to overcharge you, or they will charge dollars at a one-to-one ratio – making the food ridiculously overpriced. Verify *before* you order that you're looking at peso prices (meals will be in the 15- to 25-peso range). Sometimes peso restaurants have one menu in dollars at a reasonable rate and another in pesos.

Dollar restaurants are generally more reliable, but this isn't capitalism: just because you're paying more doesn't necessarily mean better service, more variety or more food; in fact, portions in peso restaurants tend to be larger. Pizza Nova is a good nationwide chain, as is El Rápido, with

US$1 microwave pizzas, hot dogs and sandwiches. Cuba would do well to open more La Vicarias, where the service is uniformly good, the prices fair and the food palatable. All state-run restaurant employees earn the standard US$8 to US$13 a month, so tips are highly appreciated (see the boxed text below).

Paladares

The Cuban dining scene brightened considerably with the advent of private restaurants in 1995. Legally, paladares can only have 12 seats and cannot serve beef, lobster or shrimp. In practise, however, paladares routinely offer forbidden foods and have doors leading from the kitchen to back rooms or patios where they accommodate more than 12 diners.

Because these restaurants are in private residences (and the owners pay a stiff monthly tax for the privilege), each atmosphere is different, from romantic garden dining to windowless rooms with the air-con set to 'polar cap.' Some paladares have written menus, while others don't; some take pesos, but most want dollars. If there's a menu, check how much beer costs, and if it's over $10 (dollars and pesos use the same symbol!) you can assume the menu is in pesos, which always works out cheaper. In dollar terms, a filling meal costs anywhere between US$4 and US$12. Always check prices beforehand, as some paladares are just rip-offs. If a paladar doesn't have a written menu with prices listed, it's a negative sign. Many paladares have two or three menus all listing the same dishes but with different prices, depending on how much they think you might be willing to pay (often directly related to your Spanish abilities) and whether a commission must be paid to the *jinetero* who led you there. These touts will add a few dollars to each meal.

We list as many paladares as possible in this book, but the situation is changing fast and many places close down when owners emigrate or can't pay their taxes. The government has become increasingly strict with inspections and licensing, making it more difficult than ever to maintain a paladar. There's always someone willing to cook meals clandestinely (ie non-tax paying), but this can incur heavy fines, so discretion is advised.

To allow our readers to quickly distinguish between private and state-run restaurants, we call all privately operated eateries 'paladares.' Whenever this book refers to a 'restaurant,' it means it's a government-operated place. The majority of paladares are open noon to midnight, usually daily, although some take a day off (often Monday).

Quick Eats

Like all private industry, *cafeterías* (street stalls) are government regulated, so hygiene is usually not a problem. Cuban street pizza, with its pungent

TIPPING & RESERVATIONS

Unless you've had one of those infamous Cuba experiences where you waited forever for your meal while attended by a moping waitress with a smirk and then *still* had to dispute the bill, you should leave a tip. This holds true for places in pesos or dollars, state-run or private. In Cuba, a 10% tip is sufficient, with US$1 being the appropriate minimum. Keep in mind that workers in dollar restaurants (and some paladares) are still earning pesos. Tipping in peso restaurants is not compulsory, but is greatly appreciated; these folks take home in a month what we normally spend on a movie back home. Leaving 10 pesos or US$0.50 in convertible peso change is a generous tip.

Unless you're in a large group or want to eat at one of the chic, trendy paladares (eg La Guarida in Havana), there's no need for a reservation.

cheese and great price (US$0.25), is legendary. Good standards on th street dining scene include *batidos*, *asado* (roasted) or breaded pork cutle sandwiches, fruit cocktail and ice cream. There's also a whole category o *pan con...* (bread with...) – whatever can be put inside bread, from tortill (tasty eggs) to pasta (an icky mayonnaise substance).

Keep an eye out for stalls and windows with '*comida criolla*' signs These places sell *cajitas* (literally 'little boxes'): full meals of salad, bake vegetables, *congrí* and pork cutlets are sold in little take-away boxes wit a cardboard spoon cutout on the lid for US$1.

All street food is sold in pesos. For more information see the boxe text (p50).

VEGETARIANS & VEGANS

Strict vegetarians (ie no lard, no meat bullion, no fish) will have a hard time in Cuba due to the traditionally carnivorous diet. Time of year plays a part as well: for example, fruit and veggie variety is scarce in the hottes months (June to September). Vegetarianism might also be interpreted as 'no meat chunks in the soup,' so they've been picked out just before serving. Still, a flurry of new vegetarian restaurants in Havana (see the boxed text p95) and a nationwide educational campaign mean Cubans are increasingly aware of the health benefits of a vegetarian diet. Cooks in casas particulares who may already have had experience cooking meatless dishes are more than happy to accommodate vegetarians; just ask.

Vegans have little choice but to cook for themselves. Many people rent rooms with kitchen privileges or entire self-sufficient apartments; this book makes a conscious effort to provide information about cooking options in casas particulares. Other resources for serious vegans and/or vegetarians include:

agropecuarios – vegetable markets; also sell rice, beans, fruit (for a list of Havana's best markets, see p99)

organopónicos – organic vegetable markets

yogurt de soya – soy yogurt (sold in bodegas; regular yogurt is sold in dollar stores)

proteina vegetal – dried soy protein (sold in bodegas)

spirulina – spirulina powder (an aquatic plant offering high protein and vitamins)

EAT YOUR WORDS

Managing a menu in Spanish, making special requests or maneuvering a meal in pesos – your eating options will expand if you can speak the language. For pronunciation guidelines see p443.

Useful Phrases

Is there food?   *¿Hay comida?*
ai ko·*mee*·da

What kind of food is there?   *¿Qué comida hay?*
ke ko·*mee*·da ai

Can I see the menu?   *¿Puedo ver la carta?*
pwe·do ver la *kar*·ta

Do you have a menu in English?   *¿Tiene una carta en inglés?*
tye·ne *oo*·na *kar*·ta en een·*gles*

This menu is in pesos, right?   *¿Esta carta está en moneda nacional, verdad?*
es·ta *kar*·ta es·*ta* en mo·*ne*·da na·syo·*nal* ver·*da*

Do you have a napkin?   *¿Tiene una servilleta?*
tye·ne *oo*·na ser·vee·*lye*·ta

Pardon me, but the bill is wrong.   *Disculpame, pero la cuenta tiene un error.*
dees·kool·pa·me pe·ro la *kwen*·ta *tye*·ne oon e·ror

re you open?   *¿Está trabajando/abierto?*
    es·*ta* tra·ba·*khan*·do/a·*byer*·to
What does this dish come with?   *¿Con qué sale?*
    kon ke *sa*·le
m a vegetarian.   *Soy vegetariano/a.*
    soy ve·khe·ta·*rya*·no/a

Menu Decoder

jiaco (a·*khya*·ko) – a 'kitchen sink' stew that has potatoes, squash, malanga, plantains, corn, meat, tomato paste, spices, old beer, lemon juice and whatever else is around

rroz con pollo (a·*ros* kon po·*lyo*) – rice and bits of chicken mixed together

ocadito (bo·ka·*dee*·to) – sandwich on round bread

afé cortado (ka·*fe* kor·*ta*·do) – espresso with a shot of milk

ajita (ka·*khee*·ta) – take-out meal that comes in a small box

aldosa (kal·*do*·sa) – similar to *ajiaco*; literally 'stew'

hicharitas/mariquitas (chee·cha·*ree*·tas/ ma·ree·*kee*·tas) – plantain (green banana) chips; sometimes made from potatoes or malanga

hicharrones (chee·cha·*ro*·nes) – fried pork rinds

rema de queso (*kre*·ma de *ke*·so) – heavy cheese soup that has as much flour as cheese; variations include crema Aurora and crema Virginia

ntremes (en·tre·*mes*) – finger food or appetizer, usually with ham and cheese slices and green olives; sometimes quite large servings

ilete Canciller (fi·*le*·te kan·see·*lyer*) – breaded fish stuffed with ham and cheese

ilete Monte Toro (fi·*le*·te mon·te *to*·ro) – delicately breaded fish filet, fried and stuffed with cheese

ilete Uruguayo (fi·*le*·te oo·ro·*gwai*·yo) – fried, breaded pork cutlet stuffed with ham and cheese

ordon Bleu (gor·don bloo) – chicken stuffed with ham and cheese; charming anthropomorphism of *cordon bleu*

uarnición (gwar·nee·*syon*) – side dish

ígado a la italiana (ee·ga·do a la ee·tal·*ya*·na) – liver sautéed in tomato sauce, with peppers and onions

omo ahumado (*lo*·mo a·oo·*ma*·do) – smoked pork loin

otaje (po·*ta*·khe) – subtly spiced black beans with pork bones or chunks, served in its own soupy uices

opa vieja (*ro*·pa *vye*·kha) – traditional Cuban dish of mounds of shredded beef livened with tomatoes and onions; only available in state-run restaurants

ervicio incluído (ser·*vee*·syo een·kloo·*ee*·do) – tip included

able 1, 2 etc (*ta*·ble oo·no dos etc) – different meal offers (distinguished by the numbers) that include a main dish, salad, side and dessert, usually with smaller portions

amal en cazuela (ta·*mal* en ka·*swe*·la) – ground fresh corn, boiled with meat and spices and erved in a pot; called *tamales* when wrapped in corn husks

ostones (tos·*to*·nes) – fried plantain patties

vegetales Macedonias (ve·khe·*ta*·les ma·se·*don*·yas) – a mix of carrots and green beans boiled o death or canned

vianda (vee·*an*·dah) – any root vegetable (potato, yuca, *malanga*, *boniato*, plantain etc). This appears on many menus as *vianda frita*.

Spanish-English Glossary

FRUTAS (FRUITS)

fruta bomba	*froo*·ta *bom*·ba	papaya
guayaba	gwa·*ya*·ba	guava
mamey	*ma*·me	brown-skinned fruit with orange flesh
melón	me·*lon*	watermelon
naranja (agria)	na·*ran*·kha (a·gree·a)	orange (bitter)
piña	*pee*·nya	pineapple
plátano fruta	*pla*·ta·no *froo*·ta	banana

toronja	*to·ron·kha*	grapefruit
zapote	*sa·po·te*	brown-skinned fruit with orange flesh

VERDURAS (VEGETABLES)

berenjena	*be·ren·kha*	eggplant
boniato	*bo·nya·to*	sweet potato
calabaza	*ka·la·ba·sa*	squash
champiñon	*cham·pee·nyon*	mushroom
espinaca	*es·pee·na·ka*	spinach
maíz	*mai·ees*	corn
malanga	*ma·lan·ga*	root vegetable similar to taro
papa	*pa·pa*	potato
plátano verde	*pla·ta·no ver·de*	green plantain (savory)
plátano maduro	*pla·ta·no ma·doo·ro*	green plantain (sweet)

ENSALADA (SALAD)

aguacate	*a·gwa·ka·te*	avocado
aliño	*a·lee·nyo*	oil and vinegar dressing/carafes
berro	*be·ro*	watercress
col	kol	cabbage
ensalada de estación	*en·sa·la·da de es·ta·syon*	seasonal salad
ensalada mixta	*en·sa·la·da meeks·ta*	mixed salad; usually tomatoes, cucumbers and cabbage/lettuce
habichuela	*a·bee·chwe·la*	green beans
lechuga	*le·choo·ga*	lettuce
pepino	*pe·pee·no*	cucumber
remolacha	*re·mo·la·cha*	beets
zanahoria	*sa·na·o·rya*	carrot

CARNE (MEAT)

cerdo	*ser·do*	pork
chorizo	*cho·ree·so*	sausage
jamón	*kha·mon*	ham
lechón asado	*le·chon a·sa·do*	roast pork
picadillo	*pee·ka·dee·lyo*	ground beef
pollo frito	*po·lyo free·to*	fried chicken
puerco	*pwer·ko*	pork

PESCADO & MARISCOS (FISH & SHELLFISH)

calamar	*ka·la·mar*	squid
camarones	*ka·ma·ro·nes*	shrimp
cangrejo	*kan·gre·kho*	crab
langosta	*lan·gos·ta*	lobster
mariscos	*ma·rees·kos*	shellfish
ostiones	*os·tyo·nes*	oysters
pargo	*par·go*	red snapper

POSTRES (DESSERTS)

arroz con leche	*a·ros kon le·che*	rice and milk pudding
flan	flan	baked custard with caramel glaze
helado (en pote)	*e·la·do (en po·te)*	ice cream (cup)
jimagua	*khee·ma·gwa*	two scoops of ice cream
lolita	*lo·lee·ta*	flan à la mode
natilla	*na·tee·lya*	sinful custard made almost entirely of egg yolks

pudín	poo·*deen*	bread pudding
tres gracias	tres *gra*·syas	three scoops of ice cream

SNACKS & STREET FOOD

maní en grano	ma·*nee* en *gra*·no	peanut brittle
maní molido	ma·*nee* mo·*lee*·do	peanut paste (similar to peanut butter)
pan con tortilla/ pasta/croqueta	pan kon tor·*tee*·lya/ *pas*·ta/kro·*ke*·ta	bread with egg/ mayonnaise/fritter
tortica	tor·*tee*·ka	butter cookie (often made with lard)

TÉCNICAS (COOKING TECHNIQUES)

a la plancha	a la *plan*·cha	cooked in a skillet
asado	a·*sa*·do	roasted
empanizado	em·pa·nee·*sa*·do	breaded
parrillada/grille	pa·ree·*lya*·da/*gree*·lye	on the grill
sofrito	so·*free*·to	Cuban seasoning made by sautéing onions, garlic and sweet peppers

City of Havana

Havana (La Habana) is the Caribbean's biggest city, with the entire whorl of politics, culture, education and attitude that befits a great urban center. Like Manhattan in many ways, Havana is sophisticated and dynamic, bustling and polluted. The city suffered little damage during the wars and revolutions of the past 200 years, and Habana Vieja (a Unesco World Heritage site since 1982) is easily the finest surviving colonial complex in the Americas. Although many of Havana's houses are worn – crumbling even – the heavy traffic, rampant commercialization and slums that choke other Latin American cities are absent.

Crowding the historical monuments and cobblestone streets are the resourceful, gracious and outgoing people themselves. Life isn't easy here: nearly half the housing is in bad repair, antiquated plumbing means uncertain water supplies, and some 300 buildings collapse annually. Hardscrabble as they need to be facing such challenges, Habaneros are still exuberantly friendly, leaving their indelible mark on any visit.

Sadly, Havana is also dirty. Thermoelectric and chemical plants, paper mills, tobacco factories and shipyards all sully the environment with airborne particles. Cars belch black smoke, garbage dumps emit malodorous methane fumes and the humidity sometimes makes you feel like you're wrapped in a pollution blanket.

Havana is like a temptress, inviting you to explore her charms, without ever revealing them all. For this reason so many people return; some never leave.

HIGHLIGHTS

Palacio Presidencial
Capitolio Nacional
Catedral de San Cristóbal de la Habana
Gran Teatro
Edificio Bacardí
Museo Nacional de Bellas Artes

★ Fortaleza de San Carlos de la Cabaña
★★
★ Plaza de la Revolución

■ The Architecture

Capitolio Nacional (p73) or Catedral de San Cristóbal de la Habana (p67), Edificio Bacardí (p84), Palacio Presidencial (p74), Gran Teatro (p74): the list is long

■ The Art

From home-studio visits to the stunning Cuban collection at the Museo Nacional de Bellas Artes (p74), come enjoy art for art's sake

■ The Music

Jazz, son, salsa, rock or hip hop: the hottest sounds coming from Cuba come from Havana and you're invited (p100)

■ The Revolution

Take the long view across the Plaza de la Revolución (p77) or from Che's headquarters in the Fortaleza de San Carlos de la Cabaña (p129)

■ The People

Intriguing, enigmatic, educated and so alive, it's for her people that Havana's heart beats

| ■ TELEPHONE CODE: 7 | ■ POPULATION: 2.2 MILLION | ■ AREA: 740 SQ KM |

HISTORY

In 1514 San Cristóbal de la Havana was founded on the south coast of Cuba near the mouth of the Río Mayabeque, today a swampy, sparsely inhabited area. Thankfully for us all, a few years later the settlement shifted to the mouth of the Río Almendares between present-day Vedado and Miramar. Only in 1519 did the town reestablish itself next to the mouth of the harbor, an area now world famous as Habana Vieja.

Although Havana was one of the seven original towns established in Cuba by Diego Velázquez, no-one ever intended for it to be the capital. The town's remote northwest location made it a poor site from which to administer the center and east of the island, and it's no coincidence that almost every rebellion against authorities in Havana since the early 19th century has broken out far to the east.

It took the Spanish conquest of Mexico and Peru to swing the pendulum in Havana's favor. The town's strategic location, at the mouth of the Gulf of Mexico facing a coastline washed by the northeast-bound Gulf Stream, made it a perfect gathering point for the annual treasure fleets. Its ascension was quick and in 1556 Havana replaced Santiago de Cuba as seat of the Spanish captains general. The first combined flota sailed to Spain from here in 1564, and for the next 200 years Havana was the most important port in the Americas, the 'key' to the vast Spanish colonial empire. In 1592 Havana was declared a city, and in 1607 the capital of the colony was officially moved here.

After Havana was sacked by French privateers led by Jacques de Sores in 1555, the castles of La Fuerza, La Punta and El Morro were built between 1558 and 1630. From 1674 to 1740, a strong wall was built around the city. These defenses kept out the pirates but proved ineffective when Spain became embroiled in the Seven Years' War with Britain, the strongest maritime power of the time.

On June 6, 1762, a British army under the Earl of Albemarle attacked Havana, landing at Cojímar and striking inland to Guanabacoa. From there they drove west along the northeastern side of the harbor, and on July 30 they attacked El Morro from the rear.

Other troops landed at La Chorrera, west of the city, and by August 13 the Spanish were surrounded and forced to surrender. The British held Havana for 11 months. (The same war cost France almost all its colonies in North America, including Québec and Louisiana – a major paradigm shift.)

When the Spanish regained the city a year later in exchange for Florida, they began a crash programme to upgrade the city's defenses so it would never fall again. A new fortress, La Cabaña, was built along the ridge from which the British had shelled El Morro, and by the time the work was finished in 1766, Havana had become the most heavily fortified city in the New World, the 'bulwark of the Indies.'

The British occupation resulted in Spain opening Havana to freer trade. In 1765 the city was granted the right to trade with seven Spanish cities instead of only Cádiz, and beginning in 1818 Havana was allowed to ship its sugar, rum, tobacco and coffee directly to any part of the world. The 19th century was an era of steady progress: first came the railway in 1837, and then public gas lighting in 1848, the telegraph in 1851, an urban transportation system in 1862, telephones in 1888 and electric lighting in 1890. At the end of the 16th century Havana had around 4000 inhabitants; by 1774 it had grown to 76,000, half the population of the island. The city was physically untouched by the devastating wars of independence, and by 1902 it had a quarter million inhabitants.

ORIENTATION

Completely surrounded by Havana Province, the City of Havana is divided into 15 municipalities: Habana Vieja, Centro Habana, Plaza de la Revolución, Playa, La Lisa, Marianao, Cerro, Diez de Octubre, Boyeros, Arroyo Naranjo, San Miguel del Padrón, Cotorro, Regla, Guanabacoa and La Habana del Este.

Habana Vieja, or 'colonial Havana,' sits on the western side of the harbor in an area once bounded by 17th-century city walls that ran along present Av de Bélgica and Av de las Misiones. In 1863 these walls were demolished and the city spilled west into Centro Habana, bisected by busy San Rafael (the dividing line between the two are still fuzzy). West of this lies Vedado,

MUNICIPALITIES OF CITY OF HAVANA

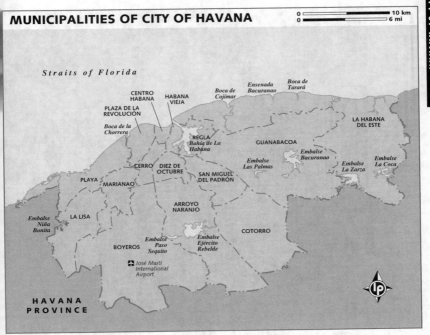

the 20th-century hotel and entertainment district that developed after independence in 1902. Near Plaza de la Revolución and between Vedado and Nuevo Vedado, a huge government complex was erected in the 1950s. West of the Río Almendares are Miramar, Marianao and Playa, Havana's most fashionable residential suburbs prior to the 1959 revolution.

Between 1955 and 1958, a 733m-long tunnel was drilled between Habana Vieja and Habana del Este under the harbor mouth, and since 1959 a flurry of high-rise housing has been thrown up in Habana del Este, Cojímar (a former fishing village), and Alamar, northeast of the harbor. South of Habana del Este's endless blocks of flats are the colonial towns of Guanabacoa, San Francisco de Paula and Santa María del Rosario. On the eastern side of the harbor are Regla and Casablanca, friendly old towns.

Totally off the beaten track for most tourists are Havana's working-class areas south of Centro Habana like Cerro, Diez de Octubre and San Miguel del Padrón. Further south still is industrial Boyeros,

with the golf course, zoo and international airport, and Arroyo Naranjo with Parque Lenin.

Visitors spend the bulk of their time in Habana Vieja, Centro Habana and Vedado. Important streets here include: Obispo, a pedestrian mall cutting through the center of Habana Vieja; Paseo de Martí (aka Paseo del Prado or just 'Prado'), an elegant 19th-century promenade in Centro Habana; Av de Italia (aka Galiano), Centro Habana's main shopping street for Cubans; Malecón, Havana's broad coastal boulevard; and Calle 23 (aka La Rampa), the heart of Vedado's commercial district.

Confusingly, many main avenues around Havana have two names in everyday use – a new name that appears on street signs and in this book, and an old name overwhelmingly preferred by locals. See the boxed text to sort it all out (p63).

This chapter starts with Habana Vieja and Centro Habana, followed by Vedado and then Outer Havana (Playa, Marianao, Parque Lenin, Santiago de las Vegas), plus all of the areas east of the harbor.

CITY OF HAVANA

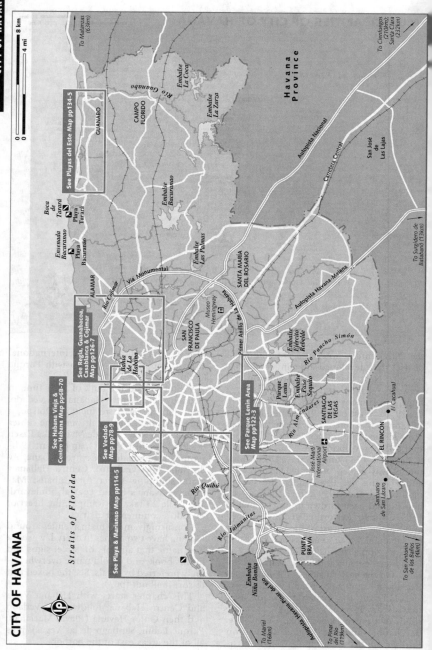

0 ___ 4 mi
0 ___ 8 km

Strait s of Florida

To Mariel (16km)

To Pinar del Río (119km)

Autopista Havana–Pinar del Río

Embalse Niña Bonita

To San Antonio de los Baños (4km)

Río Jaimanitas

Río Quibú

See Playa & Marianao Map pp114-5

See Vedado Map pp78-9

See Habana Vieja & Centro Habana Map pp68-70

Bahía de La Habana

See Regla, Guanabacoa, Casablanca & Cojímar Map pp126-7

ALAMAR

Río Cojímar

Vía Monumental

Playa Bacuranao

Ensenada Bacuranao

Playa Tarará

Boca de Tarará

See Playas del Este Map pp134-5

GUANABO

CAMPO FLORIDO

Río Guanabo

Embalse La Coca

Embalse La Zarza

Embalse Bacuranao

Embalse Las Palmas

SANTA MARÍA DEL ROSARIO

Museo Hemingway

SAN FRANCISCO DE PAULA

Río La Habana

Primer Anillo de La Habana

Autopista Havana–Matanzas

Havana Province

Autopista Nacional

Carretera Central

San José de Las Lajas

Río Pancho Simón

Embalse Ejército Rebelde

Embalse Paso Seguito

Parque Lenin

SANTIAGO DE LAS VEGAS

Río Almendares

See Parque Lenin Area Map pp122-3

José Martí International Airport

EL RINCÓN

Santuario de San Lázaro

El Cacahual

PUNTA BRAVA

To San Antonio de los Baños (4km)

To Surgidero de Batabanó (13km)

To Cienfuegos (210km); Santa Clara (232km)

To Matanzas (63km)

Maps

Your best guide to the old city is *La Habana Vieja Guía Turística*, published by the Instituto Cubano de Geodesia y Cartografía (GeoCuba). It contains 35 maps of the old town, along with 222 pages of references and helpful descriptions in Spanish, English, French and German. It is available at some hotel shops.

GeoCuba also publishes *Ciudad de la Habana Mapa Turístico*, which covers all 15 municipalities in detail, including good scale street maps of the central city and Playas del Este. The fold-out *Guía de Carreteras*, with countrywide and Havana city maps, is very useful if you'll also be exploring other provinces. Highway signs around Havana are poor to nonexistent, and these maps are almost essential for drivers. **Tienda El Navegante** (Map pp68-9; ☎ 861-3625; fax 66 67 63; Mercaderes No 115 btwn Obispo & Obrapía; ✆ 8am-noon, 1-5pm Mon-Fri, 8am-1pm Sat) has many useful maps of Cuba (including maritime charts), plus the *Mapa Biográfico de Ernest Hemingway* (US$1.20) for buffs.

HAVANA STREET NAMES

Old Name	New Name
Zulueta	Agramonte
Someruelos	Aponte
Av del Puerto	Av Carlos Manuel de Céspedes
Egido and Monserrate	Av de Bélgica
Vives	Av de España
Galiano	Av de Italia
Av de Rancho Boyeros ('Boyeros')	Av de la Independencia
Monserrate	Av de las Misiones
Cristina	Av de México
Carlos III (Tercera)	Av Salvador Allende
Reina	Av Simón Bolívar
Teniente Rey	Brasil
La Rampa	Calle 23
Av de los Presidentes	Calle G
Cárcel	Capdevila
Estrella	Enrique Barnet
Paula	Leonor Pérez
Av de Maceo	Malecón
Monte	Máximo Gómez
Belascoaín	Padre Varela
Paseo del Prado	Paseo de Martí
San José	San Martín

DOWNTOWN HAVANA

INFORMATION
Bookshops

Librería Alma Mater (Map pp78-9; ☎ 870-2060; San Lázaro & Calle L, Vedado) Next to the university steps. Has textbooks and poetry.

Librería Centenario del Apóstol (Map pp68-9; ☎ 870-7220; Calle 25 No 164 at Calle O, Vedado; ✆ 10am-5pm Mon-Sat, 9am-1pm Sun) Great assortment of used books.

Librería Grijalbo Mondadovi (Map pp68-9; O'Reilly No 4 in Palacio del Segundo Cabo, Plaza de Armas, Habana Vieja; ✆ 9am-5pm Mon-Sat) Fantastic mix of magazines, guidebooks, reference, politics and art imprints in English and Spanish.

Librería La Internacional (Map pp68-9; ☎ 861-3283; Obispo No 526, Habana Vieja; ✆ 9am-7pm Mon-Sat, 9am-3pm Sun) Good selection of guides, photo books and Cuban literature in English; next door is Librería Cervantes, an antiquarian bookseller.

Librería Luis Rogelio Nogueras (☎ 863-8101; Av de Italia No 467, btwn Barcelona & San Martín, Centro Habana) Literary magazines and Cuban literature in Spanish.

Librería Rayuela (Map pp78-9; ☎ 55 27 06; Calles 3 & G, inside the Casa de las Américas, Vedado; ✆ 9am-4:30pm Mon-Fri) Terrific for contemporary literature, compact discs; some guidebooks.

Moderna Poesía (Map pp68-9; ☎ 861-6640; Obispo 525, Habana Vieja; ✆ 10am-8pm) Perhaps Havana's best spot for Spanish-language books.

Plaza de Armas Secondhand Book Market (Obispo & Tacón, Habana Vieja) Old, new and rare books; some in English.

Cultural Centers

Alliance Française (Map pp78-9; ☎ 33 33 70; Calle G No 407 btwn Calles 17 & 19, Vedado). Free French films Mon (11am), Wed (3pm) and Fri (5pm); good place to meet Cubans (including children for French travelers with kids) interested in French culture.

Casa de las Américas (Map pp78-9; ☎ 55 27 06/07; Calles 3 & G, Vedado) Powerhouse of Cuban and Latin American culture, with conferences, exhibitions, gallery, book launches and concerts. The casa's annual literary award is one of the Spanish-speaking world's most prestigious. Pick up a schedule of weekly events in the library. Hosts international seminar on Afro-Cuban culture every August.

Casa de la Cultura Centro Habana Centro Habana (Map pp78-9; ☎ 878-4727; Av Salvador Allende No 720 near Soledad) Habana Vieja (Map pp68-9; ☎ 863-4860; Aguiar No 509) Vedado (Map pp78-9; ☎ 831-2023; Calzada No 909 at Calle 8) High quality concerts and festivals.

Fundación Alejo Carpentier (Map pp68-9; Empedrado No 215, Habana Vieja; ☉ 8am-4pm Mon-Fri) Near the Plaza de la Catedral. Check for cultural events at this baroque former palace of the Condessa de la Reunión (1820s) where Carpentier set his famous novel *El Siglo de las Luces (Explosion in a Cathedral)*.

Instituto Cubano de Amistad con los Pueblos (Map pp78-9; ICAP; ☎ 55 23 95; Paseo No 406, btwn Calles 17 & 19, Vedado; ☉ 11am-11pm) Rocking cultural and musical events in elegant mansion (1926); restaurant, bar and cigar shop also here.

Emergency
Ambulance (☎ 40 50 93/4)
Asistur (Map pp68-9; ☎ 33 85 27, 33 89 20; asisten@a sisten.get.cma.net; Paseo de Martí, No 212 in the Casa del Científico, Centro Habana; ☉ 8:30am-5:30pm Mon-Fri, 8am-2pm Sat) Someone on staff should speak English; the alarm center here is open 24 hours.
Poison Control (☎ 260-1230, 260-8751)

HAVANA IN...

Two Days

Fortify yourself with fruits, omelettes and *café con leche* before touring the **Capitolio** and choosing art or war by visiting the **Museo Nacional de Bellas Artes** or the **Museo de la Revolución**. A stroll along the **Malecón** is mandatory after which **Chinatown** stir-fries will be calling you. At night, salsa and swoon at the **Casa de la Música** in Miramar.

Habana Vieja will gobble up day two with gorgeous art and architecture; galleries in **Plaza Vieja**, books in **Plaza de Armas** and the cathedral in **Plaza de la Cátedral**. At night it's the **Tropicana Nightclub** or **Casa de la Trova**.

Four Days

Follow the two-day itinerary, visiting the **Plaza de la Revolución** and dining at a **paladar**. On day four, take a ferry across the bay to visit the **old forts** and sip sunset cocktails by the sea. Splurge on dinner at **El Paseo** in the Hotel Parque Central or at **Café del Oriente** in Plaza de San Francisco de Asís.

Immigration
Inmigración (Map pp78-9; Calle Factor al final & Santa Ana, south of Tulipán, Nuevo Vedado) This office is specifically for extensions. It has no phone, but you can direct questions to immigration proper at ☎ 203-0307.

Internet Access
Biblioteca Nacional de Ciencias y Técnica (Map pp68-9; Paseo de Martí & Brasil in Capitolio Nacional, Centro Habana; ☉ 8:15am-5pm Mon-Fri) Enter through stairs on left of main entrance.

Cibercafe Capitolio (Map pp68-9; ☎ 862-0485; Paseo de Martí & Brasil; US$5/hr ; ☉ 8am-8pm) Inside main entrance.

Citmatel Centro Habana (Map pp68-9; O'Reilly No 4 cnr of Tacón in Palacio del Segundo Cabo) Centro Habana (Map pp68-9; Paseo de Martí No 212 cnr Trocadero in Casa del Científico) Vedado (☎ 831-1321; Calle 15 No 551 btwn Calles C & D; ☉ 8:30am-5pm Mon-Sat) All these places (and the Biblioteca above) use the same card worth US$6/10/20 for one/two/five hours.

Etecsa Habana Vieja (Map pp68-9; Habana 406 cnr Obispo) Vedado (Map pp78-9; Calle 23 cnr O in Centro de Prensa Internacional; ☉ 8am-8pm) Crowded.

Hotel Business Centers (Hotel Habana Libre Map pp78-9; Calle L btwn Calles 23 & 25; Hotel Inglaterra Map pp68-9; Paseo de Martí No 416; Hotel Nacional Map pp78-9; Calles O & 21, Vedado; Hotel NH Parque Central Map pp68-9; Neptuno cnr Paseo de Martí & Zulueta, Centro Habana) Usually a couple dollars more expensive, but reliable and shorter wait times.

Laundry
Lavandería Alaska (Map pp68-9; ☎ 863-0463; Villegas No 256 at Obrapía; ☉ 6am-5pm Mon-Sat) Laundromat charging US$3 a load to wash and dry (when the dryers work).

Libraries
Foreign students with a carnet (or letter from their academic institution) can get library cards. Each library requires its own card; show up with two passport photos. The following are open to the public, except for the Casa de las Américas' closed stacks, which require a card.

Biblioteca José A Echevarría (Map pp78-9; ☎ 832-6380; Av de Presidentes No 210 in Casa de las Américas) Best art, architecture and general culture collection; books can't leave library.

Biblioteca Nacional José Martí (Map pp78-9; ☎ 55 54 42; Av de la Independencia, on the Plaza de la Revolución; ☉ 8am-5:45pm Mon-Sat) Havana's biggest library. Book and magazine launches often held here.

Biblioteca Rubén M Villena (Map pp68-9; ☎ 862-9038; Obispo No 59 at Baratillo, Habana Vieja; ☺ 8am-9pm Mon-Sat, 9am-4pm Sat) Nice reading rooms and garden.

Medical Services

Many of Cuba's specialist hospitals offering services to foreigners are based in Havana; see the site www.cubanacan.cu for details. Also consult the Playa & Marianao section of this chapter (p111) for listings of pharmacies and hospitals serving the diplomatic community.

Centro Oftalmológico Camilo Cienfuegos (Map pp78-9; Calle L No 151 at Calle 13, Vedado) Head straight here with eye problems; also has an excellent pharmacy.

Drogería Johnson (Map pp68-9; ☎ 862-6870; Obispo No 260, Habana Vieja; ☺ 24hr) Old-fashioned pharmacy in pesos.

Farmacia Homopática (Map pp78-9; Calle 23 at Calle M, Vedado; ☺ 8am-8pm Mon-Fri, 8am-4pm Sat)

Farmacia Taquechel (Map pp68-9; ☎ 862-9286; Obispo No 155, Habana Vieja; ☺ 9am-6pm) Next to the Hotel Ambos Mundos. Cuban wonder drugs like anticholesterol medication PPG sold in pesos here.

Hospital Nacional Hermanos Ameijeiras (Map pp78-9; ☎ 877-6053; fax 33 50 36; San Lázaro No 701 at Padre Varela, Centro Habana) Special hard-currency services; general consultations (US$25), hospitalization (US$75/night) and cosmetic surgery. Enter via the lower level below the parking lot off Padre Varela (ask for 'CEDA' in Section N).

Hotel Habana Libre (Map pp78-9; ☎ 55 45 93; Calle L btwn Calles 23 & 25, Vedado) Dollar pharmacy.

Money

Banco de Crédito y Comercio Habana Vieja (Map pp78-9; ☎ 862-9513; Aguiar No 310 near Obispo; ☺ 8:30am-1:30pm Mon-Fri) Vedado (Map pp78-9; ☎ 33 76 33; Línea No 705 at Paseo) Vedado (Map pp78-9; ☎ 870-2684; Calle 23 in Airline Building) Vedado (Map pp78-9; ☎ 879-2074; Av Independencia No 101 near Calle 19 de Mayo) The last – in post office between Terminal de Omnibus and Plaza de la Revolución – is most convenient to immigration for visa extension stamps. Expect lines.

Banco Financiero Internacional Centro Habana (Map pp78-9; ☎ 873-6496; Carlos III btwn Arbol Seco & Retiro in Plaza Carlos III) Habana Vieja (Map pp68-9; ☎ 860-9369; Oficios & Brasil) Vedado (Map pp78-9; ☎ 55 44 29; Calle L btwn Calles 23 & 25 in Hotel Habana Libre) Vedado (Map pp78-9; ☎ 33 34 23; Línea & Calle 0) Efficient, professional service.

Banco Metropolitano (Map pp78-9; ☎ 55 33 16/7; Línea & Calle M, Vedado) The ATM might be working.

Cadeca Centro Habana (Map Map pp68-9; Neptuno & Agramonte in Cafetería Rumbos, queue outside; ☺ 9am-noon, 1-7pm Mon-Sat); Centro Habana (Rayo No 261 at Simón Bolívar; ☺ 9am-6pm Mon-Sat, 9am-1pm Sun); Habana Vieja (Map pp68-9; Oficios & Lamparilla, facing Plaza de San Francisco de Asís; ☺ 8am-7pm Mon-Sat, 8am-1pm Sun); Habana Vieja (Map pp68-9; Obispo btwn Aguacate & Compostela; ☺ 8am-5:30pm Mon-Sat, 8am-1pm Sun); Vedado (Map pp78-9; Calle 23 btwn K & L; ☺ 7am-2:30pm, 3:30-10pm); Vedado (Map pp78-9; Calle 19 btwn Calles A & B at mercado agropecuario; ☺ 7am-6pm Mon-Sat, 8am-1pm Sun); Vedado·(Map pp78-9; Malecón cnr Calle D). Cadeca gives cash advances and changes traveler's checks at 3.5% commission Mon-Fri, 4% weekends.

Photography

Photo Service Vedado (Map pp78-9; ☎ 33 50 31; Calles 23 & 0 in Centro de Prensa Internacional; ☺ 8:30am-midnight); Vedado (Map pp78-9; ☎ 66 21 12; Calle M btwn Calles 17 & 19 below Edificio Focsa); Vedado·(Map pp78-9; ☎ 55 39 74; Calle 1 & Paseo in Galerías de Paseo; ☺ 9am-6pm) Two-hour film developing, photocopies, passport photos (US$2 for four).

Post

DHL Vedado (Map pp78-9; ☎ 832-2112; No 818 btwn Calles 2 & 4; ☺ 8am-5pm Mon-Fri); Vedado·(Map pp78-9; ☎ 55 00 04; Calles 0 & 21 in Hotel Nacional).

Post offices Centro Habana (Map pp68-9; San Martín & Paseo de Martí at the Gran Teatro); Habana Vieja (Map pp68-9; Oficios No 102 on Plaza de San Francisco de Asís); Habana Vieja (Map pp68-9; Unidad de Filatelia, Obispo No 518; ☺ 9am-7pm); Vedado (Map pp78-9; Línea & Paseo; ☺ 8am-8pm Mon-Sat); Vedado (Map pp78-9; Calle 23 cnr Calle C; ☺ 8am-6pm Mon-Fri, 8am-noon Sat); Vedado (Map pp78-9; Av de la Independencia btwn Plaza de la Revolución & Terminal de Omnibus; ☺ 24hr stamp sales). This last has many services including photo developing, a bank and Cadeca. The **Museo Postal Cubano** (☎ 870-5581; admission US$1; ☺ 10am-5pm Sat & Sun) here has a philatelic shop. The post office at Obispo, Habana Vieja also has stamps for collectors.

Radio

Cuba has a fantastic radio culture, where you'll hear everything from salsa to Supertramp, plus live sports broadcasts and soap operas. Radio is also the best source for listings on concerts, plays, movies and dances.

Radio Ciudad de la Habana (820 AM & 94.9 FM) Cuban tunes by day, foreign pop at night; great '70s flashback, 8pm on Thursday and Friday.

Radio Metropolitana (910 AM & 98.3 FM) Jazz and traditional *boleros* (ballads); excellent Sunday afternoon rock show.

Radio Musical Nacional (590 AM & 99.1FM) Classical.

Radio Progreso (640 AM & 90.3 FM) Soap operas and humor.

Radio Rebelde (640 & 710 AM, & 96.7 FM) News, interviews, good mixed music, plus baseball games.

Radio Reloj (950 AM & 101.5 FM) News, plus the time every minute of every day. 'Tick, tick, tick...Radio Reloj.'

Radio Taino (1290 AM & 93.3 FM) National tourism station with music, listings and interviews in Spanish and English. Nightly broadcasts (5pm to 7pm) list what's happening around town.

Telephone

Etecsa Habana Vieja (Map pp68-9; Habana 406 cnr Obispo); Vedado (Map pp78-9; Calle 23 cnr O in Centro de Prensa Internacional; 8am-8pm) Send and receive faxes, make international calls, use Internet and buy phonecards here.

Toilets

Biblioteca Nacional de Ciencias y Técnica (Map pp68-70; Paseo de Martí & Brasil in Capitolio Nacional, Centro Habana)

Hotel Ambos Mundos (Map pp68-70; Obispo No 153 at Mercaderes)

Hotel Habana Libre (Map pp78-9; Calle L btwn Calles 23 & 25) Upstairs and by the elevators. Spiffy!

Iglesia de Nuestra Señora de la Merced (Map pp68-70; Cuba No 806 at Merced) In the cloister.

La Lluvia de Oro (Map pp68-70; Obispo No 316 at Habana)

Terminal de Ómnibus (Map pp78-9; Av de la Independencia) Near Plaza de la Revolución, downstairs.

Tourist Information

Buró de Convenciones de Cuba (Map pp78-9; 66 20 15; Calle M btwn Calles 17 & 19, Vedado; 8am-5pm Mon-Fri, 8am-noon Sat) Conferences, special events and festival information available here.

Infotur Habana Vieja (Map pp68-70; 862-4586; Obispo cnr of San Ignacio; 10am-1pm, 2-7pm); Habana Vieja (Map pp68-70; 33 33 33; Obispo btwn Bernaza & Villegas); Airport (Map pp122-3; 66 61 01; Terminal 3 Aeropuerto Internacional José Martí; 8:30am-5:30pm) Books excursions, sells maps and phonecards, transport schedules.

Travel Agencies

Many of the following agencies also have offices in the international arrivals lounge of Terminal 3.

Agencia de Viajes Horizontes (Map pp78-9; 66-2004; fax 33-4585; www.horizontes.cu; Calle 23 No 156, btwn Calles N & O; 8:30am-5pm Mon-Fri, 8:30am-1pm Sat) Reserves Horizontes Hotels countrywide.

Cubamar (Map pp78-9; 831-3151; www.cubamar viajes.cu; Calle 3 & Malecón, Vedado; 8:30am-5pm Mon-Sat) Travel agency for Campismo Popular cabins countrywide. Also rents mobile homes.

Cubanacán (Map pp78-9; 873-2686; Calles O & 21 in Hotel Nacional; 8am-7pm) Very helpful; head here if you want to arrange fishing or diving at Marina Hemingway; also in Hotel NH Parque Central, Centro Habana.

Cubatur (Map pp78-9; 33 31 70/1; Calles 23 & M, below Hotel Habana Libre, Vedado; 8am-8pm) This agency pulls a lot of weight and finds rooms where others can't, which goes a long way towards explaining its slacker attitude.

Havanatur Vedado (Map pp78-9; 66 40 82; www.havanatur.cu; Calles 23 & M; 8am-5:30pm Mon-Sat); Vedado (33 46 51; Calle 1 & Paseo in Galerías de Paseo)

Marsub (96 13 49; Calle 3 No 34004, Tarará) Specializes in scuba diving. The bulk of its business is prearranged, but you may be able to book one of its tours on-site.

San Cristóbal Agencia de Viajes (Map pp68-9; 861-9171/2; www.sancristobaltravel.com; Oficios No 110, btwn Lamparilla & Amargura on Plaza de San Francisco de Asís, Habana Vieja; 8:30am-5:30pm Mon-Fri, 8:30am-2pm Sat, 9am-noon Sun) Habaguanex agency operates Habana Vieja's classic hotels; income helps finance restoration.

Sol y Son (Map pp78-9; 33 32 71; fax 33 51 50; Calle 23 No 64; 8:30am-7pm Mon-Fri, 8:30am-noon Sat) Sells Cubana flights.

DANGERS & ANNOYANCES

Havana is an amazingly safe city, and the heavy police presence on the streets keeps it so. You can walk through areas here in the middle of the night that you wouldn't dare enter midday in places like London or New York. However, watch out for young men on bicycles who try to snatch purses, handbags or cameras. Like anywhere in the world, pickpockets are active on crowded city buses.

Don't stop to talk to anyone offering 'Havana cigars' on the street, as these are the most persistent hustlers around.

Shops may try to overcharge or cheat you, especially if your Spanish is minimal. Verify all prices before buying, check the addition and count your change before leaving the counter.

Environmentally, crumbling sidewalks with big holes can be a problem, and the air pollution is irritating. Take care walking on La Rampa when it rains, as the slick sidewalks throw people on their asses regularly.

SIGHTS
Habana Vieja   Map pp68-70

Colonial Havana is chock-a-block with museums, memorials, art galleries, churches and other historical monuments; way too much to see in a day or three. Places and palaces are constantly being restored, so you can expect many new, interesting sites to be open by the time you arrive. For an introduction to the city, you could do one of the walking tours (pp82-3) or hire a coco-taxi for a spell and zip around to sites that grab you. Expect most of the printed information and verbal guidance along the way to be in Spanish.

PLAZA DE LA CATEDRAL

Dominated by two unequal towers, the **Catedral de San Cristóbal de la Habana** (San Ignacio & Empedrado; ☯ before noon) was described by novelist Alejo Carpentier as 'music set in stone.' It's striking baroque facade (à la Italian architect Francesco Borromini) creates unrivaled ambiance, especially at night when live music mingles with laughter in the wide open plaza. The Jesuits began construction of the church in 1748, and work continued despite their expulsion in 1767. When the building was finished in 1787 the diocese of Havana was created. A year later the city became a bishop's seat, elevating the church to a cathedral, one of the oldest in the Americas. Perhaps the best time to visit is during mass, celebrated Sunday at 10:30am; smaller services happen in the adjacent chapel Monday to Friday at 8pm.

While poking around the plaza, be sure to visit the **Centro Wilfredo Lam** (☎ 862-2611; San Ignacio No 22 cnr Empedrado; admission US$2; ☯ 10am-5pm Mon-Sat) next to the cathedral, which displays the works of one of Cuba's leading modern painters and hosts shows by local and international artists. A Cuban of Chinese and African ancestry, Lam was strongly influenced by Pablo Picasso, whom he met in 1936. Many other noble buildings face the Plaza de la Catedral, including the **Palacio de los Marqueses de Aguas Claras** (1760; San Ignacio No 54 at Empedrado), now drawing crowds as Restaurante El Patio. The outdoor tables make a nice spot for a break.

Across the square are the 18th-century **Casa de Lombillo** and the **Palacio del Marqués de Arcos** (1746), today a Telecorreo Internacional office (notorious among LP readers for price gouging on stamps). During the mid-19th century this palace served as Hav-ana's main post office and the stone mask mailbox in the wall is still in use.

The **Museo de Arte Colonial** (☎ 862-6440; San Ignacio No 61; unguided/guided US$2/3, plus camera US$2; ☯ 9am-6:30pm), on the southern side of the plaza, displays colonial furniture and decorative arts in the **Palacio de los Condes de Casa Bayona** (1720), the oldest house on the square. One of the funkiest sites around here (aside from the folkloric mulattas posing for pictures) is the **Taller Experimental de Gráfica** (☎ 862-0979; tgrafica@cubarte.cult.cu; Callejón del Chorro No 6; admission free; ☯ 10am-4pm Mon-Fri) up the alley from the southwestern corner of Plaza de la Catedral. You'll see reams of original prints freshly inked and hanging to dry; you can buy what you like. This workshop accepts serious students interested in mastering the art of engraving (see Art & Film, p412).

PLAZA DE ARMAS

This lovely plaza and book bazaar was the seat of authority and power in Cuba for 400 years. A square has existed on this site since 1582, although the present Plaza de Armas dates only from 1792. In the center of the park surrounded by stately royal palms is a marble **statue of Carlos Manuel de Céspedes** (1955), the man who set Cuba on the road to independence in 1868. Live music floats about, while the breeze flutters over from the Malecón – a nice spot to chill out.

With lots of stained glass and gigantic chandeliers, the baroque **Palacio de los Capitanes Generales**, on the western side of the Plaza de Armas, is one of Cuba's most majestic buildings. Construction began on the site of the old parochial church in 1776, and from 1791 until 1898 this was the residence of the Spanish captains general. From 1899 until 1902, the US military governors were based here, after which the building became the presidential palace. In 1920 the president moved to the building now housing the Museo de la Revolución and this palace became the city hall. The municipal authorities moved out in 1967 and since 1968 it has been home to the **Museo de la Ciudad** (unguided/guided US$3/4, plus camera US$2; ☯ 9am-6pm). Peacocks strut about the courtyard, there's a spooky crypt and an

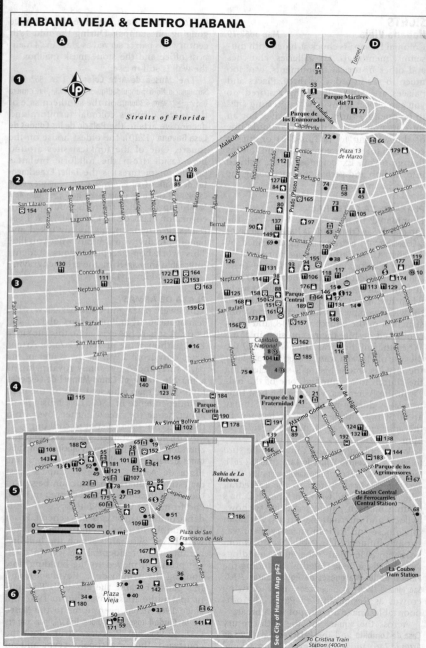

HABANA VIEJA & CENTRO HABANA

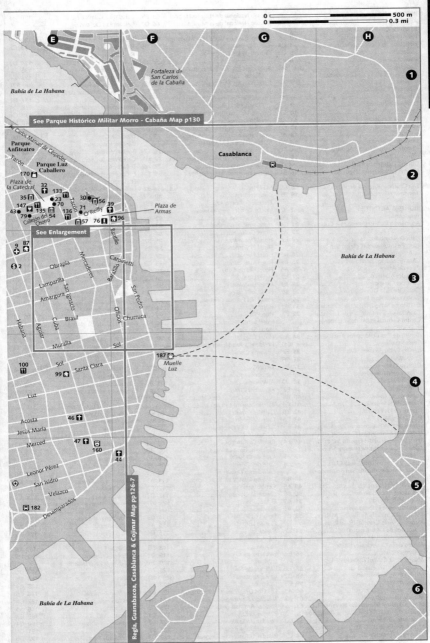

0 — 500 m
0 — 0.3 mi

E   F   G   H

1

Fortaleza de
San Carlos
de la Cabaña

Bahía de La Habana

2

Casablanca

See Parque Histórico Militar Morro – Cabaña Map p130

Parque
Anfiteatro

Parque Luz
Caballero

Plaza de
la Catedral

170

32
133
35   23
147   70
43   135   136
79   54
57   76   96

Plaza de
Armas

30   56   39

O'Reilly

Bahía de La Habana

3

See Enlargement

9   87

2

Obrapía

Mercaderes

Lamparilla

San Ignacio

Amargura

Brasil

Cuba

Aguiar

Habana

Muralla

Sol

Carpinetti

Baratillo

Oficios

San Pedro

Churruca

4

100

Sol   Santa Clara

99

187

Muelle
Luz

Luz

5

Acosta

Jesús María

Merced

46

47   160

44

Leonor Pérez

San Isidro

Velazco

182

Desamparados

6

Bahía de La Habana

Regla, Guanabacoa, Casablanca & Cojímar Map pp126-7

even more eerie Jesus. The marble bathtubs are marvelous. The guided tour gets you behind the velvet ropes and up close with the lush collection. Come early to beat the tour bus crowd.

The **Palacio del Segundo Cabo** (1772; O'Reilly No 4; admission US$1), the former headquarters of the Spanish vice-governor at the northwestern corner of the plaza, is another baroque beauty. Later it became the Supreme Court, and today it houses the **Instituto Cubano del Libro**. It's worth glimpsing into the arcaded inner courtyard and visiting the very good (with air-con) bookstore here. Pop-art fans should take a look in the **Sala Galería Raúl Martínez** (☺ 9am-6pm Mon-Sat).

On the northeastern side of the Plaza de Armas is the oldest extant colonial fortress in the Americas, the **Castillo de la Real Fuerza**, built between 1558 and 1577 on the site of an earlier fort destroyed by French privateers in 1555. The west tower is crowned by the famous bronze weather vane called **La Giraldilla**, cast in Havana in 1632 by Jerónimo Martínez Pinzón and popularly believed to be Doña Inés de Bobadilla, the wife of explorer Hernando de Soto. The original Giraldilla is in the Museo de la Ciudad and the figure also appears on the Havana Club rum label. The Spanish captains general resided in the castle for 200 years until they finally got around to constructing a palace of their own across the square. La Fuerza now shelters the **Museo de la Cerámica Artística Cubana** (☎ 861-6130; admission US$1; ☺ 9am-6pm) downstairs. Worth a look, this museum displays works by some of Cuba's leading contemporary artists. Upstairs affords a great view of the harbor entrance.

In 1519 the Villa de San Cristóbal de la Habana was founded on the spot marked by **El Templete** (admission US$1; ☺ 8:30am-6pm) a neoclassical Doric chapel erected on the eastern side of the Plaza de Armas in 1828. The first mass was held below a ceiba tree similar to the one presently in front of the building, and inside the chapel are three paintings of the event by the French painter Jean Baptiste Vermay. Adjacent to El Templete is the late-18th-century **Palacio de los Condes de Santovenia**, today the five-star, 27-room Hotel Santa Isabel. Nearby is the **Museo Nacional de Historia Natural** (☎ 863-9361; Obispo No 61; admission US$3; ☺ 9:30am-7pm Tue-Sun) which contains examples of Cuba's flora and fauna. The restaurant bar upstairs has fabulous vistas across the bay.

Just a block south of here is the small but worthwhile **Museo del Automóvil** (Oficios No 13; admission US$1; ☺ 9am-7pm), with ancient Harley Davidson motorcycles and Model Ts. Che's ride was in the shop at the time of writing.

ALONG MERCADERES & OBRAPÍA

This stretch is packed with quirky little places like the **Museo de Arte del Lejano Oriente** (☎ 863-9740; Mercaderes No 111; ☺ 10am-6pm Tue-Sat, 9am-1pm Sun) with Far Eastern art and the **Museo de Tabaco** (☎ 861-5795; Mercaderes No 120; ☺ Mon-Sat 10am-5pm), where indigenous pipes and idols feature; you can buy and smoke quality cigars at **La Casa del Habano** attached. You might glimpse a young woman celebrating her *quincñera* at **Casa de la Obra Pía** (Obrapía No 158; admission US$1, plus camera US$2; 9am-4:30pm Tue-Sat, ☺ 9:30am-12:30pm Sun) around the corner. This typical Havana aristocratic residence was originally built in the first half of the 17th century and rebuilt in 1780 soon after the British occupation. Decorative flourishes cover the exterior facade, and between the two inner courtyards is a wonderfully refreshing room. Across the street is the **Casa de África** (☎ 861-5798; Obrapía No 157) housing artifacts from Fidel Castro's 1977 African tour, plus sacred objects relating to Santería, formerly in the collection of ethnographer Fernando Ortíz. It was undergoing repairs while this book was being written.

On the corner of Mercaderes and Obrapía is a bronze **statue** of Latin America liberator Simón Bolívar, to whom a **museum** (☎ 861-3988; Mercaderes No 160; donations accepted; ☺ 9am-5pm Tue-Sun) is dedicated nearby. The **Casa de México Benito Juárez** (☎ 861-8166; Obrapía No 116 at Mercaderes; admission US$1; ☺ 10:15am-5:45pm Tue-Sat, 9am-1pm Sun) exhibits Mexican folk art in an 18th-century palace; there's a specialized library here for all things *mexicana*. Just east is the **Casa Oswaldo Guayasamín** (☎ 861-3843; Obrapía No 111; donations accepted; ☺ 9am-2:30pm Tue-Sun), the old studio, now a museum, of the great Ecuadorian painter. (Fidel sat for Guayasamín; to see the portrait, visit the Fundación Naturaleza y El Hombre, p116.) Openings and exhibits of Cuban and international art are held here.

PLAZA DE SAN FRANCISCO DE ASÍS

Another of Habana Vieja's picturesque plazas, **Plaza de San Francisco de Asís** is a seaside beauty dominated by the domed **Lonja del Comercio**, a former commodities market erected in 1909 and restored in 1996 to provide office space for foreign companies with joint ventures in Cuba. Enter the building to admire its central dome. Across from 'La Lonja' is the white marble **Fuente de los Leones** (Fountain of Lions) carved by the Italian sculptor Giuseppe Gaginini in 1836. The southern side of the square is taken up by the impressive **Iglesia y Monasterio de San Francisco de Asís**. Originally constructed in 1608 and rebuilt in the baroque style from 1719 to 1738, San Francisco de Asís was taken over by the Spanish state in 1841 as part of a political move against the powerful religious orders of the day, when it ceased to be a church. Today the church itself is a **concert hall** (starting 5pm or 6pm) hosting classical, chamber and choral music and a **museum** (☎ 862-3467; admission US$1, plus camera US$2; ☯ 9am-5:30pm) in the two large cloisters. Price of admission allows access to the tallest church tower in Havana; a dollar well spent.

MUSEO DEL RON

Even for teetotalers, the intriguing **Museo del Ron** (☎ 861-8051; San Pedro No 262 at Sol; admission incl guide US$5; ☎ 9am-5pm Mon-Fri, 10am-4pm Sat & Sun) in the Fundación Havana Club is worth a turn. The interesting bilingual guided tour shows rum-making antiquities (check out the funky terracotta flask), plus explains the entire brewing process, from cane cutting to quaffing amber Añejo Reserva in the museum's tasting room. The scale model of the Central La Esperanza, with working train, is especially cool. Check out occasional musical events in the beautiful courtyard here (☯ 9pm) or have a cocktail in the bar (☯ 9am to midnight).

PLAZA VIEJA

Certainly one of Habana Vieja's most dazzling public spaces, **Plaza Vieja**, dating from the 16th century, is surrounded by several sites not to be missed. An open-air marketplace until 1835, and hideous underground parking lot during the Batista regime, since the mid-1990s there has been a concerted effort to restore this plaza to its former grandeur. On the northwestern corner is Havana's **cámara oscura** (admission US$1; ☯ 9am-5pm Tue-Sat, 9am-1pm Sun), providing live, 360° views of the city from atop a 35m-tall tower. Sheets flap in the breeze, old cars amble by and the docent does an admirable job explaining Havana's architectural highlights in Spanish and English. In the arcade adjacent is **Fototeca de Cuba** (☎ 862-2530; Mercaderes No 307; admission free; ☯ 10am-5pm Tue-Fri, 9am-noon Sat), a photo gallery with intriguing exhibits by local and international artists.

On the southern side of the plaza is the quirky **Museo de Naipes** (Muralla No 101 cnr Mercaderes; admission US$1; ☯ 9am-6pm Tue-Sun), with a collection of every playing card imaginable. Rock stars, rum drinks, round cards – they've got 2000 of them here. Next door is **La Casona Centro de Arte** (☎ 861-8544; Muralla No 107 at San Ignacio; ☯ 10am-5pm Mon-Fri, 10am-2pm Sat), with great solo and group shows by up-and-coming Cuban artists like Abel Barroso. Also here is **Diago Galería de Arte** (☎ 863-4703). On the western side of the park is yet another gallery in another gorgeous colonial building at the **Centro de Desarollo de los Artes Visuales** (☎ 862-2611; San Ignacio No 352; admission free; ☯ 10am-5pm Tue-Sat); here you'll find good contemporary Cuban art.

Around the corner, the **Centro Cultural Pablo de la Torriente Brau** (☎ 861-6251; www .centropablo.cult.cu; Muralla No 63; admission free; ☯ Tue-Sat 9am-5:30pm) hosts a variety of expositions of substance, including poetry readings and a live acoustic music series called 'Guitarra Limpia.' Its Salón de Arte Digital is renowned for its groundbreaking digital art.

CHURCHES

South of Plaza Vieja are a string of stunning and important churches. The **Iglesia y Convento de Santa Clara** (1638-43; ☎ 866-9327; Cuba No 610; admission US$2; ☯ 9am-4pm Mon-Fri) stopped being a convent in 1920. Later this complex was the Ministry of Public Works, and today the Habana Vieja restoration team is based there. You can visit the large cloister and nun's cemetery or even spend the night (with reservations far in advance, see p88). Havana's oldest surviving church is the **Iglesia Parroquial del Espíritu Santo** (1640, rebuilt in 1674; ☎ 862-3140; Acosta 161 cnr of Cuba; ☯ 8am-noon, 3-6pm), with many burials in the crypt. The **Iglesia y Convento de Nuestra Señora de la Merced** (1755; Cuba No 806 at Merced; ☾ 8am-noon, 3-5:30pm) was reconstructed in the 19th century. Beautiful gilded altars, frescoed vaults and a number of old paintings create a sacrosanct mood; there's a quiet cloister adjacent.

The **Iglesia de San Francisco de Paula** (☎ 41 50 37; Leonor Pérez & Desamparados) is one of Havana's most attractive churches. Fully restored in 2000, this church is all that remains of the San Francisco de Paula women's hospital from the mid-1700s. Lit up at night for concerts (most notably by the medieval ensemble Ars Longa) the stained glass, heavy cupola and baroque facade are utterly romantic and inviting.

MUSEO-CASA NATAL DE JOSÉ MARTÍ
If you visit only one *casa natal* in Cuba, make it **Museo-Casa Natal de José Martí** (☎ 861-3778; Leonor Pérez No 314; admission US$1, plus camera US$2; ☾ 9am-5pm Tue-Sat), the birthplace of José Martí. The apostle of Cuban independence was born in this humble dwelling on January 28, 1853, and the museum displays letters, manuscripts, photos, books and other mementos of his life. Nearby, to the west across Av de Bélgica, is the longest remaining stretch of the **old city wall** (building began in 1674). A bronze map shows the outline of the original layout. To the west is Havana's huge Central Train Station where *La Junta*, the steam locomotive that inaugurated the line to Matanzas in 1843, is on display.

Centro Habana   Map pp68-70
CAPITOLIO NACIONAL
Washington, DC and Havana have more in common than you may think, evidenced by the dominating marble-covered **Capitolio Nacional** (☎ 863-7861; admission unguided/guided US$3/4; ☾ 9am-8pm), which is similar to the US Capitol Building, but richer in detail. This is one of Havana's divine architectural highlights. To enter, climb the monumental stairway on the eastern side of the building. The tour is highly recommended.

Initiated by the US-backed dictator Gerardo Machado in 1929, the Capitolio took 5000 workers three years, two months and 20 days to build at a cost of US$17 million. It was the seat of the Cuban Congress until 1959 and now houses the Cuban Academy

of Sciences and the National Library of Science and Technology. Entering the great domed hall through huge bronze doors (notice the important events in Cuban history they depict) imbues just how monumental this building is.

Across what seems like miles of intricately laid portico marble is the 49-metric-ton, 17m statue of the republic (a woman, don't you know?), the third-largest indoor bronze statue in the world; only the Buddha in Nava, Japan, and the Lincoln Memorial in Washington, DC are bigger. Directly below the Capitolio's 62m-high dome, a 24-carat diamond replica is set in the floor. Highway distances between Havana and all sites in Cuba are calculated from this point. Visitors are also shown the mahogany-covered library and the former chambers of the Senate and Deputies. It's an extraordinary edifice and you can spend a whole afternoon gawking at the architectural details, taking coffee at the lovely balcony café (see p97) and stealing kisses in the refugio, a lush courtyard tucked inside.

Behind the Capitolio is the **Real Fábrica de Tabacos Partagás** (☎ 862-0086; Industria No 520 btwn Barcelona & Dragones; ☾ tours every 15 min btwn 9:30am-11pm, 12:30-3pm); for tours of this and other Havana cigar factories, see the boxed text p76.

PARQUE LA FRATERNIDAD
The **Fuente de la India** (roundabout at Dragones near Máximo Gómez, east of the park) is a white Carrara marble fountain carved by Giuseppe Gaginni in 1837. Honoring heritage old and new, the sculpture is an indigenous girl seated above four dolphins, a famous symbol of Havana. She's embracing the city's coat of arms.

Just east of the sculpture across Paseo de Martí is the **Asociación Cultural Yoruba de Cuba** (☎ 863-5953; Paseo de Martí No 615; admission US$6; ☾ 9am-4pm Mon-Sat). The museum here provides a worthwhile overview of the Santería religion, the saints and their powers. There are free *tambores* (drum jams/ceremonies) here alternate Fridays at 4:30pm (when you can check out the museum for free), and you can arrange consultations as well. Note that there's a church dress code for the *tambores* (no shorts or tank tops guys).

Across the street is leafy **Parque de la Fraternidad**, originally a Spanish military parade ground. The first park was laid out here in 1892 to commemorate the fourth centenary of the Spanish arrival in the Americas, and in 1928 the park was remodeled in honor of the Pan-American Conference hosted in Havana that year. The grand ceiba tree dominating the park was planted in a mixture of soil from all the countries of the Americas, and busts of prominent Latin and North Americans were set up around the park (including Abe Lincoln, a hero in Cuba). Today this area is the terminus of numerous city bus routes, and you'll see rows of lovingly restored American cars, which are now used as collective taxis, parked in the sun-dappled streets.

GRAN TEATRO & AROUND

On the northern side of the Capitolio is the ornate neobaroque **Centro Gallego** (Paseo de Martí No 458 at San Rafael) erected as a Galician social club between 1907 and 1914. The Centro was built around the existing Teatro Tacón, which opened in 1838 with five masked carnaval dances. This connection is the basis of claims by the present 2000-seat **Gran Teatro de La Habana** (☎ 861-3077; guided tours US$2; ☽ 9am-6pm) that it's the oldest operating theater in the Western Hemisphere. Never mind the date details, this is an outrageously beautiful building inside and out. You can catch the National Ballet of Cuba and the State Opera in the Sala García Lorca here (see p104).

Just across the San Rafael pedestrian mall is **Hotel Inglaterra**, one of Havana's finest grand hotels. José Martí made a speech advocating independence at a banquet here in 1879, and much later US journalists covering the so-called Spanish-American War stayed at this hotel. Bar La Sevillana just inside the Inglaterra is a nice place for a break, as is the hotel's sidewalk terrace. **San Rafael**, a riot of ice-cream stalls, vintage clothing shops, plumbing supplies and more, is a fun detour where everything is sold in pesos.

Diminutive **Parque Central** across from the Inglaterra, was expanded to its present size after the city walls were knocked down in the late 19th century, and the marble statue of José Martí (1905) in its center was the first statue of the poet to be erected in Cuba. Nowadays, this park is the turf for Rastas and baseball fans. See those men laughing, shouting and arguing just south of the statue? That's the famous *esquina caliente*,

where ball fanatics avidly debate statistics, play-off chances and personal habits of their favorite teams and players.

MUSEO NACIONAL DE BELLAS ARTES

After undergoing a multi-year renovation and expansion completed in 2001, this museum has reopened with a collection so extensive they need two buildings to house it all. The **Colección de Arte Universal** (☎ 863-9484; www.museonacional.cult.cu; Agramonte & San Rafael; admission US$5, children under 14 free, student discounts; ☽ 10am-6pm Tue-Sat, 10am-2pm Sun) features European and Latin American paintings and ancient Greek and Roman artifacts (lots of urns). It's a beautiful eclectic building (1886), but the permanent collection can't compare to others in larger cities. Good temporary exhibits do pass through, however.

Then there's the **Colección de Arte Cubano** (☎ 861-3858; Trocadero btwn Agramonte & Av de las Misiones; admission US$5; ☽ 10am-6pm Tue-Sat, 10am-2pm Sun). If you visit one fine art museum in Cuba, make it this world-class facility and set aside an entire afternoon. Split into three floors (all handicap accessible), the museum houses a sculpture garden, café and good museum shop on the ground floor. The second floor is contemporary and modern art (look especially for works by Kcho, Raúl Martínez, Portocarrero and of course, Wilfredo Lam), while the third floor collects everything from the 16th century up to 1951. There's also a terrific art reference library here and a concert hall with varied events, including children's activities most weekends.

MUSEO DE LA REVOLUCIÓN

You can't miss the glass-encased **Pavillón Granma** facing the Colección de Arte Cubano. Since 1976, this has been the home to the 18m 'yacht' *Granma* that ushered Fidel Castro and 81 others from Tuxpán, Mexico, into Cuba and world history in 1956. Today this is one of the holiest shrines of the Cuban Revolution, the equivalent of Mao's mausoleum in Beijing. Other vehicles associated with the armed struggle surround the heavily guarded pavilion, which is accessible from the museum proper.

The **Museo de la Revolución** (☎ 862-4093; Refugio No 1; admission unguided/guided US$4/6, cameras extra; ☽ 10am-5pm) is housed in the former Palacio Presidencial (1913–20), a signature of the Havana skyline. Tiffany's of New York decorated the interior. This palace was the site of an unsuccessful assassination attempt against Fulgencio Batista in March 1957 (see History, p28). The exhibits inside provide a complete documentary and photographic account of the Cuban Revolution (from the guns shot to the bread sacks), and it's a must for anyone with a taste for history – allow yourself plenty of time. Labels are in English and Spanish and one English-speaking guide is available, which can really make the difference here. In front of the building is an SAU-100 tank used by Fidel Castro during the 1961 Battle of the Bay of Pigs, and a fragment of the former city wall.

PRADO (PASEO DE MARTÍ)

Technically it's called Paseo de Martí, but Cubans know and love it as **Prado**. Construction of this stately boulevard began outside the city walls in 1770, and the work was completed in the mid-1830s during the term of Captain-General Miguel Tacón, who ruled from 1834 to 1838. He also constructed the original Parque Central. The figures of lions along the promenade were added in 1928. You'll see happy couples arriving in 1950s convertibles at the neo-Renaissance **Palacio de los Matrimonios** (1914; Paseo de Martí No 302 cnr of Ánimas) to tie the knot. For more sights along here, see the walking tour (p83).

IGLESIA DEL SANTO ANGEL CUSTODIO

This small but important **church** (☎ 861-0469; Compostela No 2 at Av de las Misiones; ◷ 9am-noon, 3-6pm Tue, Thu, Fri, 3-6pm Wed, mass 7:15am Tue, Wed & Fri, 6pm Thu, Sat & Sun) was rebuilt in neo-Gothic style in 1871. Not only were both Felix Varela and José Martí baptized here (in 1788 and 1853 respectively), but Cirilo Villaverde also set the main scene of his novel Cecilia Valdés in this church. Don't miss the Cristo Yacente, titillating in his lacy net covering. You can hear the 1869 organ ringing out here during mass.

MUSEO NACIONAL DE LA MÚSICA

Musicians especially will dig this **museum** (☎ 863-0052; Capdevila No 1 at Aguiar; admission US$2, cameras extra; ◷ 10am-5:45pm), with its extensive collection of Cuban and international instruments. Exhibited in the ec-lectic residence (1905) of a wealthy Havana merchant, the stringed room is particularly impressive. The museum shop sells recordings of Cuban music, and concerts take place in the music room a couple of nights a week (check the schedule at the museum entrance for events). Guides (in Spanish) are available for US$1 extra.

There are two important monuments just across hectic Av de los Estudiantes from here. A surviving section of the colonial **Cárcel** (1838) where many Cuban patriots, including José Martí, were imprisoned is in Parque de los Enamorados (Lover's Park, which sees few for lack of shade). Beyond that is the **Memorial a los Estudiantes de Medicina**, a fragment of wall encased in marble where eight Cuban medical students chosen at random were shot by the Spanish in 1871 as a reprisal for allegedly desecrating the tomb of a Spanish journalist (in fact, they didn't do it). That beautiful art noveau building behind, flying the Spanish flag, is the old **Palacio Velasco** (1912), now the Spanish embassy, but on the skids with the Cuban government since they agreed to restrictive embargo-type legislation at the behest of the US in 2003.

Across the street is the picturesque **Castillo de San Salvador de la Punta**, designed by the Italian military engineer Giovanni Bautista Antonelli and built between 1589 and 1600. During the colonial era, a chain was stretched 250m to the castle of El Morro every night to close the harbor mouth to shipping. This castle has been closed for restoration for many years, but the watchman may offer to show you around for a gratuity.

That monumental **statue** of a strapping man on a huge bronze horse is the memorial to Dominican General Máximo Gómez, number one in command during the wars of independence.

Vedado   Map pp78-9

Today Vedado is the suburb it was designed to be – a place to sleep, dine and go dancing – but really, the bulk of sites are in Habana Vieja and Centro Habana. The name Vedado means 'forest reserve'; during the colonial era, felling trees was forbidden here and that's why it's so green. Havana's US community established itself in this area after 1898, and within a few decades Vedado was thick with high-rises, restaurants, nightclubs and other businesses.

Vedado boomed during the Batista era, and the East Coast Mafia of the US had a hand in it all. The Hotel Capri was a favorite haunt of Mafia bigwigs such as Lucky Luciano and Meyer Lansky, the same mob that was behind the Las Vegas-style Hotel Riviera. The cheap sex, liquor and gambling were big attractions for US tourists, and Batista's thugs made sure everything ran smoothly. The party ended in January 1959 when Fidel Castro and his *barbudos* arrived from the Sierra Maestra and set up headquarters on the 22nd floor of the 25-story Havana Hilton, now called the Hotel Habana Libre (a permanent photo exhibit on the 2nd floor documents the transition).

Beatles fans will want to make a special trip to **Parque Lennon** (Calles 15 & 17 btwn Calles 6 & 8) where a hyper-realistic bronze of John lounges on a bench. Every December 8 there are vigils and music jams here remembering his murder.

HOTEL NACIONAL

The neocolonial-style **Hotel Nacional** (☎ 873-3564; Calles O & 21) was built in 1930. In August 1933 the US-backed dictator Gerardo Machado was overthrown during a popular uprising, and a month later army sergeant Fulgencio Batista seized power. Two months later, some 300 army officers displaced by Batista's coup sought refuge in the newly opened Hotel Nacional, where the US ambassador Sumner Wells was staying. Aware that the reins of power had changed hands, Ambassador Wells found urgent business elsewhere and Batista's troops attacked the officers, many of whom were shot after surrendering. The Nacional's tiled lobby, oversized chairs and aristocratic air capture the atmosphere of a bygone era and it's a nice place for a coffee or cocktail. Stroll straight through the lobby to the gardens behind the hotel. Several huge naval guns set up by the Spanish during the late 19th century still point out to sea from this cliff-top park where benches overlook the Malecón. If you're not down with crowds, this is a good perch for those mass marches to the US Interests Section. The Nacional is also HQ for the Festival Internacional del Nuevo Cine Latinoamericano. Nonguests can use the **pool** (admission with food & drink minimum US$15; ☽ 8am-6:30pm).

CIGAR FACTORY TOURS

There are three factories presently allowing tours and the programme is largely the same: visitors check out the ground floor where the leaves are unbundled and sorted, proceeding to the upper floors to watch the tobacco get rolled, pressed, adorned with a band, and boxed. Contrary to popular belief, no one factory is responsible for any single type of cigar (Cohibas are rolled at Partagas and Montecristos at the Romeo y Julieta factory for example), so there's no cache in going to one factory over the other. However, individual visitors are sometimes tacked on to boorish tour groups (common at the world famous and over-photographed Partagas), so you might want to visit a factory more off the beaten track (like the aforementioned Romeo y Julieta). These are factories, remember, where people toil (sometimes for 12 hours a day or more) for around 200 pesos a month, and some visitors find they smack of a human zoo. Still, if you have even a passing interest in tobacco, Cuban work environments or economies of scale, you'll enjoy one of the US$10, 45-minute tours held Monday to Friday at:

Real Fábrica de Tabacos Partagás (Map pp68-70; ☎ 862-0086; Industria No 520 btwn Barcelona & Dragones; ☽ tours every 15 minutes btwn 9:30am-11pm & 12:30-3pm) The tobacco shop (☽ 9am-5pm Mon-Sat) and smoking lounge are bonuses here. This is one of Havana's oldest cigar factories (1845).

Real Fábrica de Tabacos La Corona (Map pp68-70; ☎ 862-0001; Calle Agramonte No 106 btwn Colón & Refugio; ☽ tours 9:30am-2:30pm Mon-Fri) Founded in 1842, Romeo y Julieta, Montecristo and Cohibas are rolled here. Factory shop is good for buying single smokes (☽ 9am-5pm Mon-Sat).

Romeo y Julieta (Map pp78-9; ☎ 878-1058; Padre Varela No 852 at Benjumeda; ☽ tours 10am-3pm Mon-Fri) Far removed from any tourist sites, you may get lucky here and have a personalized tour.

Cabaret, **Tropicana Nightclub** (p120), Havana

ALFREDO MAIQUEZ

RHONDA GUTENBERG

Cuban woman

Street scene, **Havana** (p58)

GREG JOHNSTON

Dominoes (p39)

Capitolio Nacional (p73), Havana

Habaneros (p59)

Paseo de Martí (p75), Havana

HOTEL HABANA LIBRE

This hotel was commandeered by triumphant revolutionaries in 1959 and promptly renamed the **Habana Libre** (☎ 55 47 04; Calle L btwn Calles 23 & 25); the art here, starting with the 670-sq-meter Venetian tile mural by Amelia Peláez splashed across the front of the building, is worth a look. Upstairs is Alfredo Sosa Bravo's *Carro de la Revolución* made from 525 ceramic pieces, plus a rotating painting exhibit. The shopping arcade has a good liquor store and pharmacy.

UNIVERSIDAD DE LA HABANA

Every great city deserves a great university and the **Universidad de La Habana** (Neptuno & San Lázaro) is just that (it even hosted anti-war protests when the US invaded Iraq in 2003). Before climbing the monumental stairs toward alma mater, head downhill to check out the **Monumento a Julio Antonio Mella**, the student leader who founded the first Cuban Communist Party in 1925. In 1929 the dictator Machado had Mella assassinated in Mexico City. More interesting than the monument, however, are the black and white **Mella portraits** permanently mounted in the wall in the little park across San Lázaro.

The university was founded by Dominican monks in 1728 and secularized in 1842. The present neoclassical complex dates from the second quarter of the 20th century, and today some 30,000 students (2000 of them foreigners), taught by 1700 professors, take courses in the social sciences and humanities, natural sciences, mathematics and economics.

Go up the stairway and through the monumental gateway into Plaza Ignacio Agramonte, the university's central square. In front of you is the **biblioteca** (library) and to your left the **Edificio Felipe Poey**, with two **museums** (admission US$1; ☼ 9am-noon, 1-4pm Mon-Fri). Downstairs, the **Museo de Historia Natural** is the oldest museum in Cuba, founded in 1874 by the Royal Academy of Medical, Physical and Natural Sciences. Many of the stuffed specimens of Cuban flora and fauna here date from the 19th century. Upstairs is the **Museo Antropológico Montané**, established in 1903, with a rich collection of pre-Columbian Indian artifacts. The most important objects are the wooden 10th-century Ídolo del Tobaco, discovered in

Guantánamo Province, and the stone Ídolo de Bayamo, but the mummies are cool, too. Keep this building on your left, and the next building on your left is the **Anfiteatro Enrique José Varona**; films are screened here during the Festival Internacional del Nuevo Cine Latinamericano.

Go down through the park on the north side of the Edificio Felipe Poey and exit the university compound via a small gate to reach the **Museo Napoleónico** (☎ 79 14 60; San Miguel No 1159 at Ronda; unguided/guided US$3/5; ☼ 10am-5:30pm Mon-Sat), containing 7000 objects associated with Napoleon Bonaparte, including his 1821 death mask. The 10,000-seat **Estadio Universitario Juan Abrahantes**, where students play soccer and baseball, is just up the hill from this museum.

MUSEUMS

Two museums farther afield in Vedado that are worthwhile if you're in the neighborhood are the **Museo de Artes Decorativas** (☎ 830-9848; Calle 17 No 502 btwn Calles D & E; admission US$2; ☼ 11am-7pm Tue-Sat), with its fancy rococo, oriental and art-deco baubles, and the **Museo de Danza** (☎ 831-2198; Línea No 365 cnr of Av de los Presidentes; admission US$2; ☼ 11am-6:30pm Tue-Sat), which collects objects from Cuba's rich dance history, including personal effects of Alicia Alonso.

PARQUE ALMENDARES

Running along the banks of the Río Almendares below the bridge on Calle 23, is this wonderful oasis of green and negative-air ions in the heart of chaotic Havana. The park has just undergone a massive (sorely needed) restoration and they've done a beautiful job: benches line the river promenade, plants grow profusely and there are many facilities here, including an antiquated **miniature golf course**, the **Anfiteatro Parque Almendares** (see Entertainment p102) and a **playground**. There are several good places to eat. Take a 20-minute stroll through old growth trees in the **Bosque de la Habana** and you'll feel transported (take a buddy though: this is a very isolated spot and is considered unsafe by locals).

Plaza de la Revolución Area Map pp78-9

PLAZA DE LA REVOLUCIÓN

Those tingles you feel may be the emotion of being in Cuba's most important public

VEDADO

	A		B		C		D

INFORMATION
Agencia de Viajes Horizontes.............1 F3
Airline Building....................................2 F2
Alliance Française...............................3 E3
Banco de Crédito Comercio.............(see 2)
Banco de Crédito y Comercio.............4 C3
Banco Financiero Internacional...........5 E2
Banco Financiero Internacional...(see 144)
Banco Financiero Internacional...(see 55)
Banco Metropolitano............................6 E2
Biblioteca José A Echevarría.........(see 26)
Biblioteca Nacional José Martí............7 E5
Buró de Convenciones de Cuba..(see 136)
Cadeca..8 D2
Cadeca..9 E3
Cadeca..10 D4
Cadeca..(see 83)
Casa de la Cultura de Plaza..............11 C3
Centro Oftalmológico Camilo
   Cienfuegos....................................12 E2
Citmatel...13 D3
Cubamar..14 B3
Cubanacán....................................(see 57)
Cubatur...15 E3
DHL...(see 57)
Etecsa...(see 28)
Farmacia Homopática.......................16 E3
German Embassy...............................17 D3
Havanatur.......................................(see 15)
Hospital Nacional Hermanos
   Ameijeiras.....................................18 G3
Inmigración.......................................19 D6
Instituto Cubano de Amistad con los
   Pueblos...20 D4
Italian Embassy.................................21 D4
Librería Alma Mater......................(see 50)
Librería Centenario del Apóstol......22 F3
Librería Luis Rogelio Nogueras....(see 26)
Photo Service...............................(see 143)
Photo Service................................(see 28)
Photo Service................................(see 81)
Sol y Son..(see 2)
US Interests Section.........................23 E2

SIGHTS & ACTIVITIES   pp67-82
Anfiteatro Enrique José Varona......24 F3
Bosque de la Habana.......................25 B6
Casa de las Américas.......................26 D2
Castillo de Santa Dolores de La Luna La
   Chorrera...................................(see 84)
Cementerio Chino.............................27 C6
Centro de Prensa Internacional......28 F3
Comité Central del Partido Comunista de
   Cuba..29 E5
Edificio Felipe Poey..........................30 F3
Edificio Focsa...............................(see 81)
Estadio Universitario Juan
   Abrahantes....................................31 F3
Holá Ola..32 F3
Mella portraits..................................33 F3
Memorial José Martí.........................34 E5
Ministerio de Relaciones Exteriores.35 D2
Ministry of the Interior....................36 E5
Monumento a Antonio Maceo........37 G3
Monumento a Calixto García..........38 D2
Monumento a José Miguel Gómez.39 E4
Monumento a Julio Antonio Mella.40 F3
Monumento a las Víctimas del
   Maine..41 E2
Museo Antropológico Montané...(see 30)
Museo de Artes Decorativas............42 D3
Museo de Danza...............................43 D3
Museo de Historia Natural...........(see 30)
Museo Napoleónico..........................44 F3
Parque Lennon..................................45 C4
Quinta de los Molinos.......................46 F4
Romeo y Julieta Cigar Factory.........47 C4
Socialist Revolution Plaque...............48 C4
Torreón de San Lázaro......................49 G3
Universidad de La Habana................50 F3

SLEEPING   🛏 pp86-92
Hotel Bruzón......................................51 F4
Hotel Capri...52 E2
Hotel Colina.......................................53 E3
Hotel El Morro...................................54 E3
Hotel Habana Libre............................55 E2
Hotel Meliá Cohiba...........................56 E2
Hotel Nacional...................................57 E2
Hotel Presidente................................58 D2
Hotel Riviera......................................59 C3
Hotel St Johns....................................60 E3
Hotel Universitario............................61 E3
Hotel Vedado.....................................62 F3
Hotel Victoria.....................................63 E3

EATING   🍴 pp92-9
Agropecuario 17 & K.........................64 E2
Agropecuario 19 & A......................(see 83)
Agropecuario 21 & J..........................65 E3
Biki Vegetarian Restaurant...............66 F3
Bim Bom..67 F2
Cafetería La Tovola Calda.................68 E3
Cafetería M en A...............................69 E3
CafeTV...70 E2
Casa Sarasua.....................................71 E3
Coppelia...72 E3

D'Oscar..73 F3
Decameron...74 C3
El Cocotero..75 D3
El Conejito...76 E2
El Gringo Viejo...................................77 D3
El Lugar...78 B6
El Recanto...79 C4
La Complaciente................................80 E2
La Torre..81 E2
Le Chansonnier..................................82 E2
Mercado Agropecuario......................83 D3
Mesón La Chorrera............................84 B4
Organoponico Plaza...........................85 D5
Pain de Paris..................................(see 22)
Pain de París......................................86 C3
Paladar El Helecho.............................87 C3
Paladar El Hurón Azul........................88 F3

Straits of Florida

Boca de la Chorrera

To Miramar

Malecón

Vedado

Necrópolis Cristóbal Colón

See Necrópolis Cristóbal Colón Map pp80-1

Río Almendares

Parque Almendares

See Playa & Mariano Map pp114-5

Nuevo Vedado

19 de Noviembre Train Station

To Viazul Terminal; Panautos

San Antonio Chiquito

Av de Colón

Lombillo

Tulipán

Av Kohly

Panamericá

E F G H

0 _____ 500 m
0 _____ 0.3 mi

23
41
122 151
152
5
124
90 12 6
Linea 80 81 70 91
82 64 76 57 2
112 61 89 52 67
127 68 63 28 115 99
16 126 88
119 118 60 98
72 15 101 62 22 110
95 9 55 140
97 146
125 154 53 33
65 132 50
3 30
116 71 24 44
93 40
31

Malecón (Av Maceo)
Caleta de San Lázaro
Parque Maceo
150
32 49
137 129 18

Principe
Vapor
Jovellar
San Lázaro
Infanta
San Francisco
San Miguel
San Rafael
San Martín

Virtudes
Concordia
Neptuno
Soledad
Hospital
Aramburo
Espada

39

Estadio Juan
Abrahantes

Zanja
Salud

128 Pocito
46 Av Salvador Allende
144 Enrique Barnet
Maloja
Sitio
Peñalver
Desagüe
Benjumeda
Santo Tomás
Clavel
Santa Marta
Arroyo (Av Manglar)

113

Av Simón Bolívar

Escobar
Lealtad
Perseverancia
Campanario
Manrique
San Nicolás
Indio

To Habana
Vieja

Figuras
Carmen
Rastro
47

Castillo del
Príncipe

Av Universidad

Av Carlos M de Céspedes
Av de la Independencia
Pozos Dulces
Zapata
Brizon
Calz de Infanta

131
153
51

111 36
130 7
34 29

Plaza de la
Revolución

Aranguren

C-39
C 19 de Mayo
Av 20 de Mayo
Calz de Ayestarán

To San Francisco
de Paula (14km)

To Estadio
Latinoamericano
(250m)

To Ciudad Deportiva (1km);
José Martí International
Airport (25km)

Calz del Cerro

See Habana Vieja & Centro
Habana Map pp68-70

Zanja
Cuchillo
Barcelona
Industria
Amistad

Padre Varela
Marqués Gonzáli
Lucena
Oquendo

Máximo Gómez
Av de México

Cristina
Train
Station

Fábrica

147

Zanja
San Carlos
Padre Varela
Av de España (Vives)
Puerta Cerrada
Diaria

Malecón

1
2
3
4
5
6

space or maybe it's the heat (it gets very hot here; visit as early or late in the day as you can). Predating the 1959 triumph, the **Plaza de la Revolución** was once called Plaza de la República. Although this gigantic square has come to symbolize the Cuban Revolution, due to the huge political rallies held here in the '60s, most buildings date from the Batista era. On important occasions Castro and others have addressed up to 1.2 million Cubans and supporters from the podium in front of the star-shaped, 142m-high **Memorial José Martí** (☎ 59 23 47; admission US$3; ☾ 9:30am-5pm Mon-Sat). Head here on May 1 or July 26 at 7am if you want to experience it yourself (most hotels offer excursions). The 17m marble Martí statue in front is by Juan José Sicre. In 1996 the memorial was renovated; you can visit the museum dedicated to Martí at the memorial's base, and for US$2 more, take the elevator to the enclosed 129m-level viewpoint – the highest structure in Cuba.

Fidel Castro's office is located in the long building behind the memorial, the heavily guarded **Comité Central del Partido Comunista de Cuba**, once the Ministry of Justice (1958).

The **Ministry of the Interior** on the northern side of the square is easily identifiable for its huge Ernesto 'Che' Guevara mural and the slogan '*Hasta la Victoria Siempre.*' West of it is the **Teatro Nacional de Cuba** (see p104).

On the western side of the Plaza de la Revolución is the **Biblioteca Nacional José Martí** (1957; admission free; ☾ 8am-9:45pm Mon-Sat), with a photo exhibit in the lobby. Downstairs is the children's library, with events and kid's art exhibits.

Quinta de los Molinos (Salvador Allende & Luaces; admission US$1; ☾ 9am-5pm Tue-Sat, 9am-noon Sun) is a former residence of General Máximo Gómez and now a museum, set in the university's former botanical gardens. There's a shady park that Cubans will warn you away from. This place is important as the site of the Asociación Hermanos Saíz, youth arm of Unión de Escritores y Artistas de Cuba (UNEAC). Concerts held at La Madriguera (lots of rock and rap) are notoriously fun (see p102).

NECRÓPOLIS CRISTÓBAL COLÓN

A mini-city of granite, marble and loved ones, this is Cuba's most important cem-

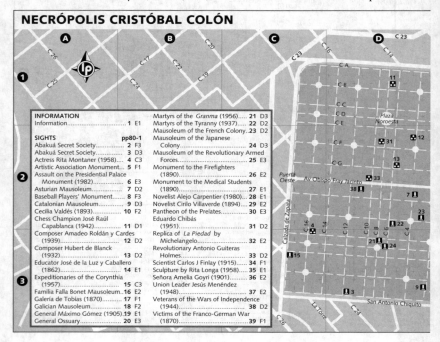

NECRÓPOLIS CRISTÓBAL COLÓN

etery (admission US$1; ⏱ 7am-5pm). It's even laid out like a metropolis of the dearly departed, with numbered streets and avenues on a rectangular grid. The Necrópolis accommodates the graves of just under a million people interred here between 1868 and today (unfortunately, they are disinterring people daily because they've run out of room). Many of the graves have impressive marble tombstones (ask to be shown the domino grave), making this the largest sculpture park in the country. Silvio Rodríguez filmed his latest video *Cita con Angeles* among all the cherubs here. A guidebook with a detailed map (US$5) is for sale at the entrance.

Soon after entering through the neo-Romanesque **northern gateway** (1870), there's the tomb of independence leader **General Máximo Gómez** (1905) on the right (look for the bronze face in a circular medallion). Further along past the first circle, and also on the right, are the **monument to the firefighters** (1890); the **Familia Falla Bonet mausoleum** (of artistic interest); and the **Capilla Central** (1886) in the center of the cemetery. Just northeast of this chapel is the tomb of

Señora Amelia Goyri (cnr Calles 1 & F), who died while giving birth on May 3, 1901. The marble figure of a woman holding a large cross with the baby in her arms is easy to find, due to the many flowers piled on the tomb and the local devotees in attendance. When the bodies were exhumed, the baby was in her arms. Señora Amelia is the focus of a miraculous cult, and its followers never turn their backs on her.

Also worth seeking out is the tomb of Orthodox Party leader **Eduardo Chibás** (Calle 8 btwn Calles E & F). During the '40s and early '50s Chibás was a relentless crusader against political corruption, and as a personal protest he committed suicide during a radio broadcast in 1951. At his burial ceremony a young Orthodox activist named Fidel Castro jumped atop Chibás' grave and made a fiery speech denouncing the old establishment – the political debut of the most influential Cuban of the 20th century.

A bronze **plaque** (cnr Calles 14 & 23), one block from the cemetery entrance, marks the spot where Fidel proclaimed the socialist nature of the Cuban Revolution on April 16, 1961, at a funeral service for those killed during a counter-revolutionary raid on a Havana air base the previous day.

For something completely different, exit the west gate of the cemetery and walk south for three blocks to the **Cementerio Chino** (Av 26 cnr of Zapata; ⏱ 6am-6pm).

Along the Malecón

Havana has become synonymous with the Malecón, its 8km seawall. Constructed during the American administration in 1901, it snakes along the coast from the Castillo de la Punta in Habana Vieja to La Chorrera, another castle at the mouth of the Río Almendares. Here two one-way tunnels dive under the river, and the main thoroughfare continues through Miramar as Av 5, eventually becoming the autopista (freeway) to Mariel. In the early spring and aggressive weather, waves splash high over the wall, soaking cars and strollers alike. Even though you've probably seen many photos of the same scene, the pastiche of architectural gems, restored or collapsing, backing the Malecón are enchanting. A new project erecting old fashioned-style street lamps make it even more attractive at night, when lovers paste themselves to the wall,

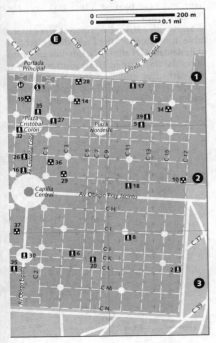

wandering troubadours sing for tips, and there's always a bottle of rum being passed your way. Hustlers here can be fierce: tell them directly and unequivocally that you're grooving on your own and they'll go away (see 'Hints on Jineterismo' p359).

The 24-story **Hospital Nacional Hermanos Ameijeiras** (1980), the highest building in Centro Habana (but not in Havana – that would be the Focsa), dominates this area. Some of the clinics specialize in treating foreigners (see Medical Services, p65). Opposite the hospital is the **Monumento a Antonio Maceo** (1916), the mulatto general who cut a blazing trail across the entire length of Cuba during the 1895 War of Independence. The nearby 18th-century **Torreón de San Lázaro** was built as a watchtower by the Spanish.

West beyond Hotel Nacional is a stretch of the Malecón known as Av Washington because the old US Embassy was here. In the center of the boulevard is the **Monumento a las Víctimas del Maine** (1926), which had an American eagle on top until the 1959 revolution. The current inscription on the side of the monument alludes to the theory that US agents deliberately blew up their own ship to create a pretext for declaring war on Spain: '*A las víctimas de el* Maine *que fueron sacrificados por la voracidad imperialista en su afán de apoderarse de la Isla de Cuba*' (To the victims of the *Maine* who were sacrificed by voracious imperialism in its desire to gain control of the island of Cuba). The incongruous seven-story building with high security fencing at the western end of this square is the **US Interests Office**. Facing this is the plaza known as Tribuna Anti-Imperialista, built during the Elián affair to host major in-your-face protests (earning it the local nickname '*protestódromo*'). Concerts, protests and marches – some one million strong – are still held here.

Another impressive memorial is the **Monumento a Calixto García** (1959; Malecón & Calle G) of the valiant Cuban general who US military leaders in Santiago de Cuba prevented from attending the Spanish surrender in 1898. Twenty-four bronze plaques around the equestrian statue provide a history of García's 30-year struggle for Cuban independence. On Calle G just behind the monument is the **Casa de las Américas** (☎ 55 27 06; Calle G btwn Calles 3 & 5; admission US$2; ⏰ 10am-4:30pm Tue-Sat, 9am-1pm Sun), a major cultural institution sponsoring

literary and artistic seminars, concerts and exhibitions. Inside there's an art gallery and a bookstore. The affiliated Galería de Haydee Santamaría features Latin American art.

Many busts and statues line Calle G (Av de los Presidentes). In the middle of the avenue is a former monument to Cuba's first president, Tomás Estrada Palma, who is now considered a US puppet. His statue was toppled and all that remains of the monument are his shoes. On the other side of Calle G is the neobaroque **Ministerio de Relaciones Exteriores**.

A large **fería de la artesanía** with handicrafts and used books is at the corner of Malecón and Calle D.

HABANA VIEJA WALKING TOUR

Map pp83

It's unlikely you'll get to both the Habana Vieja and Centro Habana walking tours in a day, unless you hop some transport halfway through. You can connect with a horse carriage (US$10/hour) on Mercaderes just off Obispo, a coco-taxi anywhere around Plaza de San Francisco de Asís (horse carriages hang out here too) or a bici-taxi near the Central Train Station.

Start with a strong espresso at an outdoor table in the heart of the Plaza de la Catedral at **Restaurante El Patio (1)**, before heading into the cathedral proper. Head southwest from the cathedral and pop into the alleyway on the right housing **Taller Experimental de Gráfica (2)** to see what prints are hot off

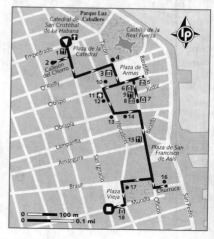

the presses. Don't linger too long though, because you'll want some time before the tour hordes arrive at the **Museo de la Ciudad (3)** on the western side of Plaza de Armas (turn left one block south of the Taller). This plaza is a bibliophile's Nirvana, with used book stalls ringing the park, a chilly **library** and two good bookstores in the **Palacio del Segundo Cabo (4)**. You might skip the stuffed animals at the Museo Nacional de Historia Natural and head straight to the 5th-floor terrace bar at **Restaurante Mirador de la Bahía (5)**, where the views are superb.

If coins, cars or the Koran interest you, turn south on Oficios beside La Mina and hit the string of small museums there, starting with the 17th-century **Casa del Obispo**, which houses the **Museo Numismático (6**; ☎ 861-5881; Oficios No 8; admission by donation; ☻ Tue-Sat 9am-1:30pm, Sun 9am-1pm) and displays Cuban coins and medals from the 16th century to today. A half block further on is the **Museo del Automóvil (7)**, with lots of cool cars and some interesting souvenir kitsch. Across the street is the **Casa de los Árabes**, (**8**; 861-5868; Oficios No 14; admission US$1; ☻ 9am-7pm) in the 18th-century **Colegio San Ambrosio**, which has objects relating to Islamic culture, but is most importantly Havana's only functioning mosque. Across the street is **Al Medina (9)**, offering Havana's best Middle Eastern cuisine if you're craving falafel (oh yeah!).

Alternatively, go south on Mercaderes, the street one block west and parallel to Oficios. Right on the corner of Obispo is **Hotel Ambos Mundos (11)**, where Ernest Hemingway stayed off and on during the 1930s. You can visit room 511 where he started writing *For Whom the Bell Tolls* (admission US$2; ☻ 9am-5pm Mon-Sat). A few doors south is the **Maqueta de la Habana Vieja (12**; no phone; unguided/guided US$1/2; ☻ 9am-6pm), a darling scale model of our favorite Unesco World Heritage site. Before turning left onto Obrapía at the next corner, check out **Habana 1791 (13**; Mercaderes No 176 at Obrapía) where floral fragrances are made and mixed by hand (you can see all the petals drying in the laboratory in back). These make a great souvenir for mom or your honey.

Halfway down Obrapía is **Casa del Abanico (14**; Obrapía No 109 btwn Mercaderes & Oficios), where hand fans are handcrafted with loads of TLC. You can even watch several compañeras painting the dainty floral work

that make these another unique souvenir (from US$6 to several hundred dollars). At the end of the block turn right onto Oficios for two blocks and you'll be dumped into **Plaza de San Francisco de Asís.** The western side of the plaza hosts several art galleries (see p106), some with little gardens out back if you need a break. Or splurge with a cappuccino at **Café del Oriente (15)**.

Train lovers will want to detour a half block south on Oficios and turn left on Churruca to check out the **Coche Mambí (16**; admission free; ☻ 9am-2pm Tue-Sat), a 1900 train car built in the US and brought to Cuba in 1912. Put into service as the 'Presidential Car,' it's a palace on wheels, with a formal dining room, louvered wooden windows and, back in its heyday, fans cooling the car with dry ice.

Otherwise, turn right at the corner of Oficios and Brasil and you're headed toward **Plaza Vieja**. This plaza is captivating: you'll get some of the city's best views from atop the tower housing the **cámara oscura (17)** on the northeastern corner, and the card collection at **Museo de Naipes (18)**, on the southeastern corner, is something to behold. Finish the tour at the cluster of galleries on the southwestern corner.

If you want to say goodbye to tourist-brochure Habana Vieja and hello to the real world, continue west on Muralla one block and then south on Cuba. Here ceilings fall without warning and power outages, water shortages and garbage-strewn streets are the norm. This is one of the roughest parts of the city, and though this author has walked these streets many times without trouble, be on your toes. (This same warning applies to Centro Habana west of Paseo de Martí and north of San Rafael.) Everyone will see at a glance that you're a tourist, but try not to look like an easy mark. If in doubt, head back toward the Plaza de Armas. Avoid these areas after dark. If you want to check out some churches and link up with the Centro Habana Walking Tour, continue six blocks south on Cuba and then go left on Leonor Pérez for five blocks.

CENTRO HABANA WALKING TOUR
Map pp84

This tour starts in the heart of matters, at the **Museo de la Revolución (1)** and **Museo Nacional de Bellas Artes (2)**. OK, so you probably won't visit both because then you would

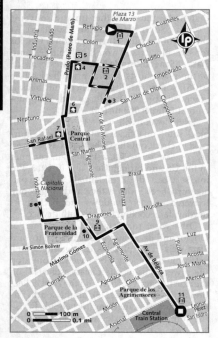

The hustlers can be fierce along here, so you'll want to make your way south at some point to **Parque Central** to admire the José Martí statue (first among thousands!) and catch the latest baseball gossip at the hot *esquina caliente*. The views of the Gran Teatro and Inglaterra are particularly luscious from the southern side of the park. If you're parched, you could take a mojito curbside at the **Hotel Inglaterra (7)** or head to the rooftop pool/bar at the **Hotel NH Parque Central (6)** on the northern side of the park. The latter is strictly five-star stuff, so slackers beware.

If you want to get off the tourist track, head up San Rafael (aka 'Bulevar'), alongside the Inglaterra. This is where Cubans shop, so have your pesos ready for anything from costume jewelry to vintage board games.

Everyone has to visit the **Capitolio Nacional** and photographers should check it out around 7am (bonus is you get to check out rush-hour Havana style with insanely crowded camellos and super long lines for the colectivos). Keep walking south on Prado and you can turn right on Dragones just at the edge of the Capitolio to take a cigar tour at the **Real Fábrica de Tabacos Partagás (8)** or continue straight past the **Fuente de la India (9)** sculpture at the crazy roundabout (cross carefully here) to the **Asociación Cultural Yoruba de Cuba (10)** with their fascinating, well laid out museum.

Jog left on Máximo Gómez for two blocks and then turn right onto chaotic Av de Bélgica and into the 'real' Havana, where peso cafeterias and one of the city's biggest markets provide cheap eating opportunities. If you don't feel like walking the five long blocks south to the **Museo Casa-Natal de José Martí (11)**, flag down a bici-taxi here.

COURSES

UniversiTUR (☎ 870-4667; eventos@rect.uh.cu; 8am-5pm Mon-Fri), upstairs in the Edificio Varona at the Universidad de La Habana, organizes Spanish language courses on the spot. Go early morning if you can; Mondays are best. With 17 universities countrywide to choose from, it's a good excuse for lingering in Cuba. For more information see Courses in Directory (p411).

Yoga classes are offered in the peaceful garden of the **Museo de Artes Decorativas** (Map pp78-9; ☎ 830-9848; Calle 17 No 502 btwn Calles D & E; admission US$2; 11am-7pm Tue-Sat). Eight

need a hammock *fast*. But cruise at least one before heading south a block and a half to the **Edificio Bacardí (3**; Av de las Misiones No 261 btwn Empedrado & San Juan de Dios), one of Havana's most striking buildings. Completed in 1930, this monument to art deco has been lovingly restored and you'll want plenty of film at the ready to capture the different granites, Capellanía limestone, mosaics and multicolored bricks in all their glory.

Retrace your steps for a few meters and head left on Ánimas. Make the first right onto Agramonte and then the next left. This is Trocadero, site of the sumptuous old **Hotel Sevilla (4)**. The former Sevilla-Biltmore (erected 1908), this is where Enrico Caruso stayed in 1920, where one of Graham Greene's characters slept (in room 510) and where the Mary Pickford cocktail was first concocted (rum, pineapple juice and grenadine). The Prado end of the lobby has a wall of interesting historic photos. A few steps more and you're on the **Prado**, that urban glade where tykes skate by and sinuous youths from the **Escuela Nacional de Ballet (5)** nurse sore muscles.

weeks of beginner or advanced classes cost 50 pesos; check at the museum for the next session. You may be able to drop in on classes held at the **Teatro Nacional** (Map pp78-9; Paseo & Calle 39 on the Plaza de la Revolución). Look for the class schedule by the box office.

Tango, salsa, mambo and other styles of dance are offered all over Havana; see Directory (p411) for details.

HAVANA FOR CHILDREN

Cubans love kids, and families traveling together will have special experiences not available to the rest of us. Staying in casas particulares is especially recommended as it provides the opportunity for cross-cultural family exchanges. Vagaries of the Cuban reality will demand patience and creativity by parents (particularly when it comes to food) but there is no lack of fun things to do here including the big aquarium in Playa (see Acuario Nacional on p116), plus the freshwater **Aquarivm** (☎ 863-9493; Calle Brasil No 9 btwn Mercaderes & Oficios; ☺ 9am-5.30pm Tue-Sun) in Habana Vieja, the fantastic **playground** right on the Malecón (at Tacón), replete with rides, **horseback riding** in Parque Lenin, and water slides and bumper cars at **Complejo Recreo** in Marina Hemingway. Head to the **beach** at Playas del Este to sail, kayak and swim.

Culturally, there are slews of things specifically for kids including **La Colmenita** children's theater (see p104), **Cinecito** with all-kids movies all the time and kids concerts, films and activities every Saturday (3pm) and Sunday (11am) at the Museo Nacional de Bellas Artes, Colección de Arte Cubano (see p74). All the **ice-cream parlors** are a kid's delight and playing a round of **miniature golf** in Parque Almendares (see p77) or seaside at **Holá Ola** (Malecón btwn Principe & Valor; mini-golf US$2; ☺ 11am-sunset) is fun for everyone. Even the transport here is kid friendly: hop in an old Chevy, grab a coco-taxi or hire a bici-taxi and discover Havana.

TOURS

Most general agencies offer the same tours, with some exceptions noted below. The regular tour diet includes a four-hour city tour (US$15), a specialized Hemingway tour (from US$20), a *cañonazo* ceremony (without/with dinner US$15/25), a botanical garden trip (US$15), a Varadero tour

(day trip from US$35; one night all inclusive US$50), and, of course, excursions to Tropicana Nightclub (starting at US$65). Other options include tours to Boca de Guamá crocodile farm (US$48), Playas del Este (US$20, includes lunch), Viñales (US$44), Cayo Largo del Sur (US$137) and a Trinidad-Cienfuegos overnight (US$129). Children usually pay a fraction of the price of adults and solo travelers get socked with a US$15 supplement. Note that if the minimum number of people don't sign up, the trip will be cancelled. Any of the following agencies (most of which also have offices in Playa/Miramar) can arrange these tours and more:

Cubatur (Map pp78-9; ☎ 33 31 70/1; Calles 23 & M, below the Hotel Habana Libre, Vedado; ☺ 8am-8pm)

Havanatur Vedado (Map pp78-9; ☎ 66 40 82; www.havanatur.cu; Calles 23 & M; ☺ 8am-5:30pm Mon-Sat); Vedado (Map pp78-9; ☎ 33 46 51; Calle 1 & Paseo in Galerías de Paseo)

Infotur Habana Vieja (Map pp68-70; ☎ 862-4586; Obispo cnr of San Ignacio; ☺ 10am-1pm, 2-7pm); Habana Vieja (Map pp68-70; ☎ 33 33 33; Obispo btwn Bernaza & Villegas); Airport (☎ 66 61 01; Terminal 3 Aeropuerto Internacional José Martí; ☺ 8:30am-5:30pm)

Paradiso (Map pp78-9; ☎ 832-9538; fax 33 39 21; Calle 19 No 560 cnr of Calle C, Vedado) Tours with art emphasis in several languages and departing from many cities. Check out Martí's Havana (US$64) or special concert tours.

Rumbos (Map pp78-9; ☎ 873-3725; Calles O & 21 in Hotel Nacional; ☺ 8:30am-5:30pm Mon-Sat) Ask about tours to Cayo Largo del Sur.

San Cristóbal Agencia de Viajes (Map pp68-70; ☎ 861-9171/2; www.sancristobaltravel.com; Oficios No 110 btwn Lamparilla & Amargura on Plaza de San Francisco de Asís, Habana Vieja; ☺ 8:30am-5:30pm Mon-Fri, 8:30am-2pm Sat, 9am-noon Sun) Offers an Havana archaeological tour (US$8) and a Buena Vista Social Club tour (US$15) with 'band members' of the famous group.

FESTIVALS & EVENTS

The major cultural events in Havana include: FolkCuba in mid-January of odd-numbered years; Festival Internacional del Libro in the last week of January; PerCuba (Festival Internacional de Percusión) every mid-April; Cubadisco and the Festival Internacional de Guitarra every May; and the Ernest Hemingway Dialog each May in odd-numbered years; the Festival Internacional de Boleros de Oro in June; Festival de Rap Cubana Hip

Hop in August; the Festival de Teatro de la Habana odd-numbered years in September; the Festival de Música Contemporanea (Festival of Contemporary Music) every October; the Internacional de Ballet Festival in October in even-numbered years; the annual Marabana Marathon in November; the Festival de Raíces Africanas Wemilere (Wemilere African Roots Festival) in Guanabacao in late November; the Bienial de la Habana in November in odd-numbered years; the Festival Internacional de Jazz in December of even-numbered years; and the Festival Internacional del Nuevo Cine Latinamericano every December.

For advance information about special events, visit AfroCuba web at www.afrocuba web.com/festivals.htm.

SLEEPING
Budget

Private rooms are readily available throughout the city. You'll pay anywhere from US$15 to US$35 per room, with those in Vedado usually better quality and more expensive than those in Centro Habana – but also more suburban, and some people find it too far removed from the action. Don't allow a room tout to lead you around; their commission will add US$5 per night to the cost. See the boxed texts for casas particulares in Habana Vieja (below), Centro Habana (p87) and Vedado (p90) for details.

CENTRO HABANA   Map pp68-70

Casa del Científico (☎ 862-4511, 863-8103; Paseo de Martí No 212 at Trocadero; s/d/tr with shared bath US$25/31/37, with private bath US$45/55/64) This elegant old building with grand stairways, marble columns, courtyards, and terraces overlooking the Prado makes an atmospheric introduction to Havana. Services abound (Internet, restaurants, bars, dancing) and it serves as a sort of social center for the neighborhood and traveler traffic (though the guard at the door tempers any hard-core mingling). The rooms are rather ordinary but adequate.

Hotel Isla de Cuba (Islazul; ☎ 57 11 29; Máximo Gómez No 169; s/d US$15/19) Housed in a beautiful building from the 1880s, elegant wrought-iron railings highlight this little-known hotel, and the 67 fan-cooled rooms with bath are dirt cheap (keep expectations to a minimum). Mostly Cubans stay here, but they'll give non-Cubans a room if they have one. Lock your luggage securely when you go out, as we've received several reports of thefts from the rooms.

Hotel Lido (Horizontes; ☎ 867-1102; www.horizontes.cu; Consulado No 210 btwn Ánimas & Trocadero; s/d low

---

CASAS PARTICULARES – HABANA VIEJA

Casa de Pepe and Rafaela (☎ 862-9877; San Ignacio No 454 btwn Sol & Santa Clara; r US$30) One of Havana's best: antiques and Moorish tiles throughout, three rooms each with balconies and gorgeous new baths, excellent location. Son also rents in charming colonial house at San Ignacio No 656 (US$25).

Juan and Margarita (☎ 867-9592; Obispo No 522 Apto 8 btwn Bernaza & Villegas; apt US$60) Two-bedroom apartment, super central, flexible and friendly hosts.

Eliberto Barrios Suárez (☎ 863-3782; eliberto62@webcorreosdecuba.cu; San Juan Díos No 112 Apto 3A btwn Aguacate & Compostela; apt US$30) Nice two-bedroom duplex apartment with kitchen.

Migdalia Carraballe (☎ /fax 861-7352; Santa Clara No 164 btwn Cuba & San Ignacio; r US$25-35) Rents three rooms, two with balconies overlooking Santa Clara convent.

Noemi Moreno (☎ 862-3809; Cuba No 611 Apto 2 btwn Luz & Santa Clara; r US$25) Simple, clean room in great location behind convent; also rent in Apto 1.

Jesús and María (☎ 861-1378; jesusmaria2003@yahoo.com; Aguacate No 518 btwn Sol & Muralla; r US$25) Rent three rooms, try for one upstairs; inviting inner patio.

Casa Alameda de Paula – Nancy Pérez (☎ 860-1898; Jesús María No 23 btwn San Ignacio & Inquisador; r US$20-25) Two rooms, only one with private bath, four flight walk up.

Pablo Rodríguez (☎ 861-2111; Compostela btwn Brasil & Muralla; r US$30) Rents two rooms with fan and fridge; bargain for longer stays.

Luis Fornaris and Mirtha García (☎ 860-0650; mfornaris@empresch.get.tur.cu; Compostela No 119 cnr Empedrado; r US$25) Basic room sleeps three, warmly reader recommended.

Ramón and Maritza (☎ 862-3303; Calle Luz No 115 btwn San Ignacio & Inquisidor; r US$25) Two big interconnecting rooms in colonial house; friendly.

CASAS PARTICULARES – CENTRO HABANA

Esther Cardoso (☎ 862-0401; Aguila No 367 btwn Neptuno 7 San Miguel; r US$25) Several rooms in artistic house; great furnishings and spectacular roof terrace with views.

Dulce Hostal – Dulce María González (☎ 863-2506; Amistad No 220 btwn Neptuno & San Miguel; r US$20) Beautiful colonial house, tile floors, soaring ceilings, quiet, friendly hostess.

Triny Vital (☎ 867-9132; Calle Aguila No 118 Bajos btwn Colón & Trocadero; apt US$50) Two-bedroom independent apartment with kitchen sleeps four to five.

Juan Carlos (☎ 863-6301, 861-8003; Crespo No 107 btwn Colón & Trocadero; r US$15-20) Big, spotless house. Cheapest room has shared bath and fan. Natural light throughout. Value.

La Casona Colonial – Jorge Díaz (☎ 870-0489; cubarooms2000@yahoo.com; Gervasio No 209 btwn Concordia & Virtudes; r US$25) Several rooms around nice courtyard, one has three beds, shared bath; good for longer stays.

Carlos Luis Valerrama Moré (☎ 867-9842; Neptuno No 404 2nd floor btwn San Nicolás & Manrique; r US$25) Big space with living/dining room and balcony.

Elsa and Julio Roque (☎ 861-8027; julioroq@yahoo.com; Consulado No 162 Apto 2 btwn Colón & Trocadero; r US$15-25) Rents three rooms with different amenities. Cheapest has shared bath, fan only and cold water. Friendly and quiet.

Elicio Fernández (☎ 861-7447; Aguila No 314 Apto 405 btwn Neptune & Concordia; r US$25) Breezy rooms with lots of natural light. Fan and shared bath. Doorman and elevator building. Rooftop views.

Casa Marta (☎ 863-3078; bienvenidoalcorazon@yahoo.com; Manrique No 362 cnr San Rafael; r US$30) Three rooms around inner patio; chance to meet other travelers.

Sandra Elso Aguilera (☎ 861-2944, 70 75 16; Consulado No 304 Apto 3E btwn Neptuno & Virtudes; r US$25) Friendly.

Alejandro Osés (☎ 863-7359; Malecón No 163 1st flr east of Hotel Deauville; r US$22) Three rooms, sea views very popular, English spoken.

Amada Pérez Güelmes and Antonio Clavero (☎ 862-3924; Lealtad No 262 Altos btwn Neptuno & Concordia; r US$25) Four rooms available in pleasant colonial house.

Rufino Añel Martín and Pilar Rodríguez Santos (☎ 862-4149; Neptuno No 556 btwn Lealtad & Escobar; r US$25) Lively, edgy area. Can cook and do laundry; helpful hosts.

Isabel Mesa Torreguitart (☎ 861-1268; San Lázaro No 119 Apto 13 btwn Crespo & Genios; r US$25) Small and simple room with shared bath. Family atmosphere. Repeatedly reader recommended.

Julio Massagué (☎ 863-1731; Escobar No 413 btwn San Rafael & San Martín; r US$20-25) Helpful. English spoken. Signposted.

Victoria Rivero Nuñez (☎ 863-7750; Consulado No 304 Apto 2D btwn Neptuno & Virtudes; r US$30) Spacious. Eighteen others renting in this building.

Martha Obregón (☎ 870-2095; marthaobregon@yahoo.com; Gervasio No 308 Altos btwn Neptuno & San Miguel; r US$20-25) Nice home, little balconies have small street views. Popular, often full.

Odales García (☎ 878-2877; Padre Varela No 307 1st flr btwn San Miguel & San Rafael; US$20-25) Super nice hostess, knows many others.

season US$21/31, high season US$23/41) One of the cheapest Havana hotels catering to foreigners, this isn't a bad choice deep inside Centro Habana (not for the timid). Expect cold water showers, frequent power outages and noise. Try for a room with balcony. Lock your valuables in a safety deposit box at reception for US$2 a day (don't leave valuables unattended in your room). The cafeteria (☯ 7am to 9:30pm) serves a reasonable breakfast. The Lido's rooftop bar (☯ 4pm to 4am) rustles up a good meal of pork, veggies and chips for US$6. There are many peso joints that will keep you well fed in the area.

Hotel Lincoln (Islazul; ☎ 33 82 09; Av de Italia btwn Virtudes & Ánimas; s/d low season US$28/37, high season US$46/35) This nine-story hotel was the second-tallest building in Havana when it was built in 1926; these days it offers 135 air-con rooms with bath and TV. A nightclub with a show is on the roof, and although most of the guests are Cuban, you'll also be welcome. Readers like this place, but caution to watch your valuables. At this price, Casa del Científico has way more atmosphere.

VEDADO   Map pp78-9

Hotel Bruzón (Islazul; ☎ 877-5684; Bruzón No 217 btwn Pozos Dulces & Av de la Independencia; s/d US$22/28; ☒) If you need to make a quick exit, consider this place next to the bus station. This four-story hotel has 46 rooms with bath, but they sell out fast. Avoid the wretched basement restaurant.

Hotel Universitario (☎ 33 34 03; Calle 17 at Calle L; s/d US$25/34) This friendly place opposite the Servi-Cupet gas station has a good location. It's basic, but you won't find another hotel in central Vedado for this price.

Hotel El Morro (Horizontes; ☎ 33 39 08; fax 33 39 07; Calle 3 at Calle D; s/d low season US$24/28, high season US$32/38) Just off the Malecón, this three-story hotel has 20 rooms with bath and TV.

Guarded parking is available across the street. It's good value, if a little out of the way.

Mid-Range

HABANA VIEJA   Map pp68-70

Hostal Valencia (Habaguanex; ☎ 867-1037; www.cuba .tc/cuhostalvalencia.html; Oficios No 53 at Obrapía; s/d incl breakfast low season US$57/67, high US$90/110) A super-popular place with only 11 rooms and stellar location, this 18th-century colonial mansion is a great place to stay if you can get a room. The upstairs units have little balconies and there's a pretty courtyard. The hotel restaurant is known for its paella (small portions). Next door with the same prices is the similar **Hotel El Comendador** (Habaguanex; ☎ 867-1037; Obrapía No 55 cnr of Baratillo; ☒).

THE AUTHOR'S CHOICE

Residencia Académica Convento de Santa Clara (Map pp68-70; ☎ 866-9327; fax 833-5696; Cuba No 610 btwn Luz & Sol; per person US$25) This is the oldest nunnery in Havana and the hushed, historic digs make for special accommodation – if you can get in. The nine rooms with bath around the side courtyard are usually booked months in advance.

Hotel Raquel (Map pp68-70; ☎ 860-8280; www.cuba.tc/raquel.html; Calle Amargura cnr San Ignacio; s/d incl breakfast US$105/180; ☒) At the time of writing, this was the newest refurbished hotel in the Habaguanex family. This time it's an Art-Deco theme, done stunningly well: the rooms feature simple cast-iron furnishings, beautiful tile floors and fine linens. The lobby, dominated by dozens of marble pillars, overwhelms. It's all very elegant and the restaurant is kosher.

Hotel NH Parque Central (Map pp68-70; Cubanacán; ☎ 860-6627; www.nh-hotels.com; Neptuno btwn Zulueta & Paseo de Martí; s/d US$185/245; P ☒ ⌨ ⌧) This is central Havana's top international hotel, with the facilities, location and service to prove it. The 277 rooms (two accommodate disabled guests) are as comfortable as you should expect from any five-star hotel. The rooftop pool has gorgeous skyline views (a gym and Jacuzzi are up there too) and does a great smoked salmon baguette sandwich. El Paseo Restaurant downstairs (open to nonguests) is dynamite.

Hotel Nacional (Map pp78-9; Gran Caribe; ☎ 55 00 04; www.grancaribe.cu; Calles O & 21; s/d/ste incl breakfast US$120/170/210; P ☒ ⌨ ⌧) An architectural stunner right on the Malecón, the Nacional has been Havana's flagship hotel since 1930. Famous former guests include Winston Churchill, Ava Gardner and Frank Sinatra (who attended a Mafia reunion here in 1946). Canadian Prime Minister Jean Chrétien stayed here during his April 1998 official visit and the few US senators that come to see Cuba for themselves usually stay here. This eight-story landmark edifice has 442 surprisingly plain rooms, but you stay here more for the history and legacy than the creature comforts. The presidential suite is US$1000. Coming here on a package deal will net a much cheaper room than these rack rates listed. The 6th floor is designated the executive floor with its own reception, telex, fax, meeting rooms and secretarial staff for business travelers. The Cabaret Parisién here is second only to the Tropicana in Marianao. The hotel's exchange office gives cash advances on Visa and MasterCard.

Hotel Meliá Habana (Map pp114-15; Cubanacán; ☎ 204-8500; www.solmeliacuba.com; Av 3 btwn Calles 76 & 80; s/d US$175/225; P ☒ ⌨ ⌧) Next to the Neptuno-Tritón. The 409 rooms in this swanky 11-story hotel all have balconies and sea or city views. Four rooms are accessible to disabled persons. You realize you're in a hotel run by private professionals rather than government functionaries as soon as you request some service. There's a business center, 14 conference rooms and an impressive lobby. Cuba's largest swimming pool is next to a desolate, rocky shore, fringed with tropical plants and secret spaces: lovely.

CENTRO HABANA   **Map pp68-70**
Hotel Caribbean (Horizontes; ☎ 860-8233; Paseo de Martí No 164 btwn Colón & Refugio; s/d low season US$33/48, high season US$36/54; ⊠) Another popular mid-range place with a terrific location on Prado, the rooms can be noisy here. Go for something on the upper floors. The price includes the use of the safe in the room.

Hotel Deauville (Horizontes; ☎ 33 88 13; www.horizontes.cu; Av de Italia No 1 & Malecón; s/d low season US$33/52, high season US$56/90; P ⊠ ⊠) This place is a mixed bag: it was recently renovated, so rooms are in fairly good shape and the seaside location is a bonus. However, it's betwixt and between everything, so you have to walk or taxi everywhere. Still, it's got lots of handy facilities, plus a disco and good city views from the cafeteria.

VEDADO   **Map pp78-9**
Hotel Colina (Horizontes; ☎ 33 40 71; Calles L & 27; s/d low season US$40/50, high season US$44/54; ⊠) Well worn rooms, bored staff and sparse facilities (there is a 24-hour sidewalk cafeteria with a decent local scene, however) mean you can usually get one of the 79 rooms here, no problem. Notice the reasonable price difference between seasons.

Hotel St John's (Horizontes; ☎ 33 37 40; Calle O No 216 btwn Calles 23 & 25; s/d incl breakfast low season US$50/67, high season US$63/80; ⊠ ⊠) The rooftop pool is small and the staff unresponsive, but the beds are good, the bathrooms clean and western facing rooms have killer Malecón views. Radio Taino is broadcast to your bedside at the touch of a button. Use the safe deposit box. The 14th-floor Pico Blanco nightclub is a local institution and the lobby bar relaxed.

Hotel Vedado (Horizontes; ☎ 832-2806; www.horizontes.com; Calle O No 244 btwn Calles 23 & 25; s/d low season US$50/67, high season US$63/80; ⊠ ⊠ ⊠) Perhaps slightly better value than the St John's, this hotel is just a touch more upscale, with a small business center, massage services and a cabaret with nightly flamenco show (US$5 drink minimum). Staff are friendly. Staying at either of these places puts you steps from Trattoría Maraka's (p96), which is super-added value.

Top End
The colonial properties administered by Habaguanex are loaded with charm, have great locations, professional staff and most

offer cribs and babysitting. What many of them lack, however, are elevators and accessible rooms for handicapped guests.

HABANA VIEJA   **Map pp68-70**
Hotel Santa Isabel (Habaguanex; ☎ 860-8201; www.cuba.tc/havana/cuhavsantaisabel.html; Baratillo No 9; s/d incl breakfast US$160/200; P ⊠ ⊠) Originally the Palacio de los Condes de Santovenia, this not quite five-star charmer on the eastern side of Plaza de Armas is loaded with architectural details, soft lighting, amenable staff and perks like views, terraces and tubs in every room. The spacious suites are especially nice, with large balconies overlooking the plaza (s/d US$315/400). We've received some complaints about frayed furnishings and lax housecleaning.

Hotel Florida (Habaguanex; ☎ 862-4127; www.cuba.tc/cuflorida.html; Obispo No 252 at Cuba; s/d incl breakfast US$80/130; P ⊠) This three-story building in the purest colonial style, with arches and pillars around the central courtyard, is a beauty. Constructed in 1836, it was recently restored with loving attention to detail; the nicely furnished rooms have high ceilings and fantastic beds. This stately old hotel also has a very elegant café with some of the plushest seating in the city, recommended for a splurge even if you're sleeping cheap elsewhere. There's dancing nightly (⊠ 8pm).

Hotel Ambos Mundos (Habaguanex; ☎ 860-9529; www.cuba.tc/havana/cuhavambosmundos.html; Obispo No 153 at Mercaderes; s/d/tr low season US$70/110/159, high season US$80/130/186; ⊠ ⊠) During his stays in Havana in the 1930s, author Ernest Hemingway put up at this five-story, pastel-pink palace, but these days it's mostly package tourists. The lobby bar is nice and the folklore shows at the roof bar are quality. Watch they don't put you in a windowless room.

Hostal Condes de Villanueva (Habaguanex; ☎ 862-9293; www.cuba.tc/villanueva.html; Mercaderes No 202 at Lamparilla; s/d US$95/150; P ⊠) Also known as El Hostal del Habano, this hotel near Plaza de San Francisco de Asís caters primarily to cigar aficionados, with a cigar shop, cigar club and cigar storage facilities. Each of the nine rooms bears the name of a different tobacco-growing area. It's not as spectacular or cozy as others in the chain.

Hotel Los Frailes (☎ 862-9383; www.hostallosfrailes.cu; Calle Brasil btwn Oficios & Mercaderes; s/d incl breakfast US$77/110; ⊠) This cozy 22-room hotel in the heart of Habana Vieja distinguishes

CITY OF HAVANA

itself with comfortable rooms with earth tones and rough-hewn furniture in keeping with the 'monkish' theme. The four rooms with balconies are best. The lobby bar is inviting.

CENTRO HABANA   **Map pp68–70**
Hotel Telégrafo (Habaguanex; ☎ 861-1010, 861-4741; www.hoteltelegrafo.cu; Paseo de Martí No 408 cnr Neptuno;

s/d from US$90/150; P ⟮⟯ ⎕) This well-located historic hotel (1888) updated to new millennium standards is a good choice if you want comfort and service at the nice price. The rooms are so modern they're almost mod – a novelty in Havana – and the lobby bar blends the old with the new successfully. The staff is efficient and professional,

---

CASAS PARTICULARES – VEDADO

Marta Vitorte (☎ 885- 7792; martavitorte@hotmail.com; Calle G No 301 Apto 14 btwn 13 & 15; r US$35-40) Several rooms in deluxe apartment with phenomenal views, great beds, wraparound terrace. English spoken.

Daysi Licor Pérez (☎ 832-6135; Calle G No 301 Apto 17 btwn Calles 13 & 15; r US$35-40; P) Beautiful views from this luxurious high-rise, antiques throughout, private. Italian spoken.

Melba Piñeda Bermudez (☎ 832-5929; lienafp@yahoo.com; Calle 11 no 802 btwn Calles 2 & 4; r US$25-30) Sweet room with nice furnishings and private terrace in beautiful colonial home. Quiet street. Helpful owners.

Made and Ernesto (☎ 830-6957; laispaz@yahoo.es; Paseo No 126 Apto 8B btwn 5 & 7; r US$25-30) Two spotless rooms with fridge and views.

Nelsy Alemán Machado (☎ 832-8467; Calle 25 No 361 Apto 1 btwn K & L; r US$20-25) Independent, laidback place. Fridge.

Basilia Pérez Castro (☎ 832-3953; bpcdt@hotmail.com; Calle 25 No 361 Apto 7 Bajos btwn K & L; r US$25) Two rooms with independent entrances, fridge, phone, TV. Mellow, good value.

Maribel y Luis Garcé (☎ 832-1619; Calle 19 No 356 upstairs btwn G & H; r US$25) Nice young couple rent smallish room, little balcony.

Eida Céspedes (☎ 832-3420; Calle 21 No 19 Apto 2 btwn N & O; r US$25) Equipped room with fridge, TV, small covered terrace.

Guillermina and Roberto Abreu (☎ 833-6401; Paseo No 126 Apto 13A btwn 5 & Calzada; r US$25) Two spacious rooms with views. Elevator here.

Celia and Rubén (☎ 833-6505; Paseo No 654 btwn 27 & Zapata; r US$25) Colonial manor with comfortable rooms, fridge, nice porch. Convenient to bus station, Plaza de la Revolución.

Angela Muñiz Rubio (☎ 879-6851; San Miguel No 1116 btwn Mazón & Basarrate; r US$20) Rents three rooms near Museo Napoleónico, two with private bath.

Julio Padilla Martín (☎ 832-5709; juliop_martin@hotmail.com; Calle K No 210 Apto 7B btwn Línea & 15; r US$30-35) Rents four rooms, good for groups. English spoken.

Pilar Palma (☎ 831-8918; Calle O No 202 Apto 9 btwn 23 & 25; r US$20-25) Prime La Rampa location; friendly.

Isabel 'Concha' Pérez (☎ 878-4871; freudmdj@yahoo.es; Mazón No 2 2nd flr cnr Neptuno; r US$15-25) Near the university steps. Friendly. Perfect for students at UH.

Conchita García (☎ 832-6187; conchitagarcia21@hotmail.com; Calle 21 No 4 Apto 74 btwn N & O; r US$30-35) Well-kept apartment with two rooms, TV, nice terrace. Numerous others in this building.

Casa Teresita (☎ 832-0777; Calle 21 No 4 Apto 54 btwn O & N; r US$25) Clean room, doting hostesses. Good for bikes.

Armando Gutiérrez (☎ /fax 832-1876; Calle 21 No 62 Apto 7 btwn M & N; r US$25-30) Nice room with balcony and fridge friendly. English spoken. Elevator.

Eddy Gutiérrez Bouza (☎ 832-5207; Calle 21 No 408 btwn F & G; r US$30; P) Fridge. Private, longstanding casa.

Francisco Rodríguez Sánchez (☎ 832-5003; Calle 17 No 558 btwn C & D; r US$25) Rents two rooms in splendid 1916 mansion. English spoken.

Iraida Carpio (☎ 832-4084; Calle 19 No 376 flr 10A btwn G & H; rUS$25) Take elevator. A splendid view.

Natalia Rodes (☎ 832-8909; Calle 19 No 376 flr 11B btwn G & H; r US$25) Shared bath, nice bed, expansive views.

María Esther Barrios 'La Superabuela' (☎ 832-3033; Calle I No 355 2nd flr btwn 17 & 19; r US$25) Small and simple room with shared bath; Superabuela is super friendly.

Casa de Jannett (☎ 831-7367; Calle F No 610 btwn 25 & 27; r US$25) Colonial house, close to university.

Ilka Picart (☎ 832-6886; Calle 19 No 606 btwn B & C; r US$30) Near the Mercado Agropecuario.

Elia León Cruz (☎ 833-7558; Calle 21 No 15 Apto 2A btwn N & O; r US$25) Independent house with little porch alongside Club 21.

which is a boon. This is the best affordable top range choice in Centro Habana at the moment; more are due to open.

Hotel Sevilla (Gran Caribe; ☎ 860-8560; fax 860-8582; Trocadero No 55 btwn Paseo de Martí & Agramonte; s/d/tr incl breakfast US$120/164/195; P X 🛋) This elegant place lives up to the Old World aura of its name. In a city brimming with unique hotels, this 1908 structure, managed by the French Accor chain, is another of the greats. Clean, safe and recommended, there's a sauna and fitness club, and the Sevilla's swimming pool is open to nonguests (US$5 at the rear entrance, Paseo de Martí and Ánimas). Its Patio Sevillano café off the lobby is open 24 hours a day, and the hotel restaurant near the front door lays out a breakfast buffet 7am to 10am daily for US$10. For an unforgettable view take the elevator up to the 9th-floor rooftop restaurant/bar.

Hotel Inglaterra (Gran Caribe; ☎ 860-8595; www.grancaribe.cu; Paseo de Martí No 416 at San Rafael; s/d/tr US$80/120/150; P X 🛋) This neoclassical hotel opposite Parque Central was erected in 1875. Given all the wonderful accommodation in Habana Vieja these days, the Inglaterra is not the prime place to stay that it once was. The rooftop La Terraza bar offers entertainment several nights a week, and rooms can be noisy. The street side bar does good mojitos and bad food. Guests beware: the hustlers are ready to pounce once you step beyond the lobby.

Hotel Plaza (Gran Caribe; ☎ 860-8592; www.grancaribe.cu; Agramonte No 267 at Neptuno; s/d/tr US$80/120/171; X) Sigh. This place routinely gets dumped upon: shabby rooms, pitiful service (staff are often overwhelmed by the big tour groups that always stay here), bad food, overbooking, you name it. The location is prime, but unless the package price is phenomenal, think twice. The Piano Bar at the Plaza opens at 10:30pm nightly except Tuesday, and the US$5 cover charge can go toward drinks. There's a 24-hour bar and rooftop terrace.

VEDADO   Map pp78-9
Hotel Habana Libre (Gran Caribe; ☎ 55 47 04; www.solmeliacuba.com; Calle L btwn Calles 23 & 25; incl breakfast s/d/tr US$80/100/142; P X 🛋 🛋) Havana's biggest hotel and skyline bully opened in March 1958 just prior to the 1959 revolution. Once part of the Hilton chain, it's now efficiently managed by Spain's Tryp Hotels. All the 574 comfort-

able rooms with small balcony are big and outfitted with modern furnishings in soothing tones. If you want a hotel with all the amenities, including a spiffy business center and shopping, this is a good choice for the price.

Hotel Meliá Cohiba (Cubanacán; ☎ 33 36 36; fax 33 45 55; Paseo btwn Calles 1 & 3; s/d US$175/225; P X 🛋 🛋) What with its winning formula of modern facilities, professional staff and overall consistency (something most Cuban hotels sorely lack), it's no coincidence that the Spanish Sol Meliá chain has two of Havana's top hotels. This property overlooking the Malecón is a blemish on the skyline, but sparkling inside, with 462 comfortable rooms in good repair (two are accessible to disabled guests). There are rooms especially for business travelers and 59 units have Jacuzzis. There's also a shopping arcade and the Habana Café here.

Hotel Victoria (Gran Caribe; ☎ 33 35 10; fax 33 31 09; Calle 19 No 101 & Calle M; s/d incl breakfast US$80/100; P X 🛋 🛋) This intimate five-story hotel off the main strip has only 31 rooms and is a good Vedado option if you want more personable service than the Nacional or Habana Libre offer. Rooms are tight, but well-equipped with fridge, safe and minibar. Built in the roaring '20s, it has style.

Hotel Presidente (Gran Caribe; ☎ 55 18 01; www.grancaribe.cu; Calzada & Calle G; s/d US$92/142; P X 🛋 🛋) Fully restored in 2000, this 160-room hotel wouldn't be out of place on a street just off Times Square in New York. Built the same year as the Victoria (1928), the Presidente is similar but larger, with gruffer staff. Unless you're a walker or are comfortable working Havana's transportation system, the location can be awkward.

Hotel Riviera (Gran Caribe; ☎ 33 40 51; fax 33 42 28; www.grancaribe.cu; Paseo & Malecón; s/d incl breakfast US$72/96) Built by US Mafia boss Meyer Lansky in 1957, this hotel oozes character – all the spacious lobby lacks is a lounge lizard in a sharkskin suit. Some of the 354 rooms have terrific sea views and balconies; two have been laid out for disabled guests. The big pool catches sea breezes and the Copa Room here hosts top bands nightly. There are lots of facilities (bank, shops, tourism desks etc), making this a decent choice, especially if you want to be by the water and not pay through the nose. The location means lots of walking, guaguas (local buses) or taxis.

Hotel Capri (Horizontes; ☎ 832-3708; www.horizontes.cu; Calle 21 No 8 at Calle N) was closed for restoration at the time of writing which is a very good thing; it had little to recommend it previously.

EATING
Paladares

Habana Vieja is notorious for overpriced, mediocre paladares and you'll generally find a better selection in Centro Habana and Vedado. Always ask to see the menu before committing and move on if you don't like what you see. For example, most of the paladares in the small streets off Plaza de la Catedral are overpriced. Some paladares add 10% 'tax' or 'servicio' to your bill without mentioning it beforehand. Others will charge extra for the rice and beans on the plate. Don't let *jineteros* (hustlers) lead you to a restaurant, unless you're happy to cover their commission (and possibly their meal!) Most places will happily arrange (illicit) lobster and shrimp plates.

HABANA VIEJA   Map pp68-70

La Julia (☎ 862-7438; O'Reilly No 506A btwn Bernaza & Villegas; ☒ noon-midnight) The pick of the Habana Vieja litter by consensus, this is *comida criolla* in a friendly, familial setting where you can get away for under US$10. It's small and popular: reservations recommended.

Paladar El Rincón de Elegguá (Aguacate No 257; ☒ noon-midnight) Just off the main Obispo drag,

---

THE AUTHOR'S CHOICE

If you're looking for a memorable dining experience in Havana, the following are recommended:

Tres Chinitos (Sue Yuen Zong; Map pp68-70; ☎ 863-3388; Dragones No 355 btwn San Nicolás & Manrique, Centro Habana; ☒ noon-midnight) The line of locals snaking down the block from this Chinatown favorite is for good reason, but it isn't the wontons. The throngs are waiting for a table in forgettable surroundings to sup on some of Havana's best pizza, lasagne and beautiful salads. It's nothing fancy mind you, but the value of that big US$4 pizza with red peppers, mushrooms, black olives and onions is unbeatable. Skip the affiliated Chinese greasy spoon downstairs and head to nearby Flor de Loto (p96), another local hot spot, if you're craving flavors from the east.

La Fontana (Map pp114-15; 3A No 305 cnr 46, Miramar) You might think you died and went to Spain, dining in the leafy, sheltered surroundings of this Mirarmar paladar. Real kalamata olives, carpaccio, smoked salmon and a cheese plate to make you swoon, this is the place to go if you want away from Cuban cooking. The wine selection is divine, perfect to wash down a delicious mixed grill or some quail eggs. Expect to pay at least US$25 per person for the memories.

La Complaciente (Map pp78-9; ☎ 831-8399; Calle 15 No 109 btwn L & M, Vedado; ☒ noon-10pm) Who knows if this humble paladar (true to the three table rule), located in an unattractive sliver of patio, will be able to handle all this publicity, but it can't go without mention because I have never found a better *lomo ahumado* in Cuba. Its succulent, smoked pork comes with a huge, delicious salad that will leave you licking your garlicky lips, mounds of congrí made just right and plantains, sweet or salty, whatever's around. There's no menu, just one thing from the classic Cuban kitchen, served daily at US$5 the meal; budget travelers should ask about the cheaper take-out *cajitas*.

El Paseo (Map pp68-70; ☎ 860-6627; Neptuno cnr of Prado & Zulueta in the NH Parque Central) Save up some money to treat yourself here, where we need only say two words: fresh mushrooms. OK, four words: blue cheese. This place adheres to the highest international standards (where the Turkish management shines) and you can get such treats as a real filet mignon and eggplant caviar (and other veggie delights), plus stellar service. Double bonus: huge breakfast buffet in the hotel's other restaurant, Mediterrane, and cocktails and appetizers by the rooftop pool. There is a breakfast buffet too.

La Torre (Map pp78-9; ☎ 55 30 89; Calle 17 cnr of Calle M in Edificio Focsa, Vedado) Just the views at this glass-enclosed restaurant 36 floors above Havana will knock your socks off. Dining on the French-inspired food here while gazing upon the Malecón drenched in a honey sunset will cost minimum US$30 a head, but you can bank on more once you see the dessert menu (tart almondine, drizzled with fresh whipped cream and raspberry coulis? I'll take it!) and extensive wine list. Budget travelers know you can get one of Havana's best veggie sandwiches – artichoke hearts baby! – with stellar sea views in the bar adjacent for US$2.50. Check out the luscious thin-cut french fries too.

this place has complete meals for US$10. It has been around awhile, but endures for its handy location, not necessarily the food.

CENTRO HABANA

Paladar La Guarida (☎ 264-4940; Concordia No 418 btwn Gervasio & Escobar; ☯ noon-3pm, 7pm-midnight) Wildly popular since the movie *Fresa y Chocolate* was partly filmed here, if you want a break from *cocina cubana* and have at least US$20 to spare, head here. It does a nice sea bass in coconut reduction and the Indian-inspired lamb is novel. Appetizer fans will be ecstatic here. Housed in a classic unrestored Centro Habana palace/tenement, the renovated dining rooms are interestingly eclectic, if cramped. The service is almost too businesslike; reservations essential.

Paladar Doña Blanquita (no phone; Paseo de Martí No 158 btwn Colón & Refugio; ☯ noon-10pm) The balcony overlooking Prado here is a romantic, if bustling, spot for classic Cuban cuisine (lots of pork, rice and beans). The service is friendly, the food reliable and the price right (everything in the US$7 to US$9 range). Enter through the narrow, unmarked doorway and go upstairs.

Paladar Las Delicias de Consulado (☎ 863-7722; Consulado No 309 btwn Neptuno & Virtudes; ☯ noon-midnight) This place in the scrappy Consulado corridor has a small upstairs terrace for dining. Dishes are the usual pork-and-bean feed for US$7. It also rents rooms.

Paladar Bellamar (Virtudes No 169 near Amistad; ☯ noon-10pm) A good standby. The amiable family here offers classic chicken, pork and fish dishes for US$6.

Paladar Amistad de Lanzarote (☎ 863-6172; Amistad No 211 btwn Neptuno & San Miguel; ☯ noon-midnight) Charges US$6 for most meals. The portions are large and English is spoken.

Paladar Doña Rosario (☎ 867-7773; San Lázaro No 260; ☯ noon-midnight) Behind the Hotel Deauville. A full meal of chicken or fish and all the fixings is US$8 – depending. There's no written menu, so the scam opportunity is there.

VEDADO

Variety is the spice of life, and Vedado has it coming and going with the paladar selection. These are some of our tried and true favorites; you're encouraged to find your own.

Decameron (☎ 832-2444; Línea No 753 btwn Paseo & Calle 2; ☯ noon-midnight) Nothing mediocre will ever pass your lips at this intimate Italian restaurant, so order from the varied menu with abandon. Veggie pizza, lasagna bolognese, a sinful calabaza soup, steak au poivre: it's all good. There's a decent wine selection and vegetarians will find heavenly options. Figure US$10 to US$12 per person.

Paladar El Hurón Azul (☎ 879-1691; Humboldt No 153 at Calle P; ☯ noon-midnight Tue-Sun) A solid central Vedado paladar with windowless but tasteful dining rooms, you'll eat well here. Meals start with a nice fruit plate, but save room for the yummy mains (try the snapper in red and green sauce or the 'La Guajira' house special). Dishes start at US$7 and top out at US$12 (plus 10% service charge). You may have to wait for a table here. (Touts will tell you that the place is closed or expensive because Hurón Azul pays them no commissions.)

Paladar El Helecho (☎ 831-3552; Calle 6 No 203 btwn Línea & Calle 11; ☯ noon-10:30pm Wed-Thu) Tucked along a leafy sidestreet in western Vedado, this romantic little place is a longtime favorite. The nice atmosphere is complemented by decent prices (US$4.75 for a pork steak, US$5.25 for the chicken) and good portions. The food is remarkably good. Try the chicken soup which a Cuban friend called 'the best I've had outside my own kitchen': high praise.

Le Chansonnier (☎ 832-1576; Calle J No 257 btwn Calles 13 & 15; ☯ 12:30pm-12:30am) You'll sup in your own elegant dining room in this Vedado mansion-turned-paladar specializing in French flavors. Rabbit in red wine sauce, chicken smothered in mushrooms, and gigantic salads for herbivores are some of the offers (nothing over US$12) in this gay-friendly establishment. Save room for dessert.

El Gringo Viejo (☎ 831-1946; Calle 21 No 454 btwn Calles E & F; ☯ noon-11pm) Locals and visitors alike swear by this place for the speedy service, fine wine list and big portions of more adventurous plates like smoked salmon with olives and gouda (US$8) or crab meat in red sauce (US$7.50). But after two meals, we're still not convinced. Chef's night off both times? You be the judge.

El Recanto (Calle 17 No 957 btwn Calles 8 & 10; ☯ noon-2am, closed Wed) Head up a rickety set of stairs, down a dingy hallway, through someone's living room, then the kitchen and out back to the funky rooftop patio paladar here. Good points: atmosphere, long hours, big portions and cheap prices (around US$4 for most mains). Bad points: long waits, brusque service and zilch for vegetarians.

Casa Sarasua (Calle 25 No 510 Apto 1 btwn Calles H & I; ☼ noon-midnight) This place is a veritable rabbit's warren of arms and armaments, and your chatty host is more than happy to enlighten you about his collection-cum-museum. Meat dominates the menu, but vegetarians will be accommodated with something or other. Conveniently located near the university.

Also recommended:

Paladar Escorpión (Calle 17 No 105 btwn Calles L & M; meals US$6-7; ☼ noon-2am) Next to El Conejito Bar.

Paladar Los Amigos (Calle M No 253 at Calle 19, out back; ☼ noon-midnight) Handy location beside the Focsa building.

Paladar Nerei (Calles 19 & L; ☼ noon-midnight Mon-Fri, 6pm-midnight Sat & Sun) Reliable place with outdoor dining.

Paladar Monopoly (☎ 832-2471; Calle K No 154 btwn Línea & Calle 11; ☼ noon-1am) Museum-quality dining digs; unsignposted, ask a neighbor if in doubt.

Spanish Clubs
Map pp68-70

Several Spanish clubs that are open to the public have excellent, inexpensive restaurants. Most are in pesos (but accept dollars at the current exchange), which makes them an attractive option if you're 'going Dutch' with Cuban friends or colleagues.

Asociación Canaria de Cuba (☎ 862-5284; Av de las Misiones No 258 btwn Neptuno & Ánimas; ☼ noon-8:30pm) Go to the second floor dining room of this club across from the Edificio Bacardí and you'll be treated to a varied menu featuring shrimp or lobster (US$6.50), fish (US$2.50) and several chicken dishes (none over US$2). The atmosphere is fluorescent lights and plastic flowers in the dining room, but the foyer is grand.

Centro Andaluz (☎ 863-6745; Paseo de Martí No 104 btwn Genios & Refugio; ☼ 6-11pm Tue-Sun) For a whopping US$11, you might splash out and try the house paella for two, or pinch some pennies and go for the fish (US$3.75) or pork filet (US$3). Regardless, try the house cocktail 'locura flamenca' (US$1.60). You can see flamenco dancing here starting at 9pm Tuesday to Sunday

or take classes yourself (see Courses in the Directory p411).

Casa de Castilla (☼ 862-5482; Neptuno No 519 btwn Lealtad & Perseverancia; ☼ noon-10pm Tue-Sun) Another fluorescent dining room with zero atmosphere has delights coming from the kitchen including a killer ropa vieja (US$2), filet Montetoro (fish with cheese, US$2.50) and filete Uruguayo (real beef, US$4.50). There are dozens of dishes (served with reliable frequency) here. The stand-up bar is good for a cold one if you're caught in the middle of Centro Habana.

Restaurants
HABANA VIEJA
Map pp68-70

Café del Oriente (☎ 860-6686; Oficios 112 at Amargura in Plaza de San Francisco de Asís; ☼ noon-11pm) It's hard to even type what's on offer at this fine dining establishment without drooling on the keyboard. Try the smoked salmon with caviar (US$12) or goose liver pate appetizer (US$8), moving on to lobster thermidor (US$27) or steak au poivre (US$19), finishing with the cheese plate (US$12) and a glass of port. Service is tux deluxe, but you can also come in just for a coffee.

Restaurante Mirador de la Bahía (Obispo No 61 south side Plaza de Armas; ☼ noon-midnight) On the fifth floor above the Museo Nacional de Historia Natural, this place has great views. Dine on cheeseburgers (US$2.25), pizza (US$3 to US$6) or go for something more substantial (like fish, US$7) while gazing over the bay at El Cristo. Live music and dancing during lunch and dinner hours.

Cafetería Torre La Vega (Obrapía No 114a near Oficios; ☼ 9am-9pm) This friendly, reliable place is hard to beat with it's outdoor tables and large bowls of spaghetti for just over US$1. Try some of the crispy, handmade chips with your cold beer. Next door is a phenomenal **batido and juice joint**.

Al Medina (☎ 867-1041; Oficios No 12 btwn Obrapía & Obispo; ☼ noon-midnight) This is Havana's top Middle Eastern place, where you can dine on lamb (US$6 to US$9) or chicken (US$5) with a spicy twist. It's especially recommended for its voluminous veggie platter that comes with hummus, taboulé, dolma, pilaf and felafel (US$10). Budget eaters will dig the US$2.50 special at the cafeteria just inside on the left (kebab, rice, salad and drink). There's live music in the courtyard.

MEAT'S NOT FOR ME

Cubans like their meat. Not only is the cuisine traditionally carnivorous, but after the leanest years of the Special Period, people are anxious to consume as much protein as possible whenever it's available. It's surprising then, that a new chain of vegetarian restaurants, plus TV cooking shows advocating healthy (and often meatless) eating habits have been such a big hit. They certainly are with foreigners and even if you're not a vegetarian, the restaurants listed below provide great and welcomed variety to the same old pork/chicken/rice and bean feed.

Biki Vegetarian Restaurant (Map pp78-9; Infanta & San Lázaro, Centro Habana-Vedado border; noon-10pm, closed Mon) This place near the university has dozens of selections daily, laid out cafeteria style; grab a tray and pick from several fresh juices and salads (four to six pesos), veggie paella, fried rice or stuffed peppers (10 to15 pesos), root vegetables (six pesos) and desserts like rice pudding. Beware that the staff at this restaurant and the branch on Calzada have developed the nasty habit of charging foreigners indiscriminate dollar prices. This is a peso restaurant; don't let them bully you into paying dollars.

Restaurant Vegetariano Carmelo (Map pp78-9; Calzada btwn Calles D & E; noon-midnight, closed Mon) This place has the same menu as Biki, but a much nicer locale opposite the Teatro Amadeo Roldán, with patio dining and a full bar. Some friends from the US were gouged here for US$27 for a meal that really cost US$3.50, so watch out. One tip is to refuse the table service they try to push upon you and just proceed cafeteria style.

Restaurante El Bambú (Map pp122-3; in the Jardín Botánico; noon-5pm, closed Mon) This is the first and finest in Havana vegetarian dining and has led the way in education efforts as to the benefits of a meatless diet. The all-you-can-eat lunch buffet is served en plein air deep in the botanical gardens, with the natural setting paralleling the wholesome tastiness of the food. For US$14 you can gorge on soups and salads, root vegetables, tamales and eggplant caviar. Herbs grown on the premises figure prominently in the dishes. Juices, desserts and coffee are on offer too. Coupled with a visit to the garden, it makes a smashing side trip.

La Lluvia de Oro (862-9870; Obispo No 316 at Habana; 24hr) An atmospheric restaurant and bar with overhead ceiling fans stirring the smoke and catching drifting notes from the live septet, this is a good place for a pizza and beer or mojito and sandwich (nothing over US$3). It's a popular traveler hang-out, which means it's a popular *jinetero* hang-out.

Restaurante El Patio (867-1034/5; San Ignacio No 54 at Empedrado; meals US$15-20; noon-midnight) You can take a full meal at this restaurant in the romantic inner courtyard of an old colonial palace on the Plaza de la Catedral or just camp out on the pleasant terrace (24 hours) facing the cathedral and have a sandwich or snack.

Restaurante La Paella (867-1037; Hostal Valencia, Oficios & Obrapía; noon-11pm) Known for its paella (US$8 to US$15), don't neglect to consider the shrimp (US$10), lobster (US$23) or fish (US$10) at this cozy and popular oldie but goodie (reservations suggested).

Hanoi (867-1029; Brasil cnr of Bernaza; noon-11pm) Disregard anything anyone tells you

about this place having a hint of Vietnamese flavor: this is straight-up creole cuisine with a couple of fried rice dishes thrown in for good measure (US$2 to US$3). It's cheap and decent, just don't get too excited. As this place is central, well signposted and in all the guidebooks, you might have to wait for a table; but we wouldn't. Live music to dine by.

Restaurante La Dominica (860-2918; O'Reilly No 108 at Mercaderes; noon-midnight) Widely considered to be Havana's finest Italian restaurant; the menu ranges from spaghetti and pizza (US$4.50 to US$7.50) to shrimp and lobster (US$10 to US$18). The foreign management is reflected in the surprisingly good service and food.

Restaurante El Castillo de Farnés (867-1030; Av de Bélgica No 361 at Obrapía; noon-midnight) This is a good pre- or post-theater place, with seafood in the US$7 to US$20 range, but don't make a special trip. The bar alongside with sidewalk tables is a good spot to cool your heels awhile.

Restaurante-Bar El Criollo (Av de Bélgica No 560 just off Apodaca; 24hr) A local and very atmospheric option worth a try. The tamale, salad and chicken special for US$1 is a steal. Wash it down with Cristal on tap. There are many other peso places along Av de Belgíca between Parque de la Fraternidad and the Central Train Station good for a fill up while you wait for your train.

Also recommended:

La Torre de Marfil (☎ 867-1038; Mercaderes No 111 btwn Obispo & Obrapía; ☽ noon-10pm Mon-Thu, noon-midnight Fri-Sun) Cantonese-type food at around US$5 a plate.

La Zaragozana (☎ 867-1040; Av de Bélgica, btwn Obispo & Obrapía; ☽ noon-midnight) Skip the food, but drop in for a drink, music and flamenco dancing from 9pm.

La Mina (☎ 862-0216; Obispo & Oficios on Plaza de Armas; ☽ 24hr) An institution with side-by-side patio restaurants. Stick to the chicken or pork (US$7 to US$8) if you're peaked, but this place is better for mojitos and coffee and people watching.

Restaurante D'Giovanni (☎ 867-1027; Tacón No 4 at Empedrado; ☽ noon-midnight) Try the pastas here (the house specialty) at US$3 to US$5 and watch the price of the side salad.

CENTRO HABANA   Map pp68-70

Restaurante Oasis (Paseo de Martí No 256 in the Centro Cultural Cubano Árabe; ☽ 2pm-3am). The Arabian-inspired menu here is reasonable and there's a floor show on Saturday at 9pm. A shop at the entrance sells bread. The disco is a *jineteras*-fest.

Los Dos Dragones (Chung Shan; ☎ 862-0909; Dragones No 311 near San Nicolás; ☽ noon-10:30pm) Away from the Cuchillo madness, this is Chinatown's most reliable restaurant, serving up tremendous portions of shrimp in red sauce (US$8) and chicken with bamboo shoots and mushrooms ($6). It does a booming business in oyster cocktails (US$1).

Flor de Loto (Salud No 313 btwn Gervasio & Escobar; ☽ noon-midnight) Chinatown's newest addition is this place specializing in grilled lobster (US$7) and interesting dishes like fish with almond sauce (US$4.50). The portions are tremendous – try a mountain of fried rice – and the kitchen opens into the dining room, giving you a sneak peak.

Restaurante Tien-Tan (☎ 861-5478; Cuchillo No 17 btwn Zanja & San Nicolás; ☽ 11am-11pm) Of all the cookie-cutter Chinese places on the Cuchillo, this is the best hands down. There are 130 dishes to choose from and you can eat several and still not owe US$10 (payable in pesos or dollars). It does an especially good

wonton soup. Expect a 20% service charge to be added to your bill.

Some of the street stalls selling *cajitas* in Chinatown's Cuchillo are better than the actual restaurants.

Also recommended:

Feria Los Fornos (Neptuno btwn Paseo de Martí & Consulado; ☽ 24 hr) Try the grilled meats (US$2 to US$6) in this open courtyard if you're not rushed.

Café del Prado (☎ 860-8241; Paseo de Martí & Colón; ☽ 7am-3am) Good post-disco snack stop or for an espresso any time.

Restaurante Puerto de Sagua (☎ 867-1026; Av de Bélgica No 603 at Acosta; ☽ noon-midnight) Nautical-themed place with super-friendly staff serving fish dishes starting at US$5 and shrimp at US$8.

VEDADO   Map pp78-9

Trattoría Maraka's (☎ 33 37 40, ext143; Calle O No 260 btwn Calles 23 & 25; ☽ 10am-11pm) Real olive oil, parmesan and mozarella cheese, plus a wood oven, mean this pizza (US$4 to US$6) is among the city's best. Also on offer are Greek salads (US$6.95), tortellini with red sauce, spinach-stuffed canelloni – the menu is long and quality, with few items over US$8.

El Lugar (☎ 204-5162; Calle 49C & 28A; ☽ noon-midnight) Even more reason to come to Parque Almendares, this restaurant just across the road from the river below the bridge is fantastic value. For US$4.50 you get a juicy pork filet, a whole heap of *congrí*, salad, *tostones*, ice cream and coffee. Add a dollar or two for *ropa vieja* or fish. There's a talented trio playing nights. The pizza place attached is good too.

Cafe TV (☎ 33 44 99; Calles N & 19; ☽ 10am-9pm) This bar-restaurant in the bowels of the Focsa Building has real breakfast: eggs, toast, juice etc, with nothing over US$1. The lunch and dinner menu is varied and cheap and at night there's live music (US$7 minimum consumption; ☽ 9pm-2am). Televisión Cubana is around the corner, hence the name and theme.

Pan.com (☎ 53 50 40; Calles 17 & 10; ☽ 10am-2am) Cuba's answer to Subway, this place does big, fresh sandwiches (turkey with cheese on a baguette for example), bacon and egg breakfast and veggie burgers heavy on the fixings. The milkshakes (real milk, creamy ice cream) are incredible. Nothing is over US$5. There's a full bar.

El Conejito (☎ 832-4671; Calle M No 206 at Calle 17; ☽ noon-midnight) The odd, Tudor-type brick building on the corner is the 'little rabbit' and that's the house specialty (in many forms for US$10). There are many other items on the menu, all done equally reliably. There's a lively bar scene here too.

Restaurante 1830 (☎ 55 30 90; Malecón No 1252; ☻ noon-10pm) One of Havana's most elegant restaurants is this old stalwart (though one reader called it 'terrible'). After the kitchen closes at 10pm there's live music and salsa dancing in the garden behind the restaurant (don't come on a windy night).

Mesón La Chorrera (☻ 10am-2am) is in the Castillo de Santa Dolores de La Luna La Chorrera (1643), the old tower nearby. It's more reasonable than the restaurant and snacks and drinks are available seaside at El Viejo Espigón.

Also recommended:

Rumbos Cafetería (Calles 23 & P; ☻ 24hr) Popular, informal place with good pastries (usually) and sandwiches.

Restaurante Bulerías (☎ 832-3823; Calle L No 414 btwn Calles 23 & 25; ☻ 11am-10pm) Don't venture into the basement here, but eat at the sidewalk tables; half a fried chicken is US$2.50.

Restaurante Wakamba (☎ 878-4526; Calle O btwn Calles 23 & 25; ☻ 24hr) Forty years and still going, this bar/counter place serving light meals hosts many late-night characters.

Cafés

Café Santo Domingo (Map pp68-70; Obispo No 159 btwn San Ignacio & Mercaderes; ☻ 9am-9pm) Tucked away upstairs beyond the very good pastry/ bread shop is this laidback café with a small balcony overlooking the street. The sandwiches and pizzas are big and tasty; this is a good hideaway.

Bar-Restaurant La Luz (☻ 24hr) Next door to Café Santo Domingo, this place offers one-peso shots of strong coffee.

El Mercurio (Map pp68-70; ☎ 860-6188; in Lonja del Comercio; ☻ 24hr) On Plaza de San Francisco de Asís, this is an elegant café-restaurant ('for businessmen and travelers') with fresh salads and sandwiches.

Cafe La Logia (Map pp68-70; ☎ 861-5657; in the Capitolio; ☻ 9am-7pm) With tropical atmosphere to spare, this breezy terrace café provides excellent views of all the classic cars and general action going on below the Capitolio. Hole up here and nosh on a good veggie sandwich (US$2.50) or sip a cappuccino (US$1.50) or mojito (US$2).

Pain de Paris Vedado (Map pp78-9; Calle 25 No 164 btwn Infanta & O; ☻ 8am-midnight); Vedado (Map pp78-9; Línea btwn Paseo & Calle A; ☻ 24hr) This chain serves reliable cappuccino, croissants (with ham and cheese if you like), napoleons and other pastries. A box of treats from here is nice to share if you're invited to a Cuban home for dinner.

Café de O'Reilly (Map pp68-70; O'Reilly No 203 btwn Cuba & San Ignacio; ☻ 11am-3am) Snacks and drinks are served here. Go up the stairway inside.

Cafe Wilfredo Lam (Map pp68-70; San Ignacio No 22 cnr Empedrado; ☻ 10am-5pm Mon-Sat) At the center of the same name, this is an arty nook for a drink. Next to the cathedral.

Ice-Cream Parlors

Havana has some fabulous ice cream, available in both dollars and pesos – just the ticket on a hot day. *Paleticas* are popsicles (usually chocolate covered), while *bocaditos* are big, delicious ice-cream sandwiches (often handmade). For more ice-cream vocab, see the Food & Drink chapter (p56). Ice-cream cones are sold on the street for three pesos. Otherwise you can try these parlors:

Bim Bom (Map pp78-9; ☎ 879-2892; Calle 23 & Infanta, Vedado) Phenomenally creamy stuff in flavors like coffee, condensed milk (sounds gross, tastes great) and rum raisins; in dollars.

Coppelia (Map pp78-9; ☎ 832-6184; Calles 23 & L, Vedado) The original. See boxed text 'Making Cents of Coppelia', p98.

Cremería Obispo (Map pp68-70; Obispo No 58 cnr of Villegas) New peso parlor in the heart of Habana Vieja; often has fruit flavors (pineapple, strawberry, etc)

Takeout

There are some great peso places sprinkled about. Some of the most outstanding **peso pizza** (Map pp78-9) is at San Rafael just off Infanta (look for the line). They make the pizza on the roof, so you have to shout up your order (there's a menu posted) and then it comes down via a rope/basket rig. This may be the only peso place offering 'pizza Hawaiiana' (ham and pineapple). Also try around Calles H and 17 where there are clusters of **peso stalls** (Map pp78-9) and Calle 21 between Calles 4 and 6 (Map pp78-9; this area is close to the hospital, so there's great variety and long hours), both in Vedado.

MAKING CENTS OF COPPELIA

Until you've gone slackjawed watching a young woman with a model's body wolf down nine scoops of ice cream followed by a cake à la mode with childish delight, you haven't eaten at Coppelia. Truly a cultural phenomenon, waiting a near eternity to enter the weirdly futuristic but retro and hallowed halls of this Havana ice institution is like riding the 4 train out to Yankee Stadium for a twilight double header. Of course, you can just hop into Coppelia's sterile dollar café, but we swear the ice cream tastes better after a 45-minute wait (and at five cents a scoop, the price is right). But there's a system to the peso part, which many foreigners don't observe or get, jumping the line, which stinks for the rest of us. Here's how it works.

There are several entrances to Coppelia, each with their own menu, line and dining area. Diehards cruise the different entrances (at Calles 23 and L, on L between Calles 23 and 21, and on the corner of L and Calle 21) to see what's on each menu (it lists the brand – more often Varadero than Coppelia, which is still good, only less creamy – the flavors and the combos available). What the menu says and what's actually on offer once you're inside is another story, but I've eaten the classic *fresa y chocolate*, coconut, banana and orange-pineapple, so it's not just vanilla (though Coppelia's vanilla is luscious). You take the *último* in the line you like and then you wait. Sections are seated all at once, so some 20 people are let in en masse and shown to their section. A server comes around, tells you what's available, you give your order and they bring you the goods. They come around afterward to collect your money. Rainy days are classically slow here, so you might minimize wait times by showing up then. The language of ice-cream love is complex here: see Food & Drink (p56) for the vocab basics. A movie at Cine Yara across the street, followed by a *jimagua* at Coppelia is the classic Havana date.

Cajitas can save your night: these complete take-out meals in cardboard boxes usually cost about US$1. Some boxes have cut-out spoons on the lid, but most don't, so you'll have to supply your own fork (or use part of the box itself as a shovel). You can usually buy *cajitas* at agropecuarios; otherwise, private cafeteria and *merendero* (snack seller) windows sell them. Chinatown is known for their *cajitas*. Try one of these on for size:

Cafetería La Primera de Aguacate (Map pp68-70; Aguacate No 12; ⊗ noon-10pm) Just north of Tejadillo and not far from the Museo de la Revolución; famous for its *cajitas*.

D'Oscar (Map pp78-9; San Lázaro No 1061) Near Infanta.

Cafetería M en A (Map pp78-9; Calle 25 No 163 btwn Calle O & Infanta; ⊗ noon-11pm Mon-Fri, noon-8pm Sat & Sun)

Cafetería La Tavola Calda (Map pp78-9; Calle 21 No 103 btwn Calles L & M)

El Cocotero (Map pp78-9; Línea & Calle F; ⊗ 11am-7pm Mon-Fri)

Self-Catering

You often have to check your bags at a '*guardabolsa*' outside of the actual store before shopping. You also have to show a security guard your receipt and open your grocery sack when leaving the store.

HABANA VIEJA   **Map pp68-70**
Fresh loaves of bread are sold at **Panadería San José** (Obispo No 161; ⊗ 24hr). **Bodegón La Lluvia de Oro** (Obispo No 314; ⊗ 9am-9pm) also has bread and some groceries.

Supermercado El Cristo (Brasil No 461; ⊗ 9am-11pm) the best-stocked supermarket in the old town, also sells bread.

CENTRO HABANA   **Map pp68-70**
The best stocked store in the entire area is **Harris Brothers** (O'Reilly No 526; ⊗ 9am-9pm Mon-Sat), just off Parque Central, with a large liquor selection (including wine), cheeses, bread, olives and other picnic goodies. Also good is **Supermercado Isla de Cuba** (Máximo Gómez & Factoría; ⊗ 10am-6pm Mon-Sat, 9am-1pm Sun) on the southern side of Parque de la Fraternidad, with yogurt, cereals, pasta etc. You have to check your bag outside, to the right of the entrance.

For a decent supermarket in Centro Habana, try **Almacenes Ultra** (Av Simón Bolívar No 109; ⊗ 9am-6pm Mon-Sat, 9am-1pm Sun), at the corner of Rayo, near Av de Italia.

La Época (Av de Italia & Neptuno; ⊗ 9am-9pm Mon-Sat, 9am-noon Sun) is a hard-currency department store with a supermarket in the basement. Check your bags outside before entering this epic Havana emporium.

Further west is **Supermercado Amistad** (San Lázaro No 1109; ⏰ 10am-6pm Mon-Fri, 9am-noon Sat), just below Infanta. The good stuff is upstairs.

VEDADO
Map pp78-9

The **supermercado** below the Edificio Focsa (Calle 17 at Calle N; ⏰ 9am-6pm Mon-Sat, 9am-1pm Sun) has good variety; plus there is a toiletry store and candy/cookie place with good chocolate here.

Supermercado Meridiano (Calle 1 & Paseo in Galerías de Paseo; ⏰ 10am-5pm Mon-Fri, 10am-2pm Sun), across the street from the Hotel Meliá Cohiba, has a good wine and liquor selection, lots of yogurt, cheese and chips. The bread is overpriced.

DRINKING
Habana Vieja
Map pp68-70

La Bodeguita del Medio (☎ 33 88 57; Empedrado No 207 off Plaza de la Catedral; ⏰ 11am-midnight) Made famous thanks to the rum-swilling exploits of Ernest Hemingway, a visit to Havana's most celebrated bar has become de rigueur, and notables including Salvador Allende, Fidel Castro, Nicolás Guillén, Harry Belafonte and Nat King Cole have left their autographs on La Bodeguita's wall. These

days the clientele is less luminous, with package tourists from Varadero and literary sycophants delighting in the bottled (some say canned) bohemian atmosphere and the US$4 mojitos. The staff claim to serve Cuba's best *lechón asado* (roast suckling pig), though at US$20 per person we weren't willing to verify.

El Caserón del Tango (Jústiz No 21 off Officios) This unpretentious place, down the street beside the Museo del Automóvil, has a nice, low-key bar where you can get sandwiches and drinks for pesos. On Wednesday and Friday at 5pm there's a special tango programme, and lessons can be arranged. There's live music and dancing from 9pm on weekends.

Cafe París (Obispo No 202 at San Ignacio; ⏰ 24hr) Jump into the mix by grabbing one of the rough hewn tables at this Habana Vieja standby, known for its live music and gregarious atmosphere. On good nights, the rum flows, talented musicians jam and spontaneous dancing and singing erupt from the crowd. Filling slices of pizza (US$0.50) are sold at a takeout window on the side of the building.

Bar La Marina (Oficios & Brasil; ⏰ 10am-11pm) The agreeable courtyard here is an inviting glen in which to take a break or nibble after

---

HAVANA'S BEST AGROPECUARIOS

These farmers markets (often called 'agros') are where you'll find all in-season fruits and vegetables; *organopónicos* are organic markets. Agros are not only good for buying raw, fresh foods, but are handy for getting pesos (every large market has a Cadeca), *cajitas*, fresh meat, bread, cut flowers and other natural products like herbs, honey, spices, beeswax candles etc. Every market also has a '*protección de consumidor*' section with a scale where they'll weigh what you've purchased. Go here if you think you've been ripped off (a merchant caught three times cheating is booted from the market). Most markets are closed Monday. Here are some of Havana's biggest:

Agropecuario Sol (Map pp68-70; Calle Sol btwn Habana & Compostela, Habana Vieja) Compact, well-stocked market; decent variety.

Mercado Agropecuario Egido (Map pp68-70; Av de Bélgica, btwn Corrales & Apodaca, Centro Habana) Gigantic market: the action is over by 2pm.

Tulipán (Map pp78-9; Av Tulipán just off Av de la Independencia, Plaza) This is a huge, 'capped' market, with prices set by the government; so it's cheap.

Organopónico Plaza (Map pp78-9; Av de Colón & Panorama, Plaza) One of Havana's biggest organic farms with a retail market.

Plaza de Marianao (Map pp114-15; Av 51 & Calle 124, Marianao) Friendly local market with produce downstairs and flowers and plants up. Head east up Av 51 for amazingly varied peso shopping.

Calle 19 & A (Map pp78-9; Calle 19 btwn Calles A & B, Vedado) Havana's 'gourmet' market with cauliflower, fresh herbs and rarer produce during shoulder seasons; prices reflect the selection.

Calle 21 & J (Map pp78-9; Calle 21 & J, Vedado) Good selection, including potted plants; watch for overcharging.

Calle 17 & K (Map pp78-9; Calle 17 & K, Vedado) Another 'capped' market with cheap prices, but limited selection.

visiting the Monasterio de San Francisco de Asís. A Cuban combo plays in the afternoons. The popcorn is very good (when the machine is working).

Bar Dos Hermanos (☎ 861-3436; San Pedro No 304 at Sol near Muelle Luz; ☯ 24hr) A wonderful old wooden dive, this was a favorite Havana hang-out of Spanish poet Federico García Lorca during his three months in Cuba in 1930. Pub snacks such as oyster cocktails, hamburgers and chicken go well with the drinks. The salty atmosphere adds to the flavor, but this is a rather seedy area late at night. For something more upscale, try the bar inside **Fundación Havana Club** (Sol & Malecón; ☯ 9am-midnight), where it's all rum all the time, plus live music.

For bars with views, try the **Restaurante Mirador de la Bahía** on the southern side of the Plaza de Armas, above the Museo Nacional de Historia Nacional, or one of the 24-hour Cristal kiosks along the Malecón (at the end of O'Reilly for instance).

If you need to kill time before a train departure, try **El Baturro** (Av de Bélgica & Merced; ☯ 11am-11pm), a Spanish bistro with a long wooden bar and an all-male – aggressively so – drinking clientele.

Centro Habana   Map pp68-70
El Floridita (☎ 867-1300; Obispo No 557 at Av de Bélgica; ☯ 11am-midnight) Hemingway was a barhopper and name maker and this place, like La Bodeguita del Medio, cashes in on the literary legend. A bartender named Constante Ribalaigua assured El Floridita's place in drinking history when he used shaved ice to make frozen daiquiris here in the 1920s. A decade later Hemingway arrived and the Papa Hemingway Special (rum with grapefruit juice, lemon juice and crushed ice) was created in his honor. If you'd like to order either at the long wooden bar, they're US$6 a pop (yowza!). The atmosphere and churlish staff leave a lot to be desired.

Rather than rubbing sunburned elbows with the tour-bus crowd in El Floridita, head south on Av de Bélgica one block to Obrapía, where you can sip a daiquiri at the **Monserrate Bar** (☎ 860-9751; Obrapía No 410) for a third of the price quoted by the red-coated waiters in El Floridita. Skip the cheap (for a reason) food. Across the street, Restaurante El Castillo de Farnés has good value, light food and an airy atmosphere. If you're feeling hassled by

the hustlers, you can retire to the terrace of the nearby Hotel Inglaterra, the 2nd-floor veranda bar at the Capitolio or the small, subdued lobby bar at the Hotel Telégrafo.

Restaurante Prado 264 (Paseo de Martí No 264; ☯ noon-10:30pm) has a long wooden bar in the back. Don't eat here if they ask you to pay dollars for peso food.

Vedado   Map pp78-9
Opus Bar (Calzada & Calle D above Teatro Amadeo Roldán; ☯ 3pm-3am) With individual candle-lit tables, overstuffed chairs and Sly and the Family Stone on the airways, this is Havana's (good) approximation of a lounge. The wall of windows make it a great sunset spot and performances in the theater downstairs are broadcast via closed-circuit TV; a good alternative if that hot concert is sold out.

Bar-Club Imágenes (☎ 33 36 06; Calzada No 602 at Calle C; drink minimum US$5; ☯ 9pm-5am) This upscale piano bar attracts something of an older crowd with its regular diet of *boleros* (ballads) and *trova* (traditional music), but sometimes there are surprise concerts by big name musicians; check the schedule posted outside. Meals are available (and affordable: shrimp for US$5).

As opposed to the previous two (where the air is likely to be sullied by ringing cell phones), a couple of local watering holes include **Cafeterías Cubanitas** (Línea btwn Paseo & A; ☯ 9am-3am), which has zero atmosphere save the raucous late-night, post-concert crowd, and **El Jardín** (Línea cnr C; ☯ 10am-2am) which has cheap beer on tap, a lively terrace and vegetarian food (in pesos).

For a more intellectual scene, check out the **bar/café** in the basement of the **Centro de Prensa Internacional** (Calles 23 & 0; ☯ 9am-7pm), where journalists and writers talk shop over coffee, whiskey and wine.

ENTERTAINMENT
One Saturday a month, the Plaza de la Catedral is closed off for a spectacular **Noche Plaza** with 100 of Cuba's finest singers, dancers and other entertainers performing on a stage directly in front of the cathedral. The staff at Restaurante El Patio should know the date of the next extravaganza. Admission is US$10/25 without/with dinner. This is also the place to come for New Year's Eve (if you can afford the US$100 ticket).

The nightly **cañonazo ceremony** at the Fortaleza de la Cabaña, when they shoot off the cannons, is another popular thing to do (see p129). Also be sure to reference the Playa and Marianao (see p120) sections as both those neighborhoods heat up nights.

Many clubs and discos charge a cover, but then offer an open bar or a certain number of drinks once you're in.

Folk & Traditional Music

Casa de la Cultura de La Habana Vieja (Map pp68-70; ☎ 863-4860; Aguiar No 509 btwn Amargura & Brasil; admission adult/child 5 pesos/free; ⏰ 9pm) Habana Vieja's active *casa* usually has something on like Afro-Cuban dancing or folk singing nightly. The programme varies every week (and it could be canceled if it's raining). The staff can arrange Cuban dancing lessons. They sometimes charge foreigners US$5 instead of five pesos, which might be worth it depending on the event.

Casa de la Trova (Map pp68-70; ☎ 879-3373; San Lázaro No 661 near Parque Maceo; admission free;

⏰ 7pm-late Tue-Sun) Headquarters of Havana's *son* sound, classic Cuban music fans will be thrilled at the atmosphere and jams that coalesce here regularly.

Salón de Ensayo Benny Moré (Map pp68-70; Neptuno No 960; ⏰ 9:30am-noon, 2-5pm Tue-Sat) Bands like Los Izquierdos, El Casino and El Prisma rehearse here and you're welcome to watch them playing boleros, *danzón*, *guaracha* or whatever comes over them. For information, ask for Pedro next door at No 958.

El Hurón Azul (Map pp78-9; ☎ 832-4551; Calles 17 & H, Vedado) The Unión Nacional de Escritores y Artistas de Cuba (UNEAC) is the nerve center of official art and intellectual life in Cuba, and this is its social club. Intellectuals associated with UNEAC are usually in attendance and you might even hobnob with hip Minister of Culture Abel Prieto (you'll know him by his mullet). Wednesday is the Afro-Cuban Peña del Ambia (US$5), Saturday it's authentic Cuban boleros (US$1; ⏰ 10pm to 2am) and alternate Thursdays there's jazz and *trova* (US$1; ⏰ 5pm).

WHAT'S HAPPENING?!

Plays, concerts, book launches, ballets, poetry readings, rap *peñas* – there's always something happening in Havana. The problem is finding out when and where. Here are some tips to get plugged in to what's on.

▪ 'Hurón Azul' – This is a select schedule of the week's biggest cultural events broadcast every Thursday night at 10:25pm on Cubavisión (Channel 6).

▪ *Cartelera de la Habana* – Broader listings (in Spanish) of things happening all over town, published biweekly by the Ministry of Culture. This is one of your best resources; sold at newspaper kiosks (20 centavos). Look for it alternate Thursdays.

▪ Bilingual English-Spanish *Cartelera* for the tourist population (www.cartelera.com; Calle 15 No 602; corner of C) comes out every Thursday, but it lists what they think you want to see. Still, good for non-Spanish speakers. Look for it in big hotels.

▪ The daily newspaper *Juventud Rebelde* has decent cultural listings.

▪ Posters – Concert flyers usually appear around La Rampa, from Calle L up to 'Rocker's Park' at Calle de los Presidentes (also known as 'G').

▪ Radio – Radio stations are constantly promoting upcoming cultural events; tune to Radio Taino (93.3 FM) or Radio Habana (94.9FM).

▪ Web – Check out www.cubarte.cult.cu and www.afrocubaweb.com for concerts, dance and fine art listings.

▪ Word of Mouth – There's nothing better. Because the state publishes *Cartelera* and produces 'Hurón Azul,' you have no chance of learning of anything underground. Also, you'll learn about spontaneous/spur of the moment happenings by talking to people.

▪ Pounding the pavement – Cubans know it's hard to get the word out, so every cinema posts the week's showings at every other city cinema (called the ICAIC *Cartelera*) and theaters post a schedule at their box office. If all else fails, make the rounds to see what's happening.

El Gato Tuerto (Map pp78-9; ☎ 66 22 24; Calle O No 14 btwn Calles 17 & 19, Vedado; drink minimum US$5; ⊕ dusk-dawn) Once the headquarters of Havana's alternative artistic and sexual scene, this chic bar with live music still packs in the folks in the old days, although now they're a little softer around the middle. It's amazing to behold on a crowded weekend night as scores of 40-somethings belt out *boleros* word-for-word with the band, shouting requests and cramming the dance floor.

Conjunto Folklórico Nacional de Cuba (Map pp78-9; Calle 4 No 103 btwn Calzada & Calle 5, Vedado; admission US$5; ⊕ promptly at 3pm Sat) Founded in 1962, this high energy ensemble specializes in Afro-Cuban dancing (all of the drummers are *santeros*). See them perform, and dance along during the regular Sábado de Rumba at El Gran Palenque at Teatro Mella. A major festival called FolkCuba unfolds here biannually during the second half of January.

Other spaces to experience rumba include the wild **Callejón de Hamel** (see p108) on Sunday from 11am and **5ta Avenida** (Map pp68-70; no phone; San Rafael & Consulado, Centro Habana; admission US$1; ⊕ 4-7pm Fri-Sun). The latter is red hot, sees few tourists and the drinks are three pesos.

Jazz   Map pp78-9

Jazz Club La Zorra y El Cuervo (☎ 66 24 02; Calles 23 & O, Vedado; admission US$5-10; ⊕ 10pm) The house band is good, and its freestyle jazz is a nice change from salsa. Thursday is blues night and this place hosts great late-night jams during the International Jazz Fest; check out the cool photos by local photographer Leslie Sinclair (and cast member of Six Degrees Havana).

Jazz Cafe (☎ 55 33 02; Calle 1 & Paseo, top flr of Galerías de Paseo; drink minimum US$10; ⊕ noon-late) This upscale joint overlooking the Malecón is like a jazz supper club, with tables and a decent menu (come here for cocktails at sunset). At night, the club swings into action with jazz, *timba* and occasionally, straight up salsa. Pity the dance floor is just a strip between the tables.

Rock, Reggae & Rap   Map pp78-9

Patio de María (Calle 37 No 262 btwn Paseo & Calle 2; admission five pesos) This legendary club near the Teatro Nacional de Cuba is run by the equally legendary María Gattorno. A great old-school venue with indoor and outdoor space, it's packed to the rafters with head-banging Habaneros; lots of black eyeliner here. Check the *cartelera* posted at the door or head to Parque de los Rockeros (Calles 23 and G) to find out what's happening. This unpretentious counterculture venue has received considerable media coverage in Cuba and abroad, partly due to Gattorno's AIDS- and drug-prevention educational work.

La Madriguera (☎ 879-8175; Salvador Allende & Luaces, Quinta los Molinos; admission five-10 pesos) Connected with the Asociación Hermanos Saíz, UNEAC's youth arm, rock, rap and reggae concerts happen at this venue in leafy Quinta los Molinos (enter via Calzada de Infanta). A very local scene, this is a good place to meet young Cuban artists and musicians.

Anfiteatro Parque Almendares (Calle 23 & Río Almendares; admission two pesos) This riverside amphitheater hosts regular musical events and special concerts by the likes of Frank Delgado and Interactivo. It's an intimate place to catch some terrific music. Regular *peñas* include reggae (8pm Friday) and rap (8pm Saturday). You can also catch a rap matinee (4pm Saturday) at Cafe Cantante (p103) and the rock cover band Los Kents (4pm Sunday).

Dance Clubs

In Cuba, a dance club usually means DJs and recorded music, with dance floor taking priority over seating (your basic disco), while a nightclub features live music and table seating. Female travelers should be prepared for lots of attention in Havana's discos, whether they're traveling solo or not. Cuban dance styles involve lots of touching, grinding and frisson in general and if you're in the mix, it's assumed you're game. Set your boundaries early.

CENTRO HABANA   Map pp68-70

El Palermo (☎ 861-9745; San Miguel & Amistad; admission US$2; ⊕ 11pm Thu-Sun) Your casa hostess will likely warn you away from this local disco. It's very much in the 'hood, with a heavy rap scene. Fun, but *fuerte*. There's also the tamer **Discoteca Ribera Azul** (☎ 833-8813; Av de Italia & Malecón; per couple US$5; ⊕ closed Tue), downstairs from the lobby of the Hotel Deauville.

VEDADO   Map pp78-9

Cabaret Las Vegas (☎ 870-7939; Infanta No 104 btwn Calles 25 & 27; admission US$5; ☽ 10pm-4am) Mostly a local scene, head here to cut loose with Cubans. There's recorded music followed by a show at midnight. The patio overlooking the street is a nice place for a beer.

El Chevere (Calles 49-A & 28-A in Parque Almendares; admission US$6-10; ☽ from 10pm) One of Havana's most popular discos, this al fresco place in a lush park setting hosts a good mix of locals and tourists.

Pico Blanco (☎ 833-4187; Calle O btwn Calles 23 & 25; admission US$5; ☽ 9pm) This disco on the 14th floor of the Hotel St John's ('the cathedral of *filin'* say fans of this soupy music) can be hit or miss. Some nights it's karaoke and cheesy *boleros*, another night it's jamming with some rather famous Cuban musicians. Check the schedule posted in the hotel window. The rooftop bar here has terrific views.

Vedado has several mixed peso-dollar discos that are great fun (especially if your budget has blown out) including **Club La Red** (☎ 832-5415; Calles 19 & L; admission US$3), and **Karachi Club** (☎ 832-3485; Calles 17 & K; admission US$3-5; ☽ 10pm-5am). As with all clubs, late night Friday and Saturday are best. Our favorite, though, is **La Pampa** (Malecón & Vapor; per couple US$2; ☽ 11pm-3am), a small dark disco with a mostly black crowd where they're laying down rap, salsa and sugar pop.

West of here are **Discoteca Amanecer** (☎ 832-9075; Calle 15 No 12 btwn Calles N & O; admission US$3; ☽ 10pm-4am) and **Club Tropical** (☎ 832-7361; Línea & Calle F; ☽ 9pm-2am). **Atelier** (☎ 830-6808; Calles 17 & 6; admission five pesos; ☽ 11pm-4am) is DJ central, with even young women manning the decks occasionally and spinning rap, pop and salsa (of course).

Cafe Cantante (☎ 879-0710; Paseo & Calle 39; admission US$10; ☽ 9pm-5am Tue-Sat), below the Teatro Nacional de Cuba (side entrance), is a disco with live salsa music and dancing. The music is good and it's a popular place, despite being in a low-ceilinged basement. The crowd is usually a decent mix, though a certain type of tourist and the local women they favor are very much in evidence. No shorts, T-shirts, hats, photos or under 18s allowed.

Nightclubs

Piano Bar Delirio Habanero (Map pp78-9; ☎ 873-5713; Paseo & Calle 39; admission US$5; ☽ from 6pm Tue-Sun)

This plush lounge upstairs in the Teatro Nacional hosts everything from young *trovadores* to aging *salseros* and when it gets hot, it rocks to the rafters. The deep red couches abut a wall of glass overlooking the Plaza de la Revolución and it's stunning at night with the Martí Memorial alluringly backlit.

Habana Café (Map pp78-9; ☎ 33 36 36; Paseo btwn Calles 1 & 3 at the Hotel Meliá Cohiba; minimum at bar/table, plus cover US$5/10; ☽ from 9:30pm) If you prefer to see big salsa acts like Pupi y Su Son Son or NG La Banda in a controlled, upscale setting, come here. (Otherwise, cut way loose at Salón Rosado Benny Moré, p121.) The layout is cabaret style, with tables and chairs surrounding a stage and dance floor, and American 1950s memorabilia, including old cars, motorcycles and gas pumps, constitute the decoration. You can eat here too.

La Casa de la Música Centro Habana (Map pp68-70; ☎ 878-4727; admission US$5-10; Av de Italia btwn Concordia & Neptuno) Edgier than its Miramar counterpart, big salsa bands play here regularly to a mixed crowd of tourists and hustlers. Special blow-out events sometimes happen too, like rap festivals and gigs by visiting musicians such as Philadelphia's Roots.

Cabarets

Cabaret Nacional (Map pp68-70; ☎ 863-2361; San Rafael No 208 & Paseo de Martí; per couple US$10; ☽ 9pm-2am) Come to this cabaret alongside the Gran Teatro de La Habana, for a mix of show (as captivating as it is camp) and dancing. The show kicks off at 11:30pm, followed by steamy dancing. Thursday to Sunday is best; there's also a matinee (admission US$5; ☽ 3-8pm) here. The Nacional maintains a couples only and minimum dress policy: definitely no shorts or T-shirts.

Cabaret Turquino (Map pp78-9; Calles 23 & L; admission US$15; ☽ opens 10pm) Some of Cuba's biggest bands play here (including Los Van Van) and superstar parties (to close the film or jazz festival, for instance) sometimes happen here too. It's a spectacular place on the 25th floor of the Hotel Habana Libre, with unsurpassable views.

Cabaret Parisién (Map pp78-9; ☎ 33 35 64; Calles 21 & 0; admission US$30; ☽ 9pm) If you want to experience Cuban cabaret but aren't quite up for the Tropicana, this room at the western end of the Hotel Nacional lobby is a good choice. You get all the feathers and fun, plus it becomes a disco after midnight and if there are any VIPs in town, they'll likely be partying here.

The **Cabaret Salón Rojo** (Map pp78-9; Calle 21 btwn Calles N & O at Hotel Capri) was closed at the time of writing.

Theater

Ballet, opera and theater performance are almost always at 8:30pm Monday to Saturday, with a matinee at 5pm Sunday for the length of the run.

CENTRO HABANA   Map pp68-70

Gran Teatro de La Habana (☎ 861-3077; Paseo de Martí & San Rafael; per person US$10; ☒ box office 9am-6pm Mon-Sat, until 3pm Sun) This magnificent theater is closely associated with its most famous resident: the acclaimed Ballet Nacional de Cuba and its founder Alicia Alonso. The National Opera performs here occasionally. You'll often hear this theater referred to as the Sala García Lorca, which is the grandest of several concert halls here (the others are the Sala Alejo Carpentier and Sala Ernesto Lecuono, where art films are sometimes shown). You can count on some type of live musical event every Friday, Saturday and Sunday (check the notices posted outside the theater).

Lighter fare is presented at **Teatro Fausto** (☎ 863-1173; Paseo de Martí No 201 at Colón). The humorous programs Friday and Saturday at 8:30pm and Sunday at 5pm are great fun. See the schedule posted outside.

The **Teatro América** (☎ 862-5695; Av de Italia No 253 btwn Concordia & Neptuno) made its name with big variety shows by talents like Roberto Carcassés, and you still might catch his jazzy act here, but this place also hosts blowout rumba, rap and drum concerts too (tickets are sold on the day of the performance).

HABANA VIEJA   Map pp68-70

The **Casa de la Comedia** across the street from **El Caserón del Tango** (Jústiz No 21 off Oficios) sometimes presents live theater in Spanish.

VEDADO   Map pp78-9

Teatro Nacional de Cuba (☎ 879-6011; Paseo & Calle 39; per person US$10; ☒ box office 9am-5pm & before performances) This modern theater on the Plaza de la Revolución hosts landmark concerts, foreign theater troupes, La Colmenita children's company and the Ballet Nacional de Cuba. The main hall is the Sala Avellaneda

and hosts big events, while the smaller Sala Covarrubias along the back side puts on a more daring programme like the recent Cuban adaptation of Eve Ensler's *Vagina Monologues*. The ninth floor is a rehearsal and performance space where the newest, most experimental stuff happens like **Teatro El Puente**. The ticket office is at the far end of a separate single-story building beside the main theater.

Teatro Mella (☎ 833-8696; Línea No 657 btwn Calles A & B) This cozy theater hosts all manner of dance, music and theater performances. The Festival Internacional de Ballet happens here and the Conjunto Folklórico Nacional calls this theater home. Travelers with kids will enjoy the children's show Sunday at 11am.

If you understand Spanish, it's well worth attending some of the cutting-edge contemporary theater that's a staple of Grupo Teatro Rita Montaner in the **Sala Teatro El Sótano** (☎ 832-0833; Calle K No 514 btwn Calles 25 & 27; ☒ 5-8:30pm Fri & Sat, 3-5pm Sun), not far from the Habana Libre. Performances are Friday and Saturday at 8:30pm, Sunday at 5pm. Also check **Café Teatro Brecht** (Calle 13 at Calle I), where varied performances take place. Tickets go on sale one hour before the performance.

Sala Teatro Hubert de Blanck (☎ 833-5962; Calzada No 657 btwn Calles A & B; per person US$5) is named for the founder of Havana's first conservatory of music (1885). The Teatro Estudio based here is Cuba's leading theater company. You can usually see plays in Spanish here Saturday at 8:30pm and Sunday at 7pm. Tickets are sold just prior to the performance.

The **Teatro Nacional de Guiñol** (☎ 832-6262; Calle M btwn Calles 17 & 19) was closed at the time of writing, but check back for quality puppet shows and children's theater.

Classical Music

Teatro Amadeo Roldán (Map pp78-9; ☎ 832-4522; Calzada & Calle D; per person US$10) This lovely modern theater is the seat of the Orquesta Sinfónica Nacional, which plays in the 886-seat Sala Amadeo Roldán (concerts on Sundays at 11am in season). Try to catch a programme conducted by master Leo Brouwer. Major concerts (eg Síntesis, Egberto Gismonti, Aldo Pérez-Gavilán) also go down here. Soloists and small groups play in the 276-seat Sala Caturla. Built in 1922, this magnificent building was destroyed by an arsonist in 1977 and only reopened in 1999 after a careful restoration.

Classical and chamber music concerts also happen nearly nightly at the **Iglesia de San Francisco de Asís** (Map pp68–70; Plaza de San Francisco de Asís) and the **Iglesia de San Francisco de Paula** (Map pp68–70).

Cinemas

There are about 200 cinemas in Havana. Most have several screenings daily and every theater posts the *Cartelera ICAIC*, which lists show times for the entire city. Tickets are usually two pesos; queue early. Hundreds of movies are screened throughout Havana during the Festival Internacional del Nuevo Cine Latinoamericano. Schedules are published daily in the *Diario del Festival*, available in the morning at big theaters and the Hotel Nacional. We've whittled the theater list down to these select few:

Acapulco (Map pp78–9; ☎ 833-9573; Avs 26 & 35, Nuevo Vedado) Concerts and special events happen here too.

Cine Payret (Map pp68–70; ☎ 863-3163; Paseo de Martí No 505) Opposite the Capitolio, this is Centro Habana's largest and most luxurious cinema, erected in 1878.

Cine El Mégano (Map pp68–70; ☎ 863-8023; Industria No 416 at San Martín) Behind the Capitolio.

Cinecito (Map pp68–70; ☎ 863-8051; San Rafael No 68 at Consulado) Films for kids behind the Hotel Inglaterra.

Cine Actualidades (Map pp68–70; ☎ 861-5193; Av de Bélgica No 262) Behind the Hotel Plaza.

Cine La Rampa (Map pp78–9; ☎ 878-6146; Calle 23 No 111 at Calle O) Catch film festivals here (DeNiro, French Cinema etc).

Cine Yara (Map pp78–9; ☎ 832-9430; Calles 23 & L) One big screen and two video 'salas' here at Havana's most famous cinema (with the best popcorn).

Cine Riviera (Map pp78–9; ☎ 830-9648; Calle 23 No 507 near Calle G) Big pop, rock and sometimes rap concerts happen here.

Cine Charles Chaplin (Map pp78–9; ☎ 831-1101; Calle 23 No 1157 btwn Calles 10 & 12) Previews and special screenings and events happen at ICAIC's theater; don't miss the poster gallery of great Cuban classic films here.

Cine 23 y 12 (Map pp78–9; ☎ 833-6906; Calles 23 & 12)

Cine Trianón (Map pp78–9; ☎ 830-9648; Línea No 706 near Paseo) Movies or live theater.

Sport

Estadio Latinoamericano (☎ 870-6526; Zequiera No 312 at Pedro Pérez) From October to April (and into May if Havana's Industriales 'Los Azules' make it into the playoffs), baseball games happen at this 58,000-seat stadium in Cerro, just south of Centro Habana. Entry costs three pesos (but they like to charge foreigners US$1). The Metropolitanos also play here, but they are to the Industriales what the Mets are to the Yankees. Games are 7:30pm Tuesday, Wednesday and Thursday, 1:30pm Saturday and Sunday. Unfortunately, getting here by public transportation is difficult. The benches are cement – painful after nine innings.

Ciudad Deportiva (☎ 54 50 00; Av de la Independencia at Vía Blanca; admission five pesos) 'Sport City' is Cuba's premier sports training center and big basketball, volleyball, boxing and track contests happen at the coliseum here. The M-2 camello from Av Bolívar in Centro Habana stops across the street.

Sala Polivalente Ramón Fonst (Map pp78–9; ☎ 881-4196; Av de la Independencia; one peso) Raucous basketball and volleyball games are held at this stadium opposite the main bus station.

For boxing, try **Kid Chocolate** (Map pp68–70; ☎ 861-1546; Paseo de Martí, next to Cine Payret), directly opposite the Capitolio, which usually hosts matches on Fridays at 7pm or **Gimnasio de Boxeo Rafael Trejo** (Map pp68–70; ☎ 862-0266; Calle Cuba No 815 btwn Merced & Leonor Pérez, Habana Vieja). Here you can see matches on Friday at 7pm (US$1) or drop by any day after 4pm to watch training. Travelers (including women) interested in boxing can find a trainer here.

SHOPPING
Shops & Markets
HABANA VIEJA   Map pp68–70

Palacio de la Artesanía (Cuba No 64 at Tacón; ☉ 9am–7pm) For one stop shopping for souvenirs, cigars, crafts, musical instruments, CDs, clothing and jewelry at fixed prices, join the gaggle of tour-bus escapees here. This building is the former Palacio de Pedroso, erected by Havana Major Mateo Pedroso in 1780. In the mid-19th century it was Havana's high court and later police headquarters.

Fería de la Artesanía (Tacón btwn Tejadillo & Chacón; ☉ Wed-Sat) Paintings, guayaberas, woodwork, leather items, Che everything, jewelry and more can be haggled over at this open-air handicraft market. If you buy paintings, make sure you arrange an export license (it's easy, see the boxed text p107) or risk losing your loot at customs upon leaving Cuba (if they're deemed 'national treasures' they'll be confiscated). Smaller artwork can easily be tucked safely in luggage.

Fondo Cubano de Bienes Culturales (☎ 860-0224; Muralla & San Ignacio; ☼ 10am-5pm Mon-Fri, 10am-2pm Sat) You'll receive receipts for whatever artwork or handicrafts you buy at this government shop in Plaza Vieja, so you should have no problem at customs. Some of the original works here are quite lovely.

Longina Música (☎ 862-8371; Obispo No 360 btwn Habana & Compostela; ☼ 10am-7pm Mon-Sat, 10am-1pm Sun) This place on the pedestrian mall has a good selection of CDs, plus musical instruments such as bongos (US$75), guitars (US$75), maracas (US$5), guiros (US$13) and *tumbadoras* (US$700). Shop around and you'll probably find cheaper instruments.

Galería Manos (Obispo No 411 btwn Aguacate & Compostela; ☼ 10am-6pm Mon-Sat) is a craft outlet that sells dolls, masks and other handmade souvenirs. For very cool Havana Club gear (US$6 martini glasses or classic mojito glasses for US$2 each), check out the **Fundación Havana Club shop** (San Pedro No 262 at Sol; ☼ 9am-9pm).

CENTRO HABANA

El Bulevar (San Rafael from Paseo de Martí to Av de Italia) This is a pedestrian mall and peso bazaar full of snacks and surprises. When you exit on to Av de Italia, you come to an equally important shopping strip for Cubans containing giant department stores including **Variadades Galiano** (San Rafael & Av de Italia; ☼ 10am-6pm Mon-Sat, 9am-noon Sun). This former Woolworth's has a great lunch and ice-cream counter and a wide selection of interesting stuff like old records and the mesh tank tops you see everyone wearing.

La Manzana de Gómez (Agramonte & San Rafael) This faded but elegant European-style covered shopping arcade built in 1910 is full of stores. La Exposición, in a downstairs corner, sells reproductions of the works of famous Cuban painters for US$3 to US$10 each. Shipping tubes are available.

Area de Vendedores por Cuenta Propia (Máximo Gómez No 259 at Suárez; ☼ 9am-5pm Mon-Sat) This is a permanent flea market where you can

pick up Santería beads, old books, leather belts and so on. More of the same is available at the large **open-air market** (crnr Av Simón Bolívar & Aguila) open daily.

VEDADO

ARTex (Calles 23 & L; ☼ 10am-11pm Mon-Sat, 10am-2pm Sun) This shop opposite the Hotel Habana Libre has a good selection of CDs, cassettes, books, crafts and postcards.

Fería de la Artesanía (Malecón btwn Calles D & E; ☼ from 10:30am, closed Wed) This artisan market has much of the same as its Habana Vieja counterpart with some key differences: the side facing Calle D is all handmade shoes and sandals, there's a whole section of numismatic interest, with old stamps, coins, bills and other ephemera and there are many more kitschy paintings for sale. It's also a better set-up allowing for easier browsing.

Cine Yara (☎ 832-9430; Calles 23 & L) A fabulous selection of old movie posters, antique postcards, T-shirts and, of course, all the greatest Cuban films on videotape are sold at this shop inside the theater.

Galerías de Paseo (Calle 1 & Paseo; ☼ 9am-6pm Mon-Sat, 9am-1pm Sun) This shopping mall across from the Hotel Meliá Cohiba is the most upscale east of the Río Almendares, with Adidas, Chanel, and even a car dealership. There's a Bim Bom ice-cream parlor too.

Plaza Carlos III (Av Salvador Allende btwn Arbol Seco & Retiro; ☼ 10am-6pm Mon-Sat) It's usually called simply 'Carlos Tercera.' Stop into this big, flashy department store on a Saturday to see the double economy working at a feverish pitch.

Art Galleries

The art scene in Havana is cutting edge and ever-changing and collectors, browsers and admirers will find many galleries in which to while away hours. Remember that you'll need official receipts or export permits to take artwork home with you (see the boxed text). For gallery events, look for the free *Arte en La Habana*, a tri-quarterly listings flyer (the San Cristóbal agency on Plaza San Francisco de Asís usually has them) or visit www.galeriascubanas.com.

HABANA VIEJA

Taller Experimental de Gráfica (☎ 862-0979; tgrafica@cubarte.cult.cu; Callejón del Chorro No 6;

10am-4pm Mon-Fri) This active workshop off Plaza de la Catedral sells engravings and prints that you can watch being made on the premises (US$15 to US$800).

Casa de Carmen Montilla (Oficios No 164; 10:30am-5:30pm Tue-Sat, 9am-1pm Sun) This gallery features a huge ceramic mural by Sosa Bravo in the pretty rear courtyard.

Estudio Galería Los Oficios (863-0497; Oficios No 166; 10am-5:30pm Mon-Sat) Pop in to this gallery to see the large, hectic, but intriguing canvasses by Nelson Domínguez, whose workshop is upstairs.

Diago Galería de Arte (863-4703; Muralla No 107 at San Ignacio; 10am-5pm Mon-Fri, 9am-2pm Sat) In a complex of galleries on Plaza Vieja, this one specializes in naive paintings but also features audio and visual installations.

Taller de Serigrafía René Portocarrero (862-3276; Cuba No 513 btwn Brasil & Muralla; 9am-4pm Mon-Fri) Paintings and prints by young Cuban artists are exhibited and sold here (from US$30 to US$150). You can see the artists at work here.

CENTRO HABANA   Map pp68-70
Galería Orígenes (863-6690; Paseo de Martí No 458; 9am-6pm) Paintings and sculptures are exhibited and sold at this gallery inside the Gran Teatro de La Habana, opposite Parque Central.

Galería La Acacia (861-3533; San Martín No 114 btwn Industria & Consulado; 10am-3:30pm Mon-Fri, 10am-1pm Sat) This important gallery behind the Gran Teatro de La Habana has paintings by leading artists like Zaida del Río, plus antiques. Export permits are arranged.

Also have a look at paintings and sculpture at **Galería Galiano** (862-5365; Av de Italia No 258 at Concordia; 10am-6pm Tue-Sat), opposite Teatro América. If you see something you like, negotiate a price directly with the artist.

VEDADO   Map pp78-9
Galería Ciudades del Mundo (832-3175; Calle 25 No 307 at Calle L; 8:30am-5pm Mon-Fri) Interesting expositions on Havana and other cities of the world are put up here. While you're waiting for an email terminal to become available, you can check out photo exhibits in the gallery of the **Centro de Prensa Internacional** (Calles 23 & 0).

Galería Habana (832-7101; Línea No 460 btwn Calles E & F; 10am-5pm Mon-Sat) This wonderful space in the heart of Vedado shows contem-

---

EXPORTING ARTWORK

When buying art at an official outlet always ask for an official receipt to show Cuban customs, especially if the object won't fit in your suitcase. To discourage private trading, officials often confiscate undocumented artwork at the airport. If you've purchased a work of art at state-run galleries and have the receipts, you shouldn't have a problem, but it's always better to have a certificate to export artwork (and you'll definitely need one if you purchase directly from the artist).

Certificates to export artwork are issued by the **Registro Nacional de Bienes Culturales** (Map pp78-9; Calle 17 No 1009 btwn Calles 10 & 12, Vedado; 9am-noon Mon-Fri). To obtain an export certificate you must bring the objects here for inspection; fill in a form; queue for two hours; pay a fee of US$10 to US$30, which covers from one to five pieces of artwork; and return 24 hours later to pick up the certificate. Don't leave this bit of business until your last day. Some artists will offer to obtain the permit for you upon payment of a deposit. However, the only way to be sure that your paintings won't be confiscated at the airport is to obtain the permit yourself in person.

---

porary Cuban art in big, bright galleries. Come here to see what's new and different from artists like Aimée García.

Galería Haydee Santamaría (Calle G next to the Casa de las Américas; admission US$2; 10am-5pm Tue-Sat, 9am-1pm Sun) and the gallery inside **Casa de las Américas** (Calles 3 & G; admission US$2; 10am-4:30pm Tue-Sat, 9am-1pm Sun) have fine exhibits featuring art from all over Latin America.

Taller Gráfica (Calle 17 No 7 btwn Calles N & 0; 9am-5pm Mon-Fri) This print shop run by artist Nelson Domínguez makes an intriguing visit. Here you'll see prints by some of Cuba's greatest contemporary artists (eg Zaida del Río, Alicia Leal, Juan Moreira and others), plus there's a good chance some of them might be there working away. The prints made here are sold at Estudio Galería Los Oficios (see above left).

Since 1990 local painter **Salvador González Escalona** has converted Callejón de Hamel, between Aramburu and Hospital, off San Lázaro, into an open-air art center with zany murals, sculpture and found-object art. Visit Salvador's **studio** (878-1661; Callejón de Hamel No 1054; 🕙 10am-6pm) to view (and perhaps purchase) his work. The studio also organizes free cultural activities along the Callejón such as the **Sunday rumba** at 11am (beware, this is jinetero city), **children's theater** (🕙 10am, third Saturday of the month), and **street theater** (🕙 7pm, fourth Thursday of the month).

Other galleries worth a peek in Vedado are the **Centro de Arte 23 y 12** (Calles 12 & 23; 🕙 10am-5pm Tue-Sat) for contemporary Cuban art and the gallery at **UNEAC** (Calles 17 & H).

GETTING THERE & AWAY
Air
Take a number at the **Cubana Airlines** (Map pp78-9; 🕿 33 49 49; Calle 23 No 64 at Infanta; 🕙 8:30am-4pm Mon-Fri, 8:30am-noon Sat) bustling head office at the Malecón end of the Airline Building, where you can buy international or domestic tickets. If it's packed, book Cubana flights for the same price a few doors down at **Sol y Son Travel Agency** (Map pp78-9; 🕿 33 02 93/4; fax 33 51 50; Calle 23 No 64 btwn Calle P & Infanta 🕙 8:30am-6pm Mon-Fri, 8:30am-noon Sat).

Other airlines worth domestic services:
Aerocaribbean (🕿 33 36 21; fax 33 38 71; Calle 23 No 64 in the Airline Building)
Aerotaxi (Map pp78-9; 🕿 53 53 48; fax 33 40 64; Calles 27 & M, Vedado) Private charters only.

Boat
Buses connecting with the hydrofoil and ferry services to Nueva Gerona on Isla de la Juventud leave at 12:30pm from the **Terminal de Omnibus** (Map pp78-9; 🕿 878-1841; Av de la Independencia & Calle 19 de Mayo), near the Plaza de la Revolución. Bus tickets are sold at the kiosk marked 'NCC' between gate Nos 9 and 10 in the middle of the departures hall (US$2). Ferry tickets are sold at the harbor at Surgidero de Batabanó, and a passport is required. See p144 for schedules.

Bus
Astro buses to all corners of Cuba depart from the **Terminal de Omnibus** (Map pp78-9; 🕿 870-9401; Av de la Independencia & Calle 19 de Mayo) near the Plaza de la Revolución. Dollar tickets are readily available at the office marked 'Venta de Boletines USD' (🕿 870-3397; 🕙 24hr), down the hall to the right of the main entrance. Four seats on each bus are available for dollar sales, and you can usually get one on any Astro bus the same day. The staff will take you right to your bus and help you board (no pushing in line). For departure information see below.

Víazul (🕿 881-1413, 881-5652; www.viazul.cu; Calle 26 & Zoológico, Nuevo Vedado) covers most destinations of interest to travelers, in deluxe, air-conditioned coaches. You can board at the inconveniently located terminal 3km southwest of Plaza de la Revolución, or at the Terminal de Omnibus. Here tickets for Víazul services are sold immediately prior to the departure in the Venta de Boletines USD office. You can get full schedules on

BUS TIMETABLE

Astro

Destination	Cost (one way)	Distance	Duration	Departure time
Cienfuegos	US$16	254km	5 hours	6:15am, noon, 4:15pm, 7:30pm, 9:15pm
Pinar del Río	US$8	162km	4 hours	8am, 12:30pm, 5pm, 7:30pm, 8:20pm
Santa Clara	US$12	276km	5 hours	6:30am, 9:40pm
Santiago de Cuba	US$42	861km	15 hours	12:15pm, 7:20pm
Trinidad	US$21	335km	7½ hours	5am
Varadero	US$8	140km	3 hours	4:35am

Víazul

Destination	Cost (one way)	Distance	Duration	Departure time
Cienfuegos	US$20	254km	5 hours	8:15am, 1pm
Pinar del Río	US$8	162km	4 hours	9am
Santiago de Cuba	US$51	861km	16 hours	9:30am, 3pm, 8pm
Trinidad	US$25	335km	6 hours	8:15am, 1pm
Varadero	US$10	140km	3 hours	8am, 8:30am, 7pm
Viñales	US$12	189km	3¼ hours	9am

CHARLOTTE HINDLE

Relaxing with a **newspaper** (p405), Havana

RICHARD I'ANSON

Art for sale (p107), Havana

La Bodeguita del Medio (p99), Havana

ALFREDO MAIQUEZ

ALFREDO MAIQUEZ

Real Fábrica de Tabacos Partagás (p73), Havana

DOMINIC ARIZONA BONUCCELLI

Along the **Malecón** (p81), Havana

DOUG McKINLAY

Getting around Havana on a motorcycle

Coco-taxi (p67), Plaza de Armas, Havana

TOM SMA

the website or at **Infotur** (Map pp68-70; Obispo No 358), which also sells tickets requiring you to board at its originating station in Nuevo Vedado.

Havana-bound, you can get off the Víazul bus from Varadero/Matanzas in Centro Habana right after the tunnel, but if you arrive from most other points you'll be let out at the Nuevo Vedado terminal. From here city bus No 27 will take you to Vedado or Centro Habana (ask). Otherwise, if your bus stops at the Terminal de Omnibus on Av de la Independencia, jump off there. The M-2 camello stops in front of the terminal along with many other buses en route to Parque Fraternidad in Centro Habana. The local buses won't accommodate backpacks. See the boxed text opposite for departure information.

The bus to Santiago de Cuba also stops at Santa Clara (US$18), Sancti Spíritus (US$23), Ciego de Ávila (US$27), Camagüey (US$33), Las Tunas (US$39), Holguín (US$44) and Bayamo (US$44).

Any of the tour buses parked near the Palacio de la Artesanía (Cuba No 64) near the cathedral, will happily take you to Varadero in the afternoon for US$10 to US$20 per person. Just ask the driver.

Buses to points in the Havana Province leave from Apodaca No 53, off Agramonte, near the main railway station. They go to Güines, Jaruco, Madruga, Nueva Paz, San José, San Nicolás and Santa Cruz del Norte, but expect large crowds and come early to get a peso ticket.

Taxi

Small Lada taxis, operated by Cubataxi, park on Calle 19 de Mayo beside the Terminal de Omnibus (bus station). They charge US$0.35 a kilometer (US$44 to Varadero, US$54 to Pinar del Río, US$72 to Santa Clara, US$88 to Cienfuegos, US$102 to Trinidad). Up to four people can go for that price. It's worth considering in a pinch and is perfectly legal. Other cars hang about the Víazul station offering to zip travelers to Varadero or Viñales for a couple dollars each less than the bus fare – great for small groups.

Unlicensed private taxis may offer to take you to Pinar del Río, Santa Clara or Cienfuegos for the equivalent of the bus fare, and it's up to you to decide if you're willing to risk getting stranded somewhere if the driver gets caught. If they offer to drive you to Varadero, they will leave you in Santa Marta, before the bridge and several kilometers from most of the hotels.

Train

Trains to most parts of Cuba depart from **Estación Central de Ferrocarriles** (Map pp68-70; ☎ 862-4971, 861-8540; Av de Bélgica & Arsenal), on the southwestern side of Habana Vieja. Foreigners must buy tickets for dollars at La Coubre station (☎ 862-1006; Av del Puerto & Desamparados; ☽ 9am-3pm Mon-Fri). If it's closed, try the Lista de Espera office adjacent which sells tickets for trains leaving immediately. Kids under 12 travel half-price. Rail services include:

Destination	Cost (one way)	Distance	Frequency
Bayamo	US$26	744km	three weekly
Camagüey	US$19/32	534km	one daily
Ciego de Ávila	US$16/22	435km	three daily
Cienfuegos	US$11	254km	three weekly
Holguín	US$27	743km	one daily
Las Tunas	US$23	652km	two daily
Manzanillo	US$28	775km	three weekly
Matanzas	US$4	105km	eight daily
Morón	US$24	446km	three weekly
Pinar del Río	US$6.50	162km	one daily
Sancti Spíritus	US$13.50	354km	one daily
Santa Clara	US$14/17	276km	four daily
Santiago de Cuba	US$30/50/62	861km	two-three daily

The above information is only a rough approximation of what should happen; services are routinely delayed or canceled. Always double-check scheduling and from which terminal your train will leave.

For information about the electric train from Casablanca to Matanzas, see p131. Suburban trains and local services to points within the Havana Province are discussed under Getting Around, below.

GETTING AROUND
To/From the Airport

José Martí International Airport is at Rancho Boyeros, 25km southwest of Havana via Av de la Independencia. There are several terminals here. Terminal No 1, on the southeastern side of the runway, handles only domestic Cubana flights. Three kilometers away, via Av de la Independencia, is the dreaded Terminal No 2, which receives Corsair flights and charters from Miami. All other international flights use Terminal No 3, a modern facility at Wajay, 2.5km west of Terminal No 2. Charter flights on Aerocaribbean, Aerogaviota, Aerotaxi etc, to Cayo Largo del Sur and elsewhere use the Caribbean Terminal (also known as Terminal No 5), at the northwestern end of the runway, 2.5km west of Terminal No 3. (Terminal No 4 hasn't been built yet.) Check carefully which terminal you'll be using.

Foreigners arriving at Terminal No 3 are expected to take a taxi to their hotel. There is no public transport except the insane M-2 camello to the airport, stopping 3km away: what a fine welcome Cuba gives budget travelers. A taxi should cost no more than US$20 in one of the new tourist taxis based at the airport, or US$12 in an older yellow-and-black Lada taxi, which could by chance be dropping someone off (don't count on it). Agree on the price beforehand as some of the drivers are greedy. It may work out cheaper if you can convince a tourist taxi driver to use the meter, but don't bother trying this with a Lada taxi driver as their meters are set at artificially low rates and they'll simply decline your business.

The closest public bus stop to Terminal No 3 is that of the M-2 Metro Bus ('camello' or 'emay dose'), 500m east of Terminal No 2. The tourist taxis at Terminal No 3 should charge US$3 to Terminal No 2, and you could easily walk from there to the bus stop. If you want to walk the 3km from Terminal No 3 to Av de la Independencia, keep right as you leave the airport, watching for signs reading Vuelos Nacionales or Terminal Doméstico. You'll need Cuban pesos to pay the fare (20 centavo) but the M-2 is not for amateurs. Cuban friends have called it 'inhumane' it's so crowded, and pickpockets glory in these close quarters. Unless you're the hardest of hard-core backpackers, you shouldn't try to follow this route upon arrival (especially at night), although you could consider getting to the airport on the M-2 if saving US$12 is a high priority and you don't have much luggage. The bus boards on Av Simón Bolívar and Aguila in Parque El Curita, in Centro Habana. When you board here, note that there are three separate lines, one for people who want seats (sentados, on the corner of Aguila), another for those willing to stand (parados, on Angeles) and one between the two for pregnant women (embarazadas). Of course, the standing line moves faster, but it's a long, hot trip (one hour) so it's best to wait for a seat. Sit near an exit door so you can make a quick escape.

If you're arriving at Terminal No 1 on a domestic Cubana flight and see all the Cuban passengers getting into a bus marked 'Aeropuerto' in front of the terminal, follow them and you'll probably get a ride into town for one peso. It generally leaves about 15 minutes after the arrival of domestic Cubana flights and takes about an hour to reach town. Otherwise walk less than a kilometer to Av de la Independencia and try catching the M-2 (see above). Attempting to use the 'Aeropuerto' bus to get to the airport is a pain as it's not intended for foreigners, and the Cubana staff will pretend they don't know anything about it. Typical tourist taxi fares from Terminal No 1 are US$2 to Terminal No 2, US$5 to Terminal No 3, or US$20 to Havana. It should be easier to find a Lada or private taxi around Terminal No 1 as the police scrutiny there is less strict.

Víazul (☎ 881-5652; www.víazul.com; Calle 26 & Zoológico, Nuevo Vedado) has a very sporadic service to the airport at noon and 6:15pm (US$3) from their Nuevo Vedado terminal and the Hotel Plaza on Parque to Terminal 3. We encourage independent travelers to call or email their office to nag them into making this a regular run.

To/From the Bus Terminal

The crowded M-2 Metro Bus from Santiago de las Vegas stops outside the Terminal de Omnibus and runs directly to Parque de la Fraternidad near the Capitolio. In the other direction ask someone where to get out, as the southbound M-2 stops across the Plaza de la Revolución, out of sight of the bus station.

Bici-taxi

Two-seater bici-taxis will take you anywhere around Centro Habana for US$1/2 for a short/long trip, after bargaining. It's a lot more than a Cuban would pay, but cheaper and more fun than a tourist taxi. A recent law prohibits bici-taxis from taking tourists and they may wish to go via a roundabout route through the back streets to avoid police controls – a cheap tour! If they get stopped, it's their problem, not yours.

Bicycle & Moped

At the time of writing we only knew of one official bike rental outlet. **Rumbos** (Map pp114-15; ☎ 203-3376; Av 3 btwn Calles 28 & 30, Playa; bikes per day US$12) had a few bikes. It also had mopeds for US$10/13/15/24 for one/two/three/24 hours. You can definitely arrange a private bicycle rental by asking around. Expect to pay US$5 to US$10 a day. Always use the ubiquitous bicycle *parqueos* and lock the bike securely. Parts are sold in front of the Tulipán market near the Plaza de la Revolución, and everyone knows a good mechanic.

Boat

Passenger **ferries** (Map pp68-70; ☎ 867-3726) shuttle across the harbor to Regla and Casablanca, leaving every 10 or 15 minutes from Muelle Luz, corner of San Pedro and Santa Clara, on the southeast side of Habana Vieja. The fare is a flat 10 centavos. Since the ferries were hijacked to Florida in 1994 (and later returned) and again in 2003 (the hijackers never made it outside Cuban waters), security has been tightened.

Car

There are lots of car rental offices in Havana, so if you're told there are no cars or there isn't one in your price range just try another office or agency. All agencies have offices at Terminal 3 at Aeropuerto Internacional José Martí. Here's a quick in-town list:

Cubacar (☎ 33 22 77) Desks at the following hotels: Meliá Cohiba, Meliá Habana, NH Parque Central, Habana Libre, Comodoro and Bello Caribe.

Gran Car (☎ 33 56 47; Vía Blanca & Palatino, Cerro) Rents mint-model classic cars.

Havanautos Vedado (Map pp68-70; ☎ 33 34 84; Calles 23 & M); Playa (☎ 204-3203; Av 5 & Calle 112) Desks at the Habana Libre, Nacional, Riviera, Sevilla, Complejo Neptuno-Tritón and Vista al Mar hotels.

Micar Playa (Map pp114-15; ☎ 204-7777; Av 3 & Calle 70); Vedado (Map pp78-9; ☎ 24 24 44; Calle 1 & Paseo in Galerías de Paseo; ☿ 24hr); Vedado (Map pp78-9; Calle 23 & Infanta) Micar has one or two super cheapie cars (US$30-35/day); go in person to get the best deal.

Panautos Playa (Map p114-15; ☎ 202-7684; Av 3 & Calle 42; ☎ 881-1413); Vedado (Map pp78-9; ☎ 55 32 55; Línea & Malecón); Nuevo Vedado (Av 26 & Zoológico at Víazul terminal)

Rex Rent a Car (☎ 33 77 88; Línea & Malecón) Fancy cars.

Transtur Vedado (Map pp78-9; ☎ 33 40 38; Calles 21 & N); Vedado (Map pp78-9; ☎ 55 32 52; Calle 25 btwn Calles K & L);·Miramar (Map pp114-15; ☎ 204-6163; Av 3 & Calle 82) Desks at the Ambos Mundos, Copacabana, Deauville, Inglaterra, Nacional, Neptuno-Tritón, Panamericano, Plaza, Riviera and Sevilla hotels. Transtur and Havanautos offices in Havana tend not to have the cheaper models you can find in other cities.

Vía Rent a Car (☎ 204-3606; Avs 47 & 36, Kohly)

There are Servi-Cupet gas stations in Vedado at Calles L and 17; Malecón and Calle 15; Malecón and Paseo, near the Riviera and Meliá Cohiba hotels; and on Av de la Independencia (northbound lane) south of Plaza de la Revolución. All are open 24 hours a day.

Municipal parking attendants watch over vehicles parked all over Havana (eg on Trocadero in front of the Hotel Sevilla, in front of the Inglaterra) charging US$0.25 an hour, or US$1 for 12 hours. The same system is used at the parking lot of the Hotel Nacional in Vedado. Guarded parking is also available at the Parqueo Parque El Curita, Av Aguila and Av Simón Bolívar in Centro Habana (US$1 a day). More of the same is at the corner of Industria and Dragones, between the Partagás cigar factory and Hotel New York.

Colectivos

All those beautiful hulks parked in front of the Capitolio are 'colectivos' – collective taxis that hold six or more people and run on fixed routes. They're not supposed to take tourists, but many will, typically asking US$2 for the Centro Habana–Vedado run; a trip that costs Cubans 10 pesos. There are different lines for Vedado, Alamar, Marianao etc. The Vedado line is toward the southern end of the line of cars. Alternatively, you can walk west on Neptuno toward Av de Italia and hail one there. This is usually less hassle and· if you speak Spanish, you might skate by on 10 pesos. From Vedado, try catching a colectivo anywhere along Calle 23; when they slow, ask 'Habana?' or 'Capitolio?' to ascertain where they're going.

Public Transport

BUS

Havana's local bus service is either improving slightly or going straight to hell, depending on who you ask. Regular city buses are called guaguas (pronounced 'WA was'), while the much larger Metro Buses are camellos (camels) for their two humps. Within the city the fare is a flat 20 centavos in a camello, and 40 centavos in a regular bus, which you must toss into a box near the driver or pay to a conductor. Unfortunately, no bus-route map is available.

There are lines (colas) at most bus stops (paradas) even though it may not appear so at first glance. To mark your place ask for el último (the last in line), and when the bus arrives get behind that person. This excellent, efficient system is (mostly) rigorously followed, with cola-breakers taken to task by their compatriots.

To take a bus to places outside of town, such as Cojímar, Guanabo and Guanabacoa, you should try to board at the originating point of the bus (listed in the sections of this book dealing with those destinations), as the buses are often so full they don't stop at subsequent bus stops.

Since 1995 the public-transport crisis in Havana has been eased by the introduction of Metro Buses. These huge 300-plus passenger buses are hauled by trucks, all have the prefix M before their number and are color-coded:

M-1	Alamar–Vedado via Parque de la Fraternidad (pink)
M-2	Parque de la Fraternidad–Santiago de las Vegas (blue)
M-3	Alamar–Ciudad Deportiva (orange)
M-4	Parque de la Fraternidad–San Agustín via Marianao (green)
M-5	Vedado–San Agustín (red)
M-6	Calvario–Vedado (corner of 21 and L) (beige)
M-7	Parque de la Fraternidad–Alberro via Cotorro (red – they ran out of colors)

As you can see, many of the Metro Buses leave from Parque de la Fraternidad on the southern side of the Capitolio in Centro Habana. At the originating places of these buses there will be two lines, one for people who want a seat (sentados) and another for those willing to stand (parados). The second line moves faster and is best if you're only going a short distance and have no luggage. There is sometimes a third line for pregnant women (embarazadas).

The camello is known as the 'Saturday night movie' because it contains sex, violence and adult language (the warning that precedes the weekend movie on Cuban TV). It can be intimidating at first. Expect to be crushed by the crowd. It's imperative that

you move toward the back exit doors as soon as you get on because you're not allowed to exit through the door where you boarded. This can be a real problem (but not impossible) if you're only going one or two stops and can't reach the exit. Be alert to pickpockets who may spot you at the bus stop and get on right behind. Before boarding, empty your pockets into a handbag you can clutch in front of you. If the bus looks impossibly crowded, just step back and wait for the next, as they run every 10 minutes and the next one may be less crowded (ha!).

To go from Centro Habana to Vedado, catch the M-1 on Agramonte beside the Museo Nacional de Bellas Artes and stay on until the last stop, which is on Calle G, near the monument to José Miguel Gómez. To get from Vedado to Centro Habana, you're better off on the regular No 200 bus (stops across from Centro de Prensa Internacional) or the P4 (stops across from Coppelia).

TRAIN

Cristina Station (Map pp68-70; ☎ 878-4971; Av de México & Arroyo, Cuatro Caminos) lies south of Centro Habana and about a kilometer southwest of the train station. It handles local trains within the city limits. Trains to Batabanó leave twice a day (2½ hours), and four trains a day go to Wajay (one hour). In July and August only, there's a train from here to Guanabo three times a day except Monday (1½ hours). There are also daily trains to Artemisa and Güines. Cristina was the first train station built in Havana, and it's worth checking out if you're spending some time in Havana and want to get around cheaply.

19 de Noviembre Train Station (☎ 881-4431; Tulipán, Nuevo Vedado) has trains to a couple of points in the Havana Province, including six to San Antonio de los Baños (one hour). There's railcar service to ExpoCuba (40 minutes) at 9:30am Wednesday to Sunday.

TAXI

Metered tourist taxis are readily available at all of the upscale hotels, with the air-con Nissan taxis charging higher tariffs than the nonair-con Ladas. The cheapest official taxis are operated by **Panataxi** (☎ 55 55 55), costing US$1 flagfall, then US$0.45 a kilometer. Tourist taxis charge US$0.80 a kilometer and can be ordered from **Havanautos Taxi** (☎ 832-3232), **Habanataxi** (☎ 53 90 86) and

Transgaviota (☎ 33 97 80). **Taxi OK** (☎ 204-0000) is based in Miramar. Drivers of the tourist taxis are government employees who work for a peso salary.

The cheapest taxis are the older yellow-and-black Ladas, which are state-owned but rented out to private operators. They won't wish to use their meters, as these are set at an unrealistically low rate, but you can bargain over the fare. They're not supposed to pick up passengers within 100m of a tourist hotel.

Private pirate taxis with yellow license plates are a bit cheaper, but you must agree on the fare before getting into the car, and carry exact change. There are usually classic car taxis parked in front of the Inglaterra.

OUTER HAVANA

PLAYA & MARIANAO

The municipality of Playa, west of Vedado across the Río Almendares, includes the prestigious residential neighborhoods of Miramar, Cubanacán, Náutico, Flores, Siboney, Atabey, Barlovento and Santa Fé. To the south is the more proletarian municipality of Marianao.

Many of Havana's foreign embassies are in Miramar, and business travelers or conference attendees could consider staying at one of the large hotels in the area to have easy access to many handy facilities. If you're interested primarily in sightseeing and entertainment, commuting to Vedado or Habana Vieja is a nuisance and an expense. However, some of the best salsa clubs, discos and restaurants are out this way and the casas particulares are luxurious.

Many of Havana's business or scientific fairs and conventions take place at Cubanacán, where there are also several specialized medical institutes. Despite the austerity of the *período especial*, vast resources have been plowed into biotechnological and pharmaceutical research institutes in this area. Yachties, anglers and scuba divers will find themselves using the Marina Hemingway at Playa's west end. Marianao was made world famous for the Tropicana Nightclub, but locally it's known as a tough, in parts rough, neighborhood with a long history of social commitment and a powerful Santería community.

Information

INTERNET ACCESS

Hotel Business Centers Palco, Neptuno-Tritón and Meliá Habana charge US$7 per half-hour for Internet access.
Tu Isla (☎ 203-337; Av 3 & Calle 28, Playa; ☼ 7am-7pm)

LAUNDRY

Aster Tintorería y Lavandería (☎ 204-1622; Calle 34 No 314 btwn Avs 3 & 5, Miramar; ☼ 9am-5pm Mon-Fri, 9am-2pm Sun) Wash and dry for US$3 or dry cleaning by the piece; efficient and reliable.

MEDIA

The best **newsstand** in Havana is in the parking lot of **Supermercado 70** (Av 3 at Calle 70; ☼ 9am-6pm Mon-Sat). *Time, Newsweek*, the *Economist, Rolling Stone* and more (US$5 to US$8 each).

MEDICAL SERVICES

Clínica Central Cira García (☎ 204-2811; fax 24 16 33; Calle 18A No 4101 cnr Av 41, Playa) Emergency, dental and medical consultations for foreigners (consultations US$25-35).
Pharmacy (☎ 204-2880; Calle 18A No 4104 cnr Av 41, Playa; ☼ 24hr) In Clínica Central Cira García; one of the city's best, along with the pharmacy across the street on Calle 20 cnr Av 41 (☼ 9am-8:45pm).
Farmacia Internacional (☎ 204-9385; Av 3 & Calle 84 in Hotel Comodoro)

MONEY

Banco Financiero Internacional Miramar (☎ 203-9762; Av 1 & Calle 0, Sierra Maestra Building); Playa (☎ 204-2058; Calle 18 No 111 btwn Calles 1 & 3); Playa (☎ 267-5500; Av 5 & Calle 92)
Cadeca Miramar (Av 5A btwn Calles 40 & 42; ☼ 9am-5pm Mon-Sat, 9am-noon Sun); Playa (Av 3 at Calle 70 in front of Supermercado 70)

PHOTOGRAPHY

Photo Club Playa (☎ 204-1969; Av 3 & Calle 84); Playa (☎ 204-4991; Av 5 & Calle 96) Developing and passport photos.

POST

DHL (☎ 204-1578; Av 1 corner Calle 26, Miramar; ☼ 8am-8pm)
Post office Miramar (Calle 42 No 112 btwn Avs 1 & 3; ☼ 8am-11:30am, 2-6pm Mon-Fri, 8am-11:30am Sat); Miramar (Calle 110 btwn Avs 3 & 5; ☼ 8am-5:30pm Mon-Sat)

TOURIST INFORMATION

Infotur (☎ 24 70 36; Av 5 & Calle 112, Playa; ☼ 8:30am-5pm Mon-Sat, 8:30am-noon Sun)

PLAYA & MARIANAO

A **B** **C** **D**

INFORMATION
Aster Tintorería y Lavandería.....1	G2
Banco Financiero Internacional...2	E4
Banco Financiero Internacional...3	G2
Banco Financiero Internacional..............(see 36)	
British Embassy..........................4	G2
Cadeca.......................................5	G2
Cadeca...............................(see 75)	
Canadian Embassy.....................6	G2
Clínica Central Cira García.........7	H2
Cubanacán Náutica.....................8	B4
Cubanacán...................................9	F3
DHL...10	G2
French Embassy........................11	G2
Havanatur.............................(see 36)	
Infotur....................................12	E4
Japanese Embassy....................13	F3
Mexico Embassy.......................14	H2
Netherlands Embassy................15	H2
Pharmacy.................................16	H2
Pharmacy...............................(see 7)	
Photo Club...............................17	E4
Photo Club...............................18	E3
Russian Embassy......................19	F3
Swedish Embassy......................20	G2
Swiss Embassy.........................21	G2
Tu Isla.....................................22	G2

SIGHTS & ACTIVITIES   pp116–7
Acuario Nacional.......................23	F3
Centro de Ingeniería Genética y Biotecnología.......................24	E6
Centro Internacional de Restauración Neurológica (CIREN)............25	E5
Centro Nacional de Investigaciones Científicas (CENIC)................26	E5
Complejo Recreo......................27	A5
Fundación Naturaleza y El Hombre.................................28	F3

Iglesia Jesús de Miramar...........29	F3
Instituto Superior de Arte (ISA).30	E4
La Aguja Marlin Diving Center..31	B4
La Maqueta de La Habana........32	G2
Museo de la Alfabetización.......33	G5
Museo del Aire.........................34	D6
Pabexpo...................................35	D5
Palacio de las Convenciones...(see 47)	
Sierra Maestra Building.............36	H1

SLEEPING   pp117–8
Complejo Neptuno-Tritón.........37	F3
Hostal Costa Sol......................38	F3
Hotel Acuario...........................39	F3
Hotel Bello Caribe....................40	E6
Hotel Chateau Miramar............41	F3
Hotel Copacabana....................42	F2
Hotel El Comodoro...................43	E3
Hotel El Viejo y El Mar.............44	B4
Hotel Meliá Habana..................45	F3
Hotel Mirazul...........................46	G2
Hotel Palco..............................47	E5
LTI-Panorama Hotel Havana.....48	F3
Novotel Miramar......................49	F3
Residencia Universitaria Ispjae..50	G2

EATING   pp118–20
Cafetería de 3 y 62..................51	F3
Don Cangrejo...........................52	G2
Dos Gardenias.........................53	F3
El Aljibe..................................54	G2
El Buganvil..............................55	D5
El Elegante..............................56	H3
El Rancho Palco.......................57	E5
El Tocororo..............................58	G2
La Cecilia................................59	E4
La Esperanza...........................60	G2
La Ferminia.............................61	D5
La Flora...................................62	G4
La Fontana..............................63	G2

La Paila...................................64	H5
Paladar Calle 10......................65	G2
Paladar La Familia....................66	H2
Paladar La Fontana..................67	F3
Paladar Los Cactus de 33.........68	H3
Paladar Mi Jardín.....................69	F3
Pan.com..................................70	G2
Panadería Doña Neli.................71	G3
Pizza Nova..............................72	B5
Plaza de Marianao....................73	F6
Restaurante El Pavo Real.........74	H2
Supermercado 70.....................75	F3
Supermercado Universo.............76	B4

ENTERTAINMENT   pp120–1
Casa de la Música....................77	H2
Estadio Pedro Marrero..............78	H3
Havana Club Disco...................79	E3
Río Club..................................80	H1
Salón Rosado Benny Moré (El Tropical)..............................81	H3
Teatro Karl Marx......................82	G1
Tropicana Nightclub.................83	G4

SHOPPING   p121
Egrem Tienda de Música...........84	G2
La Maison...............................85	H2

TRANSPORT   pp121–3
Buses Nos P1 and 100.............86	F3
Cubacar..................................87	B4
Havanautos.............................88	E4
Havanautos.........................(see 36)	
Micar......................................89	F3
Panautos.................................90	G2
Panautos.................................91	F3
Rumbos...................................92	G2
Rumbos.............................(see 45)	
Transtur..................................93	F3
Vía Rent A Car........................94	H3

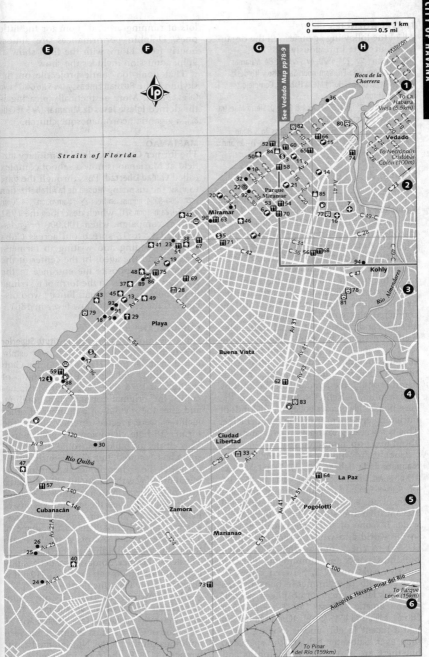

TRAVEL AGENCIES

All of the following agencies sell the organized tours listed previously (p85).

Cubanacán (☎ 204-6970; Av 3 & Calle 84, Miramar; ☷ 8am-5pm Mon-Fri, 8am-noon Sat) Also with desks at Hotel Bello Caribe, Hotel Meliá Habana, Complejo Neptuno-Tritón.

Havanatur (☎ 204-7541; Av 1 & Calle O, Sierra Maestra Building; ☷ 9am-6pm Mon-Sat)

Rumbos (☎ 204-7734; Av 3 btwn Calles 76 & 80 in Hotel Meliá Habana) Also in Complejo Neptuno-Tritón and Hotel Copacabana.

Sights
MIRAMAR

The fascinating museum at the **Fundación Naturaleza y El Hombre** (☎ 204-0438; Av 5B No 6611 btwn Calles 66 & 70; admission US$3; ☷ 10am-4pm Mon-Fri) collects artifacts from the 17,422km canoe trip from Amazon source to sea led by Cuban intellectual and nature-lover Antonio Nuñez Jiménez. There's the canoe in which they made the trip, of course, but there are also headdresses, weapons and adornments used by indigenous communities the team encountered, plus, scores of ceramic figurines in all stages and positions of sexual arousal; the 'Latin American Kamasutra.' The Fundación itself is mind-blowing, with one of Cuba's largest photography collections, plus all the titles written by Nuñez Jiménez, (he was damn prolific), the famous Fidel portrait by Guayasamín, stalactites in the foyer and 'the glass house,' glass cases collecting all kinds of intriguing ephemera from the founder's life. This is a working foundation; you must call ahead to set up a museum visit.

Cubans are wild for scale models and **La Maqueta de la Habana** (☎ 202-7303; Calle 28 No 113 btwn Avs 1 & 3; student/unguided/guided US$1/3/4; ☷ 9:30am-5pm Tue-Sat) is the biggest and best of them all: a huge 1/1000 scale model of Havana that measures 22m long and 8m wide. It's one of the largest scale models in the world and you can rent binoculars (US$1) to check out all the color-coded buildings, parks and monuments. Nearby, the two **parks** on Av 5, between Calles 24 and 26, with their immense banyan trees and dark lanes, are an atmospheric pocket.

The **Acuario Nacional** (☎ 202-5872; at Calle 62; adult/child US$5/3; ☷ 10am-10pm Tue-Sun) had a recent facelift and is looking better than ever. Saltwater fish are the specialty, but there are also sea lions, dolphins and

lots of running-around room for the little ones. Dolphin performances are almost hourly from 11am, with the final show at 9pm; admission includes the show.

That none-too-subtle projectile on the skyline is the **Russian Embassy** (Av 5 No 6402 btwn Calles 62 & 66). More aesthetically pleasing is the domed **Iglesia Jesús de Miramar** (Av 5 at Calle 82), a gigantic neoromanesque church.

MARIANAO

The former Cuartel Colombia military airfield at Marianao is now a school complex called **Ciudad Libertad**. Pass through the gate to visit the inspiring **Museo de la Alfabetización** (☎ 260-8054; admission free; ☷ 8am-noon, 1-4:30pm Mon-Fri, 8am-noon Sat), which describes the 1961 literacy campaign, when 100,000 *brigadistas* aged 12 to 18 spread out across Cuba to teach reading and writing to farmers, workers and the aged. In the center of the traffic circle, opposite the entrance to the complex, is a tower in the form of a syringe in memory of Carlos Juan Finlay, who discovered the cause of yellow fever in 1881.

CUBANACÁN

Cuba's leading art academy, **Instituto Superior de Arte** (ISA; Calle 120 No 1110 off Av 9), was established in the former Havana Country Club here in 1961, and elevated to the status of institute in 1976. The Faculty of Music occupies the original country-club building, and after the revolution a number of other facilities were erected on the site of the former 18-hole championship golf course. This cluster of buildings, some unfinished, some half-restored, but all gloriously graceful due to the arches, domes and profuse use of red brick, was the brainchild of Che and a team of architects. Among them was Richard Porro, who designed the striking Faculty of Plastic Arts (1961) with long curving passageways and domed halls in the shape of a reclining woman. Across a small stream from the main building is the Faculty of Theater and Dance. Some 800 students study here, and foreigners can too (see p412). It is accessible only from the northwest.

Also known as the Havana Convention Center, the **Palacio de las Convenciones** (☎ 20 60 11; www.complejopalco.com; Calle 146 btwn Avs 11 & 13) is one of Cuba's most dramatic modern buildings. Built for the Non-aligned Conference in 1979, the four interconnecting alls contain a state-of-the-art auditorium ith 2101 seats and 11 smaller halls. The 89-member National Assembly meets here wice a year and the complex hosts over 0,000 conference attendees annually. Not ar from here is **Pabexpo** (☎ 54 91 11; Av 17 & alle 180), just two blocks off Av 5. Opened n 1987, Pabexpo's 20,000 sq meters of exhibition space in four interconnecting pavilions are filled with about 15 business or scientific shows a year. Cubadisco (Cuba's Grammys) are held here each May.

Many of Cuba's cutting-edge scientific and medical facilities are out here including: **Centro de Ingeniería Genética y Biotecnología** (☎ 271-6022; Av 31 & Calle 190), the focus of Cuba's genetic engineering and biotechnology research; the **Centro Nacional de Investigaciones Científicas** (☎ 208-2546; Av 25 & Calle 158), where the anticholesterol wonder drug Ateromixol, or PPG, was created; and the **Centro Internacional de Restauración Neurológica** (☎ 271-6844; Av 25 & Calle 158), CIREN, where Cuba has developed breakthrough neurological treatments. All these installations are heavily guarded, so unless you're a patient, don't even think about visiting.

Museo del Aire (☎ 271-0632; Calle 212 btwn Avs 29 & 31, La Coronela; unguided/guided US$2/3, plus camera US$2; 🕑 9am-4pm Tue-Sun) has 22 planes and helicopters on display, most of them ex-military aircraft. Don't miss Che Guevara's personal Cessna 310, or the space suit used by Cuba's first cosmonaut.

Activities

There are many water activities available at Marina Hemingway in Barlovento, 20km west of central Havana. Deep-sea fishing can be arranged at **Cubanacán Naútica** (☎ 204-6848; Av 5 & Calle 248) for US$155 to US$280 for four anglers for four hours depending on the boat. Included are a captain, sailor, open bar and tackle. Marlin season is June to October. Scuba packages for US$35 per dive and tours of Havana's littoral can also be arranged. Hotel tour desks should also be able to arrange these things.

La Aguja Marlin Diving Center (☎ 204-5088), between Cubanacán Naútica and the shopping center, offers scuba diving for US$30/dive, plus US$5 for gear. It has one morning and one afternoon departure. A diving excursion to Varadero or Playa Girón costs US$70. Reader reviews have been favorable.

Sleeping

The only budget accommodation out this way is in casas particulares (see p118).

MIRAMAR

Residencia Universitaria Ispjae (☎ 203-6633, 209-2841; Av 1 at Calle 22; s/d US$27/44) Has eight rooms with baths that are usually booked up by foreigners studying with UniversiTUR. Still, with the seaside setting, bar and restaurant, it's worth a try.

Hotel Mirazul (☎ 204-0088/45; Av 5 No 3603 btwn Calles 36 & 40; s/d US$40/50) An elegant old mansion operated as a hotel by the Ministerio de Educación Superior. The eight air-con rooms with baths and TVs are all different, so look first. A restaurant/bar is available. It's excellent value compared to the larger tourist hotels found here.

Hostal Costa Sol (☎ 202-8269, 209-0828; Calle 60 No 307 at Av 3A, Miramar; s/d US$25/48). Operated by the Ministerio de Educación Superior, this is an intimate place with only 11 rooms, but is far from everything. The restaurant is cheap and decent if you happen to be out this way.

Hotel Copacabana (Gran Caribe; ☎ 204-0340; www.grancaribe.cu; Av 1 No 4404 at Calle 44; s/d incl breakfast US$75/110) A five-story, 168-room hotel complex right on the coast. Although there's no beach, a seawall creates a protected pool. The hotel also features a swimming pool, tennis courts and scuba diving, and aqua-scooters can be hired to explore the coast. It's popular with return visitors, families and laidback conference groups. The Ipanema Disco here is a good time out.

Hotel Chateau Miramar (Cubanacán; ☎ 24 19 51/2/3; www.cubanacan.cu; Av 1 btwn Calles 60 & 70; s/d US$95/120; P 🔀 🖳 🌊) Marketed as a 'boutique hotel' and considering neighboring properties, this hotel, with only five floors and 50 rooms, does have a more intimate feel. But 'chateau' and 'boutique' are a bit of a stretch. Still, professionals will appreciate the free cell phone, computer connection, direct international phone service and minibar that come with rooms.

LTI-Panorama Hotel Havana (☎ 204-0100; www.lti.de; Av 3 & Calle 70; s/d US$95/120; P 🔀 🖳 🌊) Miramar's newest hotel, which opened in spring 2003. This super-mod hotel is an architectural oddity on this bit of coast, with its obnoxious all mirrored facade, but once inside you can appreciate the wisdom of a wall of windows facing the sea. The 317 rooms here are spacious, comfortable and have delicious bathrooms. Suites have terraces and whirlpools. The pool here is fantastic and right on the ocean. Kids under 12 stay for half price.

Complejo Neptuno-Tritón (Gran Caribe; ☎ 204-0245; www.grancaribe.cu; Av 3 & Calle 70; s/d low season US$45/60, high season US$60/80; P ✗ ☐ ✑) That pair of 22-floor towers perched on the shore is the Complejo Neptuno-Tritón (one tower is the Neptuno, the other the Tritón). Fully renovated in 1999, each identical tower has its own reception area and 266 rooms; they share a sprawling pool on the rocky shore. Many memories have been made here by honeymooners, workers and UJC members who are given weekends here as incentives or rewards from the state (that's why you'll see so many Cubans here). The Neptuno has a decent lobby bar (✆ 24 hours) with Internet. The Tritón is US$10 more than the Neptuno in all price ranges shown above.

Hotel El Comodoro (Cubanacán; ☎ 204-5551; www.cubanacan.cu; Av 3 & Calle 84; s/d/tr from US$60/95/136; P ✗ ☐ ✑) Right on the coast, about 15km west of Habana Vieja. This complex is a maze of shops, restaurants and accommodation, both old and new. The 134 rooms in the main four-story building date from before the revolution; another 10 rooms in a two-story cabaña block facing the ocean cost the same. You're better off paying about 10% more for one of the Bungalows Alborada or Pleamar, which are fairly new. The hotel's small, sandy beach is protected from the

waves by a large iron seawall, and the Co modoro is a good choice for anyone lookin for real resort atmosphere within a taxi rid of the city. A beer at the hotel bar will run yo US$3 (triple what you pay normally).

Novotel Miramar (☎ 204-3584; fax 204-3583; Av at Calle 74, Miramar; s/d/tr low season US$70/85/125, hig season US$85/120/170) Business travelers familia with the worldwide chain will like this nev hotel. The Novotel has 427 rooms, a busines center and big, plush rooms, if generic.

CUBANACÁN

Hotel Palco (Cubanacán; ☎ 204-7235; Calle 146 btw Avs 11 & 13; s/d incl breakfast low season US$80/106, hig season US$97/123; P ✗ ☐ ✑) Attached t the Palacio de las Convenciones is this top business hotel with 180 rooms. There ar several bars (real espresso!), a decent cigar shop and a high-tech business center.

Hotel Bello Caribe (Cubanacán; ☎ 33 05 67; Av 31 & Calle 158; s/d US$45/64; P ✗ ✑) A couple o kilometers south of Hotel Palco, next to the huge Centro de Ingeniería Genética y Biotec nología. The 120 rooms are generally used by foreigners undergoing treatment at the nearby medical facilities. Though this place is inconveniently located, we've received favor able letters about the facilities and services; there is a good buffet and salad bar.

MARINA HEMINGWAY

Hotel El Viejo y El Mar (Cubanacán; ☎ 204-6336; fax 204-6823; s/d US$72/92; P ✗ ✑) *The Old Man and the Sea* is at the Marina Hemingway, Av 5 and Calle 248, 20km west of colonial Havana. There's not much to recommend this place unless you've been at sea awhile and want a stable bed. There's live music and a pool table in the lobby lounge. Maybe go for one of the cabanas with king-sized bed overlooking the pool (US$100). You're far from the action out here.

Hotel Acuario (Cubanacán; ☎ 204-7628; fax 204-4379; s/d/bungalow US$63/82/99) In the center of the marina. It's got a better setup than the El Viejo, as the 314 rooms are in a series of three- and four-story blocks sprinkled between the marina channels. There's a 24-hour international pharmacy here.

Eating
PLAYA & MARIANAO
Paladar Los Cactus de 33 (☎ 203-5139; Av 33 No 3405 btwn Calles 34 & 36, Playa; ✆ noon-midnight)

CASAS PARTICULARES – PLAYA & MIRAMAR

Mayda Bellón Trueba (☎ 203-4490; Av 33 No 3404 btwn C 34 & 36, Playa; r US$30) Opposite Los Cactus de 33. Palatial, private. English spoken. Nine houses renting on this tranquil block, allowing big groups to arrange casa accommodation together.

Marta Rodríguez (☎ 203-8596; Calle 42 No 914 at Av 11; r US$40; P) Rents two outfitted rooms with TV/VCR, stereo and fridge.

Rina and Geraldo (☎ 202-4112; Av 3A No 8610 btwn 86 & 88, Miramar; r US$25-30) Two clean rooms, one with sun terrace. Flexible hosts.

Suites Olimpia Jorge Pérez (☎ /fax 202-4126; Calle 96 No 535 btwn Avs 5F & 7, Miramar; r US$30-35; P) Fridge. Private.

...eviewed in international lifestyle magazines and used as a setting for TV specials, this place has impeccable service, elegant surroundings, well-prepared food and (in Cuban context) outrageous prices. A full pork meal with all the sides is US$18, the house special chicken breast with mushrooms, olives and cheese is US$22. Its humbler neighbor **El Elegante** (☎ 203-215; Av 33 No 3410 btwn 34 & 36) is better value, with meals in the US$10 to US$13 range. They're open 'whenever you want them to be.'

La Paila (☎ 267-1771; Ave 51A No 8827 btwn Calles 88B & 88C, Marianao; ☯ noon-midnight) If this place wasn't so off the beaten track, it would be in Havana's Top Five. With just a few tables ensconced in a lush garden replete with soft-lit lanterns, this is the most romantic paladar no-one knows about. And the food is infallible. They do a great *bistec* Uruguayo (US$3.75) or try one of the famous pizzas (US$1.60-US$3.60). The appetizers and sides are good too. The menu is in pesos, but they take dollars. A good pre-Tropicana spot.

La Flora (☎ 209-5889; Av 41 & Calle 68, Playa) Unique in Havana, catch a colectivo on Calle 23 in Vedado to visit this bakery selling whole wheat bread (¡sí señor!), brownies, éclairs, cinnamon-raisin buns and other sweet treats. In dollars of course. It claims to be 24 hours, but we've been duped before.

MIRAMAR
There are some stellar paladares in Miramar.

La Esperanza (☎ 202-4361; Calle 16 No 105 btwn Avs 1 & 3; ☯ 6:30-11pm, closed Thu) This lovely home on a Miramar side street is worth a special trip. The well-prepared and presented food is served by wonderfully friendly staff in antique outfitted dining rooms or a leafy backyard. Reservations are advised, but not to worry if you have to wait; the couches, coffee-table books and a glass of fine wine will keep you occupied.

Paladar Calle 10 (☎ 205-3970; Calle 10 No 314 btwn Avs 3 & 5; ☯ noon-3pm, 6-11pm) Hidden in a back garden, the specialty here is outstandingly delicious barbecue: the lamb skewers marinated in oregano (US$8) just might be the tastiest meat to pass your lips in Cuba, while the exotic red snapper stuffed with *frutas de mar* and flambéed with rum (US$9) is out of this world. The kitchen

is wide open so you can watch and learn. Italian, French and English spoken. Reservations recommended.

Paladar Mi Jardín (☎ 203-4627; Calle 66 No 517 at Av 5B; ☯ noon-midnight) It's the rare Cuban menu that offers chicken mole (US$6.50) or tacos and quesadillas (US$5), which makes this Mexican place a keeper. Dining under the vine-covered trellis in the garden is recommended, as is the house special fish Veracruz (US$9).

El Aljibe (☎ 204-1583/4; Av 7 btwn Calles 24 & 26; ☯ noon-midnight) This place gets so much press (*Cigar Aficionado*, *New York Times* etc) you might think success has gone to its head. But no, the house special roasted chicken (US$12, plus 10%) is as succulent as always and the all-you-can-eat rice, black beans, fries and salad will do you right. That distinct flavoring of the chicken and gravy is *naranja agria* (bitter orange). One of Havana's best wine lists is here, from California cabernets to Australian shiraz.

El Tocororo (☎ 202-4530; Calle 18 No 302 at Av 3; ☯ noon-midnight) Considered one of Havana's finest restaurants, be prepared to open your billfold at this spendy place. Fried fish (US$12), lobster tail (US$24) or a live lobster plucked from the tank (US$35) is just the beginning. Everything, even the bread and rice, is à la carte, and 10% is added on top. The candlelit tables and garden are plusses, but don't believe the hype.

Don Cangrejo (☎ 204-4169; Av 1 No 1606 btwn Calles 16 & 18; ☯ noon-midnight) Right on the water, this seafood restaurant (fish US$8 to US$12 or lobster US$20 to US$25) scores high points for atmosphere (love the buccaneer waitstaff!). There's a pool table and pool, an inexpensive pizza and grill menu and one of Havana's classic signs out front.

Supermercado 70 (Av 3 at Calle 70; ☯ 9am-6pm Mon-Sat, 9am-1pm Sun) Still known as the 'Diplomercado' from the days when you had to show a foreign passport to be able to shop here, this place is gigantic. One of the best in Havana with lots of selection.

If you're staying in one of the pricey hotels and want a cheaper place to eat than what the hotels offer, there's the **Cafetería de 3 y 62** (☎ 204-0369; Av 3 & Calle 62; ☯ 8am-11pm), on the eastern side of the Russian Embassy. There are also a row of simple restaurant kiosks facing Supermercado 70.

Also recommended:

Paladar La Familia (Calle 6 No 302 at Av 3; ☟ noon-midnight) On the grounds of an incredible estate, replete with pool.

Pan.com (☎ 204-4232; Av 7 & Calle 26, Miramar; ☟ 10am-midnight) Burgers, creamy milkshakes and hero sandwiches.

Dos Gardenias (☎ 204-2353; Av 7 at Calle 28; ☟ noon-midnight) Choose from grill, Chinese and pasta restaurants in this complex; also a *bolero* hot spot.

Restaurante El Pavo Real (☎ 204-6688; Av 7A & Calle 4; ☟ noon-midnight) Good, quick Chinese fill ups for around US$5; greasy, but tasty. Pizza and pasta across the street.

Panadería Doña Neli (Av 5A & Calle 42; ☟ 7am-6pm Mon-Sat, 7am-1pm Sun) Bread in dollars.

CUBANACÁN

El Buganvil (☎ 271-4791; Calle 190 No 1501 btwn Calles 15 & 17, Siboney; ☟ noon-midnight) Another solid paladar with a pleasant outdoor plant and thatch setting, this place has sterling service and good *comida criolla*. The house specialty is *loma ahumado* (US$4), but if you get a group of six together, they'll smoke a whole pig for you and put out an all-you-can-eat spread (US$10 per person; 24-hour notice).

La Cecilia (☎ 204-1562; Av 5 No 11010 btwn Calles 110 & 112; ☟ noon-midnight) Folks come to this upscale garden restaurant to feast on steak, lobster and grilled meats, but they stick around for the hot bands. Drop in on a weekend night and you might catch Moneda Dura or Buena Fe.

La Ferminia (☎ 33 67 86; Av 5 No 18207 at Calle 184) Dine in the mansion or out in the garden patio at this fine restaurant – it doesn't matter. The point is the food. A wonderful mixed grill, pulled straight from the fire onto your plate, or a thick filet mignon will set you back more than US$20, but it will be well spent. This is a good place to celebrate something special.

El Rancho Palco (Av 19 & Calle 140; ☟ noon-11pm) Another upscale place, in a forest near the Palacio de las Convenciones. Steaks, seafood and Cuban cooking are served under a thatched roof.

El Laurel (☎ 29 77 67; Av 5 No 26002 btwn Calles 260 & 262, Santa Fé; ☟ 11:30am 'until you leave') Further afield is this terrific paladar that serves smallish portions of tasty *comida criolla* in an awesome setting right on the water.

You can even fish off the pier after lunch if you like.

At Marina Hemingway is the terrific **Pizza Nova**, serving pies on the water and the well stocked **Supermercado Universo**.

Entertainment
MIRAMAR

Teatro Karl Marx (☎ 203-0801, 209-1991; Av 1 & Calle 10, Miramar) The very biggest events happen here, like the closing galas for the jazz and film fests (with Harry Belafonte and Roman Polanski in the house) and rare concerts by *trovador* Carlos Varela. Get tickets for row 20 or closer because the acoustics crumple if you're back under the balcony.

Casa de la Música (☎ 202-6147; Calle 20 No 3308 at Av 35, Miramar; admission US$5-20; ☟ 10pm Tue-Sat) One of Havana's premier venues, you're good time is almost guaranteed at this casa run by recording company Egrem. Renowned jazz pianist Chuchu Valdés, NG la Banda, Los Van Van, Aldaberto Alvarez y Su Son: all the platinum players gig here. If you can only make it out one night for live music, this is the place.

Ipanema Disco (☎ 204-0340; Av 1 No 4404 at Calle 44; admission US$5; ☟ 10pm Tue-Sun) This is the disco if you want a good disco-pop-salsa mix in a cool, nonthreatening setting. The Sunday matinee at 4pm is 'Disco de las Tembas' (the middle-aged disco); you have to be over 30 to get in and the tunes are what you'd expect: BeeGees, Zeppelin and Donna Summer.

Havana Club Disco (☎ 202-7712; Av 1 & Calle 86, Miramar; admission US$10; ☟ 10pm-3am Mon-Sat) This tremendous video disco behind the Hotel Comodoro is probably more trouble than it's worth: no posted prices, lots of *jineteras* and their over-50 benefactors and itty-bitty drinks in plastic cups. The Sunday matinee is better (US$3; ☟ 2pm to 7pm; aged 16 to 30 only).

Río Club (☎ 209-3389; Calle A No 314 btwn Avs 3 & 3A, Miramar; ☟ 10pm) This disco claims to offer *el sonida más duro de la ciudad* (the hardest sound in town). The location is reflected in the scene, which is a good mix of locals and tourists, but pricey for what it is.

MARIANAO

Tropicana Nightclub (☎ 267-1871; Calle 72 No 4504 at Av 43, Marianao; ☟ show at 10pm) Cuba's most famous nightclub. Since the Tropicana opened in 1939, famous artists such as Benny Moré,

Nat King Cole and Maurice Chevalier have appeared here. Over 200 dancers perform during Tropicana's 1950s-style cabaret show 'Paradise Under the Stars,' a spectacle not soon forgotten. The doors open at 8:30pm. Admission including one drink is from US$65 per person, depending on the table. Tropicana bookings can be made through any hotel tour desk, with hotel transfers included. The Tropicana box office opens 10am to 4pm daily, and although booking in person is no cheaper, you'll be able to choose your own table (important as we've received several complaints about switched tables and botched reservations). When bookings are light, bar seats might be available (US$25), but these can't be reserved in advance. Just turn up at 8:30pm and ask.

Order a bottle of rum and your mixers straight away to avoid fighting for your server's attention during the show. The dress code here requires that men wear long pants and shoes (important to remember if you arrive by tour bus straight from a day of sightseeing). An after-hours club called **Arcos de Cristal** is on the same premises as the Tropicana, and it has a show that starts after the one at the Tropicana finishes.

Salón Rosado Benny Moré (☎ 206-1281; Av 41 & 46, Playa; admission 10 pesos-US$10; 🕑 9pm-late) For something completely different, check out the very *caliente* action at this outdoor venue. This place (aka El Tropical) packs in hot, sexy Cuban youths dancing madly to Los Van Van, Pupi y Su Son Son or Habana Abierta. It's a fierce scene and female travelers should expect aggressive come-ons. Friday to Sunday is best. Some travelers pay pesos, others dollars – more of that Cuban randomness for you.

LA LISA

This residential neighborhood southwest of Cubanacán holds **Macumba Habana** (☎ 33 05 68/9; Calle 222 cnr of Av 37; admission US$10-20; 🕑 10pm), one of Havana's biggest venues for live salsa. The outdoor setting is refreshing and the sets long, so you'll get a lot of dancing in. You can also dine at La Giradilla in the same complex. At the time of writing it was about to launch jazz and reggae nights (US$5 cover). Hotels and Infotur (p113) sell excursions here, but you're better off getting here yourself (a dollar taxi should cost around US$8).

Sport

You can see soccer matches on weekends at 3pm at the 15,000-seat **Estadio Pedro Marrero** (Av 41 & Calle 46), near Hotel Kohly.

Shopping

For compact discs head to **Egrem Tienda de Música** (Calle 18 No 103 at Av 1; 🕑 9am-6pm Mon-Sat), which has a great selection, or visit the **Casa de la Música** (Av 35 & Calle 20; 🕑 10am-10pm).

Smokers and souvenir seekers will like **La Casa del Tabaco** (Av 5 & Calle 16; 🕑 10am-6pm Mon-Sat, 10am-1pm Sun), arguably Havana's top cigar store. There's a comfy smoking lounge.

The Cuban fashion fascination is in high gear at **La Maison** (Calle 16 No 701 at Av 7, Miramar), with a large boutique selling designer clothing, shoes, handbags, jewelry, cosmetics and souvenirs. Models strut the catwalk here in outlandish costumes nightly at 10pm (US$10 admission). La Maison's upscale unisex hairdresser works noon to 7pm (closed Sunday).

Getting There & Away

To get to Playa from Havana, take bus No 264 from Desamparados, between Picota and Compostela, near the old city wall southeast of the central train station. Other-wise try bus No 132 or 232 from Dragones and Industria beside the Capitolio. From Vedado to Playa you can catch the P1 from in front of Coppelia on Calle 23 or the P4 along Línea, just before Paseo toward Calle A. For Marianao, take bus No 34 from Dragones and Industria or the M-4 camello from Parque Fraternidad (a long, slow ride).

To reach the Marina Hemingway, take bus No 9 or 420 from near the tunnel under the Río Almendares in Miramar.

Getting Around

Havanautos (☎ 204-0646/7; 3rd flr Sierra Maestra Bldg, Av 1 & Calle 0, Miramar) Also a desk at the Complejo Neptuno-Tritón (☎ 204-3203).

Panautos (☎ 204-3605; Av 3 & Calle 84, Playa)

Cubacar (☎ 204-1707) has an office across the street from Hotel El Viejo y El Mar at the Marina Hemingway, plus at the Chateau Miramar, the Bello Caribe and the Meliá Habana, while Transtur is represented at Hotel Copacabana.

There are Servi-Cupet gas stations at Av 31, between Calles 18 and 20, in Miramar;

PARQUE LENIN AREA

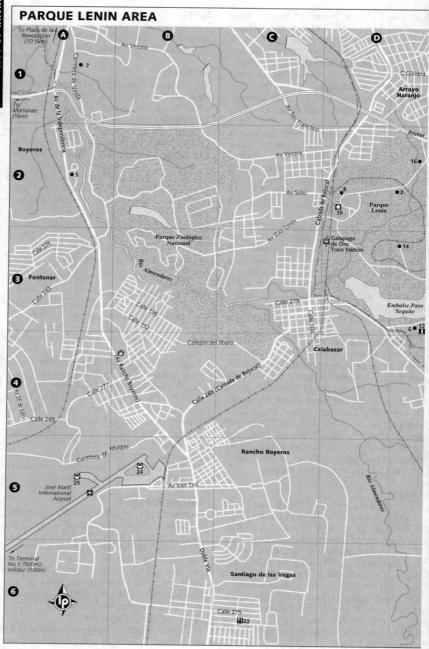

To Plaza de la
Revolución
(10.5km)

To
Marianao
(5km)

Av Verona

Carretera de Vento

Av de la Independencia

Boyeros

Fontanar

Calle 229

Calle 243

Calle 136

Calle 152

Rio Almendares

Parque Zoológico
Nacional

Callejón del Jíbaro

Av Rancho Boyeros

Calle 277

Av 26 de Julio

Calle 249

Carretera de Murgas

José Martí
International
Airport

Av Van Troi

Calle 289 (Calzada de Bejucal)

Rancho Boyeros

Doble Vía

To Terminal
No 3 (500m);
Infotur (500m)

Santiago de las Vegas

Calle 275

Av Verona

Av San Francisco

Av Soto

Av Verona

Calzada de Bejucal

Calle 104

Parque Lenin

Galápago
de Oro
Train Station

Av Zoo-Lenin

Calle 279

Calle 289 (Calzada de Bejucal)

C Güinera

Arroyo
Naranjo

Primer

Embalse Paso
Sequito

Río Almendares

7

5

25

24

22

19

8

2

16

14

6   12

A   B   C   D

1

2

3

4

5

6

Calabazar

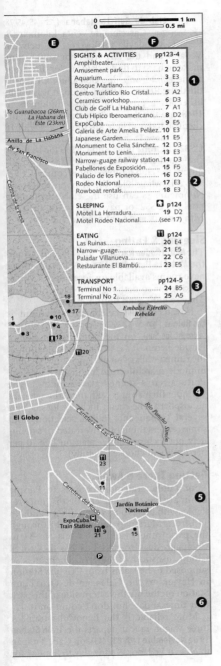

Calle 72 and Av 41 in Marianao (near the Tropicana); and on the traffic circle at Av 5 and Calle 112 in Cubanacán. Oro Negro is at Av 5 and Calle 120, Cubanacán. All are open 24 hours.

Hail colectivos (10 pesos) in Vedado to Playa along Línea; the usual route is down Av 3 to Calle 70 (ask ¿Playa?) and on Calle 23 to Marianao (ask ¿La Siguera? which will drop you on Calle 72 and Av 41, a block from the Tropicana).

PARQUE LENIN AREA

Parque Lenin, off the Calzada de Bejucal in Arroyo Naranjo, 20km south of central Havana, is the city's largest recreational area and packed with fun things to do. Constructed between 1969 and 1972, this is one of the few developments in Havana from that era. These 670 hectares of green parkland and beautiful old trees surround an artificial lake, the Embalse Paso Sequito, just west of the much larger Embalse Ejército Rebelde, which was formed by damming the Río Almendares.

Sights

The main things to see are south of the lake, including the **Galería de Arte Amelia Peláez** (admission US$1). Opposite is the **Bosque Martiano**, with a small library under a bridge. Up the hill there's a dramatic white marble **monument to Lenin** (1984) by the Soviet sculptor LE Kerbel, and west along the lake is an overgrown **amphitheater** and an **aquarium** with freshwater fish and crocodiles (admission US$1). The bronze **monument to the late Celia Sánchez** (1985), a longtime associate of Fidel Castro who was instrumental in having Parque Lenin built, is rather hidden beyond the aquarium. A **ceramics workshop** is nearby.

Most of these attractions are open 9am to 5pm Tuesday to Sunday, and admission to the park itself is free. You can rent a **rowboat** on the Embalse Paso Sequito from a dock behind the **Rodeo Nacional**. A 9km **narrow-gauge railway** with four stops operates inside the park from 10am to 3pm Wednesday to Sunday.

A visit to Parque Lenin can be combined with a trip to **ExpoCuba**, (☎ 66 42 92; admission US$1; ☼ 9am-5pm Wed-Sun) at Calabazar on the Carretera del Rocío in Arroyo Naranjo, 3km south of Las Ruinas restaurant. Opened in

1989, this large permanent exhibition showcases Cuba's economic and scientific achievements in 25 pavilions based on themes such as sugar, farming, apiculture, animal science, fishing, construction, food, geology, sports and defense. Cubans visiting ExpoCuba flock to the amusement park at the center of the complex, bypassing the rather dry propaganda displays. **Don Cuba** (☎ 57 82 87), a revolving restaurant is atop a tower. The Feria Internacional de La Habana, Cuba's largest trade fair, is held at ExpoCuba the first week of November. Parking is available at Gate E, at the south end of the complex (US$1).

Across the highway from ExpoCuba is the 600-hectare **Jardín Botánico Nacional** (☎ 54 93 65; admission US$1; ☯ 8:30am-4:30pm Wed-Sun). The **Pabellones de Exposición** (1987), near the entry gate, is a series of greenhouses with cactuses and tropicals, while two kilometers beyond is the tranquil **Japanese Garden** (1992). Nearby is the celebrated **Restaurante El Bambú**, where a vegetarian buffet is US$14 (see the boxed text p95). The tractor train ride around the park departs four times a day and costs US$3, gardens admission included. Parking costs US$2.

The extensive **Parque Zoológico Nacional** (☎ 44 76 13; adult/child US$3/2; ☯ 9am-3:30pm Wed-Sun) off Calzada de Bejucal, on Av Zoo-Lenin in Boyeros, is 2km west of the Parque Lenin riding school. Worlds apart from the inner-city zoo at Av 26 near the Víazul terminal in Nuevo Vedado, with its stagnant crocodile ponds and jail cells for cages, this is more of a zoo/safari park where rhinos, hippos and other imported fauna have free reign. A trolley bus tours the grounds all day (included in admission). The caged animals (big cats, primates etc) is more akin to Latin American zoo-style.

Activities

In the northwestern corner of Parque Lenin, behind Motel La Herradura, is the **Club Hípico Iberoamericano** (☎ 44 10 58; ☯ 9am-5pm). Horseback riding through the park on a steed rented from the club costs US$12 an hour, but horses rented from boys at the nearby **amusement park** or at the entrance to Parque Lenin proper (you'll be besieged) costs US$3/hour, guide included. The club's Escuela de Equitación offers riding classes for US$12/hour.

The **Club de Golf La Habana** (☎ 45 45 78; ☯ 8am-8pm), Carretera de Venta, kilometer 8, Reparto Capdevila in Boyeros, lies between Vedado and the airport. Poor signposting makes it hard to find: ask locals for directions to the 'golfito' or 'Dilpo Golf Club.' Originally titled the Rover's Athletic Club, it was established by a group of British diplomats in 1948 and the diplomatic corps is largely the clientele today. There are nine holes with 18 tees to allow 18-hole rounds. Green fees are US$20 for nine holes and US$30 for 18 holes, clubs and cart US$10, caddie US$10. In addition, the club has five tennis courts (US$2) and a bowling alley (open noon to 11pm). Nonmembers can use the club's swimming pool for US$2, or pay US$5 to use the pool with a drink and light meal included.

Sleeping & Eating

The **Motel Rodeo Nacional** (☎ 44 30 26 ext 242) and the **Motel La Herradura** (☎ 44 28 10) sometimes have rooms available for foreigners if you're looking for something completely different. They're both rock-bottom budget.

Havana's most celebrated restaurant is **Las Ruinas** (☎ 57 82 86; Cortina de la Presa; ☯ 11am-midnight Tue-Sun), on the southeastern side of Parque Lenin. It's a striking combination of the ruined walls of an old sugar mill engulfed in modern architecture highlighted by René Portocarrero's stained-glass windows. The antique furnishings enhance the elegant atmosphere. The menu includes lobster plus several Cuban and Italian selections, but some readers thought it overrated (it's definitely not a cheap date – plan on US$30 per person if you choose carefully).

Getting There & Away

Your public transport choices to Parque Lenin are bus or train. The first is more reliable, with bus No 88 from Víbora and No 113 from Marianao running right through the park; otherwise, there's bus No 31 to Galápago de Oro and bus No 473 to El Globo, just south of the park. There are also supposed to be trains from Cristina Station in Havana to the Galápago de Oro Train Station on the northwestern side of the park four times a day, but don't count on it.

More reliable is the ExpoCuba train. A three-wagon railcar departs the **Train Station 19 de Noviembre** (☎ 881-4431) on Calle Tulipán in Nuevo Vedado, Wednesday to Sunday for

he exhibition at 9:30am (one peso), and returns at 5:30pm. This train passes Boyeros,
Parque Lenin and El Rincón.

Getting Around

There's a Servi-Cupet gas station at Av de
la Independencia and Calle 271 in Boyeros,
north of the airport. It's accessible only
from the northbound lane and is open 24
hours a day.

SANTIAGO DE LAS VEGAS AREA

On a hilltop at El Cacahual, 8km south of José
Martí International Airport via Santiago de
las Vegas, is the open-air mausoleum of the
hero of Cuban independence, General Antonio Maceo, who was killed in the Battle
of San Pedro near Bauta on December 7,
1896. An open-air pavilion next to the mausoleum shelters a historical exhibit.

There is no pilgrimage more powerful
or disturbing in Cuba than the devotional
crawl to the Santuario de San Lázaro, (1917) at
El Rincón, 4km southwest of Santiago de
las Vegas. Up to 50,000 Cubans come here
on bloodied knees, dragging themselves
prostrate along the asphalt or walking
barefoot for kilometers during the night of
December 16 to exorcise evil spirits and pay
off debts for miracles granted. Along the
several-kilometer route, flowers, candles
and coin offerings are made to Lazarus,
a Christian saint known for his ministra-
tions to lepers. San Lázaro is paralleled in
Afro-Cuban Santería by Babalú Ayé, the
Yoruba god of sickness; look for the statue
wearing a bright red cape on the western
side of the church. Devotees come from afar
to fill their bottles with holy water from a
fountain in front of the leprosy sanatorium
directly behind the church.

Another feature of this area is the well-
kept AIDS sanatorium 'Los Cocos,' which
opened in 1986, occupying buildings on
both sides of the road midway between
Santiago de las Vegas and El Rincón.
Cubans found to be HIV-positive were
once required to stay here indefinitely, but
the norm is now a couple of weeks, after
which they're free to leave provided they're
considered sexually responsible. In practice
many stay because medical and housing
conditions here are often better than at
home. The scene on December 16, with
many patients pressed against the fence

flirting and conversing on living with HIV
with passersby is what the Cuban character
is all about, as it's socializing, questioning,
joking and educating all in one.

Paladar Villanueva (☎ 683-4508; Calle 182 No
39511 btwn 395 & 397; ☿ noon-11:30pm), off the
Doble Vía toward Cacahual, provides a
detailed menu with reasonable prices. A
carnaval atmosphere prevails on December
16 with food, drink and smokes sold along
the pilgrimage route.

To get here, take the M-2 Metro Bus from
Parque de la Fraternidad in Havana to San-
tiago de las Vegas. Bus No 476 between San-
tiago de las Vegas and La Ceiba passes both
the AIDS sanatorium and the sanctuary.
On December 16, trains run all night from
Train Station 19 de Noviembre, on Calle
Tulipán in Nuevo Vedado (one peso).

REGLA

pop 42,390

The old town of Regla, just across the harbor from Habana Vieja, is an industrial-
port town known as a center of Afro-Cuban
religions, including the all-male secret society Abakúa. Several babalawo (Santería
priests) reside in Regla, and it's not hard
to find one if you're in need of advice (in
Spanish). You'll probably be presented
with protective beads and/or prescriptions
for treatment. A donation left on the altar
in the living room is expected (US$5). One
famous Regla babalawo is Eberardo Marero
(Ñico López No 60, btwn Coyola & Camilo Cienfuegos),
and others live nearby.

Long before the triumph of the 1959
revolution, Regla was known as the Sierra
Chiquita (Little Sierra, after the Sierra
Maestra) for its revolutionary traditions.
This working-class neighborhood is also
notable for a large thermoelectric power
plant and shipyard. Regla is almost free of
tourist trappings, and makes a nice afternoon out of the city; the skyline views from
this side of the harbor offer perspective.
There are lots of little peso food items for
sale along Martí, a good vegetable market
and lots of local street scenes.

Sights

Beyond a huge ceiba tree on Santuario, in
front of you as you get off the ferry, is the
Iglesia de Nuestra Señora de Regla (☎ 97 62 88;
☿ 7:30am-6pm) with La Santísima Virgen de

REGLA, GUANABACOA, CASABLANCA & COJIMAR

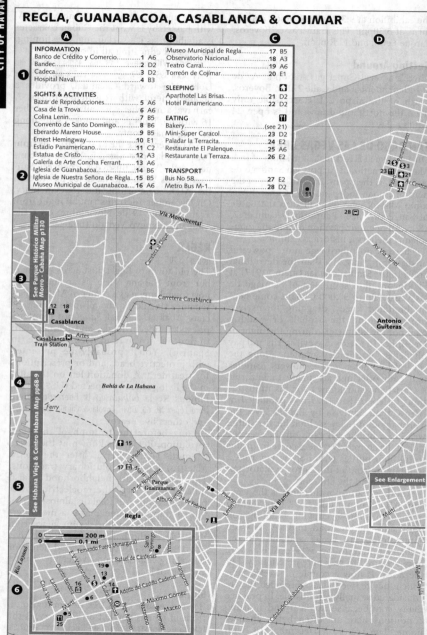

A   **B**   **C**   **D**

INFORMATION
Banco de Crédito y Comercio............1 A6
Bandec...2 D2
Cadeca..3 D2
Hospital Naval....................................4 B3

SIGHTS & ACTIVITIES
Bazar de Reproducciones...................5 A6
Casa de la Trova................................6 A6
Colina Lenin.......................................7 B5
Convento de Santo Domingo............8 B6
Eberardo Marero House......................9 B5
Ernest Hemingway...........................10 E1
Estadio Panamericano......................11 C2
Estatua de Cristo.............................12 A3
Galería de Arte Concha Ferrant.......13 A6
Iglesia de Guanabacoa.....................14 B6
Iglesia de Nuestra Señora de Regla..15 B5
Museo Municipal de Guanabacoa....16 A6

Museo Municipal de Regla................17 B5
Observatorio Nacional......................18 A3
Teatro Carral....................................19 A6
Torreón de Cojímar..........................20 E1

SLEEPING 🛏
Aparthotel Las Brisas.......................21 D2
Hotel Panamericano........................22 D2

EATING 🍴
Bakery...(see 21)
Mini-Super Caracol..........................23 D2
Paladar la Terracita..........................24 E2
Restaurante El Palenque...................25 A6
Restaurante La Terraza.....................26 E2

TRANSPORT
Bus No 58..27 E2
Metro Bus M-1.................................28 D2

See Parque Histórico Militar
Morro - Cabaña Map p130

See Habana Vieja & Centro Habana Map pp68-9

Vía Monumental

Carretera La Dique

Carretera Casablanca

Av Vía Túnel

Antonio Guiteras

Casablanca

Casablanca Train Station

Artes

Bahía de La Habana

Ferry

La Piedra

Martí

27 de Noviembre

Parque Guaicanamar

Albuquerque

24 de Febrero

Presno

Lenin

Vía Blanca

See Enlargement

Martí

Regla

Paseo Panamericano

Av Central

Miguel Coyula

0 ——— 200 m
0 ——— 0.1 mi

Río Luyanó

Calle Verde

Lima

Quintin Banderas

Martí

E. Fernando Fuero (Amargura)

E. V. Valiente

Rafael de Cárdenas

Santo Domingo

Venus

Adolfo del Castillo Cadenas

Calle Rabel

Aranguren

Máximo Gómez

Pepe Antonio

Nazareno

Bertematti

Maceo

Calzada Guanabacoa

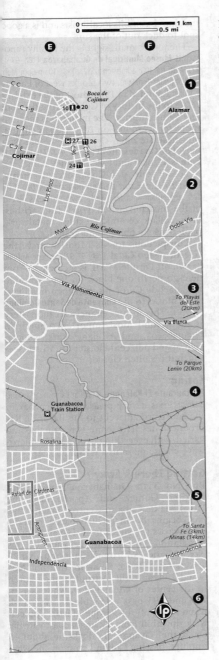

Regla on the main altar. This black Madonna is associated with Yemayá, the orisha (spirit) of the ocean and patron of sailors (always represented in blue). Legend claims this image was carved by St Augustine 'The African' in the 5th century, and that in the year AD 453 a disciple brought the statue to Spain to safeguard it from barbarians. The small vessel in which the image was traveling survived a storm in the Strait of Gibraltar, so the figure was recognized as the patron of sailors. These days, rafters attempting to reach the US also evoke the protection of the Black Virgin.

In the early 17th century a hut was built at Regla to shelter a copy of the image, and when this was destroyed during a hurricane, a new Virgen de Regla was brought from Spain in 1664. In 1714 Nuestra Señora de Regla was proclaimed patron of Bahía de La Habana. A pilgrimage is celebrated here on September 7, when the image is taken out for a **procession** through the streets. **Mass** is said at 8am Tuesday, Wednesday, Friday, Saturday and Sunday, and on Sunday a second mass is said at 5pm. There is no better (public) place to see the layering and transference between Catholic beliefs and African traditions than in this church. A branch of the Museo Municipal de Regla is next door.

The main outpost of the **Museo Municipal de Regla** (☎ 97 69 89; Martí No 158; admission US$2; ☼ 9am-5pm Mon-Sat, 9am-1pm Sun) is a couple of blocks straight up the main street from the ferry. Recording the history of Regla and its Afro-Cuban religions, there's an interesting, small exhibit on Remigio Herrero, first *babalawo* of Regla, complete with his shackles of slavery and *elegguá*. An **Observatorio Astronómico** was established in the museum building in 1921. Price of admission includes both museum outposts and the Colina Lenin exhibit.

From the museum head straight (south) on Martí past **Parque Guaicanamar**, and turn left on Albuquerque and right on 24 de Febrero, the road to Guanabacoa. About 1.5km from the ferry you'll see a high metal stairway that gives access to **Colina Lenin**. In 1924 Antonio Bosch, the socialist mayor of Regla, created a monument to Lenin's death, one of the first of its kind outside the USSR. Above the monolithic image of Lenin is an olive tree planted by Bosch surrounded by seven lithe figures; unlike many other Soviet-inspired homages you'll find in Cuba, this one imbues hope. Maybe it's the fine harbor views from here. A small exhibition on the history of Colina Lenin is in a pavilion on the back side of the hill (it's often closed).

Getting There & Away

Regla is easily accessible on the regular passenger ferry that departs every 10 minutes (10 centavos) from Muelle Luz, San Pedro and Santa Clara, in Habana Vieja. Bicycles are readily accepted via a separate line that boards first. Bus No 29 runs to Guanabacoa from Parque Maceo between the ferry terminal and the Museo Municipal de Regla, but the boat is much more fun.

GUANABACOA
pop 106,374

In the 1540s the Spanish conquerors concentrated the few surviving indigenous people at Guanabacoa, 5km east of central Havana. A town was founded here in 1607, and this later became a center of the slave trade. In 1762 the British occupied Guanabacoa, but not without a fight from its mayor, José Antonio Gómez Bulones, better known as Pepe Antonio, who attained almost legendary status by conducting a guerrilla campaign behind the lines of the victorious British.

Guanabacoa today is a lively, colorful and friendly town. (Guanabacoa is also the name of the municipality that surrounds the town.) Though there are no hotels here, access on public transport is not easy, and the town is surrounded by ugly industrial suburbs, it's still worth making the effort to visit if you have time.

Sights

The **Iglesia de Guanabacoa** (Pepe Antonio at Adolfo del Castillo Cadenas), on Parque Martí in the center of town, is also known as the Iglesia de Nuestra Señora de la Asunción, and was designed by Lorenzo Camacho and built between 1721 and 1748. The gilded main altar and nine lateral altars are worth a look, and a painting of the Assumption of the Virgin is at the back. Notice the Moorish-influenced wooden ceiling. The main doors are usually closed, but knock at the **parochial office** (Enrique Guiral; 8am-11am, 2pm-5pm Mon-Fri) on the back side of the church. The **Galería de Arte Concha Ferrant** (97 98 04; Martí No 8A; admission free; 9am-5pm Tue-Sat, 10am-2pm Sun) across Parque Martí from

the church exhibits local artists and is a good spot to duck out of the sun.

The town's main sight is the freshly renovated **Museo Municipal de Guanabacoa** (97 91 17; Martí No 108; admission US$2; 10am-6pm Mon, Wed-Sat, 9am-1pm Sun), two blocks west of Parque Martí. Founded in 1964, most of the exhibits relate to the history of Cuba during the 18th and 19th centuries. The museum is most famous for its rooms on Afro-Cuban culture, but these are often closed (ask before paying). The **Casa de la Trova** (97 76 87; Martí No 111) here is as local and folksy as they come.

For all your Afro-Cuban accoutrements, head to the **Bazar de Reproducciones** (Martí No 175; 10am-6pm Mon-Sat), two blocks west of the museum, where you'll find orishas, dolls, collars, ceramics, textiles, metalwork, papier-mâché objects and graphics.

Conspicuous for its Moorish arch, the eclectic **Teatro Carral** (97 92 33; Pepe Antonio No 362), off Parque Martí, is a cinema. From here go north one block on Pepe Antonio to Rafael de Cárdenas, and then head east three blocks to the **Convento de Santo Domingo** (1748). This former Franciscan monastery is the second most important church in Guanabacoa, and its eight altars, wooden ceiling and adjacent cloister are worth seeing, but it's often closed.

Eating

Restaurante El Palenque (Martí at Lamas; 10am-midnight) has a very pleasant garden bar in the courtyard adjacent to the Bazar de Reproducciones. The menu is reasonable and varied, with everything from a US$1 microwave cheese pizza to a US$23 lobster.

Getting There & Away

Bus No 3 to Guanabacoa leaves from Máximo Gómez and Aponte near the Hotel Isla de Cuba in Centro Habana. Bus No 5 begins its run to Guanabacoa from the park across the street from Havana's main bus station. You can also get there on bus Nos 195 and 295 from Vedado. Bus No 29 arrives from Regla. Be aware that bus Nos 5 and 29 stop right in front of the church in the center of Guanabacoa, while Nos 3, 195 and 295 pass a few blocks away (ask when to get off for Parque Martí). You can walk downhill from Guanabacoa to Regla, where the Havana ferry docks, in about 45 minutes, passing Colina Lenin on the way.

SAN FRANCISCO DE PAULA

In 1939 US novelist Ernest Hemingway rented a villa called Finca la Vigía on a hill at San Francisco de Paula, 15km southeast of central Havana. A year later he bought the house (1888) and property and lived there continuously until 1960, when he moved back to the US. Each morning Hemingway would rise at dawn and spend six hours standing in oversized moccasins before a typewriter and full-length mirror, writing. In the evening he'd receive personal friends over cocktails.

The villa's interior has remained unchanged since the day Hemingway left (there are lots of stuffed trophies), and the wooded estate is now the **Museo Hemingway** (Map p62; ☎ 91 08 09; unguided/guided US$3/4, plus camera/video US$5/25; ☼ 9am-4:30pm, closed Tue). To prevent the pilfering of objects, visitors are not allowed inside the house (though a US$5 tip might bend that rule), but there are enough open doors and windows to allow a proper glimpse into Papa's universe. There are books everywhere (including beside the toilet), a large Victrola and record collection and an astounding number of knickknacks. Don't come when it's raining as the house itself will be closed. A stroll through the garden is worthwhile to see the surprisingly sentimental dog cemetery, Hemingway's fishing boat *El Pilar* and the pool where actress Ava Gardner once swam naked. You can chill out on a chaise lounge below whispering palms and bamboo here.

To reach San Francisco de Paula, take Metro Bus M-7 (Cotorro) from Industria, between Dragones and Av Simón Bolívar, on Parque de la Fraternidad, in Centro Habana. You'll go eight stops to San Miguel del Padrón.

SANTA MARÍA DEL ROSARIO

☎ 6820

Santa María del Rosario, 19km southeast of central Havana, is an old colonial town founded in 1732. Unlike most other towns from that period it has not become engulfed in modern suburbs, but stands alone in the countryside. The charms of this area were recognized by one of Cuba's greatest living painters, Manuel Mendive, who selected it for his personal residence. You can also see the countryside of this area in Tomás

Gutiérrez Alea's metaphorical critique of slavery in his movie *La Última Cena*.

The **Iglesia de Nuestra Señora del Rosario** (☼ 5:30-7:30pm) also called the Catedral de los Campos de Cuba, on Santa María del Rosario's old town square, was built in 1720 by the Conde de Casa Bayona near the Quiebra Hacha Sugar Mill, of which nothing remains today. Inside are a gilded mahogany altar and a painting by Veronese.

On a rear wall of the **Casa de la Cultura**, opposite the church, is a great mural by Manuel Mendive depicting the legends of this region.

From Havana take the Metro Bus M-7 to Cotorro and then bus No 97, which runs from Guanabacoa to town.

PARQUE HISTÓRICO MILITAR MORRO-CABAÑA

The sweeping views of Havana from the other side of the bay are lovely and a trip to the two old forts of the **Parque Histórico Militar Morro-Cabaña** is worthwhile. It gets very hot around midday with the sun pounding down; beat the heat with a drink at one of the shoreline bars or restaurants or come at sunset – sensational. All the Havana travel agencies offer tours here; the **cañonazo ceremony** is especially popular (without/with dinner US$15/25).

The **Castillo de los Tres Santos Reyes Magnos del Morro** (per person incl museum entrance US$3) was erected between 1589 and 1630 on an abrupt limestone headland to protect the entrance to the harbor. In 1762 the British captured El Morro by attacking from the landward side and digging a tunnel under the walls. The castle's gallant Spanish commander, Don Luís de Velasco, was killed in the battle, and the British buried him with full military honors. In 1845 a lighthouse was added to the castle, the first in Cuba. Since 1986 the castle has hosted a **maritime museum** (☎ 863-7941; guide US$1, plus camera US$2; ☼ 8am-8pm). To climb to the top of the lighthouse is an additional US$2.

The **Fortaleza de San Carlos de la Cabaña** was built between 1763 and 1774 to deny the long ridge overlooking Havana to attackers. It's one of the largest colonial fortresses in the Americas, replete with grassy moats, ancient chapel, cobblestone streets and shops inside. It cost so much to build, Carlos III of Spain supposedly tried to spy it through a telescope, convinced it must be visible from Madrid. During the 19th century, Cuban patriots faced firing squads in the **Foso de los Laureles** outside La Cabaña's southeastern wall. Dictators Machado and Batista used the fortress as a military prison, and immediately after the revolution, Che Guevara set up his headquarters there. Be sure to visit the creative Havana skyline **mirador** (viewpoint) on the other side of the **Museo de Comandancia del Che** here. Later it served as a military academy.

Visitors are welcome to see the collection of armaments at the **Museo Fortificaciones y Armas** (☎ 862-0617; admission US$3, plus camera/video US$2/5; ⏰ 10am-10pm). Nightly at 9pm a cannon is fired on the harbor side of La Cabaña by a squad attired in 19th-century uniforms, a hold-over from Spanish times when such a shot signaled that the city gates were closing. The **cañonazo** begins at 8:30pm and is included in the regular admission price (as is the concert following by Moncada, a locally famous geriatric rock band). A smaller cannon, with equally overdressed young men, is shot off daily at 3pm.

Surprisingly, almost no tourists visit the more interesting La Cabaña, while El Morro is usually jammed (tour buses unload their masses at El Morro but never have time for La Cabaña). Around midmorning it's especially chaotic at El Morro, as the tour buses from Varadero stop there on their way to Havana, so plan accordingly. The annual Feria Internacional del Libro is held here each January.

Eating

Parts of the fortresses have been converted into good restaurants and atmospheric bars. The **Restaurante Los Doce Apóstoles** (☎ 863-8295; ⏰ noon-11pm) below El Morro, so named for the battery of 12 cannons atop its ramparts, serves *comida criolla*. It's a better-than-average government-run kitchen, and the prices are fair. **Bar El Polvorín** (☎ 860-9990; ⏰ 10am-4am) just beyond Los Doce Apóstoles, offers drinks and light snacks on a patio overlooking the bay. There's zero shade, but it's perfect for those famous Havana sunsets.

Back below La Cabaña, just beyond the Dársena de los Franceses, is another battery

PARQUE HISTÓRICO MILITAR MORRO - CABAÑA

0 ———— 100 m
0 ———— 0.1 mi

Straits of Florida

Via Monumental

To Playas del Este (13km)

INFORMATION
Ticket Booth............................1 B1
Ticket Booth............................2 B1

SIGHTS & ACTIVITIES pp129-30
Baluarte de Austria...................3 A2
Baluarte de San Ambrosio.......4 C2
Baluarte de Tejada....................5 A1
Batería de la Divina Pastora....6 B2
Batería de los Doce Apóstoles..7 A2

Castillo de los Tres Santos Reyes Magnos del Morro

Military Cantonment

Dársena de los Franceses

Fortaleza de San Carlos de la Cabaña

Tunnel

See Habana Vieja & Centro Habana Map pp68-9

Bahía de La Habana

La Habana Vieja

To Casablanca; Estatua de Cristo

Batería de Velasco.....................8 A1
Cañonazo....................................9 C3
Entrance....................................10 B2
Entrance....................................11 A2
Former Toll Gates.....................12 B1
Foso de los Laureles................13 C3
Lighthouse................................14 A2
Luneto de San Julián................15 C3
Luneto de San Leopoldo..........16 C3
Maritime Museum.....................17 A1
Mirador de los Pescadores......18 A2
Mirador......................................19 C3
Museo de Comandancia del
  Che..20 C3
Museo Fortificaciones y
  Armas......................................21 C3
Plaza de Armas.........................22 C3
Semibaluarte de San Francisco.23 B2
Semibaluarte de San Lorenzo..24 C3
Tenaza de San Antonio.............25 C2
Tenaza de San Agustín.............26 C3

EATING pp130-1
Bar El Polvorín..........................27 A2
Restaurante La Divina Pastora.28 B2
Restaurante Los Doce
  Apóstoles................................29 A2

of huge 18th-century cannons. The upscale but approachable **Restaurante La Divina Pastora** (☎ 860-8341; noon–11pm) behind the guns, offers well prepared seafood, including lobster and fish. You can also just sit and soak in the views with an icy Cristal and some crisp *tostones*.

Getting There & Away

Cyclists can get to the fortresses from Havana with the specially designed CicloBus leaving from Dragones and Águila on Parque El Curita. This seatless bus is accessible via small ramps that lead to the doors. Cyclists are obliged to use it to get to La Habana del Este as riding a bicycle through the tunnel is prohibited. If you don't have a bicycle, you can walk to the head of the line and get on the first bus (ask the person selling bus tickets). Get off at the first stop after the tunnel; it's only a 10-minute walk back to either fortress. You can also get there on the pink M-1 Metro Bus, (get off at the first stop after the tunnel), but make sure you're near an exit as very few other people get out there. Otherwise, a metered tourist taxi from Habana Vieja should cost around US$3.

An interesting way to return to Havana is via the Casablanca ferry. From the entrance to La Cabaña, go down into the moat and follow it around to a gate just below the huge Christ statue.

Parking costs US$1 at the fortresses.

CASABLANCA

Casablanca, just across the harbor from Habana Vieja, is best known for its towering white marble **Estatua de Cristo**, created in 1958 by J Madera. As you disembark the harbor ferry, keep going straight up the stairway in front of you. Follow the road on the left to the impressive, but discordant, statue – an easy 10-minute walk. There's a splendid view of Havana from the statue (a popular night-time hang-out spot), and a 24-hour snack bar at its base. You can reach the fort-ress of La Cabaña from this side via a red gate at the switchback in the road on your way up to the statue. Behind the statue is the **Observatorio Nacional** (closed to tourists).

The **Hospital Naval** (☎ 62 68 25), off the Vía Monumental in La Habana del Este, northeast of Casablanca, has a recompression chamber accessible 24 hours a day.

Passenger ferries to Casablanca depart Muelle Luz, San Pedro and Santa Clara, in Habana Vieja, about every 15 minutes (10 centavos). Bicycles are welcome.

The **Casablanca Train Station** (☎ 862-4888), next to the ferry wharf, is the western terminus of the only electric railway in Cuba. In 1917 the Hershey Chocolate Company of the US state of Pennsylvania built this line to Matanzas, and trains still depart for Matanzas five times a day (currently at 4:46am, 8:35am, 12:48pm, 4:38pm and 8:46pm). The 8:35am service is an 'express.' You'll travel via Guanabo (US$0.80, 25km), Hershey (US$1.45, 46km), Jibacoa (US$1.65, 54km), and Canasí (US$1.95, 65km) to Matanzas (US$3, 90km). The train usually leaves Casablanca on time but often arrives an hour late. We've heard that bicycles aren't allowed on this train, but try anyway. It's a scenic four- to five-hour trip, and tickets are easily obtainable at the station (except on weekends and holidays when it could be crowded).

COJÍMAR AREA

Ten kilometers east of Havana is the little port town of Cojímar, famous for harboring Ernest Hemingway's fishing boat *El Pilar* in the 1940s and '50s. This picturesque harbor community served as the prototype for the fishing village in Hemingway's novel *The Old Man and the Sea*, which won him the Nobel Prize for Literature in 1954. Cojímar native and fishing tar Gregorio Fuentes (recently deceased) inspired Hemingway's 'Old Man.' Founded in 17th century at the mouth of the Río Cojímar, in 1762 an invading British army landed here and in 1994, thousands of 'rafters' split from here, lured to Florida by US radio broadcasts and promises of political asylum.

If you're not a Hemingway devotee or particularly enamored of nondescript seaside villages, there's little reason to visit here.

Information

Bandec (☒ 8:30am–3pm Mon-Fri, 8:30–11am Sat), which is just down the Paseo Panamericano from Aparthotel Las Brisas, changes travelers checks and gives cash advances. For Cuban pesos there's **Cadeca**, just down the side street, across the avenue from Bandec.

Sights

The huge 55,000-seat **Estadio Panamericano**, on the Vía Monumental between Havana and Cojímar, was built for the 1991 Pan-American Games. There are also tennis courts, Olympic-sized swimming pools and other sport facilities nearby.

Overlooking the harbor is the **Torreón de Cojímar**, an old Spanish fort (1649) presently occupied by the Cuban coast guard. Next to this tower and framed by a neoclassical archway is a gilded **bust of Ernest Hemingway** erected by the residents of Cojímar in 1962.

Ernest Hemingway's old captain, Gregorio Fuentes, lived in the green-and-white house at Calle 98 No 209, at the corner of 3D, five blocks up the hill from Restaurante La Terraza.

East across the river from Cojímar is Alamar, a large housing estate of prefabricated apartment blocks built by *microbrigadas* (small armies of workers responsible for building much of the post-revolutionary housing) beginning in 1971. Form trails way behind function in Cuban public housing, but it beats living on the streets.

Sleeping

Hotel Panamericano (Horizontes; Av Central; ☎ 95 10 00/10; s/d incl breakfast low season US$45/59, high season US$54/71; P 🍴 🏊) At the entrance to Cojímar, 2km from the Hemingway bust, this four-story hotel was built in 1991 to house athletes attending the 11th Pan-American Games. There's a large swimming pool and a disco (closed Monday). Excellent services nearby include a 24-hour pharmacy, car-rental agencies, banks, restaurants and shops. The two- (low/high season US$48/55) and three-bedroom apartments (low/high US$58/68) can sleep four and six people respectively and come with fridges – good value for a family or small group. This hotel is far from the coast but it offers a free shuttle to the Hotel Caribbean and Hotel Capri in Havana four times a day between 9am and 6pm.

Eating

Restaurante La Terraza (☎ 93 92 32; Calle 152 No 161; 🕐 noon-11pm) Specializes in seafood like stuffed squid (US$7) and paella (US$7 to US$15). The terrace dining room overlooking the bay is pleasant. More atmospheric, however, is the old bar out front

(🕐 10:30am to 11pm) where a mojito is just US$1.75. Check out the classic wooden refrigerators and don't miss the B&W photos of Hemingway in the terrace dining room.

For good *comida criolla* served on an upstairs patio head to **Paladar La Terracita** (☎ 65 71 18; Calle 3C No 9606 btwn Calles 96 & 98), where the portions are huge. Try a flaky filet Montetoro (US$2.25) or the house special *bistec mixto* (US$4), payable in pesos or dollars.

Beside the Aparthotel Las Brisas is a **bakery** (🕐 8am-8pm). Across the Paseo Panamericano is a grocery store, the **Mini-Super Caracol** (🕐 9am-8pm).

Getting There & Away

Bus No 58 from Av de la Independencia and Bruzón, near Havana's main bus station, reaches Cojímar. In Centro Habana, get this bus at Paseo de Martí No 59, near the Malecón. You can catch it back to Havana from Calle 92 in Cojímar, though it's sometimes full and won't stop.

Alternatively, catch the Metro Bus M-1 (Alamar) at the corner of Calles G and 27 in Vedado, or at Paseo de Martí No 563 opposite the Capitolio in Centro Habana, and get out at the third stop after the tunnel. Cross the highway to the Hotel Panamericano, from which it's around 2km on foot downhill through the village to the Hemingway bust. Bus Nos 195 and 265 from Havana also service the Hotel Panamericano.

PLAYAS DEL ESTE

Havana's pine-fringed Riviera, Playas del Este, begins at Bacuranao, 18km east of central Havana, and continues to the east through Tarará, El Mégano, Santa María del Mar and Boca Ciega to the town of Guanabo, 27km from the capital. This is where all of Havana comes to lounge on soft white sands and bathe in aquamarine waters. About a dozen large resorts are scattered along this 9km stretch of beach, with the largest concentration at Santa María del Mar (Santa María). For a more affordable and local experience here, you can rent a private room in Guanabo (where most Cubans stay) or a little beach house in Boca Ciega. The latter is great for families, as are the spacious houses at Villa Marina Tarará.

The hotel area of Santa María is now heavily patrolled by uniformed security guards to keep prostitution in check, and they've withdrawn to the western end of El Mégano and Guanabo. If you come to Santa María with Cuban friends, expect the police to ask for their identification. If everything isn't in order, it's trouble. The heavy security presence makes this area safe and hassle-free, but it also eliminates much of the local color, and at times Santa María can be like a graveyard. You'll find Cuban families on the beach at Guanabo, Cuban holidaymakers at Boca Ciega, foreign tourists and their friends at Santa María, and men and women in search of each other at the western end of El Mégano. A very pretty part of Santa María is accessible from the parking area on Calle 13.

Cheap tour packages to Santa María are readily available in Canada and Europe, and the resorts provide a base from which you can visit Havana while enjoying a seaside holiday. Alternatively, these beaches provide an easy and effortless escape from Havana should you need it. Access is simple: the Vía Blanca runs right along the back side of the seaside strip, and there are buses between Havana and Guanabo. However, those interested mostly in museums and historical sites would do better to stay in Havana itself.

Some 13,500 radiation-affected children and 2500 adults from Ukraine have received medical treatment at a sanatorium at Tarará since February 1989. Cuba has provided more assistance to the victims of the 1986 Chernobyl accident than all the wealthy member nations of the Group of Seven combined.

Information

MEDICAL SERVICES

Clínica Internacional Habana del Este
(☎ 204-9385; Av de las Terrazas west of Calle 9, Santa María) Consultations (US$25-30), hotel visits (US$50) and hospitalization (US$10/hr). There's a well-stocked dollar pharmacy here; the closest recompression chamber is at the Hospital Naval in La Habana del Este (see p131).

MONEY

Banco Popular de Ahorro (☎ 96 22 69; Av 5 No 47810 btwn Calles 478 & 480, Guanabo; ☻ 8:30am-5:30pm Mon-Fri) Changes travelers checks.
Cadeca Guanabo (Av 5 No 47614 btwn 476 & 478; ☻ 8am-6pm); Santa María (Edificio Los Corales, Av de las Terrazas btwn Calles 10 & 11)

PHOTOGRAPHY

Photo Service (in Hotel Tropicoco btwn Avs del Sur & de las Terrazas)

POST

Post office Guanabo (Av 5, btwn Calles 490 & 492; ☻ 8am-6pm Mon-Sat); Santa María (Edificio Los Corales, Av de las Terrazas btwn Calles 10 & 11; ☻ 7:30am-6:30pm)

TRAVEL AGENCIES

Cubatur and **Havanatur** both have desks at Hotel Tropicoco, between Avs del Sur and de las Terrazas in Santa María. Their main business is booking bus tours, though they might be willing to help with hotel reservations in other cities. Rumbos is in Aparthotel Las Terrazas, on Av del Sur between Calles 9 and 10.

TELEPHONE

Etecsa Guanabo (Av 5C btwn Calles 490 & 492); Santa María (Edificio Los Corales, Av de las Terrazas btwn Calles 10 & 11)

TOURIST INFORMATION

Infotur Guanabo (☎ 96 68 68; Av 5 btwn Calles 468 & 470; ☎ 96 11 11); Santa María (Av Las Terrazas btwn Calles 10 & 11)

Activities

Yacht charters, deep-sea fishing and scuba diving are offered by **Cubanacán Naútica Tarará** (☎ 96 15 08/9; VHF channels 16 & 77; Av 8 & Calle 17, Tarará), 22km east of Havana. Ask about this at your hotel tour desk.

Restaurante Mi Cayito (☎ 97 13 39), at the eastern end of Santa María del Mar, has a *base naútico* renting paddle boats (US$1.50/hour), rowboats (US$1/hour) and kayaks (US$1/hour). A paddle around here exploring the mangrove-choked canals is a pleasure. They'll drive you around the Laguna Itabo in a motorboat for 30 minutes (US$10, maximum eight people).

Beach toys like windsurfers (US$6/hour), catamarans (US$12/hour), water bikes (US$8/hour) and badminton (US$3/hour) can be rented at **Club Mégano** (☻ 10am-6pm) at Playa El Mégano. It also rents umbrellas, beach chairs (US$2/3 hours), snorkel gear (US$6/hour) and do scuba diving, but there's not much (healthy) reef out this way. Many people rent similar equipment all along the beach to Guanabo, but check any water vessels and gear carefully

CITY OF HAVANA

as we've received complaints about faulty equipment. Consider leaving a deposit instead of prepaying in full, should anything go awry.

On weekends local kids go wild on a **go-cart track** called 'Karting,' in El Mégano on Av de las Banderas just before Av del Sur.

Sleeping

GUANABO

Villa Playa Hermosa (Islazul; ☎ 96 27 74; Av 5D btwn Calles 472 & 474; s/d low season US$21/26, high US$25/33; **P** ✖ ⚅) This villa has 47 rooms in small single-story bungalows with shared bath and TV. It's a popular spot with vacationing Cubans, so expect music, dancing and drinking to all hours; the beach is nearby.

Hotel Gran Vía (Islazul; ☎ 96 22 71; Av 5 & Calle 462; s/d low season US$22/26, high season US$25/31; **P** ✖ ⚅) A good budget choice, but because there are only 10 rooms, it's hard to get in. Not all are the same, so if you can look at a few, go for it. The hotel restaurant has a dirt-cheap menu, and a pleasant open-terrace bar is next to the hotel.

PLAYA BOCA CIEGA

Islazul Rent House (☎ 96 27 71; Av 1 btwn Calles 438 & 440) Rents houses from one to five bedrooms with air-con, kitchen and TV for US$22/31/43/62/54 (the five bedroom is cheaper because only three of the rooms have air-con). Though none of these houses are right on the beach, they're all within a few hundred meters. It's tough to get one of these high-demand units (also rented to Cubans, so forget about July and August), but you might get lucky in the off-season.

PLAYA SANTA MARÍA DEL MAR

Some of the places listed here offer 'all-inclusive' rates that include meals, drinks, accommodation, water toys and (sometimes) bicycles.

Hotel Arenal (Horizontes; ☎ 97 15 20; www.horizontes.cu; s/d all inclusive low season US$85/130, high season US$95/150; **P** ✖ ⚅) A modern hotel on the Laguna Itabo, between Boca Ciega and Santa María del Mar. It has 166 rooms set around the pool. Ground-floor rooms have patios. Suites are much larger and cost about 20% more. The beach is just 150m

PLAYAS DEL ESTE

away via a wooden footbridge suspended over the lagoon (which you can explore by rowboat). If you want a resort atmosphere, this is a good choice.

Club Atlántico (Gran Caribe; ☎ 97 10 85; fax 96 15 32; Av de las Terrazas & Calle 11; s/d all inclusive US$85/145 P ⚅ ⚄ ⚅) Right on the beach. Higher quality than most of the properties out here, it's more like something you might find in Varadero. The 92 rooms are well equipped with fridge, satellite TV and little balconies.

Aparthotel Atlántico (Horizontes; ☎ 97 14 94; Av de las Terrazas btwn Calles 11 & 12; 1/2/3-bedroom apts low season US$30/40/52, high season US$36/48/60; P ⚄ ⚅) This hotel is just across the street from Club Atlántico. Families make up most of the clientele here. There are 60 apartments with cooking facilities in this four-story development. The two-bedroom units sleep four people and the three-bedrooms accommodate six, so it's great for a group. Ask specifically if your unit will have a fridge, as not all of them do. At this price, this is a decent-value choice that is just 100m from the beach.

Aparthotel Las Terrazas (Horizontes; ☎ 97 13 44; Av del Sur btwn Calles 9 & 10; 1/2/3-bedroom apts low season US$36/54/63, high season US$50/75/88; P ⚄ ⚅) A bit more upscale than the Atlántico, the 154 apartments here also have cooking facilities, fridges and TVs. The split-level pool is kind of cool and it's only 100m from the beach. The disco, apart from the hotel, is a popular night spot.

Hotel Tropicoco (Horizontes; ☎ 97 13 71; btwn Av del Sur & Av de las Terrazas; s/d all inclusive low season US$40/70, high season US$50/80) This big blue hotel is more a landmark than somewhere to stay. The food pretty much stinks, the pool is indoors and the disco has shut. The prices are cheap, it has that going for it. Actually, it's been renovated recently and if the package is right, you might consider taking it. There are tennis courts and many agency desks here.

PLAYA EL MÉGANO
Villa Los Pinos (Gran Caribe; ☎ 97 13 61; fax 97 15 24; Av de las Terrazas No 21 btwn Calles 5 & 7; 2-bedroom house low/high season US$120/160) A terrific option if you're after private accommodation with

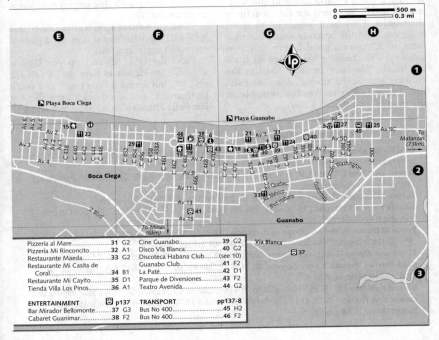

style. The collection of houses here have kitchens, TVs and a personal feel (these were holiday getaways before the revolution); the majority also have swimming pools, making them a great option for families when price isn't important. Three-(US$170/210) and four-bedroom (US$220/250) houses are also available.

Villa El Mégano (Horizontes; ☎ 97 13 27; s/d incl breakfast low season US$57/74, high season US$65/90; P 🍴 🍷) Opposite the Campamento de Pioneros José Martí, this place is up the hill from the beach. The 73 cabañas here have had a recent facelift and the shady grounds are welcoming. It's also removed from the rest of the Playa Santa María action, which has a certain appeal.

PLAYA TARARÁ
Villa Marina Tarará (Puertosol; ☎ 97-1616/17; 2-bedroom houses low/high season from US$50/60) Reached through the Campamento de Pioneros José Martí off the Vía Blanca, 22km east of Havana. The entrance is poorly marked, so be alert. You have to show your passport and receive a pass before you can enter. This is truly a gated community and the well-maintained quiet streets are almost eerie in their order. They have houses up to seven bedrooms and the beach is small, but nice here, so it makes a good family or group getaway. The cheapest houses are far from the beach. You have to pay US$1/day for cooking gas. Scuba diving, deep-sea fishing, and yachting are readily available at the marina, and there's a disco.

PLAYA BACURANAO
Villa Bacuranao (Islazul; ☎ 65 76 45; s/d cabañas low season $US33/38, high season US$38/44) On the Vía Blanca, 18km east of Havana, this is the closest beach resort to Havana. There's a long sandy beach between the resort and mouth of the Río Bacuranao, across which is the old Torreón de Bacuranao (inside the compound of the Military Academy and inaccessible). The beach here isn't as nice as its more easterly counterparts, but the price is nice. Smaller cabañas are even cheaper (low season US$23/25, high season US$25/30).

Eating
GUANABO
El Brocal (☎ 96 28 92; Av 5 cnr Calle 500; ⏱ noon-11pm) Want a nice surprise? Then check out this place, which serves up tacos (US$1.50 to US$3), *quesadillas* and a big combo of shrimp cocktail, fish, rice, salad and dessert (US$7.50) in a little ranch house. There are porch tables here.

Restaurante Maeda (Av Quebec near Calle 476; ⏱ noon-midnight) Guanabo's *paladar* scene is going strong with this restaurant hidden away on the hill.

The local **mercado agropecuario** (Calle 492 btwn Avs 5B & 5C) has what's in season; try a glass of *guarapo* (sugarcane juice).

Pizza for US$1.50 and up per slice is available at **Pizzería al Mare** (Av 5 & Calle 482; ⏱ 24hr), but spend a little more and you'll be treated to real wood-brick oven slices at **Don Pedro Pizzería** (Calle 482 No 503 btwn Avs 5 & 5D;

CASAS PARTICULARES – GUANABO
La Gallega and Teresa (☎ 96 68 60; Calle 472 No 7B07A btwn Calle 7B & 9; apts US$25-30; 🍴) Three nice independent apartments with kitchen.

Teresa and Edel (☎ 96 32 94; Av 5C No 49816 btwn Calles 498 & 500; r US$25; 🍴) Eastern end of Guanabo. Meals served. Family atmosphere.

Teresa Carmona (☎ 96 30 69; Calle 476 No 703 btwn Avs 7A & 7B; r US$30; 🍴) Upstairs.

Sonnia Mujica Amargós (☎ 96 48 50; Calle 476 No 706 btwn Avs 7A & 7B; r US$25; P 🍴) Can cook here, also at Nos 7B04 and 7B10 nearby.

Pablo M Durán Jubiel and Rosario Redonda (☎ 96 52 81; Calle 476 No 905 btwn Avs 9 & 9B; r US$25; P 🍴) Little house with kitchen and patio, also at Nos 906 and 9B01 nearby.

Elena and Aimeé González (no phone; Calle 472 No 7B11 btwn Avs 7B & 9; r US$20-25; 🍴) Leafy patio here.

Casa Olivia – Amada V Lois Correa (☎ 96 28 19; Calle 468 No 714 btwn Avs 7 & 9; r US$40; 🍴 🍷) Breakfast, nice house, huge salon.

Rolando del Rey (☎ 96 36 16; Calle 470A No 9B09 btwn Calles 9B & 11; r US$25; 🍴) About 500m from the beach.

Nancy and Tomás (☎ 96 41 57; Calle 444 No 701 btwn Avs 7 & 7A; r US$25, entire house US$50; 🍴) Two-bedroom house, cooking, big porch.

☼ 11am-11pm). For ice cream, head to **Bim Bom** (Av 5 cnr of Calle 464; ☼ 11am-1am). **Panadería O'Prisa** (Av 5 No 47802 at Calle 478; ☼ 24hr) is the place for pastries and light snacks.

Cafetería Rumbos Park (Av 5 at Calle 476; ☼ 24hr) Has chicken, snacks, and drinks, plus a cool open terrace.

PLAYA BOCA CIEGA
Mini-Super Caribe Caracol (☼ 9am-6:45pm) at the Puente de Boca Ciega near Hotel Arenal sells groceries.

Pan.com (Av 5 btwn Calles 456 & 458; ☼ 11am-midnight) sells the same fresh, tasty sandwiches, hamburgers and milkshakes at this beach outpost as it does in Havana proper.

The **Casa del Pescador** (Av 5 & Calle 442; ☼ noon-10:45pm) is a good medium-priced seafood restaurant worth seeking out if you like to dine in style.

PLAYA SANTA MARÍA DEL MAR
Restaurante Mi Cayito (☎ 97 13 39; ☼ 10am-6pm) On a tiny island in the Laguna Itabo, serves lobster, shrimp and grilled fish in an open-air locale. A pork filet is only US$2.50 to US$4.50. There's a live show here every Saturday and Sunday at 3pm, which you can enjoy for the price of a drink.

Restaurante Mi Casita de Coral (Av del Sur & Calle 8; ☼ 10am-11pm) A good seafood restaurant with reasonable prices; more upscale than most here. Another finer choice is **Costarenas** (Av de las Terrazas; ☼ 10am-midnight) across from Hotel Tropicoco, specializing in seafood dishes like paella (US$6) and a mixed grill with lobster, shrimp and fish (US$17). The upstairs terrace is a good place to catch a beer and breeze. Fishermen sell their catch nearby for US$1/pound; terrific if you've got cooking facilities.

Among the many small grocery stores at Santa María del Mar are **El Grocery Caracol** (Av del Sur; ☼ 9am-6:30pm) behind Aparthotel Atlántico; **Mini-Super Santa María** (Av de las Terrazas & Calle 7; ☼ 9am-6:45pm) opposite Hotel Tropicoco and **Tienda Villa Los Pinos** (Av del Sur btwn 5 & 7; ☼ 9am-6:45pm). The **Sylvain kiosk** next to Mini-Super Santa María has ample supplies of bread, as does **Mini-Super Las Terrazas**.

PLAYA EL MÉGANO
Cafetería Pinomar (Av del Sur & Calle 7; ☼ 24hr, they claim) The least expensive place to eat in this part of Playas del Este. Hamburgers, chicken, hot dogs and beer are served on its outdoor terrace and inside.

Pizzería Mi Rinconcito (Av de las Terrazas & Calle 4; ☼ noon-9:45pm) Near Villa Los Pinos, it has pizza (US$2 to US$3), cannelloni, lasagna, salads and spaghetti (US$2 to US$3.50). A Dutch traveler said this was the best pizza she had in Cuba (thin crust and lots of fresh toppings).

Entertainment
GUANABO
Disco Vía Blanca (Av 5 at Calle 486; males/couples US$1/3; ☼ 9pm-2:30am) Below Hotel Vía Blanca, this disco bar is best weekends and all summer.

Cabaret Guanimar (☎ 96 29 47; Av 5 & Calle 468; per couple US$10; ☼ 9pm-3am Tue-Sat) An outdoor club with a show at 11pm. If you want to be in the front rows, you'll pay US$16 a couple.

Guanabo Club (☎ 96 28 84; Calle 468 btwn Avs 13 & 15; per person US$2; ☼ 10pm-2am). On a hillside with sea views, five blocks straight up the hill from the Guanimar. The open-air disco here is one of the best local scenes in town. The club's **bar** (☼ 10am-1pm) has a down-home atmosphere too.

An even better view of Guanabo is obtained from the **Bar Mirador de Bellomonte** off the Vía Blanca high above the town.

A children's park and playground, the **Parque de Diversiones**, (Av 5 btwn Calles 468 & 470) will get the kids laughing, as will the **children's matinees** (☼ 3pm Sat & Sun) at **Teatro Avenida** (☎ 96 29 44; Av 5 No 47612 btwn Calles 476 & 478).

For a movie try **Cine Guanabo** (☎ 96 24 40; Calle 480 off Av 5; ☼ films at 5:30pm except Wed).

PLAYA SANTA MARÍA DEL MAR
Discoteca Habana Club (☎ 97 13 44; Av de las Terrazas btwn Calles 9 & 10; admission US$5; ☼ 10pm-3am) At the Aparthotel Las Terrazas. Attracts a good, mixed local and tourist crowd.

Playas del Este's gay scene revolves around a beach bar called **La Paté**, near Restaurante Mi Cayito, at the east end of Santa María del Mar. You might also check all the way west on Playa El Mégano for cruising opportunities.

Getting There & Away
BUS & TAXI
Private blue buses (five pesos) from Gloria and Agramonte, near Havana's central train

station, will bring you to Guanabo, though they don't pass through Santa María del Mar. Colectivos here will quote you US$8 for the trip to Guanabo (Cubans pay 20 pesos); don't pay more than US$5.

Bus No 400 to Guanabo leaves every hour or so from Taya Piedra, a park two blocks east of Cristina Station in Havana. Going the other way, it stops all along Av 5, but it's best to catch it as far east as possible. Bus No 405 runs between Guanabacoa and Guanabo.

A tourist taxi from Playas del Este to Havana will cost around US$20 for the car (US$80 to Varadero).

TRAIN
From June through August you can catch a train from Havana's Cristina Station, south of Centro Habana, to the train station next to the road to Campo Florido, at the far east end of Guanabo (once a day except Monday, 1½ hours).

Getting Around
A large guarded parking area is off Calle 7, between Av de las Terrazas and Av del Sur, near Hotel Tropicoco (US$1 a day from 8am to 7pm). Several other paid parking areas are along Playa Santa María del Mar.

Havanautos (Calle 500 btwn Avs 5C & D, Guanabo; ☎ 96 38 45) Also has an office at Hotel Tropicoco and next door to the **Servi-Cupet** (☎ 96 38 58; Rotonda de Guanabo Av 5 & Calle 464).

Transtur Guanabo (Calle 478 & Av 9A); Santa María del Mar (Av de las Terrazas; ☎ 97 15 35) The main office is between Aparthotel Atlántico and Aparthotel Las Terrazas in Santa María del Mar. It also has desks at the Tropicoco and Arenal resorts, and another office in Guanabo, next to Hotel Gran Vía, across the street from the Servi-Cupet on Av 5.

Servi-Cupet Guanabo (☎ 96 38 58; Rotonda de Guanabo Av 5 & Calle 464; ☼ 24hr); west of Bacuranao (Vía Blanca; ☼ 24hr) Both gas stations have snack bars. The gas station west of Bacuranao is opposite the military academy.

Havana Province

HAVANA PROVINCE

Havana
Province

Squashed between Pinar del Río and Matanzas Provinces, with the city of Havana cut out of its northern heart, Havana Province is only glimpsed in passing by most tourists. Yet, it has its charms. Cabin camping at Villa El Abra or crisscrossing back roads into Matanzas through the Valle de Yumurí parts the veil for peeks into the 'real' Cuba. Havana Province is where independent travelers will find little beach houses to rent, single-track for cycling and charming pockets inviting discovery.

Along the north coast, from Puerto Escondido to Santa Cruz del Norte, is an uplifted limestone ridge offering excellent views. To the south lie the plains of western Cuba, extending into Pinar del Río and Matanzas. The swampy south coast faces Golfo de Batabanó, where ferries and hydrofoils motor to Isla de la Juventud.

Dairy cows dot the hills, and potatoes, mangos, tomatoes and cucumbers destined for market cover the plains. During the 16th and 17th centuries, the lowlands' fertile red soil was used to cultivate tobacco, but in the 18th and 19th centuries, sugarcane became king.

Havana Province has 19 municipalities, the most of any province. In 1837 a 72km railway line was laid southeast from Havana to Güines via Bejucal, the first in the Western hemisphere outside the US. More recent historical events, such as the 1896 independence campaign led by Antonio Maceo and the 1980 Mariel boat lift, appear only as footnotes in Cuban history. Overshadowed by the city of Havana, this province is off the beaten track.

HIGHLIGHTS

■ **The Anti-Varadero**
  Hiking and snorkeling (p142) at local hot spot Playa Jibacoa

■ **Horizon Broadener**
  Enjoying fabulous views from Mirador de Bacunayagua (p141)

■ **Funky Transport**
  Riding the rails on the historic Hershey Electric Railway (p142)

■ **Local Festival**
  Watching dazzling floats and booty shaking at Charangas de Bejucal (p145)

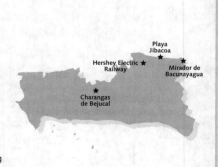

■ TELEPHONE CODE VARIES ■ POPULATION: 711,590 ■ AREA: 5731 SQ KM

PLAYA JIBACOA AREA

☎ 692

Little beaches, clusters of campismos and good offshore snorkeling make Playa Jibacoa, 60km east of Havana and 50km west of Varadero, the preferred getaway for Cubans of ordinary means. It doesn't have the white sand (or high price tag) of Playas del Este or Varadero, but the lofty limestone terrace overlooking the coast provides terrific views and hiking. Travelers with children will find interesting things to do in the surrounding area and the popularity of the region with Cuban families means fast friends are made wherever you go. The Vía Blanca, with beguiling sea and oil derrick vistas from Havana to Matanzas, runs along this coast; just inland are picturesque farming communities linked by the Hershey Electric Railway. Although Playa Jibacoa is a good pit stop between Havana and Matanzas, getting there will be difficult without your own transport (or catching rides Cuban-style). This area is changing fast and there are already two deluxe resorts at Arroyo Bermejo at the east end of the beach.

Sights

Above the Vía Blanca on the border of Havana and Matanzas Provinces is the **Mirador de Bacunayagua**, an outlook over Cuba's longest (313m) and highest (100m) bridge. This is one of the best views in Cuba, with densely wooded valley chasms backed by blue waves. It's certainly the best vista from any pool table we've seen lately (US$0.25 a rack), plus the beer is cold and the juice freshly squeezed. All tour buses between Varadero and Havana stop here.

West of here is **Santa Cruz del Norte**, an important factory town. The most famous plant is the Ronera Santa Cruz, producer of Havana Club rum, one of the largest plants of its kind in Cuba. Havana Club, founded in 1878 by the Arrechabala family of Cárdenas, opened its first distillery at Santa Cruz del Norte in 1919, and in 1973 a new factory was erected with the capacity to produce 30 million liters of rum a year. Unfortunately, for whatever reason (industrial espionage?), tourist visits are prohibited. A thermoelectric power station burning oil extracted from the coastal wells near Boca de Jaruco is just to the west. These and other oilfields west of Santa Cruz del Norte have been heavily exploited in recent years.

Five kilometers south of Santa Cruz del Norte is one of Cuba's largest sugar mills, the **Central Camilo Cienfuegos**, formerly owned by the US-based Hershey Chocolate Company.

HAVANA PROVINCE

HOW 'BOUT A LITTLE SUGAR
THE SUGAR MILLING PROCESS

In the mid-18th century, sugar replaced tobacco as Cuba's main crop. During the harvest season (zafra), from January to May, the country's sugar mills are working 24-7 cutting, chipping, shredding and crushing the cane. Like almost everything in Cuba, the process wastes nothing: the leaves are fed to animals, the fibers (or bagasse) are used as fuel to make cardboard, and a centrifuge spins off molasses used to make rum or animal feed.

It's a labor-intensive business. The harvested cane must be brought to the mill within two days of being cut, or it ferments – hence all those overloaded, double-hitch trailers hauling the stuff along the Carretera Central. Once at the *central* (sugar mill), the cane is crushed between huge rollers that squeeze out the juice. Milk of lime is added to the juice, and the mixture is fed into a clarifier and heated. Evaporators remove excess water from the purified juice and sugar crystals begin to form in a vacuum pan after further boiling under pressure. Once the molasses is spun off, hot air dries the raw sugar crystals that are now ready for export or refining into white sugar. In Cuba, white sugar is somewhat of a luxury, with brown or raw sugar being what is usually dispensed on the ration card. It's ironic in light of the raw-sugar chic that is sweeping cafés worldwide.

In 2000, Cuba shut over half the 156 sugar mills in recognition of the industry's inefficiencies, signifying a shift away from the sugar dependency that has typified Cuba for over a century. Out-of-work mill workers were given the opportunity to attend university or technical college. Though many took advantage, sugar towns throughout the country once reliant on the mill are struggling to adjust to their new, less sweet reality.

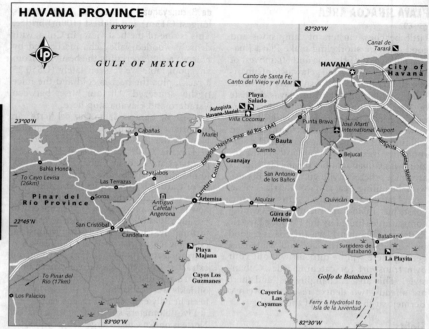

In cane-crushing season it's discernible from the Vía Blanca by its cloud of black smoke. Headquarters of the Casablanca–Matanzas electric railway (**Hershey Electric Railway**), built by Hershey in 1917, is here. Five daily trains between Havana (Casablanca Station) and Matanzas cross nearby; there are also three trains from Hershey (as Camilo Cienfuegos is commonly called) to Santa Cruz del Norte and six from Hershey to Jaruco.

Activities

Cubanacán Naútica (☎ 96 15 08; nauhab@cbcan.cyt.cu) has a water-sports center at Puerto Escondido, 1.5km off the Vía Blanca, 7km east of Arcos de Canasí. It offers scuba diving at US$25/35 for one/two dives (two-person minimum), while two-hour snorkeling trips cost US$10 (four-person minimum), both including gear. Four hours of deep-sea fishing cost US$75/150 for two/four people. The center arranges transfers from Villa El Abra (see p143) at US$3 per person round-trip.

Take any signposted side road heading toward the coast and you'll end up at one of the 10 national campismos that dot the

landscape here. They all have their attractions and for an entry fee of US$1, you can explore at will. There is good **snorkeling** from the beach facing Villa El Abra and heading westward along the coast you'll find unpopulated pockets where you can don a mask or relax under a palm.

You'll need your own wheels to get to **Ranchón Gaviota** (⊙ 9am-6pm), 12km inland from Puerto Escondido; it's a pretty drive through verdant countryside sprinkled with palms and sugar cane. This hilltop ranch overlooking a reservoir offers horseback riding, kayaking and a massive feast of *ajiaco* (meat stew), roasted pork, *congrí* (rice with beans), salad, desert and coffee, all-included in the US$8 entry fee. To get here take the inland road for 2km to Arcos de Canasí, turn left at the fork for another 10km to the sign.

Sleeping & Eating

Villa Loma de Jibacoa (Islazul; ☎ 8-5316; s/d US$29/38; **P** **⊠**) stands on a hill overlooking a small beach near the mouth of the Río Jibacoa, just off the Vía Blanca. The perfect place for a family or group beach vacation, this hotel is

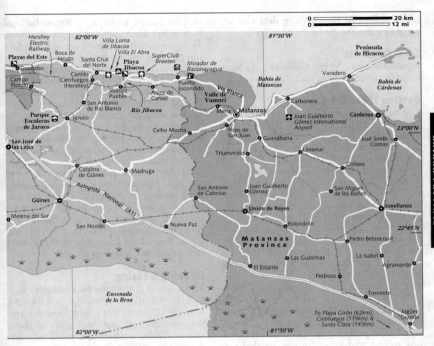

actually 13 individual houses of one to four rooms each sharing a TV, fridge and bath. As each one is different, you should look at a few before deciding – not always possible at this popular, heavily booked place.

East of Villa Loma are two resorts for Cubans, **Villa Los Júcaros** (☎ 8-5107; Vía Blanca), with wooden A-frame huts, and a collection of cabanas called **Campismo Las Caletas** (☎ 8-5238; Playa Jibacoa).

Backpackers and foreigners on budget 'ecotours' often stay at **Villa El Abra** (Cubamar; ☎ 8-5224; s/d incl breakfast US$25/35). The 87 simple concrete bungalows with AC here are sparse, but good value. The food in the restaurant is predictably poor. The bar overlooks an Olympic-size swimming pool, and there's good snorkeling on the reef just off the beach. Hiking trails scale the hills right behind the resort. It's a good destination for nature lovers. El Abra starts getting crowded in May and remains so through August. This is a full service Campertour installation.

Next to El Abra on the east side is **Campismo La Laguna** (☎ 8-5200; Playa Jibacoa), with more concrete cabins for Cubans and a large swim-ming pool. A hiking trail runs directly up the hill from opposite the main entrance.

Five hundred meters east of El Abra is **Villa El Trópico** (Gran Caribe; ☎ 8-4203), an all-inclusive resort marketed exclusively to Italians as 'VentaClub' and closed to individual tourists.

SuperClub Breezes (☎ 8-5122; www.superclubscuba .net; s/d from US$121/220), just east of El Trópico, opened in 1999. The overwhelming majority of guests arrive on air-hotel packages and unless you're one of them, you probably won't even get close to its artificial sandy beach. Children under 16 are not accepted here. SuperClub has a reputation for good food, entertainment and activities. Coming from Matanzas, the turnoff is 13km west of the Bacunayagua Bridge – you can't miss it.

Eating is a grim prospect over this way: there's a bar opposite reception at Villa El Abra with microwave pizza. Alternatively, limited groceries are available at **Caracol Tienda** (⏱ 9am-4:30pm Mon-Fri, 9am-6:30pm Sat & Sun). It's on the inland side of the road 3km east of El Abra, just before the turn-off to Villa Loma. Striking up a friendly conversation with the locals pulling in their fishing nets and arranging a meal is the best way to go.

Entertainment
Discoteca Jibacoa (🕑 9pm-4am Tue-Sun) is a local disco between El Abra and Villa Loma.

Getting There & Away
The most interesting way to get to Playa Jibacoa is on the Hershey Electric Railway from Casablanca Station in Havana to Jibacoa Pueblo. There's no bus to the beach from there and traffic is sporadic, so you'll probably end up walking the 5km to Villa Loma or 9km to El Abra. The electric train also stops at Arcos de Canasí, but that's still 6km from El Abra and it's not as nice a walking road (though the hitchhiking might be easier).

Another option is to take crowded bus No 669 from outside Estación La Coubre on Desamparados, just south of Havana's Central Train Station, to Santa Cruz del Norte. Unfortunately, this bus only operates three times a day and you'd still have to hitchhike or take a taxi 9km further east to Villa Loma (for information on the risks associated with hitching see p433). Your best bet is probably to go to the Havana bus station and take any bus headed for Matanzas along the Vía Blanca. Talk to the driver to arrange a drop-off at Playa Jibacoa, just across a long bridge from Villa Loma.

JARUCO
☎ 64 / pop 20,400

Jaruco, halfway between Havana and Matanzas but inland, is a good day trip for travelers with transport who value the journey over the destination. The **Parque Escaleras de Jaruco**, 6km west of Jaruco village, features interesting forests, caves, rock formations and limestone cliffs, but the picturesque countryside on unmarked roads along the way to Jaruco is what recommends this trip. It's a scenic 32km drive southeast from Guanabo via Campo Florido, and you can make it a loop by returning through Santa Cruz del Norte, 18km northeast of Jaruco via Central Camilo Cienfuegos. This is a good moped or bicycle adventure from Playas del Este or Jibacoa.

SURGIDERO DE BATABANÓ
☎ 62 / pop 22,587

The small town of Batabanó, 51km south of central Havana, has few attractions for visitors except, perhaps, its **Museo Municipal** (Calle 64 No 7502; 🕑 9am-5pm Tue-Sun, closed Mon). The real reason to come here is to explore the pleasant fishing village of Surgidero de Batabanó, 5km south, and board a boat for Isla de la Juventud ('La Isla'). Fidel Castro and the other Moncada prisoners disembarked here on May 15, 1955, after Fulgencio Batista granted them amnesty.

Surgidero de Batabanó is a surprisingly picturesque settlement of ramshackle wooden houses with covered porches. There are lots of little eateries, many specializing in fried fish. If you miss the daily ferry to Isla de la Juventud, it's a congenial place to hang around for the night. If you feel like exploring, head east from the dock along the shore for just under 2km to la **Playita** ('Little Beach'), a small but pretty patch of sand where you might catch one of those fluffy cloud sunsets Cuba does so well.

Sleeping & Eating
The old four-story **Hotel Dos Hermanos** (☎ 8-8975; Calle 68 No 315), in Surgidero de Batabanó, is a huge 29-room peso hotel looming near the port and train station. Expect no water unless it rains, in which case you'll get some through the ceiling.

Better situated are the 20 small prefabricated cabanas with baths on the beach at la **Playita**, 2km east by road from the ferry terminal (or less on foot via the beach). How foreigners are received at these places and how much they're charged varies. Ask around for a private room; delicious fresh fish meals will find you.

Getting There & Away
The train station is just down the street from the Hotel Dos Hermanos and less than a kilometer from the ferry terminal. Trains from the Cristina train station in Havana (2½ hours) should arrive/depart here twice a day, but they're often canceled.

The hydrofoil *(kometa)* from Surgidero de Batabanó to Isla de la Juventud leaves daily at 5pm (US$11, two hours). In addition, a normal ferry leaves at 7:30pm on Wednesday, Friday and Sunday (US$7, five hours). With US dollars you can buy ferry or boat tickets right at the wharf; otherwise, check the office controlling the ferry waiting list *(lista de espera)* next to the post office between the train station and Hotel Dos Hermanos. Call the

gencia de Pasajes (☎ 8-5355) in Surgidero de
atabanó for hydrofoil or ferry reservations.
or information on direct bus connections
om Havana, see Boat on p108.

Vehicles are shipped by barge daily and
ad at 1pm (US$20 each way). One passen-
er per vehicle is allowed on the cargo barge.
's time-consuming and not always guaran-
ed to come off. For information on the car
arge, call the **Empresa Naviera** (☎ 8-4455).

There's a Servi-Cupet gasoline station in
e center of Batabanó town at Calle 64 No
110 between 71 and 73. The next Servi-
:upet station to the east is in Güines.

AN ANTONIO DE LOS BAÑOS
☎ 650 / pop 37,059

an Antonio de los Baños, 35km southwest
f central Havana, is famous for the Escuela
nternacional de Cine y Television. Founded
vith generous donations from supporters of
:uban culture like Gabriel García Marquez,
1e world-class facilities at this film school
1clude an Olympic-size pool for practicing
nderwater shooting techniques. Despite
eing the hometown of musical giant Silvio
.odríguez, friendly San Antonio de los Baños
founded in 1775) doesn't warrant a special
rip, but the riverside Hotel Las Yagrumas is
nice escape from Havana's kinetic pace.
'he surrounding countryside is more citrus
nd tobacco than anything else; the region's
artidos brand is among Cuba's finest.

The post office is at the corner of Calles 41
nd 64. Photo Service is across the street.

ights

an Antonio de los Baños has several attrac-
ve squares, like the one with the old church
t the corner of Calles 66 and 41. Nearby is
1e **Museo Municipal** (☎ 2539; Calle 66 No 4113 btwn
alles 41 & 43; admission free; �‌ 10am-6pm Tue-Sat,
am-noon Sun).

Unique in Cuba is the collection of car-
oons, caricatures and other ha-ha objects at
1e **Museo del Humor** (Calle 60 at Av 45; admission US$2;
�‌ 10am-6pm Tue-Sat, 9am-1pm Sun). Among the
rawings exhibited in this colonial house are
aucy and satirical cartoons which capture
1e best of Cuban humor. If you like to laugh,
ead here in April for the International
fumor Festival; winning entries remain on
isplay for several weeks following.

The work of local artists is displayed at
1e **Galería Provincial Aduardo Abela** (☎ 4224;

Calle 58 No 3708 btwn Calles 37 & 39; admission free;
�‌ 1-5pm Mon-Fri).

Sleeping & Eating
Hotel Las Yagrumas (Islazul; ☎ 38 44 60/61/62;
s/d/t US$30/40/48; ℗ 🍴 🛉) overlooks the
picturesque Río Ariguanabo, 3km north of
San Antonio de los Baños. Each of the 120
damp rooms has a balcony or terrace. Take
a room facing the river for maximum peace
and quiet. All meals are (surprisingly decent) buffets. You can poke along the river
in a rowboat (US$1 per hour per person),
take a 6km river exploration in a motor-
boat (US$12 per boat) or rent a bicycle for
a zoom into town (US$2 per hour). There's
table tennis, a gigantic pool and hilarious
karaoke. Families will groove on this place.

Av 41 is the main shopping strip, and
there are numerous places to snack on peso
treats along this street.

Entertainment
The **Taberna del Tío Cabrera** (Calle 56 No 3910 btwn
Calles 39 & 41; �‌ 2-5pm Mon-Fri, 2pm-1am Sat & Sun) is
an attractive garden nightclub where you can
unwind with a cocktail in the courtyard.

La Quintica, a local peso restaurant, is just
past the baseball stadium alongside the river
2km north of town. There's live music Friday and Saturday nights (closed Monday).

A footbridge across the river leads to a
hiking area.

Getting There & Away
There are supposedly four trains a day to
Havana's Estación Tulipán (one peso) from
the train station at Calles 53 and 54 on the
south side of town. The other option is to
take a 30-peso car from the Intermunicipal
Terminal in 'El Lido', Av 41 in Marianao.

BEJUCAL
☎ 66 / pop 20,442

This teeny town right on the edge of Havana City Province is recommended for one
reason: the **Charangas de Bejucal** that takes
over every December 24. A cross between
Carnaval and the more famous Parrandas
in Remedios, this festival – dating from the
1800s – sends 10,000 people into the streets,
laughing, dancing and singing amongst
outrageously large, dazzling floats and
countless brass bands. Things heat up at
midnight in the central plaza. Trains shuttle

between here and Havana's Cristina train station day and night on December 24.

ARTEMISA

☎ 63 / pop 60,477

Artemisa is a bustling sugar town 60km southwest of Havana. If you're passing this way, it's worth a quick stopover – at least for a little pizza. Beside the Carretera Central between Artemisa and Guanajay is a restored section of the Trocha Mariel-Majana, a defensive wall erected by the Spanish during the wars of independence.

Revolution buffs may want to peel off the Carretera Central to visit the **Mausoleo a las Mártires de Artemisa** (☎ 3-3276; Av 28 de Enero; admission US$1; ⏲ 9am-6pm Tue-Sun). Of the 119 revolutionaries who accompanied Fidel Castro in the 1953 assault on the Moncada Barracks, 28 were from Artemisa or this region. Fourteen of the men presently buried below the cube-shaped bronze mausoleum died in the actual assault or were killed soon after by Batista's troops. The other Moncada veterans buried here died later in the Sierra Maestra. Guides are available.

The **Antiguo Cafetal Angerona**, 17km west of Artemisa on the road to Cayajabos and the Autopista Havana–Pinar del Río (A4), has been preserved as a museum. Angerona was erected between 1813 and 1820 by Cornelio Sauchay, who had 450 slaves tending 750,000 coffee plants. Behind the ruined mansion lie the slave barracks and an old watchtower, from which the slaves' comings and goings were monitored. The estate is mentioned in novels by Cirilo Villaverde and Alejo Carpentier, and James A Michener devotes several pages to it in *Six Days in Havana*.

Seriously good **peso pizza** is dished up at the corner of Calles 31 and 54, a block west of Artemisa's bus station. Try a *batido* (fruit milkshake).

The train station is four blocks east of the bus station along Av Héroes del Moncada. Only two trains a day pass through Artemisa, one around noon to Havana and another at midnight to Pinar del Río.

The bus station is on the Carretera Central in the center of town.

MARIEL

☎ 63 / pop 31,922

Mariel, 45km west of Havana, is known mostly for the 125,000 Cubans who left here for Florida in April 1980. Once you see it you'll want to flee too. Founded in 1762 Mariel is a major industrial town and por with the largest cement factory in Cuba, a huge thermoelectric power plant, militar airfield and shipyards. There's also a new duty-free industrial zone adding to the action. It sits on the Bahía de Mariel a Cuba's narrowest point, just 31km nort of the Caribbean at Playa Majana.

After Moa in Holguín Province, Marie is Cuba's most heavily polluted town The filthy cement factory at Mariel (onc belonging to American cement produce Lone Star) is now run by the Mexican ce ment giant Cemex as a joint venture with the Cuban government.

The local **Museo Histórico** (☎ 9-2954; Calle 13 No 6926) is opposite the church at the entranc to town. A huge castlelike mansion, now naval academy, stands on a hilltop overlook ing Mariel.

Motel La Puntilla (☎ 9-2548; Calle 128; r US$5 ⛏ ⛁), on the beach near the center o town, has 21 rooms with baths. If you don' feel like pushing on to Havana, this friendly hotel is OK for a night.

Twenty-two kilometers east of Mariel or the Autopista is **Playa Salado**, a popular beach that swarms with locals in summer, but i largely deserted at other times. The shore line is rocky instead of sandy, but the wate is mostly clean and you'll have the optio of staying at one of the cute cabins at **Villa Cocomar** (Cubanacán; ☎ 37 82 93) once it reopens Even while they're renovating you can stil use the pool (US$5 incl lunch; ⏲ 9am-6pm daily) which has pretty palm-fringed views. This i promoted as a snorkeling spot and the Blu Reef Marlin Dive Center next to Cocoma sometimes opens, but we're doubtful.

A few kilometers east of Playa Salad is the more developed **Playa Baracoa**. Com here for the local party atmosphere rathe than the surf and sand (crowded, dark and limited). Imagine West Side Story meet West Palm Beach, with swarthy men and their beautiful dates hanging about big ol American cars drinking beer while fisher men throw lines from the rocky shore There are two BBQ restaurants (*parrilladas*) and the more upscale El Yunque in a big thatched hut. Alternatively, you can nosh or the best *chicharitas* (plantain chips) in Cuba (five pesos a box). It's a nice sunset spot.

Isla de la Juventud (Special Municipality)

CONTENTS

ISLA DE LA JUVENTUD

ISLA DE LA JUVENTUD

At turns known as Siguanea, El Evangelista, Parrot Island, Treasure Island and Isla de Pinos, Isla de la Juventud is famous for its prisons (both José Martí and Fidel Castro were imprisoned here), exclusive resort island Cayo Largo del Sur, fantastic scuba diving, and grapefruit. Cuba's second-largest island after the main island, 'La Isla' (as Cubans know it) is the least populated and touristy region. It's as off the beaten track as you'll find in Cuba and a beautiful natural setting in which to slow down, poke around and make some friends.

The Golfo de Batabanó separates the 350-island Archipiélago de los Canarreos from the main island of Cuba, which lies about 100km north. Nueva Gerona is the administrative center and most of the population lives here amongst the grapefruit plantations and towering marble hills. Dedicated trailblazers should check out La Fe or Cueva de Punta del Este in the eastern part of the Ciénaga de Lanier, Cuba's second-largest swamp. This largely uninhabited southern half of Isla de la Juventud contains Cuba's greatest concentration and variety of animals, including crocodiles, iguanas, jutías and innumerable birds. Clearly, this is the next frontier for adventure ecotourism in Cuba.

One of the few parts of Cuba that doesn't cultivate cane (instead it's citrus and fish), there's a thriving construction material industry here, including marble and ceramics (from kaolin). Many of the glossy ceramic knickknacks crowding Cuban homes come from La Isla. Famous native sons include celebrated artist Kcho and Habana Abierta frontman Kelvis Ochoa.

HIGHLIGHTS

- **The Journey**

  Crossing the Golfo de Batabanó in modern hydrofoil or lumbering on the slow barge (p155)

- **Jail Break**

  Exploring the eerily empty Presidio Modelo, where Fidel Castro and other Moncada Barrack rebels were imprisoned (p156)

- **Indigenous Art**

  Admiring the 'Sistine Chapel' of primitive cave paintings in Cueva de Punta del Este (p157)

- **Going Deep**

  Scuba diving the wrecks, walls, coral gardens and caves off Punta de Pedernales (p157)

- **Beach Comb**

  Relaxing on the white, soft sands of Playa Sirena on Cayo Largo del Sur (p158)

- TELEPHONE CODE: 46
- POPULATION: 80,625
- AREA: 2398 SQ KM

HISTORY

Cuba's pre-Columbian inhabitants called this island Siguanea, but when Columbus arrived in June 1494, he renamed it El Evangelista. From the 16th to the 18th century, Isla de la Juventud was a hideout for pirates, including Francis Drake, John Hawkins, Thomas Baskerville and Henry Morgan. They called it Parrot Island, and their exploits here inspired Robert Louis Stevenson's *Treasure Island*. In December 1830 the Colonia Reina Amalia (now Nueva Gerona) was founded, and throughout the 19th century the island served as a place of exile for independence advocates and rebels, including José Martí. Twentieth-century dictators Gerardo Machado and Fulgencio Batista followed this Spanish example by sending political prisoners – Fidel Castro included – to what was then called Isla de Pinos (Isle of Pines).

The English-speaking world has left its mark here: in the late 19th century, some fishing families from the British colony of the Caiman Islands established a settlement called Jacksonville (now Cocodrilo) on the southwest tip of Isla de Pinos and you'll still meet an English-speaking local occasionally. Additionally, just prior to Cuban independence in 1902, the US forced on Cuba the one-sided treaty known as the Platt Amendment, which included a provision placing Isla de Pinos outside the boundaries of the country. Some 300 US colonists established themselves here soon after, and only in March 1925 did the US recognize the island as an integral part of Cuba.

Before the revolution, Isla de Pinos was sparsely populated. In the 1960s and 1970s, however, tens of thousands of young people volunteered to study here at specially built 'secondary schools' in the countryside, which now dot the plains in the northern part of the island. Students at these schools worked the fields in shifts, creating the vast citrus plantations of today. In 1978 their role in developing the island was officially recognized when the name was changed from Isla de Pinos to Isla de la Juventud (Isle of Youth). Numerous young people from Africa have also studied here, and foreign students still come to the island today, though in smaller numbers.

ISLA DE LA JUVENTUD

The island of Isla de la Juventud (as opposed to the special municipality) is one of the most welcoming places you'll come across in Cuba. The laid-back pace and opportunities for getting (way) off the beaten track will appeal to chilled out artists and adventure types alike. What's more, the casas particulares hosts are genuinely warm, generous people that open both their homes and hearts to guests, making a stay here memorable. Hopefully the southern area, with its preserved ecosystem and rich wildlife, will be opened up to careful tourism

ISLA DE LA JUVENTUD (SPECIAL MUNICIPALITY)

Pinar del Río Province

To Surgidero de Batabanó (82km)

Ferry & Hydrofoil

Havana Province

Ciénaga de Zapata

Islas de Mangles

Cayos Alacranes

22°00'N

Archipiélago de los Canarreos

Matanzas Province

Cayos de los Inglesitos

Golfo de Batabanó

Nueva Gerona

Cayos Los Indios

Cayo San Juan

La Fe

Cayo Rico

Cayo Largo del Sur

Dársena

Punta del Este

Cayo Matías

Cayo Campos

Cayo Cantiles

Cayo del Rosario

21°30'N

Isla de la Juventud

CARIBBEAN SEA

83°00'W 82°30'W 82°00'W 81°30'W

0 — 24 km
0 — 14 mi

ISLA DE LA JUVENTUD

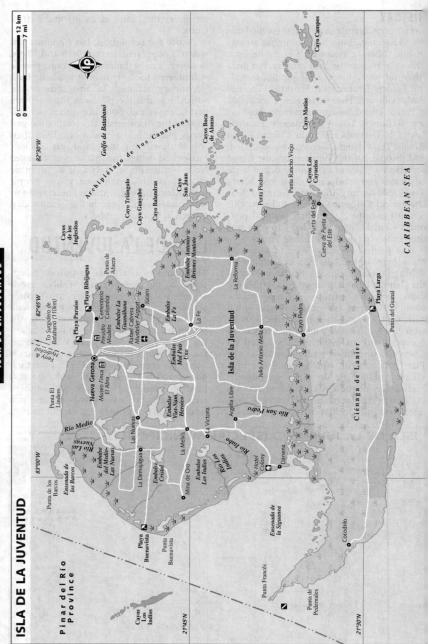

ISLA DE LA JUVENTUD

Pinar del Río Province

Cayos Los Indios

Punta de los Barcos
Ensenada de los Barcos

Punta El Lindero

To Surgidero de Batabanó (110km)

Ferry & Hydrofoil

Río Medio

Río Las Nuevas

Embalse del Medio-Las Nuevas

La Demajagua

Embalse Cristal

Mina de Oro

Río Los Indios

Playa Buenavista
Punta Buenavista

Las Nuevas

Nueva Gerona
Museo Finca El Abra

Embalse Viet-Nam Heroico

La Melvis

La Victoria

Embalse Los Indios

Ensenada de la Siguanea

Punta Francés
Punta de Pedernales

Playa Paraíso
Cementerio Colombia
Presidio Modelo
Embalse La Guayabma
Rafael Cabrera
Musteller Airport

Playa Bibijagua
Punta de Afuera

Júcaro

Embalse Mal País Uno

Embalse La Fe

La Fe

Argelia Libre

Río Itabo

Río San Pedro

Hotel Colony

Dársena

Cocodrilo

Cayos de los Inglesitos

Cayo Triángulo

Cayo Guayabo

Cayo Balandras

Archipiélago de los Canarreos

Golfo de Batabanó

Cayos Campos

Cayo Matías

Cayo Boca de Alonso

Cayo San Juan

Embalse Antonio Briones Montoto

La Reforma

Isla de la Juventud

Julio Antonio Mella

Ciénaga de Lanier

Cayo Piedra

Punta del Guanal

Punta Piedras

Punta Rancho Viejo

Cayos Los Cayuelos

Punta del Este

Cueva de Punta del Este

Playa Larga

CARIBBEAN SEA

12 km
7 mi

83°00'W
82°45'W
82°30'W

21°45'N
21°30'N

the future. The southwestern part of the land around Punta Francés is known for its magnificent scuba diving.

NUEVA GERONA

☎ 46 / pop 37,300

Flanked by the Sierra de Las Casas to the west and the Sierra de Caballos to the east, Nueva Gerona huddles on the left bank of the Río Las Casas, the island's only large river. It's an incredibly friendly place and you could easily be the only foreign face around. It's also much cheaper than Havana, so you could conceivably hole up here to save cash. Public transport is spotty at best. It's useful to note that Calle 39 is more often called Calle Martí.

Information

IMMIGRATION

Inmigración (cnr Calles 34 & 35; ☺ 8am-noon & 1-5pm Mon & Wed) Probably not the greatest place to seek an extension.

MEDIA

Radio Caribe Broadcasts varied musical programs on 270AM.

Victoria Local paper published on Saturday.

MEDICAL SERVICES

Farmacia Nueva Gerona (☎ 32 60 84; cnr Calles 39 & 24; ☺ 8am-11pm Mon-Sat)

Hospital General Héroes de Baire (☎ 32 30 12; Calle 39A) Recompression chamber here.

Policlínico Provincial de Emergencia (☎ 32 22 36; Calle 41 btwn Calles 32 & 34)

MONEY

Don't rely on credit cards on La Isla as the phone lines go down, machines bust and banks are sometimes finicky.

Banco de Crédito y Comercio (☎ 32 48 05; Calle 39 No 1802 at Calle 18; ☺ 8am-3pm Mon-Fri)

Banco Popular de Ahorro (☎ 32 27 42; Calle 39 at Calle 26; ☺ 8am-noon & 1:30-5pm Mon-Fri)

Cadeca (☎ 32 34 62; Calle 39 No 2022 at Calle 20; ☺ 8:30am-6pm Mon-Sat, 8:30am-1pm Sun)

PHOTOGRAPHY

Photo Service (☎ 32 47 66; Calle 39 No 2010 btwn Calles 20 & 22) Buy or develop film.

POST

Post office (☎ 32 26 00; Calle 39 No 1810 btwn Calles 18 & 20; ☺ 8am-6pm Mon-Sat)

TELEPHONE & INTERNET ACCESS

Etecsa (Calle 41 No 2802 btwn Calles 28 & 30; ☺ 6am-10pm)

TOILETS

Public toilets (Calle 39 btwn Calles 26 & 28)

TOURIST INFORMATION

There's no tourist information office in Nueva Gerona. Travelers wishing to visit the Cueva del Punta del Este must arrange permits and a guide through Havanautos (see p156).

TRAVEL AGENCIES

Oficina de Campismo (☎ 32 45 17; Calle 37 No 2208 btwn Calles 22 & 24; ☺ 8am-4pm Mon-Fri, 8am-noon Sat) Handles reservations for Cabañas Playa Paraíso, Campismo Arenas Negras (may not accept foreigners) and Motel Los Codornices.

Sights

This is a good area to discover on bicycle, with beaches, Museo Finca El Abra and the Presidio Modelo all several kilometers from Nueva Gerona. Ask at your casa particular about rentals.

DOWNTOWN

The **Museo Municipal** (☎ 32 37 91; Calle 30 btwn Calles 37 & 39; ☺ 9am-1pm & 2-6pm Mon-Sat, 9am-noon Sun) is in the former Casa de Gobierno (1853). It houses a small historical collection with a few pirate tidbits mixed in with the usual bones and birds. The art school on the west side of Parque Central is the former **Centro Escolar**, built in 1928.

On the northwest side of Parque Central is the church of **Nuestra Señora de los Dolores** (1929; ☎ 32 18 35). This Mexican colonial-style church was built in 1926, after the original was destroyed by a hurricane. In 1957 the parish priest, Guillermo Sardiñas, left Nueva Gerona to join Fidel Castro in the Sierra Maestra, the only Cuban priest to do so. Sardiñas was eventually promoted to the rank of *comandante*.

On Calle 28, two blocks east of Parque Central, you'll see a huge ferry painted black and white and set up as a memorial next to the river. This is **El Pinero** (☎ 32 41 62), the original boat used to ferry passengers between La Isla and the main island from the 1920s until 1974. On May 15, 1955, Castro and the other prisoners released from Moncada returned to the main island on El Pinero.

NUEVA GERONA
0 500 m
0 0.3 mi
INFORMATION
Banco de Crédito y Comercio... 1 B1
Banco Popular de Ahorro........ 2 C2
Cadeca........ 3 B1
Etecsa........ 4 B2
Farmacia Nueva Gerona........ 5 C2
Hospital General Héroes de Baire........ 6 B1
Inmigración........ 7 C3
Oficina de Campismo........ 8 C2
Photo Service........ 9 B2
Policlínico Provincial de Emergencia........ 10 B3
SIGHTS & ACTIVITIES pp151-3
Casa de Gobierno (Museo Municipal)........ 11 C2
Centro Escolar........ 12 C2
El Pinero........ 13 C2
Museo de la Lucha Clandestina........ 14 B2
Nuestra Señora de los Dolores.. 15 C2
Planetario y Museo de Historia Natural........ 16 C4
SLEEPING p153
Hotel Bamboo........ 17 C4
Hotel La Cubana........ 18 B1
EATING pp153-4
Cafetería El Avión........ 19 B4
Cafetería La Cocinita........ 20 B1
Coppelia........ 21 C2
Cubalse Supermarket........ 22 C2
El Cochinito........ 23 C2
El Corderito........ 24 B2
Mercado Agropecuario........ 25 C2
Pizzería La Gondóla........ 26 C2
Restaurante El Dragón........ 27 C2
Restaurante La Vajilla........ 28 C1
DRINKING p154
Cabaret El Patio........ 29 C2
Café Nuevo Virginia........ 30 C2
Casa de los Vinos........ 31 B1
ENTERTAINMENT pp154-5
Casa de la Cultura........ 32 C2
Cine Caribe........ 33 C2
Disco La Movida........ 34 C1
SHOPPING p155
Centro Experimental de Artes Aplicadas........ 35 C4
Galería de Arte Gerona........ 36 C2
TRANSPORT pp155-6
Bus No 4 & 38........ 37 C1
Bus No 431 & 441........ 38 B1
Havanautos........ 39 C3
New Ferry Terminal........ 40 C2
Old Ferry Terminal........ 41 C2
OTHER
Cemetery........ 42 B1
To Sierra de Las Casas (1km)
To Estadio Cristóbal Labra
To Presidio Modelo (5km); Campismo Arenas Negras (10km)
Parque Central
Río Las Casas
Carretera a La Fe
To Marble Quarry (3km)
To Museo Finca El Abra (3km); La Demajagua (21km); Hotel Colony (46km)
To Villa Isla de Juventud (2.5km); Super Disco (2.5km); Motel El Rancho El Tesoro (3.5km); Motel Las Codornices (5km)
To Airport (5km), La Fe (10km)
C 39 (Martí)
C 39A
C 41A

In terms of the revolution, the most important museum here is the **Museo de la Lucha Clandestina** (☎ 32 45 82; Calle 24 btwn Calles 43 & 45; admission US$1; 9am-5pm Tue-Sat, 8am-noon Sun), which is crammed with both boring (reams of correspondence) and fascinating (cool photos of Fidel and La Isla rebels) information about the underground struggle against Batista.

More interesting for the average visitor is the **Planetario y Museo de Historia Natural** (☎ 32 31 43; cnr Calles 41 & 52; admission US$2; 8am-5pm Tue-Sat, 9am-noon Sun), showcasing the natural history, geology and archaeology of the island. There's a replica of the Cueva Punta del Este cave paintings here if you can't make it out there (see p157). You might gain access to the planetarium (and use of the telescope therein) by talking to the guard.

MUSEO FINCA EL ABRA

This **museum** (Carretera Siguanea Km 2; 9am-5pm Tue-Sun) is 3km southwest of Nueva Gerona, off the road to La Demajagua (the continuation of Calle 41). Coming from Motel El Rancho El Tesoro, go southwest from the motel a few hundred meters on a dirt road to another highway. Turn right and cross a bridge over the Río Las Casas. At the next junction, turn right again, and you'll soon come to a sign indicating the access road to Finca El Abra.

The teenage José Martí arrived at Finca El Abra on October 17, 1870, to spend nine weeks of exile on this farm, prior to his deportation to Spain. Legend has it that the shackles he wore here were forged into a ring by his mother, which Martí wore to his death. The old hacienda is directly below the Sierra de Las Casas and it's worth coming as much for the surroundings as for the museum. Cuban oaks and eucalyptus trees line the access road, and a huge ceiba tree stands next to the museum. A sundial (1868) is outside the museum. The adjacent house is still occupied by Omar Sarda, whose ancestor Giuseppe Girondella hosted Martí here.

To loop back to town, look for the dirt road just before the museum. This road leads north to the island's former **marble quarry**, which is clearly visible in the distance. The quarry is moderately interesting (if you dig big holes in the ground), but the real attraction is the climb up the hill, from where there are lovely views. After descending, continue north between a garbage dump and several rows of pig pens (not very attractive, but any loop has got to be better than backtracking, right?) to Calle 54 on the right. This street will bring you into town via the planetarium and natural history museum, six blocks to the east.

Activities
HIKING
It's possible to climb the **Sierra de Las Casas** from the west end of Calle 22. A few hundred meters along a dirt track, you will see a trail on the left toward the hills. At the very foot of the hill is a deep cave with a concrete stairway leading down to the local swimming hole. The trail beyond this is fairly obvious, but mark your way mentally so you can return without a worry. A stone on the mountaintop is inscribed 'pilot's seat,' and from here you can see most of the north of the island.

PARAGLIDING
The Club de Parapente organizes paragliding from the hills around Nueva Gerona. It costs US$1 per minute, or US$30 for a 30-minute glide. Contact **Reynaldo Prendes Montes** (☎ 32 35 52; Calle 49 No 1615 btwn Calles 16 & 18). Reynaldo is sometimes gliding around Cayo Coco, so call ahead if this is something you're hell-bent on doing.

Festivals & Events
Fiesta de la Toronja (Grapefruit Festival) is on Isla de la Juventud every March. Pucker up for this one.

Sleeping
Many people offering private rooms meet the arriving ferries. This is the best way to go, as you'll have a room right in town, and your hosts will feed you filling meals. See the 'Casas Particulares – Isla de la Juventud' boxed text (p154) for suggestions. Otherwise, most of Nueva Gerona's state-run hotels are located south of town.

Hotel La Cubana (☎ 32 35 12; Calle 39 No 1417 btwn Calles 14 & 16) This is the only hotel right in town and does not accept foreigners.

Hotel Bamboo (☎ 32 49 24) Located about 2km southeast of town, off the road to the airport. Also reserved for Cubans only, but there's a restaurant and bar that might interest guests staying at nearby Villa Isla de Juventud.

Villa Isla de Juventud (aka Villa Gaviota; ☎ 32 32 90; Autopista Nueva Gerona-La Fe Km 1; s/d/tr incl breakfast US$29/33/40; P 🅿 🗶 🗷) Located 5km from the airport and 2.5km from Nueva Gerona, this is the nicest hotel with friendly staff. There are 20 rooms with fridges in two-story, four-unit blocks. Framed by the island's twin marble mountains, Villa Isla de Juventud has a surprising amount of atmosphere, enhanced by a suspension bridge behind the hotel that crosses the Río Las Casas. It's not a bad spot, especially around sunset, provided you're well lathered with insect repellent.

Motel El Rancho El Tesoro (Islazul; ☎ 32 30 35; s/d US$31/36). This friendly motel lies in a wooded area near the Río Las Casas, 3km south of town, just off the Autopista Nueva Gerona La Fe. The 60 rooms are in five long blocks of 10 rooms each, with another 10 rooms upstairs in a two-story building near the entrance.

Motel Los Codornices (☎ 32 49 81; Antigua Carretera a La Fe Km 4½; s/d/tr US$20/25/31; P 🅿 🗶 🗷) This far-flung motel, 2km north of the airport and 5km southeast of Nueva Gerona, is patronized mostly by Cubans. The cabanas are better than the rooms, but this place is so far removed it's an 'only if desperate' option.

Eating
Casas particulares (most of which are licensed to serve food) serve better value meals than

ISLA DE LA JUVENTUD

CASAS PARTICULARES – ISLA DE LA JUVENTUD

Elda Cepero (☎ 32 27 74; Calle 43 No 2004 btwn Calles 20 & 22; r US$15) Nice backyard and meals; ask about bikes.

Villa Mas – Jorge Luis Mas Peña (☎ 32 35 44; Calle 41 No 4108 Apt 7 btwn Calles 8 & 10; r US$15) Outside town center behind hospital; friendly hosts and rooftop terrace.

Alcides Taureaux Nieves (☎ 32 43 10; Calle 35 No 1813 btwn 18 & 20; r US$15) Near the ferry; meals served and friendly service.

Odalis Peña Fernández (☎ 32 23 45; Calle 10 No 3710 at Calle 39; r US$10, with air-con US$15; [⊠]) Three blocks north of Hotel La Cubana, signposted 'Peña Village.'

Elena Martínez Naranjo (☎ 32 32 43; Calle 8 No 3528 btwn Calles 35 & 37; r US$15) Meals served.

---

any of the state-run restaurants. You might try El Doblón, the restaurant in Villa Isla de Juventud.

RESTAURANTS

El Cochinito (☎ 32 28 09; Calle 39 at Calle 24; ⏱ noon-11pm, closed Wed) Get your pork steaks here; shamelessly charges US$3.75 for a piece of meat and no sides.

Restaurante El Dragón (☎ 32 44 79; Calle 39 at Calle 26; ⏱ noon-10pm, closed Wed) Specializes in Chinese food costing US$3 or less, but there's little selection and it's not recommended for vegetarians. There's sometimes live music after 8pm and there's always a big gong to beat if the inspiration hits.

El Corderito (☎ 32 24 00; cnr Calles 39 & 22; ⏱ 11am-10pm) Specializes in lamb, which is a nice change of pace. Nothing costs over US$5.50.

Pizzería La Góndola (cnr Calles 30 & 35; ⏱ noon-10pm) Also offers a break from the pork-chicken-*congrí* cycle. The pizza here is on par with other Cuban pizza places.

Restaurante La Vajilla (☎ 32 46 92; Calle 37 btwn Calles 20 & 22; ⏱ noon-9pm, closed Thu) For cheap *comida criolla* (Creole food) try this large hangar-like building that becomes a disco at night. Main plates cost around US$3.

Cafetería La Cocinita (☎ 32 46 40; Calles 18 & 41; ⏱ 24 hr) Across the park from Hotel La Cubana, this is a good place for peso sandwiches and juice or more substantial meals in the nicer sit-down section in the back.

Cafetería El Avión (☎ 32 29 70; Calle 41 A; ⏱ 10am-7pm) Another peso place. The adjacent snack counter is open 24 hours.

Coppelia (☎ 32 22 25; Calle 37 btwn Calles 30 & 32; ⏱ noon-10pm Tue-Sun). You wouldn't be in Cuba if there wasn't a Coppelia. Head here to sate that ice-cream craving.

SELF-CATERING

Mercado agropecuario (cnr Calles 24 & 35) Try this large market for fresh vegetables and meat. A smaller market is at the corner of Calles 24 and 35.

Cubalse Supermarket (Calle 35 btwn Calles 30 & 32; ⏱ 9:30am-6pm Mon-Sat) Sells groceries and sundries.

Drinking

Casa de los Vinos (Calle 20 at Calle 41; ⏱ 1-10pm Mon-Wed, 1pm-midnight Fri-Sun, closed Thu) A nice local drinking hole with 'ahoy matey!' nautical decor. Aside from ham sandwiches, you can get glasses of wine made from grapefruit, grapes and melon.

Café Nuevo Virginia (Calle 39 at Calle 24; ⏱ closed Wed) This café makes an OK second choice for a drink if you don't mind sitting indoors.

Entertainment

Evening events are often held at the **Casa de la Cultura** (☎ 32 35 91; Calle 37 at Calle 24). Also ask about the famous local *sucu-sucu* (a variation of *son*) group led by Mongo Rives, which sometimes plays at the Casa de la Cultura in **La Fe** (☎ 39 74 68; cnr Calles 7 & 8).

DANCE CLUBS

Disco La Movida (Calle 18; ⏱ 11pm onwards) For a little atmospheric booty shaking, join the throngs of locals dancing casino in an open-air locale hidden among the trees near the river.

Cabaret El Patio (☎ 32 23 46; Calle 24 btwn Calles 37 & 39; per couple US$3; ⏱ 10pm-2am Thu-Sun) Next door to the Casa de la Cultura, this venue has an entertaining floorshow at 11pm. Show up early to get in; official policy is couples only.

Restaurante El Dragón (Calle 39 at Calle 26; 🕑 10pm onwards Tue & Wed, 8pm Thu-Sun) Disco dancing in the rear courtyard.

Super Disco (admission US$1; 🕑 10pm onwards Thu-Sun) You've got to love a place with a name like this. The locals do: this club next to Villa Isla de Juventud is always packed.

CINEMAS

For a film or video, check **Cine Caribe** (☎ 32 24 16; Calle 37 at Calle 28) on Parque Central.

SPORT

Nueva Gerona's baseball stadium, **Estadio Cristóbal Labra** (☎ 32 10 44; cnr Calles 32 & 53), is six blocks west of the Policlínico Provincial de Emergencia. From October to April, the local team usually plays here at 1:35pm daily except Monday and Friday, though not every week.

Shopping

Calle 39, also known as Calle Martí, is a pleasant pedestrian mall interspersed with small parks.

Galería de Arte Gerona (cnr Calles 39 & 26) This local art gallery exhibits and sells paintings, ceramics and sculpture.

Centro Experimental de Artes Aplicadas (Calle 40; 🕑 8am-4pm Mon-Fri, 8am-noon Sat) This center, near the planetarium, makes and sells artistic ceramics.

Getting There & Away

AIR

Rafael Cabrera Mustelier Airport (airport code GER) is 5km southeast of Nueva Gerona. Cubana flies here from Havana daily except Saturday (US$64 round-trip). There are no international flights. Aerotaxi offers charter flights (you have to buy all the seats on the plane) and you could arrange passage in Havana if you have about US$500 to blow. For contact details see p108.

There's no regular air or sea connection from Isla de la Juventud to Cayo Largo del Sur. It's possible to charter an 11-passenger Aerotaxi biplane for a day trip at US$470, including waiting time. Otherwise, you must return to Havana to go to Cayo Largo del Sur.

BOAT

You have four choices for crossing the 118km from the mainland to La Isla: hydrofoil (aka *la lancha* or the Kometa; two hours), catamaran (two hours, but only leaves when there's sufficient demand), ferry (*el barco*; five hours) and car barge (eight hours or more). All boats leave from Surgidero de Batabanó in Havana Province and land in one of Nueva Gerona's two terminals.

Most people reach Nueva Gerona on one of the Soviet-made Kometa hydrofoils that have been used here since 1980. The Kometa is speedy and holds 106 passengers (in Eastern Europe, identical hydrofoils ply the Danube, Volga and Black Sea). Sadly, in 1997, two Kometas collided at full speed and were destroyed; the captain of one had been drinking. There's an open observation area in the middle where you can stand and it's a nice ride when the weather cooperates. You are strictly limited to 20kg on the Kometa (which sometimes presents a problem for cyclists). The Kometa usually uses the new **Naviera Cubana Caribeña (NCC) ferry terminal** (☎ 32 49 77; Calle 31 at Calle 24), beside the Río Las Casas. It leaves for Surgidero de Batabanó daily at 9am (US$11), returning to La Isla at 5pm.

Overflow passengers are accommodated on a 113-passenger catamaran formerly used in Quebec, Canada, and purchased by Cuba. The catamaran has a large, open upper deck and an air-con salon downstairs where videos are shown, making for a pleasant voyage. There are no scheduled departures for the catamaran.

There's also the 500-passenger regular *el barco*. This ferry leaves Nueva Gerona at 7am (US$7) on Wednesday, Friday and Sunday, returning to La Isla at 7:30pm. You must check in at least 90 minutes before departure time. No baggage-weight limit is enforced on the catamaran or ferry.

Lastly, a barge carries vehicles and other cargo (US$20, one departure daily), but only one passenger can accompany the vehicle, and it's time-consuming.

The catamaran, ferry and cargo barge use the older **Terminal de Pasajes** (🕑 32 44 15), at the end of Calle 22, half a block north of the new terminal. You can buy Kometa tickets here at the **NCC ticket office** (🕑 6am-4pm); book a day or two before you go. Because you're paying in dollars, it should be an easy process, facilitated by staff. You can often get on the catamaran via the *lista de espera* (waiting list), whereas the Kometa is always full.

All vessels are less crowded at the beginning or middle of the week.

Before reserving tickets, ask if there's a bus connection from Surgidero de Batabanó to Havana, as some northbound catamaran departures have no connection at all, whereas the Kometa always does. This connecting bus costs US$2 and you should make a reservation as you buy your boat ticket. Otherwise, large passenger trucks with rows of benches often meet the ferries at Surgidero de Batabanó, charging 10 pesos per person to go to the Havana bus station. There's also the train to Cristina Station, which only costs two pesos, but it's slow and usually late.

In Havana, bus tickets are sold at the **NCC kiosk** (☎ 878-1841) in the main bus station, and you pay for the ferry at the wharf. In either direction you'll need to show your passport, both when buying the ticket and boarding the vessel. See Surgidero de Batabanó (p144) and Havana City (p108) for more.

Getting Around
TO/FROM THE AIRPORT
From the airport, look for the bus marked 'Servicio Aereo,' which will take you into town for one peso. To get to the airport, catch this bus in front of **Cine Caribe** (cnr Calles 28 & 37). A taxi to town will cost about US$5, or US$30 to Hotel Colony.

BUS
Bus No 431 to La Fe (35 centavos, 26km) and No 441 to the Hotel Colony (two pesos) leave from a stop opposite the cemetery on Calle 39A, just northwest of the hospital.

Bus No 38 leaves from the corner of Calles 18 and 37, a block behind Hotel La Cubana, departing for Chacón (Presidio Modelo), Playa Paraíso and Playa Bibijagua at 7:30am Monday to Saturday. It makes four additional trips throughout the day. Bus No 4 also leaves from this stop, but it only goes as far as Chacón.

CAR
Havanautos (☎ 32 44 32; cnr Calles 32 & 39; ☽ 7am-7pm) rents cars (they might insist you take a 4WD, citing bad roads, but it's not necessary) and arranges passage beyond the checkpoint at Cayo Piedra (see p157). For this you'll need a permit, transport and guide. Havanautos provides all three for US$78; the

vehicle will only hold four or five people maximum.

The Servi-Cupet gasoline station is at the corner of Calles 30 and 39 in the center of town.

HORSE CARTS
Horse carts (coches) often park next to the Cubalse Supermarket on Calle 35. You can easily rent one at US$10 per day for excursions to the Presidio Modelo, Finca El Abra, Playa Bibijagua and other nearby destinations.

EAST OF NUEVA GERONA
The island's most impressive but depressing sight is the **Presidio Modelo** at Reparto Chacón, 5km east of Nueva Gerona. Built between 1926 and 1931, during the repressive regime of Gerardo Machado, the prison's four five-story, yellow circular blocks were modeled after those of a notorious penitentiary in Joliet, Illinois, and could hold 5000 prisoners at a time. During WWII, assorted enemy nationals who happened to find themselves in Cuba (including 350 Japanese, 50 Germans and 25 Italians) were interned in the two rectangular blocks at the north end of the complex.

The Presidio's most famous inmates, however, were Fidel Castro and the other Moncada rebels who were imprisoned here from October 1953 to May 1955. They were held separately from the other prisoners, in the hospital building at the south end of the complex. After heckling Batista during a February 1954 prison visit, Castro was thrown into solitary confinement. In 1967, the prison was closed and the section where Castro stayed was converted into a **museum** (☎ 32 51 12; admission US$2; ☽ 8am-4pm Tue-Sat, 8am-noon Sun). Admission includes a tour, but cameras/videos are US$3/25 extra. Bring exact change. Admission to the circular blocks is free.

Cementerio Colombia, with the graves of Americans who lived and died on the island during the 1920s and 1930s, is about 7km east of Presidio Modelo. Bus No 38 passes here.

Cabañas Playa Paraíso (☎ 32 52 46), on a beach 2km north of Chacón (about 6km northeast of Nueva Gerona), usually doesn't rent rooms to foreigners, but the **bar and restaurant** are open to all (☽ noon-8pm). Playa Paraíso itself is no paradise, but more a dirty brown beach. Still, it's in a scenic spot, with a high hill behind and a small island offshore. The wharf here was originally used to unload prisoners for the Presidio Modelo. If you're driving around up this way, there are several prettier pocket beaches, some good for snorkeling, east and west of this one.

Campismo Arenas Negras (☎ 32 52 66), 5km on from the Presidio Modelo, has 28 low-budget cabanas with baths. The amount you pay could vary. Before heading here or to the Cabañas Playa Paraíso, ask at the **Oficina de Campismo** (☎ 32 45 17) in Nueva Gerona (see p151).

HOTEL COLONY

The **Hotel Colony** (Puertosol; ☎ 39 81 81; fax 39 84 28; s/d incl breakfast US$30/56) on the Ensenada de la Siguanea, 46km southwest of Nueva Gerona, originated in 1958 as part of the Hilton chain but was confiscated by the revolutionary government before it got off the ground. Today it's a bit run down with plaster falling from the walls, but at least the 77 rooms with fridges are cheap. The 23 triple cabanas are a bit more expensive. You might save a few cents by taking a package which includes three meals and scuba diving.

The Colony's pool is pleasant, but the water off the hotel's white-sand beach is shallow, with sea urchins littering the bottom. A long wharf (with a bar perfect for sunset mojitos) stretches out over the bay, but snorkeling in the immediate vicinity of the hotel is mediocre. The diving, however, is to die for (and the deep-sea fishing isn't bad either). A Havanautos car-rental office is at the hotel.

Scuba Diving

The **Puertosol International Diving Center** (☎ 39 82 82/84) at the Hotel Colony (see above) is dive central. Diving costs US$60 for two tanks, and anything additional costs extra; lunch costs US$12 and the price of any beers you are 'offered' will be added to your bill. Snorkelers can go along for US$8. Scuba certification courses are offered. The dive boats actually leave from the Dársena de Siguanea, a 15-minute walk from the hotel. A recompression chamber is near the dock.

You have to earn the brilliant diving here: the prime immersion sites are 25km

from the Colony by boat, and commutes of an hour in each direction aboard Puertosol's less-than-luxury fleet can be a bit of a drag. In fact, your experience will hinge on where you're taken, which can depend on whether the guides know/like you. If you're staying at the hotel for any length of time and have regularly tipped the right people, you'll have no problems, but those who just drop in from Nueva Gerona for a day of diving could be disappointed. Also, remember that this whole area was declared a marine reserve, so diving is allowed only with an official guide; those with their own gear must join one of the organized trips at the rates quoted above. Thanks to this the marine life is profuse and daring (plentiful sea turtles, and tarpon up to 2m!) and the visibility and light are fantastic for underwater photography. Some dives are in the 30m to 40m range.

Divers come for the caves, crevices, tunnels and passages along the 'Pirate Coast' between Punta Francés and Punta de Pedernales. Among the 56 named dive sites are the Valle del Coral near Punta Francés, the Pasaje Escondido and Cueva del Misterio off Punta de la Playita, and the Túnel del Amor, Valle de los Guacamayos, and Pared de Coral Negro near Punta de Pedernales at the south end of the reef. Three groups of sunken ships are northeast of Punta Francés, victims of pirate attacks centuries ago.

CUEVA DE PUNTA DEL ESTE

The Cueva de Punta del Este, a national monument 59km southeast of Nueva Gerona, has been called the 'Sistine Chapel' of Caribbean Indian art. Long before the Spanish conquest (experts estimate around AD 800), Indians painted some 235 pictographs on the walls and ceiling of the cave. The largest has 28 concentric circles of red and black, and the paintings have been interpreted as a solar calendar. Discovered in 1910, they're considered the most important of their kind in the Caribbean. Smaller, similar paintings can be seen in the Cueva de Ambrosio in Varadero (p202). The long, shadeless white beach nearby is another draw (for you and the mosquitoes – bring insect repellent).

The entire area south of Cayo Piedra was unexpectedly closed in June 2003. Although the authorities were not sure when it was going to reopen (nor divulging why it was closed to begin with), it will hopefully be accessible by the time you read this. When it does reopen, foreigners will still need a special permit to go south of the police checkpoint at Cayo Piedra. **Havanautos** (☎ 32 44 32) in Nueva Gerona offers a full-day package tour of the southern part of the island (p156). The Hotel Colony also does these tours (p157). You'll visit a crocodile farm (extra admission fee), a turtle hatchery and the Punta del Este cave. No food or drink is sold south of Cayo Piedra.

Cocodrilo, 50km southwest of Cayo Piedra, is a friendly village of 750 residents, still untouched by tourism. Through the lush vegetation beside the potholed road one catches glimpses of cattle, birds, lizards and bee hives. The rocky coastline, with its natural inlets and small, white sandy beaches lapped by crystal-blue water, is magnificent. Someday this area will be thick with hotels, but at present it's completely virgin.

CAYO LARGO DEL SUR

☎ 45

Cayo Largo del Sur is 26km of glittering white sands, luminous turquoise waters at near bathtub temperatures, teeming coral reefs, plus several fabulous resorts – a tropical paradise. What Cayo Largo del Sur is not, is Cuba. Here, women sunbathe topless, you can throw your toilet paper into whatever toilet bowl, and an inordinate number of people speak a language (or several) other than Spanish. If you're looking for fun in the sun, spectacular scuba diving and all the creature comforts upmarket resorts are famous for, then you'll love this little idyll. Packages from Havana are relatively affordable if you just want to jump over for a couple of days. In winter especially, the weather tends to be warmer and more stable than at resorts along Cuba's north coast.

Cayo Largo del Sur is the second-largest (38 sq km) and easternmost island of the Archipiélago de los Canarreos. It lies between the Golfo de Batabanó and the Caribbean Sea, 177km southeast of Havana, 114km east of Isla de la Juventud, 80km south of the Península de Zapata and 300km due north of Grand Cayman Island. Though 26km long, this sandy coral key is never more than a couple of kilometers wide. Due to the island's isolation, there's a profusion of turtles, iguanas and birdlife including cranes, bee hummingbirds and flamingos.

Information

The **Cubatur** (☎ 34 80 18) and Transtur offices **bank** (☎ 34 82 25) and medical clinic are all at Hotel Isla del Sur (p159), and the telephone center is across the street. Euros are accepted at all the tourist installations here.

Due to dangerous currents, swimming is occasionally forbidden. This will be indicated by red flags on the beach, and care should be taken with waves, which can suddenly throw snorkelers into the reef. Mosquitoes can be a nuisance here, too, so bring repellent.

Sights & Activities

Cayo Largo del Sur's finest beach is the broad westward-facing **Playa Sirena**, where 2km of powdery white sand is well protected from the waves and wind. Tourists on day trips from Havana and Varadero are often brought here. Various nautical activities are available, including scuba diving and certification courses with Puertosol. A dive shop and restaurant are at Playa Sirena. All of Cayo Largo del Sur's hotels offer day excursions to Playa Sirena for around US$25, or you can walk there in less than two hours from Hotel Pelícano via **Playa Paraíso**, a nude beach (several stretches of sand on this island are clothing optional).

The island's other big day-trip destinations are **Cayo del Rosario** and **Cayo Rico** between Cayo Largo del Sur and Isla de la Juventud. Boat excursions to these beaches from the hotels cost around US$35 per person. **Cayo Iguana**, off the northwest tip of Cayo Largo del Sur, is home to hundreds of friendly iguanas; unfortunately, many perished in Hurricane Michelle – the worst tropical storm to hit Cuba in 50 years – in 2001.

You can also rent a bicycle and head east to **Playa Los Cocos**, where there's good snorkeling, or continue further northeast to **Playa Tortuga**, where sea turtles lay their eggs in the sand. A **turtle farm** (*granja de las tortugas*) is at Combinado, on the northwest end of the island beyond the airstrip.

Sporting activities available on the island include snorkeling, scuba diving, windsurfing, sailing, kayaking, tennis, horseback riding, cycling and volleyball. The best selections of these are at the Pelícano and Isla del Sur hotels.

CAYO LARGO DEL SUR

Barceló Cayo Largo Beach Resort......1 C2	Villa Capricho..............................6 C2
Discoteca Iguana Azul......................2 B2	Villa Coral....................................7 C2
Hotel Isla del Sur..............................3 C2	Villa Iguana..................................8 C2
Sol Club Cayo Largo........................4 B2	Villa Lindamar..............................9 B2
Sol Pelícano.......................................5 B2	Villa Soledad..............................10 B2

There's also deep-sea fishing from powerboats for marlin, dorado, snapper and bonito. Two international fishing tournaments are held here in September.

Sleeping & Eating

All of Cayo Largo del Sur's hotels face the 4km beach on the south side of the island. It's said that these white sands are unique, in that they aren't heated up by the sun's rays. This permits barefoot (and bare-bottomed – Cayo Largo is known for its naturism) traffic along the shore and kind of compensates for the lack of shade.

This resort island is unique in Cuba in that you buy an all-inclusive package with Gran Caribe or Sol Meliá and your color-coded bracelet allows you to use whatever facilities belong to that chain. At the time of writing, Sol Meliá owned Sol Club Cayo Largo and Sol Pelícano and was constructing the Meliá Linda Arena; while Gran Caribe Club had Villas Coral, Soledad, Lindamar, Hotel Isla del Sur, Iguana and Capricho. The Barceló Cayo Largo Beach Resort was preparing to open at the time of research. Virtually everyone arrives on prepaid package tours, with transport, accommodation and meals included. Rack rates for the Gran Caribe properties are single/double US$78/126 all-inclusive, or US$160 per person for the Sol Meliá properties. Check at Cubatur in Havana for better deals.

Sol Pelícano (☎ 34 82 60; www.solpelicano.solmelia cuba.com; P 🖳 🗷 🗷) This Spanish-style

resort on Playa Lindamar, 5km southeast of the airport, has 203 rooms in a series of three-story buildings and two-story duplex cabanas built in 1995. This is the island's largest resort and facilities include a nightclub. A small bridge links the complex to the beach.

Sol Meliá's other property is the five-star **Sol Club Cayo Largo** (☎ 34 82 60; www.solmeliacuba.com; P 🖳 🗷 🗷) on the northwestern nub of the island. The beach out here is fantastic and every room comes with a terrace or balcony. To date, it's Cayo Largo's most exclusive resort (but watch for Meliá's Linda Arena, still under construction at the time of writing).

Villa Coral (☎ 34 81 11; fax 34 81 60; P 🗷 🗷) Also known as 'El Pueblito,' this villa consists of 10 two-story buildings outfitted to look like colonial villas (eg faux terracotta roofs, wooden balconies) arranged around a swimming pool. There are 60 rooms here.

Villa Soledad (☎ 34 81 11; fax 34 81 60; P 🗷) This adjacent cluster of single-story, plainer bungalows has another 43 rooms (but no restaurant – you have to go to one of the neighboring hotels held by Gran Caribe).

Villa Lindamar (☎ 34 81 11; fax 34 81 60; P 🗷 🗷) These 63 thatched bungalows are the only four-star rooms in this chain – love the hammocks. The Piazzoletta Italian Restaurant on the premises offers pizza and more.

Hotel Isla del Sur (☎ 34 81 11; fax 34 81 60; P 🗷 🗷) This hotel has 59 rooms with mini-fridges in a long, two-story building. Built in 1981 on the point between Playa Lindamar and Playa Blanca, this was the first hotel on Cayo Largo del Sur. All meals here are served buffet style, and there's a poolside entertainment nightly. A small shopping arcade is opposite the hotel, and guests at Villa Coral and Villa Iguana must come here for sporting activities such as horseback riding, tennis, deep-sea fishing and scuba diving. Bicycle rentals are available and there's a Transtur and Cubatur desk here.

Villa Iguana (☎ 34 81 11; 🖥) This villa has 114 rooms with fridges in 10 two-story blocks. The swimming pool (also used for scuba instruction) sits in the center of the resort and the beach is just 200m away down a flight of steps. Buffet-style meals are served in the Gavilán restaurant.

Villa Capricho (☎ 34 81 11; P 🍴 🖥) Just east of Villa Iguana, this place has 62 nice, individual wooden cabins, each with a porch and hammock. Windsurfing, kayaking and sailing are possible off its beach, and its Restaurante Blue Marlin specializes in paella and seafood.

Entertainment
After 11pm, there's a minibus service between the hotels and the **Discoteca Iguana Azul**, near the airport.

Getting There & Away
Several charter flights arrive directly from Canada weekly, and Cubana has weekly flights from Montreal and Milan. Condor also arrives from Frankfurt weekly (with connections to other German cities) in the winter.

You could get yourself independently from Havana to Cayo Largo del Sur with Cubana (US$70 one way), but it would be hard getting around once you arrived and you would probably end up spending as much (or more) as you would if you took a tour. Day trips to Cayo Largo del Sur are offered from Havana and Varadero for US$137, including airport transfers, return flights and a sumptuous barbecue lunch. Just don't expect to see much of the island on this bus-plane-boat-beach whirlwind upon arrival you'll be taken by boat to Playa Sirena, where you'll spend the day. If you want to take the excursion to see iguanas on an offshore island, it costs extra. For a little more money (single/double US$159/286) you can arrange an all-inclusive tour and hotel package that allows you to spend one night on Cayo Largo del Sur. All the Havana agencies offer this (see p66).

Pinar del Río Province

CONTENTS

Tobacco leaves drying in the sun, stretches of pine trees and sugar cane soaring beside bright carpets of rice: come to Pinar del Río Province when you're ready for some green. With rock climbing, caving, diving and birding sprinkled throughout two Unesco Biosphere Reserves and one World Heritage site, outdoor-adventure types fall hard for Pinar.

Valle de Viñales is famous for its *mogotes* (limestone hills like misshaped marshmallows). Embraced by two arms of the Guaniguanico, the Sierra de los Órganos to the west and the Sierra del Rosario to the east, the valley and environs are one of Cuba's most photogenic and protected areas. Nestled in the Sierra del Rosario are picturesque Las Terrazas and Soroa, Cuba's first designated Unesco Biosphere Reserve and a popular day trip from Havana.

To the east of the 112km Río Cuyaguateje (Pinar's longest) is the tobacco-growing region of San Juan y Martínez and the Vuelta Abajo plantations, where the world's finest tobacco thrives in the sandy soil. The majority of export-quality tobacco – including Hoyo del Monterrey, which has been producing cigars here since 1865 – comes from here. The best time to visit is as the harvest starts, from January to March.

West of here, tobacco gives way to the scrubby Parque Nacional Península de Guanahacabibes. This wonderful area boasts remote beaches (with ace scuba diving), and mangrove swamps excellent for bird-watching and hiking. It is difficult, but not impossible, to hitchhike to the peninsula (for information on the risks associated with hitching see p433).

HIGHLIGHTS

- **Adrenaline Rush**
  Rock climbing in Viñales (p176)

- **Underwater Odyssey**
  Scuba diving at lovely Playa María la Gorda (p172)

- **Wildlife Watching**
  Watching birds, iguanas and those damn crabs on Península de Guanahacabibes (p170)

- **Hot Water Hedonism**
  Soaking up mineral waters and scenery in San Diego de los Baños (p180)

- **Eco-Zone**
  Waterfall romping and exploring around Las Terrazas (p182) and Soroa (p181)

■ TELEPHONE CODE VARIES   ■ POPULATION: 739,473   ■ AREA: 10,924 SQ KM

HISTORY

The conquistadors left rugged Pinar del Río largely to its own devices, and the area developed lackadaisically only after Canary Islanders started arriving in the late 1500s. It was originally called Nueva Filipina (New Philippines), but the province was renamed Pinar del Río in 1778, supposedly for the pine forests crowded along the Río Guamá. Tobacco plantations and cattle ranches quickly sprung up in the rich soil and open grazing land that typifies the area and even today Pinar del Río is stereotyped as an agricultural hinterland populated by hicks from the sticks (see the boxed text below). By the mid-1800s, Europeans were hooked on the fragrant weed and the region flourished. Sea routes opened up and the railway was extended to facilitate shipping the perishable product. These days, tobacco, along with tourism, keep the province flush.

In October 2002, Pinar del Río Province got hit by Lili and Isidore – back-to-back hurricanes.

PINAR DEL RÍO

☎ 82 / pop 148,295

Pinar del Río, 162km southwest of Havana via the Autopista, is a bustling town that is jammed with bicycles and horse carriages and has a reputation for aggressive *jine-teros* (touts). While you'll find interesting sites hiding behind the long, neoclassical colonnades lining the city streets, the best the province has to offer is beyond here, so the city is best used as a stopover or springboard to the wonderful countryside surrounding.

Pinar del Río was founded in 1669, one of the last of the major cities of Cuba to be established. In 1896 General Antonio Maceo brought the Second War of Independence to Pinar del Río. This town was once sadly neglected by the central government, but since the revolution, an excellent Autopista from Havana has been built and much new development followed.

Orientation

Martí is Pinar del Río's main street, and there are also many facilities on Máximo Gómez and Antonio Maceo, which run parallel to Martí just to the south. An important cross street is Isabel Rubio, which becomes the Carretera Central north of the city toward Havana and on the road to San Juan y Martínez to the southwest.

To avoid going the wrong way when you're looking for addresses, it's important to know that the street numbering begins at two base streets: Gerardo Medina divides the numbering of east–west streets between Este and Oeste, while Martí marks

---

ANOTHER CHANCE FOR THE GUAJIRO

Every country has its jabbing stereotypes about bumpkins from country backwaters. In the US, southern 'rednecks' bear the brunt, while in France, French Canadians are so burdened. In Cuba, it's Pinareños, folks from the fair province of Pinar del Río who suffer the label. Called *guajiros*, this term can be used disparagingly or endearingly, as in *Guajiro Natural*, the hit record by well-loved musician and Pinareño Polo Montañez. Here's one of the jokes (or *'cuentos'*) making the rounds:

It's the seventh-inning stretch at packed Estadio Capitán San Luis in a close game between the hometown heroes of Pinar del Río and their rivals, the Industriales from Havana. Pinar is up by a run and the crowd is pumped when the announcer comes to the stands to hold a competition. Something fun to invigorate the crowd further, the winner gets a bottle of rum.

Announcer: OK, we have here Paco Pérez from Macagua ready to compete. Are you ready? Great. Here's your question *compañero*: what's two plus two?

Paco (looking nervous): Uh, five?

Crowd in unison: Give him another chance! Give him another chance!

Announcer: Wrong. Let's try again. What's two plus two?

Paco (with all eyes on him, nervous as hell): Six?

Crowd in unison: Give him another chance! Give him another chance!

Announcer: Sorry Paco. Two plus two is not six. This is your last try: what's two plus two?

Paco (with conviction): Four!

Crowd in unison: Give him another chance! Give him another chance!

PINAR DEL RÍO PROVINCE

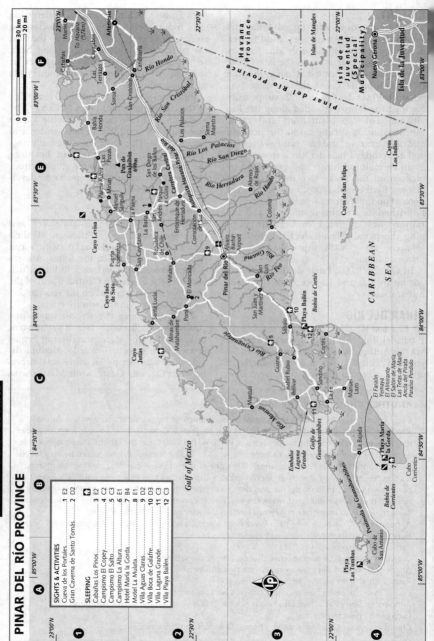

SIGHTS & ACTIVITIES
Cueva de los Portales	1 E2
Gran Caverna de Santo Tomás	2 D2

SLEEPING
Cabañas Los Pinos	3 E2
Campismo El Copey	4 C2
Campismo El Salto	5 C3
Campismo La Altura	6 E1
Hotel María la Gorda	7 B4
Motel La Mulata	8 E1
Villa Aguas Claras	9 D2
Villa Boca de Galafre	10 D3
Villa Laguna Grande	11 C3
Villa Playa Bailén	12 C3

30 km
20 mi

0
0

PINAR DEL RÍO STREET NAMES

Locals stick to the old street names; this chart should help:

old name	new name
Recreo	Isabel Rubio
Caubada	Commandante Pinares
Calzada de la Coloma	Rafael Ferro
Vélez Caviedes	Gerardo Medina
Rosario	Germanio Arenado
San Juan	Rafael Morales
Virtudes	Ceferino Fernández

the division between the Norte and Sur portions of the north–south streets.

Information

BOOKSHOPS

Havanatur (☎ 77 84 94; cnr Martí & Colón; ☼ 8am-noon & 1:30-6pm Mon-Fri, 8am-noon & 1-4pm Sat) Best selection of maps, books in English and office supplies.

Librería La Internacional (cnr Colón & Martí; ☼ 8am-4pm Mon-Fri, 8am-noon Sat) Sells mostly books in Spanish.

INTERNET ACCESS

Etecsa (cnr Gerardo Medina & Juan Gómez; ☼ 24hr; US$0.10/min)

Rumbos (cnr Martí & Colón; ☼ 8am-noon & 1-5pm Mon-Fri, 8am-noon Sat; US$5/3h)

LEFT LUGGAGE

Downstairs at the bus station you can talk your way into leaving your bag(s) at the luggage storage window for US$1.

MEDIA

Guerrillero Publishes on Fridays.
Radio Guamá Airs on 1080AM or 90.2FM.

MEDICAL SERVICES

Farmacia Martí (Martí Este No 50 at Isabel Rubio; ☼ 8am-11pm daily)
Hospital Provincial León Cuervo Rubio (☎ 75 44 43; Carretera Central) Two kilometers north of town.

MONEY

Banco Financiero Internacional (☎ 77 81 53; Gerardo Medina Norte No 46) Opposite Casa de la Música.
Bandec (☎ 75 26 07; Martí Este No 32; ☼ 8:30am-noon & 1:30-3:30pm Mon-Fri)
Cadeca (☎ 77 83 57; Martí No 46; ☼ 8:30am-5:30pm Mon-Sat)

POST

Post Office (Martí Este No 49 at Isabel Rubio; ☼ 8am-8pm Mon-Sat)

TELEPHONE

Etecsa (cnr Gerardo Medina & Juan Gómez; ☼ 24hr)

TRAVEL AGENCIES

Campismo Popular (☎ 75 26 77; Isabel Rubio Norte No 20A near Adela Azcuy; ☼ 8am-noon & 1-5pm Mon-Fri, 8am-noon Sat) Makes reservations at the province's eight campismos.
Havanatur (☎ 77 84 94; cnr Martí & Colón; ☼ 8am-noon & 1:30-6pm Mon-Fri, 8am-noon & 1-4pm Sat)
Islazul (☎ 75 56 62; Martí Oeste No 127A) Check for information on Laguna Grande fishing resort here.
Rumbos (☎ 77 14 02; cnr Colón at Martí; ☼ 8am-noon & 1-5pm Mon-Fri, 8am-noon Sat) Books all provincial hotels, including María la Gorda; rents mopeds.

Annoyances

Young men will do their damndest to attach themselves to you as a paid guide or to lead you to a private room or paladar. You may also be chased by youths on bicycles as you arrive in town by car, or accosted when you stop at the first traffic light after the Autopista. If the light is green, they'll swerve dangerously in front of you to try to get you to stop. Keep your windows closed and ignore them if they point to one of your tires, pretending it's flat. Several readers said they drove straight through Pinar del Río without stopping after that reception and this author was grabbed on the sidewalk – what a drag.

Sights

The most interesting sight is the **Museo de Ciencias Naturales Sandalio de Noda** (☎ 77 94 83; Martí Este No 202 at Commandante Pinares; admission US$1, plus camera US$1; ☼ 9am-6pm Mon-Sat, 9am-1pm Sun). In a wild, neogothic-meets-Moorish mansion built by local doctor and world traveler Francisco Guasch, this museum (called Palacio de Guasch by locals) has everything from a concrete T-Rex to a stuffed baby giraffe. Come for the flowering garden, architectural details and friendly specialist staff.

Nearby is the **Museo Provincial de Historia** (☎ 75 43 00; Martí Este No 58 btwn Colón & Isabel Rubio; admission US$1; ☼ 8:30am-6:30pm Mon-Fri, 9am-1pm Sat), collecting the history of the province from pre-Columbian times to the present. Look for the Enrique Jorrín (creator of the cha-cha-cha) ephemera.

PINAR DEL RÍO

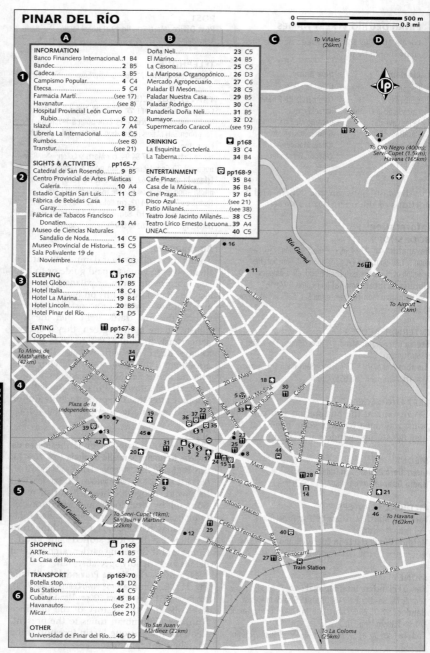

0 —————— 500 m
0 —————— 0.3 mi

To Viñales (26km)

A   **B**   **C**   **D**

INFORMATION
Banco Financiero Internacional.....**1** B4
Bandec..**2** B5
Cadeca...**3** B5
Campismo Popular............................**4** C4
Etecsa...**5** C4
Farmacia Martí...........................(see 17)
Havanatur....................................(see 8)
Hospital Provincial León Currvo
   Rubio..**6** D2
Islazul...**7** A4
Librería La Internacional..................**8** C5
Rumbos.......................................(see 8)
Transtur......................................(see 21)

SIGHTS & ACTIVITIES   **pp165-7**
Catedral de San Rosendo..................**9** B5
Centro Provincial de Artes Plásticas
   Galería......................................**10** A4
Estadio Capitán San Luis..................**11** C3
Fábrica de Bebidas Casa
   Garay.......................................**12** B5
Fábrica de Tabacos Francisco
   Donatien...................................**13** A4
Museo de Ciencias Naturales
   Sandalio de Noda.....................**14** C5
Museo Provincial de Historia..**15** C5
Sala Polivalente 19 de
   Noviembre.................................**16** C3

SLEEPING   **p167**
Hotel Globo....................................**17** B5
Hotel Italia.....................................**18** C4
Hotel La Marina..............................**19** B4
Hotel Lincoln..................................**20** B5
Hotel Pinar del Río.........................**21** D5

EATING   **pp167-8**
Coppelia...**22** B4

Doña Neli.......................................**23** C5
El Marino..**24** B5
La Casona.......................................**25** C5
La Mariposa Organopónico..........**26** D3
Mercado Agropecuario...................**27** C6
Paladar El Mesón...........................**28** C5
Paladar Nuestra Casa.....................**29** B5
Paladar Rodrigo..............................**30** C4
Panadería Doña Neli.......................**31** B5
Rumayor..**32** D2
Supermercado Caracol...............(see 19)

DRINKING   **p168**
La Esquinita Coctelería................**33** C4
La Taberna.....................................**34** B4

ENTERTAINMENT   **pp168-9**
Cafe Pinar......................................**35** B4
Casa de la Música...........................**36** B4
Cine Praga......................................**37** B4
Disco Azul..................................(see 21)
Patio Milanés.............................(see 38)
Teatro José Jacinto Milanés..........**38** C5
Teatro Lírico Ernesto Lecuona..**39** A4
UNEAC...**40** C5

To Oro Negro (400m);
Servi-Cupet (1.5km);
Havana (165km)

To Airport (2km)

To Minas de
Matahambre
(42km)

To Servi-Cupet (1km);
San Juan y Martínez
(22km)

To Havana
(162km)

SHOPPING   **p169**
ARTex...**41** B5
La Casa del Ron.............................**42** A5

TRANSPORT   **pp169-70**
Botella stop....................................**43** D2
Bus Station.....................................**44** C5
Cubatur..**45** B4
Havanautos...............................(see 21)
Micar..(see 21)

OTHER
Universidad de Pinar del Río....**46** D5

To San Juan y
Martínez (22km)

To La Coloma
(25km)

Four blocks south is the **Fábrica de Bebidas Casa Garay** (admission US$1; Isabel Rubio Sur No 189, btwn Ceferino Fernández & Frank País; 9am-3:30pm Mon-Fri, 9am-12:30pm Sat). Erected in 1892, this factory uses a secret recipe to distill sweet and dry versions of the famous Guayabita del Pinar guava brandy. Factory tours are offered in Spanish, English and French, topped off by a taste of the brew in the sampling room. There's a shop adjacent (US$4 for a bottle).

You can observe people busily rolling cigars at the **Fábrica de Tabacos Francisco Donatien** (Maceo Oeste No 157; admission US$5; 9am-noon & 1-4pm Mon-Fri). Until 1961 this building was a jail. Unless you're really interested, it's not worth the price of admission, as the guides are untrained and the workers want extra money for photos. Check out their cigar store, however. The top brand produced here is called Vegueros.

On Plaza de la Independencia around the corner from the cigar factory is the **Centro Provincial de Artes Plásticas Galería** (Antonio Guiteras near Alameda; admission free; 8am-9pm Mon-Sat), which presents good local art. The **Taller Provincial del Grabado**, a large engraving workshop welcoming visitors, is adjacent.

The wooden, 500-seat **Teatro José Jacinto Milanés** (cnr Martí & Colón) is a gorgeous venue from 1845; too bad it has been undergoing restoration since 1991.

Festivals & Events

Carnaval in early July features a procession of carriages (carrozas) through the streets with couples dancing between the floats. It's a big drunken, dance party.

Sleeping

IN TOWN

Hotel Pinar del Río (Islazul; 50 70 74; s/d/tr incl breakfast US$29/38/46; cnr Gonzales Alcorta & Autopista; P [X] [Z]) is at the eastern end of town, where tourists are supposed to stay (and many do). The 136 rooms have bright spots like refrigerators and radios, but the bad lighting and dizzying decor cast a shadow. The other hotels in town are quite basic, so if you're looking for a hotel atmosphere (as opposed to a private house), this is the size of it. The disco is popular with locals who can afford it.

The cheapest regular hotel that accepts foreigners is the three-story **Hotel Italia** (77 61 20; Gerardo Medina Norte No 213; s/d US$15/20)

opposite a monument to José Martí at the start of the Carretera Central. It's a serviceable place; the 2nd-floor nightclub opens nightly.

The 14-room **Hotel La Marina** (75 25 58; Martí Oeste No 56 btwn Rafael Morales & Ormani Arenado; r 16 pesos) is a friendly peso place that may be willing to take you, while the attractive 12-room **Hotel Lincoln** (75 46 43; Ormani Arenado Sur No 52 at Máximo Gómez) may not.

The **Hotel Globo** (Martí Este at Isabel Rubio) is a colorful hotel (1917) with intricate Spanish tiles lining the lobby. Unfortunately, they stopped accepting foreigners, but it's still worth a peek.

For a capital city, Pinar del Río has few private rooms. See the boxed text for recommendations.

OUTSIDE TOWN

Villa Aguas Claras (Cubamar; 77 84 27; s/d low season US$20/26, high season US$26/32 incl breakfast; [P] [Z]) is 8km north of town on the Viñales Hwy. The 50 bungalows with hot showers sleep two (10 have air-con). The rooms are adequate, the landscaping lush and the staff congenial, making this a better overall choice than Hotel Pinar del Río. They offer horseback riding and day trips. Insect repellent is essential here. Aguas Claras is accessible from Pinar del Río by bus No 7 six times a day.

Eating

PALADARES

Paladar El Mesón (Martí Este No 205; noon-10pm Mon-Sat) is a long-standing paladar opposite the Museo de Ciencias Naturales that serves chicken, pork and fish in a pleasant colonial atmosphere. Main plates start at US$4.50 with side dishes extra; the service is efficient and friendly.

Two other good, private eateries a bit out of the center are **Paladar Nuestra Casa** (77 51 43; Colón Sur No 161 btwn Ceferino Fernández & Primero de Enero), which serves fish all ways including filet (US$7) and canciller (fish stuffed with ham and cheese, US$8), and **Paladar Rodrigo** (Colón Norte No 167 btwn Mariana Grajales and Emilio Núñez; noon-10pm). This last one might be the better value, with big portions at US$5 to US$7.

RESTAURANTS

Specializing in seafood, **El Marino** (Martí Este No 52 at Isabel Rubio; 6:30-9pm Mon-Tue & Thu-

---

CASAS PARTICULARES – PINAR DEL RÍO

Mr. Aquino (no phone; Av Comandante Pinares Sur No 56-A cnr Máximo Gómez; r US$20) Fully-equipped independent apartment with kitchen, super friendly hosts, quiet, good value.

Martí 51 – Laura González Valdés (☎ 2264; Martí Este No 51 Altos btwn Colón & Isabel Rubio; r US$20; ⊠) Central, balcony overlooking street, awesome private library, colonial atmosphere, meals.

Gladys Cruz Hernández (☎ 77 96 98; Av Comandante Pinares Sur No 15 btwn Martí & Máximo Gómez; r US$15) Near train, sleeps three, big patio and fridge, TV, nice bath.

Mayda Martínez (☎ 2110; Isabel Rubio Sur No 125; r US$15-20; ⊠) Apartment with kitchen, meals.

Herminia & Sixto (no phone; Ceferino Fernández Este No 143 near Colón; r US$20; ⊠) Clean, shared bath, friendly.

Anna Maria García & Salvador Reyes (☎ 77 31 46; Alameda No 24 Bajos btwn Volcán & Avellaneda; r US$20; ⊠) Clean, German spoken, good house for cyclists, helpful.

Colonial House – José Antonio Mesa (☎ 3173; Gerardo Medina Norte No 67 btwn Adela Azcuy and Isidro de Armas; r US$10-15) Good for groups; courtyard.

Carmen Puentes (☎ 2309; Av Comandante Pinares Norte No 157 btwn Roldán and Emilio Núñez; r US$20; P ⊠) Friendly, signposted.

Fernández Rent Room (☎ 3158; Colón Norte No 73 btwn Juan Gualberto Gómez & Adela Azcuy; r US$10) Shared bath, meals served, signposted.

Fri, 8pm-midnight Sat) does a decent fish filet for US$4.50. Further down the street, the colonial-style **La Casona** (☎ 77 82 63; cnr Martí & Colón; ☽ 11am-11pm) has steak, chicken and pasta. Atmosphere hovers around zero at both these state-run places, but the food isn't bad.

The best government-operated restaurant in Pinar del Río is Islazul's **Rumayor** (☎ 76 30 51; ☽ noon-midnight), 1km north of the town center, off the Viñales Hwy. Justly famous for its succulent *pollo ahumado* (smoked chicken), you'll pay a little extra here (US$10 to US$15), but it is definitely worth it. There is a cabaret here as well (see p169).

Coppelia (Gerardo Medina Norte No 33; ☽ noon-midnight Tue-Sun) requires line-waiting skills, but the two peso a scoop ice cream (when there *is* ice cream) is dreamy.

SELF-CATERING

Pinar del Río's colorful open-air **mercado agropecuario** (Rafael Ferro; ☽ 8am-6pm Mon-Sat, 8am-1pm Sun) is almost on top of the train tracks near the railway station. **La Mariposa Organopónico** (cnr Carretera Central & Av Aeropuerto) is a conveniently located organic fruit and vegetable market; a good place to stop en route to Viñales.

Panadería Doña Neli (Gerardo Medina Sur at Máximo Gómez; ☽ 7am-7pm) sells bread. The adjacent cafeteria is open until 10pm and has pastries and drinks. A second branch of **Doña**

Neli (cnr Colón & Adela Azcuy; ☽ 7am-12:30am) serves burgers, sandwiches, snacks and soda on a little terrace; it's handy to the bus station. **Supermercado Caracol** (Martí Oeste No 56 btwn Morales & Arenado; ☽ 9am-5pm Mon-Sat, 9am-noon Sun) is the best supermarket in town.

Drinking

La Esquinita Coctelería (Isabel Rubio Norte at Juan Gómez; ☽ noon-midnight) is a darling cocktail place where tropical foliage gone haywire creates semi-private nooks in the back patio. Pesos only, please. If you're looking for the local crowd, grab some drinks at **La Taberna** (González Coro No 101; 6-10pm Tue-Sun), a large, dark Spanish-style pub.

Entertainment

A welcome addition to Pinar's nightlife repertoire is **Cafe Pinar** (☎ 77 81 99; Gerardo Medina Norte No 34; admission US$1-4; ☽ 10-2am). Live bands play nightly in this intimate patio space and there's a light menu with pasta, chicken and sandwiches (US$1 to US$2). Come here if you want to meet some other travelers. Across the street is the **Casa de la Música** (Gerardo Medina Norte No 21; admission US$1; concerts start at 9pm nightly), which also has live concerts in a cozy patio.

Disco Azul (cnr Gonzales Alcorta & Autopista; admission US$2; ☽ 10pm Tue-Sun), in Hotel Pinar del Río, is Pinar del Río's most popular dance spot. Entry for nonguests is from outside the hotel.

Teatro Lírico Ernesto Lecuona (Antonio Maceo Oeste No 163), near the cigar factory, presents plays in Spanish.

Cine Praga (☎ 75 32 71; Gerardo Medina Norte No 31), next to Coppelia, shows mostly subtitled films; also look here for the video schedule at **UNEAC** (Antonio Maceo No 178 btwn Rafael Ferro & Comandante Pinares; ☽ movies at 8:30pm & 10:15pm). **Patio Milanés** (cnr Martí & Colón), alongside the Teatro José Jacinto Milanés, has nightly cultural activities; check the schedule that's posted outside.

From Tuesday through Sunday nights, **Rumayor** (p168) functions as a cabaret, with a floor show starting at 11pm (US$5 cover). It's not the Tropicana, but it ain't half bad.

From October to April, exciting baseball games happen at the **Estadio Capitán San Luis** (☎ 75 38 95; one peso), on the north side of town. Pinar del Río is one of the country's best teams.

The **Sala Polivalente 19 de Noviembre**, on nearby Rafael Morales, is the venue for boxing, volleyball and basketball.

Shopping

ARTex (☎ 77 83 67; Martí Este No 36; ☽ 9am-5pm Mon-Sat, 9am-noon Sun) sells souvenirs, compact discs and T-shirts. **La Casa del Ron** (Antonio Maceo Oeste No 151; ☽ 9am-4:30pm Mon-Fri, 9am-1pm Sat & Sun), near the cigar factory, sells the same, plus rum.

Getting There & Away

BUS

Whatever transport needs you have, they can likely be met at the **bus station** (Adela Azcuy btwn Colón & Comandante Pinares). Because Víazul from Havana only goes as far as Viñales, travelers interested in exploring other parts of the province will have to rely on **Astro** (☎ 75 25 72), passenger trucks, hitching and colectivos (for information on the risks associated with hitching see p433). Astro serves the destinations below:

Guane is as close as you can get to the Península de Guanahacabibes on Astro; alight at Isabel Rubio 5km before Guane and hitch a ride or hire a colectivo (taxi) from there. You really only need to reach La Bajada, from where any car with an empty seat will take pity on you and give you a lift to Playa María la Gorda, 14km down the road.

To get to Cayo Levisa, board the 6:20pm bus to Bahía Honda via Viñales and alight at Mirian, 4km from the Palma Rubia coast guard station, from where boats leave for the Cayo; you'll have to overnight at the station.

Víazul leaves for Viñales daily at 11:15am (US$6) and for Havana at 1:30pm (US$12). Tickets in dollars are purchased at the window upstairs (☽ 8am to 7pm).

A better bet are the colectivos parked in front of the bus station that take passengers to Havana for US$7 a seat. Lately they've been skittish about taking foreigners (resident students excluded). You could also hire a car and driver here for a day in Viñales for US$35 and up (or US$15 one way). A private taxi to María la Gorda will cost you US$35; expect to drive on some back roads to avoid detection (private, unlicensed taxis are technically prohibited from carrying foreigners).

TRAIN

Before planning any rail travel, check the blackboards at the station for cancelled, suspended and rescheduled services. From the train station (☎ 75 57 34; Ferrocarril & Comandante Pinares Sur; ☽ ticket window 6:30am-noon & 1-6:30pm) there's a daily train to Havana (US$6.50, 5½ hours, 162km, 8:45am). You can buy your ticket for this train the day of departure; be at the station between 7am and 8pm. Local trains go southwest to Sábalo (US$1.75, two hours, 47km, 7:25am and 6:30pm). From Sábalo a bus takes passengers to Isabel Rubio and Guane; this is the closest you can get by train to the Península de Guanahacabibes.

destination	cost (one-way)	distance	duration	departure time
Guane	US$4	65km	3h	6:15pm
Havana	US$8	162km	4h	3am, 5:20am, 7:20am, noon, 4pm
Puerto Esperanza	US$3	52km	2h 40min	7:30pm
Santa Lucía	US$3	80km	2h 20min	9pm
Viñales	US$2	27km	1h	5:30pm (bus for La Palma), 6:20pm (bus for Bahía Honda)

Getting Around

There are **Micar** (☎ 77 14 54), **Transtur** (☎ 77 81 78) and **Havanautos** (☎ 77 80 15) car rental offices at the Hotel Pinar del Río. You can also rent mopeds at Transtur (US$20/day).

Servicentro **Oro Negro** is two blocks north of the Hospital Provincial on the Carretera Central. **Servi-Cupet** is 1.5km further north on the Carretera Central toward Havana; another is on Rafael Morales Sur at the south entrance to town.

Horse carts (one peso) on Isabel Rubio near Adela Azcuy go to the Hospital Provincial and out onto the Carretera Central. **Bici-taxis** cost five pesos around town.

It's not difficult to catch a **botella** (ride) from the outskirts of Pinar del Río to Viñales (10 pesos): wait at the junction of the Viñales Hwy and the northern extent of Rafael Morales.

SOUTHWEST OF PINAR DEL RÍO

You're escorted southwest out of Pinar del Río city by rows of royal palms lining the roadside. Before long, you're dipping into the picturesque tobacco-growing area around the town of San Juan y Martínez. Large thatched drying houses float in a sea of tobacco leaves and farmers in signature straw hats tend to the delicate plants. Campismo El Salto, just north of Guane, is a good budget mountain resort. To the west is the freshwater Embalse Laguna Grande stocked with largemouth bass.

Sleeping & Eating

Two local, not terribly pretty, beach resorts are on the Bahía de Cortés. They're not bad places to end up, especially for a fresh fish meal. First is the **Villa Boca de Galafre** (☎ 829-8592; 3/6 beds US$15/20) with 32 cabins with bath, fans, TV and fridge. The turn-off from the main highway is on the left, 36km southwest of Pinar del Río; then it's 3km down to the beach. The train to Guane stops on the access road 2km from the resort. It might be closed outside the peak summer season.

Villa Playa Bailén (☎ 829-6145; bungalow US$15) is further along, 44km from Pinar del Río. It's 8km off the main highway and 6km from the nearest train station on the Pinar del Río–Sábalo railway. The basic A-frame bungalows here sleep four people and are right on the beach.

Campismo El Salto (☎ 849-7347; cabins US$5) 5km north of Guane on the interior road to Pinar del Río, is a basic crash pad in a pretty location next to Río Los Portales at the southwestern end of the Cordillera de Guaniguanico. It's below a high hill with hiking trails to various caves. Each of the 46 four-bunk cabins at El Salto has a private bath. Ask about pitching your tent by the river. There are great swimming spots here and a disco in a cave. Unless you have serious ride *ache* (luck), you'll have to walk the 6km from the train or bus station in Guane.

The pleasant fishing resort of **Villa Laguna Grande** (Islazul; ☎ 84 24 30; s/d low season US$19/27, high season US$20/29) is 29km southwest of Guane and 18km off the highway to María la Gorda. The resort has 12 thatched cabins located directly below the dam that created the Embalse Laguna Grande, which is presently stocked with bass, but the fishing facilities are unreliable. If fishing is your goal, inquire at the Islazul office in Pinar del Río before coming here. It's a quiet, good value place to stay.

Good private rooms (US$15 to US$20) are available in Sandino, 6km southwest of the Laguna Grande turn-off and 89km from Pinar del Río. Try **Motel Alexis** (☎ 84 32 82; Zona L No 33; r US$15-20), or nearby **Casa de Estrella**; both are signposted just off the main highway.

Getting There & Away

Two trains a day travel between Pinar del Río and Sábalo (two hours, 47km). A bus shuttles train passengers to Isabel Rubio and the center of Guane from the Sábalo station. Passenger trucks run periodically between Guane and Sandino, but southwest of there, public transportation is sparse. Be sure to tank up at the **Servi-Cupet** gas station in Isabel Rubio if you intend to drive to Cabo de San Antonio, as this is the last gasp for gas.

PENÍNSULA DE GUANAHACABIBES

The flat Península de Guanahacabibes begins at La Fe, 94km southwest of Pinar del Río. In 1987, the 101,500 hectares of this tail end of Cuba were declared a Biosphere Reserve by Unesco. The reserve's submerged 89km north coast features broad mangrove swamps, while the 108km south coast is an uplifted shelf of alternating white sand and coral rock – idyllic. The reserve's 172 species of birds include parrots, the *tocororo*

CUBAN CIGARS

On his first visit to Cuba, Christopher Columbus encountered Indian medicine men puffing a reed pipe called a *tobago* to inhale smoke from the burning dried leaves of the *cohiba* (tobacco) plant. Part of a fortune-telling ritual, the Spaniards began rolling the leaves into cigars. Tobacco *(Nicotiana tabacum)* was grown commercially in Cuba after 1580, and by 1700 it was the largest export.

Tobacco plants require fastidious care, involving as many as 150 visits during the growing season. The fields *(vegas)* are plowed using oxen to avoid the compacting that would result if tractors were employed. Corn is often rotated with tobacco to maintain the fertility of the soil.

After seeding at a nursery, it takes about 45 days until the tobacco seedlings are between 15cm and 20cm tall and ready for transplanting. Planting takes place from October to December, and in two months the plants grow to about 1.5m high, with leaves 30cm long and 25cm wide. When the plant has reached the desired height, the central bud is removed to stimulate the growth of the leaves. The finest Corojo tobacco, intended for the outer covering of cigars, is grown under cheesecloth coverings to protect the leaves from the sun's rays. Criollo tobacco, used for filler, is grown in full sunlight. A fully grown plant has six to nine pairs of leaves, and the pairs at each level of the plant must be gathered individually by hand at intervals of about a week as it attains maturity from January to March.

The harvested leaves are sewn together in pairs and hung to dry for about 50 days over wooden poles in special curing barns *(secaderos)*, which are oriented to catch the maximum amount of sunlight. At first the leaves turn yellow, then reddish gold. The cured leaves are then bound together and piled in stacks half a meter high for a first fermentation that lasts about 30 days. This reduces the resin in the leaves and produces a more uniform color. The leaves are then moistened and classified, and the thickest parts of the stems are stripped out. The leaves are stacked again in higher bales and left for two months for a second fermentation. After this, they are unpacked and dried on racks, then packed again in special bales called *tercios*, which are covered with *yagua* bark from the royal palm tree. After varying periods of aging, the bales are shipped to cigar factories in Havana.

At the factory the tobacco is shaken out, moistened, and dried again in a special room. The next day the leaves are flattened and their central veins removed, dividing them in two. After sorting, the leaves go to a mixing room where a master blender combines several types to form the filler tobacco *(tripa)* for the desired brand of cigar. The mix of filler determines the flavor of the cigar. The product is then sent to the rolling tables *(galeras)*, where each worker makes around 120 cigars a day. To create a cigar, a roller encloses a body of cut filler in a binder leaf *(capote)* and puts it in a press for half an hour. He then covers the cigar by hand, wrapping it in a high-quality wrapper leaf *(capa)*. The result is something money can't buy in the US. In Cuba, cigars are called, simply, tobacco or *habanos*.

(Cuba's national bird), woodpeckers, owls, tody flycatchers and bee hummingbirds. Because 70% of the birds here are migratory, the best time of year for a visit is in November or March. In addition, there are 600 species of plants, 30 types of mammals, 21 reptiles, 19 amphibians and 16 orchid species. Sea turtles come ashore at night in summer to lay their eggs. If you're here between March and May, you'll smell the crushed *cangrejos colorados* (red and yellow crabs) before you see them. Swarms of them move over the road inevitably getting smashed by passing tires, sending a steaming stench off the tarmac.

At La Bajada the road splits, with the left fork going to María la Gorda (14km) and the right to Cabo San Antonio (54km). To enter this reserve and drive to remote Cabo de San Antonio, where the Caribbean Sea becomes the Gulf of Mexico, you must pay US$10 per person and be accompanied by an official guide (easily arranged at the Estación Ecológica Guanahacabibes, see p172). A chain is strung across the road at a checkpoint 300m below La Bajada, where permits and passports are given the once over. The virgin sands of luscious Playa Las Tumbas near Cabo de San Antonio are truly memorable. The waters off this cape are always rough as the Caribbean Current squeezes through the Estrecho de Yucatán into the Gulf of Mexico.

There's no charge to visit Hotel María la Gorda (Fat Maria; p172) and its splendid beach, both named after a voluptuous Venezuelan who was marooned here by pirates and turned to prostitution to survive. Divers can drop in on El Salón de María and gaze upon Las Tetas de María (Maria's breasts). All the scuba diving here is quality (not just Maria's charms) and it's also one of Cuba's prime yachting venues. Luckily, the nearest international airport is far away in Havana, so you won't be overwhelmed by the packaged tourists who engulf so many of this country's other beauty spots.

Activities

The **Estación Ecológica Guanahacabibes** (☎ 84 32 77; www.ecovida.pinar.cu/Png/index.htm ; ☉ 7:30am-3:30pm), opposite the meteorological station at La Bajada, arranges guides, specialized visits and the five-hour tour to Cuba's western tip at Cabo de San Antonio. You have to supply transport for the latter and should carry everything you'll need – particularly sufficient gas, water, sunscreen, insect repellant and a hat. During most of the 108km roundtrip you'll have dark, rough *diente de perro* (dog's teeth) rock on one side and the brilliant blue sea on the other. Iguanas will lumber for cover as you approach and you might see small deer, *jutía* (an edible tree rat) and lots of birds.

Of the two **hiking trails**, Cueva las Perlas (Pearl Cave, US$8, two hours, 3km) is superior. Immediately as you enter the trail you'll see and hear loads of birds, including *tocororos*, *zunzuncitos* (bee hummingbirds) and woodpeckers. After 1.5km you come to Pearl Cave, a multi-gallery cave system of which 300m is accessible to hikers. The Del Bosque al Mar trail (US$6, 1½ hours, 1.4km) is interesting for about five minutes. Too much of this 'hike' is on the blazing road to Cabo de San Antonio. The guides here are highly trained and knowledgeable; tours can be in Spanish, English or Italian. There were seven more proposed trails snaking their way through the maze of bureaucracy as this book was being written – a decent loop hike would be nice. To enjoy unparalled **views**, you can climb to the top of the meteorological tower across from the park office (US$1).

The **Puertosol International Dive Center** (☎ 77 13 06) at the Hotel María la Gorda sends out their scuba-diving boat at 9am and 3pm daily. Diving costs US$35 per dive (night diving US$40), plus US$7.50 for equipment. The center offers a full CMAS scuba certification course (US$300; four days) and snorkelers can hop on the dive boat for US$12. The dive center also offers four hours of deep-sea fishing for US$200 for up

to four people and line fishing/trolling at US$30 per person, four max.

Among the 30 identified dive sites in the vicinity, divers are shown El Valle de Coral Negro, a 100m-long black-coral wall, and El Salón de María, a cave 20m deep containing feather stars and Technicolor corals. The concentrations of migratory fish can be incredible. The furthest entry is only 30 minutes by boat from shore. Yachties are not allowed to scuba-dive on their own and must join the organized dive groups at the rates quoted above.

Sleeping & Eating

Clean, comfortable rooms are offered at the **Radar Meteorológico La Bajada** (☎ 84 32 77; per person US$8; ☒), opposite the Estación Ecológica Guanahacabibes. Each of the four well-screened rooms inside the weather station has two twin beds and private bath. The very simple **cafeteria** here may be able to serve you some rice and beans, but it's best to bring your own food (plus extra to share with the kind staff). This place is excellent value. Backpackers can probably pitch camp for a small fee.

At the time of writing they were constructing a pair of 'eco-villas' across the road at the Estación Ecológica Guanahacabibes. Once completed, they'll certainly be in the budget range and might include kitchen facilities. Just next to the meteorological station is **Restaurante La Bajada** (☉ 8:30am-10:30pm) with (you guessed it) fried chicken, pork filets, french fries and loud music.

The **Hotel María la Gorda** (Puertosol; ☎ 827-8131; fax 827-8077; s/d/tr low season US$25/50/72, high season US$38/56/81 incl breakfast; ℗ ☒) is on the Bahía de Corrientes, 150km southwest of Pinar del Río (2½ hours by car if you haul ass). From the park office at La Bajada, where the highway meets the Caribbean, Hotel María la Gorda is 14km to the left. This is the most remote hotel on the main island of Cuba. It's right on a palm-fringed beach and there's a dive site with a vertical drop-off just 200m from the hotel. There are lots of nice picnic and aqua-blue snorkeling spots along the road to the hotel if you want to make it a day trip. Camping is also possible along this stretch.

At the time of writing, all rooms were priced equally, but not all are the same. There are three pink-concrete, motel-type

JERRY ALEXANDER

Catedral de San Cristóbal de la Habana (p67)

JERRY ALEXANDER

Habaneros (p59)

Traditional painted **fans** (p83)

RICHARD I'ANSON

Political mural, **Vedado** (p75), Havana

Capitolio Nacional (p73), Havana

Playing **baseball** (p38), Havana

Camello (p112), Havana

buildings where two rooms (each with private entrance) share a common TV, bath and fridge. Another 18 rooms have private bath and fridge. Construction of 20 new cabins set back from the beach was proceeding at a breakneck pace and several were already being rented when we visited. The privacy and comfort afforded by these cabins is quite a step above the older units, so expect higher prices soon. Buffet meals cost US$15 for lunch or dinner; reports on the food vary. Water in the hotel shop is expensive (US$2/1.5L), so bring your own or purify the tap water. Credit cards are not accepted at María la Gorda. Far from a posh resort, hammocks strung between palm trees, cold beers at sunset and dive talk over rum highballs on the beach is what this place is about.

Travel agencies in Pinar del Río offer good dive deals: US$105 includes one night at Hotel María la Gorda with all meals and two dives; nondivers can tag along for US$50.

Getting There & Away

Havanautos (☎ 827-8131) has an office at Hotel María la Gorda, but you'll be lucky if the staff appears. They offer a jeep taxi service with driver to Cabo de San Antonio at US$50 for up to four persons. They'll also do transfers to/from Pinar del Río at US$50 one way for the whole car (or US$120 to/from Havana).

VIÑALES
☎ 8 / pop 14,279

Tucked within the Sierra de los Órganos, 27km north of Pinar del Río, is one of Cuba's most magnificent natural settings. Parque Nacional Viñales is a fertile plain of several valleys separated by pincushion or haystack hills called mogotes, reminiscent of the limestone hills of Quilin in southern China. Rising above fields of green tobacco run through with rich red earth, these bulbous mounds play host to a healthy rock-climbing scene.

This whole area was once several hundred meters higher, but during the Cretaceous period 100 million years ago, a network of underground rivers ate away at the limestone bedrock, creating vast caverns. Eventually the roofs collapsed leaving only the eroded walls we see today. In 1999, Valle de Viñales was declared a Unesco World Heritage site. (Viñales is also the name of the main valley village).

Bus tourism to the province focuses almost exclusively on this area and the brochure hype is such that some travelers consider it overrated. To avoid this fate, get out and explore: rent a moped and poke through the Valle Ancón or take the 43km back route to San Diego de los Baños for a sulfur soak; try rock climbing or hike deep into the Gran Caverna de Santo Tomás; drive or hitch up to the beach at Cayo Jutías; or arrange a horse and guide to show you spots still unpublished in any guidebook. The area around Viñales has Cuba's largest pine forests and 64 bird species, making for fragrant, melodic adventures. This is a great area to discover by bike.

If you intend to stay in casas particulares in Viñales or coastal points north, you must have your passport with a visa or tourist card attached, photocopies are not acceptable; they are very strict about this and even resident students with a carnet may encounter problems. Mixed foreign-Cuban couples without marriage papers won't be rented rooms here.

Information

The **Parque Nacional Viñales visitors center** (Carretera a Pinar del Río Km 2) had everything but the roof and displays in place at the time of writing. Once finished, hiking information and guides will be on hand. If it's still not open when you arrive, check the **Museo Municipal** (Salvador Cisneros No 115) for park information.

IMMIGRATION
Inmigración (cnr Salvador Cisneros & Ceferino Fernández; 🕑 8am-5pm weekdays)

INTERNET ACCESS & TELEPHONE
Cubanacán (Salvador Cisneros No 63C; 🕑 9am-7pm Mon-Sat; US$5/3hr with Tu Isla card)
Etecsa (Ceferino Fernández No 3; US$0.10/min & international calls) Across from the post office.

MONEY
Banco de Crédito y Comercio (☎ 79 31 30; Salvador Cisneros No 58; 🕑 8am-noon & 1:30-3pm Mon-Fri, 8am-11am Sat)
Cadeca (☎ 79 63 64; Salvador Cisneros & Adela Azcuy; 🕑 8:30am-5:30pm Mon-Sat)

POST
Post Office (Ceferino Fernández No 14 ; 9am-6pm Mon-Sat) Just off the main square.

VIÑALES

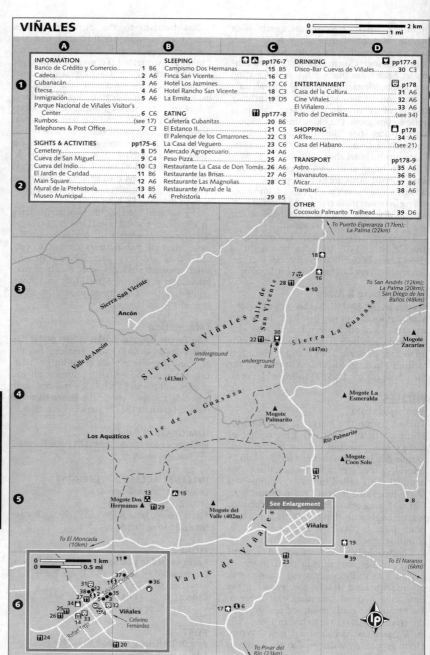

INFORMATION	
Banco de Crédito y Comercio	**1** B6
Cadeca	**2** A6
Cubanacán	**3** A6
Etecsa	**4** A6
Inmigración	**5** A6
Parque Nacional de Viñales Visitor's Center	**6** C6
Rumbos	(see 17)
Telephones & Post Office	**7** C3

SIGHTS & ACTIVITIES	pp175–6
Cemetery	**8** D5
Cueva de San Miguel	**9** C4
Cueva del Indio	**10** C3
El Jardín de Caridad	**11** B6
Main Square	**12** A6
Mural de la Prehistoria	**13** B5
Museo Municipal	**14** A6

SLEEPING	☐ ☐ pp176–7
Campismo Dos Hermanas	**15** B5
Finca San Vicente	**16** C3
Hotel Los Jazmines	**17** C6
Hotel Rancho San Vicente	**18** C3
La Ermita	**19** D5

EATING	☐ pp177–8
Cafetería Cubanitas	**20** B6
El Estanco II	**21** C5
El Palenque de los Cimarrones	**22** C3
La Casa del Veguero	**23** C6
Mercado Agropecuario	**24** A6
Peso Pizza	**25** A6
Restaurante La Casa de Don Tomás	**26** A6
Restaurante las Brisas	**27** A6
Restaurante Las Magnolias	**28** C3
Restaurante Mural de la Prehistoria	**29** B5

DRINKING	☐ pp177–8
Disco-Bar Cuevas de Viñales	**30** C3

ENTERTAINMENT	☐ p178
Casa de la Cultura	**31** A6
Cine Viñales	**32** A6
El Viñalero	**33** A6
Patio del Decimista	(see 34)

SHOPPING	☐ p178
ARTex	**34** A6
Casa del Habano	(see 21)

TRANSPORT	pp178–9
Astro	**35** A6
Havanautos	**36** B6
Micar	**37** B6
Transtur	**38** A6

OTHER	
Cocosolo Palmarito Trailhead	**39** D6

TRAVEL AGENCIES

Cubanacán (☎ 79 63 93; Salvador Cisneros No 63C; 🕑 9am-7pm Mon-Sat) Moped rentals and tours, but you can arrange your own tour for less money (p176).

Rumbos (☎ 79 63 39) In Hotel Los Jazmines.

Sights

The village of Viñales was founded in 1875. The **Casa de la Cultura**, in an old mansion next to the church on the main square, has a full program of cultural activities; an art gallery is next door. The **Museo Municipal** (☎ 79 33 95; Salvador Cisneros No 115; 🕑 8am-5pm daily) occupies the former home of independence heroine Adela Azcuy (1861–1914).

Look to your left just past the Servi-Cupet on the road north out of town and you'll see a funky, vine-choked gate with fresh fruit hanging from it. This is the entrance to **El Jardín de Caridad** (donations accepted; 🕑 8am-5pm), a sprawling garden almost a century in the making. Cascades of orchids bloom alongside plastic doll heads, thickets of orange lilies grow in soft groves and turkeys run amok. One of the ancient sisters tending the place will likely offer you some conversation and a plate of fruit.

Four kilometers west of the village is the **Mural de la Prehistoria** (US$1). On a cliff at the foot of the 617m-high Sierra de Viñales, the highest portion of the Sierra de los Órganos, this 120m-long painting on the side of Mogote Dos Hermanas was designed in 1961 by Leovigildo González Morillo, a follower of Mexican artist Diego Rivera (the idea was hatched by Celia Sáncez, Alicia Alonso and Antonio Nuñez Jiménez). It took 15 people five years to complete it. The huge snail, dinosaurs, sea monsters and humans on the cliff symbolize the theory of evolution and are either impressively psychedelic or monumentally horrific, depending on your point of view. You don't really have to get up close to appreciate the mural, but the admission fee is waived if you take the delicious US$15 lunch at the site restaurant (see p178). Horses are usually available here at US$1 for a short ride around the park or US$5 for an hour through the valley.

A kilometer beyond the turn-off to Dos Hermanas, a dirt road leads toward the mountain community of **Los Aquáticos**. Los Aquáticos was founded in 1943 by followers of visionary Antoñica Izquierdo, who discovered the healing power of water when the

campesinos (country folk) of this area had no access to conventional medicine. They colonized the mountain slopes and several families still live there. Unfortunately, the last patriarch practicing the water cure died in 2002, taking the tradition with him, but you can still visit. Los Aquáticos is accessible only by horse or on foot. Ask at your casa for guide contacts; horses can be hired from farmers living near the trailhead (US$10 per person for a three-hour tour with Spanish-speaking guide). From the main road it's 1km inland to the trailhead (just across the stream) of La Ruta de las Aguas. After your visit, you can make this a loop by continuing on this road (fork left at the same stream, re-crossing it a few hundred meters to the east), another 3km to Campismo Dos Hermanas and the cliff paintings, a wonderfully scenic route (the complete Los Aquático/Dos Hermanas circuit totals 6km from the main highway).

The Cueva de San Miguel, 4km north of Viñales village, is now **Disco-Bar Cuevas de Viñales** (admissin US$5 incl 1 drink; 🕑 11am-2am) with a cabaret show at night. During the day it's a nice cool bar. There's a lit passageway 150m through the mogote to El Palenque de los Cimarrones (see Eating, p178).

North from the **Cueva del Indio** (☎ 79 62 80; US$5; 🕑 9am-5:30pm) is the prettiest part of Viñales, but the cave itself, 5.5km north of Viñales village, is a shameless tourist trap. An ancient indigenous dwelling, it was rediscovered in 1920 and motor boats now ply the underground river through the electrically lit cave. Souvenir vendors crowd the entrance, while cheesy musicians serenade you and tour buses roll in belching out large groups.

Activities

If you're looking to go for a **swim**, La Ermita has a seriously beautiful poolside view (admission US$3; open 8am to 10pm) taking in large swaths of the valley. You can also get a **massage** (US$20 to US$35) here. Hotel Los Jazmines has a pool too (admission US$5 including three drinks; open 9am to 7pm) and an even better view, but the coming and going of sightseers kills the tranquility.

HIKING

The folks at Parque Nacional Viñales are working hard to open up new hiking trails, including a nine-day trek that will take in all of the national park; those interested in longer hikes should inquire at the Museo Municipal (p175) or, once it's open, the new visitor center (p173). Already open is the Cocosolo Palmarito hike, which starts on a spur road just before La Ermita hotel. This 11km walk takes in several mogotes, including Coco Solo and Palmarito, before passing by the Mural de la Prehistoria and through tobacco *fincas* (ask about lunch with one of the families there), dropping you on the main road back to Viñales.

The Maravillas de Viñales trail is a 4km loop beginning one kilometer before El Moncada, 13km from the Dos Hermanas turn-off. This hike takes in endemic plants, orchids and the biggest ant cutter hive in Cuba (so they say). A caretaker at the trailhead collects the US$1 entry fee. Both of these hikes are intended to be guided either by a park ranger or on an organized tour (see p176).

ROCK CLIMBING

If local buzz and recent articles in *Rock & Ice* magazine are any indication, Viñales is getting a reputation as one of the premier rock-climbing spots in the Western hemisphere. At last count there were 150 routes opened, with more being mapped all the time. With all levels of difficulty – and names like Rompe los Dedos (Finger Breaker) and Cuba Libre (Free Cuba) – the rock climbing here is outstanding. Of all the outdoor adventure in Cuba, this is the most DIY by far. Climbers should head to www.cubaclimbing.com for the skinny and bring extra gear to share (local supplies are ridiculously limited).

Tours

You can arrange hikes in and around Viñales Valley (US$8 to US$14), as well as tours to Gran Caverna de Santo Tomás or Cayo Levisa, at **Rumbos** (☎ 93 63 39). Service here is professional and friendly, with English-speakers on staff. **Cubanacán** (Salvador Cisneros No 63C; ☼ 8:30am-5:30pm Mon-Sat) is conveniently located in the center of Viñales village and is often overwhelmed as a result. **Campismo Dos Hermanas** organizes hikes (check at the front desk) or you can arrange your own tailored tour with the taxis lining the main square. A day trip around Viñales taking in El Jardín de Caridad, the mural, a visit to a tobacco *finca* and several caves will cost US$30.

Sleeping

There are some 200 houses renting rooms in Viñales, so shop around. Also try bargaining here.

The setting of **Campismo Dos Hermanas** (Cubamar; ☎ 79 32 23; s/d US$11/15; ☒), among the mogotes directly opposite El Mural de la Prehistoria, can't be beat. The 54 two- and four-bed concrete cabins are popular with campers, climbers and cyclists; it's a good place to meet other travelers. There's a restaurant as well as horseback riding and other excursions. Several caves are accessible on foot nearby and you can hike back into the valley. An archaeological museum is on the premises. It's good value and a pretty place to stay, but fills fast (especially on weekends). This is a full Campertour facility.

Hotel Rancho San Vicente (Horizontes; ☎ 79 62 01; s/d low season US$34/43, high season US$39/48 incl breakfast; P ☒ ☒), just 7km north of Viñales village and 1km north of the Cueva del Indio, is nestled in a grove and will make you go ahhhhh. Skip the 20 older cabins and go straight for the new wooden units (Nos 6 to 43) with lovely natural furnishings, delicious baths and sliding glass doors onto a porch. Put up your feet and look for the 30 to 50 bird species that frequent the grounds or go for a sulfur soak (25°C to 28°C; US$5/30 minutes) or massage (US$9 to US$15). Highly recommended for exhausted guidebook writers.

La Ermita (Horizontes; ☎ 79 60 71; www.horizontes.cu; s/d low season US$45/58, high season US$50/65 incl breakfast; P ☒ ☒) is a top mid-range pick, with its dazzling views, cozy furnishings and friendly staff, 2km east of Viñales village. Go for a room with a valley view. Breakfast on the patio can't be beat and *mojitos* poolside are also highly recommended (have a staff member point out the endangered cork palm there). This modern hotel offers tennis courts, an excellent shop, horseback riding (US$5 per hour) and excursions. This is the only government hotel within easy walking distance of the village. Two caveats: the walls are thin and construction of 50 new cabins in the near future might disturb the peace.

Hotel Los Jazmines (Horizontes; ☎ 79 62 05; www .horizontes.cu; s/d low season US$49/61, high season US$57/71 incl breakfast; P ☒ ☒), with the best valley views, lies 4km south of Viñales on the road to Pinar del Río (also known as the Viñales Hwy) and sees a lot of traffic. Still, conscientious renovations and professional staff keep the 48 rooms looking spiffy. The 16 rooms in a long block facing the valley offer the best vistas and the most privacy. The postcard-perfect (literally) view of the Valle de Viñales from the hotel means the pool area and viewpoint are crowded with sightseers all day. Several readers have recommended the walking tours offered here. Horseback riding can also be arranged (US$5/hour).

Travelers with children will like **Ranchón y Finca San Vicente** (Rumbos; ☎ 79 61 10; bohío US$15; cabins US$50), a working farm just beyond the Cueva del Indio exit. Trails, orchards (eat as much as you can pick), horses, birds and plenty of room to run around will delight kids and at night there is folkloric music and dancing. The rustic *bohío* is thatch and wood, sleeps two and has a private bath. The cabin sleeps four in two rooms and has a bath, kitchen and TV.

Three rooms are for rent at **Restaurante Las Magnolias** (☎ 79 60 62; d US$25 incl breakfast; P), a little house directly across the highway from the Cueva del Indio. Only one of the rooms has a private bath, but kitchens and satellite TV are nice perks.

Eating & Drinking
IN TOWN
Because so many casas particulares provide meals for guests, Viñales is short on paladares. While you're out hiking, you might get an invitation to eat with *campesinos*: take it and you'll dine fabulously on fresh roasted pork, the best *congrí* (rice with beans) you're likely to have, *yuca con mojo* and salad.

Restaurante La Casa de Don Tomás (☎ 79 63 00; Salvador Cisneros No 140; 10am-9:30pm) is the oldest house in Viñales. You'll know this restaurant by the terra cotta roof and exuberant flowering vines bursting from the balcony. This place has atmospheric patio dining out the back, where you can try '*las delicias de Don Tomás*,' the house specialty with rice, lobster, fish, pork, chicken and sausage with an egg crowning it all (US$10). Chicken and fish dishes are cheaper.

El Estanco II (10am-11pm) is a simple pizza and beer place a kilometer out of town on the road north, and a decent pit stop. A pizza costs US$1, a plate of spaghetti twice that.

Other, simpler places include **Restaurante Las Brisas** (☎ 79 33 53; Salvador Cisneros No 96; 11am-2pm & 6-9pm), a not half bad peso restaurant where you can fill up for under US$4, and takeout **peso pizza** (Salvador Cisneros No 130).

Cafetería Cubanitas (Adela Azcuy & Rafael Trejo; 9:30am-10pm) has a nice terrace for sandwiches and snacks.

Viñales' **mercado agropecuario** is about 100m from town at the west end of Salvador Cisneros down the road toward Dos Hermanas. Get your peso rum and dollar bread here. **El Viñalero** (Salvador Cisneros No 105; 7:30am-midnight) has early-morning espresso.

CASAS PARTICULARES – VIÑALES

Eloy Hernández Rodríguez (no phone; Salvador Cisneros No 198; r US$15-20;) Private house in backyard, meals to fatten you.

Nena Paula (☎ 93 60 18; Camilo Cienfuegos No 56; r US$15;) Friendly, many others on this block.

Ubaldo Chirino Suárez (☎ 9-3226; Adela Azcuy No 35; r US$20;) Private, meals served.

Villa Chicha (no phone; Camilo Cienfuegos No 22; r US$10) Basic room in home of gracious señora, value.

Teresa Martínez Hernández (☎ 9-3267; Camilo Cienfuegos No 10; r US$15;) Nice porch and small garden, good meals.

Casa Lucy – Lucy & Bartolo (☎ 9-3214; Orlando Nodarse No 9; r US$15;) Quiet street behind school, mogote views from porch.

Casa La Prieta & Mario (☎ 9-3267; Adela Azcuy No 21; r US$15;) Clean, comfortable room, patio with people-watching.

Villa Nelson (☎ 9-3268; Camilo Cienfuegos No 4; r US$12-15) Private, independent room in backyard; meals for nonguests.

Oscar Jaime Rodríguez (☎ 9-3381; Adela Azcuy No 43; r US$15;) Climbers hangout, enthusiastically reader recommended.

Casa Emilia Díaz (Nenita) (no phone; Calle Salvador Cisneros Interior 6-1; r US$20;) Fantastic setting on valley edge with bold mogote views; sleeps four, good bathroom, meals, off main road behind policlínico.

OUTSIDE TOWN

La Casa del Veguero (☎ 97 60 80; ☾ 10am-5pm daily), just outside Viñales toward Pinar del Río, serves a complete (and tasty) criollo lunch for US$10. Adjacent to the restaurant is a drying house (*secadero*) where tobacco leaves are cured from February to May. Visitors are welcome in the *secadero* and you can buy loose cigars here at discount prices.

Of all the places clustered within spitting distance of Viñales serving *asado* (roast), the **restaurant** (☎ 79 62 60; ☾ 11:30am-7pm) at the Mural de la Prehistoria has the recipe mastered. The pork is roasted and smoked over natural charcoal, giving it a sublime melt-in-your-mouth flavor. You'll have to roll from the table after the US$15 complete lunch with all the fixings; try the house piña colada. Also on the tour bus circuit, the more intimate **Ranchón y Finca San Vincente** (☎ 79 61 10; ☾ noon-5pm), near the Cueva del Indio exit, runs a close second with its succulent smoke-roasted pork (US$11). You may get live salsa music at either place.

El Palenque de los Cimarrones (☎ 79 62 90; ☾ noon-4pm), entered through the Cueva de San Miguel north of town, is an odd combination of folklore show, restaurant and plantation slavery museum. The complete Cuban-style lunch (US$11) is tasty, but the young Cubans dressed as *cimarrones* (runaway slaves) somehow fails to stimulate the appetite.

The coziest place to eat near the Cueva del Indio is **Restaurante Las Magnolias** (☎ 79 60 62; ☾ 10am-6pm) across the highway from the cave. They offer lobster in their attractive back garden for US$15, but most of the other dishes are around US$6.

Entertainment

There are two places in town to party: **Patio del Decimista** (Salvador Cisneros No 102; admission free; ☾ music at 9pm), serving live music nightly and cold beers on its swinging patio next to ARTex, and **El Viñalero** (Salvador Cisneros No 105) across the street. Darker and less of an established hangout, this place also has live music and sidewalk tables. The disco in the courtyard next to the Casa de la Cultura begins at 9:30pm on Saturday and Sunday. **Cine Viñales** (Ceferino Fernández & Rafael Trejo) is a block south of the main square.

Shopping

You can get postcards, T-shirts and compact discs at **ARTex** (Salvador Cisneros No 102) and cigars at **Casa del Habano** (Carretera de Puerto Esperanza Km 1; ☾ 9am-5pm).

Getting There & Around

BUS

The **Astro ticket office** (Salvador Cisneros No 63A; 8am-noon & 1-3pm) is opposite the church on Viñales' main square. The daily Astro bus to Havana leaves at 2:30pm (US$8, 189km), and a comfortable Víazul bus for Havana via Pinar del Río departs at 1:30pm daily (US$12). A long 'transporte popular' bus leaves for Pinar del Río from a stop beside the church opposite Salvador Cisneros No 59 at 8am daily (one peso), but it's not reliable. It should leave Pinar del Río bus station for the round-trip to Viñales at 11am. Taxis park alongside the main square in Viñales.

CAR & MOPED

To reach Viñales from the south, you take the nauseatingly curvy road from Pinar del Río; the roads from the north coast are not as sinuous, but are pretty drives. The wildly scenic mountain road from the Península de Guanahacabibes through Guane and Pons is one of Cuba's most spectacular routes. Allow a lot of travel time for all these routes (especially if you're relying on public transport).

The following agencies have offices in Viñales:

Cubanacán (☎ 79 63 93; Salvador Cisneros No 63C; ☾ 9am-7pm) Mopeds/motorcross US$17/24 per day.
Havanautos At the Servi-Cupet; rents mopeds.
Micar (☎ 79 63 30; Salvador Cisneros final)
Rumbos (☎ 79 63 39; Salvador Cisneros No 140; ☾ 8am-4pm) Has cheapest mopeds in town (US$15/day including gas).
Transtur (☎ 79 60 60; Salvador Cisneros) Beside the church; rents mopeds.

A **Servi-Cupet** gas station is at the northeast end of Viñales town. **Taxis** parked alongside the square will take you to Pinar del Río (US$10), Palma Rubia for the boat to Cayo Levisa (US$25) or Gran Caverna de Santo Tomás (US$16).

BICYCLE

There are several places renting bicycles, including Cubanacán, the kiosk on the main square and Rumbos alongside Restaurante la Casa de Don Tomás. This last is the cheapest with bikes at US$6 per day or US$20 per week.

WEST OF VIÑALES

At El Moncada, 14km west of the Dos Hermanas turn-off and 1.5km off the road to Minas de Matahambre, is **Gran Caverna de Santo Tomás** (admission US$8; ☼ 8:30am-5pm), Cuba's largest cave system. There are over 46km of galleries on eight levels; 1km on the sixth level, 42m above the valley, is accessible to visitors. There's no artificial lighting, but headlamps are provided for the 90-minute guided tour. At the time of writing, the speleologists here were developing guided hikes of four to seven hours ranging in difficulty from medium to hard (involving ropes and level changes). Specialists should contact the **Escuela de Espeleológica** (☎ 79 31 45) for more information. Near the cave entrance is a massive poured-concrete **monument** erected in 1999 to Los Doce Malagones, 12 locals who eliminated a counterrevolutionary band in the hills in 1959, giving rise to today's Cuban militias. A **museum** (admission US$1; ☼ 10am-10pm) with a veteran docent is on site.

In the late 1990s, **Cayo Jutías**, off northwestern Pinar del Río, was linked to the mainland by a massive causeway (*pedraplén*) that offers a dramatic view of the province's mountains in profile. The access road begins 4km west of Santa Lucía. At the beginning of the causeway, 4.5km off the coastal road, you have to pay a US$5 per person entry fee (one drink included). Nine kilometers from the main highway is a metal lighthouse, the **Faro de Cayo Jutías**, erected by the US in 1902. The route ends at a picturesque white beach caressed by crystal-clear water, 12.5km from the coastal highway. Rumbos runs **Restaurante Cayo Jutías** (☎ 9am-5pm) here. It's a nice picnic, camping and swimming spot, though the snorkeling is poor. Get here before 11am to have a few hours to yourself before the tour buses roll in. A tour from Pinar del Río costs US$53/45 with/without guide. The fastest, prettiest route to Cayo Jutías is via El Moncada and Minas de Matahambre.

Santa Lucía is a small town known mostly for its huge thermoelectric power plant and sulfuric acid factory. However, two nice private rooms are available at **Casa Nelida González** (☎ 3-8314; Calle José R Trujillo No 88; r US$15). Further

afield near Río del Medio is **Campismo El Copey** (☎ 3-8398; per person US$5), 3km off the coastal highway 10km west of the Cayo Jutías access road. Osf the 30 concrete duplex cabins here, two are officially designated for foreigners. The beach here is only so-so but you can swim off the long pier. A cafeteria is on the beach. This place may be full of Cubans on the weekends and closed at other times.

PUERTO ESPERANZA

☎ 8

Puerto Esperanza, 6km north of San Cayetano and 25km north of Viñales, is a sleepy little port often visited by yachts sailing around the country. According to town lore, the giant mango trees lining the entrance to town were planted by slaves in the 1800s. A long pier pointing out into the bay is decent for a jump in the ocean.

There's not much to do here but get to know the locals. The super nice couple at **Villa Leonila Blanco** (☎ 9-3843; Calle Hermanos Caballeros No 41; r US$15; ✗) rent two big rooms with shared bath, garage and meals served. They also have an independent house. Another good option is **Villa Maribel** (☎ 9-3845; Calle Maceo No 56; r US$15), which rents two interconnecting rooms that can sleep up to six; meals served. **Omayda Delgado** (☎ 9-3803; Amejeira No 12) has rooms closer to the water than the previous two; meals are served here too.

There's a handy **Servi-Cupet** gas station at San Cayetano. The road to Santa Lucía and Cayo Jutías detoriates to dirt outside of San Cayetano: expect a throbbing ass if you're on a bike or moped.

EAST OF VIÑALES

A lovely, little-known road runs through the mountains from Viñales to San Diego de los Baños. Three kilometers north of Viñales, take the road toward La Palma via República de Chile. Eight kilometers along, turn right toward La Baria, which is 17km straight ahead. Turn right again at La Baria and go 6km up and over the ridge to the access road to San Andrés, where you turn left. Eight kilometers from the San Andrés junction, turn left again. The signposted turn-off to the Cueva de los Portales (see San Diego de los Baños & Around, p180) will be just 500m ahead. This entire route is paved, though potholes force you to slow down and enjoy the scenery. Spectacular cliffs and picturesque farms will be with you almost all the way.

CAYO LEVISA

Three kilometers of white sand and sapphire waters distinguish this small coral key off the north coast of Pinar del Río. Part of the Archipiélago de los Colorados, thick mangroves, swarms of mosquitoes, abundant seabirds, red snapper, sea bass, lobster and marlin frolic here.

From the early 1940s, American author and avid outdoorsman Ernest Hemingway had a fishing camp on Cayo Paraíso, a smaller coral island 10km east, giving you an idea how they bite up this way.

Hotel Cayo Levisa (Horizontes; ☎ 66-6075; s/d low season US$55/71, high season US$63/81; ✸) has 20 cozy cabañas with private bath; the room price includes transport to the island and a welcome drink. This is a terrific place to kick off your shoes for a few days and relax, if the tour groups and mosquitoes don't overwhelm you. Havanatur or Cubatur offices around Cuba sell excursions to Cayo Levisa. Scuba diving is offered at US$26 for one to four dives, including gear and transport to dive site.

The landing for Cayo Levisa is 21km northeast of La Palma or 40km west of Bahía Honda. Take the turn-off to Mirian and proceed 4km through a large banana plantation to reach the coast-guard station at Palma Rubia, from which the boat to the island departs. The Cayo Levisa boat leaves at 11am and returns at 5pm, and costs US$19 per person round-trip without lunch, or US$25 including a seafood lunch. For US$4 extra dollars you can go snorkeling. From the Cayo Levisa dock you cross the mangroves on a wooden walkway to the resort and gorgeous beach along the island's north side.

BAHÍA HONDA & AROUND

The scenic, winding road to Havana through northern Pinar del Río province is a pretty, relaxing alternative to the Autopista. Rice paddies lie in the river valleys and you pass a succession of picturesque thatched farmhouses.

Motel La Mulata (r US$10), 27km west of Bahía Honda and 1km off the main road, has six duplex units with bath in a long single-story block. A pleasant terrace overlooks the bay, but there's no swimming beach.

Campismo La Altura (☎ 8-6470; r US$5) is 400m back from a long white beach, 12km off the coastal highway. The signposted turn-off is 11km west of Bahía Honda and 4km east of Las Pozas. The 50 rooms are usually full on weekends. The beach here isn't bad.

SAN DIEGO DE LOS BAÑOS & AROUND
☎ 8

San Diego de los Baños, 130km southwest of Havana, is a friendly little town nestled between two mountain ranges and is perfect for a day of indulgence if you like hot soaks and massages. The Spanish established a spa under medical supervision here in 1891. The Río San Diego, on which this lowland village sits, separates the Sierra de los Órganos to the west from the higher Sierra del Rosario to the east. The Sierra de Güira to the west of San Diego de los Baños is a nature reserve with pine, mahogany and cedar forests, and is a favorite bird-watching area.

Sights & Activities

The **Balneario San Diego** (☎ 3-7812; ◷ 8am-4pm) is a modern bathing complex where thermal waters of 30°C to 40°C are used to treat muscular and skin afflictions. Mud from the mouth of the Río San Diego is used here for mud baths (US$20). The sulfurous waters of these mineral springs are potent and immersions of only 20 minutes per day are allowed (US$4/6 for collective/private pools). Massage is available at US$25 and many other health services are offered. These facilities are among the finest of their kind in the country and many Cubans are prescribed treatment here by their family doctors – which explains the sweet little old ladies everywhere.

If you're looking for cold water, you can swim at the Hotel Mirador **pool** (adult/child US$1/0.50; ◷ 9am-6pm).

Five kilometers west of San Diego de los Baños is **Parque La Güira**, the former Hacienda Cortina, a large sculpture park built during the 1920s and '30s by wealthy lawyer José Manuel Cortina. There are artificial ruins, a Chinese pavilion and clusters of bamboo. A huge state-operated restaurant is just above Parque La Güira, but the cabins here are reserved for vacationing military personnel.

During the October 1962 Cuban Missile Crisis, Ernesto 'Che' Guevara transferred headquarters of the Western Army to **Cueva de Los Portales**, 11km west of Parque La Güira and 16km north of Entronque de Herradura on the Carretera Central. The cave is in a pretty area, 1km off the main road, and the Río Caiguanabo runs right through it. Three other caves called El Espejo, El Salvador and Cueva Oscura are up on the hillside. Together they make a cool sidetrip.

Sleeping

IN TOWN

Private rooms are available from **Julio Gil Marquez** (☎ 3-7845; Calle 29 No 4009 btwn 40 & 42; r US$20), directly across the park from the bathing complex. A small patio runs in front of the big room, which has a private bath and fridge. Passable meals are served for US$7. Another option is **Villa Carmen** (Calle 34 No 2310; r US$20 incl breakfast), two blocks down from the Hotel Mirador, with one room in a cute house on a quiet block.

Foreigners usually stay at the attractive, two-story **Hotel Mirador** (Islazul; ☎ 7-8338; s/d/tr US$29/38/45; P ✗ ✿), adjacent to the hot springs. The Mirador is a modernized hotel dating from 1954, with comfortable rooms with fridge (some with views). A suite costs US$47.

Two blocks over from the Hotel Mirador is the gracious old **Hotel Saratoga** (1924), complete with columns, mosaic tiling and elderly Cubans working the rocking chairs on the porch. Unfortunately the 35 rooms are for Cubans only.

WEST OF TOWN

Motel Las Palmas, inside Parque La Güira, has nine air-con rooms at US$17 with bath, fridge and TV (US$14 without TV). Mostly Cubans stay here.

Like a faded Hollywood starlet with a habit, **Cabañas Los Pinos** is beautiful, but hit the skids long ago. Located in the Sierra de Güira, 12km west of San Diego de los Baños via Parque La Güira, it's a terrific camping spot if you've got gear. Los Pinos was built in the early 1960s by Castro's secretary (and respected revolutionary leader in her own right), the late Celia Sánchez, whose circular cabin stands in the center of the eerie, shuttered complex. It's an idyllic location, standing on a ridge below the mountain peaks, and it's an excellent bird-watching base. Los Pinos would make a perfect ecotourism resort were it ever restored. Until that happens you'll probably have the place to yourself.

At **Cueva de Los Portales** (☎ 3-2749), 5km west of Los Pinos, are six basic cabañas (US$5 per person) or you can pitch a tent (US$3 per person) in the forest near the cave, but the mosquitoes are fierce.

Eating

The en-plein-air *parrillada* (grill restaurant) at the **Hotel Mirador** is quite good, with complete meals for US$6. There is also a proper restaurant at the hotel serving Cuban cuisine.

Getting Around

There's a **Servi-Cupet** at the entrance to San Diego de los Baños from Havana. Horse carts shuttle between San Diego de los Baños and Parque La Güira for a couple of pesos. If you're planning to cycle over the mountain to Cabañas Los Pinos and Guevara's cave, beware of dangerous potholes and loose gravel on the steep downhill stretches.

SOROA
☎ 82

Soroa, 95km west of Havana, is the closest mountain resort area to the capital and makes a popular day trip. It's above Candelaria in the Sierra del Rosario, the easternmost and highest section of the Cordillera de Guaniguanico. Soroa is nicknamed the 'rainbow of Cuba,' and the region's heavy rainfall (more than 1300mm annually) promotes the growth of tall trees and orchids. The area gets its name from Jean-Pierre Soroa, a Frenchman who owned a 19th-century coffee plantation in these hills. One of his descendants, Ignacio Soroa, created the park as a personal retreat in the 1920s, and only since the revolution has this luxuriant area been developed for tourism. This is another great area to explore by bike.

Sights & Activities

All Soroa's sights are conveniently near Hotel & Villas Soroa, a large motel complex offering horseback riding. Next door is **Orquidearo Soroa** (☎ 77 25 58; admission US$3, plus US$3 camera; ⏱ 9am-5pm), built between 1943 and 1953 by Spanish lawyer Tomás Felipe Camacho in memory of his wife and daughter. There are 700 orchid species (most voluminous blooming from December to March), 6000 ornamentals and various growing houses and research facilities. Visits are well guided in Spanish or English; enthusiasts should inquire about on-site live-study arrangements.

Just down the road is the entrance to a park featuring the **Salto del Arco Iris** (admission US$3), a 22m waterfall on the Arroyo Manantiales. It's at its most impressive in the May to October rainy season, otherwise it's a trickle. You can swim at the foot of the falls. Entry is free for Villa Soroa guests.

On the opposite side of the stream from the waterfall parking lot are the **Baños Romanos** (US$5/h; 🕐 9am-4pm), a stone bathhouse with a pool of cold sulfurous water. It's a half-hour scramble up the hill from the bathhouse to the **Mirador**, a rocky crag with a sweeping view of all Soroa.

Castillo de las Nubes is a romantic castle with a circular tower on a hilltop above the Orquideario. There are good views of the Valle de Soroa and the coastal plain beyond from the ridge beyond the bar. The restaurant has the liveliness of a crypt, but you might grab a drink from the bar (🕐 10am to 5pm).

Sleeping & Eating

Several signposted houses on the road from Candelaria to Soroa, 4km below the Hotel & Villas Soroa, rent rooms. Westbound you first reach the home of **Virginia and Rolando González Méndez** (r US$25) who have a private bungalow in their backyard and serve good meals. Half a kilometer west toward Soroa, **Pepe Hernández** (r US$25) rents rooms in his house and there's parking, but at this price the first place is better. Because the greatest profit margin is in the food, both families will expect you to order meals.

Hotel & Villas Soroa (Horizontes; ☎ 77 82 18; www .horizontes.cu; s/d low season US$34/43, high season US$45/55 incl breakfast; 🅿 🍴 🈁) nestles in a valley on spacious grounds amid stately trees and verdant hills. The 80 rooms have fridges, good beds and nice touches like incandescent light. Try for a room on the front row above the swimming pool. A fabulous alternative is to take one of the private villas (US$43 to US$85 low season, US$50 to US$92 high season) in the wooded slope above the Orquideario administered by the hotel. They sleep one to five people, have kitchens, fridges and satellite TVs; six have swimming pools, which may be dry: great for boarders!

Campismo La Caridad (☎ 9-8487; per person US$5) is near the Arroyo Manantiales, 2.5km west

of Hotel & Villas Soroa. The 23 tiny four bed cement cubicles are on a nice grassy expanse with mango and coconut palm trees. A large cave is about 1km away. Like the others countrywide, this campismo fills on Friday and Saturday nights; other times it might be closed.

Getting There & Away

The only easy access to Soroa and the surrounding area is with wheels: car, bicycle or moped. The nearest train station is at Candelaria, 10km southeast of Villa Soroa. The station is on Calle 34, a few blocks south of Candelaria's central square, but only one train a day in each direction arrives from Havana's Central Station or Pinar del Río. You may be able to find a horse cart (three pesos) from Candelaria out to the Autopista, but from there you'll have to hitch a ride to Villa Soroa (for information on the risks associated with hitching see p433). Any Astro or Víazul bus will drop you at Candelaria as well. Official taxis are not available, but you might be able to resolve a ride privately.

Servi-Cupet is on the Autopista at the turn-off to Candelaria, 8km below Villa Soroa.

LAS TERRAZAS
☎ 82

The quaint, leafy community of Las Terrazas in eastern Pinar del Río, near the border of Havana province, dates back to a reforestation project in 1968. The surrounding mountains had been denuded by fire and shortsighted agricultural techniques, and the inhabitants lived in poor conditions. A reservoir was created in 1971, and beside it a model settlement was built, taking its name from the hillside terraces planted with pines. The experiment was so successful that in 1985 this area was declared the Reserva Sierra del Rosario, Cuba's first Unesco-sanctioned Biosphere Reserve.

In 1990, then minister of tourism Osmani Cienfuegos (brother of revolutionary hero Camilo Cienfuegos) approved an upmarket ecotourism resort here as a means of providing employment for the 890 inhabitants. Between 1992 and 1994 a hotel was built with workers drawn from Las Terrazas. A vibrant art community with open studios, woodworking and pottery workshops has taken hold – a great opportunity to get to know the artists and purchase their work

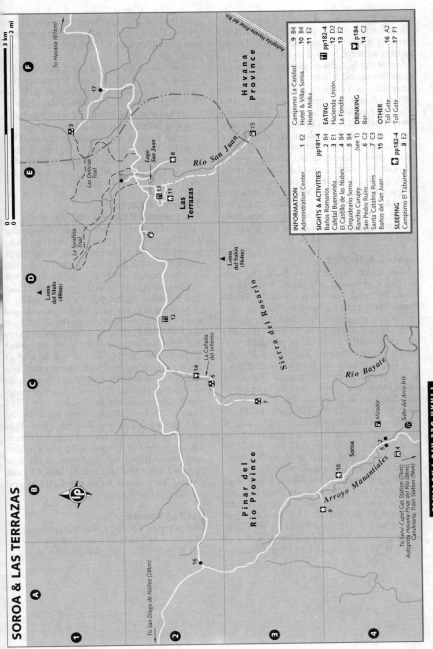

SOROA & LAS TERRAZAS

0 ___ 3 km
0 ___ 2 mi

To Havana (61km)

Havana Province

Pinar del Río Province

To San Diego de Núñez (28km)

To Servi-Cupet Gas Station (7km);
Autopista Havana–Pinar del Río (8km);
Candelaria, Train Station (9km)

Río San Juan

Río Bayate

Arroyo Manantiales

Lago San Juan

Las Terrazas

Sierra del Rosario

Loma del Salón (564m)

Loma del Mulo (486m)

La Serafina Trail

Las Delicias Trail

La Cañada del Infierno

Salto del Arco Iris

Mirador

Soroa

Autopista Havana–Pinar del Río

PINAR DEL RÍO PROVINCE

INFORMATION	
Administration Center.................1 E2	

SIGHTS & ACTIVITIES	pp181-4
Baños Romanos.................2 B4	
Cafetal Buenavista.................3 E1	
El Castillo de las Nubes.................4 B4	
Orquideario Soroa.................5 B4	
Rancho Curujey.................6 C2	
San Pedro Ruins.................7 C3	
Santa Catalina Ruins.................15 E3	
Baños del San Juan.................(see 1)	

SLEEPING	pp182-4
Campismo El Taburete.................8 E2	

Campismo La Caridad.................9 B4	
Hotel & Villas Soroa.................10 B4	
Hotel Moka.................11 E2	

EATING	pp182-4
Hacienda Unión.................12 D2	
La Fondita.................13 E2	

DRINKING	p184
Bar.................14 C2	

OTHER	
Toll Gate.................16 A2	
Toll Gate.................17 F1	

directly. Cienfuegos, who had a hand in the original reforestation project, is still heavily involved in Las Terrazas and regarded as the motivating force behind its success.

Las Terrazas is 20km northeast of Hotel & Villas Soroa and 13km west of the Havana–Pinar del Río Autopista at Cayajabos. There are toll gates at both entrances to the reserve (US$3 per person). The reserve's **administrative center** (☎ 77 29 21) is next to Rancho Curujey, a bar overlooking a bulrush-fringed lake, a few hundred meters east of the Hotel Moka access road. Here you can arrange guided hikes on La Serafina and Las Delicias trails, costing US$20 for one or two persons (two to three hours). Hotel Moka also organizes these hikes. Unfortunately these trails are poorly marked (deliberately?), so you really do need a guide. It's said that 83 species of birds can be seen in the reserve.

Sights & Activities

About 1.5km up the hill from the gate on the Cayajabos side, 6km from Hotel Moka by road, are the ruins of the **Cafetal Buenavista**, a coffee plantation built in 1802 by French refugees from Haiti. During the 19th century there were 54 similar coffee estates around Las Terrazas, although coffee isn't grown commercially here anymore. The huge grindstone (*tajona*) at the back of the property once extracted the coffee beans from their shells. Next the beans were sun-dried on huge platforms. Ruins of the quarters of some of the 126 slaves held here can be seen alongside the driers. The attic of the master's house (now a restaurant) was used to store the beans until they could be carried down to the port of Mariel by mule. There are decent views from here.

From just below Hotel Moka, a 3km road runs down the Río San Juan to small falls and natural swimming holes called the Baños del San Juan (US$3 extra). This popular spot has naturally terraced rocks with clean, bracing waters cascading into a series of pools. If it's too crowded for your taste, you

can bushwhack downriver to more private pools. There's a simple restaurant here serving palatable plates of fried chicken, rice and salad for US$3.

Hacienda Unión, 3.5km west of the Hotel Moka access road, features a country-style restaurant, horses available for riding (US$6/ hour) and a set of old coffee-estate ruins.

At **La Cañada del Infierno** ('the trail to hell'), midway between the Hotel Moka access road and the Soroa side entrance gate, a road follows the Río Bayate down to the 19th-century San Pedro and Santa Catalina coffee-estate ruins. A kilometer off the main road, a bar overlooks a popular swimming spot.

Sleeping & Eating

The **Campismo El Taburete** (☎ 77 86 70; US$5) access road begins on the east side of the bridge a few hundred meters east of the Hotel Moka access road, the campismo is 700m south. Attractively set on a hill, it has 11 concrete two-bed cabins and 36 four-bed units. It will be fully occupied by Cuban groups on Friday and Saturday nights, but it's good value.

Melting into the surrounding woods and with a tree growing through the airy lobby, the **Hotel Moka** (☎ 77 86 00; hmoka@teleda.get.cma .net; s/d/tr low season US$100/129/157, high season US$114/150/186; P X R) is one of Cuba's most interesting and well-maintained hotels. The 26 bright, spacious rooms have fridge and satellite TV and activities ranging from mountain biking (rentals US$1 per hour) to fishing. Horseback riding and guided hikes are also on offer. This place regularly receives recommendations. Through the hotel front desk, you can also rent the darling two-bedroom bungalow perched over the lake called **Casa del Lago**. Guests have access to all the facilities and services at the hotel.

Getting Around

The Essto gas station, 1.5km west of the Hotel Moka access road, sells especial gasoline for just slightly more than Servi-Cupet prices.

Matanzas Province

CONTENTS

Matanzas
Province

Matanzas Province hosts much of Cuba's tourist industry, both at Playa de Varadero and around the Bahía de Cochinos (Bay of Pigs). Varadero is Cuba's biggest resort center, with more than 50 hotels and all the facilities you could hope for. If anything, it's overbuilt. Gran Parque Natural Montemar in the south, contains the gigantic Ciénega de Zapata Unesco Biosphere Reserve, with terrific bird-watching. Scuba divers and history buffs will love Playa Girón on the Bahía de Cochinos. Other towns such as Matanzas and Cárdenas have museums and colonial buildings but little in the way of accommodation and are visited mostly by tourists in transit.

Matanzas is Cuba's second-largest province in area, and has Havana Province to the west, and Villa Clara and Cienfuegos Provinces to the east. In the 18th and 19th centuries, this was the heartland of the Cuban sugar industry, and towns like Matanzas and Cárdenas were built with sugar money. Since the 1959 revolution, huge grapefruit and orange plantations have been created in the province between Varadero and the Bahía de Cochinos. Fruit from the 300 sq km of orange trees around Jagüey Grande is processed into boxed juices.

The province's highest point is the Pan de Matanzas (381m), west of the city of Matanzas, which is mostly cattle country. Cane fields fill the fertile plains of western Matanzas. The southern half of the province is mostly marsh and bog; the Ciénaga de Zapata around the Bahía de Cochinos is Cuba's largest swamp.

HIGHLIGHTS

■ **Cityscape**

Picturesque bayside Matanzas, the 'city of bridges' (p187)

■ **Beach Adventures**

Skydiving, sailing, golf and scuba diving at Varadero (p202)

■ **Wildlife**

Amazing bird-watching and watching crocodiles hatch in the Ciénega de Zapata (p217)

■ **Scuba Cuba**

Underwater wonderworld (p220) between Playa Larga and Playa Girón

■ **Hidden Delights**

Old Varadero coastal road (p193), hiding out in the Valle del Yumurí's lovely Casa del Valle (p194) and exploring the Río Canímar (p192)

MATANZAS PROVINCE

| ■ TELEPHONE CODE: 45 | ■ POPULATION: 665,419 | ■ AREA: 11,978 SQ KM |

MATANZAS

☎ 45 / pop 126,220

Right on the Bahía de Matanzas at the confluence of the Ríos San Juan and Yumurí, Matanzas is a striking capital known as the 'city of bridges' for the six spans enriching the landscape. There's a pretty scoop of local beach on the eastern extent of town, with large industry huffing in the distance. Rather than a destination, Matanzas is more of a drive by on the way to Varadero, the lovely Valle del Yumurí or the coastal beaches just over the border in Havana Province. Still, Matanzas has an ambience and cultural vibe that enchants if you give it the chance. Public transport is quite good to and from Matanzas (see p196).

History

In 1508 Sebastián de Ocampo sighted a bay that the Indians called Guanima. Now known as the Bahía de Matanzas, it's said the name recalls the massacre (matanza) of a group of Spaniards during an early indigenous uprising. In 1628 the Dutch pirate Piet Heyn captured a Spanish treasure fleet carrying 12 million gold florins in this bay. Later, Carlos II of Spain ordered that a settlement be established, so on October 30, 1693, 30 families from the Canary Islands arrived to found the town of San Carlos y Severino de Matanzas. The earliest fort has long since disappeared, but the original Plaza de Armas remains as Plaza de la Vigía.

Matanzas only began to flourish after large sugar mills were established in the region between 1817 and 1827. Coffee also began to be exported, and in 1843 the railway arrived from Havana. By the second half of the 19th century, this was the second-largest city in Cuba, boasting a newspaper, public library, high school, theater and philharmonic society. Due to the number of artists, writers, musicians, and intellectuals living here at that time, Matanzas came to be known as the 'Athens of Cuba.' The most famous 19th-century resident was the mulatto poet Gabriel de la Concepción Valdés, better known as Plácido, who was executed by the Spanish in 1844.

Orientation

The compact old town lies between the Río Yumurí and the Río San Juan, with the historic Versalles quarter just to the north.

Most of the industry is east of Versalles. The Hershey Railway terminates in Versalles, but all other transport facilities are south of the Río San Juan.

Matanzas is on the Vía Blanca between Varadero and Havana, 42km west of Varadero and 98km east of central Havana. The Carretera Central from Pinar del Río to Santiago de Cuba also passes through the city.

The streets of Matanzas suffer from a capricious numbering system. In the old town the north-south streets bear even numbers, beginning at Calle 268 near the bay and rising. The streets on either side of the main square, Parque Libertad, are 288 and 290. The east-west streets increase from Calle 75 at the Yumurí bridge (Puente de la Concordia) to Calle 97 along the banks of the San Juan. House numbers give an indication of the location: Building No 28813 on Calle 85 is west of Calle 288, and shop No 8311 on Calle 288 is south of Calle 83.

Matanzas residents just ignore these arbitrary numbers and continue using the old colonial street names. However, we use the numbers because that's what you'll see on street corners (see the boxed text below).

Information

BOOKSHOPS

Librería Viet Nam (Map pp190-1; Calle 85 No 28612, near Calle 288; ☼ 9am-5pm Mon-Fri, 10am-2pm Sat)

INTERNET ACCESS

Etecsa (Map pp190-1; Calle 83 at Calle 282; US$6/hour; ☼ 9am-9pm)

LIBRARIES

Biblioteca Gener y Del Monte (Map pp190-1; ☎ 24 41 34; Calles 79 & 290; ☼ 8:30am-10pm Mon-Fri, 8:30am-3:30pm Sat, 8:30am-12:30pm Sun), on Parque Libertad,

MATANZAS STREET NAMES	
old name	new name
Contreras	Calle 79
Daoíz	Calle 75
Maceo	Calle 77
Medio/Independencia	Calle 85
Milanés	Calle 83
San Luis	Calle 298
Santa Teresa	Calle 290
Zaragoza	Calle 292

MATANZAS PROVINCE

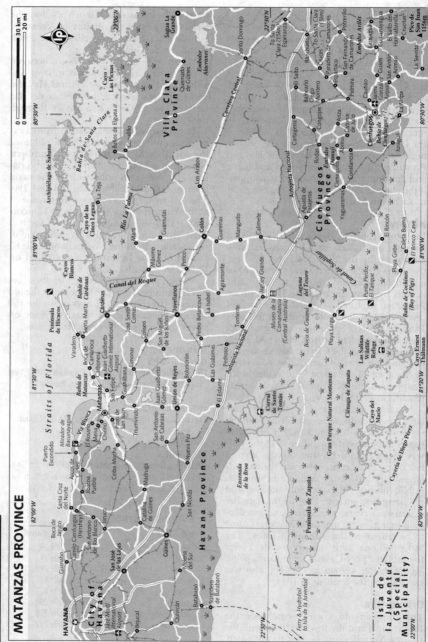

is one of the oldest libraries in Cuba (1835). Housed in the former Casino Español, this beautiful place is a must for bibliophiles.

MEDICAL SERVICES
Farmacia Principal (Map pp190-1; Calles 298 & 85; ☻ 8am-10pm)
Servimed (Map pp190-1; ☎ 25 31 70; Hospital Faustino Pérez, Carretera Central Km 101) Clinic just southwest of town.

MONEY   Map pp190-1
Banco Financiero Internacional (☎ 25 34 00; Calles 85 & 298)
Bandec (☎ 24 27 81; Calle 85 No 28604 btwn 286 & 288)
Cadeca (Calle 286; ☻ 8am-6pm Mon-Sat, 8am-noon Sun) Two portable kiosks here behind the cathedral.

PHOTOGRAPHY
Photo Service (Map pp190-1; Calle 288 No 8311, btwn Calles 83 & 85)

POST
Post Office (Map pp190-1; Calle 85 No 28813 at Calle 290; ☻ 24hr)

TELEPHONE
Etecsa (Map pp190-1; Calle 83 at Calle 282; ☻ 9am-9pm) International calls, fax and Internet.

TOURIST INFORMATION
Infotur (Map pp190-1; ☎ 25 35 51; cnr of Calle 290 & 83; ☻ 8am-11pm Mon-Sat, 11am-11pm Sun) Sells phonecards on Parque Libertad.

TRAVEL AGENCIES
Dirección Provincial de Campismo Popular (Map p0190-1; ☎ 24 39 51; Calle 290, btwn Calles 83 & 85; ☻ 8am-5pm Mon-Fri) Makes reservations for Canímar Abajo, Faro de Maya and Victoria de Girón.

Dangers & Annoyances
Matanzas doesn't have the heavy jinetero presence like some other Cuban cities, but 'characters' will try to latch onto you around Parque Libertad. It's not safe to park on Parque Libertad overnight (unless you pay said characters a dollar or two to mind said car).

Sights & Activities
IN TOWN   Map pp190-1
The steel **Puente Calixto García** (1899) spans the Río San Juan and leads directly into **Plaza de la Vigía** from the south. Three centuries ago the original settlement of Matanzas was established on this site. The Matanzas fire brigade still has its headquarters in the neoclassical **Parque de los Bomberos** (1897) just opposite.

Across the plaza is **Ediciones Vigía** (☎ 24 48 45; ☻ 8am-4pm Mon-Fri), one of Matanzas' most intriguing attractions. Founded in 1985, this unique institution produces handmade paper and first-edition books on a range of topics. The books are typed, stenciled, and pasted in editions of 200 copies. Visitors are welcome in the workshop and you can purchase numbered and signed copies for US$5 to US$15 each. They're genuine collector's items. Next door is the fine **Galería de Arte Provincial** (Calle 272, btwn Calles 85 & 91; admission US$1; ☻ 10am-2pm Mon, 10am-6pm Tue-Sat).

The **Teatro Sauto** (☎ 24 27 21), diagonally across Plaza de la Vigía from the art gallery, is one of Cuba's finest neoclassical buildings (1862) and famous for its superb acoustics. The lobby is graced by marble Greek goddesses and the main hall ceiling bears paintings of the muses. Three balconies enclose this 775-seat theater, which features a floor that can be raised to convert the auditorium into a ballroom. A work of art, the original theater curtain is a painting of the Puente de la Concordia over the Río Yumurí. Enrico Caruso performed here, as did the Soviet dancer Anna Pavlova in 1945. Your best chance of catching a performance is Friday, Saturday or Sunday at 8:30pm.

A few blocks directly west is **Parque Libertad** with several more of Matanzas' most stimulating sights, including a bronze statue (1909) of José Martí in the center. Head to the south side to grab a beer in the atmospheric old Hotel El Louvre (1894) before visiting the **Museo Farmacéutico** (☎ 25 31 79; Calle 83 No 4951; admission US$2; ☻ 10am-5pm Mon-Sun). Formerly Botica La Francesa, founded in 1882 by the Triolett family, this antique pharmacy has been a museum since 1964 and is crowded with all the odd bottles and instruments, porcelain jars and medical recipes used in the trade. The eastern side of the park is dominated by the orderly **Palacio de Gobierno** (1853), now the seat of the *Poder Popular* (Popular Power). On the northern side are the defunct Hotel Velazco and the former **Casino Español** (Calles 79 & 290), where the first performance of the danzonette *Rompiendo La Rutina* by Anceto Díaz took place. It's now the **Biblioteca Gener y Del Monte**.

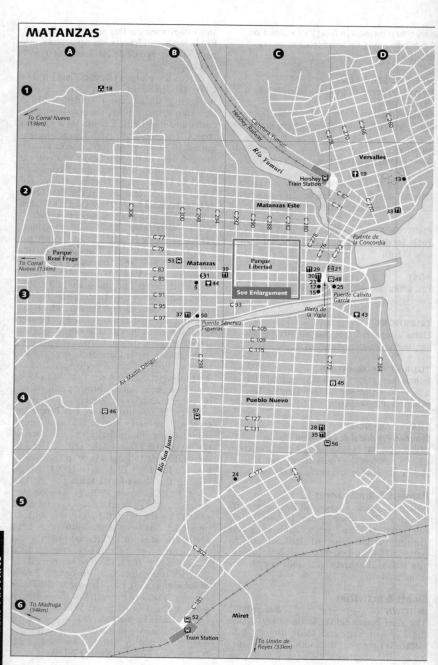

MATANZAS

To Corral Nuevo
(13km)

Hershey Railway
Carretera Yumuri
Río Yumuri

Versalles

Hershey
Train Station

Matanzas Este

Puente de
la Concordia

Parque
René Fraga

To Corral
Nuevo (13km)

Matanzas

Parque
Libertad

See Enlargement

Puente Calixto
García

Puente Sánchez
Figueras

Plaza de
la Vigía

Pueblo Nuevo

Av Martín Dihigo

Río San Juan

To Madruga
(34km)

Train Station

Miret

To Unión de
Reyes (33km)

MATANZAS PROVINCE

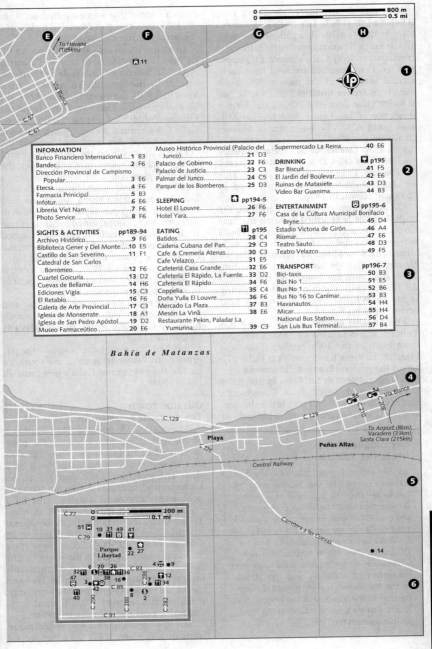

0 800 m
0 0.5 mi

To Havana (105km)

INFORMATION
Banco Financiero Internacional.....1 B3
Bandec..2 F6
Dirección Provincial de Campismo
  Popular.....................................3 E6
Etecsa..4 F6
Farmacia Prinicipal......................5 B3
Infotur.......................................6 E6
Librería Viet Nam........................7 F6
Photo Service..............................8 F6

SIGHTS & ACTIVITIES   pp189-94
Archivo Histórico........................9 F6
Biblioteca Gener y Del Monte.....10 E5
Castillo de San Severino.............11 F1
Catedral de San Carlos
  Borromeo................................12 F6
Cuartel Goicuría........................13 D2
Cuevas de Bellamar....................14 H6
Ediciones Vigía..........................15 C3
El Retablo.................................16 F6
Galería de Arte Provincial...........17 C3
Iglesia de Monserrate.................18 A1
Iglesia de San Pedro Apóstol......19 D2
Museo Farmacéutico...................20 E6

Museo Histórico Provincial (Palacio del
  Junco)....................................21 D3
Palacio de Gobierno...................22 F6
Palacio de Justicia.....................23 C3
Palmar del Junco.......................24 C5
Parque de los Bomberos.............25 D3

SLEEPING   pp194-5
Hotel El Louvre..........................26 F6
Hotel Yara.................................27 F6

EATING   p195
Batidos.....................................28 C4
Cadena Cubana del Pan..............29 C3
Cafe & Cremería Atenas..............30 C3
Cafe Velazco.............................31 E5
Cafetería Casa Grande................32 E6
Cafetería El Rápido, La Fuente....33 D2
Cafetería El Rápido.....................34 F6
Coppelia...................................35 C4
Doña Yulla El Louvre..................36 F6
Mercado La Plaza.......................37 B3
Mesón La Viña..........................38 E6
Restaurante Pekin, Paladar La
  Yumurina...............................39 C3

Supermercado La Reina..............40 E6

DRINKING   p195
Bar Biscuit................................41 F5
El Jardin del Boulevar.................42 E6
Ruinas de Matasiete....................43 D3
Video Bar Guanima.....................44 B3

ENTERTAINMENT   pp195-6
Casa de la Cultura Municipal Bonifacio
  Bryne....................................45 D4
Estadio Victoria de Girón............46 A4
Riomar.....................................47 E6
Teatro Sauto..............................48 D3
Teatro Velazco...........................49 F5

TRANSPORT   pp196-7
Bici-taxis..................................50 B3
Bus No 1..................................51 E5
Bus No 1..................................52 B6
Bus No 16 to Canímar................53 B3
Havanautos...............................54 H4
Micar..55 H4
National Bus Station...................56 D4
San Luis Bus Terminal................57 B4

Bahía de Matanzas

Via Blanca

To Airport (8km);
Varadero (33km);
Santa Clara (215km)

Playa

Peñas Altas

Central Railway

Carretera a las Cuevas

0 200 m
0 0.1 mi

Parque
Libertad

Parque
Libertad

Kids and theater lovers shouldn't miss **El Retablo** (☎ 61 70 38; Calle 288 No 8313; admission US$1; ☻ 10am-6pm Mon-Sat), a gallery filled with all the fantastic costumes, marionettes and creations made by Cuba's masterful puppet makers. Performances are held here every second Saturday of the month. Nearby is the city's **Archivo Histórico** (☎ 24 42 12; Calle 83 No 28013 btwn Calles 280 & 282), in the former residence of local poet José Jacinto Milanés (1814–63). A bronze statue of Milanés stands on the Plaza de la Iglesia in front of the nearby **Catedral de San Carlos Borromeo** (Calle 282, btwn Calles 83 & 85; donation suggested; ☻ 8am-noon, 3-5pm Mon-Fri, 9am-noon Sun). This neoclassical cathedral was constructed in 1693 and rebuilt in 1878.

Other impressive buildings include the imposing **Palacio de Justicia** opposite the Teatro Sauto, first erected in 1826 and rebuilt between 1908 and 1911. Also on Plaza de la Vigía is the **Museo Histórico Provincial** (Calles 83 & 272; admission US$2; ☻ 10am-noon & 1-5pm Tue-Sun). This large museum housed in the Palacio del Junco (1840) contains exhibits relating to Matanzas history. Free concerts are held here at 4pm on Saturday.

The **Versalles quarter**, north of the Río Yumurí, was colonized by French refugees from Haiti in the 19th century. From the Plaza de la Vigía head north on Calle 272 across the graceful **Puente de la Concordia**. The neoclassical **Iglesia de San Pedro Apóstol** (Calles 57 & 270) is worth seeking out. Four blocks east at Calles 63 and 260 stands the sinister-looking **Cuartel Goicuría**, a former barracks of

Batista's army that was assaulted on April 29, 1956, by a group of rebels led by Reinold T García. Today it's a school.

In an industrial area above the port, a little over 1km northeast of Cuartel Goicuría, is the 18th-century **Castillo de San Severino**, erected by the Spanish. To get there from Versalles, walk northeast to the end of Calle 57 and cross the highway. Entry is via the Centro Politécnico Ernest Thälmann on Calle 230. Continue straight, past the school, on a potholed dirt track and around the corner is the castle on the right. The guard of the adjacent warehouse will unlock the gate and give you a complete tour for a US$2 tip. Slaves were brought directly into the castle from nearby boats and held in sinister dungeons below. Later, Cuban patriots were imprisoned within these walls. A plaque recalls 61 persons executed here between 1895 and 1897. San Severino remained a prison until the 1970s. Three cannons, one dated 1775, and the central square are well preserved, and plans exist to turn the castle into a tourist center.

For an excellent view of Matanzas and the picturesque Valle del Yumurí, march north up Calle 306 to the ruined **Iglesia de Monserrate** (1875).

Baseball fans might want to make the pilgrimage to **Palmar del Junco** in the southern part of the city, site of Cuba's first baseball field (1904).

OUTSIDE TOWN   Map p193

The **Cuevas de Bellamar** (☎ 25 35 38; admission US$3, cameras US$2; ☻ 9am-6pm), 5km southeast of Matanzas, are promoted as *the* place to visit while in Matanzas. These 2500m-long caves were discovered in 1850 by a shepherd searching for a lost sheep. An underground stream is inside; a restaurant, pool and playground outside. One-hour visits into the cave leave every 45 minutes. To get there, take bus No 16, 17 or 20 east toward Canímar and ask the driver to let you out near Calle 226. From there it's a 30-minute walk uphill to the caves; a tiny railroad tunnel makes this road impassable for anything larger than a jeep or compact car. Other vehicles must follow a confusing, roundabout route via Calle 276, south from Calle 171, near the old railway station.

The Río Canímar, 8km east of Matanzas, feeds into the bay. It's one of the deepest

---

THE ORIGIN OF THE VALLE DEL YUMURÍ

An old Indian legend tells of a maiden named Coalina who was hidden away by her father after the prophesy of a terrible disaster that would befall the community if she ever fell in love. In due course a young chief of Camagüey named Nerey heard of Coalina's beauty and resolved to find her. Of course, they fell in love at first sight, whereupon an earthquake split apart the mountains of Matanzas and the waters of the Río Yumurí rushed toward the sea, destroying the village and carrying off the lovers. Coalina's last words were 'Yu murí,' archaic Spanish for 'I die.'

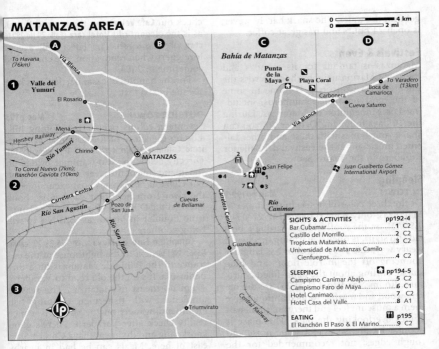

MATANZAS AREA

SIGHTS & ACTIVITIES	pp192–4
Bar Cubamar	1 C2
Castillo del Morrillo	2 C2
Tropicana Matanzas	3 C2
Universidad de Matanzas Camilo Cienfuegos	4 C2

SLEEPING	pp194–5
Campismo Canímar Abajo	5 C2
Campismo Faro de Maya	6 C1
Hotel Canimao	7 C2
Hotel Casa del Valle	8 A1

EATING	p195
El Ranchón El Paso & El Marino	9 C2

rivers in Cuba. Just before the highway bridge a road runs 1km down the western (ocean) side of the river to a cove where the four guns of the **Castillo del Morrillo** (1720) overlook a small beach. This castle is now a **museum** (admission US$1; 9am-4pm Tue-Sun) dedicated to the student leader Antonio Guiteras Holmes (1906–35), who founded the revolutionary group Joven Cuba (Young Cuba) in 1934. After serving briefly in the post-Machado government, Guiteras was forced out by army chief Fulgencio Batista. On May 8 1935, he and 18 others came to Matanzas to find a yacht that would take them into exile in Mexico. Before they could board, Guiteras and Venezuelan revolutionary Carlos Aponte Hernández (1901–35), who had served with Sandino in Nicaragua, were discovered by Batista's troops and shot. Bronze busts of the pair now mark the spot where they were executed, under a caoba (mahogany) tree down some steps from a cement gate back near the bridge. The shore behind the castle isn't a bad place for a swim.

Boat trips 12km up the jungle-clad **Río Canímar** depart from **Bar Cubamar** (26 15 16),

below the bridge on the inland side. Varadero tour companies offer this excursion with lunch, horseback riding, fishing and snorkeling for US$45, but you can work out something cheaper by showing up at the landing before noon. Rowboats are for rent at the bar any time.

The old coastal road to Varadero is great on a moped, providing better scenery and a mellower pace than the Autopista. There are some OK swimming spots en route and **Playa Coral** has 2km of offshore reef with terrific snorkeling. The airport access road is just beyond Playa Coral at the small crossroads town of Carbonera (a fresh fish lunch can be arranged here; ask around). One kilometer south of the Vía Blanca on this road is the **Cueva Saturno** (25 32 72; admission incl snorkel gear US$5; 8am-6pm). It's promoted as a snorkeling spot and Varadero companies include it on many tours, but don't believe the hype: it's really just a ho-hum cave with limited access (except for experienced cave divers who can explore tunnels leading to caverns thick with stalactites and stalagmites) and screaming crowds clamoring to get into the water. The snack bar, however, is open 24 hours and has great coffee.

Festivals & Events

Matanzas is famous for its rumbas and the spicy Marina neighborhood across the Puente de la Concordia is home to some of the most renowned rumberos, including Los Muñequitos de Matanzas. During the 10 days following October 10, you can shake your bones with these and other talented musicians at the Festival del Bailador Rumbero in the Teatro Sauto.

Sleeping

IN TOWN   Map pp190-1

Of the three colorful hotels in the center of Matanzas, only **Hotel El Louvre** (☎ 24 40 74; r US$18/25), on the south side of Parque Libertad (no sign), is open. Charming in a world weary way, this 1894 mansion has laughter bouncing off the marble floors and blue smoke curling about the palm-filled courtyard. Room Nos 1 to 4 (US$25) are divine: rare wood and marble-topped antiques give them a museum feel and there are small balconies overlooking the park. This place is popular locally, so expect some noise and rough edges; not recommended for the fastidiously clean.

Closed for what seems like forever (going on five years), the old-fashioned, 18-room Hotel Velazco on the north side of Parque Libertad is still shuttered to guests (but

---

CASAS PARTICULARES – MATANZAS

Ana Lilia Triana Abad (☎ 26 15 76; ana .triana@yumuri.mtz.sld.cu; Calle 129 No 21603 btwn 216 & 218; r US$25; ✗) Seaside house with two rooms, one with full kitchen; great back lawn and swimming; top choice if you have wheels.

Enriqueta & Exposito (☎ 24 51 51; Calle 79 No 29016 btwn Calles 290 & 292; r US$15-20) Two big rooms in center, both with bath & fridge, one with AC; friendly.

Hostal Alma – Alberto Hernández (☎ 24 78 10; Calle 83 No 29008 btwn Calles 290 & 292; r US$20; ✗) Two rooms in colonial house, one with shared bath, terrace, meals.

Roberto Chaves Llerena & Margarita Romero (☎ 24 25 77; Calle 79 No 27608 btwn Calles 276 & 278; r US$20) Big colonial house, meals, bike storage.

---

check out **Café Velazco** on the ground floor), as is the elegant old **Hotel Yara** (Calle 79 No 28216 btwn Calles 288 & 282). The latter will accept foreigners when renovations are completed sometime in 2004.

For the handful of casas particulares here see the boxed text.

OUTSIDE TOWN   Map p193

Seventeen cabins pepper the sloping hillside on the shore of Río Canímar at **Campismo Canímar Abajo** (☎ 26 15 16; cabins US$10). Directly below the Río Canímar bridge on the inland side of the river, it's a pretty spot. Bar Cubamar organizes boat excursions on the river from here. For easy entry, book ahead at the Dirección Provincial de Campismo Popular in Matanzas. Bus No 16 will bring you here.

Campismo Faro de Maya (☎ 26 31 29; cabins US$5; ✗) is next to the lighthouse at the entrance to the Bahía de Matanzas on a tiny peninsula. It's on the old road to Varadero, 17km northeast of Matanzas. The seaside ambience, with fishermen cleaning fish and mending nets on the shore, is a nice reality check after Varadero. There's good snorkeling and diving at Playa Coral 1.5km east of here. Meals can be had in nearby Carbonera; there's no restaurant here. Book ahead through the Dirección Provincial de Campismo Popular in Matanzas.

The **Hotel Canimao** (Islazul; ☎ 26 10 14; s/d low season US$24/30, high US$32/36; P ✗ ☎), high above the Río Canímar 8km east of Matanzas on the way to Varadero, has 120 comfortable rooms with little balconies catering to Cubans. It does excursions on the Río Canímar (US$15, including lunch) and the Cuevas de Bellamar (US$8). Bus No 16 from Calle 300 at Calle 83, in Matanzas, will drop you at the bridge downhill from the hotel. Nonguests can use the pool (US$3) and the Tropicana nightclub (p196) is next door.

Further afield is the tranquil **Hotel Casa del Valle** (Horizontes; ☎ 25 35 84; www.horizontes.cu; s/d low season US$28/37, high US$33/44), 7km northwest of Matanzas in the beautiful Valle del Yumurí. Go west on Calle 79 and take the road to Corral Nuevo, turning right (north) just past Mena. Another road leads from Vía Blanca through El Rosario. You can also get there on the Hershey Railway; the Mena station is only 2km from the hotel. The 40 newer rooms with fridge, satellite

TV and hot water are comfortable and have valley views. Horseback riding (US$3 per hour per person) and massages are also on offer. The restaurant is good and the staff very friendly. Hidden in a forest, this hotel makes a good base for visiting the Valle del Yumurí.

Eating

RESTAURANTS IN TOWN   Map pp190-1
While Matanzas has no paladares, there's a wide selection of state-run peso restaurants that, if you're willing to select from a limited menu, provide good fill-ups for US$1 to US$2. The pick of the litter is **Doña Yulla El Louvre** (cnr of Calles 83 & 288; ☉ noon-11pm) right on Parque Libertad. It does a simple tomato salad and veggie stuffed potatoes for six pesos. Another good choice is **Paladar La Yumurina** (Calle 83 No 29202 at Calle 292; ☉ 8am-9pm), which serves the house special egg sandwich in a bright dining room.

Most tourists eat at **Café Atenas** (☎ 25 34 93; Calles 83 No 8301; ☉ 10am-11pm), opposite the Teatro Sauto on Plaza de la Vigía. It offers pizza (try the four-way at US$2.50), spaghetti, sandwiches, chicken, beer and coffee. Watch for overcharging. Next door, ice-cream junkies will find their fix at **Cremería Atenas** (☉ 9am-9pm).

RESTAURANTS OUT OF TOWN   Map p193
There are two quite nice options outside of town en route to Varadero. **El Ranchón El Paso** (☉ 10am-11pm) is a simple, breezy place high above the Río Canímar, 8km east of Matanzas. Good pork or chicken meals cost under US$3. There's a full bar. Next door, the fancier, reader-recommended **El Marino** (☎ 26 14 83; ☉ noon-9pm) specializes in reasonably priced seafood, including lobster (US$7 to US$23) and shrimp (US$3 to US$6). There are egg dishes and soups for vegetarians.

CAFETERIAS   Map pp190-1
Cafetería El Rápido (Calles 85 & 282), next to the cathedral, is big, but bogus. Better is the **branch** (Calles 262 & 75; ☉ 24hr), just down from the Cuartel Goicuría in Versalles, with a nice terrace. Lots of cheap peso take-out windows exist on Calle 272 in Versalles, just across the bridge from Matanzas.

Privately operated **Cafetería Casa Grande** (Calle 83 No 29010 btwn Calles 290 & 292; ☉ 10am-8pm) sells good cajitas for pesos.

For ice cream it's the one, the only **Coppelia** (Calle 272 at Calle 127; ☉ 10am-10pm), near the bus station. Nearby is a private house doing a booming business in fresh **batidos** (Calle 272 btwn Calles 131 & 127).

CAFÉS   Map pp190-1
Mesón La Viña (Calles 83 & 290), next to the Museo Farmacéutico on the southern side of Parque Libertad, is a 19th-century grocery store turned café. Lots of worn wood and soaring ceilings lend it atmosphere. It's a nice setting for a cold beer; now if they could only do something about the grouchy staff. In the early morning, small take-out windows opposite the cathedral sell fresh peso coffee.

SELF-CATERING   Map pp190-1
Cadena Cubana del Pan (Calle 83 btwn Calles 278 & 280; ☉ 24hr) has loaves of 10 peso bread you can watch being kneaded and baked; they sometimes have the yummy round rolls too.

Groceries are available at **Supermercado La Reina** (Calle 85 No 29006 btwn Calles 290 & 292; ☉ 8:30am-4:30pm Mon-Sat, 8:30am-12:30pm Sun).

Mercado La Plaza (Calles 97 & 298), Matanzas' colorful vegetable market, is near the Puente Sánchez Figueras (1916). Many peso stalls selling fried things are here.

Drinking   Map pp190-1

Bar Biscuit (Calles 79 & 288), facing Parque Libertad, sells beer and little shots of rum. **El Jardín del Boulevar** (Calle 85 No 28805 btwn Calles 288 & 290) offers a nice open garden in which to sit and drink.

Video Bar Guanima (Calle 85 No 29404 btwn Calles 294 & 298; ☉ 10am-6pm & 8pm-2am). Only couples are allowed entry here, but singles will find willing partners at the door.

Ruinas de Matasiete (☎ 25 33 87; ☉ 24hr) is a dollar bar housed in the ruins of a 19th-century warehouse, next to the bay. It's near the entrance to town if you're coming from Varadero. Drinks and grilled meats are served on an open-air terrace, but a better reason to come is to hear live music (9pm Friday, Saturday and Sunday).

Entertainment   Map pp190-1

The **Teatro Sauto** (☎ 24 27 21), across Plaza de la Vigía, is a national landmark and one of Cuba's premier theaters; performances have been hosted here since 1862, where you might catch the Ballet Nacional de Cuba or the Conjunto Folklórico Nacional de Cuba. Performances are at 8:30pm with Sunday matinees at 3pm (see p189). The **Teatro Velazco** (Calle 79 at Calle 288), on Parque Libertad, shows movies.

The **Casa de la Cultura Municipal Bonifacio Bryne** (☎ 29 27 09; Calle 272 No 11916 btwn Calles 119 & 121), in Pueblo Nuevo, has cultural programmes most evenings at 9pm.

For the disco, karaoke and rum mix, check out **Ríomar** (Calle 85 No 29003 btwn Calles 290 & 292; couple US$3; ☯ 9pm-2:30am). Reasonably priced meals are also served here.

Capitalizing on its success in Havana and Santiago de Cuba, the **Tropicana Matanzas** (Map p193; ☎ 26 53 80; per person US$40; ☯ 10pm-2am Tue-Sat) has a branch 8km east of Matanzas, next to the Hotel Canimao. It's the same entertaining formula of lights, flash, tits and ass in an open-air performance space like the other Tropicanas.

From October to April, baseball games take place at the **Estadio Victoria de Girón**, near the Río San Juan, 1km southwest of the market. The schedule varies, so ask when the local team, Citricultores, will be playing. Don't expect Cuba's best ball here: this is equivalent to a farm team.

Shopping

The **Casa de Bienes Culturales La Vigía** (Map pp190-1; Calle 272 No 8501 at Calle 85), located on Plaza de la Vigía, has Cuban handicrafts, and there's also a small bar attached. For highly original handmade books that make unique souvenirs, head to Ediciones Vigía, which can be found at the other end of the same block (see p189).

Getting There & Away

AIR

Matanzas is connected to the outside world through Juan Gualberto Gómez International Airport, 20km east of town. See p211 for details.

BUS

Long-distance buses use the **National Bus Station** (Map pp190-1; ☎ 9-2923) in the old train station at Calles 131 and 272 in Pueblo Nuevo south of the Río San Juan. Matanzas has good connections to the rest of the country. Víazul has departures to Havana (US$7, 105km, 8:50am, 4:50pm and 6:

50pm) and Varadero (US$6, 35km, 10:05am, 10:35am and 6:05pm). Astro buses leave this station for the following destinations:

destination	cost	distance	departure time
Camagüey	US$19	474km	9am alt days
Cárdenas	US$4	51km	10:45am
Cienfuegos	US$7	194km	8am
Havana	US$5	105km	5:35am, 1:30pm
Santa Clara	US$8	217km	4:45pm
Santiago de Cuba	US$32	801km	10:40am alt days

Two seats on each bus are reserved for dollar-paying tourists, and tickets are sold the same day one hour prior to departure. When buses arrive full, the staff will try to get you on. Colectivos go to Havana for US$3 to US$4 per person, but unless you're a resident student, they won't take you.

Buses within Matanzas Province use the **San Luis Bus Terminal** (☎ 29 27 01; Calle 298 at Calle 127) for the following services:

destination	cost	distance	departure time
Canasí	US$1	21km	5am, 5pm
Cárdenas	US$2.75	51km	1:40pm Mon, Wed & Fri
Colón	US$2.65	89km	7:30am, 3:10pm, 3:55pm
Jagüey Grande	US$2.85	90km	1:30pm Tue & Thu
Jovellanos	US$1.65	54km	1:45pm
Varadero	US$1.50	35km	9am, 10am, noon, 2pm

Except for Varadero departures, you may be able to pay in pesos on these services, but forget about catching one of the private colectivos parked outside: fines are stiff for carrying nonresident foreigners.

HITCHHIKING

Catch rides to Havana from opposite the Cuartel Goicuría, Calles 63 and 260, in Versalles. For Varadero, take bus No 16 or 17 from Calle 300, between Calles 81 and 83, to Canímar and hitch from there (for information on the risks associated with hitching see p433).

TRAIN

The **train station** (Map pp190-1; ☎ 29 16 45; Calle 181) is in Miret, at the southern edge of the city. Foreigners must pay the peso price in dollars to the *jefe de turno*. All trains between Havana and Santiago de Cuba stop here. In theory, there are eight daily trains to Havana beginning at 3:21am (US$4, 105km, 1½ hours) and a Cienfuegos departure at 5:30am (US$6, 194km, three hours). Eastbound, there's a 10:03pm train to Bayamo (US$23, 684km, 24 hours), a 7:48am train to Manzanillo (US$25, 696km, 24 hours) and an 8:38pm train to Holguín (US$26, 683km, 13 hours). The Santiago de Cuba train (US$27, 764km, 13 hours) leaves daily at 4:41pm, 6:51pm and 7:30pm, stopping at:

destination	cost	distance	departure time
Camagüey	US$22	474km	7 hours
Ciego de Ávila	US$14	366km	5 hours
Las Tunas	US$20	602km	9 hours
Santa Clara	US$6.50	217km	3½ hours

In practice, these services are usually delayed or cancelled.

The **Hershey Railway Station** (Map pp190-1; ☎ 24 48 05; Calles 55 & 67) is in Versalles, an easy 10-minute walk from Parque Libertad. There are five trains a day to Casablanca Station in Havana (US$3, 90km, four hours) via San Antonio (US$0.40), Canasí (US$0.85, 25km), Jibacoa (US$1.10, 36km), Hershey (US$1.40, 44km), and Guanabo (US$2, 65km). Departure times from Matanzas are 4:33am, 8:30am, 12:43pm, 4:33pm, and 8:34pm (the 12:43pm train is an express and takes three hours instead of four). Ticket sales begin an hour before the scheduled departure time and, except on weekends and holidays, there's no problem getting aboard. Bicycles may not be allowed (ask). The train usually leaves on time, but it often arrives in Havana one hour late. There was a time when this train went right to the La Coubre train station, which is way more convenient than Casablanca; check if this is a possibility. This is the only electric railway in Cuba, and during thunderstorms the train doesn't run. It's a scenic trip if you're not in a hurry.

Getting Around

Buses within Matanzas are scarce. To get to the train station from the center, Bus No 1 leaves from Calle 79 between Calles 290 & 292. If all else fails, hail a bici-taxi just before the Puente Sánchez Figueras. A **horse carriage** between the bus and train stations costs one peso, a private taxi US$1. The **Oro Negro gas station** is at Calles 129 and 210, 4km outside the city of Matanzas on the road to Vara-

dero. There's also a Micar rental office here. Servi-Cupetand **Havanautos** (Map pp190-1; ☎ 25 32 94; Calles 129 & 208) are a block further on. A soda bar with snacks is attached. If you're driving to Varadero, you will pay a US$2 highway toll between Boca de Camarioca and Santa Marta (no toll between Matanzas and the airport).

VARADERO
☎ 45 / pop 18,000

At the end of the Vía Blanca, 140km east of Havana, is Varadero, the largest resort complex in the Caribbean. It's massive, with over 50 hotels and resorts, nearly 15,000 rooms and 50 weekly flights coming in from Canada alone. In December 2002, Varadero broke its own record when it received 21,337 visitors in one day. One foreign tourist in three comes to Cuba specifically to vacation in Varadero and with reason: the sun, sand and aquamarine sea combine with the all-inclusive resorts to deliver the perfect tropical getaway. And yet, Varadero lacks a certain intimacy. Cuba has such an intimate, embracing culture and while Varadero has 20km of superb beach, scads of top hotels and activities galore, it's got that generic resort feel; budget travelers (who are *technically* prevented from renting private rooms) might come away disappointed.

Although a Cuban holiday center existed here as early as 1872, international development only began in 1930, when the US chemical millionaire Irénée Dupont de Nemours built an estate, complete with a large mansion, golf course, airstrip and yacht harbor. Other wealthy Americans soon followed and Varadero became a millionaires' hideaway. Even Chicago Mafia boss Al Capone used to frolic here.

Orientation

Varadero begins at the western end of the Península de Hicacos, where a channel called the Laguna de Paso Malo links the Bahía de Cárdenas to the Atlantic Ocean. After crossing the Puente Bascular (Lift Bridge) over this waterway, the Vía Blanca becomes the Autopista Sur and runs up the peninsula's spine to Marina Gaviota at Varadero's easternmost point. From the same bridge Av Kawama heads west along the channel toward several big resorts. In general the Atlantic side of the peninsula (with the 20km of bright white sands for which Varadero is famous) is devoted to tourism, while the Bahía de Cárdenas side is where locals live (another Cuban community is in Santa Marta at the western end of the peninsula). The largest and most expensive resorts are to the east on Punta Hicacos. The quietest section of beach in the center of Varadero is between Calles 46 and 65.

The hotel, restaurant, entertainment, shopping and other listings that follow are roughly organized in geographical order from west to east, from one end of the peninsula to the other. Beginning around Calle 13, everything from hotels to groceries, becomes progressively more expensive the further east you go.

Information

AIRLINE OFFICES   Map pp200-1
Aerocaribbean Av 1 (☎ 61 14 70; Av 1 btwn Calles 54 & 55); Aeropuerto Juan Gualberto Gómez (☎ 61 47 23; Aeropuerto Juan Gualberto Gómez)
Air France (☎ 66 82 85; Av 1 cnr Calle 30)
Air Transat (☎ 66 75 95; Calle 30 & Av 3ra, in Apartamentos Mar del Sur No 13)

Cubana Av 1 (☎ 61 18 23/24/25; Av 1 btwn Calles 54 & 55); ⏱ 8am-8pm); Aeropuerto Juan Gualberto Gómez (☎ 61 30 16; Aeropuerto Juan Gualberto Gómez)

BOOKSHOPS
Librería Hanoi (Map pp200-1; ☎ 61 26 94; Av 1 & Calle 44; ⏱ 9am-9pm) has a good selection of books in English, poetry & politics.

CONSULATES
Canadian Consulate (Map pp200-1; ☎ 61 20 78; Calle 13 No 422, btwn Av 1 & Camino del Mar) also represents Australia.

EMERGENCY
Asistur (Map pp200-1; ☎ 66 72 77; Calle 31 No 101, btwn Avs 1ra & 3; ⏱ 9am-4:30pm Mon-Fri)

IMMIGRATION
Inmigración (Map pp200-1; Av 1 & Calle 39; ⏱ 8am-3:30pm Mon-Fri), where you extend your tourist visa.

INTERNET ACCESS
Most hotels have Internet access at US$5 to US$7/hour.
Tu Isla (Map pp200-1; Av 1 & Calle 13; US$5 for 3 hr)

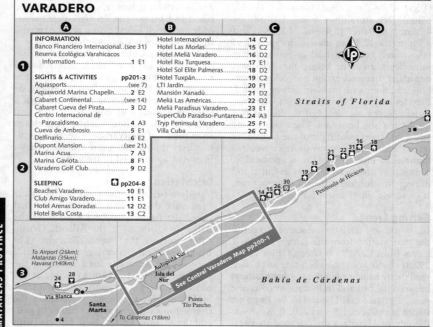

VARADERO

INFORMATION	
Banco Financiero Internacional..(see 31)	
Reserva Ecológica Varahicacos Información...................................**1** E1	

SIGHTS & ACTIVITIES	pp201-3
Aquasports..................................(see 7)	
Aquaworld Marina Chapelín.........**2** E2	
Cabaret Continental.................(see 14)	
Cabaret Cueva del Pirata........... **3** D2	
Centro Internacional de Paracaidismo.............................**4** A3	
Cueva de Ambrosio......................**5** E1	
Delfinario....................................**6** E2	
Dupont Mansion......................(see 21)	
Marina Acua................................**7** A3	
Marina Gaviota...........................**8** F1	
Varadero Golf Club......................**9** D2	

SLEEPING	pp204-8
Beaches Varadero.......................**10** E1	
Club Amigo Varadero..................**11** E1	
Hotel Arenas Doradas................**12** D2	
Hotel Bella Costa........................**13** C2	

Hotel Internacional.....................**14** C2	
Hotel Las Morlas.........................**15** C2	
Hotel Meliá Varadero..................**16** D2	
Hotel Riu Turquesa.....................**17** E1	
Hotel Sol Elite Palmeras.............**18** D2	
Hotel Tuxpán..............................**19** C2	
LTI Jardín....................................**20** F1	
Mansión Xanadú.........................**21** D2	
Meliá Las Américas.....................**22** D2	
Meliá Paradisus Varadero............**23** E1	
SuperClub Paradiso-Puntarena....**24** A3	
Tryp Peninsula Varadero..............**25** F1	
Villa Cuba **26** C2	

Straits of Florida

Peninsula de Hicacos

To Airport (26km);
Matanzas (35km);
Havana (140km)

Av 1
Autopista Sur
Isla del Sur

See Central Varadero Map pp200-1

Bahía de Cárdenas

Via Blanca
Santa Marta
Punta Tío Pancho
To Cárdenas (18km)

LIBRARIES

Biblioteca José Smith Comas (Map pp200-1; ☎ 61 23 58; Calle 33 No 104, btwn Avs 1 & 3; ☺ 9am-8pm Mon-Fri, 9am-5pm Sat) Present your hotel guest card to withdraw books (free); book donations happily accepted.

MEDICAL SERVICES

Many large hotels have infirmaries that provide free basic first-aid.

Clínica Estomatológico (Map pp200-1; ☎ 61 27 67; Av 1 & Calle 49) Dental clinic for Cubans, but tooth pain knows no nationality.

Clínica Internacional Servimed (Map pp200-1; ☎ 66 77 10; Av 1 & Calle 60; ☺ 24hr). Medical or dental consultations cost US$25 (US$30 after 4pm); hotel calls are US$50 (US$60 after 11pm). It's US$10 an hour if you're hospitalized on these premises; serious and specialist (eg ophthalmology) cases are referred to the hospital in Matanzas. There's a good dollar **pharmacy** (☺ 24hr) here.

Policlínico Dr Mario Muñoz Monroy (Map pp200-1; ☎ 61 34 64; Calle 27, near Av 1; ☺ 24hr) Intended for Cubans, but they don't generally turn sick people away.

Servimed Farmacia Internacional (Map pp198-9; Plaza América, Av Las Américas & Calle 61; ☺ 9am-7pm) Well-stocked dollar pharmacy.

MONEY

In Varadero, European visitors can pay for hotels and meals in Euros. If you change money at your hotel front desk, you'll sacrifice 1% more than at a bank.

Banco de Ahorro Popular (Map pp200-1; Calle 36, btwn Av 1 & Autopista Sur; ☺ 8:30am-4pm Mon-Fri) Probably the slowest option.

Banco de Crédito y Comercio (Map pp200-1; Av 1 at Calle 36; ☺ 9am-1:30pm & 3-5pm Mon-Fri) Changes traveler's checks; expect queues.

Banco Financiero Internacional Av 1 (Map pp200-1; ☎ 66 70 02; Av 1 & Calle 32; ☺ 9am-3pm Mon-Fri, 9am-5pm Sat & Sun); Plaza América (Map pp200-1; ☎ 66 82 72; Plaza América at Av Las Américas & Calle 61; ☺ 9am-noon & 1-6pm Mon-Fri, 9am-6pm Sat & Sun) Travelers checks and cash advances on Visa and MasterCard.

Cadeca (Map pp200-1; Av de la Playa & Calle 41; ☺ 8:30am-6pm Mon-Sat, 8:30am-noon Sun) If you're not venturing beyond Varadero or the tour bus circuit, you won't need moneda nacional, as foreign tourists can buy very little for pesos around here.

PHOTOGRAPHY   Map pp200-1

Film is cheaper in one of these outlets than in hotel shops. Five new Photo Clubs are slated to open in 2004.

Agfa Image Center (Av 1 & Calle 42) Most professional selection and services.

Photo Service (☎ 66 72 91; Calle 63, btwn Avs 2 & 3; ☺ 9am-10pm)

POST   Map pp200-1

Many of the larger hotels have branch post offices in the reception area.

DHL (☎ 61 44 52; Av 1 & Calle 42, upstairs, enter from rear; ☺ 8am-noon & 1-5pm Mon-Fri, 8am-noon Sat)

Post Office (Av 1 at Calle 36; 8am-6pm Mon-Sat)

TELEPHONE

Centro Telefónico Internacional (Map pp200-1; Calle 64, btwn Avs Las Américas & 2; ☺ 8am-10pm)

Cubacel Av 1 (Map pp200-1; ☎ 66 72 22; Av 1 & Calle 42, upstairs, enter from rear; ☺ 8am-5pm Mon-Fri); Aeropuerto Juan Gualberto Gómez (☎ 880-9280; Aeropuerto Juan Gualberto Gómez; ☺ 8am-7pm)

Etecsa Av 1 (Map pp198-9; Av 1 & Calle 30); Plaza América (Plaza América at Av Las Américas & Calle 61; 24hr) Sells telephone cards, international calls.

TRAVEL AGENCIES

Almost every hotel has a tourism desk where staff will book adventure tours, skydiving, scuba diving, whatever. It's almost always cheaper, however, to go directly to the tour agency or outfit.

Cubatur (Map pp200-1; ☎ 61 44 05; fax 66 70 48; Av 1 & Calle 33; ⏰ 8:30am-6pm) Reserves hotel rooms nationally, Varadero excursions, and bus transfers to Havana hotels (US$25).

EcoTur (Map pp200-1; ☎ 61 48 84; Calle 26 btwn Avs 2ra & 3ra) Jeep safari (per person US$59), snorkeling at Playa Coral, Valle del Yumurí tours.

Havanatur Tour & Travel Av de la Playa (Map pp200-1; ☎ 66 70 26; Av de la Playa, btwn Calles 36 & 37; ⏰ 8am-6pm); Av Las Américas (Map pp198-9; ☎ 66 77 08; Av Las Américas near Hotel Tuxpán; ⏰ 8am-8pm); Av Las Américas (Map pp200-1; ☎ 66 72 03; Av Las Américas; ⏰ 8am-8pm). Hotel rooms booked and bus transfers arranged to Havana (US$20) or the Havana airport (US$25), plus sightseeing excursions.

Rumbos (Map pp200-1; ☎ 66 75 67; Av 1 at Calle 13; ⏰ 8am-8pm) Sells excursions tickets and maps.

Dangers & Annoyances

Watch for mismatched electrical outlets in hotels. In some rooms, a 110 volt socket might sit right next to a 220 volt one. They should be labelled, but aren't always.

A red flag on the beach means no swim-

ming allowed due to the undertow or some other danger. A blue jellyfish known as the Portuguese man-of-war will leave burning welts across your body if you come in contact with its long tentacles. They're most common in summer when you'll see them washed up on the beach; tread carefully. Theft of unguarded shoes, sunglasses and towels is routine along this beach.

Twenty-four hours a day, long tongues of flame shoot up from two tall chimneys just southwest of Varadero, as excess natural gas from oil wells in the vicinity is burned off. Coming into town from Cárdenas and points west, you'll notice a nauseating smell as sulfurous gas is released from the wells. The offending odor sometimes drifts over to hotels on Varadero's western side. Persons with asthma especially should avoid staying anywhere west of Hotel Bellamar. We've received reports that Sherritt International was engaged in a project to clean the gas and convert it into electricity, but the stench lingers. Varadero itself may be sitting on top of the richest oilfield of all, and wells may one day sprout from the hotel gardens.

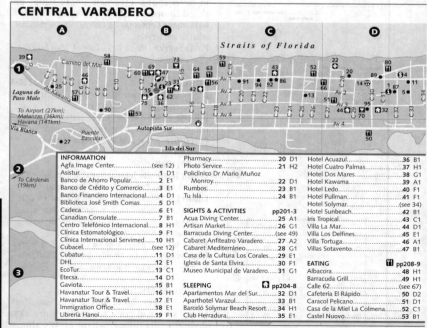

INFORMATION		
Agfa Image Center..............(see 12)	Pharmacy..............................**20** D1	Hotel Acuazul............................**36** B1
Asistur..............................**1** D1	Photo Service..........................**21** H2	Hotel Cuatro Palmas................**37** H1
Banco de Ahorro Popular..........**2** E1	Policlínico Dr Mario Muñoz	Hotel Dos Mares.......................**38** G1
Banco de Crédito y Comercio....**3** E1	Monroy...............................**22** D1	Hotel Kawama.........................**39** A1
Banco Financiero Internacional....**4** D1	Rumbos.................................**23** B1	Hotel Ledo..............................**40** F1
Biblioteca José Smith Comas......**5** D1	Tu Isla..................................**24** B1	Hotel Pullman.........................**41** F1
Cadeca....................................**6** E1		Hotel Solymar......................(see 34)
Canadian Consulate...................**7** B1	**SIGHTS & ACTIVITIES** pp201-3	Hotel Sunbeach.......................**42** B1
Centro Telefónico Internacional....**8** H1	Acua Diving Center....................**25** A1	Iris Tropical............................**43** C1
Clínica Estomatológico.............**9** F1	Artisan Market..........................**26** G1	Villa La Mar............................**44** D1
Clínica Internacional Servimed....**10** H1	Barracuda Diving Center.........(see 49)	Villa Los Delfines......................**45** E1
Cubacel................................(see 12)	Cabaret Anfiteatro Varadero.......**27** A2	Villa Tortuga...........................**46** A1
Cubatur.................................**11** D1	Cabaret Mediterráneo................**28** C1	Villas Sotavento.......................**47** B1
DHL.......................................**12** D1	Casa de la Cultura Los Corales.....**29** E1	
EcoTur..................................**13** C1	Iglesia de Santa Elvira................**30** F1	**EATING** pp208-9
Etecsa..................................**14** D1	Museo Municipal de Varadero.....**31** G1	Albacora.................................**48** H1
Gaviota.................................**15** B1		Barracuda Grill.........................**49** H1
Havanatur Tour & Travel............**16** B1	**SLEEPING** pp204-8	Calle 62...............................(see 67)
Havanatur Tour & Travel............**17** E1	Apartamentos Mar del Sur..........**32** D1	Cafetería El Rápido....................**50** D2
Immigration Office....................**18** E1	Aparthotel Varazul...................**33** B1	Caracol Pelicano.......................**51** D1
Librería Hanoi........................**19** F1	Barceló Solymar Beach Resort.....**34** H1	Casa de la Miel La Colmena........**52** C1
	Club Herradura.......................**35** E1	Castel Nuovo...........................**53** B1

Sights

The Parque Central and adjacent Parque de las 8000 Taquillas host the biggest **artisan market** (Map pp200-1; btwn Calles 44 & 46) in town and through the *uva caleta* (sea grape) trees is a pretty part of the public beach. Just east is the colonial-style **Iglesia de Santa Elvira** (Map pp200-1; Av 1 & Calle 47) and a monument to fallen revolutionary heroes across the street.

Around 1km east, the friendly **Museo Municipal de Varadero** (Map pp200-1; Calle 57, off Av 1; admission US$1; ☯ 10am-7pm) displays period furniture and Varadero history in a large, two-story mansion erected in 1921. Don't miss the two-headed baby shark and the fine beach view from the upstairs balcony.

Parque Josone (Map pp200-1; Av 1 & Calle 58; admission free; ☯ 9am-midnight) is Varadero's Central Park. The expansive, shady grounds feature an attractive lake with quaint bridges and geese flitting about, lots of lovely trees and a tranquil vibe. Girls celebrating their quinceñeras often hold their photo shoots here. The park dates back to 1940, when the owner of the Arrechabala rum distillery in nearby Cárdenas built a romantic mansion

here, the Retiro Josone. It's now a restaurant, and the family's guesthouse is Restaurante La Campana. For US$2 an hour you can float about in a rowboat. Also ask about the '**Noche de Santería**' (admission US$3; ☯ 9pm Fri & Sat) shows on the terrace between the mansion and lake. There's a public **swimming pool** (admission US$2) in the southern part of the park that's surprisingly uncrowded.

Everything east of the stone gate on Av Las Américas, near Hotel Las Morlas, once belonged to the Dupont family. Here they built a three-story mansion called Xanadu overlooking the coast and laid out a nine-hole golf course. Today the **Dupont Mansion** (Map pp198-9) is a B&B abreast Varadero's 18-hole golf course, with a restaurant downstairs and a bar on the top floor. Nearby, **Plaza América** (btwn Meliás Las Américas & Varadero) is Varadero's top shopping mall.

Beyond Marina Chapelín, 5km northeast of the Dupont Mansion along Autopista Sur, is Varadero's **Delfinario** (Map pp198-9; ☎ 66 80 31; admission US$10, camera/video camera US$5/10 extra; ☯ 9am-5pm). Dolphin shows happen here daily at 11am, 2:30pm and 4:30pm.

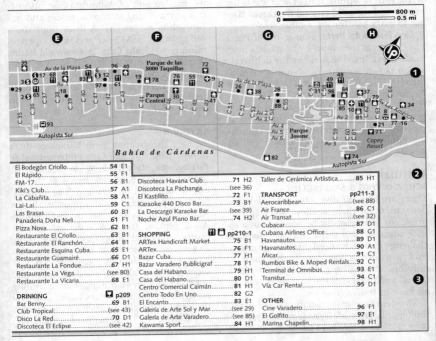

Swimming with the dolphins costs US$65. You're allowed to grab the dolphin's fin and let it drag you around.

East on Autopista Sur and 500m beyond the Club Amigo Varadero is the **Cueva de Ambrosio** (Map pp198-9; admission US$3; ☺ 9am-4:30pm). In 1961 some 47 pre-Columbian drawings were discovered in this 300m cave. The black and red doodles feature the same concentric circles seen in similar paintings on the Isla de la Juventud, perhaps a form of solar calendar. The cave was also used as a refuge by escaped slaves.

A few hundred meters beyond the cave is the entrance to the **Reserva Ecológica Varahicacos** (Map pp198-9; ☺ 9am-4:30pm). A gratuitous bit of greenwashing: the ubiquitous bulldozers making way for more hotels and the shrinking patch of protected land out here belie the purpose of an ecological reserve. There are three short trails (US$3 each, 45 minutes each), the highlight of which are a couple of caves and a giant cactus tree nicknamed 'El Patriarca.' **Playa Las Calaveras**, 800m of beach promoted as 'virgin' by tourist brochures is dotted with massage shacks and drink stands. At the time of writing, tons of land was being moved and removed around the **Laguna Mangón** to make way for yet another resort.

Cayo Piedras del Norte, 5km north of Playa Las Calaveras (one hour by boat), has been made into a 'marine park' by the deliberate sinking of an assortment of military equipment in 15m-30m of water. The yacht *Coral Negro* was sunk here in 1997, followed by frigate 383 in 1998. Also scuttled for the benefit of divers and glass-bottom boat passengers are a towboat, a missile launching gunboat (with missiles intact) and an AN-24 aircraft.

Activities
SCUBA DIVING & SNORKELING
There are over 30 dive sites around Varadero, many of them shallow dives appropriate for snorkelers or beginners, but also with some sunken ships and cave dives to challenge more advanced divers. One drawback with diving Varadero is that there is only one shore dive (20km away at Playa Coral) and the rest of the boat dives require an hour in transit (one way).

Varadero's top scuba facility is the friendly, multilingual **Barracuda Diving Center** (Map pp200-1; ☎ 61 34 81; fax 66 70 72; Av 1 & Calle 58; ☺ 8am-6pm).

Diving is US$35 per dive (US$30 if you bring your own equipment). Cave diving or night diving costs US$50, and packages of four/five/six dives are US$105/130/150. Snorkelers can join the divers for US$25. A scuba excursion to the Bahía de Cochinos is US$45/70 with one/two tanks, equipment included. Barracuda conducts introductory resort courses for US$70 and ACUC open water certification courses for US$365, plus many advanced courses. At last report, it was having a recompression facility installed with on-site doctor. A popular seafood restaurant is on the center's premises.

As a secondary option you have Puertosol's **Acua Diving Center** (Map pp200-1; ☎ 66 80 64; Av Kawama btwn Calles 2 & 3) in western Varadero. It charges much the same prices as Barracuda, but doesn't have quite the facilities, nor volume. When a north wind is blowing and diving isn't possible in the Atlantic, you can be transfered to the Caribbean coast in a minibus (90 minute drive); this costs a total of US$45/65 for one/two dives. Certification courses are possible.

Marina Gaviota (Map pp198-9; ☎ 66 77 55), at the eastern end of Autopista Sur, also offers scuba diving at similar prices and has snorkeling excursions. A three-hour snorkeling trip is US$35 per person (six-person minimum). **Scuba Cuba** at **Aquaworld Marina Chapelín** (Map pp198-9; ☎ 66 75 50; fax 66 70 93) also has snorkeling and diving trips.

Until Barracuda opens its chamber, a recompression chamber is available in nearby Cárdenas.

SKYDIVING
Perhaps the greatest thrill Varadero offers is skydiving with the **Centro Internacional de Paracaidismo** (Map pp198-9; ☎ 66 72 56, 66 72 60; skygators@cubairsports.itgo.com), based at the old airport just west of Varadero. The terminal is 1km up the dirt road, opposite Marina Acua. Skydivers take off in an Antonov AN-2 biplane (of WWII design, but recently built) and jump from 3000m using a two-harness parachute with an instructor strapped in tandem to your back. After 35 seconds of free fall the parachute opens and you float another 10 minutes before landing on the beach. It also offers tamer (but still thrilling) ultralight flights over the beach.

The price is US$150 per person, including hotel transfers. You can pay another US$45 to have photos taken of yourself during the dive or get a video of it all for US$50. Four pairs of divers jump from a single flight.

The parachuting center opened in 1993 and, although there's about 250 jumps a month, there have been no accidents. Jumps are only scheduled in good weather when the wind is exactly right, so start inquiring as soon as you get to Varadero and go at the first opportunity.

DEEP-SEA FISHING

Varadero's three marinas offer a variety of nautical activities and facilities. Many outfits are at **Aquaworld Marina Chapelín** (Map pp198-9; ☎ 66 75 50; www.aquaworldvaradero.com), where five hours of deep-sea fishing costs US$270 for four people (price includes hotel transfers and open bar; nonfishing companions pay US$30). **Marina Gaviota** (Map pp198-9; ☎ 66 77 55), at the eastern end of Autopista Sur and **Marina Acua** (Map pp198-9; ☎ 66 80 62), just west of Varadero, have similar packages. Book the latter through the **Acua Diving Center** (Map pp200-1; ☎ 66 80 64; Av Kawama, btwn Calles 2 & 3).

GOLF

While it's no Pebble Beach, golfers will certainly have a swinging session at the uncrowded and nicely laid out **Varadero Golf Club** (Map pp198-9; ☎ 66 77 88; www.varaderogo lfclub.com; green fees for 9/18 holes US$45/65; ⏰ 7am-7pm). The original nine holes created by the Duponts are between Hotel Bella Costa and the Dupont Mansion, and in 1998 the course was extended to 18 holes (par 72) by adding another nine holes along the southern side of the three Meliá resorts. Bookings are made through the Pro-Shop next to the Dupont Mansion (now a cozy B&B with free, unlimited tee time). A twilight nine holes after 4:30pm costs US$25. Club rentals are US$12, and an electric cart and caddie another US$27 (plus tip). A nine-hole lesson costs US$100 for one or two people, 18 holes is US$200. A bucket of 30 balls at the driving range is US$3.

It's also fun to play miniature golf at **El Golfito** (Map pp200-1; Av 1 & Calle 42; per person US$3; ⏰ 24hr).

OTHER ACTIVITIES

Kids love the **bolera** (bowling alley) inside the **Centro Todo En Uno** (Map pp200-1; per game US$2.50; Calle 54 & Autopista Sur; ⏰ 24hr), a complex with a giant, modern playground adjacent

and lots of junk food, making this a good family destination away from the resorts.

Windsurfers are for rent all over the beach (US$10 per hour) as are small catamarans, parasailing, banana boats, sea kayaks etc. The upmarket resorts usually include these water toys in the all-inclusive price.

Tours

Tour desks at the main hotels book most of the nautical or sporting activities mentioned earlier and arrange organized sightseeing excursions from Varadero. You'll pay a surcharge (usually US$5 per person) if you book at these desks instead of going directly to the tour operator.

Among the many tours offered are a half-day trip to the Cuevas de Bellamar near Matanzas (US$25/$49 with lunch, horseback riding, fishing and snorkeling); a 10-hour bus tour to the Bahía de Cochinos and the crocodile farm at Boca de Guamá (US$51, including lunch); bus tours to Santa Clara (US$52), Trinidad (US$69) and Viñales (US$139 including lunch); an 18-hour tour of Havana, including the evening show at the Tropicana Nightclub (US$129, including lunch and dinner); and an overnight Havana trip (US$159, including the Tropicana show and accommodation). One-day excursions by air go to Cienfuegos with a hike to El Nicho (US$149), Trinidad (US$126), Santiago de Cuba (US$168) and Cayo Largo del Sur (US$136). An overnight tour to Guama, Cienfuegos, Trinidad and Santa Clara is US$135. Solo travelers pay a single supplement (US$15 to US$25) on all overnight tours.

A visit to colonial Havana (US$63 including lunch) is a must and it operates daily. The other trips are often canceled if the minimum number of participants fails to sign up, so it's wise to decide early and make advance bookings. The day before your scheduled departure date, reconfirm that the tour will actually operate. Groups of four or more should be able to arrange a private guided tour for only slightly more than the prices listed above (ask at your hotel tour desk). This is much better because the guide won't have to translate everything into two or three languages, nor will you have to stick to a rigid schedule.

Gaviota (Map pp200-1; ☎ 61 23 67; Av 1 & Calle 13) has 25-minute helicopter tours in Russian M1-8 choppers over Varadero and the wonderfully scenic Valle del Yumurí. The excursion (adult/child US$79/68) includes a visit with a campesino family and a huge, delicious meal at Ranchón Gaviota on the shores of a reservoir, where horseback riding and paddle boats are available. There is also a similar tour in jeeps for US$68/51.

BOAT TOURS

The 48-passenger *Varasub* offers 90-minute underwater viewing possibilities six times a day (adult/child US$25/20), including unlimited soda or rum drinks and transfers. You sit on benches at the bottom of the air-con vessel and peer out through glass windows, though the boat itself doesn't actually submerge. Trips on Varasub can be arranged at any Havanatur office (see p200). The boat leaves from the Super Clubs Puntarenas in west Varadero.

El Galeón is a nocturnal boat excursion from **Aquaworld** (Map pp198-9; www.aquaworldvaradero.com; ☎ 66 88 86; adult/child US$49/free) including transfers, lobster dinner and a show or US$29 without the dinner. **Aquasports** (Map pp198-9; ☎ 66 71 66), at Marina Acua, also offers three-hour, glass-bottom boat trips at 9am and 2pm (US$27, including hotel transfers) and a four-hour yacht tour to the reef at 9am (US$30).

'Jolly Roger' (☎ 66 77 57; www.jollyrogervaradero.com; per person US$70; ⊙ 10am-4.30pm) is Aquaworld's best-known catamaran safari to Cayo Blanco, which includes the dolphin show at the Delfinario, open bar, buffet lunch (served aboard), two snorkeling stops, live music and hotel transfers. This comes with a free sunset cruise that includes dancing and a cash bar; you can split the Cayo Blanco excursion and sunset cruise over two days or just do the sunset cruise (US$25; ⊙ 4:45pm). Watch out in case you're told it's a lobster lunch and then it's US$10 more on board.

A similar cruise from Aquaworld is the **'Seafari Cayo Blanco'** (US$65). You get the same package as you would on the Jolly Roger, but have lunch on Cayo Blanco itself. Several readers said these trips were the highlight of their stay. There are cheaper catamaran tours that are less heavily promoted, but still great fun, with the same excellent snorkeling. Try the stripped down tour (US$40) that has no music and dancing, and a chicken, rather than seafood lunch. There's also a two-hour

guided **'Jungle Tour'** (☎ 66 84 40; www.jungletourcuba.com; per person US$39; ⊙ 9am-4pm) by two-person jet ski from here (bear-hugging crocodiles optional). Bookings for any of these can be made directly at Aquaworld or at hotel tour desks (for a surcharge).

Marina Gaviota has a seven-hour catamaran tour (US$70), which includes a chance to swim with dolphins held in an enclosure on a coral key called Rancho Cangrejo, followed by a lobster lunch on Cayo Blanco. The same tour on a yacht without the dolphins is US$65. Included are hotel transfers, snorkeling, swimming and line fishing.

Festivals & Events

The carnaval formerly held at Varadero in late January and early February is now irregular. Golf tournaments are held at the Varadero Golf Club in June and October and the annual regatta is in May. Varadero also hosts the annual tourism convention the first week in May when accommodation is tight and some places are reserved solely for conference participants.

Sleeping

Varadero is an extremely popular destination, so if you're picky about your digs make reservations. Of course, the cheapest and easiest way to come for a beach holiday is to buy a package tour with the airfare included.

The state authorities maintain their tourism monopoly at Varadero by prohibiting individuals from renting rooms. Since early 1998 this rule has been strictly enforced. In practice, people still do rent rooms (US$20 to US$25) and you'll be approached at the bus terminal or as you traipse down the street with luggage. This is the cheapest way to stay in Varadero, but it usually involves plenty of subterfuge as the owners try to avoid detection since big fines or even confiscation of their homes could result. It's frustrating that a billion dollar tourist complex should be unwilling to compete with a few locals renting out spare rooms. Independent budget travelers, especially, will chafe at the irksome guided hikes, escorted excursions and general handholding that typifies tourism in Cuba.

Hotels with low-occupancy levels often slash their rates to fill rooms. If you are traveling independently, you're better off in one of the places in central Varadero,

Overleaf:
Sunset, **Isla de la Juventud**
(p149)
GREG JOHNSTON

CHARLOTTE HINDLE

Che Guevara mural, **Plaza de la Revolución**
(p80), Havana

ANDREW MARSHALL & LEANNE WALKER

Gran Teatro de La Habana (p104)

Musicians, Santa María del Mar, **Playas del Este** (p132)

RHONDA GUTENBERG

between Calles 7 and 53. Many of the more expensive, all-inclusive resorts are east of Hotel Internacional. Head to any of these if you don't care too much about the price and want a quality beach vacation. Foodies, especially, will want to consider them as the food at more modest places is often anaemic. Take care selecting your resort as you could end up far from the action.

It's officially prohibited to invite Cubans back to your room. All-inclusive resorts are difficult for any nonguest, Cuban or no, to gain access. In fact their guests must wear color-coded plastic wristbands. This results in a rather sterile environment, with nothing happening beyond the tightly controlled precincts of hotel and beach. Eastern Varadero is also one of the most expensive corners in Cuba, but a pre-booked package can net you a US$200 single room for US$95. Travel agencies in Havana (p66) offer good deals if you want to arrange a Varadero getaway once you're in Cuba.

Among the many large resorts in eastern Varadero, several do stand out. The Hotel Internacional is an admirable choice. The location and facilities are good, the atmosphere lively and prices are lower than anything east of here. The Tuxpán and Bella Costa have commendable service and facilities, if you feel the package price is right. The three Meliá resorts offer top facilities, striking architecture, a relaxed atmosphere, great food, easy access to the golf course, and an excellent shopping mall. The area east of the Meliás is undergoing constant development; furthest east on the peninsula are the most luxurious resorts. All of the budget and mid-range hotels discussed here are west of the Hotel Internacional.

Accommodations listings here have been arranged west to east. In Varadero, 'budget' edges into the mid-range category and mid-range into top end, but once you figure in the food and drink that comes with the all-inclusive deals, some are quite good value.

BUDGET
Map pp200-1

Villa La Mar (Islazul; ☎ 61 39 10; Av 3 and Calle 29; s/d/tr low season US$26/34/35, high US$33/42/45; 🔀) Located 200m from the beach and without a swimming pool, this is among the cheapest hotels in Varadero. Breakfast is a couple of extra dollars, but skip the all-inclusive deal unless you drink a hell of a lot of beer. The

260 rooms in a series of newish, four-story blocks are patronized mostly by Cuban groups, which gives it a more boisterous atmosphere than most hotels here. It has an unreasonable 10am checkout time.

Hotel Ledo (Cubanacán; ☎ 61 32 06; Av de la Playa & Calle 43; s/d US$18/20) This two-story motel in a lively, local area in central Varadero, has 20 rooms with fridge. You can add breakfast/lunch or dinner for US$2/6. The beach is just across a park.

Hotel Pullman (Horizontes; ☎ 66 71 61; www.horizontes.cu; Av 1, btwn Calles 49 & 50) This intimate Spanish castle-style pension has long been a favorite for its fair value and good location. It's in an untourist area with some local atmosphere and a quiet section of beach just 150m away. It is being renovated and new prices are not yet set.

Hotel Dos Mares (Horizontes; ☎ 61 27 02; www.horizontes.cu; Av 1 & Calle 53; s/d incl breakfast low season US$35/45, high US$42/54). A good option if you can't get into the Pullman, this attractive old three-story building is about 70m from a nice beach. Rooms are dark, however.

MID-RANGE
Map pp200-1

Villa Tortuga (Horizontes; ☎ 61 47 47; www.horizontes.cu; Calle 7, btwn Camino del Mar & Av Kawama; s/d all-inclusive low season US$53/80, high US$58/90; 🅿 🔀 🖳 🕿) This very good value resort in western Varadero is squeezed between the beach and the canal, meaning even the cheap rooms have a view. The pool is big, there are tons of activities and all the rooms have balconies and satellite TV. The food is not bad given the price.

Hotel Acuazul (Horizontes; ☎ 66 71 32; www.horizontes.com; Av 1, btwn Calles 13 & 14; s/d incl breakfast low season US$35/48, high US$45/60; 🔀 🕿) You can't miss this eight-story blue high-rise with 78 rooms (all with balcony) on Primera Avenida. It's two blocks from the beach, and Disco La Pachanga is in a corner of the hotel (get a room well away from it).

Villas Sotavento (☎ 66 71 32; Calle 13, btwn Av 1 & Camino del Mar; s/d low season US$39/58, high US$47/67) If you prefer a little house to a hotel set-up, try one of these 25 older two-story villas, each with three or four double units. The 108 simple rooms vary considerably as these were once privately owned holiday homes, and the front door, living room, fridge and patio will be shared with other guests.

Aparthotel Varazul (Av 1, btwn Calles 14 & 15; s/d low season US$33/45, high US$40/55) Another decent choice for independent-minded travelers is one of these one-bedroom apartments with kitchenette and small balcony. Cooking your own food is possible (check that the kitchen has proper cooking gear). You can use the pool at the adjacent Hotel Acuazul, but the beach is some distance away. The Varazul is popular for long stays.

Apartamentos Mar del Sur (Horizontes; ☎ 66 74 81; www.horizontes.cu; Av 3 & Calle 30; 1/2 room d incl breakfast low season US$48/76, high US$58/86, hotel s/d low season US$38/52, high US$46/62; ☒ ☲) Affording some semblance of independence, the one- and two-bedroom apartments in this scattered complex have cooking facilities and living rooms. It's all several hundred meters away from the beach, but is decent value.

Club Herradura (Horizontes; ☎ 61 37 03; Av de la Playa, btwn Calles 35 & 36; s/d incl breakfast low season US$42/50, high US$58/67) This four-story, crescent-shaped hotel is right on the beach, which gets swallowed up at high tide. Accommodation is spacious, nicely outfitted with wicker furniture and those facing the beach have great balcony views. A few rooms have shared bath; ask.

Villa Los Delfines (Horizontes; ☎ 66 77 20; www.horizontes.cu; Av de la Playa & Calle 38; s/d incl breakfast & dinner low season US$51/65, high US$75/97; ☒ ☲) One of Varadero's best values, the 100 rooms here were recently restored and come packed with extras like satellite TV, minibar and safe deposit box. This smart resort with its own protected beach area is friendly and cozier than the big sprawling complexes nearby in central Varadero. Nonguests can use the pool here.

TOP END

Rates in these resorts are all-inclusive, and discounted if you take a package.

Hotel Kawama (Map pp200-1; Gran Caribe; ☎ 61 44 16/17/18/19; www.grancaribe.com; Calle 0 (zero), near Av Kawama; s/d start at US$89/149; ☐ ☒ ☲ ☲) This graceful old hacienda-style building from the 1930s was Varadero's first large hotel. The property is huge, so some of the 235 colorful rooms are a fair distance from the pool/beach/restaurant/tennis courts; the cheaper your room, the more removed you'll be.

Hotel Sunbeach (Map pp200-1; Horizontes; ☎ 66 74 90; www.horizontes.cu; Calle 17 btwn Avs 1 & 2; s/d low season US$60/96, high US$73/116; ☒ ☲) Formerly known as Hotel Bellamar (locals still call it that), this place is one block from the beach. The 282 recently renovated rooms are comfortable and serviceable, but overpriced unless you secure a sweet package deal (they abound). The small pool gets crowded and after a few meals you'll probably be hunting and gathering elsewhere.

Club Tropical (Map pp200-1; Horizontes; ☎ 61 39 15; www.horizontes.cu; Av 1, btwn Calles 22 & 23; s/d low season US$55/100, high US$67/110; ☒ ☲) Right on a nice piece of beach, this activities-oriented hotel attracts youthful package tourists. It's well located right in the center. Ask about cheaper two-bedroom apartments with shared facilities in the Iris Tropical annex nearby.

Hotel Cuatro Palmas (Map pp200-1; Gran Caribe; ☎ 66 70 40; www.accorhotels.com; Av 1 btwn Calles 60 & 62; s/d low season US$80/100, high US$100/135; ☐ ☒ ☲ ☲) This friendly resort right on the beach is run by the French Accor chain. Rooms are in a huge Spanish-style complex enclosing a swimming pool. Rooms No 1241 to 1246 were once part of dictator Fulgencio Batista's personal residence. Jammed together across the street are a series of shared two-story villas with another 122 rooms with fridges and toilet only (shower is shared). Odd perk: pets are allowed.

Barceló Solymar Beach Resort (Map pp200-1; Gran Caribe; ☎ 61 44 99; www.iberostarcaribe.com; Av Las Américas & Calle 64; s/d low season US$102/162, high US$133/204; ☐ ☒ ☲ ☲) A sprawling complex hotel block and two-story bungalows, this brand new resort is a good choice for families. There are kids activities, on-site babysitting, a playground and pools. All the rooms have a balcony or terrace and the bungalows are quite nice.

SuperClub Paradiso-Puntarena (Map pp198-9; Cubanacán; ☎ 66 71 20/21/22/23/24; www.superclubscuba.net; Av Kawama Final; s/d start at US$112/187; ☐ ☒ ☲ ☲) A mammoth place with 532 rooms in two eight-story towers, the impressive two-level atrium lobbies, a huge freshwater swimming pool (one of the biggest free form pools in Cuba), a sauna and gym are some of the attractions here. There are special kid's activities, a kiddy pool and ice-cream parlor on-site. SuperClubs maintain a strict no-tipping policy and the all-inclusive deals cover everything from bicycles to boogie boards.

Hotel Internacional (Map pp198-9; Gran Caribe; ☎ 66 70 38; www.grancaribe.cu; Av Las Américas; s/d low season

US$70/100, high US$90/130; (P ⊠ ☐ ☒) Opened in December 1950 as a sister hotel to Miami's Fontainebleau, the four-story Internacional is Varadero's most famous and fabulously retro resort. While it retains its '50s charm, the rooms are modern-ish and the facilities extensive, including a cabaret, tennis courts and massages. It's right on the beach. Restaurante Universal here is a teaching restaurant meaning conscientious service and extra effort. Bonuses include cool art (there's a large René Portocarrero mural in the lobby) and super-friendly staff.

Hotel Las Morlas (Map pp198-9; Gran Caribe; ☎ 66 72 30/31/32/34/35; www.grancaribe.cu; Av Las Américas & Calle; (P ⊠ ☐ ☒) Before the revamp this hotel was undergoing at the time of writing, the rooms were cluttered, but had nice terraces. With a facelift, this will be an affordable top-end option near the golf course.

Villa Cuba (Map pp198-9; Gran Caribe; ☎ 66 82 80; Av 1 & Calle C; s/d/tr low season US$79/139/199, high US$109/189/269; (P ⊠ ☐ ☒) Interesting architecture, a variety of accomodation and loads of activities make this a good choice. Families and groups of friends should investigate the two- to six-bedroom **villas** (low season US$127/189/239/299/339) which all feature communal living areas, fridge, TV and a patio. There are four rooms designed for disabled guests with bathtubs in the bathrooms.

Hotel Tuxpán (Map pp198-9; Cubanacán; ☎ 66 75 60; www.cubanacan.cu; Av Las Américas; s/d low season US$85/120, high US$95/140; (P ⊠ ☐ ☒) There are often phenomenal packaged deals (including from Havana) to this 233-room resort right on the beach. Don't be fooled by the blah building and lobby: all rooms have a terrace or balcony, the food is reportedly good and there's a welcoming pool and hot tub.

Hotel Bella Costa (Map pp198-9; Cubanacán; ☎ 66 72 10; www.cubanacan.cu; Av Las Américas; s/d starting at US$100/140; (P ⊠ ☐ ☒) Managed by the Spanish Iberostar chain, this all-inclusive resort was recently renovated and is a good choice for travelers with children. There's a kid's club, a separate pool for the under seven set and individual villas that provide a bit of familial privacy/bonding. This hotel abuts the golf course.

Mansión Xanadú (Map pp198-9; ☎ 66 84 82; fax 66 84 81; Av Las Américas; s/d low season US$120/150, high US$160/210; (P ⊠ ☐) Rated by many as Vara-

dero's most intriguing and intimate lodging are the six deluxe rooms in the Dupont Mansion. This was a museum until recently and the five-star rooms retain the 1930s furniture and decor from Dupont's days. Rates here include unlimited tee time. Built on a small bluff, beach access is just alongside.

Meliá Las Américas (Map pp198-9; Cubanacán; ☎ 66 76 00; www.solmeliacuba.com; s/d from US$140/180; (P ⊠ ☐ ☒) Parked on the eastern side of the golf course, this upscale resort is on a choice stretch of beach with terrific views. The rooms are big, the pool overlooks the beach and the meals are lavish. Golfers, especially, will be happy here. Kids under 12 stay free with their parents.

Hotel Meliá Varadero (Map pp198-9; Cubanacán; ☎ 66 70 13; www.solmeliacuba.com; s/d from US$210/270) This stunning resort has a seven-story central atrium dripping with vines creating a natural curtain from the open dome down to the lobby. Rooms overlook the golf course or the beach and it's a popular honeymoon spot. The Meliá Varadero sits on a rocky headland, so you have to walk a bit to reach the beach. Kids aged 12 and under stay here for 50%.

Hotel Sol Elite Palmeras (Map pp198-9; Cubanacán; ☎ 66 70 09; www.solmeliacuba.com; standard s/d from US$180/240; (P ⊠ ☐ ☒) Opened in 1990, this was the first joint venture between a foreign company and the Cuban government. The main horseshoe-shaped building fronts the best section of beach or there's the one/two room bungalows (from US$200/270) set in luxuriant, heavily wooded grounds. The hotel's huge lobby, with its bars, restaurants, caged birds, vegetation and many places to sit down, is well worth a walk around. There's a 24 hour pharmacy here (unit No 314).

Hotel Brisas del Caribe (Cubanacán; ☎ 66 80 30; ventas@bricar.var.cyt.cu; s/d/tr low season US$100/170/225, high US$115/195/243; (P ⊠ ☐ ☒) Another massive resort, this is distinguished by its intense programming for kids and a whopping 78 handicap-accessible rooms.

Hotel Riu Turquesa (Map pp198-9; Gran Caribe; ☎ 66 84 71; fax 66 84 95; s/d from US$87/132; (P ⊠ ☐ ☒)), near Aquaworld Marina Chapelín, is the first resort in a chain of quality, but largely indistinguishable, places including **Hotel Arenas Doradas** (Map pp198-9; Gran Caribe; ☎ 66 81 50; www.hotelesc.com; s/d low season US$105/165, high US$135/220; (P ⊠ ☐ ☒)); **Beaches Varadero**

(Map pp198-9; ☎ 66 84 70; varadero@beaches.var.cyt.cu; s/d from US$121/238; P ⊠ ⬜ ⬛), which has a party atmosphere (only guests 16 and over allowed), and **Club Amigo Varadero** (Map pp198-9; Cubanacán; ☎ 66 82 43; fax 66 82 02; s/d US$160/190; P ⊠ ⬜ ⬛), which is the former Gran Hotel.

The eastern tip of the peninsula at Punta Hicacos is five-star territory with **Meliá Paradisus Varadero** (Map pp198-9; Gaviota; ☎ 66 87 00; www.solmeliacuba.com; s low season US$170, high US$220; P ⊠ ⬜ ⬛), the lovely **Tryp Peninsula Varadero** (Map pp198-9; ☎ 66 88 00; www.solmeliacuba.com); and **LTI Jardín** (Map pp198-9; Gaviota; ☎ 66 88 82; www.lti.de; s/d from US$95/153; P ⊠ ⬜ ⬛), a good family choice with pro child care and lots of kids stuff. They all deliver the beauty, services and style you would find at any top Caribbean resort.

Eating
Map pp200-1

Since private restaurants are banned at Varadero, all of the restaurants that follow are government-owned. You can eat well for under US$10 and the variety (Chinese food one night, fondue the next) is unlike any you'll find anywhere in Cuba (including Havana). As elsewhere, we suggest you approach these state-run restaurants with caution. If they don't have many customers seated at their tables, it could be for a good reason.

Touts along Av 1 may offer you a lobster meal in a private home for about US$10 a plate. They're often better value but these arrangements are sometimes rip-offs. Clarify the price of virtually everything before sitting down.

There are lots of unpretentious places in central Varadero where you can eat light meals and socialize over beers to live music. Most places post their menu (with prices) outside, so you can decide (unpressured) whether to sally forth.

A good place for pizza is **Kiki's Club** (☎ 61 41 15; Av 1 & Calle 5; ☾ noon-midnight), where the terrace overlooks Laguna Paso Malo. **Castel Nuovo** (☎ 66 78 45; Av 1 and Calle 11; ☾ noon-11pm) is a good, solid pizza and pasta place, that also has chicken, beef and fish dishes, plus enough choice to satisfy vegetarians. Another terrific pizza place is **Pizza Nova** (☎ 61 48 06; Av 1 cnr of Calle 13; ☾ 10am-midnight). It also delivers!

The atmospheric stretch of Camino del Mar between Calles 9 and 14 is full of places to eat. On the beach is **La Cabañita** (Camino del Mar & Calle 9; ☾ noon-9pm) specializing in shellfish and meat dishes. **Las Brasas** (Camino del Mar & Calle 12; ☾ noon-11pm) has grilled meats.

Restaurante El Ranchón (Av 1, btwn Calles 16 & 17; ☾ 10am-10pm) A pleasant thatched dining hall overlooking the beach opposite Hotel Sunbeach. It's a simple, reasonable menu done well: shrimp with garlic, pork chops and fish filets each for under US$5.

FM – 17 (☎ 61 48 31; Av 1 & Calle 17; ☾ 8am-2am) With more local vibe than most Varadero visitors ever see, this simple place has sandwiches and burgers for US$1 to US$1.50, plus a free cabaret show nightly at 9pm.

One of the more enjoyable state-run places is **Restaurante El Criollo** (☎ 61 47 94; Av 1 & Calle 18; ☾ noon-midnight), which has typical Cuban dishes. **Lai-Lai** (☎ 66 77 93; Av 1 & Calle 18; ☾ noon-11pm) in a two-story mansion on the beach has set menus with several courses (won tons, soup, shrimp, rice and desert) for US$5.50 to US$8.

Casa de la Miel La Colmena (Av 1 & Calle 26) has a dozen different ice-cream dishes, plus fish filets (US$6) and greasy, garlicky shrimp. Also here is **La Góndola Pizzería** (meals US$2-4) with yummy pizzas, lasagna and tortellini with bolognese sauce. Head to the romantic dining room in the back.

For something different, **Restaurante Guamairé** (☎ 61 18 93; Av 1 btwn Calles 26 & 27; ☾ noon-11:45pm) dishes up frogs legs (US$5 to US$7) and pineapple and crocodile kebabs (US$14) reared at the Boca de Guamá crocodile farm. A small zoo with Ciénaga de Zapata fauna is next door.

Restaurante La Vega (☎ 61 47 19; Av de la Playa & Calle 36; ☾ noon-11pm) Finally! A Cuban restaurant with ambience. Dark wood, leather chairs, a wrap around porch and interesting art and architecture make this place special. Stick to the delicious vegetable (US$4.25) or seafood (US$7) paella and save room for flan al ron (US$2.25). Connected to the Casa del Habano, there's an upstairs cigar lounge for after dinner smokes (replete with beach views).

Restaurante Esquina Cuba (☎ 61 40 19; Av 1 cnr of Calle 36; complete meal US$12; ☾ noon-11:45pm) Made famous by its most illustrious diner Compay Segundo, this place has since been winning fans with its pork/chicken/ropa vieja special. Great Cuban ephemera lines the walls, including B&W photos of Varadero in its mafia hang-out heyday. You'll eat well here.

Restaurante La Vicaria (☎ 61 47 21; Av 1 & Calle 38; meals US$2-3.50; ☯ 10:30am-10pm) Set meals of fish, pork or chicken include a beer – like all La Vicarias, the price and service make this one of the most popular places in town. There's also a nice garden.

El Bodegón Criollo (☎ 66 77 84; Av de la Playa btwn Calles 40 & 41; ☯ noon-11pm) This takeoff located on La Bodeguita del Medio in Havana, has better prices and a beach view. Try the US$6.75 special, a typical huge plate of *comida criolla*.

There are several upscale restaurants in **Parque Josone** (Av 1 btwn Calles 56 & 59). These include **El Retiro** (☎ 66 73 16; ☯ noon-10pm) with international cuisine and good lobster, **Dante** (☎ 66 77 38) with Italian food and **Restaurante La Campana** (☎ 66 72 24) with Cuban dishes. On the edge of the park is **La Casa de Antigüedades** (Av 1 & Calle 59), an old mansion crammed with antiques where beef, fish, and shellfish dishes are served beneath chandeliers.

The popular **Barracuda Grill** (Calle 58 off Av 1; complete meals US$7; ☯ 11am-7pm), in a thatched pavilion overlooking the beach on the grounds of the Barracuda Diving Center, has terrific fish and shellfish offers. Fish, squid, shrimp, and lobster are also on the menu at beachside **Albacora** (☎ 61 36 50; Av 1 & Calle 59; buffet US$9; ☯ 10am-11pm). Check out the open bar offer (US$5; ☯ noon to 4pm).

A few more upscale restaurants are opposite the Hotel Cuatro Palmas, Av 1 and Calle 62, including **Restaurante La Fondue** (☎ 66 77 47; ☯ noon-11pm) with surprisingly good Swiss French cuisine for US$10 to US$20. Next door, **Calle 62** is a fun, open air bar with tasty light meals like omelettes, hot dogs and hamburgers. Live music happens here nightly from 9pm to midnight.

Heladería Coppelia (Av 1 btwn Calles 44 and 46; ☯ 3pm-11pm) tucked back in Parque de las 8000 Taquillas, serves ice-cream sundaes for US$1. If you're craving hazelnut, coffee, tiramisu or other exotic ice-cream flavors, go straight to **Bim Bom** (Av 1 btwn Calles 24 and 25; ☯ 10am-11pm). This is high-quality, creamy stuff.

SELF-CATERING
There are **grocery stores** (Map pp200-1; Calle 13 No 9, btwn Av 1 & Camino del Mar; ☯ 9am-6:45pm); beside **Aparthotel Varazul** (Map pp200-1; Calle 15, off Av 1; ☯ 9am-7pm); at **Caracol Pelicano** (Map pp200-1; Calle

27 & Av 3; ☯ 9am-7:45pm); at **Club Herradura** (Map pp200-1; Av de la Playa & Calle 36; ☯ 9am-7pm) and at **Cabañas del Sol** (Map pp198-9; Av Las Américas; ☯ 9am-7:45pm) near Hotel Internacional. Always check prices at these places, so the cashier doesn't overcharge you. Shops in the large resorts gouge their guests for mineral water etc.

The only place where you can always find bread and pastries is **Panadería Doña Neli** (Map pp200-1; Av 1 & Calle 43; 24hr).

Drinking
Bar Benny (Map pp200-1; Camino del Mar, btwn Calles 12 & 13; ☯ noon-midnight) A tribute to the 'Barbarian of Rythym' Benny Moré, this place has a kicking, jazz-den energy, with B&W photos of the legendary musician lining the walls and his velvety voice oozing from the sound system. Post-playa cocktails and olives recommended here.

Bar Dragón (Map pp200-1; Av 1 & Calle 18; ☯ 6pm-2am), connected to the Lai-Lai mansion-restaurant, is good for a drink or three.

Noche Azul Piano Bar (Map pp200-1; Calle 60 at Av 3; ☯ from 9pm), at the entrance to Hotel Atabey, is nice for a nightcap.

Bar Mirador (Map pp198-9; Av Las Américas; admission incl 2 drinks US$2), on the top floor of the Dupont Mansion, has a happy hour from 5pm to 7pm daily. Head up to enjoy the sunset and a poke around this historic house.

Entertainment
TROVA & TRADITIONAL MUSIC
Casa de la Cultura Los Corales (Map pp200-1; ☎ 61 25 62; Av 1 & Calle 34) has an open-air theater. Local folk singers perform at its Café Cantante every Thursday at 10pm (US$5 admission). You can also catch 'filin' ('feeling') matinees, where singers pour their heart into Neil Sedaka–style crooning. You can hire an instructor here for Cuban music or take dance lessons for around US$2 an hour.

DANCE CLUBS
Several places located in central Varadero are foreigner and Cuban friendly. **Discoteca La Pachanga** (Map pp200-1; ☎ 61 45 71; Av 1 & Calle 13; ☯ 11pm-3am), at Hotel Acuazul, is one of Varadero's hottest clubs. Nearby **Karaoke 440 Disco Bar** (Map pp200-1; Camino del Mar btwn Calles 14 & 15; admission US$2; ☯ 10:30pm-3am) mixes up drunk, warbling wannabes with disco dancing. **Discoteca El Eclipse** (Map pp200-1; Av 1 & Calle 17) is on the 14th floor at Hotel Sunbeach.

You can check the mic, one, two at **La Descarga Karaoke Bar** (Map pp200-1; admission US$3; 🕑 10pm-5am) in the strip mall next to the Hotel Kawama.

When people actually turn out, good local atmosphere is to be had at **Disco La Red** (Map pp200-1; ☎ 61 31 30; Av 3, btwn Calles 29 & 30; admission US$1; 🕑 from 11pm). Unrivaled for sexy, sweaty dancing is **El Kastillito** (Map pp200-1; ☎ 61 38 88; Av de la Playa & Calle 49; admission US$1; 🕑 8pm-3am, Sun matinee 2pm) on the beach. Barefoot, synchronized couples scuffing sand beneath their feet add to the five-star local energy here. The beach bar serves drinks and meals all day.

Discoteca Havana Club (Map pp200-1; ☎ 61 18 07; Av 3 at Calle 62; admission US$5) at the Centro Comercial Copey, is another tourist disco, which welcomes Cubans. Expect big, boisterous crowds, including possessive, aggressive men in stereotypical style.

Discoteca La Salsa (Map pp198-9; 🕑 11pm-3am daily) above the reception desk at SuperClub Paradiso-Puntarena, at the western end of Varadero, attracts a foreign crowd.

Varadero's most modern video disco is **Discoteca La Bamba** (Map pp198-9; guests/nonguests free/US$10; 🕑 10pm-4am) at Hotel Tuxpán, in eastern Varadero. It plays mostly Latin music (and we've heard that for security reasons the fire escapes may be locked).

Since the Palacio de la Rumba was shut down, **Club Mambo** (Map pp198-9; ☎ 66 86 65; Av Las Américas; open bar, admission US$10; 🕑 10am-2am Mon-Fri, 10am-3am Sat & Sun) next to Club Amigo Varadero in the eastern part of town, has been Varadero's hippest nightclub. The quality live music attracts all types, but at this price to get in, don't expect many Cubans. There's a pool table if you don't feel like dancing.

Some of these discos have a youth disco on Sunday afternoon with a low admission fee. Although these are intended mostly for Cuban teens, you'll be admitted if they think you'll fit in.

Disco Splash (Map pp198-9) in western Varadero was closed for renovations but is worth checking out.

CABARETS

The **Cabaret Anfiteatro Varadero** (Map pp200-1; ☎ 61 99 38; Vía Blanca & Carretera Sur), just west of the bridge into Varadero, has a gala open-air floor show similar to that of the Tropicana. It's used mostly for special occasions and doesn't open every week.

A cabaret show is presented on a stage below the restaurant at **Hotel Kawama** (Map pp200-1; Calle 0, near Av Kawama; admission incl 2 drinks US$5; 🕑 11pm nightly except Sun).

Cabaret Mediterráneo (Map pp200-1; Islazul; ☎ 61 24 60; Av 1 & Calle 54; admission US$10; 🕑 doors 8:30pm, show 10pm) presents a professional two-hour show in an open-air location beneath thatched roofs nightly at 10pm. On a good night, it's worth the money.

Hotel Internacional's **Cabaret Continental** (Map pp198-9; Av Las Américas; admission incl drink US$25; 🕑 show 10pm) stages a 2½ hour floor show Tuesday to Sunday involving 40 singers and dancers. It costs US$40 for dinner (8pm) before the show. After midnight the cabaret becomes a disco (US$5), and Sunday afternoon there's a youth disco for teens. Make reservations through your hotel tour desk.

A few blocks east of the Caberet Continental is **Habana Café** (Map pp198-9; Av Las Américas; admission US$10; 🕑 9pm-2am) that has a talented floor show followed by disco dancing. It's an older crowd than the Cueva del Pirata set.

Cabaret Cueva del Pirata (Map pp198-9; ☎ 66 77 51; Autopista Sur; open bar US$10; 🕑 10pm-3am daily except Sun) 1km east of the Hotel Sol Elite Palmeras, presents scantily clad dancers in a Cuban-style floor show with a buccaneer twist (eye patches, swashbuckling moves etc). This cabaret is inside a natural cave and once the show is over, the disco begins. Most hotel tour desks can arrange return hotel transfers. It's a popular place, attracting a young crowd.

CINEMAS

Cine Varadero (Map pp200-1; Av de la Playa, btwn Calles 42 & 43; admission US$2; 🕑 6:30pm) When film festivals are on, there's a second showing at 8:30pm.

Shopping

Av 1, from the Laguna to Parque Josone, is strung with **artisan markets**, all selling the same wide selection of souvenirs and handicrafts, including items (particularly leather work) you won't find in the Havana markets. For one stop shopping, the big market at Parque Central is good, while the smaller, friendly market at Av 1 between Calles 51 and 52 is recommended for browsing. The **ARTex Handicraft Market** (Map pp200-1; Av 1 & Calle 12; 🕑 9am-9pm) is conveniently located next to a proper ARTex store, with an excellent selection of compact discs, cassettes, T-shirts and even a few musical instruments.

For cigars, the **Casa del Habano** Av 1 btwn Calles 31 & 32 (Map pp200-1; 9am-6pm); Av 1 & Calle 63 (Map pp200-1; 66 78 43; 9am-7pm) is warmly recommended for its top-quality merchandise and helpful service. Here you can buy cigars as they're rolled or head inside for more exclusive smokes. This is a good place for novice smokers or gift seekers to learn about this wonderful weed. Beware of guys on the street peddling black-market cigars, as the sealed boxes are often full of sand or low-quality cigars. Always insist on a receipt to prove to Cuban customs that you purchased your cigars at an official outlet.

Unique keepsakes and treasures are to be had at **Galería de Arte Varadero** (Map pp200-1; Av 1 btwn Calles 59 & 60; 9am-7pm) where antique jewelry, museum-quality silver and glass, paintings and other heirlooms from Varadero's by-gone bourgeois days are sold. As most items here are of patrimonial importance, everything is already conveniently tagged with export permission. Next door, you can buy fine artistic pottery made on the premises at the **Taller de Cerámica Artística** (Map pp200-1; 9am-7pm). Most items are in the US$200 to US$250 range.

Caracol shops in the main hotels sell souvenirs, postcards, T-shirts, clothes, alcohol and some snack foods. The prices are usually as good as those elsewhere. In the same vein but with a more cultural angle is the **Galería de Arte Sol y Mar** (Map pp200-1; Av 1 & Calle 34; 9am-6pm) at the Casa de la Cultura Los Corales, with musical instruments, compact discs, paintings and souvenirs.

For merchandise a bit more distinctive, try the **Bazar Varadero Publicigraf** (Map pp200-1; Av 1 & Calle 44; 9am-7pm) in Parque Central. It's good for ceramics, reproductions of famous paintings, artistic postcards, dolls, wall hangings, T-shirts and books. A clothing boutique is adjacent.

El Encanto (Map pp200-1; Av 1 & Calle 41; 9am-5pm Mon-Sat, 9am-noon Sun) is a dollar department where Cubans go on a shopping frenzy. This is the place to come for everyday clothes, radios, school supplies etc.

For the largest selection of compact discs and cassettes, try **ARTex** (Map pp200-1; Av 1 btwn Calles 46 & 47). **Kawama Sport** (Map pp200-1; Av 1 & Calle 60; 9am-8pm) sells beach clothing, snorkeling gear and occasionally bicycles.

One of Varadero's main shopping malls is the **Centro Comercial Caimán** (Map pp200-1; Av 1 & Calle 62; 9am-8pm), opposite Hotel Cuatro Palmas. For American-style consumerism and useful services, head to **Plaza América** (Map pp198-9), Varadero's largest shopping complex. Here you'll find fancy boutiques, music shops, cigar store, bars, restaurants, bank, post office, a **mini-market** (10am-8:30pm), car rental desks, absolutely everything and the Varadero Convention Center. The parking lot is a rip-off at US$4 a day.

Bazar Cuba (Map pp200-1; Av Las Américas & Calle 64) has the greatest selection of souvenirs and crafts in Varadero. It also sells beach clothing, jewelry and books.

Getting There & Away

AIR
Juan Gualberto Gómez (airport code VRA) International Airport is 20km from Varadero toward Matanzas and another 6km off the main highway. Airlines here include Cubana from Buenos Aires and Toronto; LTU International Airways from Düsseldorf and four other German cities; Martinair from Amsterdam; and Air Transat and Skyservice from various Canadian cities. The check-in time at Varadero is 90 minutes before flight time.

At the time of writing, Cubana had suspended domestic flights to Varadero.

BUS
Terminal de Omnibus (Map pp200-1; 61 26 26; Calle 36 & Autopista Sur) has daily long-distance Astro bus services to Havana at 8:20am (US$8, 140km, three hours), Santa Clara at 2:15pm (US$12, 182km, 3½ hours) and Cienfuegos at 8:45am (US$14, 181km, four hours). Aircon **Víazul** (61 48 86; 7am-noon & 1-7pm) buses leave for Havana at 8am, 4pm and 6pm daily (US$10). On either bus, ask to be let out at the first stop after the tunnel in Havana; from there Astro goes to the Terminal de Omnibus near the Plaza de la Revolución (convenient if you're staying in Vedado), while the Víazul bus goes to the boondocks on Av 26 in Nuevo Vedado. Víazul also has a daily bus to Trinidad at 7:30am (US$20, 262km, six hours), stopping in Sancti Spíritus (US$16, 265km, five hours) and Santa Clara (US$11, 182km, 3½ hours).

There are 10 daily bus departures to Matanzas (US$2, 35km) from here. If you have the time, you can get to Havana by taking

MATANZAS PROVINCE

this bus to Matanzas and continuing on the Hershey Railway from there, although it's not possible to do this in a day trip.

The collective taxis (*colectivos*) to Matanzas outside the bus station are not allowed to take foreigners (who are supposed to use tourist taxis). Private drivers who carry tourists are subject to heavy fines.

Getting to Cárdenas by local bus is fairly straightforward if you're prepared to wait. Bus No 236 departs every hour or so from next to a small tunnel marked 'Ómnibus de Cárdenas' outside the main bus station. You can also catch this bus at the corner of Av 1 and Calle 13 (US$1). This bus runs the length of the peninsula.

It's possible to use the rather frequent hotel employee buses marked Ómnibus Bellamar to get to Cárdenas (US$1) and Matanzas (US$2). These stop in front of the **Banco de Crédito y Comercio** (Map pp200-1; Av 1 at Calle 36) and you pay the driver as you board. The public buses use the regular stop a block west on the corner of Calle 35, but they're irregular due to the shortage of fuel. You could take any bus headed for Santa Marta and try again there, but follow the advice of any Cubans you find waiting at either stop.

The easiest way to get to Havana is on one of the regular tour buses booked through the tour desk at your hotel or at any Havanatur office. It's possible to buy just transport between Varadero and Havana for US$25/30 one way/round trip. These buses collect passengers right at the hotel doors.

CAR

Cars are available from **Havanautos** (Map pp200-1; ☎ 61 37 33; Av Kawama btwn Calles 8 & 9; Map pp200-1; ☎ 61 44 09; Av 1 & Calle 31). Other offices are at **Hotel Cuatro Palmas** (Map pp200-1; ☎ 66 70 40, ext 51), **Villa Tortuga** (Map pp200-1; ☎ 66 71 39), **Hotel Las Morlas** (Map pp200-1; ☎ 66 72 30, ext 35) and **Hotel Internacional** (Map pp198-9; ☎ 66 70 38).

Transtur (Map pp200-1; ☎ 61 31 49; Calle 10 No 703; Map pp200-1; ☎ 66 73 32; Av 1 & Calle 21) also has rental desks at or near the following hotels: Paradiso-Puntarena, Tropical, Internacional, Cuatro Palmas, Copey, Las Morlas, and Arenas Doradas.

Cubacar (Map pp200-1; ☎ 61 18 19; Calle 32 No 108 btwn 1ra & 3ra) also has desks at the Túxpan, Sol Palmerasa and Bella Costa hotels. **Vía Car Rental** (Map pp200-1; Av 3 & Calle 30) is opposite Apartamentos Mar del Sur.

Many of these companies also have desks at Plaza América, although we've received complaints about agents there who demanded kickbacks. **Havanautos** (☎ 25 36 30), **Transtur** (☎ 25 36 21), **Vía** (☎ 61 47 83) and **Cubacar** (☎ 61 44 10) all have car rental offices in the airport parking lot. Expect to pay at least US$65 a day for the smallest car (or US$50 daily on a two-week basis).

The cheapest cars are available from **Micar** (Map pp198-9; ☎ 66 85 52; in Villa Cuba; Map pp200-1; ☎ 61 18 08; Av 1 & Calle 20), which has tiny Fiats starting at US$35 a day, including 100km, plus US$5 insurance. Call ahead as the affordable cars go fast. Luxury cars are available at **Rex** (Map pp198-9; ☎ 66 77 39; Hotel Meliá Las Américas; ☎ 66 75 39; Aeropuerto Juan Gualberto Gómez). It rents Audi and automatic transmission (rare in Cuba) cars starting at US$99 per day.

There's a **Servi-Cupet gas station** (Map pp200-1; Autopista Sur & Calle 17; ☼ 24hr) on the Vía Blanca at the entrance to Marina Acua near Hotel Sunbeach; and one at **Centro Todo En Uno** (Map pp200-1; Calle 54 & Autopista Sur).

If heading to Havana, you'll have to pay the US$2 toll upon leaving.

TRAIN

The nearest train stations are 18km southeast in Cárdenas and 42km west in Matanzas. See those sections for details.

Getting Around
TO/FROM THE AIRPORT

Varadero and Matanzas are each about 20km from the spur road to Juan Gualberto Gómez International Airport; it's another 6km from the highway to the airport terminal. A tourist taxi costs US$20 to Matanzas and around US$25 from the airport to Varadero, but only US$20 from Varadero to the airport. Convince the driver to use the meter and it should work out cheaper. The closest point to the airport served by regular public transport to the city of Matanzas is near the Río Canímar bridge, 13km away. Otherwise, the drivers of the Varadero tour buses will probably be happy to take you for around US$10 per person. Unlicensed private taxis are prohibited from picking up or delivering passengers to the airport. All Víazul buses bound for Havana call at the airport, so you might try catching a ride with them.

BUS

Varadero Beach Tour (all-day ticket US$2; ☉ 9:30am-5pm) is a handy double-decker tourist bus with 42 'hop-on, hop-off' stops linking all the resorts and shopping centers the length of the peninsula. It passes every hour at well-marked stops with route and distance information. You can buy tickets at your hotel tourism desk or at Transtur on Calle 10. There's also a free shuttle connecting the three large Meliá resorts.

There are two local bus routes costing 20 centavos a ride: No 47 and 48 from Calle 64 to Santa Marta, south of Varadero on the Autopista Sur; and No 220 from Santa Marta to the east end of the peninsula. You'll spend a lot of time waiting for these to show up. The No 236 bus to and from Cárdenas (US$1) runs the length of the peninsula and is useful. Most municipal buses around Varadero don't bear a number, and many are special services for hotel employees only. If you're able to converse in Spanish, get information from the Cubans waiting at the bus stops.

MOPED & BICYCLE

Mopeds can broaden your horizons beyond the resort grounds, and rentals are available everywhere (hour/day costs US$8/22). Weekend specials from noon Friday to 9am Monday are US$55 and there's also a twilight 5pm to 9am special available at most places for US$15. Gas is included in hourly rates, but on a 24-hour basis you may be charged US$6 extra for fuel (ask). The **Rumbos rental post** (Map pp200-1; Av 1 btwn Calles 22 & 23) is located in the center of town; it also has bikes here. You can expect to pay a few dollars more if you rent mopeds at your resort. No insurance or helmets are available and a motorcycle license is not required.

Bicycles are another great way to explore Varadero. Even the mid-range resorts usually include free bikes in their all-inclusive packages, but if not, the Rumbos at Av 1 and Calle 30 and the stand outside Parque Josone have bicycles for US$2/4/6/15 for one/two/three/24 hours. Make sure the bike comes with a lock so you can frolic on the beach carefree.

TAXI

Tourist taxis charge a US$1 starting fee plus US$0.75 per kilometer (same tariff day and night). Coco-taxis (*coquitos* or *huevitos* in Cuban) charge only US$0.50 per kilometer and no starting fee. A taxi to Cárdenas/Havana will be about US$15/75 one way. You can phone order taxis by calling **Transtur** (☎ 61 44 44), **OK Taxi** (☎ 61 16 16), **Cuba Taxi** (☎ 61 05 55) or **Transgaviota** (☎ 61 97 62). The last uses large cars if you're traveling with a bike or big luggage. Tourists are not supposed to use the older Lada taxis.

Unofficial taxis with yellow 'particular' license plates face a 1500-peso fine if caught carrying foreigners. Thus you'll seldom be propositioned by private taxi drivers in Varadero itself.

A state-owned horse and buggy around Varadero costs US$5 per person for a 45-minute half tour or US$10 for a full two-hour tour, which is plenty of time to see the sights.

CÁRDENAS

☎ 45 / pop 98,644

The small city of Cárdenas was made famous by two monumental events: it was where the Cuban flag was raised for the first time (by General Narciso López in 1850) and it's the hometown of Elián and Juan Miguel González, the key figures in the 1999–2000 immigration trauma-drama (see boxed text, p216). Also the birthplace of revolutionary hero José Antonio Echeverría, Cárdenas ('Flag City') stands on the Bahía de Cárdenas, 18km southeast of Varadero. Founded in 1828, this was the heart of Cuba's richest sugar-growing area in the 19th century and period houses with stained-glass windows still grace the tattered streets. If you want to see real Cuban life, Cárdenas makes a good outing from Varadero. Otherwise, it's not worth the trip. Incidentally, most of Varadero's service staff hails from Cárdenas, explaining why so many people speak English here.

Orientation

The northeast–southwest streets are called avenidas and streets running northwest–southeast are calles. Av Céspedes (Av Real) is Cárdenas' main drag; the avenues to the northwest are called oeste, and those to the southeast are called este. The city's main northwest–southeast street is Calle 13 (Calzada); calles are numbered consecutively beginning at the bay.

Information

BOOKSHOPS
Librería La Concha de Venus (Av Céspedes & Calle 12; ✪ 9am-5pm Mon-Fri, 8am-noon Sat) Has a decent selection of books in Spanish.

MEDICAL SERVICES
Centro Médico Sub Acuática (☎ 52 21 14; channel 16 VHF; Calle 13; US$80/hr; ✪ 8am-4pm Mon-Sat; doctors on-call 24hr) It's 2km northwest on the road to Varadero at Hospital Julio M Aristegui. Has a Soviet recompression chamber dating from 1981.
Pharmacy No 12 (☎ 52 15 67; Calle 12 No 60; ✪ 24hr)

MONEY
Bandec (☎ 52 26 36; Céspedes No 252) Next to Etecsa, might change travelers checks.
Cadeca (☎ 52 41 02; Av 1 Oeste, cnr Calles 12)

PHOTOGRAPHY
Photo Service (Av Céspedes No 568)

POST
Post Office (Av Céspedes cnr of Calle 8; ✪ 8am-6pm Mon-Sat)

TELEPHONE
Etecsa (Av Céspedes cnr Calle 12; ✪ 7am-11pm)

Sights

Cárdenas has several major sights related to its famous history and hometown heroes. At the northeast end of Av Céspedes is the monument with a huge **flagpole** commemorating the first raising of the Cuban flag on May 19, 1850. It's a simple, but moving memorial with good views of the bay and Varadero. To the northwest near the port is the **Arrechabala Rum Factory** where Varadero rum is distilled. The Havana Club rum company was founded here in 1878; no tours were happening at the time of writing.

From here, make your way southwest to pretty Parque Echeverría where you'll find the **Museo Casa Natal de José Antonio Echeverría** (Av 4 Este No 560; admission free, but tip the guide; ✪ 10am-5pm Tue-Sat, 9am-noon Sun). The rich historical collection includes the original garrote used to execute Narciso López by strangulation in 1851. Objects relating to the 19th-century independence wars are downstairs, while the 20th-century revolution is covered upstairs. A spiral staircase with 36 steps links the two floors of this house dating from 1703. In 1932 Echeverría was born

here, and a monument to this student leader slain by Batista's police in 1957 is outside on Parque Echeverría. The nearby **Museo Oscar María de Rojas** (Av 4 Este & Calle 12), one of Cuba's oldest museums, was being renovated at the time of research; hopefully the flea dressed in a teeny wedding gown and veil will still be in residence when it reopens.

Around the corner is the new **Museo de Batalla de Ideas** (Av 6 btwn Calles 11 & 12; admission US$2; ✪ 9am-5pm Tue-Sun), with a well designed and organized overview of the history of US–Cuban relations, replete with sophisticated graphics. The entire Elián González incident is covered in detail and there are good city views from the mirador on the third floor. Jineteros will offer to show you Elián's house for a small tip.

Parque Colón is a small square containing the **Catedral de la Inmaculada Concepción** (1846; Av Céspedes btwn Calles 8 & 9), noted for its stained glass, and the oldest statue of Christopher Columbus in the Western Hemisphere. Dating from 1862, it's ironic and poignant that the world should be dropped so casually at his feet.

Like something from the zany brain of PT Barnum, **Plaza Molocoff** (Av 3 Oeste & Calle 12) is a whimsical two-story cast-iron market hall with a glittery 16m-high silver dome built in 1859. Now it's the city **vegetable market** (✪ 8am-5pm Mon-Sat, 8am-2pm Sun).

Sleeping

The only functioning hotel in Cárdenas is the classic **Hotel Dominica** (☎ 52 15 51; Av Céspedes at Calle 9; s/d US$15/25) on Parque Colón. This faded old hotel has 25 rooms with bath – a few even have air-con. It's not set up as a tourist hotel, so electricity/water failures are routine. The **restaurant** (✪ 7-9am, noon-2pm & 6pm-midnight) is only worth it if you can pay in pesos (they might try to squeeze some dollars out of you). The bar here is open until 1am.

Eating   Map pp200-1

The restaurant choices here are pretty grim, and you're largely looking at fast food, self-catering and pesos stalls. One exception is **Espriu** (Calle 12 btwn Avs 4 & 6; dishes US$1-2.50; ✪ 24hr) on Parque Echeverría. This Rumbos restaurant has espresso, shrimp cocktails, fish filets, burgers and sandwiches. It's probably the best game in town. Another simple cafeteria is **El Colonial** (Av Céspedes cnr of Calle 12; ☷ 8am-3pm), which serves burgers, beer and pork dishes on a cute patio.

Next to El Colonial is **Panadería Doña Neli** (Av Céspedes No 580 at Calle 12) selling a startling selection of breads including sweetish white loaves, crackers and rolls.

Restaurante Las Palmas (Av Céspedes & Calle 16; ☷ 8am-2am) Housed in a Spanish-style mansion. You can eat here, but you're better off with the cheap Cristal on tap served on the porch. From 9pm to 2am on Friday, Saturday and Sunday, Las Palmas becomes a cabaret with a show at 10:30pm (admission US$5).

For sandwiches and beer there's always **Cafetería El Rápido** (Calle 12 cnr Av 3 Oeste; ☷ 24hr;

Calle 8 cnr Av Céspedes; ☷ 24hr), an open-air snack bar with fast food at low dollar prices.

Cheap peso eateries include **Pio Pio** (Av Céspedes & Calle 12; ☷ 11am-midnight), a recommended choice for breaded pork cutlets, with congrí and tomato salad for 25 pesos and **Pizzería La Boloñesa** (Av Céspedes No 901 at Calle 19; ☷ 10am-10pm) for peso pizza.

Many dollar supermarkets and stores are along Av 3 Oeste near Plaza Molocoff. You can get cheap peso snacks in the market itself and the area surrounding, where merchants peddle everything from fake hair to plastic Buddhas. **Cafetería La Cubanita** (Av 3 Oeste & Calle 13; ☷ 24hr), near Plaza Molocoff, has a pleasant outdoor setting where you can consume drinks for dollars.

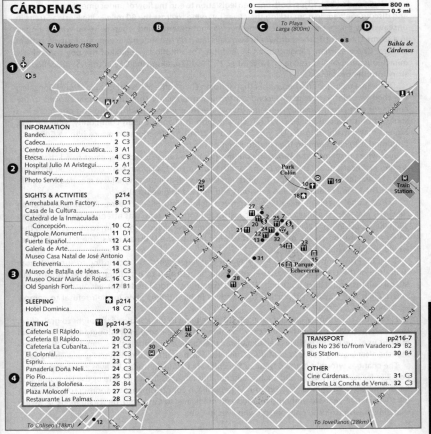

CÁRDENAS

INFORMATION	
Bandec	1 C3
Cadeca	2 C3
Centro Médico Sub Acuática	3 A1
Etecsa	4 C3
Hospital Julio M Aristegui	5 A1
Pharmacy	6 C2
Photo Service	7 C3

SIGHTS & ACTIVITIES	p214
Arrechabala Rum Factory	8 D1
Casa de la Cultura	9 C3
Catedral de la Inmaculada Concepción	10 C2
Flagpole Monument	11 D1
Fuerte Español	12 A4
Galería de Arte	13 C3
Museo Casa Natal de José Antonio Echeverría	14 C3
Museo de Batalla de Ideas	15 C3
Museo Oscar María de Rojas	16 C3
Old Spanish Fort	17 B1

SLEEPING	🛏 p214
Hotel Dominica	18 C2

EATING	🍴 pp214-5
Cafetería El Rápido	19 D2
Cafetería El Rápido	20 C2
Cafetería La Cubanita	21 C3
El Colonial	22 C3
Espriu	23 C3
Panadería Doña Neli	24 C3
Pio Pio	25 C3
Pizzería La Boloñesa	26 B4
Plaza Molocoff	27 C2
Restaurante Las Palmas	28 C3

TRANSPORT	pp216-7
Bus No 236 to/from Varadero	29 B2
Bus Station	30 B4

OTHER	
Cine Cárdenas	31 C3
Librería La Concha de Venus	32 C3

0 .... 800 m
0 .... 0.5 mi

To Varadero (18km)
To Playa Larga (800m)
Bahía de Cárdenas
Park Colón
Train Station
Parque Echeverría
To Coliseo (18km)
To Jovellanos (28km)

Entertainment

The **Casa de la Cultura** (☎ 52 12 92; Av Céspedes No 706 btwn Calles 15 & 16) is housed in a beautiful, but faded colonial building with stained glass, iron awning and interior patio with rockers. Look here for rap peñas, theater and literature events.

Cine Cárdenas (Av Céspedes & Calle 14) has daily screenings.

Getting There & Away

BUS

Transport services are thin out of Cárdenas and you're much better off making your way to Varadero and then hooking up with something there. Astro buses depart the **bus station** (Av Céspedes & Calle 22) to Havana at 1:45pm (US$7, 152km) and Santa Clara at 2:40pm (US$7.50, 174km), but they're

---

THE POLITICS OF A CHILD

When Elizabeth Broton González, a young divorcee from Cárdenas, decided to join her boyfriend and 11 others in an overcrowded boat bound for Florida, and to take her five-year-old son Elián with her, she set in motion a chain of events no-one could have imagined and which she would not live to see. Within weeks Cuba and the USA would be screaming at each other. Within months they would be on the same side. Within the year, there would be significant changes in the way Americans felt about Cuba.

The USA and Cuba had just both enacted legislation to end the flow of undocumented immigrants and discourage people from risking their lives by trying to cross the 90 mile–wide Florida Straits in unseaworthy boats. However, Elián's mother was not deterred and when her boat was swamped in a storm, she and 10 others drowned. Two days later, US fishermen plucked three survivors from the sea. One was Elián, clinging to an inner tube. The emotional appeal of the boy's seemingly miraculous survival and rescue on November 25, 1999 (Thanksgiving Day in the US) propelled the story into the headlines.

The drama heightened when, rather than sending Elián home to his father Juan Miguel González, the child was placed in care of second cousins living in Miami. They immediately applied to the courts for permanent custody. In Cuba, this was seen as a virtual kidnapping and one more in a series of US provocations. Feelings ran equally high in Miami's Cuban community, where it was argued that remaining in the US was Elián's one chance at freedom; to return him to Cuba was tantamount to condemning the child to life in prison.

Just when it seemed the situation couldn't get more tense, it did. The court ruled that there was no justification for removing Elián from the custody of his Cuban father, who by all accounts was a model father. US family and immigration law as well as international law required the child's return. The Miami relatives defied the court and refused to give up Elián.

Across Cuba, massive rallies were organized demanding Elián's return. The largest, held on Havana's Malecón in a plaza especially constructed for the event, was attended by an estimated 300,000 people in April 2000. The Cuban government flew a mediating team to Miami. When that failed to secure the child's release, Elián's father flew to the United States. The Miami relatives would not allow him to visit his son.

Then US President Bill Clinton, Attorney-General Janet Reno, and (according to surveys) more than 70% of the US public felt that Elián should be returned to his father and his country. But Miami Cubans would have none of it. Anti-Castro demonstrators lined the street outside the house where Elián was staying, supporting the relatives in high-drama style in their refusal to comply with the court decision.

Finally the US attorney-general sent a SWAT-type team in the middle of the night to grab Elián. He was reunited with his father and they remained in a safe house in Washington, DC for several months until the Miami relatives had exhausted their appeal options. In the summer of 2000, seven months after leaving Cuba, Juan Miguel González was permitted to return to Cuba with his son.

The changes wrought in the psyche of the child are unknown (today he lives as normal a life as possible for having experienced such a trauma), but changes in the psyche of the US public and its lawmakers were immediately obvious. A Republican congressman who sponsored a bipartisan bill to lift the 42-year-old embargo on food and medicines to Cuba said 'he [Elián] made us aware that Fidel Castro isn't the only person who lives in Cuba.'

often full upon reaching Cárdenas. Trucks to Jovellanos/Perico leave at 10:30am and 3pm (three pesos, 52km), which puts you 12km from Colón and possible onward transport to the east. The ticket office is at the rear of the station.

Reliable Bus No 236 to/from Varadero leaves hourly from the corner of Av 13 Oeste and Calle 13 (50 centavos, but they like to charge tourists US$1). Máquinas to places such as Coliseo (10 pesos per person, 16km) leave from Av Céspedes in front of the main bus station. Usually they won't take tourists, but it's worth a try. They certainly won't take you to Varadero, but might agree to go as far as Santa Marta just before the bridge into Varadero for US$5 for the car, provided you can negotiate in Spanish.

HITCHHIKING
To hitch to Varadero from Cárdenas, take a horse cart to the hospital, where almost any passing bus will stop to pick you up for US$1 as far as Santa Marta. Alternatively, you can park yourself a ways up Calle 13 and wait; other tourists are usually willing to help out their compadres for this short ride (for information on the risks associated with hitching see p433).

TRAIN
You could be very lucky and catch one of the frequently cancelled rail cars from **San Martín Train Station** (Av 8 Este) near the bay, to Unión de Reyes via Jovellanos (daily), Guareiras via Colón (daily) and Los Arabos (twice daily).

Getting Around
The main horse-cart (one peso) route through Cárdenas is northeast on Av Céspedes from the bus station and then northwest on Calle 13 to the hospital, passing the stop of bus No 236 (to Varadero) on the way.

The gas station **Servi-Cupet** (Calle 13 & Av 31 Oeste) is opposite an old Spanish fort on the northwest side of town, on the road to Varadero.

PENÍNSULA DE ZAPATA
☎ 459 / pop 8267
Most of the 4520 sq km Península de Zapata in southern Matanzas is included in Gran Parque Natural Montemar, formerly known as Parque Nacional Ciénaga de Zapata. In 2001, it was declared a Unesco Biosphere

Reserve. It's the largest swamp (ciénaga) in Cuba, and one of the country's most diverse ecosystems, with vast wetlands of mangroves and marshes supporting over 190 bird species, 31 types of reptile, and 12 species of mammal, plus countless amphibians, fish and insects (including the insatiable mosquito). There are more than 900 plant species here, some 115 of them endemic. This is the habitat of the manatee (manatí) and the alligator gar (manjuarí, Atractosteus tristoechus), Cuba's most primitive fish.

The Zapata is the place to come to see bee hummingbirds (the world's smallest bird), cormorants, cranes, ducks, flamingos, hawks, herons, ibis, owls, parrots, partridges, sparrows, tocororos (Cuba's national bird) and wrens. Numerous migratory birds from North America winter here, making November to April the best birding season. It's also the number-one spot in Cuba for catch-and-release sport fishing and fly fishing, where the palometa, sábalo and robalo are jumping (bonefish too!).

The municipality of Ciénega de Zapata is Cuba's biggest in area, but with the smallest population. The land is unsuitable for agriculture, and until the revolution, communications were almost nonexistent and poverty was the rule. Charcoal makers burn wood from the region's semideciduous forests, and turba (peat) dug from the swamps is an important source of fuel. The main industry today is tourism and ecotourists are arriving in increasing numbers. From sunset to sunrise in April and May, tens of thousands of red land crabs swarm across the one road through the swamp. They're impossible to dodge entirely, so be mindful of tire punctures when you hear the sickening crunch.

Information
The **Rumbos Península de Zapata** (☎ 2277; ☯ 9am-noon & 1-5pm Mon-Sat), just before the turn-off towards Playa Larga from the Autopista, arranges **bird-watching tours** (per person US$15) along Río Hatiguanico and books rooms at the Villa Guamá; anglers should inquire about multi-day fishing trips in the Ciénaga here. Arrangements for the popular bird-watching excursions to the Las Salinas Wildlife Refuge are better made at park HQ in Playa Larga (p219).

Etecsa, the post office and dollar stores are across the Autopista in bustling Jagüey

Grande. Insect repellant is absolutely essential on the peninsula and while Cuban repellant is available locally, it's like wasabi on sushi for the ravenous buggers here.

Museo de Comandancia

About 1.5km south of the Autopista Nacional on the way to Boca de Guamá, is the large Central Australia sugar mill, built in 1904. During the 1961 Bahía de Cochinos (Bay of Pigs) invasion, Fidel Castro had his headquarters in the former office of the sugar mill. Today it's the **Museo de la Comandancia** (☎ 2504; admission US$1; ☾ 8am-5pm Tue-Sun). This municipal museum contains a few stuffed birds and animals, and a good historical collection ranging from prehistory to the present; tip your guide. Outside is the wreck of an invading aircraft shot down by Fidel's troops. The concrete memorials lining the road to the Bahía de Cochinos mark the spots where defenders were killed in 1961.

Sleeping & Eating

The **Motel Batey Don Pedro** (☎ 2825) is just south of the turn-off to the Península de Zapata from Km 142 on the Autopista Nacional at Jagüey Grande. The eight thatched double units were closed at the time of writing due to a lightning strike. The motel is designed to resemble a peasant settlement, and a large tourist restaurant/bar with good, reasonably priced food called 'Finca Fiesta Campesina,' with a mini-zoo (free, but parking costs US$1) is nearby.

If you just can't drive any further, two legal casas particulares in the area include **Carmelo Abreu** (☎ 2775, 3429; Calle 26 No 14 btwn 43 & 45; r US$20; ℗ ☒), at the Central Australia sugar mill, with small, clean rooms and the more convenient **Casa de Zuleida** (☎ 3153; Calle 15A No 7211 btwn 72 & 74; r US$15-20; ℗ ☒) in Jagüey Grande behind the hospital.

The fanciest restaurant in these parts is **Pío Cuá** (☎ 3343; Carretera de Playa Larga Km 8; meals US$6-20; ☾ 9am-9pm), where bus tour groups are treated to shrimp, lobster or chicken meals in a big structure that somehow manages to combine thatch and stained glass successfully. Otherwise, there's **Rumbos Península de Zapata** (☎ 2277; ☾ 7:30am-11pm) just before the turn-off from the Autopista to Playa Larga with decent burgers, nice sandwiches and fresh juice for reasonable prices. Don't miss the quote wall.

BOCA DE GUAMÁ

The main center for visitors to this area is Boca de Guamá, about halfway between the Autopista Nacional at Jagüey Grande and the famous Bahía de Cochinos (Bay of Pigs). It's a whole lot of tourist claptrap, with a restaurant, expensive snack bar, knick-knack shop, ceramics workshop, crocodile 'farm' and boats waiting to take you across the Laguna del Tesoro to a resort built to resemble an Indian village. There are more interesting sights around this abyss, however.

Sights

Don't confuse the real **Criadero de Cocodrilos** (guided visit US$5; ☾ 8am-5pm) with the faux farm inside Boca de Guamá's tourist complex. On your right as you come from the Autopista, the Criadero de Cocodrilos is an actual breeding facility run by the Ministerio de Industrias Pesqueras where two species of crocodiles are raised: the native Rhombifer (cocodrilo) and the Acutus (caimán), which is found throughout the tropical Americas. On an informative guided visit (in Spanish), you'll see every stage of the breeding programme, from eggs and hatchlings to big, bad-ass crocs. Prior to the establishment of this programme in 1962 (considered the first environmental protection act undertaken by the revolutionary government), these two species of marsh-dwelling crocodiles were almost extinct.

The breeding has been so successful that across the road in the Boca de Guamá complex you can buy stuffed baby crocodiles or dine on crocodile steak (US$5/10 for a tiny/small portion; lunch only). Ironic, no?

The **park/zoo** (adult/child US$5/3; ☾ 9am-6pm) has two crocodiles that are often under water trying to beat the stifling 85% humidity. There are other caged animals here.

If you buy anything made from crocodile leather at Boca de Guamá, be sure to ask for an invoice (for the customs authorities) proving that the material came from a crocodile farm and not wild crocodiles. A less controversial purchase would be one of the attractive ceramic bracelets sold at the nearby **Taller de Cerámica** (☾ 9am-6pm Mon-Sat) where you can see five kilns in operation.

Aside from the crocodile farm, the main attraction is the **Laguna del Tesoro**, 8km east of Boca de Guamá via the Canal de la Laguna and accessible only by boat (see the

Getting Around section, p219). On the east side of this 92 sq km lake is a tourist resort named Villa Guamá, built to resemble a Taino village, on a dozen small islands. A sculpture park next to the mock village has 32 life-size figures of Taino villagers in a variety of idealized poses. The lake is called 'treasure lake' due to a legend about a treasure the Taino are said to have thrown into the water just prior to the Spanish conquest (not disimilar to South American El Dorado legends). The most important part of the whole scenario is Guamá himself – a rebel chief who fought bravely against the Spanish. All of this has a strong appeal to Cuban honeymooners who flock to Villa Guamá, and if you're into kitsch, you're all over it. There's freshwater fishing for largemouth bass here.

Sleeping & Eating

Villa Guamá (Rumbos; ☎ 5515; d US$40) was built in 1963 on the east side of the Laguna del Tesoro, about 5km from Boca de Guamá by boat (cars can be left at the crocodile farm; US$1). The 50 thatched cabañas with bath and TV are on piles over the shallow waters. The six small islands bearing the units are connected by wooden footbridges to other islands with a bar, cafeteria, overpriced restaurant and a swimming pool containing chlorinated lake water. Rowboats are for rent. Noise from the disco occasionally cancels some of the nocturnal tranquillity, and day-trippers come and go by speedboat throughout the day. Birding at dawn however, is reputedly fantastic. You'll need insect repellent if you decide to stay. The ferry transfer is not included in the room price (see Getting Around below).

The **restaurant** (meals US$12) at the boat dock for Laguna del Tesoro has big, set meals.

Getting There & Away

In theory the public bus between Jagüey Grande and Playa Girón passes once in the morning and there's service to/from Havana (178km) on Friday, Saturday and Sunday afternoon. If you're without your own transport, you can hitch into Playa Girón or out to the Autopista and jump on a Víazul, Astro or tour bus at the Rumbos restuarant there (most buses going in either direction pit stop there). Tours from Varadero to Boca de Guamá occur daily,

and if you're traveling independently, you can probably negotiate a ride back there by speaking to the driver (US$10 per person should be plenty).

Getting Around

A passenger ferry (adult/child US$10/5, 20 minutes) departs Boca de Guamá for Villa Guamá across Laguna del Tesoro four times a day. Speedboats (also US$10/5) depart more frequently and whisk you across to the pseudo-Indian village in just 10 minutes any time during the day for US$10 per person round trip (with 40 minutes waiting time at Villa Guamá, two-person minimum. In the morning you can allow yourself more time on the island by going one way by launch and returning by ferry.

PLAYA LARGA

Continuing south from Boca de Guamá you reach Playa Larga, on the Bahía de Cochinos (Bay of Pigs), after 13km (or 32km from where you left the Autopista Nacional). US-backed exiles took a beating trying to invade Cuba through this bay on April 17, 1961 and the museum dedicated to these events at Playa Girón, 35km further south, captures the drama pretty well. While the best accomodation is in Playa Girón, the national park office is here in Playa Larga and there is a good scuba diving outfit.

Bird-Watching

About 21km southwest of Playa Larga is the **Laguna de las Salinas**, now part of Las Salinas Wildlife Refuge, where large numbers of migratory waterfowl can be seen from November to April: we're talking 10,000 pink flamingos at a time, plus 190 other feathered species. The first half of the road to Las Salinas is through the forest, while the second half passes swamps and lagoons. Here, aquatic birds can be observed. Guides are mandatory to explore the refuge and must be arranged at the **national park office** (☎ 7249, 7128; ☉ 8am-4:30pm Mon-Fri, 8am-noon Sat), beside the highway at the north entrance to Playa Larga from Boca de Guamá. The 22km visit lasts over four hours and costs US$10 per person. The guides are ornithologists and know the Ciénaga well; specialists should ask here about longer trips to Los Sábalos, Santo Tomás and Bermejas. You'll need a rental car with a spare seat for your guide,

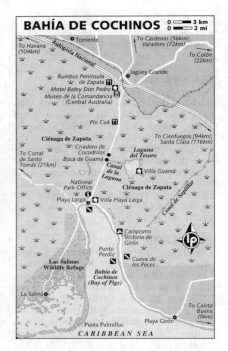

BAHÍA DE COCHINOS

the darker, spookier parts of the cenote with snorkel gear (US$3). Local dive shops bring scuba divers here if you'd rather explore the depths of Cuba's deepest flooded fault. Hammocks swing languidly around the cenote and the beach facing has good snorkeling too, making it a nice afternoon jaunt. There's a handy restaurant, with premium prices.

Just beyond the Cueva is **Punto Perdiz,** another phenomenal snorkeling (US$3 per hour) and scuba diving (US$25 per dive) spot with on-site diving outfit. The shallow water is gemstone blue here and there's good snorkeling right from the shore. It costs US$1 to use the thatched umbrellas, beach chairs and showers and there's a decent restaurant.

Sleeping & Eating

Villa Playa Larga (Horizontes; ☎ 7225, 7294; s/d low season incl breakfast US$32/40, high US$38/50; P ⊠) On an artificial white sand beach by the road, just east of the village, this hotel has huge rooms with bath, sitting room, fridge and TV. There are also eight two-bedroom family bungalows, but the restaurant is bleak. Transtur has a car rental desk here. If you must choose, Villa Playa Girón is in a much nicer location (see p221).

Campismo Victoria de Girón (☎ 5621; per person US$5) About 7km southeast of Playa Larga and 28km from Playa Girón, it has 25 simple cabins sleeping four people each. It's right on a small beach and foreigners are accepted; it will be full on weekends, holidays and in July and August.

Self-sufficient campers will find plenty of beach space between Playas Larga and Girón for pitching camp. Note that the 10km just before Playa Girón is an official off-limits military zone. The sunsets are beautiful but we challenge you to decide which is worse: the mosquitoes or the sand fleas.

The open-air **Palmares restaurant** (meals US$2-7), across the road from Villa Playa Larga, has hearty ham-and-cheese sandwiches, fish meals and can hook up a respectable vegetarian plate.

Getting There & Away

The hypothetical bus between Playa Girón and Jagüey Grande is supposed to pass here in the morning, but don't be surprised if it doesn't. Another bus should run to and from Havana (191km) on Friday, Saturday and Sunday afternoon.

as the park supplies no transport. Transtur at Villa Playa Larga rents chauffeur-driven jeeps. Early morning is the best time, with March being the absolute top time to visit.

Scuba Diving & Snorkeling

If you prefer fish to birds, the **Club Octopus International Diving Center** (☎ 7225; 200m west of Villa Playa Larga) offers full scuba facilities at US$25 per dive or US$35 for an orientation session and introductory dive (to 8m). There are 12 rich dive sites just offshore between Playa Larga and Playa Girón (you'll know them by the international scuba symbol painted on the asphalt) and both this outfit and the one in Punta Perdiz visit them. This area is great for first time divers. There's a bar and restaurant overlooking the beach here.

More underwater treasures can be seen at the **Cueva de los Peces** (admission US$1; ☺ 9am-6pm) a flooded tectonic fault, or cenote, about 70m deep on the inland side of the road, almost exactly midway between Playa Larga and Playa Girón. There are lots of bright, tropical fish, plus you can explore back into

PLAYA GIRÓN

Playa Girón, on the eastern side of the Bahía de Cochinos, 48km south of Boca de Guamá, is named for a French pirate who frequented the area centuries ago. The CIA-sponsored landing here, on April 17, 1961, is a modern twist on the old David and Goliath tale. It all started on April 14, when some 1400 obstinate émigrés sailed in six ships from Puerto Cabeza in Nicaragua bound for Cuba. US henchman and Nicaraguan dictator Luis Somoza bid them bon voyage, requesting they bring back a few hairs from Fidel's beard. Despite their airfields being bombed and seven airmen killed, the Cubans would not succumb. President Kennedy cancelled US air cover and within 72 hours the Cubans had triumphed and the rum was flowing. In all, 200 invaders were killed, 1197 captured, and 11 hostile planes shot down. You really get the feel of reliving history by coming here, and the clear Caribbean waters washing these shores make Playa Girón a favorite destination for scuba divers and snorkelers.

In addition to some nice private houses, Playa Girón's main resort is rather pleasant, despite the huge ugly seawall providing a protected swimming area. Long, shady Playa Los Cocos, where the snorkeling is good, is just a five-minute walk south along the shore. Remember, however, that this is the south shore, meaning there's more *diente de perro* (dog's tooth) than soft white sands like you find in the north. Distances are long and public transport is poor, so unless you've rented a car, you'd better be prepared to rough it.

Information

There's a tourist post office at the hotel and a regular Cuban post office next to the museum. This is a tiny two road town, so if you need any goods or service, the hotel is the most likely place to look.

Museo Girón

This **museum** (unguided/guided US$2/3, cameras US$1; ☼ 9am-5pm), across the street from Villa Playa Girón, offers two rooms of Bahía de Cochinos artifacts and photos with (some) bilingual captions. The mural of victims and their personal items is moving and the tactical genius of the Cuban forces comes through in the graphic depictions of how the battle unfolded. The 15-minute film about the 'first defeat of US imperialism in the Americas' is US$1 extra. A British Sea Fury aircraft used by the Cuban Air Force is parked outside the museum and round the back are other various vessels used in the battle.

Scuba Diving & Snorkeling

The **International Scuba Center** (☎ 4118), at Villa Playa Girón, charges US$25 per dive. Its scuba initiation course, held in the resort's swimming pool, costs US$10. Special features of the diving in this area are underwater caves with a blind species of fish, although a shortage of diving lamps means this activity is usually canceled. Most ocean dives are beach dives and the possibilities for snorkelers are endless.

Eight kilometers southeast of Playa Girón is **Caleta Buena** (☼ 10am-6pm) a lovely protected cove perfect for snorkeling with abundant coral and small fish. Admission is US$12 and includes an all-you-can-eat lunch buffet and open bar (enter after 3pm and it's US$6 with open bar only). There are beach chairs and thatched umbrellas dotting the rocky shoreline and enough space in this remote place to have a little privacy. The scuba-diving company at Villa Playa Girón has a kiosk here, charging the same rates; snorkel gear is US$3.

Sleeping & Eating

Villa Playa Girón (Horizontes; ☎ 4110; s/d all-inclusive low season US$45/60, high US$55/70; P ⓧ ⓡ) This unpretentious resort is a good option if you want the services of a hotel, but the privacy of an individual house. Skip the rooms in long blocks near the pool and go for one of the concrete bungalows (some are huge, two-bedroom spreads with kitchen – good for groups). The expansive grounds face the beach.

Budget travelers will like the selection of private rooms available here (see boxed text on p222). Most places serve meals, but double check because the choices in Girón are dire. Bargain in the off season.

Rumbos 24 Horas (south of Villa Playa Girónis) is an open-air terrace bar behind Tienda Imagen Cuba at the beginning of the road to Caleta Buena. It's a popular drinking hole for Cubans and backpackers.

CASAS PARTICULARES – PLAYA GIRÓN

Daisy Leyva & Julián Pérez (☎ 4176; down road to Cienfuegos; r US$15-20; 🔀) Nice patio with hammocks and rocking chairs.

Villa Merci – Mercedes Blanco Pérez (☎ 4304; on road to Caleta Buena; r US$20; P 🔀) Clean rooms, friendly couple.

Hostal Luis (☎ 4121; first house on road to Cienfuegos; r incl breakfast US$25; 🔀) Two spotless rooms in warm family atmosphere; look for the lions on the fence.

Silvia Acosta (☎ 4237; road to Cienfuegos; r US$15-20; P 🔀) Tremendous shell entry way, nice rooms with private entrance.

KS Abella (☎ 4260; road to Cienfuegos in front of apartments; r US$20; 🔀) Friendly, yummy meals.

Getting There & Away

The bus to/from Jagüey Grande supposedly leaves Playa Girón at 7:30am daily. On Friday, Saturday and Sunday afternoon there should be a bus to/from Havana (215km, eight hours). If any tour buses are at the hotel, find the driver and try to arrange a ride for a negotiable fee.

A single passenger truck operates daily between Playa Girón and Cienfuego (US$4, 94km), leaving Playa Girón at 5am and departing Cienfuegos bus station at 12:30pm for the return. A taxi should cost US$30 for this trip. From Playa Girón to Playa Larga, a taxi might cost US$15.

Getting Around

Transtur and Havanautos have car-rental offices at Villa Playa Girón.

Servi-Cupet gas stations are on the Carretera Central at Jovellanos and Colón and Jagüey Grande, and on the Autopista Nacional at Aguada de Pasajeros in Cienfuegos Province.

East of Caleta Buena (southeast of Playa Girón), the coastal road toward Cienfuegos becomes very bad and is only passable by a tractor, so you must backtrack and take the inland road via Rodas.

Cienfuegos
Province

Cienfuegos Province proves the old saying that good things come in small packages: the smallest province, after the City of Havana, and the least populated, Cienfuegos is a hidden treasure. The capital is charming and within easy reach of cool mountain treks, attractive beaches and memorable diving. What's more, its central location makes it a perfect base for day trips into the Sierra del Escambray, over to Playa Girón (p221) or up to the Che Memorial (p240) in Santa Clara. Most travelers don't give Cienfuegos a sidewards glance as they zoom along the Autopista, lending it an undiscovered feel.

Though most of central Cienfuegos is thick with sugarcane, cows dot the northwest plains and the Balneario Ciego Montero to the north of the capital is Cuba's finest source of mineral water (responsible for all that bottled water and soda in the dollar markets). Coffee is grown among the mountains of the Sierra del Escambray, not far from Pico San Juan (aka 'La Cuca', 1156m), the range's highest peak.

HIGHLIGHTS

- **Architect's Delight**
  Outlandish Palacio de Valle (p228)
- **Traditional Trova**
  At Casa de la Música, Salón de Minerva or Jardines de la UNEAC (p231)
- **Chilling Out**
  Bayside, in a Punta Gorda casa particular (p229)
- **Cooling Down**
  Hike to bracing waterfalls at El Nicho (p234)
- **Scuba Cuba**
  Coral gardens and shipwrecks near Rancho Luna (p233)

Casa de la Música
Salón de Minerva
Jardines de la UNEAC
★ Palacio de Valle
Punta Gorda
Rancho Luna ★
El Nicho

■ TELEPHONE CODE: 043   ■ POPULATION: 398,569   ■ AREA: 4180 SQ KM

HISTORY

Columbus explored Bahía de Cienfuegos (Cuba's third largest, with a surface area of 88 sq km) on his second voyage in 1494. By 1745, the Castillo de Jagua (p234), the most important colonial fortress on Cuba's south coast, was guarding the mouth of the bay. The province started to boom when the railway arrived from Havana in 1850, transferring passengers from train to ferry en route to Santiago de Cuba. These days, travelers with some patience and luck can still travel to and from the provincial capital by train.

Sugar has always played an important role in this part of Cuba, and by 1895 the port of Cienfuegos was exporting 15% of the country's sugar. After the US supplanted Spain as Cuba's main trading partner in the early 20th century, Cienfuegos became secondary to the northern ports. Still, the very much active Tricontinental sugar-exporting facility is believed to be the world's largest today.

In 1975, Cienfuegos was split from Las Villas and made its own province.

CIENFUEGOS

☎ 0432 / pop 139,137

Big enough to offer art, entertainment and action but small enough to retain charm, Cienfuegos is a manageable city perched on the Bahía de Cienfuegos. A lovely curve of water that opens into the Caribbean Sea, the bay is largely responsible for the city's 'pearl of the south' nickname and Punta Gorda, the knife of land slicing into its southern waters, has some of Cuba's prettiest casas particulares. Easily reached either by bus or car from Havana via the Autopista or along the coast from Trinidad, Cienfuegos is where you should head if you want to drop into one of Cuba's pockets for a few days.

While the city's 19th-century architecture and tranquil seaside setting help create a pleasant atmosphere, the churn of outlying industry does not. Ringing the Bahía de Cienfuegos is a giant shipyard, the bulk of Cuba's shrimp fishing fleet, a nitrogen fertilizer factory, a cement works, a paper mill, an oil refinery and a thermoelectric power plant. Still, the city and surroundings are

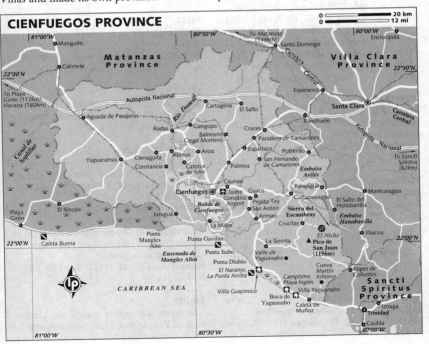

CIENFUEGOS PROVINCE

large enough that a visit won't be adversely affected by this industrial presence.

History

Cienfuegos was founded in 1819 as Fernandina de Jagua, but had to be rebuilt two years later after it was razed by a hurricane. In 1830 the settlement's name was changed to Cienfuegos for Captain-General José Cienfuegos, who ruled from 1816 to 1819. The bay, originally called Bahía de Jagua, was also renamed Bahía de Cienfuegos. You'll see the legacy of the original French colonists from Bordeaux, and French refugees from the territory of Louisiana (which the US purchased from Napoleon in 1803), in the light skin, blue eyes and blond hair of many residents.

Orientation

Cienfuegos is on a well-laid out grid system. East–west streets are evenly-numbered avenidas, while north–south streets are odd-numbered calles. Downtown Cienfuegos, or 'Pueblo Nuevo,' is the area bounded by Avs 46 and 62, bisected by Calle 37. Avenida 54 is often called 'El Bulevar' and is a pedestrian mall from Calle 37 to Parque Martí. Calle 37 (popularly called Prado) runs 3km south to seaside Punta Gorda (where it's called Malecón). Rancho Luna is 18km south via Av 5 de Septiembre and is where you'll find the beach, resorts and diving.

Information

BOOKSHOPS

Librería Bohemia (Map p227; ☎ 52 51 63; Av 56 No 3318 btwn Calles 33 & 35)
Librería Dionisio San Román (Map p227; ☎ 52 55 92; Av 54 No 3526 at Calle 37)

EMERGENCY

Ambulance (☎ 185)
Asistur (Map p227; ☎ 51 32 65; www.asistur.cubaweb .com; Calle 25 No 5405 btwn Avs 54 & 56)

IMMIGRATION

Inmigración (Map p227; ☎ 52 10 17; Av 46 btwn 29 and 31)

INTERNET ACCESS

Cybercafé En Mi Cuba (Map p227; ☎ 51 18 77; Av 54 No 3518 btwn 35 & 37; US$3/hr; ☺ 9am-10pm)
Etecsa (Map p227; ☎ 51 92 66; Calle 31 No 5402 btwn Avs 54 & 56; US$6/hr; ☺ 24hr – they claim)

MEDIA

Radio Ciudad del Mar (1350 AM & 98.9 FM)

MEDICAL SERVICES

Clínica Internacional (Map p227; ☎ 55 16 23; Calle 37 No 202, Punta Gorda) Caters to foreigners, handles dental emergencies and has a 24-hour dollar pharmacy.
Farmacia Principal Municipal (Map p227; ☎ 51 57 37; Av 54 No 3524 btwn Calles 35 & 37)
Óptica Miramar (Map p227; ☎ 55 12 78; Av 54 No 3504) Optometrists, contact lenses and solution are all here.

MONEY

Banco de Crédito y Comercio (Map p227; ☎ 51 57 47; Av 56 at Calle 31)
Banco Financiero Internacional (Map p227; ☎ 55 16 57; Av 54 at Calle 29)
Cadeca (Map p227; ☎ 55 22 21; Av 56 No 3314 btwn Calles 33 & 35)

PHOTOGRAPHY

One Hour Photo (Map p227; ☎ 55 22 98; Calle 37 No 5217 btwn Avs 52 & 54; ☺ 8am-10pm) Well-stocked with digital camera and lithium batteries and Agfa film.
Photo Service (Map p227; Av 54 No 3118 btwn Calles 31 & 33) Another outlet is across from Hotel Jagua.

POST

DHL (Map p227; ☎ 51 10 31; Av 54 No 3514 btwn Calles 35 & 37)
Post Office Av 56 and Calle 35 (Map p227; ☎ 51 82 84); Av 54 No 3514 (Map p227; btwn Calles 35 & 37)

TELEPHONE

Etecsa (Map p227; ☎ 51 92 66; Calle 31 No 5403 btwn Avs 54 & 56) Supposedly open 24 hours; also with a kiosk at Calle 37 and Av 2 in Punta Gorda.

TRAVEL AGENCIES

There is no proper tourist office; these agencies provide information and make reservations:
Cubatur (Map p227; ☎ 55 12 42; Calle 37 No 5399 btwn Avs 54 & 56)
Havanatur (Map p227; ☎ 51 11 50; fax 55 13 70; Av 54 No 2906 btwn Calles 29 & 31)
Reservaciones de Campismo (Map p227; ☎ 51 94 23; Calle 37 No 5407 btwn Avs 54 and 56) For camping cabins throughout the province.
Rumbos (Map p227; ☎ 51 83 67; Calle 25 No 5405 btwn Avs 54 & 56)

Sights

The most interesting sights are clustered around Parque José Martí and 3km south in the Punta Gorda section of town. You can see

CIENFUEGOS

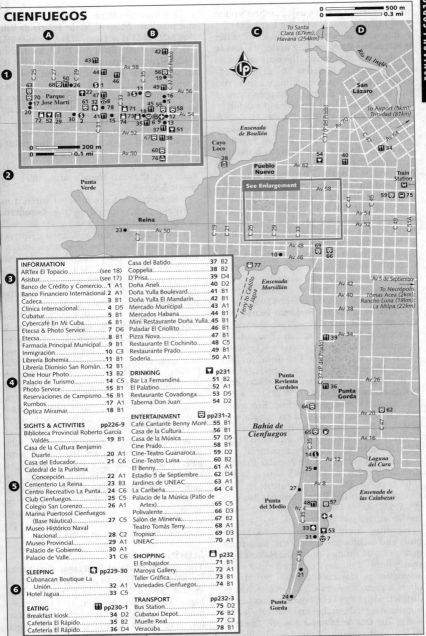

0 — 500 m
0 — 0.3 mi

To Santa
Clara (67km);
Havana (254km)

Río El Inglés

San
Lázaro

To Airport (5km);
Trinidad (81km)

Ensenada
de Boullón

Cayo
Loco

Pueblo
Nuevo

Train
Station

Punta
Verde

Reina

INFORMATION
ARTex El Topacio.................(see 18)
Asistur.................................(see 17)
Banco de Crédito y Comercio...1 A1
Banco Financiero Internacional..2 A1
Cadeca...................................3 B1
Clínica Internacional.................4 D5
Cubatur..................................5 B1
Cybercafé En Mi Cuba...............6 B1
Etecsa & Photo Service..............7 D6
Etecsa....................................8 B1
Farmacia Principal Municipal.......9 B1
Inmigración...........................10 C3
Librería Bohemia.....................11 B1
Librería Dionisio San Román.......12 B1
One Hour Photo.......................13 B2
Palacio de Turismo..................14 C5
Photo Service.........................15 B1
Reservaciones de Campismo......16 B1
Rumbos.................................17 A1
Óptica Miramar.......................18 B1

SIGHTS & ACTIVITIES   pp226-9
Biblioteca Provincial Roberto García
  Valdés.................................19 B1
Casa de la Cultura Benjamín
  Duarte................................20 A1
Casa del Educador...................21 C6
Catedral de la Purísima
  Concepción..........................22 A1
Cementerio La Reina.................23 B3
Centro Recreativo La Punta........24 C6
Club Cienfuegos......................25 C5
Colegio San Lorenzo.................26 A1
Marina Puertosol Cienfuegos
  (Base Náutica).....................27 C5
Museo Histórico Naval
  Nacional.............................28 C2
Museo Provincial.....................29 A1
Palacio de Gobierno.................30 A1
Palacio de Valle......................31 C6

SLEEPING   pp229-30
Cubanacan Boutique La
  Unión.................................32 A1
Hotel Jagua............................33 C5

EATING   pp230-1
Breakfast kiosk.......................34 D2
Cafetería El Rápido...................35 B2
Cafetería El Rápido...................36 D4

Casa del Batido.......................37 B2
Coppelia...............................38 B2
D'Prisa.................................39 D4
Doña Aneli.............................40 D2
Doña Yulla Boulevard................41 B1
Doña Yulla El Mandarín..............42 B1
Mercado Municipal...................43 B1
Mercados Habana....................44 B1
Mini Restaurante Doña Yulla.......45 B1
Paladar El Criollito...................46 B1
Pizza Nova............................47 B1
Restaurante El Cochinito...........48 C5
Restaurante Prado...................49 B1
Sodería.................................50 A1

DRINKING   p231
Bar La Fernandina....................51 B2
El Palatino.............................52 A1
Restaurante Covadonga.............53 D5
Taberna Don Juan...................54 D2

ENTERTAINMENT   pp231-2
Café Cantante Benny Moré..........55 B1
Casa de la Cultura....................56 B1
Casa de la Música....................57 D5
Cine Prado.............................58 B1
Cine-Teatro Guanaroca..............59 D2
Cine-Teatro Luisa....................60 B2
El Benny...............................61 A1
Estadio 5 de Septiembre............62 D4
Jardines de UNEAC...................63 A1
La Cariñeba...........................64 C4
Palacio de la Música (Patio de
  Artex)................................65 C5
Polivalente............................66 D3
Salón de Minerva.....................67 B2
Teatro Tomás Terry..................68 A1
Tropisur...............................69 D3
UNEAC.................................70 A1

SHOPPING   p232
El Embajador..........................71 B1
Maroya Gallery.......................72 A1
Taller Gráfica.........................73 B1
Variedades Cienfuegos..............74 B1

TRANSPORT   pp232-3
Bus Station............................75 D2
Cubataxi Depot.......................76 B2
Muelle Real...........................77 C3
Veracuba..............................78 B1

To Necrópolis
Tomás Acea (2km);
Rancho Luna (18km);
La Milpa (22km)

Ensenada
Marsillán

Av 5 de Septiembre

Punta
Revienta
Cordeles

Punta
Gorda

Bahía de
Cienfuegos

Laguna
del Cura

Punta
del Medio

Ensenada de
las Calabazas

Punta
Gorda

most of Cienfuegos in a day, but there's often good nightlife worth catching (see p231).

Start your wanderings in the town center at **Parque José Martí**, passing under the **Arco de Triunfo** (arch of triumph, the only one of its kind in Cuba) dedicated to Cuban independence. This impressive monument ushers you into the heart of the park, dropping you at the feet of José Martí rendered in marble.

Teatro Tomás Terry (Map p227; ☎ 51 33 61; Av 56 No 270 btwn Calle 27 & 29; tours $1; ☺ 9am-6pm), on the northern side of Parque Martí, is one of Cienfuegos' most famous buildings. To honor their father, sons of Venezuelan industrialist Tomás Terry built this 950-seat auditorium between 1887 and 1889 and graced the lobby with a Carrara marble statue of dad. In 1895 the theater opened with a performance of Verdi's *Aïda*. Famous artists who tread the boards here include Enrico Caruso, Anna Pavlova and Sarah Bernhardt. The seats are carved from Cuban hardwoods and there's an impressive ceiling fresco by Camilo Salaya.

On the western side of Parque Martí is the former Palacio de Ferrer (1918), now the **Casa de la Cultura Benjamin Duarte** (Map p227; ☎ 51 65 84; Calle 25 No 5401; admission free; ☺ 8:30am-midnight) where you can climb up the *mirador* (tower) for killer views (US$0.50). Check the schedule at the door for live music happenings. On the opposite side of the park is the neoclassical **Catedral de la Purísima Concepción** (Map p227; ☎ 52 52 97; Av 56 No 2902; donations accepted; ☺ 7am-noon). Erected in 1869, it has twin towers and French stained-glass windows. The southern side of Parque Martí is dominated by the red dome of the **Palacio de Gobierno**, where the provincial government, called the Poder Popular Provincial, holds forth (no visitors). Unless you're into turn of the century furniture, you can easily skip the **Museo Provincial** (Map p227; ☎ 51 97 22; Av 54 & Calle 27; admission US$2; ☺ 10am-6pm Tue-Sat, 10am-noon Sun) nearby.

Heading south for 3km on Prado, you cross into Cienfuegos' aristocratic, waterfront quarter called Punta Gorda. The **Malecón** here shares none of the sexy extracurricular characteristics of Havana's seawall, but it still offers a pretty bay vista. The architecture is distinct, with bright clapboard homes boasting sun-dappled porches and intricate lattice work. The **Casa del Educador** (Map p227; Calle 35 No 26) is a great example of these beach villas.

Continue south on this spit of land to the fabulous Moorish-style **Palacio de Vall** (Map p227; ☎ 51 12 26; Calle 37 at Av 2; admission US$1; ☺ 9:30am-11pm). Built in 1917 by Oclic[?] Valle Blanco, a Spaniard from Asturias, it's an outrageous jumble of tiles and turrets, crenellated edges and scalloped arches. Batista planned to convert the palace into a casino, but today it's an upscale restaurant with a terrace bar (p231).

The **Centro Recreativo La Punta** (Map p227; ☺ 10am-10pm) has a gazebo on the point's extreme southern tip and is a great spot to watch the sunset. You can grab a beer or *mojito* at the bar; there's sometimes live music here.

Cienfuegos has a couple of interesting outlying sights including the **Cementerio La Reina** (Map p227; Av 50 & Calle 7; ☺ 8am-6pm). Founded in 1837, this rundown cemetery is lined with the graves of Spanish soldiers who died in the independence wars and has a marble statue called 'Bella Durmiente:' a tribute to a 24-year-old woman who died in 1907 of a broken heart. It's an evocative place if you're into graveyards.

If you're out this way, tour around the **Museo Histórico Naval Nacional** (Map p227; ☎ 51 91 43; Av 60 & Calle 21; admission US$1; ☺ 9am-6pm Tue-Fri, 9am-noon Sun). Housed in the former headquarters of the Distrito Naval del Sur (1950), this important museum covers archaeology, natural history, naval history, navigation and art. The museum's central theme is the abortive naval revolt against Fulgencio Batista that took place here on September 5, 1957.

A monument to marine martyrs who died in that revolt is nestled in the **Necrópolis Tomás Acea** (Map p233; Carretera de Rancho Luna Km 2; admission US$1; ☺ 8am-6pm), a mammoth cemetery entered through a huge neoclassical pavilion (1926) flanked by 64 Doric columns. This cemetery, 2km east of town via Av 5 de Septiembre, makes a good pit stop en route to Rancho Luna.

Activities

The **Marina Puertosol Cienfuegos** (Base Náutica; Map p227; ☎ 55 12 41; fax 55 12 75; Av 8 & Calle 35; ☺ 7am-5pm), a few blocks north of Hotel Jagua, rents motorboats at US$35 for two hours (up to eight persons); this is an easy, fun way to get to the Castillo de Jagua (p234). Fishing trips are also possible from here for US$30 per hour for trolling or US$20 per hour for bottom fishing, minimum four hours, maximum four people. Also ask about sailboat and jet ski rentals.

Nearby, the new **Club Cienfuegos** (Map p227; ☎ 52 65 10; Calle 35 btwn Avs 10 & 12; ☽ 9am-1am Sun-Fri, 9am-2am Sat) has a pool and beach, with many watersports including kayaks and windsurfers. There's also an amusement park with bumper cars, go carts and video games (US$0.50 to US$1).

If you're into billiards or bowling, go to **La Bolera** (Calle 37 btwn Avs 46 & 48; US$1-2/hr; ☽ 11am-2am), where there's an ice-cream parlor and occasional live music. Nonguests can use the nice **swimming pool** at Hotel la Unión (Av 54 and Calle 31) for US$5.

Tours
Rumbos arranges tours to **El Nicho** (p234) for US$28 per person (minimum seven people) including lunch.

Festivals & Events
Local festivals include the cultural events marking the foundation of the city on April 22, 1819, carnaval in August and the Benny Moré International Festival of Popular Music in September of odd-numbered years.

Sleeping
Cienfuegos has licensed private rooms to spare – your best bet for budget accommodation (see boxed text). Those at Punta Gorda are more removed, but generally

---

CASAS PARTICULARES – CIENFUEGOS

Town Center
Friendship Home – Armando y Leonor (☎ 51 61 43; Av 56 No 2927 btwn Calles 29 & 31; r US$15-20) Colonial house just off Parque Martí, balcony, patio dining, legendary food, chatty hosts.
Elías Álvarez Hernández (☎ 51 75 85; Av 52 No 4312 btwn Calles 43 & 45; r US$10-20; ☒) Two clean rooms, independent, English spoken, friendly.
Carmen y Felipe (☎ 51 28 85; Av 60 No 4703 btwn Calles 47 & 49; r US$15-20; ☒) Near bus and train stations, private bath, small balcony, hospitable; also rent at No 4707
Casa de Armando (☎ 51 52 99; Av 60 No 3703 btwn Calles 37 & 39; r US$15-20; ☒) Sleeps 3, private bath, good location, friendly.
Miriam and Gladys Fernández Portillo (☎ 51 58 16; Av 54 No 4919 btwn 49 & 51; r US$15) Near bus station, also at No 4923, retired teachers.
Pepe and Isabel Martínez Cordero (☎ 51 82 76; Av 52 No 4318 btwn 43 & 45; r US$15) Interconnecting rooms, meals served, friendly.
Ulises Jaureguí (☎ 51 98 91; Calle 37 No 4202 btwn Avs 42 & 44; r US$15; ☒) Flexible set up, interconnecting rooms, share dining room, ideal for groups.
Carmen Rosa Tapiro (☎ 51 63 65; Calle 45 No 3801 btwn 38 & 40) Good house, garage parking.
Deliz Sierra (☎ 51 66 38; Calle 37 No 3806 btwn Avs 38 & 40; r US$15-20)

Punta Gorda
Angel e Isabel (☎ 51 15 19; Calle 35 No 24 btwn Av 0 & Litoral; r US$20-25; ☒) Three nicely furnished rooms in waterfront garden, mountain views, friendly, meals, roof terrace; also rent at No 22.
Maylin y Tony (☎ 51 99 66; Calle 35 No 4B btwn 0 & Litoral; r US$25; ☻) Two rooms with private bath, balcony, sea views and access; friendly, good meals.
Jorge A Piñeiro Vásquez (☎ 51 38 08; Calle 41 No 1402 btwn Avs 14 &16; r US$25; ℗) Meals served, secluded, upscale.
Luis Felipa Alberto Fernández (☎ 51 75 55; Av 12 No 3902 btwn Calles 39 & 41; r US$20; ☒) Three rooms with refrigerator; wraparound porch with rocking chairs; another at No 3904.
Clara Martha (☎ 51 70 57; Calle 39 No 1204 btwn Avs 12 & 14; r US$20-25; ☒) Two rooms, independent entrance.
Jorge de la Peña Castellanos (☎ 51 90 15; Calle 39 No 1206 btwn Avs 12 & 14; r US$20; ℗) English spoken.
Happy Pete's – Pedro A Febles (☎ 51 75 55; Av 12 No 3904 btwn Calles 39 & 40; r US$20-25; ☒) Also at No 3902.
Miriam Aguilera Díaz (☎ 51 80 85; Calle 37 No 1006 btwn 10 & 12; r US$15-20)

more atmospheric. At the time of writing there were only three hotels in Cienfuegos, though check out the grand old **Palacio de Turismo** (Map p227; Calle 37 No 201 btwn Avs 12 & 14) once it reopens as a boutique hotel.

Hotel Jagua (Map p227; Gran Caribe; ☎ 55 10 03; fax 55 12 45; Calle 37 No 1; low season s/d/tr US$55/65/93, high season US$75/90/128; 🏋 🖳 🗩) This hotel in Punta Gorda is located 3km south of the center. Erected in the 1950s by Batista's brother, it's one of central Cuba's top hotels. The 145 rooms are good value and kids aged 12 and under stay for half price. A decent choice for families, there are on-site babysitters, tennis courts, dance classes and jet skis. A cabaret show (US$7) happens at 9:30pm Tuesday to Friday and 10pm Saturday.

Hotel Punta La Cueva (Map p233; Islazul; ☎ 51 39 56; d US$26; 🅿 🏋 🗩) This place is east across the bay from Hotel Jagua via a 3.5km access road that begins just east of Necrópolis Tomás Acea. The 67 rooms are a bit rundown, but still good value. There's a small beach, but it doesn't compensate for such a removed location.

Cubanacán Boutique La Unión (Map p227; Cubanacán; ☎ 55 10 20; www.cubanacan.cu; Av 54 & Calle 31; s/d US$80/90; 🏋 🖳 🗩) This gem, in the heart of town, reopened recently after a major restoration by Cubanacán, so everything from the beds to the poolside loungers are fresh and new. The 46 antique-furnished rooms have balconies opening to the street or a colonial patio lined with mosaics; chill by the pool and get a relaxing massage, which will set you back US$5.

Eating

Snacking and dining in pesos is largely confined to the center of Cienfuegos (with many places along Prado), while Punta Gorda to the south has many fast food and finer dining dollar options.

TOWN CENTER

Pizza Nova (Map p227; ☎ 55 20 20; Calle 31 No 5418 btwn Avs 54 and 56; 🕑 noon-midnight) Living up to its reputation for reliable, tasty food, this place has pizzas starting at US$3.85 (with toppings like mushrooms, black olives or sausage additional) and lasagne at US$7. The big salads, bruschetta and soups make this a good vegetarian option.

Paladar El Criollito (Map p227; Calle 33 No 5603 btwn Avs 56 & 58) This friendly spot is one of the last private restaurants remaining here. Fresh, filling criollo meals cost US$6 to US$8, depending on whether you come solo or with a *jinetero*.

Mini Restaurante Doña Yulla (Map p227; Av 54 No 3507 btwn Calles 35 & 37; 🕑 11am-3pm & 6:30-10:30pm) This is among the best of the many Doña Yullas here, with tablecloths, friendly service and an inexpensive dollar menu (all items are under US$3). Try the pork steak (US$2.25).

Sodería (Map p227; Av 56 No 2703 btwn Calles 27 & 29) This dollar cafe on Parque Martí serves espresso (US$1) and café con leche (US$2), plus ice-cream sundaes (US$2). The flowering patio looks out on the park – nice!

If you feel like cooking or having a picnic, head to the **Mercado Municipal** (Map p227; Calle 31 No 5805 btwn Avs 58 & 60) for fruits and vegetables in pesos; prepackaged food and drinks are sold at the **Mercados Habana** (Av 58 No 3102 at Calle 31) dollar store.

For a quick and inexpensive breakfast, check out **Casa del Batido** (Map p227; Calle 37 No 5211 btwn Avs 52 & 54; 🕑 6am-11pm) with wonderful fruitshakes like banana and papaya (one peso) or **Doña Aneli** (Map p227; Calle 41 cnr of Av 62; 🕑 9am-10:15pm) for pastries and bread in dollars. Nearby, a **breakfast kiosk** (Map p227; Ave 64 cnr of Calle 47) sells amazing fried egg and chive sandwiches (three pesos).

Also recommended:

Restaurante Prado (Map p227; Calle 37 at the cnr of Av 56; mains US$2-4) Brand new vegetarian place.

Doña Yulla El Mandarín (Map p227; ☎ 51 74 90; Calle 37 No 5813 btwn Avs 58 & 60; everything under US$3) The Chinese option.

Doña Yulla Boulevard (Map p227; Av 54 No 3106 btwn Calles 31 & 33) Passable food and cheap draft beer (10 pesos).

El Rápido (Map p227; Av 54 & Calle 35) As always, pizza, sandwiches and snacks (US$1).

Coppelia (Map p227; Calle 37 & Av 52) Peso ice cream for two pesos a scoop.

PUNTA GORDA

Of the few cheap places out in Punta Gorda, try **Restaurante El Cochinito** (Map p227; ☎ 51 86 11; Calle 37 & Av 4; 🕑 noon-3pm & 7-10pm, closed Tue) with pork and chicken dishes for under US$4. Good old **El Rápido** (Map p227; Calle 37 Av 26) has a nice terrace overlooking the bay where you can eat your US$1 microwave pizza. Bonus: air hockey. **D'Prisa** (Map p227; Calle 37 near Av 34) is similar.

La Lobera (Map p227; ☎ 52 65 10; Calle 37 btwn Avs 10 & 12; ⌚ noon-3pm & 6-9pm) A new addition to the Cienfuegos dining scene, this upscale, affordable restaurant at the Club Cienfuegos is a local favorite. You won't pay more than US$10 for a steak with all the fixings. The fantastic wraparound dining terrace with sea views make it memorable. There's also a **cafeteria** upstairs and one of the best bars in town downstairs (see below).

Palacio de Valle (Map p227; ☎ 51 12 26; Calle 37 at Av 2) It's unfortunate the food and service here are no match for the beautiful building housing this restaurant. Despite it's promising menu of varied lobster and shrimp dishes (US$12 to US$25), both locals and travelers give this place a thumbs down (one reader called it 'a complete disaster'). Give dinner a miss and grab a cocktail at the rooftop terrace bar.

Towards the southern point of Punta Gorda is **Restaurante La Cueva del Camarón**, (☎ 55 11 28; Calle 37 and Av 2) with fish dinners at US$9 and lobster for US$20.

EAST OF TOWN
Finca La Isabela (Map p233; ☎ 51 70 06; Carratera de Rancho Luna Km 3; lunch US$8) This 'typical' country estate run by Rumbos serves the ample spit-roasted pork lunches the Cuban *campo* (countryside) is known for. Though designed as a tour bus stopover, this is a good option for hungry travelers who don't want to dawdle in Cienfuegos proper. Horseback riding is offered.

Drinking
Cienfuegos has quite a good drinking scene, with everything from sticky-floor peso dives to luxurious bars with views.

Bar Terrazas (☎ 55 10 20; Av 54 and Calle 31) This watering hole upstairs at the Hotel Unión is a good central option. Sip a *mojito* and enjoy fine city views; live music starts at 10pm.

Billiards Club (Map p227; ☎ 52 65 10; Calle 37 btwn Avs 10 & 12; ⌚ 9am-1am Sun-Fri, 9am-2am Sat) This downstairs bar with bay views at the new Club Cienfuegos has several pool tables (US$2.50 per hour) and a big city atmosphere.

Taberna Don Juan (Map p227; Calle 37 cnr of Av 62; ⌚ 9am-11pm) A good, local peso bar with sidewalk tables and rawhide chairs, head here to load up on cheap beer and rum; good Prado people watching.

Restaurante Covadonga (Map p227; ☎ 59 64 20; Calle 37 btwn Av 2 & 0) This restaurant with a terrific waterfront locale is a relaxing place for a sunset cocktail; skip the food.

El Palatino (Map p227; Av 54 No 2514) On the southern side of Parque Martí, this place is popular on the tour bus circuit. Impromptu jazz sets sometimes erupt here. Prepare to be hit up for alms.

The **terrace bar** at the Palacio de Valle scores for its views and ambiance.

Entertainment
LIVE MUSIC
Drop by any of these places to see what's on, as most have a *cartelera* (schedule) posted out front.

Jardines de la UNEAC (Map p227; ☎ 51 61 17; Calle 25 No 5413 btwn Avs 54 & 56; admission US$2) It's hard to beat this outdoor patio venue with its AfroCuban *peñas* (musical performances) and guest *trovadores* (troubadours) like Vicente Feliú.

Casa de la Música (Map p227; ☎ 55 23 20; Calle 37 btwn Avs 4 & 6; ⌚ shows start 10pm Fri & Sat, 5pm Sun) This big, new outdoor venue in Punta Gorda hosts everyone from Los Van Van and '70s cover bands to feisty rap groups.

Salón de Minerva (Map p227; Av 52 No 3512 btwn Calles 35 & 37; admission US$1; ⌚ 10pm Thu-Sat, 3pm Sun) Live boleros, salsa and *trova* (traditional poetic singing/songwriting) are all featured at this popular spot; bring your dancing shoes.

Patio de Artex (Map p227; ☎ 55 12 55; Calle 35 at Av 16) Another recommendable patio place in Cienfuegos, you can catch *son* in the evenings and live ensembles at the 2pm Sunday matinee.

Traditional music is also a staple at **Café Cantante Benny Moré** (Map p227; Av 54 at Calle 37), a rough peso place not for shrinking violets.

DANCE CLUBS
El Benny (Map p227; ☎ 55 11 05; Av 54 No 2907 btwn Calles 29 & 31; admission per couple US$8; ⌚ 10pm-3am Tue-Sun) The entrance fee to this sharp place includes a bottle of rum, two Cokes and enough salsa and sugar pop to make you drop.

Two open-air discos with a local vibe are the friendly **Tropisur** (Map p227; Calle 37 & Av 48; ⌚ Sat only), with the pink-and-white wall around it (no sign), and **La Caribeña** (Map p227; ☎ 51 70 16; Calle 35 btwn Avs 20 & 22; ⌚ Fri & Sat) in Punta Gorda. Both of these places are the real deal.

THEATER

Teatro Tomás Terry (Map p227; ☎ 51 33 61) This architectural showpiece on the northern side of Parque Martí stages premier performances; box office is open 11am to 3pm daily and 90 minutes before showtime.

Also check the cultural calendars at the **Casa de la Cultura Benjamín Duarte** (Map p227; Calle 25 No 5403; admission US$2) on Parque Martí, which shows movies daily at 2pm and 8:30pm, and the **Casa de la Cultura** (Map p227; Calle 37 No 5615 at Av 58).

CINEMAS

Cienfuegos has three movie houses: **Cine-Teatro Luisa** (Map p227; Calle 37 No 5001 at Av 50); **Cine Prado** (Map p227; Calle 37 No 5402 at Av 54) and **Cine-Teatro Guanaroca** (Map p227; Calle 49 at Av 58) opposite the bus station.

SPORT

From October to April, baseball games take place at **Estadio 5 de Septiembre** (Map p227; ☎ 51 36 44; Av 20 btwn Calles 45 & 55), while weekend boxing matches and other sporting events occur at **Polivalente** (Map p227; Calle 37 & Av 48).

Shopping

Whatever you desire can be found on the stretch of Avenue 54 between Calle 37 and Parque Martí; known as El Bulevar, it's chock-a-block with stores.

Variedades Cienfuegos (Map p227; Av 54 No 3308 btwn Calles 33 & 35) A peso emporium with used clothes and books (in Spanish), jewelry and other randomness, this is a fun place to poke around.

ARTex El Topacio (Map p227; Av 54 No 3510 btwn Calles 35 & 37) The compact disc and book selection here is good.

Taller Gráfica (Map p227; Ave 54 btwn Calles 35 & 37, upstairs; 8am-4pm Mon-Fri) Meet the artists and browse or buy their wonderful prints in this funky studio workshop.

El Embajador (Map p227; Av 54 cnr of Calle 33) La Casa del Habano, with an adjoining café, is where you can buy Cuban cigars, rum or coffee, plus enjoy a cocktail or espresso while you smoke.

Maroya Gallery (Map p227; ☎ 55 12 08; Av 54 No 2506 on Parque Martí; 9am-6pm) Fabulous collections of paintings, folk art and hand painted clothing are for sale here, and director Miguel Angel Rodgríguez can arrange studio visits with local artists.

Getting There & Away

AIR

No air services were available at the **Jaime González Airport** 5km northeast of Cienfuegos at the time of writing. The closest air connection is in Havana.

BUS

The **bus station** (☎ 51 57 20) is on Calle 49 between Avs 56 and 58. There are buses to Havana twice a day (US$20, five hours) and Trinidad twice a day (US$6, two hours). To reach any other destinations from Cienfuegos, you have to connect in Trinidad, but since the two regular daily departures to Trinidad leave too late to connect, there's a 6:30am minibus to Trinidad (US$10). Tickets must be purchased from the *jefe de turno* (shift manager) downstairs.

For local buses to Rancho Luna (US$1), Pasacaballo (US$1) and Playa Girón (US$4), check the blackboard downstairs. Outside the station, collective taxis may be willing to take you to Santa Clara (US$3) and Cumanayagua (US$1) en route to El Nicho.

Astro (☎ 52 54 95) has departures from the bus station to the following cities (details are for one way):

Camagüey (US$16; 7 hours; 1 daily)
Havana (US$16; 5 hours; 5 daily)
Santa Clara (US$2.50; 2 hours; 2 daily)
Santiago de Cuba (US$31; 2 hours; alt days)
Trinidad (US$5; 2 hours; 2 daily)

TRAIN

The **train station** (☎ 52 54 95; Av 58 & Calle 49; ticket window 8am-3:30pm Mon-Fri, 8am-11:30am Sat) is across from the bus station. Trains are often canceled. When running, the schedule is:

Havana (US$11; 10 hours; alternate days)
Santa Clara (US$2.10; 2 hours; daily but Sunday)
Sancti Spíritus (US$5.50; 5 hours; once a week)

Getting Around

BOAT

When there's gas, a 120-passenger ferry runs to the Castillo de Jagua (40 minutes, US$1) from the **Muelle Real** (Map p227; Av 46 and Calle 25). It leaves Cienfuegos at 6:30am, 8am and 10:30am and noon, 2pm and 3pm, returning from the castle 20 minutes after arrival. The wharf is near the castle. Beware of ferries leaving early. Two ferries also make this trip from just below the Hotel Pasacaballo (p234).

CAR & MOPED

Transtur Hotel Jagua (☎ 51 79 82); Hotel Rancho Luna (☎ 45 11 72)

Havanautos Punta Gorda (☎ 56 24 91; Calle 37 at Av 16); Hotel Rancho Luna (Map p233; ☎ 54 81 43)

VeraCuba (Map p227; ☎ 55 17 00; Calle 31 btwn 54 & 56) Rents cars, Jeeps and mopeds for about US$15/day.

The **Servi-Cupet** gas station is on Calle 37 at the corner of Av 16, in Punta Gorda. There's another station 5km northeast of Hotel Rancho Luna.

HORSE & CARRIAGE

Horse carts ply Calle 37 charging Cubans one peso a ride, foreigners US$1 (though Spanish speakers might be able to 'pass' and pay a peso). It's a pleasant way to travel between town and Punta Gorda.

TAXI

Cubataxi (Map p227; ☎ 51 91 45, 51 84 54; Av 50 No 3508 at Calle 37) has taxis 24 hours a day. Citroen/Lada taxis cost US$0.40/35 a kilometer, cheaper than the tourist taxis outside Hotel Jagua. Agree on the price first.

AROUND CIENFUEGOS
Rancho Luna

Rancho Luna is a picturesque bend of beach 18km south of Cienfuegos. Aside from three large hotels, it's also possible to stay in private rooms, one of the few resort areas in Cuba where this is allowed. The entire coast is protected by a coral reef that you can swim out to in some places. The local post office is in Hotel Rancho Luna. In the small village facing Hotel Club Amigo Faro Luna is a disco and beach bar.

SIGHTS & ACTIVITIES

There's a secluded little beach (Map p233) in the crook east of Punta Colorados that's a superb picnic or camping spot; access it from the dirt track just before the lighthouse.

Like most Cuban resort areas, Rancho Luna has its **Delfinario** (Map p233; ☎ 54 81 20; adult/child US$3/5; ☼ 9am-5pm Tue-Sun) where you can see the creatures jump through hoops or swim with them for an extra US$20/35.

Scuba diving is possible with dive centers at hotels Rancho Luna and Club Amigo Faro Luna, which visit 32 sites within a 20-minute boat ride. Caves, sunken ships, profuse marine life and dazzling coral gardens are among the attractions. From August to

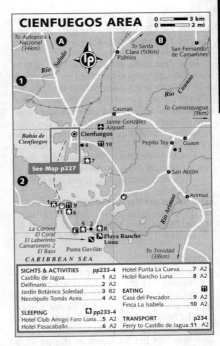

CIENFUEGOS AREA

SIGHTS & ACTIVITIES	pp233-4		Hotel Punta La Cueva	7	A2
Castillo de Jagua	1	A2	Hotel Rancho Luna	8	A2
Delfinario	2	A2			
Jardín Botánico Soledad	3	B2	EATING		
Necrópolis Tomás Acea	4	A2	Casa del Pescador	9	A2
			Finca La Isabela	10	A2
SLEEPING	pp233-4				
Hotel Club Amigo Faro Luna	5	A2	TRANSPORT		p234
Hotel Pasacaballo	6	A2	Ferry to Castillo de Jagua	11	A2

November harmless whale sharks frequent these waters. Good **snorkeling** is also possible with:

Whale Shark (Puerto Sol; ☎ 54 80 12; mpsolcfg@ip.etecsa.cu; at Hotel Rancho Luna) 1/2 dives US$25/40; for night dives US$36.

Cubanacán Náutica (☎ 54 80 40; dcfluna@acuc.cfg.cyt.cu; in Hotel Club Amigo Faro Luna) Dives US$30; open water certification US$365.

SLEEPING

Hotel Club Amigo Faro Luna (Map p233; Cubanacán; ☎ 54 81 39; www.cubanacan.cu; Carretera de Rancho Luna Km 18; s/d low season US$44/55; high US$52/66; ⓟ 🅧 🅡) This intimate resort on a bluff overlooking the sea is the pick of the litter. Not all rooms are the same and the newer units in the 200 and 300 block have tubs. The pool (with separate kiddie unit) is sweet. A long beach is only a few minutes walk away.

Hotel Rancho Luna (Map p233; Horizontes; ☎ 54 81 31; www.horizontes.cu; Carretera de Rancho Luna Km 16; s/d low season US$55/70, high US$65/80; ⓟ 🅧 🅡) This recently refurbished resort is a favorite of Canadian package tourists, who dig the all-inclusive deal, private beach and big pool. A horse and buggy can be hired at US$5 per person for rides along the coast. **Rumbos** (☎ 54 80 12) organizes tours to El Nicho from here.

Hotel Pasacaballo (Map p233; Islazul; ☎ 54 80 13; www.islazul.cu; Carretera de Rancho Luna Km 22; low season s/d/tr US$23/30/40; high season US$29/38/48; P 🍽 🍹) This five-story monster has 188 rooms hosting a mixed Cuban and international clientele. Sitting on a headland opposite the strait from the Castillo de Jagua, there are good views from the 6th-floor terrace. There's a reasonable cafeteria in the basement and a disco (open Wednesday to Sunday).

Recommended private rooms in the village include:

Finca Nelson and Marisol Rumbao (☎ 55 76 30; r US$15-20) Opposite the turn-off to Hotel Rancho Luna.

Manuel Busto Solis (in Santa Clara ☎ 42-21 80 25; Av del Golfo No 11; r US$15-20) Friendly, familial place.

EATING
Aside from the hotels, your dining options are limited (try the beach snack bar). The Servi-Cupet station 5km north of town serves microwave pizza 24 hours a day; **Casa del Pescador** (Map p233; ☎ 51 81 60; Carretera de Pasacaballo) near the ferry landing is probably you best bet for lunch or dinner (fish of the day is US$6).

GETTING THERE & AWAY
Theoretically, there are local buses from Cienfuegos seven times a day (five times on Sunday). The Jagua ferry to Cienfuegos calls at the dock directly below Hotel Pasacaballo several times daily. A one-way taxi to Cienfuegos should cost around US$8; bargain. Private persons face heavy fines if caught driving you around.

The best way to get here, though, is zipping along from Cienfuegos on a rented moped (p233).

Castillo de Jagua
The **Castillo de Nuestra Señora de los Ángeles de Jagua**, west of the mouth of Bahía de Cienfuegos, was designed by José Tontete in 1738 and completed in 1745 (long before the city of Cienfuegos was founded). At the time it was the third most important fortress in Cuba, after those of Havana and Santiago de Cuba. Built to keep pirates out, the castle now shelters a fickle government-run seafood restaurant open occasionally for lunch.

You can get to the castle via a roundabout road from Cienfuegos, but it's easier to take the ferry from a landing just below the Hotel Pasacaballo. It operates frequently throughout the day, charging one peso one way. Tourists pay US$1. Otherwise, take the ferry from Cienfuegos.

Jardín Botánico Soledad
The 94-hectare **Jardín Botánico Soledad** (Map p233; admission US$5; ☉ 8am-5pm), near the Pepito Tey sugar mill, 17km east of Cienfuegos, is one of Cuba's biggest gardens. It houses 2000 species of plants, including 23 types of bamboo, 65 of fig and 280 different palms. The botanical garden was founded in 1901 by US sugar baron Edwin F Atkins who intended to use the garden to study different varieties of sugarcane, but began planting exotic tropical trees from around the world.

Only three buses a day pass near Pepito Tey on their way from Cienfuegos to Cumanayagua, and a visit to the gardens is only practical if you have your own transportation. Coming from Cienfuegos, turn right (south) at the junction to Pepito Tey.

El Nicho
Waterfalls with small bathing pools and gorgeous mountain vistas: **El Nicho** (Map p225; admission US$5; ☉ 8:30am-6:30pm), just 90 minutes from Cienfuegos via the rough road at Crucecitas, is (was!) one of central Cuba's best kept secrets. You can swim, horseback ride to Hanabanilla (US$2 per hour) and camp here; there's a simple Rumbos restaurant. Tucked into the Sierra del Escambray, you'll need a 4WD (VeraCuba in Cienfuegos rents Jeeps for US$65 or you can take a tour with Rumbos, minimum seven persons), to reach these chilly cascades. Patient, hardy travelers can get a *colectivo* to Cumanayagua (US$1) from the bus station in Cienfuegos and then connect with a very local truck (☉ 5:30am and 5pm) to El Nicho. The falls are best (but coldest) from January to April before the rains and Cuban crowds come.

TOWARD TRINIDAD
The **Cueva Martín Infierno** in the Valle de Yuaganabo, 56km from Cienfuegos and 21km from Trinidad via the shore hamlet of Caleta de Muñoz, contains a 67m stalagmite said to be the tallest in the world, five interconnecting salons and unique formations.

This cave is not open for general tourism, but speleologists should contact Angel Graña at the **Sociedad Espeleológica de Cuba in Havana** (☎ 209-2885; angel@fanj.cult.cu). This valley is also a good bird-watching area.

Campismo Playa Inglés (Map p225; ☎ 54 09 01; Carretera de Trinidad Km 52; per person US$5) These 32 concrete cabins sleeping four to six people are right on the beach and a good budget choice en route to Trinidad. You can barbecue and horseback ride here.

Villa Guajimico (Map p225; Cubamar; ☎ 54 09 46; toll free from USA or Canada ☎ 800-645-1179; www.cubamarviajes.cu; Carretera de Trinidad Km 42; low season s/d/tr US$32/38/54, high US$35/46/66; P ⊠ ⊇)

Dotted with 51 little cabins (eight right on the beach), this picturesque dive base 42km southeast of Cienfuegos is a terrific seaside alternative halfway between Cienfuegos and Trinidad, with excellent scuba opportunities. Two to four dives are US$30 each, with US$20 initiation lessons available. This is a good place to learn to dive and is a fully-equipped Campertour site.

Villa Yaguanabo (Map p225; Islazul; ☎ 54 00 99; www.islazul.cu; low season s/d US$16/21; high US$20/26), 26km west of Trinidad and 3km east of the Playa Inglés, has 30 cabins and a new two-story block perched above the beach. There's a restaurant/bar.

Villa Clara
Province

Mention Villa Clara to Cubans and they say 'Che.' Most visitors do too, as the awesome Che Memorial in the provincial capital of Santa Clara is a tourism mecca and a mere 2½-hour drive from Havana. The dramatic turning point of the Cuban Revolution went down in and around Santa Clara, so history buffs will enjoy the museums, monuments and sites associated with Fulgencio Batista's ouster.

The colonial town of Remedios is highly recommended as one of Cuba's best detours. Once you've been enchanted by Remedios, you're just a hop skip from the super-soft, white sands of Cayo Santa María. If it's fresh H_2O you're after, head to the Embalse Hanabanilla in Villa Clara's mountainous south.

HIGHLIGHTS

■ **Historical Highs**
Inspiring Che Memorial (p240) in Santa Clara

■ **Architecture & Ambiance**
Unspoiled colonial pocket of Remedios (p246)

■ **Fireworks & Festivities**
Flying sparks, shaking hips and flowing rum: December 24 means Parrandas (p247) in Remedios

■ **Paradise Found**
Deserted beaches of Cayo Santa María (p248)

■ **Mountain Retreat**
Bass fishing the Embalse Hanabanilla (p246) in the scenic Sierra del Escambray

Cayo Santa María ★

Remedios ★

Che Memorial ★

Embalse Hanabanilla ★

| ■ TELEPHONE CODE: 42 | ■ POPULATION: 836,350 MILLION | ■ AREA: 8662 SQ KM |

VILLA CLARA PROVINCE

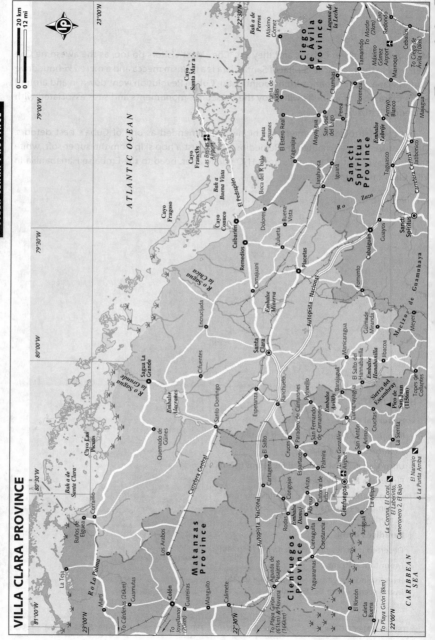

HISTORY

The most important date in Villa Clara's history was December 28, 1958, when a guerrilla force under the command of Ernesto 'Che' Guevara descended on Santa Clara from the Sierra del Escambray to do battle with Batista's troops. Despite overwhelming odds, (300 guerrillas vs 3000 of Batista's men), the rebels took control of the heavily armored train (p240) Batista had dispatched to reinforce troops in Santa Clara and points east. This victory rang the death knell for Batista, who fled the country two days later.

Villa Clara also shared in the drama of the 1962 Cuban Missile Crisis, as the four Soviet rocket launchers that sparked the incident were constructed in Sagua la Grande in the north. The Río Sagua la Grande is the largest river on Cuba's northern watershed and it drains the Embalse Alacranes, Cuba's second largest artificial reservoir. Like much of central Cuba, the economy focuses on sugarcane, with cows peppering the grazing lands south of the capital. Villa Clara is Cuba's fifth-largest province, bordering Matanzas Province to the west, Cienfuegos Province to the southwest, and Sancti Spíritus to the east.

SANTA CLARA

☎ 422 / pop 210,680

The city of Santa Clara has tons of history, but unless that's your thing, you might find yourself yawning (read: few colonial monuments and a dull sleeping/eating scene). On the upside, the Universidad Central de Las Villas, 8km east of town, is one of Cuba's most important universities and the student presence adds a young, intellectual energy.

History

Midway between Havana and Camagüey and 196km southeast of Varadero, Christopher Columbus believed that Cubanacán (or Cubana Khan), an Indian village once located near Santa Clara, was the seat of the khans of Mongolia. Hence, his misguided notion that he was exploring the Asian coast. Santa Clara proper was founded in 1689 by settlers from Remedios who wanted to distance themselves from pirates; the town grew quickly after a fire emptied Remedios in 1692. In 1867 Santa Clara became the capital of Las Villas Province, and

SANTA CLARA STREET NAMES	
old name	**new name**
Caridad	General Roloff
Sindico	Morales
Nazareno	Serafín García
San Migue	9 de Abril
Candelaria	Maestra Nicolasa

in 1873 the railway from Havana arrived. Santa Clara was the first major city to be liberated from Batista's army in December 1958.

Orientation

Monuments relating to the culminating battle of the Cuban Revolution are on the east and west sides of the city. The train station is seven blocks north of Parque Vidal; the two bus stations are less conveniently located on the Carretera Central west of town.

Santa Clara has a dual street naming system: the old names used by locals and new names that appear on signs and our maps. See the boxed text above if you're confused.

Information

BOOKSTORES

Librería Viet Nam (Independencia Este btwn Plácido & Luis Estévez) Sells books in dollars and pesos.

Proyecto Ateneo Pepe Medina (Parque Vidal No 18) Books in Spanish, plus some English and German titles; small reading area with air-con.

IMMIGRATION

Inmigración (Av Sandino cnr of Sexta; ⊗ 8am-noon & 1-3pm Mon-Thu) Three blocks east of Estadio Sandino.

INTERNET ACCESS

InfoInternet (Marta Abreu No 55 btwn Máximo Gómez & Villuendas; US$0.10/min)

LAUNDRY

Lavandería (☎ 20 35 66; Bonifacio Martínez No 12) Peso laundry at El Mundo de la Fantasía.

MEDIA

Radio CMHW Broadcasting on 840 AM and 93.5 FM.

Vanguardia Santa Clara Newspaper published Saturday.

MEDICAL SERVICES

Farmacia Campa (Independencia Este & Luis Estévez; ⊗ 8am-8:30pm)

Farmacia Homeopática (Independencia Oeste at Villuendas) Sells homeopathic and herbal remedies.

Óptica Miramar (☎ 20 80 69; Colón No 106 btwn 9 de Abril & Maestra Nicolasa) Contact lenses and solution available.

Policlínico Docente José R Leon Acosta (☎ 20 22 44; Serafín García Oeste No 167 btwn Alemán & Carretera Central)

MONEY

Banco Financiero Internacional (☎ 20 74 50; Cuba No 6 & Rafael Trista)

Bandec (☎ 21 81 15; Rafael Tristá & Cuba; ☽ 8am-2pm Mon-Fri, 8am-11am Sat)

Cadeca (☎ 20 56 90; Rafael Trista & Cuba on Parque Vidal; ☽ 8:30am-6pm Mon-Sat, 8:30am-12:30pm Sun)

PHOTOGRAPHY

Photo Service (Independencia Oeste No 55 btwn Villuendas & Zayas)

Photo Club (Marta Abreu No 10)

POST

DHL (☎ 20 89 76; Cuba btwn Rafael Tristá & Eduardo Machado; ☽ 8am-6pm Mon-Sat, 8am-noon Sun)

Post Office (Colón No 10; ☽ 8am-6pm Mon-Sat, 8am-noon Sun)

TELEPHONE

Etecsa (Cuba cnr Eduardo Machado; ☽ 8am-10pm)

TRAVEL AGENCIES

Cubatur (☎ 20 89 80; Marta Abreu No 10; ☽ 9am-6pm) Near Máximo Gómez.

Havanatur (☎ 20 40 01; Máximo Gómez No 9B; ☽ 8:30am-noon & 1-5:30pm Mon-Fri, 8:30am-12:30pm Sat) Near Independencia.

Reservaciones de Campismo (☎ 20 49 05; Maceo Sur No 315 btwn Av 9 de Abril & Serafín García) Book cabins in Villa Clara's seven campismo resorts.

TOILETS

There are 24-hour **public toilets** on Plaza de Intercambio Cultural, Independencia Este and Luis Estévez.

Dangers & Annoyances

Santa Clara has earned an unsavory reputation for its bicycle-mounted *jineteros* (hustlers) who dive-bomb rental cars at the entrance to the town. They're more aggressive than most. The same types hang around outside the front of the Hotel Santa Clara Libre offering various services and stories.

Sights & Activities

The **Monumentos a Ernesto Che Guevara** and **Tren Blindado** are within walking distance of the Parque Vidal if you have good legs; otherwise catch a taxi or horse carriage.

MONUMENTO ERNESTO CHE GUEVARA

This monument, mausoleum and museum **complex** (Av de los Desfiles; admission free; ☽ 8am-9pm Tue-Sat, 8am-6pm Sun), 2km west of Parque Vidal via Rafael Tristá, is in a vast square guarded by a bronze statue of 'El Che.' The statue was erected in 1987 to mark the 20th anniversary of Guevara's murder in Bolivia and the sublime mausoleum below (entry from the rear) contains 38 stone-carved niches dedicated to the other guerillas killed in that failed revolutionary attempt. In 1997 the remains of 17 of them, including Guevara, were recovered from a secret mass grave in Bolivia and reburied in this memorial. Fidel Castro lit the eternal flame on October 17, 1997. The adjacent museum collects the details and ephemera of Che's life and the Battle of Santa Clara.

To get here, hop a 'Terminal' or 'Riviera'-bound horse carriage (one peso) on Marta Abreu or catch a bici-taxi (US$1).

MONUMENTO A LA TOMA DEL TREN BLINDADO

This **boxcar museum** (admission US$1; ☽ 8am-6pm Tue-Sat, 8am-noon Sat), east on Independencia just over the river, marks the spot where 18 men under the command of Che Guevara, equipped with rifles and grenades, captured a 22-car armored train containing 408 heavily armed Batista troops. Amazingly, this battle, which took place on December 29, 1958, only lasted 90 minutes. The bulldozer that the guerrillas used to cut the railway line is on a pedestal nearby. Some travelers love this place, others find it uninspiring.

MUSEO PROVINCIAL ABEL SANTAMARÍA

Strictly for enthusiasts or for walkers who like to get lost, this small **museum** (☎ 20 50 41; admission US$1; ☽ 9am-5pm Mon-Fri, 9am-1pm Sat) is a former military barracks where Batista's troops surrendered to Che Guevara on January 1, 1959. Not easy to find, it's on a hilltop north of the center at the north end of Esquerra, just across the Río Bélico in Reparto Osvaldo Herrera.

SANTA CLARA

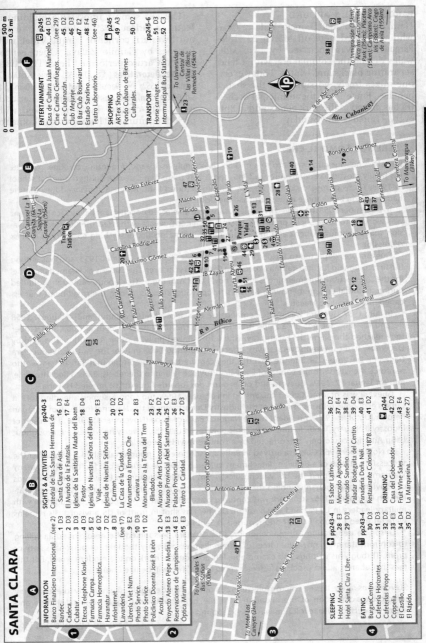

0   500 m
0   0.3 mi

INFORMATION
Banco Financiero Internacional........(see 2)
Bandec..................................1 D3
Cadeca..................................2 D3
Cubatur.................................3 D3
Etecsa Telephone Kiosk.................4 D3
Farmacia Campa.........................5 E2
Farmacia Homeopática...................6 D2
Havanatur..............................7 D2
Infotur................................8 D3
Infotrnet............................(see 7)
Lavandería.............................9 E2
Libreria Viet Nam.....................10 D3
Photo Service.........................11 D3
Photo Service
Policlínico Docente José R León
   Acosta.............................12 D4
Proyecto Ateneo Pepe Medina...........13 E3
Reservaciones de Campismo.............14 E3
Óptica Miramar........................15 E3

SIGHTS & ACTIVITIES   pp240-3
Catedral de las Santas Hermanas de
   Santa Clara de Asís................16 D3
Cine Camilo Cienfuegos................17 E4
El Mundo de la Fantasía...............18 D4
Iglesia de la Santísima Madre del Buen
   Pastor.............................18 D4
Iglesia de Nuestra Señora del Buen
   Viaje..............................19 E3
Iglesia de Nuestra Señora del
   Carmen.............................20 D2
La Casa de la Ciudad..................21 D2
Monumento a Ernesto Che
   Guevara............................22 B3
Monumento a la Toma del Tren
   Blindado...........................23 F2
Museo de Artes Decorativas............24 D3
Museo Provincial Abel Santamaría......25 C1
Palacio Provincial....................26 E3
Teatro La Caridad.....................27 D3

SLEEPING   pp243-4
Hotel Modelo..........................28 E3
Hotel Santa Clara Libre...............29 D3

EATING   pp243-4
BurgueCentro..........................30 D3
Cafetería Horizontes..................31 D3
Cafeterías Piropo.....................32 D2
Coppelia..............................33 E3
El Castillo...........................34 D4
El Rápido.............................35 D2
El Sabor Latino.......................36 D2
Mercado Agropecuario..................37 E4
Mercado Sandino.......................38 F4
Paladar Bodeguita del Centro..........39 D4
Panadería Doña Neli...................40 E3
Restaurante Colonial 1878.............41 D3

DRINKING   p244
Casa del Gobernador...................42 D2
Fruit Wine Sales......................43 E4
La Marquesina.......................(see 27)

ENTERTAINMENT   p245
Casa de Cultura Juan Marinello........44 D3
Cine Camilo Cienfuegos..............(see 29)
Cine Cubanacán........................45 D2
Club Mejunje..........................46 D3
El Bar Club Boulevard.................47 E2
Estadio Sandino.......................48 F4
Teatro Laboratorio..................(see 46)

SHOPPING   p245
ARTex Shop............................49 A3
Fondo Cubano de Bienes
   Culturales.........................50 D2

TRANSPORT   pp245-6
Horse carriages.......................51 D3
Intermunicipal Bus Station............52 C3

PARQUE VIDAL & AROUND

Named for Colonel Leoncio Vidal y Caro, who was killed here on March 23, 1896, **Parque Vidal** was encircled by twin sidewalks during the colonial era, with a fence separating blacks and whites. Today everyone mixes freely, gossiping on the shaded benches. Since 1902, the municipal orchestra has played in the park bandstand at 8pm every Thursday and Sunday.

The city's most impressive building is **Teatro La Caridad** (1885; Máximo Gómez), in the northwestern corner of Parque Vidal, with frescoes by Camilo Zalaya. Opera singer Enrico Caruso performed here. The **Museo de Artes Decorativas** (☎ 20 53 68; Parque Vidal No 27; admission US$2; ☾ 9am-6pm Wed & Thu, 1-10pm Fri & Sat, 6-10pm Sun), just east of Teatro La Caridad, is an 18th-century building packed with period furniture and luxurious knick-knacks

---

'SEREMOS COMO EL CHE'

Ernesto 'Che' Guevara was born to a middle-class family in Rosario, Argentina, on June 14, 1928. His family moved to Buenos Aires in 1945, and it was there that Guevara finished medical school in 1953. The widespread poverty he saw traveling around Latin America convinced him that he had a mission in life more important than medicine.

In December 1953, he arrived in Guatemala, where an elected government led by Jacobo Arbenz was working to solve social problems. Six months later Guevara witnessed the CIA-backed invasion that overthrew Arbenz and installed a military dictatorship, unleashing 45 years of pitiless repression.

Guevara was deported to Mexico City where he met Fidel Castro in mid-1955, and was among the first to sign up for the Granma expedition to Cuba a year later. The Cubans nicknamed him 'Che' for the interjection che (meaning 'say!' or 'hey!') that Argentines toss about. Although wounded during an initial engagement with Batista's troops, Guevara was among the small band that escaped into the Sierra Maestra.

In July 1957 Guevara was made comandante of a second rebel column, and in August 1958 he and his men set out on an epic trek to spread the revolution to central Cuba. In October they reached the Sierra del Escambray, where they linked up with other revolutionaries, and by December had captured several towns, effectively splitting Cuba in two. The Battle of Santa Clara began on December 28, and the next day they captured an armored train that Batista had sent to reinforce the city. With the capital of Las Villas Province falling to the rebels, Batista fled into exile, and on January 2, 1959, Guevara and other barbudos (bearded guerrillas) entered Havana.

Guevara was granted Cuban citizenship in February 1959, and soon assumed a leading role in Cuba's economic reforms as head of the Industry Department of the National Institute of Agrarian Reform (October 1959), president of the National Bank of Cuba (November 1959), and Minister of Industry (February 1960). In time he became convinced that the poverty he witnessed throughout Latin America could only be corrected by a continent-wide revolution.

In November 1966 Guevara arrived in Bolivia, and there his group established a base. After the successful ambush of a Bolivian detachment in March 1967, he issued a call for 'two, three, many Vietnams.' This alarmed the US, which quickly sent military advisors to Bolivia. Soon, thousands of Bolivian troops began combing the area where Guevara's small band of guerrillas was operating. On October 8, 1967, Guevara was captured by the Bolivian army, and after consultation with military leaders in La Paz and Washington, DC, he was shot in front of US advisors. His remains were returned to Cuba in 1997 and reburied in Santa Clara.

Despite a debilitating asthma condition, Che Guevara personified the heroic guerrilla willing to confront the most powerful forces of imperialism without any thought for personal safety or profit. Through his writings and example he left an indelible mark on the modern world. For this reason, Cuban children proclaim 'seremos como El Che' (we will be like Che).

'Revolutions rarely, if ever, emerge fully ripe, and not all their details are scientifically foreseen. They are products of passion, of improvisation by human beings in their struggle for social change, and are never perfect. Our revolution was no exception.'

Ernesto 'Che' Guevara, 1961

donated by poet Dulce María Loynaz. The inner patio is a treat. On the eastern side of Parque Vidal is the neoclassical **Palacio Provincial** (1902–12). It houses the provincial library (with a rare books collection).

West of the park is **La Casa de la Ciudad** (Independencia & JB Zayas; admission US$1; ☼ 8am-5pm), housed in a building representative of the 1860s. It shows the history of Santa Clara; check here for night-time cultural activities.

Uncharacteristically, the churches are scattered around the city rather than on or near the main square. South of the center is the colonial-style **Iglesia de la Santísima Madre del Buen Pastor** (EP Morales No 4 btwn Cuba & Villuendas).

On the way to the train station north of the center, is the **Iglesia de Nuestra Señora del Carmen** (Carolina Rodríguez), built in 1748, with a tower added in 1846. A large monument facing the church commemorates the foundation of Santa Clara in 1689. The **Iglesia de Nuestra Señora del Buen Viaje** (Pedro Estévez & Pardo) is an eclectic mix of gothic, Romanesque, and neoclassical architecture.

You can get a massage (25 pesos, 90 minutes), facial (23 pesos), or pedicure (five pesos) at **El Mundo de la Fantasía** (☎ 20 35 66; Bonifacio Martínez No 12; ☼ 8am-7pm Tue-Sat, 8am-noon Sun). It has a 17-page menu of unisex spa services.

If you have an extra day, consider renting a moped and jamming to Remedios, Embalse Hanabanilla or all the way to Cayo Santa María.

Sleeping

IN TOWN

Hotel Santa Clara Libre (Islazul; ☎ 20 75 48; fax 68 63 67; Parque Vidal No 6; s/d low season US$22/29, high season US$26/32; ⚡) You can't miss the tall, minty green façade of this 168-room hotel right on the park. Hosting Cuban honeymooners and economic package tours, this is a decent, central choice. Nonguests can check out the pleasant restaurant on the 10th floor and the rooftop bar (good views on the 11th). The front of this hotel is still pocked with bullet holes from one of the last battles of the revolution.

Hotel Modelo (☎ 20 75 81/82; Maceo Sur No 210) is a four-story hotel that was being renovated at the time of writing. It should be a decent, budget place to stay when they're done some time in 2004.

OUTSIDE TOWN

Campismo Arco Iris (Cubamar; ☎ 21 46 24; s/d US$9/14; ⚡) Just outside Santa Clara, off the Carretera Central toward Placetas, Arco Iris has 14 concrete cabins that sleep two to eight people. This facility overlooks a reservoir. Bus No R2, marked 'José Martí Arco Iris,' runs from Santa Clara to El Arco Iris Amusement Park, 3km before the Campismo, every 1½ hours.

Carrusel la Granjita (Cubanacán; ☎ 21 81 90; www.cubanacan.cu; Carretera de Maleza Km 21.5; s/d low season US$38/50, high season US$42/55; P ⚡ ⚡ ⚡) The 75 thatched units of this motel, 6km northeast of town, are sprinkled among a scenic orange grove. It's quiet and a decent value if you don't mind being outside town. The moderately priced restaurants (à la carte, buffet or grill) are good deals. Horseback riding is offered.

Motel Los Caneyes (Horizontes; ☎ 20 45 12; Av de los Eucaliptos & Circunvalación de Santa Clara; s/d low season US$38/50, high season US$45/58; P ⚡ ⚡) Sort of hokey, this motel has 91 thatched bungalows built in 'pre-Columbian' style, updated for the package tourists that frequent it. It's well located 2km due west of the Monumento Che Guevara and has nice grounds, but is pricey for what you get. Hunting and fishing tours are done from here and there's an Havanautos desk.

Eating

Most casas particulares here serve meals, which is generally a better value than the dollar paladares.

Paladar Bodeguita del Centro (☎ 20 43 56; Villundas Sur No 264 btwn 9 de Abril & Serafín García; dishes from US$6; ☼ 1-5pm & 7-11pm Mon-Sat, 7-11pm Sun) The dimly lit atmosphere and graffiti-covered walls here mimic Havana's Bodeguita.

El Castillo (9 de Abril No 9 btwn Cuba & Villuendas; ☼ noon-11pm) This peso find cooks up quality meals of pork, chicken or liver with *congrí* (rice flecked with black beans) and salad for 35 pesos (US$1.35). Take it away in a *cajita* or eat standing at the counter flanked by marble pillars, stained glass and mosaic tiles.

El Sabor Latino (☎ 20 65 39; Esquerra No 157 btwn Julio Jover & Berenguer; ☼ noon-midnight) An off-the-beaten track paladar with complete pork or chicken meals with rice, salad, tostones and bread for US$10 (or fish for US$12); you can eat here late.

CASAS PARTICULARES – SANTA CLARA

The short street of Bonifacio Martínez between Serafín García and the Carretera Central is a traveler's ghetto with nearly every other house renting rooms; head here if you want to find something fast and easy.

Hostal Florida Center (☎ 20 81 61; Maestra Nicolasa Este No 56 btwn Colón & Maceo; r US$20; ✗)
Beautiful colonial house with airy rooms with refrigerator and TV, generous meals served in lush patio.

Héctor Martínez (☎ 21 74 63; R Pardo No 8 btwn Maceo & Parque Vidal; r US$15-20; ✗) Terrific big room with dining area, kitchen and refrigerator; all new.

Luisa Costa Pérez (☎ 29 41 67; Maceo Sur No 326 btwn Av 9 de Abril & Serafín García; r US$15-20; ✗) Run by a sweet couple; big meals.

Ernesto & Mireya (☎ 27 35 01; Cuba No 227 Altos btwn Pastora & EP Morales; r US$15-20; ✗) Nice spacious room, common balcony overlooks church; neighbor rents in Apt 3.

Rolando Sacercio Díaz (☎ 20 67 25; Maceo No 355A btwn Serafín García & EP Morales; r US$15-20) Simple, spotless room with three beds; English spoken.

Jorge García Rodríguez (☎ 20 23 23; Cuba No 209 Apt No 1 btwn Serafín García & EP Morales; r US$15-20; ✗) Friendly place that rents two rooms; meals served.

Elida Ramírez Herrera & Sergio Proenza González (☎ 21 59 14; Independencia No 266 btwn Pedro Estévez & M Gutierrez; r US$15-20) This friendly place has a room with three beds; there's a small patio.

María Rodríguez Fariñas (Mujica No 14 btwn Colón & Maceo; r US$15; ✗) Good location across from Coppelia.

Orlando García Rodríguez (☎ 20 67 61; R Pardo No 7 btwn Maceo & Parque Vidal; r incl breakfast US$15-20; ✗) Shared bathroom.

Yadin & José (☎ 20 67 54; Bonifacio Martínez No 60 btwn EP Morales & General Roloff; r US$15; ✗) Also at No 18.

Omelio Moreno Lorenzo (☎ 21 69 41; Eduardo Machado Este No 4 btwn Cuba & Colón; r US$20; ✗) English & French spoken.

Martha Artiles Alemán (☎ 20 50 08; Marta Abreu No 56 btwn Villuendas & Zayas; r US$15-20; ✗) Big, serviceable rooms. Bargain hard here.

Casa Mercedes – Mercedes Águila (☎ 20 22 27; Máximo Gómez No 51 Altos btwn Martí & Independencia; r US$15-20) Popular kitsch-filled home.

For a cheap 'burger,' try **BurgueCentro** (Parque Vidal No 31; ✆ 24 hrs); the patio bar upstairs is a good drinking perch. For a pick me up, head next door to **Cafetería Horizontes**, (Parque Vidal cnr Colón; ✆ 24hr), a great stand-up peso coffee place with shots of the sweet stuff for 20 centavos.

Stock up on peso ice cream at **Coppelia** (Calle Colón cnr Mujica; ✆ 10:30am-midnight Tue-Sun) or head to **Cafeterías Piropo** (Lorda & Independencia; ✆ 10am-10pm) for a large choice of dollar ice cream. Across the street is **El Rápido**.

Several peso bars and cafeterias are near the corner of Independencia Oeste and Zayas around Cine Cubanacán.

SELF-CATERING

Santa Clara's largest *agropecuario* (vegetable market), **Mercado Sandino** (9 de Abril), is on the western side of the Estadio Sandino. Another small, but well-stocked **mercado agropecuario** (Cuba No 269 btwn EP Morales & General Roloff) is in the center. **Panadería Doña Neli** (Maceo Sur at 9 de Abril; ✆ 7am-6pm) sells fruit cakes and bread; the **bar** (✆ 9am-10pm) adjacent has a smoky, local atmosphere and sandwiches (US$1 to US$2).

Drinking

Santa Clara has some fun bars with occasional live music.

La Marquesina (✆ 9am-1am) This lively bar in a corner of the Teatro La Caridad building is a winner. Bonus: chanteuse belting boleros to Casio keyboard accompaniment.

Casa del Gobernador (✆ noon-11pm) Check out the colonial patio of this hard-drinking peso place with live music, or duck into the dining room for a US$4 pork filet. Similar is **Restaurante Colonial 1878** (Máximo Gómez btwn Marta Abreu & Independencia; ✆ noon-2pm & 7-10:30pm).

You can buy home-made **fruit wine** (Morales No 10 btwn Cuba & Colón) at the winemaker's door for five (500ml) or eight (750ml) pesos; bring your own bottle.

Entertainment

Club Mejunje (Marta Abreu No 107; ☽ 4pm-1am Tue-Sun) The heart of Santa Clara's hip culture scene, this bar and performance space is set among the ruins of an old building. There are regularly scheduled trova, bolero and son concerts, children's theater and disco nights. You might even catch the occasional drag show.

El Bar Club Boulevard (☎ 21 62 36; Independencia No 2 btwn Maceo & Pedro Estévez; admission US$2; ☽ 9:30pm-2am Tue-Sun) Humor shows and live bands get this fun cocktail lounge laughing, dancing and swinging from 11pm on.

Cine Camilo Cienfuegos, below the Santa Clara Libre, and **Cine Cubanacán** (Independencia Oeste No 60), show large screen films.

Also recommended:

Casa de la Cultura Juan Marinello (☎ 20 71 81; Parque Vidal No 5) Concerts and art exhibits in a colonial casa.
Teatro Laboratorio (Marta Abreu No 111; ☽ performances 8pm) Cutting-edge theater Santa Clara–style.

SPORT

The **Estadio Sandino**, east of the center via Av 9 de Abril, is the venue for baseball games from October to April. Villa Clara ('La Villa') plays a central role in the history of Cuban baseball, but they're like the Boston Red Sox of Cuba: they have rabid fans and are super fun to watch, but they can't seem to win at all lately.

Shopping

Independencia, between Maceo and Zayas, is the pedestrian shopping mall called the Boulevard. It's littered with dollar stores and has good second-hand clothes and consignment shops.

The **Fondo Cubano de Bienes Culturales** (Luis Estévez Norte No 9 btwn Parque Vidal & Independencia) sells Cuban handicrafts and the large **ARTex** (Carretera Central) near the Che Guevara Monument has a good compact disc selection.

Getting There & Away

When this book was being researched, Santa Clara's Abel Santamaría Airport was dormant. Until it reopens, the closest connection is in Havana.

BUS

The **Nacionales Bus Station** (☎ 20 34 70) is 2.5km out on the Carretera Central toward Matanzas, 500m north of the Che monu-ment. There are **Astro** (☎ 29 21 14) buses to the following destinations:

destination	cost (one way)	distance	frequency
Cienfuegos	US$2.50	67km	two daily
Havana	US$7	276km	three daily
Trinidad	US$6	88km	three daily
Santiago de Cuba	US$22.50	590km	alt days

Tickets for air-con Víazul buses are sold at a special ticket window for foreigners next to the station entrance. If it's closed, go to the 'Lista de Espera' window at the back of the station. There are daily departures to:

destination	cost (one way)	distance	frequency
Havana	US$18	276km	three daily
Trinidad	US$8	88km	one daily
Varadero	US$11	182km	one daily
Santiago de Cuba	US$590	590km	one daily

The Santiago de Cuba–bound bus also stops at Bayamo (US$26), Camagüey (US$15), Ciego de Ávila (US$9), Holguín (US$26), Las Tunas (US$22) and Sancti Spíritus (US$6).

The **intermunicipal bus station** (Carretera Central) is just west of the center via Marta Abreu and has daily buses to Remedios (US$1.45, 45km).

TRAIN

The **train station** (☎ 20 28 95) is straight up Luis Estévez from Parque Vidal on the north side of town. The **ticket office** (Luis Estévez Norte No 323), across the park from the train station. In theory, there are trains to the following destinations:

destination	cost (one way)	distance	frequency
Bayamo	US$22	473km	daily
Camagüey	US$9-13	263km	daily
Cienfuegos	US$2.50	67km	Mon-Sat
Havana	US$14	276km	four nightly
Holguín	US$17	472km	daily
Matanzas	US$8	217km	five nightly
Morón	US$5	170km	alt days
Sancti Spíritus	US$4	83km	alt days
Santiago de Cuba	US$33	590km	two daily

Getting Around

You'll notice from the manure stench that local transport is mostly horse and carriage (one peso), with an important route along Marta Abreu toward the bus stations. Bici-taxis cost US$1 a ride; catch them on the northwestern side of the park.

CAR & MOPED

Agencies renting wheels around the town include:

Cubatur (☎ 20 89 80; Marta Abreu No 10; 🕑 9am-6pm) Near Máximo Gómez; moped rentals for US$17/day.

Havanautos (☎ 20 58 95; Motel Los Caneyes)

Transtur (☎ 20 81 77; Hotel Santa Clara Libre)

Micar (☎ 20 45 70; Carretera Central & Av 9 de Abril) At Servicentro Oro Negro; usually has the cheapest cars.

Parque Vidal is closed to traffic (and cyclists must also dismount and walk their bikes).

The **Servi-Cupet gas station** (Carretera Central cnr General Roloff) is south of the center. Just north is **Servicentro Oro Negro** (Carretera Central & Av 9 de Abril).

TAXI

Taxis congregate in front of the national bus station northwest of the center. There you can hire a car and driver for trips to Remedios (US$7 one way) or Caibarién (US$9). A taxi to Havana should cost around US$45 for the car. Drivers also hang around Parque Vidal or you can call **Cubataxi** (☎ 20 68 56).

EMBALSE HANABANILLA

The Sierra del Escambray is the highest mountain range in central Cuba and has great hiking opportunities. Tucked into the northern foothills, 9km below Barajaguá, is the Embalse Hanabanilla, a 36-sq-km reservoir supplying Cuba's largest hydro-electric generating station. A tourist hotel stands on the lake's northwestern shore and there's good fishing for largemouth bass and trout. Hanabanilla is a centrally located stopover between Cienfuegos, 58km to the west; Santa Clara, 80km to the north; Sancti Spíritus, 80km to the east; or Trinidad, 58km to the south. Theoretically there are buses from Manicaragua, but the only practical access is by car.

Hotel Hanabanilla (Islazul; ☎ 49-1125; s/d/tr US$23/30/38; 🅿 ⛶ 🖭) This four-story hotel has 125 rooms with fridges, balconies and lake views. The Bar Mirador on the top floor also has good vistas. It's a peaceful spot except on the weekends when it's packed with Cubans making merry. You can rent speed boats, horses or choose from half a dozen hikes, including to **El Nicho** (p234), or a 17km loop with incredible views and a stop at the 600m Cueva del Brollo.

Campismo Río Seibabo (☎ 24 98 32; per person US$5) South of Güinía de Miranda near the border with Sancti Spíritus Province, Río Seibabo has 35 cabins. The lush grounds abut the Río Seibabo.

PRESA MINERVA

Campismo Presa Minerva (☎ 28 15 74; per person US$5; 🖭) Between Santa Clara and Cama-juaní, Minerva has 22 concrete cabins. To get there, turn right about 20 km out of Santa Clara. If you're out this way Decem-ber 24, don't miss the parrandas in Cama-juaní, a smaller version of the blowout in Remedios (p247).

REMEDIOS

☎ 42 / pop 48,908

Aaaaah, Remedios – where historic homes line cobblestone streets and you can lounge in the leafy central park with nary a hust-ler to hassle you. Certainly one of Cuba's prettiest towns, the laid-back, colonial air of Remedios shatters every December 24 when the citizens take sides and face off with floats, fireworks and dancing competi-tions. Within easy reach of Santa Clara and Cayo Santa María, this makes a good base for exploring the province.

The energetic Vasco Porcallo de Figueroa was famous for founding San Juan de los Remedios (1524), but also for fathering more than 200 children. The town served as the regional center until Santa Clara was founded in 1689, and after a fire in 1692 the town's importance declined.

Sights

The **Parroquia de San Juan Bautista de Remedios** (Camilo Cienfuegos No 20 on Parque Martí; 🕑 9am-11am Mon-Sat), is one of Cuba's finest churches. Though a church was founded here in 1545, this building dates from the late 18th century, the campanile was erected between 1848 and 1858 and its famous gilded high altar and mahogany ceiling are thanks to a restoration project (1944–46) financed by millionaire Eutimio Falla Bonet. The pregant Inmaculada Concepción on the first ide altar to the left of the entrance is said o be the only one of its kind in Cuba – the earl teardrops are a nice touch. If the front loors are closed, go around to the rear or ttend 7:30pm mass.

Also on Parque Martí, but lighter on he gold leaf, is the 18th-century **Iglesia de Nuestra Señora del Buen Viaje** (Alejandro del Río No 6). Between these churches is the **Museo de Música Alejandro García Caturla** (Parque Martí No ; ☺ 9am-noon & 1-6pm Mon-Thu, 7-11pm Fri, 2pm-midnight Sat), commemorating García Caturla, a Cuban composer who lived here from 1920 until his murder in 1940. Look for occasional concerts and plays here.

Visiting the **Museo de las Parrandas Remedianas** (Máximo Gómez No 71; admission US$1; ☺ 9am-5pm), two blocks off Parque Martí, is the next best thing to partying here on December 24 (see Festivals & Events, below). The downstairs photo gallery recaps last year's fanfare, while the upstairs rooms show the intriguing history of this tradition, including scale models of floats and graphic depictions of how the fireworks are made. Another room is jammed with feathers, headdresses and tassels from the year previous.

The friendly staff and interesting exhibitions make the **Galería del Arte Carlos Enríquez** (Parque Martí No 2; admission free; ☺ 9am-noon & 1-5pm) worth a peek. A gifted painter hailing from Zulueta, Enriquez' called his studio 'Hurón Azul,' a name adopted by Uneac's cultural space (p101) and a tasty paladar (p93), both in Havana.

Fourteen kilometers south of Remedios on the nice country road to Placetas is **Zulueta**, 'la cuna del futbol' (the birthplace of soccer). In the sleepy square there, you'll find Cuba's only monument to the sport – a big, mounted soccer ball. You might catch an afternoon match at the town's showpiece stadium. This is a good alternate route for (motor)cyclists between Santa Clara and Cayo Santa María.

Festivals & Events

For weeks leading up to the extravaganza, two competing neighborhoods secretly create gigantic floats and costumes in preparation for the **Parrandas**. A tradition that dates back to 1820, Remedios splits solidly into San Salvador from the west and El Carmen from the east as the competitions.

With spectacular *carrozas* (floats) that could sashay proudly into Rio de Janeiro's sambadrome, these are fantastic, glittery works of art. The flowing beer, maniacal fireworks and hot rumba music rounds out the party. The action begins around 9pm on December 24. In true socialist style, there aren't any judges and which neighborhood wins depends on who you ask.

Sleeping & Eating

Remedios is a small town, reflected in the limited accommodation and eating options. Casas particulares usually offer meals.

Hotel Mascotte (☎ 39 51 44; Parque Martí; s/d US$30/38) This beautiful colonial building dates from 1869 and is the only hotel in town. The nicest of the 14 rooms are No 1 and No 5; some rooms have balconies. The hotel restaurant **Las Arcadas**, serving standard meat and seafood fare, is the only game in town for a real meal.

Aside from the hotel, there are a few very basic peso cafeterias serving drinks and snacks like **La Fé** (Máximo Gómez No 126), directly opposite the Parroquia's façade; don't miss the impressive stone counter snaking through the place. **Driver's Bar** (Jose' A Peña No 61; ☺ 8am-10pm) serves peso meals on one side and is a no-nonsense saloon on the other.

Entertainment

El Louvre (Máximo Gómez No 122) on the south side of the square, is a Rumbos bar and cafeteria in dollars. If you're looking for a room/paladar/taxi, park yourself here, have a drink and wait for offers.

CASAS PARTICULARES – REMEDIOS

Hospedaje El Chalet – Jorge Rivero Méndez (☎ 39 53 31; Brigadier González No 29 btwn Independencia & José A Peña; r US$20-25; Ⓟ) Elegant house, spacious rooms that sleep three or more with fridges, patio and terrace.

Gladys Aponte Rojas (☎ 39 53 98; Brigadier González No 32A btwn Independencia & Py Margall; r US$25) Run by a *santera* with altars abounding, it's nicer inside than out. OK room and good meals served.

Cecilio Acosta Herrera & Ania González Lozano (☎ 39 56 24; José A Peña No 75C btwn Maceo & La Pastora; r US$20-25; ☒) Two attic rooms with negligible natural light sharing bath.

A block east of the park is the elegant old **Teatro Rubén M Villena** (Cienfuegos No 30) with dance performances, plays and Theater Guiñol for kids. The schedule is posted in the windows and tickets are in pesos. Check the **Casa de Cultura Agustín J Crespo** (José A Peña No 67), opposite the Parroquia, for evening activities. If you feel like dancing, head to **Bar Juvenil** (Adel Rio No 47; ⏰ 9pm-1am Sat & Sun), near Máximo Gómez (enter via park), a courtyard disco with palms, pillars and Moorish tiles. During the day there's table tennis and dominoes; despite the name, this peso place is alcohol-free, making it even more of a novelty than its colonial ambiance.

Getting There & Away

The bus station is on the southern side of town at the beginning of the excellent 45km road to Santa Clara. Theoretically there is one daily bus to and from Santa Clara (US$1.45, one hour), twice daily service to Caibarién (US$1.20, 20 minutes) and two departures Monday, Wednesday and Friday to Zulueta (US$1.10, 30 minutes).

A taxi from the bus station to Caibarién will cost US$3 one way, and US$5 to Santa Clara if you bargain. A bici-taxi from the bus station to Parque Martí is two pesos.

CAIBARIÉN

☎ 42 / pop 40,798

Caibarién, on the coast 9km east of Remedios, is Villa Clara's main Atlantic port with a large fishing fleet. It's a colorful little town, retaining its quaint, ramshackle feel despite the massive tourism development on nearby Cayo Santa María. **Havanatur** (☎ 35 11 71; Ave 9 btwn Calle 8 & 10) can arrange accommodation on Cayo Santa María. Cadeca and Banco Popular de Ahorro are nearby.

You can find a private room if you hang around the main square looking foreign. **Hotel Brisas del Mar** (☎ 36 42 14; Mar Azul on Punta Brava; s/d US$12/17) This hotel is 4km east of town and has 16 basic rooms patronized mostly by Cubans.

Campismo Popular Cayo Conuco (r per person US$5) This place is 6km from Caibarién along a road that begins beside Hotel España. Of the 24 cabins, No 9 is the nicest. You get good views from the rocky shore here, though this place is super basic.

There are a couple of good places to eat including **Cafetería La Riqueza** on the main drag, which serves ample portions of fried chicken or grilled fish for 20 pesos or the **Villas las Brisas** (Avenida 9), which is a Rumbo restaurant; it's got a nice, palm-filled setting. There's an **agropecuario** (Calle 6) near the train station.

Surprisingly, Caibarién has a hot, happening disco near the train station known generically as the **piste de baile** (dance floor; Calle 4; admission two pesos). This en plein air place jumps with hundreds of young locals on weekends.

Four buses a day go to Remedios (US$1, 20 minutes), the 4:30am and 2pm departures go all the way to Santa Clara (US$1.80, 90 minutes) and three go to Yaguajay (US$1.25, 45 minutes) from Caibarién's old blue-and-white **bus and train station** (Calle 6) on the western side of town. There's also a daily phantom train to Santa Clara via Remedios (US$1.30, 90 minutes), leaving Caibarién in the morning and returning in the afternoon. The Servi-Cupet gas station is at the entrance to town from Remedios, behind the huge crab statue by Florencio Gelabert Pérez (1983).

CAYO SANTA MARÍA

Brilliant Cayo Santa María lies at the western end of the Archipiélago de Sabana-Camagüey, 25km west of Cayo Guillermo. Between 1989 and 1996, a massive 48km causeway called **'El Pedraplén'** was constructed across the Bahía Buena Vista from the port of Caibarién at a cost of 100 million pesos. Included in the design were 45 bridges to allow an exchange of tidal waters, an improvement over the earlier Cayo Coco causeway that caused serious environmental damage. Still, when asked what might happen if a fish trying to swim to the other side of the *pedraplén* couldn't locate one of these 'eco-bridges', an aqueduct worker on the cays shrugged and said, 'he's stuck.' Paving was completed in 1999, just as Las Brujas Airport was being built on Cayo Las Brujas, 45km northwest of Caibarién.

The future plan is to have 10,000 rooms, and the resorts are mushrooming as this description is being typed. Despite various precautions included in the project planning, the environmental impact of such intense building activity is likely to be severe. The so-called 'smokeless industry' called tourism does have its price.

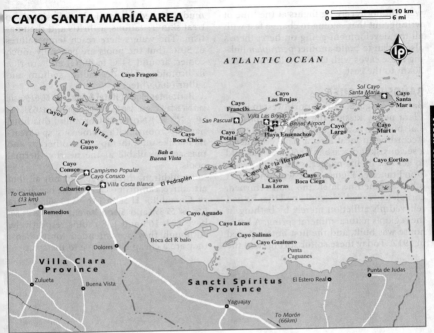

CAYO SANTA MARÍA AREA

0 ————— 10 km
0 ————— 6 mi

ATLANTIC OCEAN

Cayo Fragoso

Cayos de la Viraz n

Cayo Guayo

Cayo Conuco
Campismo Popular Cayo Conuco
Villa Costa Blanca
Caibarién

To Camajuani (13 km)

Remedios

Cayo Boca Chica

San Pascual

Cayo Francés

Cayo Potala

Cayo Las Brujas
Villa Las Brujas
Las Brujas Airport
Playa Ensenachos

Sol Cayo Santa María

Cayo Santa Mar a

Cayo Largo

Cayo Mart n

Cayo Cortizo

Bah a Buena Vista

El Pedraplén

Cayos de la Herradura

Cayo Boca Ciega

Cayo Las Loras

Villa Clara Province

Dolores

Zulueta   Buena Vista

Cayo Aguado

Cayo Lucas

Boca del R balo

Cayo Salinas

Cayo Guainaro

Punta Caguanes

Sancti Spíritus Province

El Estero Real

Punta de Judas

Yaguajay

To Morón (66km)

Gaviota operates **Villa Las Brujas** (☎ 20 75 99; s/d low season US$34/45, high season US$43/54; P ✖) along a coral ridge overlooking the crystalline sea at Punta Periquillo on Cayo Las Brujas, 3km from the airport. These 21 cabañas make a great escape to one of Cuba's prettiest areas. A large restaurant with a lookout above its thatched roof surveys the white sands of Playa La Salina just beyond the resort.

Sol Cayo Santa María (☎ 35 15 00; solmeliacuba.com; s/d/tr low season 85/120/165, high season US$100/145/200; P ✖ ⬚ ⬚) The first of the fancy resorts to colonize the further-flung caves, Sol Cayo Santa María is 8km further out. It's a 300-room, four-star resort with all the amenities. Scoop up a cheap online deal or book a room with Havanatur in Caibarién to avoid the exorbitant rack rates.

Day-trippers can easily zoom from Caibarién (56km), Remedios (65km) or Santa Clara (110km) to kick it in Cayo Santa María's white sand for an afternoon. **Playa Ensenachos** is a picture-perfect kilo-meter of virgin beach backed by sparkling turquoise water, accessible by an access road just before the airport. You can pitch a tent here,

but the mosquitoes and *jején* (sand fleas) are ferocious at dusk. There's good snorkeling around a beached ship some 50m out from shore where you'll see lobsters, tangs, grunts and wrasses.

Five kilometers away on the opposite side of Cayo Francés is the wreck of the *San Pascual*, a San Diego tanker built in 1920 and beached here in 1933. Later the ship was used to store molasses, and it still emanates a strong smell of the substance. The ship has been maintained, and these days Rumbos rents the 10 **cabins** (s/d/tr US$20/30/40) aboard ship. Meals at **Restaurante La Guasa** on the *San Pascual* cost extra. Boat transfers or day trips here from Villa Las Brujas are US$6 per person round trip.

The causeway is accessed from Caibarién and there's a toll booth (US$2 each way) 15km along. You may encounter problems if you have Cuban passengers with you (normally Cubans are denied access to these and most other cayos nationwide so if you just show up with Cuban friends in your car to enter the cayo, you'll likely be turned away). The airport at Las Brujas was still not receiving flights at the time of writing, but that's going to change fast with all the development going on here; there's also a plan to build another *pedraplén* linking these cayos with Cayo Guillermo, some 30km to the east.

BAÑOS DE ELGUEA

Baños de Elguea, 136km northwest of Santa Clara nearly kissing the Matanzas provincial border, is a legendary health resort. According to local lore, a slave contracted a serious skin disease in 1860 and was told to get lost by his master, sugar mill owner Don Francisco Elguea, so he wouldn't infect others. Sometime later, the man returned, completely cured. He explained that he had relieved his affliction merely by bathing in the region's natural mineral spring. A bathhouse was built, and the first hotel opened in 1917. Today these sulfur springs and the mud are used by medical professionals to treat skin irritations, arthritis and rheumatism. The waters here reach temperatures of 50°C (but the pools are generally much cooler, around 34°C to 48°C) and are rich in bromide, chloride, radon, sodium and sulfur (400g/liter).

Horizontes Elguea Hotel & Spa (☎ 68 62 90; s/d incl breakfast low season US$30/40, high season US$36/48; P ✗ 🛋) North of Corralillo, this hotel has 139 rooms with numerous spa treatments like mud therapy, hydrotherapy and massages available at the nearby thermal pools.

In addition, three large, but not all that attractive, campismos are on the beach east of Corralillo. **El Salto** (☎ 68 63 30), **Ganuza** (☎ 68 65 35) and **Sierra Morena** (☎ 68 21 80) have 193, 165 and 138 cabins respectively. Although they are intended for Cubans, they are a cheap alternative to the spa.

Sancti Spíritus Province

Tucked into the historical heartland of central Cuba, the coastal and mountain regions of Sancti Spíritus Province are some of the most popular destinations in the country. The fastidiously preserved colonial town of Trinidad and the adjacent Valle de los Ingenios (together a Unesco World Heritage site) are near both the white sands of Playa Ancón and the lush slopes of Topes de Collantes. With outdoor activities and natural wonders abounding, this is an invigorating area to explore. The provincial capital of Sancti Spíritus is a lovely colonial city in its own right.

The Carretera Central, Autopista and railway all meet in Sancti Spíritus Province, with Villa Clara and Cienfuegos Provinces to the west and Ciego de Ávila Province to the east, making it supremely accessible. The scenery is a bit of a yawn, with cows, sugarcane, more cows and even more cane. Rice is raised near the coast in the far south and tobacco (while inferior to that grown in Pinar del Río), is still an important crop in the center of the province. In the southwest, two branches of the Sierra del Escambray are divided by the Río Agabama, the former railway route from Trinidad to Santa Clara.

HIGHLIGHTS

- **Coolest Town You Never Heard Of**
  Hustle- and hassle-free Sancti Spíritus (p253)

- **Cobblestones & Culture**
  Colonial vibe and vibrant music in Trinidad (p259)

- **Green Scene**
  Luxuriant Valle de los Ingenios (p270)

- **Beach Break**
  Soft sands and blue bathtub waters of Playa Ancón (p268)

- **Take a Hike**
  Good trails, camping and views in the beautiful Topes de Collantes (p271)

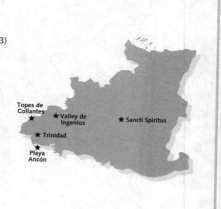

Topes de Collantes ★

Valley de Ingenios ★

★ Sancti Spíritus

★ Trinidad

Playa Ancón ★

| ■ TELEPHONE CODE: 41 | ■ POPULATION: 463,258 | ■ AREA: 6744 SQ KM |

ANCTI SPÍRITUS

☎ 41 / pop 105,815

It's as if colonial Sancti Spíritus – with its enchanting pastel facades and cobblestone streets – couldn't be bothered with tourism. Founded in 1514 on the banks of the Río Tuinicú, Sancti Spíritus is the oldest town in the Cuban interior. It was moved to its present spot on the Río Yayabo in 1522, and sacked by pirates in 1665. The Río Yayabo has lent its name to two items utterly Cuban: the dapper guayabera shirt, invented in this area, and the *guayaba* (guava), a fruit that still grows along the river's banks. The bridge spanning this river is a national landmark.

Located near Cuba's geographic center, between Santa Clara and Ciego de Ávila on the Carretera Central, Sancti Spíritus became the provincial capital in 1976. Just southeast of Sancti Spíritus is the 127-sq-km Embalse Zaza, Cuba's largest reservoir, created by damming the Río Zaza. The 1020 million cubic meters of water in this vast reservoir are stocked with largemouth bass.

Orientation

The bus and train stations are on opposite sides of town. Of the two, the train station is more convenient. It's an easy five-minute walk to the old Puente Yayabo and then another five minutes to Parque Serafín Sánchez in the heart of the town. The bus station is a couple of kilometers east of the center on the Carretera Central (called Bartolomé Masó as it passes through Sancti Spíritus).

Av de los Mártires divides the streets of Sancti Spíritus into Norte and Sur, while Independencia divides Este from Oeste, useful to know when looking for addresses. Narrow cobblestone streets, unexpected one-way arteries and pedestrian malls make for nerve-wracking driving here.

Information

BOOKSHOPS

Librería Julio Antonio Mella (☎ 2-7416; Independencia Sur No 29; ☽ 8am-5pm Mon-Sat) Near the post office; good used bookstore nearby at No 25.

J Menéndez Used Books (Av Jesús Menéndez No 6, on Plaza Honorato) Terrific used books (US$1) from private collection; Spanish and English.

IMMIGRATION

Inmigración (☎ 2-4729; Independencia Norte No 107; ☽ 8:30am-noon & 1:30-3:30pm Mon-Thu)

INTERNET ACCESS

Etecsa (M Solano; ☽ 8am-10pm) Kiosk in front of Cine Serafín Sánchez, with phones and one computer (when it works).

INDICT (cnr Carretera Central & Av de los Mártires; ☽ 8am-5:30pm Mon-Fri; US$0.10/minute)

LIBRARIES

Biblioteca Provincial Rubén Martínez Villena (☎ 2-7717; Máximo Gómez Norte No 1 on Parque Serafín Sánchez) Gorgeous building (1929) with magnificent interior dome worth a look.

MEDIA

Radio Sancti Spíritus CMHT Airing on 1200AM and 97.3FM.

MEDICAL SERVICES

Farmacia Especial (☎ 2-4660; Independencia Norte No 123 on Parque Maceo; ☽ 24hr)

Hospital Provincial Camilo Cienfuegos (☎ 2-4017; Bartolomé Masó s/n) Five hundred meters north of Plaza de la Revolución.

Policlínico Los Olivos (☎ 2-6362; Circunvalación Olivos No 1) Near the bus station.

MONEY

Banco Financiero Internacional (☎ 2-7578; Independencia Sur No 2 on Parque Serafín Sánchez)

Cadeca (☎ 2-8536; Independencia Sur No 31; ☽ 8am-6pm Mon-Sat, 8am-noon Sun) Lose your youth in this line.

PHOTOGRAPHY

VideCuba (Independencia Norte No 50; ☽ 9am-9pm)

POST

Post Office (Independencia Sur No 8; 9am-6pm Mon-Sat) There's another branch on Bartolomé Masó No 167 in the Etecsa building.

PHONE NUMBER CHANGES

The year-long project to digitalize Cuba's phone system was ongoing as this book went to print. Eventually, all numbers in Sancti Spíritus will have six digits; this usually means adding one or two digits in front of existing numbers. The project is well coordinated, and taped messages detailing the changes play for several months before and after the changeover each time you dial an affected number. If you're in doubt, drop into any Etecsa office or call 113 (national information) for the latest.

SANCTI SPÍRITUS PROVINCE

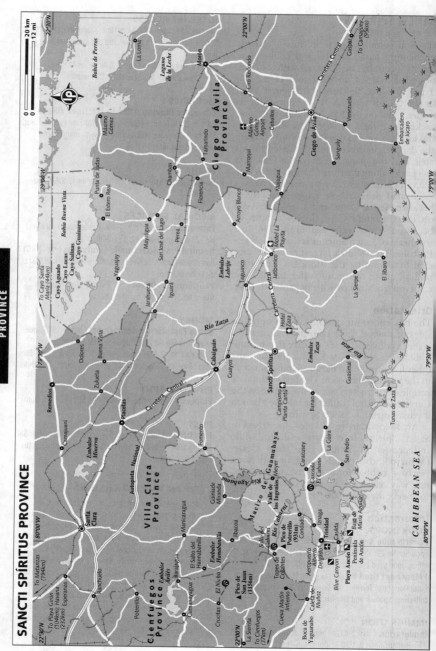

TELEPHONE

Etecsa (M Solano; ✆ 8am-10pm) In front of Cine Serafín Sánchez. There's another branch at Bartolomé Masó No 57, opposite Hospital Provincial Camilo Cienfuegos.

TRAVEL AGENCIES

Campismo Popular (✆ 2-5401; Independencia Norte No 201 off Parque Maceo) Reserves cabins at the province's six campismo resorts.

Cubatur (✆ 2-8518; Máximo Gómez Norte No 7 on Parque Serafín Sánchez; ✆ 9am-5pm Mon-Sat)

Sights

The city's most famous sight is the **Puente Yayabo**, a quadruple-arched brick bridge built by the Spanish in 1815, now a national monument. The **Teatro Principal** alongside the bridge dates from 1876, and the old cobbled streets radiating downhill were restored in the late 1980s. Tucked back here, old ladies peddle live chickens, neighbors gossip in front of their coral or lemon yellow houses and provincial city life thrums along undisturbed by tourism.

Up the hill from the Teatro Principal is the **Museo de Arte Colonial** (✆ 2-5455; Plácido Sur No 74; admission US$2; ✆ 9am-5pm Tue-Sat, 8am-noon Sun), with 19th-century furniture and decorations displayed in an imposing 17th-century building. Curve up this same way and you come to the charming yellow **Iglesia Parroquial Mayor del Espíritu Santo** (Agramonte Oeste No 58 on Plaza Honorato; ✆ 9-11am & 2-5pm Tue-Sat). Originally constructed of wood in 1522 and rebuilt in stone in 1680, it's said to be the oldest church in Cuba still standing on its original foundations (and one of the few with a working clock in its tower!). There's a splendid ceiling inside, but this church is often closed; try entering for mass (5pm daily and 9am Sunday).

The most interesting museum in town is the small collection at the **Fundación de la Naturaleza y El Hombre** (✆ 2-8342; Cruz Pérez No 1; admission US$1; ✆ 10am-5pm Mon-Fri, 10am-noon Sat) on Parque Maceo. Here you'll learn the fascinating tale of the 17,422km canoe odyssey 'from the Amazon to the Caribbean' in 1987 led by Cuban writer and renaissance man Antonio Nuñez Jiménez (1923–98). Some 432 expeditionaries made the journey through 10 countries, from Ecuador to the Bahamas, in the twin dugout canoes Simón Bolívar and Hatuey. The latter measures over 13m and is the collection's central,

prized piece. Across from the Fundación is the handsome old **Iglesia de Nuestra Señora de la Caridad** (Céspedes Norte No 207), with sparrows nesting above the altar.

Four blocks south is pretty Parque Serafín Sánchez with hundreds of metal chairs hosting cigar-smoking grandpas and flirty young couples. Sports and coin fans might like the **Museo Provincial** (Máximo Gómez Norte No 3 on Parque Serafín; admission US$1; ✆ 9am-6pm Mon-Thu, 9am-6pm & 8-10pm Sat, 8am-noon Sun), with its dedicated numismatic and athletic collections. Nearby, the **Museo de Ciencias Naturales** (✆ 2-6365; Máximo Gómez Sur No 2, off Parque Serafín Sánchez; admission US$1; ✆ 8:30am-5pm Tue-Fri, 8-10pm Sat, 8:30am-noon Sun) has stuffed animals, shiny rocks and a small planetarium. A few blocks north of the park is the **Museo Casa Natal de Serafín Sánchez** (Céspedes Norte No 112; admission US$0.50; ✆ 8am-5pm). Serafín Sánchez was a local patriot who participated in both wars of independence and went down fighting in November 1896.

The **Galería de Arte** (Céspedes Sur No 26; admission free; ✆ 8am-noon & 2-5pm Tue-Sat, 8am-noon Sun), next to the mercado agropecuario, houses 86 works by local painter Oscar Fernández Morera (1890–1946).

Sleeping

IN TOWN

The new **Hostal del Rijo** (Cubanacán; ✆ 2-8588; www.cubanacan.cu; Calle Honorato No 12; s/d/ste US$29/35/60; ✖ ▣) is a boutique hotel in a beautifully restored 1818 mansion. On Plaza Honorato facing the Parroquial Mayor, each of the 16 plush, clean rooms are different. Rooms Nos 5, 6, 7 and 9 have balconies with plaza views and one room is handicap accessible. The teeny rooftop pool is more like a puddle, but the city views are unbeatable. This place fills fast; if you can't get a room, head to the rooftop bar for a sunset cocktail.

The two-story **Hotel Plaza** (Islazul; ✆ 2-7102; Independencia Norte No 1; s/d low season US$20/28, high season US$24/32; ✖ ▣) has 28 rooms, a mirador and a great parkside location, but is a distant second choice behind the Hostal del Rijo.

The three-story **Hotel Perla de Cuba**, on Parque Serafín Sánchez, was being refurbished at the time of writing, but is a beautiful building with loads of potential.

See the boxed text (p257) for casa particular recommendations.

SANCTI SPÍRITUS

0 _____ 200 m
0 _____ 0.1 mi

INFORMATION
Banco Financiero Internacional..1 C1
Biblioteca Provincial Rubén Martínez
Villena...............................2 C1
Cadeca.................................3 C3
Campismo Popular....................4 B1
Cubatur................................5 C1
Etecsa.................................6 C2
Farmacia Especial....................7 B2
INDICT..................................8 D2
Inmigración...........................9 B2
J Menéndez Used Books............10 B4
Librería Julio Antonio Mella....11 C3
Pharmacy.............................12 B4
VideCuba.............................13 B2

SIGHTS & ACTIVITIES   p255
Fundación de la Naturaleza y El
Hombre.............................14 B2
Galería de Arte......................15 C3
Iglesia de Nuestra Señora de la
Caridad..............................16 B1
Iglesia Parroquial Mayor del Espíritu
Santo...............................17 B4
Museo Casa Natal de Serafín
Sánchez............................18 B2
Museo de Arte Colonial...........19 B4
Museo de Ciencias Naturales..20 C2
Museo Provincial....................21 C1
Parque de Diversiones.............22 D3
Plaza de la Revolución.............23 D1
Teatro Principal.....................24 B4

SLEEPING   pp255-7
Hostal del Rijo......................25 B3
Hotel Perla de Cuba................26 C1
Hotel Plaza...........................27 C1

EATING   p257
Cafetería El Rápido................28 C2
La Época.............................(see 13)
Mercado Agropecuario............29 C3
Mesón de la Plaza..................30 B3
Quinta Santa Elena.................31 B4
Restaurante 1514....................32 C2

DRINKING   p257
Taberna Don Pepe..................33 B4

ENTERTAINMENT   pp257-8
Cafe ARTex...........................34 C2
Casa de la Cultura..................35 C2
Casa de la Trova Miguel
Companioni.......................36 B3
Casa del Joven Creador...........37 B2
Cine Conrado Benítez.............38 C1
Cine Serafín Sánchez.............39 C3
UNEAC................................40 C3

SHOPPING   p258
Casa de las Comisiones...........41 C4
Fondo Cubano de Bienes
Culturales.........................42 C4

TRANSPORT   pp258-9
Horse Carts to Bus Station.....43 C3

Parque
Serafín
Sánchez

See Enlargment

Train Station
To Trinidad (70km)

To Hospital Provincial
Camilo Cienfuegos (300m);
Etecsa (300m); Rancho
Hatuey (4km); Villa
Los Laureles (5km);
Santa Clara (83km)

To Bus Station (2km);
Policlínico Los Olivos (2km);
Estadio José A Huelga (3km);
Ciego de Ávila (76km)

NORTH OF TOWN

Two agreeable hotels are along the Carretera Central as you head north toward Santa Clara; either one makes a good choice if you don't want to bother with the city center.

Villa Los Laureles (Islazul; ☎ 2-7016; Carretera Central Km 383; s/d/tr low season US$26/34/42, high season US$30/38/47; P ✕ ✦) This lively, attractive motel 5km north of town is popular with Cubans. There are 70 rooms, split between a classic motel block and separate cabins. The big, bright rooms have fridge, satellite TV and hot water, plus a patio or balcony. Cabaret Tropi has a nightly 9pm show.

Villa Rancho Hatuey (Cubanacán; ☎ 2-8315/16/17; www.cubanacan.cu; Carretera Central Km 384; s/d/tr low season US$30/40/63, high season US$32/45/75; P ✕

☐ ✦) This modern complex on a grassy hilltop is accessible from the southbound lane of the Carretera Central, 4km north of town. The 76 rooms, spread out on landscaped grounds, are popular with government officials and party leaders (you'll know them by their plaid shirts and jeans). People on bus tours are also frequently accommodated here, where all the services you would expect in a mid-range hotel are available.

EAST OF TOWN

Hotel Zaza (Islazul; ☎ 2-8512; s/d incl breakfast US$30/40; P ✕ ✦) Overlooking the huge Embalse Zaza 10km southeast of Sancti Spíritus, most tour groups overnight here. The 128 rooms are scruffy around the edges, but those numbered in the 400s have nice reservoir views. The swimming pool (US$3 for nonguests) is refreshing on a hot day and the entertainment – with music loud enough to hear underwater – is a gas. In early September, the Copa Internacional de Pesca de Black Bass is held here. Go east 5km on the Carretera Central toward Ciego de Ávila, then south 5km to the lake.

Motel La Playita (☎ 8-2422; s/d US$8/10; **P** ☒) This low-key choice is 24km east of the Hotel Zaza turn-off and just west of the large iron bridge on the Carretera Central at the exit from Jatibonico toward Sancti Spíritus. The big rooms aren't perfect, but you can't beat the price.

SOUTHWEST OF TOWN

Campismo Planta Cantú (☎ 2-9698; cabin US$30; **P** ☒) Off the beaten track, you'll need a car to get to this place near Banao, but the swimming and setting are worth it. The cute cabins below the foothills sleep four and are only good value for groups as you have to pay for the whole unit. Horses can be hired (US$3 per hour). The real draw here, though, are the revitalizing waterfalls of the crystal clear Río Cayajaná. To reach them, take the left fork before the campismo entrance and go until the road ends (about 1km). A worn path leads to the falls and swimming holes. There is a good, level camping spot here. To get to the campismo, go 16km southwest of Sancti Spíritus on the road to Trinidad, turn inland at the sign and go 6km further.

Eating

There are a couple of state-run places with decent atmosphere and food, but the best value and food is, once again, at casas particulares.

Quinta Santa Elena (☎ 2-9167; P Quintero No 60; ☒ 10am-midnight) The riverside patio with bridge views, live music at lunchtime and fair prices here are a winning combination. Good portions of shrimp in red sauce (US$7.50) or the house shrimp and pork special (US$5.50) make this the best choice in town. Salad selection for vegetarians.

Mesón de la Plaza (☎ 2-8546; Máximo Gómez Sur No 34; ☒ noon-2:30pm & 6-10pm). Facing Plaza Honorato with nice church views, this restaurant is routinely recommended by locals. Meat-heavy menu.

Restaurante 1514 (☎ 2-3514; Céspedes Norte No 52; ☒ noon-2pm & 6:30-8:30pm) Hidden in a regal colonial palace, they may be reticent to show you a menu here.

There's a big **Cafetería El Rápido** (☒ 9am-11pm) on the south side of Parque Serafín Sánchez and many street stalls sell **peso pizza** along Av de los Mártires beside Parque de Diversiones. The **mercado agropecuario** (Céspedes Sur No 28 at Valdés Muñoz) is a couple of blocks from Parque Serafín Sánchez. **La Época** (Independencia Norte No 50C) has groceries.

Drinking

Good places for a drink include **Taberna Don Pepe** (Plácido No 72; ☒ 9am-midnight), with a nice open patio next to the Museo de Arte Colonial, and the lobby bars at the Hostal del Rijo and Hotel Plaza.

Entertainment

The **Casa de la Cultura** (☎ 2-3772; M Solano No 11), diagonally opposite the library on Parque Serafín Sánchez, hosts various events. Cultural events also occur at **UNEAC** (2-6375; Independencia Sur No 10) near the post office; they show two movies daily as well. Check the **Casa del Joven Creador** (Céspedes Norte No 118), near the Museo Casa Natal de Serafín Sánchez, for rock and rap concerts.

For folk music, head to the **Casa de la Trova Miguel Companioni** (☎ 2-6802; Máximo Gómez Sur No 26) off Plaza Honorato. **Cafe ARTex** (M Solano; admission US$1; ☒ 10pm-2am Tue-Sun), on the southern side of Parque Serafín Sánchez, has dancing, live music and karaoke nightly and a Sunday matinee at 2pm.

The city's two main cinemas are **Cine Conrado Benítez** (☎ 2-5327; Máximo Gómez Norte No 13) and **Cine Serafín Sánchez** (☎ 2-3839; M Solano No 7), both on Parque Serafín Sánchez. The **Teatro Principal** (☎ 2-5755; Av Jesús Menéndez No 102) has weekend matinees (☿ 10am) with kids theater.

From October to April, baseball games are scheduled at the **Estadio José A Huelga** on Circunvalación, 1km north of the bus station. The Sancti Spiritus Gallos made it to the championship in 2002 and the games here are raucous.

Shopping

Anything you might need – from batteries to frying pans – is sold in street stalls along the pedestrian mall on Independencia Sur. The **Casa de Comisiones** (Independencia Sur No 6; ☿ 9am-4pm), a combination pawn shop–flea market, is a riot of Brownie cameras, rhinestone tiaras and vintage jewelry, watches, purses and furniture.

The **Fondo Cubano de Bienes Culturales** (☎ 2-7106; Independencia Sur No 55) has Cuban crafts and paintings.

Getting There & Away
BUS

The provincial bus station (☎ 2-4142; Carretera Central) is 2km east of town. **Astro** serves these destinations:

destination	cost (one way)	distance	departure
Camagüey	US$7	184km	7am alt days
Ciego de Ávila	US$3	76km	7am alt days
Havana	US$16	354km	9:35pm daily, 7:20am alt days
Santa Clara	US$2.50	83km	6am, 2pm
Santiago de Cuba	US$20	511km	8:40pm

With deluxe Víazul buses, you can choose from:

destination	cost (one way)	distance	departure
Havana	US$23	354km	2am, 6am, 8pm
Santiago de Cuba	US$28	511km	1am, 9:30am, 3:10pm, 8:40pm
Trinidad	US$6	70km	5:30am, 12:30pm
Varadero	US$16	265km	4pm

The Santiago de Cuba departure also stops in Ciego de Ávila (US$6, 76km), Camagüey (US$10, 184km), Las Tunas (US$17, 312km), Holguín (US$21, 393km) and Bayamo (US$21, 464km). The Havana bus stops at Santa Clara (US$6, 83km).

TRAIN

Train travel is tricky out of Sancti Spíritus. Luckily, the **train station** (☎ 2-4790; Av Jesús Menéndez final; ticket window ☿ 7am-2pm Mon-Sat), southwest of the Puente Yayabo, is an easy 10-minute walk from town so you can check schedules and status. The only departures from Sancti Spíritus proper are to Havana (US$13.50, 354km, eight hours, 9pm alternate days), stopping in Santa Clara (US$4, 83km, two hours) and to Cienfuegos (US$5.50, 151km, four hours, 5:05am Monday).

Points east are served out of Guayos, 15km north of Sancti Spíritus, including Holguín (US$14, 9:30am), Bayamo (US$13, 394km) and Santiago de Cuba (US$21, 8:45am). If you're on the Havana–Santiago de Cuba cross country express and going to Sancti Spíritus or Trinidad, you have to get off at Guayos. To disembark at Guayos you must generally move to the first carriage on the train (ask the conductor). Watch for other travelers willing to share a taxi to Sancti Spíritus (US$6) or Trinidad (US$20).

The ticket office at the Sancti Spíritus train station can sell you ticket for the trains from Guayos. You must find your own way to Guayos. If you try to buy a ticket at Guayos itself, you may be told that the day's tourist quota has been filled and you should come back in 24 hours. All in all, Guayos is an inconvenient place to board a train but OK if you're arriving from the east.

TRUCKS & TAXIS

Trucks to Trinidad, Jatibonico and elsewhere also depart from the bus station. Colectivos parked outside the station will take you to Trinidad at US$16 for the whole car, but it's technically illegal for foreigners to take them. Colectivos also go to Havana (US$60), Matanzas or Varadero (US$42), Santa Clara (US$16) or Cienfuegos (US$24).

Getting Around

Horse carts on the Carretera Central, opposite the bus station, run to the Parque Serafín Sánchez when full (one peso).

These turn around at the corner of Av de los Mártires and Adolfo del Castillo.

The Servi-Cupet gas station is 1.5km north of Motel Los Laureles, on the Carretera Central toward Santa Clara. At last report, you could safely and legally park a car around Parque Serafín Sánchez. The bypass road (Circunvalación) to Trinidad begins next to the bus station.

TRINIDAD

☎ 419 / pop 52,896

In 1988 Trinidad and the nearby Valle de los Ingenios were declared a World Heritage site by Unesco. Bumping and stumbling over the cobblestone streets as you enter town you'll see why: the beautifully restored homes, stately churches and cool, tiled courtyards ooze colonial atmosphere. Indeed, the striking architecture combines with the natural setting – squeezed between the coast and the Topes de Collantes mountains – to create an unrivalled ambiance. It's not surprising then that Trinidad is one of the most visited towns in Cuba.

But while some destinations absorb tourists well, Trinidad isn't one of them. As a result, the narrow, colonial streets teem with foreigners, the hustlers are working overtime and it sometimes feels like a Hollywood set with Cubans hired from central casting. OK, it's not that bad, but if you feel besieged, you might settle into a friendly casa particular in the small towns of La Boca or Casilda, just a quick 4km or 6km jaunt respectively from Trinidad. Alternatively, consider a casa that's outside of the historic center mayhem.

History

In 1514 the first governor of Cuba, Diego Velázquez, founded La Villa de la Santísima Trinidad. It was the third settlement established in Cuba, after Baracoa and Bayamo. It's claimed that the first mass was said here by none other than Fray Bartolomé de las Casas, 'Apostle of the Indians.' In 1518 the future conqueror of Mexico, Hernán Cortéz, recruited people here for his expedition. Despite this early start, Trinidad remained a backwater frequented by smugglers until the late 18th century. Slaves and goods were surreptitiously imported from British-controlled Jamaica, and cattle ranching and tobacco cultivation were the main agricultural activities.

Things changed in the early 19th century. Trinidad became the capital of the Departamento Central and hundreds of French refugees fleeing a slave rebellion in Haiti arrived, setting up more than 50 small sugar mills in the Valle de los Ingenios northeast of town. Sugar soon replaced leather and salted beef as the most important product, and by the mid-19th century the region around Trinidad was producing a third of Cuba's sugar, generating the wealth that financed the lovely townscape you see today.

The boom ended during the two wars of independence, when the sugar plantations around Trinidad were devastated. By the late 19th century, the focus of the sugar industry and trade had shifted to Cienfuegos and Matanzas Provinces. Trinidad wallowed in a time warp, and its baroque church towers, Carrara marble floors, wrought-iron grills, red-tile roofs and cobblestone streets have changed little in a century and a half.

Orientation

Trinidad turns on two hubs. The museums and churches of the old town (casco histórico) are focused around the Plaza Mayor, while the everyday facilities serving the local people are on or near Parque Céspedes. The bus station is a bit west of Plaza Mayor.

Be aware that most of the streets in Trinidad have two names, the new one used on the street sign (and in this book) and an old colonial name still preferred by many locals (see boxed text).

TRINIDAD STREET NAMES

old name	new name
Gutiérrez	Antonio Maceo
Jesús María	José Martí
Alameda	Jesús Menéndez
Carmen	Frank País
Santo Domingo	Camilo Cienfuegos
Rosario	Zerquera
Desengaño	Simón Bolívar
Boca	Piro Guinart
Gloria	Gustavo Izquierdo
San Procopio	General Lino Pérez
Guaurabo	Pablo Pichs Girón

TRINIDAD

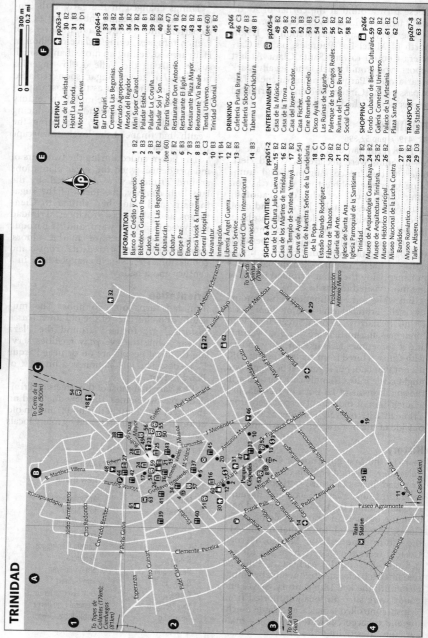

Information

BOOKSTORES
Librería Ángel Guerra (☎ 3748; José Martí No 273 btwn Colón & Zerquera; ◔ 8am-3pm Mon-Sat)

IMMIGRATION
Inmigración (Julio Cueva Díaz off Paseo Agramonte; ◔ 8am-5pm Tue-Thu) Office is south of the train station; stamps available at Banco de Crédito y Comercio.

INTERNET ACCESS
Etecsa (General Lino Pérez & Francisco Pettersen; ◔ 7am-11pm) Kiosk with one computer.
Cafe Internet Las Begonias (Antonio Maceo No 473 at Simón Bolívar; ◔ 9am-9pm; US$6/hr) Crowded.

LIBRARIES
Biblioteca Gustavo Izquierdo (José Martí No 265 btwn Colón & Zerquera; ◔ 8am-9pm Mon-Fri, 8am-6pm Sat, 8am-1pm Sun)

MEDIA
Radio Trinidad Broadcasts over 1200AM.

MEDICAL SERVICES
Servimed Clínica Internacional Cubanacán
(☎ 6240; General Lino Pérez No 103 at Anastasio Cárdenas; ◔ 24hr) Consultations cost US$25 (US$30 after 4 pm). On-site dollar pharmacy.
General Hospital (☎ 3201; Antonio Maceo No 6) Southeast of the center.

MONEY
Banco de Crédito y Comercio (☎ 2405; José Martí No 264)
Cadeca (☎ 6263; Martí No 164) Between Parque Céspedes and Camilo Cienfuegos.

PHOTOGRAPHY
Photo Service (José Martí No 192 btwn Camilo Cienfuegos & General Lino Pérez)

POST
Post Office (Antonio Maceo No 418 btwn Colón Zerquera)

TELEPHONE
Etecsa (☎ 4129; General Lino Pérez No 274) On Parque Céspedes.

TRAVEL AGENCIES
Cubanacán (☎ 6142; cnr José Martí & Zerquera)
Cubatur (☎ 6314; Antonio Maceo No 447 at Zerquera; ◔ 9am-8pm) Good for general tourist information, plus hotel bookings, car rentals and taxis; changes travelers checks and does cash advances.

Havanatur (☎ 6390; fax 6183; General Lino Pérez No 366)
Paradiso (☎ 6486; fax 6308; General Lino Pérez No 306) Cultural and general tours in English, Spanish and French.

Sights & Activities
The Plaza Mayor is the heart of the *casco histórico* (historical core) and Trinidad's loveliest spot.

Trinidad's showpiece museum is the lush **Museo Histórico Municipal** (☎ 4460; Simón Bolívar No 423; admission US$2; ◔ 9am-5pm Sat-Thu), just off Plaza Mayor, housed in a mansion that belonged to the Borrell family from 1827 to 1830. Later the building passed to a German planter named Kanter or Cantero, and it's still called Casa Cantero. Reputedly Dr Justo Cantero acquired vast sugar estates by poisoning an old slave trader and marrying his widow, who also suffered an untimely death. Cantero's ill-gotten wealth is well displayed in the stylish neoclassical decoration of the rooms. The view of Trinidad from the top of the tower alone is worth the price of admission. Visit before 11am, when the tour buses start rolling in.

The **Iglesia Parroquial de la Santísima Trinidad** (◔ 11am-12:30pm Mon-Sat) on the northeastern side of Plaza Mayor, was rebuilt in 1892 on the site of an earlier church. The venerated Christ of the True Cross (1713), on the second altar from the front to the left, is among the many sacred objects sheltered inside. Your best chance of seeing it is during mass at 8pm weekdays, 4pm Saturday, and 9am and 5pm Sunday.

Near the church is the **Museo Romántico** (☎ 4363; Echerri No 52; admission US$2; ◔ 9am-5pm Tue-Sun) in the Palacio Brunet, the ground floor of which was built in 1740, the upstairs in 1808. In 1974 the mansion was converted into a museum with 19th-century furnishings, a fine collection of china and other period pieces. Pushy museum staff will materialize at your side to guide you for a tip. The shop adjacent has a good selection of photos and books in English.

Another public display of wealth is in the **Museo de Arquitectura Trinitaria** (admission US$1; ◔ 9am-5pm Sat-Thu), on the southeastern side of Plaza Mayor, showcasing upper-class domestic architecture of the 18th and 19th centuries. The museum is housed in buildings erected in 1738 and 1785 that were joined together in 1819.

On the northwestern side of Plaza Mayor is the **Museo de Arqueología Guamuhaya** (☎ 3208; Bolívar No 457), being renovated at the time of writing.

Admission is completely free at the 19th-century Palacio Ortíz, which today houses the **Galería de Arte** (Rubén Martínez Villena at Bolívar; ☼ 9am-5pm), on the southwestern side of Plaza Mayor. Worth a look for its quality local art, particularly the embroidery, pottery and jewelry, there's also a nice courtyard and spiffy bathroom.

The **Casa Templo de Santería Yemayá** (Rubén Martínez Villena No 59 btwn Bolívar & Piro Guinart), contains a Santería altar to Yemayá, Goddess of the Sea, and the *santeros* in attendance are available for consultations. On the saint's anniversary, March 19, ceremonies are performed here day and night. Ask about carnaval routine practices and *parranda* dancing in the adjacent courtyard.

Perhaps the most photographed building in Trinidad, the **Museo Nacional de la Lucha Contra Bandidos** (☎ 4121; Echerri No 59 at Piro Guinart; admission US$1; ☼ 9am-6pm Tue-Sun) is housed in the 18th-century former convent of San Francisco de Asís; you'll know it by its yellow bell tower, the only part remaining from the original building. The displays are mostly photos, maps, weapons and other objects relating to the struggle against the various counterrevolutionary bands that operated in Sierra del Escambray between 1960 and 1965. The fuselage of a US U-2 spy plane shot down over Cuba is also on display. Here, too, you can climb the tower for good views.

Casa de los Mártires de Trinidad (Zerquera No 254 btwn Antonio Maceo & José Martí; unguided/guided free/US$1; ☼ 9am-5pm) is dedicated to 72 Trinidad residents who died in the struggle against Batista, the campaign against the counter-revolutionaries, and the war in Angola.

There's small **Fábrica de Tabacos** (Antonio Maceo No 403 at Colón), but tours were suspended at the time of writing.

Additional sights on the east side of town make a good goal for a stroll around or as you leave Trinidad for points north. Only the shell remains of the **Iglesia de Santa Ana**, but just across the square, on Calle Camilo Cienfuegos, is a former Spanish prison (1844) that has been converted into a tourist center, the **Plaza Santa Ana** (admission free; ☼ 11am-10pm). The complex includes an art gallery, handicraft market, ceramics shop, bar and restaurant.

Five blocks south is the **Taller Alfarero** (Call Andrés Berro; admission free; ☼ 8am-noon & 2-5pm Mon-Fri), a large factory where teams of worker make ceramics using the traditional potter' wheel.

For a bird's-eye view of Trinidad, wall straight up Simón Bolívar, the street be tween the Iglesia Parroquial and the Museo Romántico, to the destroyed 18th-century **Ermita de Nuestra Señora de la Candelaria d la Popa**, part of a former Spanish militar hospital. It's on a hill to the north of the ol town, a favorite sunset-watching spot (use repellant). There's also a route directly her from Motel Las Cuevas. Disco Ayala, behind the Ermita de la Popa, is a nightclub buil in a natural cave, **Cueva de Ayala** (admission US$1) From here it's a 30-minute hike up the hill t the radio transmitter atop 180m-high **Cerro de la Vigía**, which delivers broad vistas of Trini dad, Playa Ancón and the entire littoral.

The **Finca de Recreo María Dolores** (☎ 6481 6394/5; Carretera de Cienfuegos Km 1.5) is a farm and recreation complex along the Río Guaurabo. It runs sunset boat tours to the beach at La Boca (US$5 per person) and horseback riding tours to Cascada E Cubano (US$10 per person for two hours) The guide Rodolfo Bravo Pedarja has been warmly reader recommended here. It also rents rooms and hosts *fiesta campesinas* (see Hotels on p263).

At **Las Ruinas del Teatro Brunet** (Maceo No 461 btwn Simón Bolívar & Zerquera) you can take drumming lessons (☼ 9am to 11am Saturday) and dance lessons (1pm to 4pm Saturday). You might also check the **Social Club** (R Martínez Villena No 57), which holds salsa lessons (US$5 per two hours) in its courtyard.

Tours

Cubatur runs day tours to Topes de Collantes that cost US$25/37 per person for a five/seven-hour tour (three-person minimum) including hiking and swimming. Its horseback riding tours to the Cascada El Cubano include the park entrance fee, swimming, lunch and guide for US$18/12 with/without transport (horses are stabled at Finca de Recreo María Dolores; you can make your own way there and do the tour for less). Cubanacán offers much of the same excursion menu, with a slightly cheaper Topes tour (US$19) and a Ciénega de Zapata tour (US$63).

Paradiso has a great-value day tour to the Valle de los Ingenios for US$5 per person and an artist studio tour in Trinidad for US$6 per person. If you take lunch with either, it will tack on another US$10. It also runs day trips to the Che Memorial (see p240) in Santa Clara (US$24 for a seven-hour tour). Tours are in English or French.

If you're staying in a private house, your hosts will know someone renting horses for a trip around the Valle de los Ingenios or Cascada El Cubano. The first takes in a waterfall and both are through beautiful countryside. Your guide should be happy with US$7/15 per person for three/six hours. (Note that with a private guide, you have to pay an additional US$6.50 park entry fee for Cascada El Cubano.) The saddles on the horses are often poor and, unless you're an experienced rider, three hours will be plenty. A tour to Topes de Collantes by private car shouldn't cost more than US$25.

For diving, fishing, sailing and snorkeling tours, see Playa Ancón (p268); any of Trinidad's agencies can organize the same excursions.

Festivals & Events

The three-day Fiestas Sanjuaneras is a sort of local carnaval held during the last weekend in June. Rum-filled horsemen galloping through the streets is about the size of it: take cover. The Semana de la Cultura Trinitaria (Trinidad Culture Week) is at the beginning of January.

Sleeping

Trinidad has over 300 casas particulares (see the boxed text, p264) and competition is fierce: arriving by bus or walking the streets with luggage, you'll be besieged by hustlers working for commissions and desperate casa owners. With so many beautiful homes and hospitable families renting here, there's no reason to stay somewhere you're not comfortable. The houses around the bus station are convenient for new arrivals, but may not be your best choice for an extended stay, as it's not the nicest part of town.

If you're led to a house, it's preferable to do so with the actual owners rather than a *jinetero* (tout). Not only do touts jack up the room price (their commission is passed on to you, the consumer), they're doing very little work for a 25% to 50% cut, which is unjust and unnecessary given the plethora of rooms around town.

CAMPING

Along a small stream 8km out on the road to Topes de Collantes, the basic **Base de Campismo Manacal** (Map p269; ☎ 2168; per person US$3.25) has 43 small cabins with two, four or six beds. It's crowded with Cubans on Friday, Saturday and Sunday nights but empty the rest of the time. Tent campers will find good space at the camping ground in Topes de Collantes proper (p273).

HOTELS

Hotel La Ronda (Islazul; ☎ 2248; Martí No 238; s/d low season US$15/22, high season US$19/26) An acceptable, well-located option right on Parque Céspedes, this restored hotel has 19 rooms arranged around a central courtyard. The quieter rooms are at the back. The hotel restaurant is large, airy and good for breakfast (from 7:30am). There's a 'jazz' bar here.

Casa de la Amistad (amistur@ceniai.inf.cu) This hostel run by the Instituto Cubano de la Amistad is popular among visitors politically sympathetic to Cuba. At the time of writing it was moving to new, renovated digs (Zerquera between Martí & Frank Pais), which will likely provide the comfortable, intimate accommodation it's known for.

Motel Las Cuevas (Horizontes; ☎ 4013; www.horizontes.cu; s/d incl breakfast low season US$49/61, high US$57/71; P ⊠ ⊠) Bus tours inevitably stay at this place with city and sea views beyond the Iglesia de Santa Ana, 1km northeast of town. The best rooms are in newer two-story units overlooking the valley. Cueva La Maravillosa is accessible down a stairway, where you'll see a huge tree growing out of a cavern (entry US$1). When there are vacancies, nonguests can use the small pool for a small fee.

Casa del Campesino (☎ 6481, 6394/5; s/d/tr US$45/50/60; P ⊠ ⊠) If you're driving or want to get an early riding or hiking start, consider one of the rooms at the Finca de Recreo María Dolores, 1.5km west on the road to Cienfuegos and Topes de Collantes. Go for a room overlooking Río Guaurabo (cute porch included). On nights when groups are present, there's a *fiesta campesina* with country-style Cuban folk dancing at 9:30pm, (free/US$5 for guests/nonguests, including one drink). There are boat and horseback riding tours (US$10 for two hours). One kilometer west of the Casa del Campesino is a monument to Alberto Delgado, a teacher murdered by counter-revolutionaries.

Eating

Since so many casas particulares cook for their guests, you will probably end up eating in most nights. Dinners usually cost from US$5 to US$8, depending on what you eat. Vegetarians might find this a better

CASAS PARTICULARES – TRINDAD

Trinidad has the most varied casas particulares selection in Cuba. Bargain here and you could get a room for US$10 per night. Most places serve meals and have air-conditioning.

Araceli Reboso Miranda (☎ 3538, 3389; Lino Pérez No 207 btwn Frank Pais & Miguel Calzada; r US$15-20) Two spotless rooms off lush veranda; plus roof terrace, dangerously delicious meals, English spoken.

Escobar – Julio & Rosa (☎ 6688; www.trinidadphoto.com; José Martí No 401 at Santiago Escobar; r US$25; P ⊠) Lux colonial house with antiques, patio and roof terrace; English spoken.

Carlos Gil Lemes (☎ 3142; Martí No 263 btwn Zerquera & Colón; r US$20) Museum-quality colonial manor with courtyard, shared bath, friendly.

Marisol Herrera & Arnaldo Peña (☎ 3048; P Pichs Girón No 251 btwn Independencia & Vicente Suyuma; r US$15-20) Two rooms, one off roof terrace with views; flexible, spunky hostess.

Casa Arandia – Aurelio Arandia (☎ 3240; Antonio Maceo No 438 btwn Colón & Zerquera; r US$20-25) Gorgeous loft room with two double beds in colonial house with terrace, views, fridge.

Hostal Mercedes – Mercedes Padrón Jiménez (☎ 3068; Manuel Solano No 7 btwn Zerquera & Lumumba; r US$15) Independent house in back patio, clean and relaxing.

Nelson Fernández (☎ 3849, 4300; Piro Guinart No 228; r US$10-20) Near bus station. Upstairs rooms off roof terrace, good for groups, nice host.

Carmelina de la Paz (☎ 3620; Piro Guinart No 239 btwn Independencia & Vicente Suyuma; r US$15-20) Colonial house with huge rooms, ceilings to the clouds, roof terrace.

Elisa Margot Silva Ortíz (☎ 4332; Piro Guinart No 246 near Gustavo Izquierdo; r US$20) Grand room with balcony, original wood ceilings/floors, sweet sisters hosting.

Hostal Sandra y Victor (☎ /fax 2216; sandraorbea@yahoo.com; Antonio Maceo No 613 btwn Piro Guinart & P Pichs Girón; r US$20-25) Two rooms each with two double beds, nice outside/terrace space.

Beatriz Sotolongo (no phone; Antonio Maceo No 305 btwn Camilo Cienfuegos & General Lino Pérez; r US$15-20) Simple room off patio sleeps three, friendly.

Hostal El Albertico – Albertico Duarte Reyes (☎ 3721; Ernesto V Muñoz No 75A btwn Zerquera & Lumumba; r US$15-25) Spacious, quiet rooms, views; you'll eat well here.

Hostal Casa Margely (☎ 2550; Piro Guinart No 360A; r US$20) In front of the Museo Nacional de la Lucha Contra Bandidos. Good location, popular.

Ramona Hernández de la Pedraja (☎ 3637; C Cienfuegos No 68 btwn Frank País & Pedro Zerquera; r US$15-20) Quiet room in colonial house, small patio, friendly.

Mariene Ruíz Tapanes (☎ 4255; Simón Bolívar No 515; r US$15-20) Large, clean rooms above Plaza Mayor.

Balbina Cadahía (☎ 2585; Antonio Maceo No 355; r US$20) Two rooms, patio.

Hostal Cocodrilo – José Boggiano (☎ 2108; C Cienfuegos No 28 btwn Pedro Zerquera & Anastasio Cárdenas; r US$20) Busy intersection.

Rogelio Inchausti Bastida (☎ 4107; Simón Bolívar No 312; r US$15-20) Comfortable, popular, good for groups.

Ruth Martín Rodríguez (☎ 4396; Frank País No 38 btwn Eliope Paz & Manuel Fajardo; r US$15/20; P) Friendly, one/two rooms in separate house.

Casa de Ines (☎ 3241; eleusiscu@yahoo.com; José Martí No 160 btwn C Cienfuegos & General Lino Pérez; r US$20; P) Big room; kind owners.

Hospedaje Yolanda – Yolanda María Alvarez (☎ 3051; yolimar56@yahoo.com; Piro Guinart No 227; r US$15-20) Good for groups.

Nancy Ortega López (☎ 3068; Manuel Solano No 17 btwn Zerquera & Lumumba; r US$15-20) Quiet street, helpful host.

olution than picking around a restaurant r paladar menu.

PALADARES

aladar Sol y Son (Simón Bolívar No 283 btwn Frank aís & José Martí; noon-2pm & 7:30-11pm). The ood is good at this popular paladar (US$6 o US$8), but staff sometimes get overvhelmed (expect to wait for a table). The vaiting room is elegant and you dine in a ourtyard to the sound of music. English is poken. Skip the fish.

Paladar Estela (☎ 4329; Simón Bolívar No 557; 2-11:30pm) Choose the dining room or pretty rear garden to take your meals in this place above the Plaza Mayor. A voluminous meal served by friendly staff will cost from US$6 to US$8.

Paladar La Coruña (José Martí No 428 at Fidel Claro; 11am-11pm) We're unsure why graffiti is o popular in paladar decor, but it does add something to the ambiance here; meals cost US$6 and up.

RESTAURANTS

With so much tourist traffic, it's not surprising that Trinidad has some fairly good state-run places for the dollar crowd.

Trinidad Colonial (☎ 6473; Antonio Maceo No 402 at Colón; 11:30am-10pm). Here you'll dine on good portions of Cuban cuisine in the elegant 19th-century Casa Bidegaray. Meals are reasonable, with smoked pork topping out at US$5. The store attached has a good book selection.

Restorante Vía Reale (Rubén Martínez Villena No 74 btwn Piro Guinart & Pablo Pichs Girón; noon-4pm). Break the chicken and pork grind at this Italian place with pizza and spaghetti lunches for under US$4. Good vegetarian option.

Restaurante El Jigüe (☎ 6476; Rubén Martínez Villena at Piro Guinart; 11am-10pm) Back on the chicken trail, the house specialty here is *Pollo al Jigüe* (US$6); it's baked at least, offering savory flavors distinct from the usual grease fry.

Restaurants crowded with tour groups at luncheon include the **Mesón del Regidor** (☎ 64 56; Simón Bolívar No 424; 10am-10pm), specializing in grilled meats; and **Restaurante Plaza Mayor** (☎ 6470; Rubén Martínez Villena & Zerquera; 11am-10pm), with everything from spaghetti (US$3) to lobster (US$20). Live trios often strum while you dine at these places and they're quiet spots for dinner.

SELF-CATERING

Trinidad's **mercado agropecuario** (Pedro Zerquera & Manuel Fajardo; 8am-6pm Mon-Sat & 8am-noon Sun) is sad, but you should still be able to get basic fruits and vegetables. **Tienda Universo** (José Martí), near Bolívar in the Galería Comercial Universo, is Trinidad's best (and most expensive) grocery store. Head here for yogurt, cheese, even nuts and raisins. **Mini Super Caracol** (Gustavo Izquierdo & Zerquera; 9am-9pm) has a decent selection of groceries, plus cheap bottled water.

SNACKS

Bar Daiquirí (General Lino Pérez No 313 at Francisco Codanía off Parque Céspedes; 24hr) Lively place with cheap drinks and dollar fast food, the sidewalk terrace here is a popular meeting spot for locals and backpackers. The house across the street sells rocking batidos.

Cremería Las Begonias (☎ 6404; Antonio Maceo No 473 at Simón Bolívar; 9am-10pm) Ice cream, sandwiches and drinks are sold here, but the real draw is the pool tables. Across the street is another branch of this popular cafeteria (24 hour), with burgers, sandwiches and espresso. Always packed with folks using the Internet; good place to meet other travelers.

The stretch of Martí around Lino Pérez and C Cienfuegos is crowded with stalls selling peso meals, including **Pizzería Tosca** (José Martí No 226) on Parque Céspedes, with peso pizza. Other good areas for peso food include the corner of Piro Guinart and Antonio Maceo, not far from the bus station, and around the Cienfuegos, Paseo Agramonte, Cárdenas intersection on the road south out of town.

Entertainment

In addition to all the fun stuff mentioned in the boxed text (p266), the **Casa de la Música** (☎ 3414; admission free), up the wide stairway off the Plaza Mayor (you can also enter from Juan Manuel Márques), has *trova* (traditional poetic singing/songwriting) during the day, while the **Casa de la Cultura Julio Cueva Díaz** (☎ 4308; Zerquera No 406 at Ernesto Valdés Muñoz) presents various cultural activities by night.

Disco Ayala (☎ 6615; admission US$10, open bar; 10:30pm) feels gimmicky because it's inside a huge cave on the hill directly behind the Ermita de la Popa. Still, it can be fun. If you're driving, the disco's parking lot is accessible via Motel Las Cuevas.

Cine Romelio Cornelio (🕓 8pm Tue-Sun) on the southwestern side of Parque Céspedes, shows films nightly.

The **Estadio Rolando Rodríguez**, on Eliope Paz, at the southeastern end of Frank Paí's, hosts baseball games from October to April.

Shopping

There's an excellent open-air **arts and crafts market** on Jesús Menéndez, in front of the Casa de la Trova. This is the place to buy souvenirs, especially crochet work – just avoid the black coral and turtle-shell items that are endangered and forbidden entry into many countries. You can see local painters at work (and buy their painting at the **Casa de la Cultura Julio Cueva Díaz** (Zerqu No 406).

The **Fondo Cubano de Bienes Culturales** (Sim Bolívar No 418; 🕓 9am-5pm Mon-Fri, 9am-3pm Sat Sun), just down from the Plaza Mayor, h a good selection of Cuban handicraf The **Palacio de la Artesanía** (Piro Guinart No 22 located opposite the bus station, also se handicrafts.

The **Casa de la Música**, up the stairw beside the Iglesia Parroquial, has an exce lent selection of compact discs and a so-s variety of musical instruments. The **Casa** **la Trova** (Echerri No 29) sells a fine selection CDs as well.

TRINIDAD TROVA & PUB CRAWL

The Trinidad music scene might not be as polished as Santiago de Cuba's or as sexy as Havana's, but musicians here can still play. Stick around long enough and you'll discover your own jam spaces and dance places. Here are a few ideas for a night-time crawl around some of Trinidad's most popular spots (bring dollar bills to tip the musicians).

Start off with some 10-peso beer at **Cafetería Siboney** (José Martí No 208) on Parque Céspedes or cheap shots of rum at nearby **Cafetería Punta Brava** (Antinio Maceo & C Cienfuegos). The locals at either of these liquor counters will know if something hot is happening tonight. Kick off things at **Casa Fischer** (General Lino Pérez No 312 btwn José Martí & Francisco Codania; admission US$1), which cranks up at 10pm with a salsa orchestra (Tuesday to Sunday) or a folklore show (Friday). If you're early, kill time at its art gallery (free) or head to **Las Ruinas del Teatro Brunet** (Antonio Maceo No 461 btwn Simón Bolívar & Zerquera; admission US$1), which has an athletic AfroCuban show in its pleasant patio at 9:30pm nightly. En route you might check the schedule at the **Casa del Joven Creador** (José Martí No 321), where local youth might be having a rap *peña* or rock jam.

Swing by the **Cremería Las Begonias** (Antonio Maceo No 473 at Simón Bolívar), to pick up friends, chug an espresso or fortify yourself with a sandwich before diving into the heart of things. Following Bolívar up towards the Plaza Mayor, you can take a quick detour left on R Martínez Villena to see if Grupo los Pinos has swung into practice in the **Social Club** (R Martínez Villena No 57) courtyard or try the yummy *cancháchara* (US$2) at atmospheric **Taberna La Cancháchara** (R Martínez Villena at Ciro Redondo). This eponymous house cocktail is made from rum, honey, lemon and water. The local musicians that frequent this popular hang-out are often quite good, and it's not unusual for the upbeat crowd to break into spontaneous dancing.

Turn right on Ciro Redondo, round the corner and follow Echerri south and east around the Plaza Mayor and you'll come to a string of places that could take up an entire evening if things are hopping. The steps leading up to the **Casa de la Música** (🕿 3414; admission free) beside the Iglesia Parroquial off the Plaza Mayor are always crowded with people taking in the 10pm salsa/ dance show. Alternatively, full-on salsa concerts are held in the casa's rear courtyard (also accessible from Juan M Márques; cover US$2). Next door is the **Palenque de los Congos Reales** (Echerri at J Menéndez; free), an open patio with a lively scene and a full menu of salsa and *son*, heavy on the AfroCuban beat. Down the street is the famous **Casa de la Trova** (Echerri No 29; admission US$1; 🕓 9pm-2am), which can be exhilarating or bogus depending on the package-tourist-to-Cuban ratio. Give a listen at the door before shelling out the cover. Finally, a block north brings you to **Las Ruinas de Sagarte** (Jesús Menéndez near Galdós; admission free; 🕓 24hr) an intimate outdoor club with a good house band and high energy, low pressure dance scene.

If you still haven't had enough, drag your ass to **Bar Daiquirí** (Lino Pérez No 313 at Codanía off Parque Céspedes; 🕓 24hr) for a snack and a nightcap.

Getting There & Away

AIR

Alberto Delgado Airport is a kilometer south of Trinidad, just off the road to Casilda from the Servi-Cupet gas station. The only flights here are by private charter with Aerotaxi (see Air on p425).

BUS

The **bus station** (☎ 2404; Piro Guinart No 224 at Gustavo Izquierdo), has provincial buses to the following destinations:

destination	cost (one way)	distance	frequency
Cienfuegos	US$3	81km	daily
La Boca	US$1	4km	5 departures weekends only
Playa Ancón	US$1	12km	4 departures weekends only
Sancti Spíritus	US$1	70km	twice daily

Tickets are sold at a small window marked 'Taquilla Campo' near the station entrance. Check the blackboard for the current schedule. Service to Topes de Collantes was suspended at the time of writing, but double check as this should change.

The **Astro/Víazul ticket office** (☎ 4448; 🕙 8-11:30am & 1-5pm) is further back in the station. It sells Astro tickets to Cienfuegos (US$3, 81km, 9am daily), Santa Clara (US$6, 88km, 5:15pm daily) and Havana (US$21, 335km, 1:30pm daily). Four seats are available to dollar-paying tourists on any of these services (the quota on the Santa Clara service is often full, so try to book ahead).

In addition, there are air-con Víazul buses to:

destination	cost (one way)	distance	departure
Cienfuegos	US$6	81km	7:45am, 3:15pm
Havana	US$25	335km	7:45am, 3:15pm
Santa Clara	US$8	88km	2:40pm
Santiago de Cuba	US$33	581km	8:15am
Varadero	US$20	262km	2:40pm

The Varadero or Havana departures can leave you at Sancti Spíritus (US$6, 70km) or Jagüey Grande (US$15, 182km). The Santiago de Cuba departure goes through Ciego de Ávila (US$9, 146km), Camagüey (US$15, 254km), Las Tunas (US$22, 382km) and Bayamo (US$26, 463km) or Holguín (US$26, 463km).

CAR

Private cars can be contracted to Havana (US$20 per person) or Sancti Spíritus (US$5 per person).

TRAIN

The local train goes as far as Meyer, 8km north of Condado and 19km north of Trinidad. This train leaves daily at 9:30am, stopping at Iznaga, Condado and arriving in Meyer at 10:10am. The return train to Trinidad leaves Meyer at 1:30pm, giving you a few hours to explore the Valle de los Ingenios; you can also hop on the return train at Condado. Tourists are charged US$3 for a round trip. The terminal in Trinidad (☎ 4223) is in a small pink house across the train tracks on the western side of the station. (For information on train tours, see the Valle de los Ingenios p271.)

Getting Around

BICYCLE & HORSE CART

There are no official bicycle rentals in Trinidad, but your casa owner should be able to connect you with a bike for US$3/day. Horse carriages (two pesos) leave for Casilda from Paseo Agramonte at the southern end of town. Alight at Casilda, cross the train tracks and start out on the road to Playa Ancón; someone is bound to pick you up on this hot, deserted road (for information on the risks associated with hitching see p433).

BUS

The **Trinibus** shuttles between Trinidad and the Península de Ancón hourly with the first departure from Trinidad at 9am and the last return from Ancón at 6pm (US$2 one way, buy tickets on the bus). In theory, you can catch the bus in Trinidad at the Plaza Santa Ana and in front of Cubatur (Antonio Maceo No 447 at Zerquera), but sometimes they don't go at all.

CAR & TAXI

The rental agencies at the Playa Ancón hotels rent mopeds (US$27 per day), as does Transtur at Cubatur and another desk at Las Ruinas del Teatro Brunet (see p626).

Havanautos (☎ 6301; at Servi-Cupet near the airport) also has a branch in Hotel Costasur, Playa Ancón (☎ 6112).

Transtur (☎ 6257; cnr Maceo & Zerquera), in Cubatur office, is also at Hotel Ancón.

Servi-Cupet, 500m south of town on the road to Casilda, is open 24 hours and has El Rápido snack bar attached. The Oro Negro gas station is at the entrance to Trinidad from Sancti Spíritus, 1km east of Plaza Santa Ana.

Guarded parking is available on the corner of Pablo Pichs Girón and Vicente Suyuma near La Cancháchara (US$1/2 for 12/24 hours). You can also park near Plaza Santa Ana.

A coco-taxi costs US$4 to Playa Ancón.

PLAYA ANCÓN & AROUND

Playa Ancón, 12km south of Trinidad, is a luscious ribbon of white beach lapped by tranquil, blue waters. Over the centuries, ocean currents have built up 4km of soft beach here, and a few hundred meters offshore is an excellent reef for snorkeling and scuba diving.

Playa Ancón makes an ideal base from which to explore the architectural treasures of nearby Trinidad and the forested Sierra del Escambray. Not as overwhelmed by tourism as Varadero or Guardalavaca, it's a good resort choice for a Cuban holiday. It also makes a great bike trip from Trinidad. Beach bums who want to be near the water, but don't have the money or inclination to stay at one of the resorts, might consider a private home in Casilda or La Boca. The sand fleas are ferocious here at sunrise and sunset.

Sights & Activities

From Hotel Ancón, it's 18km to Trinidad via Casilda, or 16km on the much nicer coastal road via La Boca. The loop makes a pleasant bicycle trip. (Bicycles are available at Hotel Ancón and in Trinidad.) The Hotel Ancón pool is also open to nonguests.

The old fishing port of **Casilda**, 6km due south of Trinidad, is a friendly village with one paved road. On August 17 the **Fiesta de Santa Elena** engulfs little Casilda, with feasting, competitions, horse races and loads of rum. The road from Ancón to Casilda crosses a tidal flat, its abundant bird life visible in the early morning.

FISHING

The **Marina Puertosol Trinidad** (☎ 6205) is few hundred meters north of Hotel Ancón Four hours of deep-sea fishing, includin transport, gear and guide costs US$30 pe person (minimum six people). Fly fishin is also possible around the rich mangrov forests of Península de Ancón (US$7 per person for four hours, maximum tw people).

SNORKELING & SCUBA DIVING

Cayo Blanco, a reef islet 25km southeast o Playa Ancón, has eight marked scuba site where you'll see black coral and bountiful marine life. Marina Puertosol Trinida runs a seven-hour snorkeling and beacl tour to Cayo Blanco for US$20 person o US$27 with lunch. Arranging this trip a your resort will jack the price by US$5.

Diving with Marina Puertosol Trinida costs US$27/30 a dive in low/high season Snorkeling the reef with this professiona outfit costs US$5 per person, includin gear. Its **sunset catamaran cruise** (US$25/12 with without dinner) has been recommended. Ther is a minimum of eight passengers.

SAILING

The **Windward Islands Cruising Company** (in US ☎ 954-941-1335, in France ☎ 1 45 22 26 52 www.caribbean-adventure.com) charters crewed and bareboat monohulls and catamarans out ol the Marina Puertosol to the Jardines de la Reina. You can sail with or without guides on a partial package or all-inclusive tour.

Sleeping & Eating
HOTELS

Hotel Costasur (Horizontes; ☎ 6174; www.horizontes.cu; s/d incl breakfast low season US$34/45, high US$41/54; P ⊠ ⊠) Playa Ancón's oldest and humblest resort, this hotel is at the base of the peninsula, 9km from Casilda. For about US$10 more, you can upgrade to a superior room, which gives you better location and views (but not decor unfortunately). There are also 20 rooms in duplex bungalows starting at US$52/68, which are better still. From here you can scuba dive and horseback ride (US$5 an hour). The hotel faces a rocky shore, but a white sandy beach is just to the right. Swimming is difficult on the shallow reef. This place is popular with Canadian package tourists.

María la Gorda (p171), Pinar del Río Province

María la Gorda (p171), Pinar del Río Province

Reef scene, **María la Gorda** (p171), Pinar del Río Province

Diving (p407), María la Gorda, Pinar del Río Province

ALFREDO MAIQUEZ

Tobacco plantations, **Pinar del Río Province** (p161)

Tobacco farmer, **Pinar del Río Province** (p161)

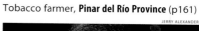

Valle de Viñales (p173), Pinar del Río Province

TRINIDAD AREA & PLAYA ANCÓN

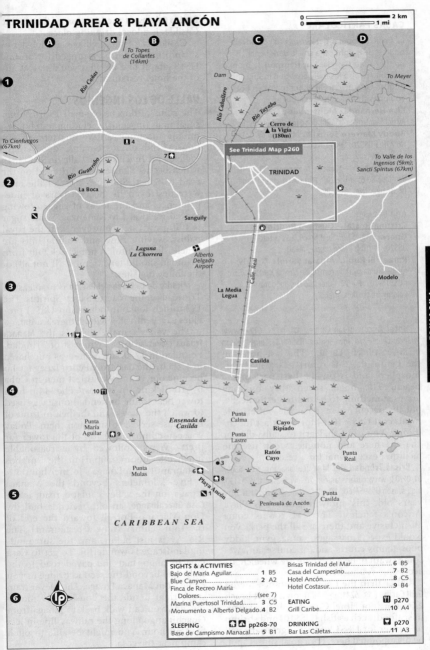

SANCTI SPÍRITUS PROVINCE

SIGHTS & ACTIVITIES
Bajo de María Aguilar...............**1** B5
Blue Canyon............................**2** A2
Finca de Recreo María
 Dolores.................................(see 7)
Marina Puertosol Trinidad.......**3** C5
Monumento a Alberto Delgado.**4** B2

SLEEPING pp268-70
Base de Campismo Manacal.....**5** B1

Brisas Trinidad del Mar...................**6** B5
Casa del Campesino.......................**7** B2
Hotel Ancón.................................**8** C5
Hotel Costasur..............................**9** B4

EATING p270
Grill Caribe.................................**10** A4

DRINKING p270
Bar Las Caletas............................**11** A3

CASAS PARTICULARES

La Boca, a popular getaway, is full of private houses. It is right on a small, dark beach. It's prettier than Casilda, but transport is more difficult. It's also insanely crowded in July and August. Casa owners in either town can hook you up with a bicycle. In La Boca:

Elsa Hernández Monteagudo (☎ 3236; Av del Mar No 5; r US$20) Good meals, friendly.

Ruddy Marrero Seijo (☎ 4586; Av del Sol No 75B; r US$20; P) Luxuriant terrace, English spoken, parking.

Villa Río Mar – Nestor Manresa (☎ 3108; San José No 65; r US$20; P) Two rooms in large house near river, friendly.

And in Casilda:

Cristina Hostal – Gustavo Rodríguez Guerra (☎ 5126; Real No 69, across tracks; r US$20; P) Nice couple, meals.

Rafael 'El Rubio' Albalat Sariol (☎ 5119; rubiopcasilda@yahoo.com; Calle Iznaga No 125; r US$15-20; P) Quiet house, good meals, yummy fruitshakes, friendly.

Hotel Ancón (Gran Caribe; ☎ 6123, 6127; www .grancaribe.cu; s/d low season US$60/85, high season US$85/90; P) The last hotel on the peninsula, this resort has a lively atmosphere and is on the best part of the beach. The huge, seven-story building leaves something to be desired esthetically, but it's decent value. Palatable buffet-style meals cost US$5/10/14 for breakfast/lunch/dinner. You can fish, learn to scuba dive or cha-cha here and nonguests can use the facilities; exceptional for a resort.

Brisas Trinidad del Mar (Cubanacán; ☎ 6500/01/02/03; www.cubanacan.cu; s/d low season US$75/130, high season US$95/160; P) Just a few years old, this sprawling resort is Playa Ancón's fanciest. The 241 rooms come all-inclusive and there are all the perks you would expect: massages, sauna, gym, kiddy pool, tennis courts and, of course, an awesome swath of beach. There are wheelchair-accessible rooms here.

Other than the hotel restaurants, there's **Grill Caribe** (☎ 6241; 24hr), on a quiet beach 2km north of Hotel Costasur. It specializes in seafood, such as fish (US$10) and shrimp or lobster for US$12. Strict vegetarians will be disappointed here. It's a great sunset spot.

Bar Las Caletas, at the junction of the road to Casilda, is a local drinking place.

Casilda is a fishing village and lobster or shrimp meals can be arranged for around US$8, about half of what you'd pay at any of the hotel restaurants.

VALLE DE LOS INGENIOS

The ruins of dozens of small 19th-century sugar mills *(ingenios)*, including warehouses, milling machinery, slave quarters, manor houses and other remains, dot verdant Valle de los Ingenios (or Valle de San Luis), which begins 8km east of Trinidad on the road to Sancti Spíritus. Most of the mills were destroyed in the two wars of independence, and the focus of sugar-growing moved westward to Matanzas. Some sugar is still grown here however, and the royal palms, waving cane and rolling hills are timelessly beautiful. A horseback tour from Trinidad should take in most (if not all) of the following sites.

Mirador de La Loma del Puerto is 6km east of Trinidad on the road to Sancti Spíritus. The 192m-high lookout (admission US$1) provides excellent valley views; there's a bar.

The valley's main sight is the **Manaca Iznaga** (admission US$1) 16km east of Trinidad. Founded in 1750, the estate was purchased in 1795 by the dastardly Pedro Iznaga, who became one of the wealthiest men in Cuba by trafficking in slaves. The 44m-high tower next to the hacienda house was used to watch the slaves, and the bell in front of the house served to summon them. Today you can climb to the top of the tower for pretty views, followed by a reasonable lunch (noon-2:30pm) in the Rumbos restaurant/bar in Iznaga's former house.

Five kilometers beyond the Manaca Iznaga, on the valley's inland road, is the **Casa Guachinango**, an old hacienda built by Don Mariano Borrell toward the end of the 18th century (now a restaurant). The Río Ay is just below, and the surrounding landscape is wonderful. To get to Casa Guachinango, take the paved road to the right just beyond the second bridge as you come from Manaca Iznaga. The Meyer train stops just beside the house every morning, and you can walk back to Iznaga from Guachinango along the railway line in less than an hour. You might be able to pitch camp near the casa.

Seven kilometers east of the Manaca Iznaga turn-off, then 2km south, is the **Sitio Guáimaro**, the former main estate of Don Mariano Borrell. The seven stone arches on the facade lead to frescoed rooms, now used as a restaurant.

Getting There & Away

It's easy for those without their own transport to visit the valley. These days, the daily local train from Trinidad (see p267) is more reliable than the 'tourist' train, which has been silenced recently due to engine problems. When it functions, the reconstructed railway carriage takes tourists on a 2½-hour trip through the valley (US$10; ☉ 9:30am). The train is pulled by steam engine No 52204, built by the Baldwin Locomotive Company of Philadelphia in August 1919. Passengers pay for their own lunch separately at the Manaca Iznaga and visit the Casa Guachinango. Cubatur in Trinidad (see p261) will know when the next tourist train trip is scheduled. Tour desks at the Ancón hotels sell the same train tour for US$17, including bus transfers to Trinidad.

Tours on horseback can be arranged at any of the tour agencies in Trinidad or Playa Ancón, or contract a horse and guide privately in Trinidad for US$15 for six hours.

TOPES DE COLLANTES

☎ 42 / elevation 771m

The rugged 90km-long Sierra del Escambray just northwest of Trinidad culminates in Pico de San Juan (1156m), also called 'La Cuca,' in neighboring Cienfuegos Province. The largest settlement in the range is Topes de Collantes, a health-resort town 20km northwest of Trinidad. En route to Topes de Collantes, your car will just about give out as you crest 600m and come upon **El Mirador**, a

CAMILO CIENFUEGOS

Ernesto 'Che' Guevara called him *la imagen del pueblo* (the image of the people), and despite his untimely death in a 1959 plane crash, the charisma of Camilo Cienfuegos continues to exemplify the Cuban Revolution. Born into a humble Havana family in 1932, Camilo was forced to drop out of art school for economic reasons and began working in a tailor's shop. In 1953 he left for the US, where he participated in various anti-Batista activities. Arrested by the American immigration authorities in 1955 and deported back to Cuba, Cienfuegos was subsequently beaten during a student demonstration in Havana. He returned to the US, where he learned of Fidel Castro's promise to liberate Cuba. Cienfuegos traveled to Mexico and became one of the last volunteers accepted for the Granma expedition.

After the disastrous battle of Alegría de Pío, Cienfuegos was among the dozen revolutionaries who managed to reach the Sierra Maestra Mountains. Castro promoted him to the rank of comandante in April 1958, and a few months later Cienfuegos led a guerrilla column on an arduous six-week march to Las Villas Province. His group became the revolution's nucleus in the north of the province, while Guevara led the fighting further south. With the success of the revolution, Cienfuegos became the military chief of Havana, and later the revolutionary army's chief of staff. In October 1959, Castro sent him to Camagüey to arrest Huber Matos, who had been plotting a counter-revolution. A week later, as Cienfuegos was returning to Havana, his Cessna aircraft plunged into the sea. His remains were never found.

Although a Havana man, Cienfuegos is most closely associated with Yaguajay in Sancti Spíritus Province, where he and his men fought one of the final battles of the revolution. Some 350 Batista troops, led by Captain Alfredo Abon Lee, had fortified themselves in a barracks between the town and the sugar mill. Eleven days of bitter fighting were required to secure their surrender. At one point the Dragon I, a homemade tank fitted with a flamethrower, was used to attack the barracks but the defenders hit it with a rocket. A train loaded with dynamite was sent toward the building along tracks meant to transport sugarcane, but it derailed. Cienfuegos dearly wanted to join Guevara in the assault on Santa Clara, but was prevented from doing so by the soldiers' stubborn resistance. Finally, on the afternoon of December 31, 1958, with numerous wounded around him and conditions deteriorating, Abon Lee ordered the white flag raised. Every October 28, on the anniversary of Cienfuegos' death, tens of thousands of schoolchildren stream down to the Cuban coast to toss 'a flower for Camilo' into the sea.

snack bar (good *mojitos*), with great views. A few hundred meters along you pass Pico de Potrerillo (931m), the highest peak in Sancti Spíritus Province. Coniferous forests, vines, lichens, mosses and giant ferns flourish in this cool, foggy climate, and Arabica coffee thrives on the slopes.

Topes de Collantes was founded in 1937 by dictator Fulgencio Batista, who built the road from Trinidad. That year he started work on the hideous building that is now the Kurhotel, but it was still unfinished when he lost the 1944 presidential elections. When he seized power anew in 1952, Batista ordered the work to continue and in 1954 it opened as a TB sanatorium. The sanatorium closed with the revolution and during the early 1960s the building housed militias fighting counterrevolutionaries in the Escambray Mountains. In 1989 the Gaviota chain reopened the Kurhotel as a spa.

Topes de Collantes has two hotels open to foreigners, plus good unguided hiking and an established camping ground. The **Carpeta Central information office** (☎ 54 02 31; ⏲ 8am-5pm), near the sundial at the entrance

to Topes de Collantes, sells a topographic map of the area for US$2.50.

It's very difficult to get here without a ca (and the steep ascent will test even nativ San Franciscan drivers) and harder still t get around to the various trailheads.

Hiking

The most popular hike is to the 62m **Salt del Caburní**, cascading over rocks into coc swimming holes before plunging int a chasm where macho locals dare eacl other to jump. At the height of the dr season (March to May), you may be dis appointed by these falls. A US$6.50 pe person entry fee is collected at the toll gat to Villa Caburní, just down the hill fron the Kurhotel near the Carpeta Central (it' a long approach on foot). Allow an hou down and an hour and a half back up fo this 2.5km hike. Some slopes are rathe steep and can be slippery after rain.

The trail to **La Batata**, a large cave containing an underground river, begins at a parking sign just up the hill from Parque La Represa. Admission is free. When you reach another highway, go around the righ side of the concrete embankment in front o you and down the hill. Always keep straight or right after this point (avoid trails to the left). Allow an hour each way. It's possible to swim in pools within the cave.

A US$7 per person guide from the Carpeta Central is required to visit **Parque La Represa** on the Río Vega Grande below Hotel Los Helechos. This park contains 300 species of trees and ferns, including the largest *caoba* (mahogany) tree in Cuba. The restaurant here is in a villa built by Fulgencio Batista's wife.

The **Salto de Vegas Grandes** trail begins at the apartment blocks known as Reparto El Chorrito on the southern side of Topes de Collantes, near the checkpoint at the entrance to the resort as you arrive from Trinidad. Allow a bit less than an hour each way to cover the 2km. It's possible to continue to the Salto del Caburní from this side, though hiring a guide would be advisable.

Another possible destination is **Hacienda Codina**. The 3.5km jeep track to the Hacienda begins on a hilltop 2.5km down the road toward Cienfuegos and Manicaragua, a kilometer before the point where these roads divide. There's a much shorter trail

TOPES DE COLLANTES

To Salto del Caburní (2km)

To Hacienda Codina (3.5km); Manicaragua (37km); Cienfuegos (65km)

Toll Gate

Kurhotel Escambray

Campground

Carpeta Central

Peso Cafeteria

Hospital Rural

To Trinidad (30km)

Hotel Los Helechos

To La Batata (1km)

Río Vega Grande

Parque La Represa

To Salto de Vegas Grandes (500m); El Mirador (11km); Trinidad (19km)

To Hacienda Codina (1km)

the Hacienda from below Hotel Los
elechos, but a guide would be required to
se that route. However, you might be able
· find your own way back, if you wanted
· make it a circle trip. Orchid and bamboo
ardens, nature trails, the Cueva del Altar,
ud baths and a scenic viewpoint are the
ttractions here.

leeping & Eating

he eight-story **Kurhotel Escambray** (Gaviota;
☎ 54 03 04; fax 54 02 28; s/d/tr low season US$40/55/75,
gh US$45/65/90) is too incongruous in this
eautiful hilltop setting. It's as if Batista
nticipated the Russians were coming way
ack when and built a dictator's dream pal-
ce to welcome his comrades. As ugly as it is,
riends swear by the facilities and treatment
f various ailments this hotel provides.

Better is the three-story **Hotel Los Helechos**
aviota; ☎ 54 03 30/1/2; fax 54 01 17; s/d US$22/31).
he rooms aren't much, but the thermal
ool, sauna and steam baths add value.

Self-sufficient campers will delight in the
amping ground (per person US$3), in a pine copse
n a spur road just below. A wacky aviary
roject of Batista's, the giant, abandoned
irdcages make great cooking areas and
here's a young, communal atmosphere as
t's a popular getaway for university students.
'ay the fee at the Carpeta Central. There are
o toilets. Several meters up the road from
he camping ground is a **cafeteria** usually sell-
ng egg sandwiches and coffee in pesos.

etting There & Away

'eople wax nostalgic when you ask them
about bus service between Trinidad and
Topes de Collantes. Theoretically, there's
supposed to be public transport, but in
practice it rarely materializes. Any of the
numerous hitchhikers along the road will
confirm this.

The road between Trinidad and Topes de
Collantes is paved, but it's very steep and
could present problems for a fully loaded
compact car. When wet, it becomes slippery and should be driven with caution.
There's also a spectacular 44km road that
continues right over the mountains from
Topes de Collantes to Manicaragua via
Jibacoa. It's also possible to drive to and
from Cienfuegos via San Blas on a partly
paved, partly gravel road.

NORTHERN SANCTI SPÍRITUS

For most visitors, the province's narrow
northern portion is only a transit corridor
between Remedios, in Villa Clara Province,
and Morón, in Ciego de Ávila Province. It's
worth stopping, however, to visit the **Museo Nacional Camilo Cienfuegos** (admission US$1;
☺ 8am-4pm Tue-Sat, 9am-1pm Sun), at Yaguajay,
36km southeast of Caibarién. In 1989 a 5m
bronze figure of Camilo Cienfuegos, reminiscent of Che Guevara in Santa Clara, was
placed atop an imposing memorial opposite the Hospital Docente General between
Yaguajay and the local sugar mill. The museum directly below this monument contains mementos of the battle fought here
on the eve of the revolution's truimph. At
that time the hospital was an army barracks
that Camilo and his band captured the day
before Batista fled the country. A replica of
the small tank Dragon I, converted from a
tractor for use in the battle, stands in front
of the hospital.

Ciego de Ávila Province

CIEGO DE ÁVILA PROVINCE

Ciego de Ávila's claim to fame is the Archipiélago de Sabana-Camagüey off the northern coast, those idyllic coral keys that include the world-class resort destinations Cayos Coco and Guillermo. Cuba's first governor, Diego Velázquez, called these islands Los Jardines del Rey ('the king's gardens'), a catchy name favored in many tourist brochures. It's not the world's second-largest reef as is sometimes claimed (that would discount the 500km-plus reefs off both coasts of New Caledonia in the South Pacific). But why dicker with details? Ciego de Ávila has a damn big stretch of reef and if you're after a resort vacation, this is the place. The Archipiélago de los Jardines de la Reina ('the queen's gardens'), off the southern coast, has more glorious beaches and excellent diving.

The provincial capital is interesting in that it's one of the least touristed cities in the country, offering a good local perspective. The saline Laguna de la Leche (67 sq km), north of Morón, is Cuba's largest lake. Sea water flows in the lake through three natural channels, causing the fine, white-clay bottom to foam up to the water's surface, creating the milky appearance that gives the lake its name. There's good trout fishing here and deep-sea fishing off both coasts. There are also mangrove swamps on both the Atlantic and Caribbean coasts and pineapple and citrus plantations through the middle, plus the usual sugarcane and cattle.

CIEGO DE ÁVILA PROVINCE

HIGHLIGHTS

Regal Beaches

Romping in the white sand and azure surf of Los Jardines del Rey (p282)

Scuba Cuba

Far-out diving on a live-aboard in the secluded Archipiélago de los Jardines de la Reina (p285)

Sport Challenge

Angling for a legendary bonefish from the shores of the Archipiélago de los Jardines de la Reina (p285)

Local Flavor Savor

Exploring pockets of the capital city, Ciego de Ávila (p276)

★ Los Jardines del Rey

★ Ciego de Ávila

★ Archipiélago de los Jardines de la Reina

| TELEPHONE CODE: 33 | POPULATION: 413,447 | AREA: 6910 SQ KM |

HISTORY

The province's name derives from a type of forest-fringed savanna called a ciego found on the original estate of Jacomé de Ávila, a Spaniard who was granted the *encomienda* (indigenous workforce) of San Antonio de la Palma in 1538. The province was a late bloomer, and towns like San Fernando de Morón only began appearing in this region in the 17th century.

During the independence wars of the latter half of the 19th century, Morón was the terminus of a defensive line built by the Spanish to prevent Cuban patriots from carrying their struggle to western Cuba. The line extended 67km from Morón in the north to Júcaro in the south. Despite this, rebel forces under Antonio Maceo and Máximo Gómez managed to break through in 1896, a feat that was repeated 62 years later by Che Guevara and Camilo Cienfuegos during their historic march on Santa Clara. In 1975, Ciego de Ávila was separated from Camagüey, becoming its own province.

GETTING THERE & AWAY

For information on getting to, from and around the province of Ciego de Ávila, refer to the Getting There & Away section of Ciego de Ávila city (p280).

CIEGO DE ÁVILA

☎ 33 / pop 104,850

With no famous colonial buildings, standout museums or natural wonders, there's little to specifically recommend this capital city and it's no surprise few foreigners stop here. Still, 'Ciego' has its charms and they're often in the details, like the giant projector mounted outside Cine Carmen (p280) or the coffee culture at La Fontana (p280). Ciego de Ávila was founded in 1840 and you can still glimpse its humble, agricultural roots.

Orientation

The streets of Ciego de Ávila divide between Norte (north) and Sur (south) at Independencia. Marcial Gómez marks the transition from Este (east) to Oeste (west). This is important to remember, as the cardinal points are often part of an address. The Carretera Central turns into Chicho Valdés as it cuts across town.

Information

AIRLINE OFFICES

Cubana (☎ 26 66 27; Chicho Valdéz No 83 btwn Maceo & Honorato del Castillo; ☾ 8am-3pm Mon-Fri, 8am-noon Sat)

BOOKSHOPS

Bookstore (Independencia Oeste No 153 at Simón Reyes)

IMMIGRATION

Inmigración (Independencia Este No 14; ☾ 8am-noon & 1-5pm Mon & Tue, 8am-noon Wed-Fri)

INTERNET ACCESS

Etecsa (Ground flr Doce Plantas; ☾ 8am-noon & 1-5pm Mon-Fri, 8am-noon Sat)

MEDIA

Radio Surco Broadcasting over 1440 AM and 98.1 FM.

MEDICAL SERVICES

General Hospital (☎ 22 24 29; Máximo Gómez No 257) Not far from the bus station.

MONEY

Banco de Crédito y Comercio (☎ 22 31 09; Independencia Oeste No 152 at Simón Reyes)
Bandec (☎ 22 23 32; Independencia Oeste and Maceo)
Banco Financiero Internacional (☎ 26 63 10; Joaquín Agüero Oeste & Honorato del Castillo)
Cadeca (☎ 26 66 15; Independencia Oeste No 118, btwn Maceo & Simón Reyes; ☾ 8:30am-6pm Mon-Sat, 8:30am-12:30pm Sun)

PHOTOGRAPHY

Photo Service (Maceo No 9 btwn Joaquín Agüero & Independencia)
VideCuba (Independencia Oeste No 173, btwn Simón Reyes & Agramonte) Developing, but light on film.

POST

DHL (☎ 26 20 96; Chicho Valdés & Marcial Gómez)
Post Office (Chicho Valdés & Marcial Gómez)

TELEPHONE

Cubacel (☎ 26 68 22; Hotel Ciego de Ávila, Carretera a Ceballos, ste 102; ☾ 8am-5pm Mon-Fri, 8am-noon Sat)
Etecsa (Ground flr Doce Plantas; ☾ 8am-noon & 1-5pm Mon-Fri, 8am-noon Sat)

TOURIST INFORMATION

Oficina de Jardines del Rey (Máximo Gómez Oeste No 82 at Maceo; ☾ 9am-5pm Mon-Fri) General information, plus interesting map showing past, present and future development on the keys.

CIEGO DE ÁVILA PROVINCE

0 — 20 km
0 — 12 mi

ATLANTIC OCEAN

Cayo Fragoso
Cayo Las Brujas
Las Brujas Airport
Cayo Santa María
Bahía Buena Vista
Caibarién
Cayo Guillermo
El Peñón
La Jaula 1, 2, 3 & 4
Archipiélago de Sabana-Camagüey
Cayo Coco
Cayo Coco Airport

79°30'W
79°00'W
78°30'W
78°00'W

22°30'N

Dolores
Cayo Romano
Buena Vista
Punta de Judas
Máximo Gómez
Bahía de Perros
El Estero Real
Yaguajay
Mayajigua
Jarahueca
San José del Lago
Iguará
Perea
Chambas
Laguna de la Leche
Laguna La Redonda
Cayo Judas
Bahía de Jigüey

Sancti Spíritus Province

Florencia
Tamarindo
Morón
Bolivia
Cabaiguán
Embalse Lebríje
Máximo Gómez Airport
Ciro Redondo
Guayos
Taguasco
Arroyo Blanco
Marroquí
Primero de Enero

22°00'N

Sancti Spíritus
Jatibonico
Ceballos
Caonao
Esmeralda
Embalse Zaza
Majagua
Ciego de Ávila
Carretera Central
Pablo
To Nuevitas (100km)
Guasimal
La Sierpe
Sanguily
Venezuela
Gaspar
Embalse Porvenir
El Jíbaro
Embalse Caonao
Embarcadero de Júcaro
Carlos Manuel de Céspedes
Florida

21°30'N
To Camagüey (2km)
Cayo Ana María
Embalse Muñoz
La Tomatera
Vertientes
Embalse Jimaguayú

Golfo de Ana María

Camagüey Province

21°00'N

Archipiélago de los Jardines de la Reina

Farallón
Pipín
Avalon
Meseta de los Meros
Faisy
La Cueva del Pulpa
Cabezo de Coral Negro
Laberinto de las Doce Leguas
Santa Cruz del Sur

CARIBBEAN SEA

79°30'W
79°00'W
78°30'W
78°00'W

Carretera de Morón

To Santa Clara (59km)

CIEGO DE ÁVILA PROVINCE

Reservaciones de Campismo Calle H Castillo (☎ 22 27 08; btwn Independencia & Libertad, ground flr of Doce Plantas; ☒ 8-11:30am & 1:30-4pm Mon-Fri, alt Sat) Chicho Valdés Oeste (☎ 22 25 01; No 113; ☒ 9am-5pm Mon-Fri) Reservations in five installations, including Cayo Coco.

Agencia de Reservas Islazul (☎ 22 53 14; Joaquín Agüero Oeste No 85 btwn Antonio Maceo & Honorato de Castillo; ☒ 9am-5pm Mon-Fri) Make reservations for Islazul properties in the province here.

Sights & Activities

Manageable and friendly, Ciego de Ávila engenders a leisurely pace. Check out **Parque Martí** – with the inevitable monument to José Martí (1925) – around which is the old Ayuntamiento (1911; no visitors), now the provincial government headquarters and

the **Museo de Artes Decorativas** (☎ 20 16 61; US$; ☒ 8am-5pm Mon-Tue, 8am-10pm Wed-Sat, 8am-noon 6-10pm Sun). This thoughtful collection ca be seen in 45 minutes and has quirky item from a bygone age, like a working Victro (Benny Moré serenades your visit), antiqu pocket watches and ornate canopy bed with mother-of-pearl inlays. A US$1 ti gets you a super guide (in English or Spar ish). The only other notable building is th grand **Teatro Principal** (1927; ☎ 22 20 86; Joaqu Agüero Oeste at Honorato del Castillo).

If you have time, you could visit the **Cer tro Raúl Martínez Galería de Arte Provincial** (Cal Independencia Oeste No 65 btwn Honorato del Castillo Maceo; ☒ 8am-noon & 1-5pm Mon & Wed, 1-9pm Th & Fri, 2-10pm Sat, 8am-noon Sun), where works b

CIEGO DE ÁVILA

0 ———— 500 m
0 ———— 0.3 mi

INFORMATION
Agencia de Reservas Islazul........1 B4
Banco de Crédito y Comercio....2 B3
Banco Financiero Internacional..3 B4
Bandec..4 B4
Bookstore....................................5 B3
Cadeca.......................................6 B3
Cubana.......................................7 B4
DHL..8 B4
Etecsa..9 B3
General Hospital........................10 D4
Inmigración...............................11 B4
Oficina de Jardines del Rey.......12 B3
Photo Service............................13 B4

Reservaciones de Campismo........14 B4
Reservaciones de Campismo..(see 19)
Transtur.................................(see 25)
VideCuba.................................15 B3

SIGHTS & ACTIVITIES pp278-9
Ayuntamiento............................16 B4
Centro Raúl Martínez Galería de Arte
  Provincial...............................17 B4
Constitutional Court Site.............18 A3
Doce Plantas.............................19 B3
Estadio José R Cepero.................20 A2
Museo de Artes Decorativas.......21 B4
Museo Provincial........................22 A3

Parque Zoológico.......................23 C4
Teatro Principal..........................24 B4

SLEEPING 🏠 p279
Hotel Ciego de Ávila...................25 B2
Hotel Santiago-Habana................26 B4
Hotel Sevilla..............................27 B4

EATING 🍴 pp279-80
Panadería Doña Neli...............(see 19)
Coppelia....................................28 B3
El Cabildo..................................29 B3
El Rápido...................................30 B3
Empresa Cubana del Pan.............31 A3
La Vicaria..................................32 D4
Mercado Agropecuario................33 A3
Paladar El Flamingo....................34 C4
Restaurante Don Pepe.................35 B3
Restaurante El Colonial...............36 B3
Restaurante La Romagnola...........37 B4
Supermercado Cruz Verde...........38 B4

DRINKING 🍷 p280
La Fontana.................................39 B3
Restaurante Moscú.....................40 B4

ENTERTAINMENT 🎭 p280
Casa de la Cultura......................41 B3
Casa de la Trova Miguel Angel
  Luna......................................42 B3
Cine Carmen.............................43 B4
Cine Iriondo..............................44 B4
Sala Fiesta Galaxia.....................45 B4

TRANSPORT pp280-1
Bus Station................................46 D4
Cubacel..................................(see 25)
Micar & Taxis.............................47 A3

uba's papa of pop art are on permanent
isplay, along with new works by local art-
ts. Or visit the **Parque Zoológico** (Independencia
te; admission free; ☼ Tue-Sun).

The **Museo Provincial** (☎ 22 87 07; Jose Antonio
hevarría No 25; admission US$1; ☼ 8am-noon & 1-5pm
on-Sat) is across the train tracks in a former
chool building marked 'Instituto de Segunda
nseñanza.' The exhibits recount the student
truggle against Fulgencio Batista. On the
orner of Independencia and Agramonte a
laque marks the site of the **constitutional court**
eld on June 14, 1952 by students and work-
rs protesting Batista's coup d'état.

From October to April, ask about base-
all games at the **Estadio José R Cepero** (☎ 22
2 83) on Máximo Gómez, northwest of the
enter.

Sleeping

Ciego has some decent, well-signposted
casas particulares and not much demand.

Hotel Sevilla (☎ 22 56 03; Independencia Oeste No
7 btwn Maceo & Honorato de Castillo; s/d US$24/31) This
elegant building just off Parque Martí, dates
from 1929 and had a facelift in 1999. Some
rooms have balconies, but none have hot
water. The open bar on the 3rd floor offers
great views and the ground-floor restaurant, decorated in a classic, old-fashioned
style is a fine, inexpensive dining option.

Hotel Ciego de Ávila (Islazul; ☎ 22 57 72; Carretera a Ceballos; s/d US$22/30 low season, US$27/36 high
season; P ⊠ ⊠) Bus tours usually stay at
this modern four-story hotel. Others won't
likely find a need to drop in except to visit
the Batanga Disco, rent a car, or eat at the
US$2.50 breakfast buffet (not bad; decent
coffee), which is free for guests.

Another option in the town center is
the five-story **Hotel Santiago-Habana** (Islazul;
☎ 22 72 62; Chicho Valdés & Honorato del Castillo;
s/d/tr US$22/30/38), with 76 rooms favored by
vacationing Cubans; it's rough around the
edges. Disco Centro Nocturno La Cima is
on the top floor.

Eating

RESTAURANTS

La Vicaria (☎ 26 64 77; Carretera Central near Máximo
Gómez; ☼ 8am-midnight) It's hard to go wrong
with this national chain, known for its tasty,
affordable food and professional, even efficient (!) service. This outlet across from the
bus station is particularly good, with a full

CASAS PARTICULARES – CIEGO DE ÁVILA

Miriam Marzabal Gómez (☎ 20 32 95;
Marcial Gómez No 58 btwn Joaquín Agüero &
Chicho Valdés; r US$15-20; ⊠) Spacious, comfort-
able rooms with TV and patio.

Gladys Luis Marrero (no phone; Calle Independencia No 205 btwn Onelio Hernández & 4ta;
r US$20; ⊠) Nice independent place with patio,
TV, perks, near hospital.

Leonarda Guitierrez (☎ 20 27 22; Honorato
del Castillo No 64 btwn Chiccho Valdés & Joaquín
Agüero; r US$15-20; ⊠) Friendly, knows others.

María del Carmen (☎ 20 12 02; Honorato
del Castillo cnr of Independencia; r US$20; ⊠)
Central, rents room in apartment.

---

meal of juicy pork steak, fries, salad, soda
and ice cream costing US$4.

Candelario Agüero (☎ 22 54 29; Candelaria
Gómez No 234 btwn Independencia & Máximo Gómez) A
veritable museum of kitsch, you'll dine well
in this private home surrounded by a dizzy-
ing clutter of porcelain figurines, campy
photos and faux gold leaf. An abundant
chicken or pork dinner with all the trim-
mings costs US$8.

Restaurante Don Pepe (☎ 22 37 13; Independencia Oeste No 103, btwn Maceo and Simón Reyes; ☼ 8-
11:45pm Wed-Mon) A bartender named Eladio
invented the Coctel Don Pepe (two shots
of orange juice, 1½ shots of white rum, and
half a shot of creme de menthe, stirred) here
back in the day. They're still serving them,
along with the good old pork and chicken
dishes found everywhere. There's live music
nightly.

There are two seatings (6pm and 8pm)
Friday to Wednesday for Italian food in
the drawn curtain setting of **Restaurante La
Romagnola** (☎ 22 59 89; Chicho Valdés at Marcial
Gómez); queue early.

Also recommended:

Restaurante El Colonial (☎ 22 35 95; Independencia
Oeste No 110; ☼ 6-11:30pm) For the regular pig and
pollo; nice courtyard is a plus.

El Cabildo (Calle Libertad No 20A cnr of Castillo) Sidewalk
tables, parkside locale and cheap beer.

El Rápido (☎ 26 61 16; Libertad cnr of Castillo;
☼ claims 24hr) Fast food Cuban style.

Coppelia (Independencia Oeste & Simon Reyes;
☼ 10am-10pm) Ice cream, you scream, we all scream
when there's no ice cream, often the case here.

SELF-CATERING

The **mercado agropecuario** (Chicho Valdés Oeste btwn Agramonte & Calle 1) is located in a blemished part of town below the overpass. **Supermercado Cruz Verde** (Independencia and Máximo Gómez; �9am-6pm Mon-Sat, 9am-noon Sun) sells groceries.

For bread, it's either **Panadería Doña Neli**, (northeastern cnr of Doce Plantas on Parque Martí) in dollars or **Empresa Cubana del Pan** (☎ 22 58 40; Independencia cnr of Agramonte) in pesos.

Drinking

La Fontana (☎ 20 21 79; Independencia cnr of A Maceo; � 6am-2:30pm & 4pm-midnight) If you've been missing 'café culture,' this place is the ticket. Choose from a menu of a dozen coffee drinks, including the spiked variety, while catching up on the daily news (a copy of *Granma* is at every table). You'll have to shout *¡último!* when you get in the line here, as it's a popular place.

Restaurante Moscú (☎ 22 53 86; Chicho Valdés No 78; � 6-10pm Tue-Thur) Walk left, past the scale model of the Kremlin, and down a fluorescent-lit hall. Push through the door in the back and step into the hushed red hues (what else?!) of the Moscu lounge.

Entertainment

Sala Fiesta Galaxia (Chicho Valdés & Maceo; � 10pm-2am Tue-Sun) Ciego heats up at this al fresco peso disco with dancing nightly and Sunday rap peñas (2pm).

Cuban folk-singing is the staple at the **Casa de la Trova Miguel Angel Luna** (Libertad No 130 at Simón Reyes). **Casa de la Cultura** (☎ 22 39 74; Independencia No 76, btwn Maceo & Honorato de Castillo), usually has something interesting on; check the *cartelera* (culture calendar) out front.

For a film, try **Cine Carmen** (☎ 22 33 87; Maceo No 51 at Libertad), with big screen and video offerings daily (don't miss the big movie projector spilling film on the Libertad side of the building), or **Cine Iriondo** (☎ 22 33 04; Joaquín Agüero Oeste & Maceo).

Getting There & Away

AIR

Ciego de Ávila's Máximo Gómez Airport (airport code AVI) is at Ceballos, 23km north of Ciego de Ávila and 23km south of Morón. Cubana (☎ 3-2525/4) has weekly flights to Havana (US$74 one way, one hour).

During the high winter season (December to April), both Air Transat and Skyservice have weekly charter flights to Ciego de Ávila from Toronto, Montreal and a few other Canadian cities. There are also weekly flights in winter from Frankfurt with Condor.

BUS

The **bus station** (☎ 22 24 07), about 1.5km east of the center on the Carretera Central, has Astro buses to the following destinations:

destination	cost (one way)	distance	departs
Camagüey	US$4	108km	5am & 4:40pm Mon-Fri, additional 10:30am Sat & Sun
Cienfuegos	US$9	227km	6:30pm, alt days
Havana	US$19	426km	8:25pm daily
Manzanillo	US$14	327km	7:30am alt days
Matanzas	US$14	366km	10:50pm alt days
Niquero	US$17	399km	8am alt days
Sancti Spíritus	US$3	76km	8:30am alt days

Tickets for these buses are sold for dollars at the regular ticket window, but most long-distance Astro buses are already full once they reach Ciego de Ávila. *Colectivos* (collective taxis) outside the station leave occasionally for Sancti Spíritus or Camagüey (US$20 for the car to either). Colectivos to Havana charge US$80.

Víazul has daily services to the following:

destination	cost (one way)	distance	departs
Camagüey	US$6	108km	11am
Havana	US$27	426km	6pm, 12:40am, 4:40am
Santiago de Cuba	US$24	435km	4:40pm, 10:05pm, 2:20am

The Santiago de Cuba departure also stops at Las Tunas (US$13), Holguín (US$17) and Bayamo (US$17). The Havana bus stops at Sancti Spíritus (US$6) and Santa Clara (US$9). For Víazul tickets, see the *jefe de turno* (shift manager), the office is right near the normal ticket window.

TRAIN

The **train station** (☎ 22 33 13) is six blocks southwest of the center. There are nightly trains to the following:

destination	cost (one way)	distance	departs
Bayamo	US$11	318km	3am, alt days
Camagüey	US$3	108km	4:50am, 2:40pm
Guantánamo	US$17	479km	9pm
Havana	US$16	426km	2am, 4am
Holguín	US$11	317km	4:45pm
Manzanillo	US$12	368km	3am, alt days
Santiago de Cuba	US$14	435km	9pm

In addition, there's a daily *expreso* (express) train to Havana (US$22) and three daily trains to Morón (US$1, 39km, one hour).

TRUCK

Private passenger trucks leave from the Ferro Omnibus bus station adjacent to the train station. They might take you to Morón, Camagüey, or Jatibonico.

Getting Around
CAR & MOPED

Havanautos Hotel Ciego de Ávila (☎ 26 63 45); airport (☎ 26 63 15)

Micar (Echevarría No 20 btwn Independencia & Libertad)

Transtur (☎ 26 62 29; at the Hotel Ciego de Ávila) Rents mopeds for US$18 a day, not including gas.

The Carretera a Morón gas station is on Carretera de Morón just before the bypass road, northeast of the center. The Oro Negro gas station is on the Carretera Central near the bus station.

You can park safely in front of the Hotel Santiago-Habana overnight.

TAXI

A taxi to the airport will cost around US$12; bargain if they're asking more. There's a **taxi stand** (Echevarría No 20 btwn Independencia & Libertad) next to Micar.

MORÓN

☎ 335 / pop 59,194

Morón is an uneventful place about 40km north of Ciego de Ávila via a flat road through cane fields. Founded in 1643, two centuries before Ciego de Ávila, it's called the *'ciudad del gallo'* for a verse about a cock that continued to crow after being defeathered. Locals love pointing out the feathered bronze rooster on a pedestal at the entrance to the Carrusel Morón. Pronounced mor-*own* (not *more*-on, so hold the dumb blond jokes), this town is a plausible base for day

---

---

trips to the beaches at Cayo Coco and is a favorite among fishers and hunters.

Travel agency **Cubanacán** (☎ 5-3168; Cristobal Colón No 49) has information about resorts and tours to Cayo Coco.

Sleeping & Eating

Thankfully there are sufficient private homes in Morón (see the boxed text), because the state-run scene isn't inspiring.

Carrusel Morón (Cubanacán; ☎ 3901; www.cubanacan.cu; Avenida de Tarafa; s/d US$39/45; P 🐾 🚗) Presently this modern-ish, four-story hotel at the south entrance to town is the only place in Morón accommodating groups. Package tourists are the main clientele. The pool is inviting; nonguests should ask about day passes. Maintain low expectations for the restaurant and you might be pleasantly surprised.

The surest bet for a solid meal in Morón is **Las Fuentes** (☎ 5758; Martí No 169 btwn Agramonte & Libertad; ☎ 11am-11pm), where you can get everything from a nice salad to grilled lobster. Fish dinners start at US$5.50 if you want to break away from fried chicken (US$1.50). Across the street is **Las Delícias** (☼ noon-midnight), a clean, friendly peso place with protein like chicken soup or egg sandwiches for two pesos.

Other recommendations:

Cafetería Mi Café (Martí No 294 btwn Calleja & S Sánchez; ☼ 9am-10pm Mon-Sat) Morón coffee junkies line up for tables.

Doña Neli-Dulcería (Serafín Sánchez No 86 btwn Narcisso López & Martí) Bread and sweets.

Los Balcones Commercial Center (Av Tarafa and Línea) A well-stocked grocery store, with wine, in the center of town.

Entertainment

The **Casa de la Trova Pablo Bernal** (Calle Libertad No 74, btwn Martí & Narciso López) is frequented by local folk singers and musicians. The **Batanga Disco** (☉ 9:30pm-2am) at the Carrusel Morón is a favorite of young locals starved for action.

Getting There & Away

Five buses a day leave from the hectic **train station** (☎ 3683; Martí & JF Poey) for Ciego de Ávila. You might be able to convince a collective taxi parked in front of the station to do this trip, but most are wary of carrying foreigners. Trains depart for Santiago de Cuba (US$22, alt days) via Ciego de Ávila (US$1, twice daily) and Camagüey (US$4, twice daily). The line from Santa Clara (US$5, alt days) to Nuevitas (US$3, alt days) also passes through Morón via Chambas. A coche motor railcar to Havana (US$24) operates on alternate days. Train travel from here is unreliable as many trains are canceled; if you want to ride the rails, Ciego de Ávila is a better bet.

Getting Around

The roads from Morón northwest to Caibarién (112km) and southeast Nuevitas (168km) are both good.

Havanautos (☎ 5-2114; Av de Tarafa s/n) is between Carrusel Morón and Hotel Perla del Norte. **Transtur** (☎ 2222) at the Carrusel Morón rents mopeds. **Micar** (☎ 5-5245; Av Tarafa & Línea) at the Los Balcones Commercial Center has fancy autos.

The Servi-Cupet gas station near Carrusel Morón is open 24 hours.

Yellow and blue buses start shuttling workers to the Cayo Coco resorts from about 6:30am, returning to Morón late in the afternoon. You might get lucky at the intersection leading to the causeway at the northwestern end of town, otherwise there's no transport to the Cayo.

NORTH OF MORÓN

There's terrific fishing for largemouth bass and trout at the **Marina Fluvial La Redonda** on Laguna La Redonda, 18km north of Morón, off the road to Cayo Coco. The mangroves surrounding this 4-sq-km lake are prime romping grounds for freshwater fish and the per square kilometer density of trout here is greater than anywhere in Cuba. Four/eight hours of fishing costs US$40/70. Fishing licenses are US$20 extra. There's also a nice bar-restaurant combo here if you only want to stop for a drink with a lake view.

El Pueblo Holandés, a small community with 49 red-roofed, Dutch-style dwellings, is on a hill next to the highway, 4km north of La Redonda. It was built by Celia Sánchez in 1960 as a home for area cattle workers. It's an interesting blip on the landscape, but not worth a detour.

CAYO COCO

☎ 33

At 370-sq-km, Cayo Coco is Cuba's fourth largest island and the main tourist destination of the Archipiélago de Sabana-Camagüey, or 'Los Jardines del Rey.' Nine kilometers of snowy white beach lapped by a batik of aqua, green and blue water runs along the Atlantic side, while the south coast is mostly mangroves (the source of Cayo Coco's 24-7 mosquito population). The 37km-long coral key is undergoing rabid development (in 2003 there were 3000 rooms out here; planners aim to triple that number) and opinions are divided on whether this is a good thing. LP readers weighed in with comments ranging from 'it was the most perfect beach and swimming that I have experienced anywhere' to a 'beautiful setting utterly wasted.'

Obviously, this type of vacation isn't for everyone: guests at all-inclusive resorts wear color-coded wrist bands and there are guards on the beach to prevent outsiders from wandering in. Furthermore, only Cubans working on Cayo Coco or staying at the national tourist installations are allowed access to the island, limiting contact to hotel staff. One misconception about Cayo Coco is there's no accommodation for independent travelers, which isn't true (see p284 for ideas). Still, the resorts *have* snatched up the best beach frontage and, at 60km from Morón and 100km from Ciego de Ávila, there are other gorgeous beaches in Cuba (eg Playa Ensenachos, p249) with better attractions nearby.

Since 1988, Cayo Coco has been connected to the mainland by a 27km causeway slicing across the Bahía de Perros (Bay of Dogs). There are also causeways from Cayo Coco to Cayo Guillermo in the west and to Cayo Romano in the east. The impact of these synthetic barriers on the environment has been severe. Circulation of seawater and marine life in the fragile coastal areas has been effectively blocked, to varying degrees, and waters east of the Cayo Coco causeway are deprived of nutrients. Dolphins are sometimes visible from the causeways, vainly searching for a way to get from one side to the other.

Information

Rumbos has an information office (but more of a) snack bar called **Parador La Silla** halfway along the causeway, 17km north of the toll gate and 16km south of the Servi-Cupet gas station on the Cayo Coco roundabout. **Havanatur** (☎ 30-1329) travel agency is at Servi-Cupet, as is Banco Financiero Internacional. There's a small, handy store (read: insect repellant) and an El Rápido too. Euros are accepted in all the Cayo Coco and Cayo Guillermo resorts.

Sights & Activities

The old airport has been converted to the **Parque Natural El Bagá**, which is better than the amusement park project that was first rumored. This 769-hectare park gives the resorts here 'added value' according to industry publications. It's a dense, green space with mangroves, lagoons, trails and a mirador.

La Cueva del Jabalí (☎ 30 12 06; admission US$5; ☷ 10pm Tue-Sat), 5km west of the Tryp complex, is a natural cave featuring a cabaret show. It's free all day to visit the bar.

East of Cayo Coco, a road crosses Cayo Romano and turns north to Cayo Paredón Grande and **Faro Diego Velázquez**, a 52m-working lighthouse that dates from 1859. The caretaker might let you up; if not, enjoy the fine beaches. The **Marina Marlin Aguas Tranquilas** (☎ 30 13 24), near the Hotel Meliá Cayo Coco, offers deep-sea fishing outings for US$250 for four hours.

The **Marlin Dive Center** (☎ 30 12 21), on the west side of Hotel Tryp Cayo Coco, is accessible via a dirt road to the beach. Scuba diving costs US$30 plus US$5 for gear. The open-water certification course costs US$365, less in low season. Snorkelers can ride on the boat for US$10. You can also rent a horse here for US$5 an hour. **Blue Diving** (☎ 30 81 79; enzoblue@ip.etecsa.cu) in Hotel Meliá Cayo Coco and **Coco** (☎ 30 13 23) at Hotel Tryp Cayo Coco, both with Cubanacán Náutica, offer similar services. Dive masters are multilingual and there are live-aboard options here.

CAYO COCO & CAYO GUILLERMO

INFORMATION
Banco Financiero Internacional...	(see 12)
Banco Financiero Internacional...	(see 7)
Havanatur...	(see 12)
Parador La Silla...	1 B2

SIGHTS & ACTIVITIES
Blue Diving...	(see 8)
Coco...	(see 5)
La Cueva del Jabalí...	2 B1
Marina Marlin Aguas Tranquilas...	(see 8)
Marinas Puertosol...	(see 11)
Marlin Dive Center...	3 B1

SLEEPING
Campismo Cayo Coco...	4 B1
Hotel Tryp Cayo Coco...	5 B1
Hotel Tryp Club...	6 B1
Iberostar Daiquiri...	7 A1
Meliá Cayo Coco...	8 C1
Meliá Cayo Guillermo...	(see 11)
Sitio La Güira...	9 B1
Sol Club Cayo Coco...	10 C1
Sol Club Cayo Guillermo...	11 A1

EATING
Cafetería El Rápido...	12 B1
Rumbos...	(see 9)

TRANSPORT
Cubacar...	13 B1
Havanautos...	(see 10)
Havanautos...	(see 5)
Toll Gate...	14 B2
Transtur...	(see 7)

Sleeping

Mosquitoes don't discriminate: whether you're in the dirt cheap camping ground or a luxurious all-inclusive resort, bring plenty of insect repellant.

BUDGET

Sitio La Güira (Rumbos; ☎ 30 12 08; r/cabaña US$20/25) This small farm 8km west of Servi-Cupet rents two rooms sharing a bath and a couple of Cuban *bohíos* (thatched huts) with private bath. A reasonable restaurant and bar are on the shady grounds and horseback riding is available. It's a mellow place until 11:30am when resort crowds pour in; the plethora of animals and extensive grounds make this a good budget place to take the kids. It's a hike (or a horse ride) from the beach, however.

Campismo Cayo Coco (☎ 30 10 39; US$13) There are 10 cabins and another five under construction available for foreigners here on the small, but pretty Playa Uva Caleta, 7.5km west of Sitio La Güira. Each cabin sleeps four. You can rent sea kayaks and there's a real Cuban atmosphere here that's absent from the international resorts. From May to August, this super friendly place is usually booked. Check for availability at the reservation offices in Ciego de Ávila (see p278) or Morón (see p281) before driving all the way out here.

TOP END

While most travelers arrive at the following resorts on a package tour, it's possible to book yourself by phone or via the website (though you'll pay premium prices). Any of the following can be checked out on the Web at www.solmeliacuba.com. Prices shown are for standard rooms; prices go up for views, junior suites, bungalows etc. You can expect all the amenities, activities and entertainment that comes with all-inclusive resorts.

Meliá Cayo Coco (☎ 30 11 80; r all-inclusive from US$190; P X X 🔲 🏊) This resort on stellar Playa Las Coloradas at the eastern end of the hotel strip, was erected in 1999 by the Spanish Meliá hotel chain. The sweet bungalows perched in the lagoon have porches and lots of sun. There are tons of romantic pockets here and the rooms are muted, tasteful and comfortable.

Sol Club Cayo Coco (Gran Caribe; ☎ 30 12 80; r all-inclusive from US$150; P X X 🔲 🏊) Also on Playa Las Coloradas, this family-friendly complex is another Meliá property. The programming is intensive and kid-friendly, including all the water sports you can imagine and day trips around the archipelago.

Hotel Tryp Cayo Coco (Cubanacán; ☎ 30 13 11; r all-inclusive from US$170; P X X 🔲 🏊) Part of a sprawling complex (this hotel and the neighboring **Hotel Tryp Club** have over 1000 rooms combined), these resorts are the older, humbler cousins to the other Meliá's here. A long pool meanders through the complex and there's snorkeling in the clear waters in front of the resorts. There's a disco, a Banco Financiero Internacional branch and Clínica Internacional at the Hotel Tryp Cayo Coco, but they're accessible only to hotel guests.

At the time of writing, El Breeze was being built by Gaviota just east of Campismo Cayo Coco.

Eating

All of the large resorts here are all-inclusive, so there are few nonhotel restaurants.

Cafetería El Rápido, at the Servi-Cupet gas station on the roundabout at the entrance to Cayo Coco, dispenses cheap drinks and snacks 24 hours. The **Rumbos** (🕙 9am-10pm) restaurant at Sitio La Güira has a varied menu with big, fresh sandwiches for US$1.50, shrimp plates for US$12 and a full bar.

Upon arrival at your resort, you may be told not to drink the tap water, only bottled water sold at the resort shop, which may be open for limited hours. The small store at the Servi-Cupet sells chlorine drops to make potable water if you have doubts.

Getting There & Around

You can't fill the rooms without an international airport, and Cayo Coco has a brand new 3000m-runway facility that can process 1.2 million visitors annually. Cubana has weekly flights from Montreal and Buenos Aires. Aerocaribbean has three flights a week from Havana (US$68).

There are no public buses to Cayo Coco, but you may be able to hitch a ride out of Morón with other tourists or on one of the buses transporting workers to the keys. Once you leave the road and enter onto the causeway proper, there's a US$2 toll (both ways).

You can rent a car (US$60 to US$80 a day) or moped (US$20 a day) at the following places on Cayo Coco:

Cubacar (☎ 30 12 75) On the second roundabout between the Meliá and Tryp complexes.

Havanautos Sol Club Cayo Coco (☎ 30 12 28) Hotel Tryp Cayo Coco (☎ 30 13 11)

CAYO GUILLERMO

Just west of Cayo Coco is 13-sq-km Cayo Guillermo, a much smaller coral key connected to Cayo Coco by a causeway. The mangroves off the south coast of Cayo Guillermo are home to pink flamingos and pelicans, and there's a great diversity of tropical fish and crustaceans on the key's Atlantic reef. The same feverish building activity seen on Cayo Coco is evident here, too.

This was a favorite fishing spot of writer Ernest Hemingway, who mentioned Cayo Guillermo in his book *Islands in the Stream*, and the best (public) beach is Playa Pilar, named after Hemingway's boat. Cayo Guillermo is probably the number one sport fishing destination in Cuba. The deep-sea fishing facilities are good, and several freshwater lakes on the mainland are within commuting distance.

A Banco Financiero Internacional branch and Transtur rental car office are on the premises of Iberostar Daiquirí (see Sleeping & Eating below).

Activities

The **Marinas Puertosol** (☎ 30 17 38; fax 30 17 37) offers deep-sea fishing for mackerel, pike, barracuda, red snapper and marlin on large boats that depart from a pier right at the hotel. It's US$250/450 for a half/full day, and you can keep some of the fish. A professional dive center charging US$35 a dive is also here. It is best to go directly to the pier and book the dive in person. Also, note that trips are cancelled when it's too windy. **Cubanacán Náutica** (Meliá Cayo Guillermo ☎ 30 16 27; Sol Club Cayo Guillermo ☎ 30 17 60) has two dive centers doing dives for US$35.

Playa Pilar is a lovely, unspoiled beach at the far western end of this key where you can sail (US$10) and snorkel (US$3).

Sleeping & Eating

Iberostar Daiquirí (Gran Caribe; ☎ 30 16 50; fax 30-1643; s/d low season US$95/130, high US$110/160; P   X   ▣ ▣) This hotel has 312 rooms in a series of three-story buildings, all brightly painted like Las Vegas casinos. Extensive gardens are a bonus, also check out the kids' packages.

Sol Club Cayo Guillermo (Gran Caribe; ☎ 30 17 60; www.solmeliacuba.com; r from US$210; P   X   ▣   ▣ ▣) Another all-inclusive managed by the Spanish Sol Meliá chain, this resort is on another blindingly white stretch of beach 2km west of VentaClub. There's a giant free-form pool snaking through the grounds and the bungalows are roomy and have terraces, though they're crowded together.

Hotel Meliá Cayo Guillermo (Gran Caribe; ☎ 30 16 80; www.solmeliacuba.com; r from US$130; P   X   ▣ ▣ ▣) Near the Sol Club Cayo Guillermo this is wickedly luxurious, with lots of high-quality linens in yummy pastels and balconies with beach views.

There's a kicking café at Playa Pilar where you can get an espresso for US$0.50.

Getting There & Around

Access information is the same as for Cayo Coco (see p284). Unless you're on a tour, the usual way to get here is by rental car. **Transtur** (☎ 30 11 75) has offices at VentaClub Cayo Guillermo and at the Iberostar Daiquirí.

LOS JARDINES DE LA REINA

The Archipiélago de los Jardines de la Reina, in the Caribbean Sea, is a 160km-long chain of low coral keys located about 80km south of the main island of Cuba. Mangroves cover much of the shoreline of these keys, and the beaches are generally small. The boundary between Ciego de Ávila and Camagüey Provinces cuts the group in two. Tourism is slowly being developed on the Ciego de Ávila side, and Marinas Puertosol uses the **Hotel Flotante Tortuga** (☎ 33-9-8104), a two-story houseboat, as a base for scuba divers. The reefs are pristine, and shark feeding is an attraction here. From shore, you can cast for macabí (bonefish), a fighting fish that has a dedicated following among anglers worldwide.

Access is via the **Embarcadero de Júcaro** (☎ 9-8126), 24km south of Ciego de Ávila. **Marsub** (☎ 96 13 49/69; marsub@ceniai.inf.cu; Tarará, Havana) used to book cruises from Trinidad, but had suspended this excursion at the time of writing. Until they start up again, interested divers should contact **Havanatur** (☎ 204-2906; www.havanatur.cu; Calle 1ra btwn O & 2, Edificio Sierra Maestra) in Havana, or check out the dive packages offered by UK-based outfit **Scuba en Cuba** (www.scuba-en-cuba.com), which has a 10-day dive trip (six are spent on board the Tortuga) for UK£1260.

Camagüey Province

Welcome to Camagüey, Cuba's largest province, biggest beef producer (nearly a million cows graze here) and home to the provincial capital of Camagüey, the country's third largest city. This might be Cuba's most atmospheric city, with its winding streets that twirl you unexpectedly into quaint colonial plazas, a happening performing arts scene, and churches, churches, churches. However, at 534km from Havana and 327km from Santiago de Cuba, surprisingly few foreigners manage a visit: for independent travelers, this is one city not to miss.

The province of Camagüey also boasts Playa Santa Lucía, a 20km ribbon of sand with warm water, inspiring scuba diving and a variety of resorts. At just 112km north of Camagüey, this makes a terrific day trip on moped or getaway splurge spot. Cayo Romano and Cayo Sabinal, the sprawling coral keys off the north coast offer some off the beaten track beach opportunities.

A long swamp extends along the south coast, facing the shallow Golfo de Ana María, itself bounded on the south by the uninhabited eastern half of the Archipiélago de los Jardines de la Reina, also a part of Camagüey.

HIGHLIGHTS

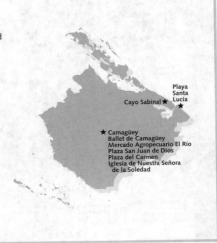

- **Colonial Cartography**
  Getting lost in Camagüey's wickedly twisted streets (p288)
- **Neverending Photo Ops**
  Plazas San Juan de Dios (p292) and del Carmen (p292) and Iglesia de Nuestra Señora de la Soledad (p292)
- **Big City Charms**
  Talented Ballet de Camagüey (p295) and fascinating Mercado Agropecuario El Río (p292)
- **Beach Bumming**
  In Playa Santa Lucía, scuba diving wrecks, reef, caves and walls (p299)
- **Far Out, Baby**
  Cayo Sabinal (p299). Huh? Where? Exactly.

- TELEPHONE CODE: 32   ■ POPULATION: 791,815   ■ AREA: 15,990 SQ KM

CAMAGÜEY

☎ 32 / pop 309,977

Approximately midway between Santa Clara and Santiago de Cuba, Camagüey enchants on sight. With its colonial buildings hiding colorful stained glass and lush inner courtyards, pastel painted churches, and outgoing locals ready with a smile, this is one of those places that hijacks your itinerary. Camagüey is known as the city of *tinajones* for the large clay pots originally kept in courtyards to provide a supply of cool water during droughts. According to the old legend, whomever drinks from the *tinajones* will fall in love with Camagüey, forever returning.

The Universidad de Camagüey, founded in 1975, is one of Cuba's largest universities and accepts foreign students wishing to study Spanish, culture or literature (see p292).

History

In February 1514 Santa María del Puerto Príncipe was founded near the site of present-day Nuevitas, one of the seven original towns established by Diego Velázquez. Not long after, the town was moved twice, mainly because of Indian rebellions and the poor farmland around Nuevitas. In 1528, the present site was selected because it was less vulnerable to attack, and Camagüey was deliberately laid out in a confusing, irregular way to disorient marauding pirates. It didn't work: English pirate Henry Morgan attacked the town in 1668, followed

CAMAGÜEY PROVINCE

in 1679 by the French buccaneer François Granmont.

Cuban national poet Nicolás Guillén hailed from Camagüey, as did Carlos J Finlay, the doctor who discovered the cause of yellow fever.

Orientation

The irregular street layout makes getting around Camagüey as confusing to visitors as it was to pirates. Luckily, friendly Camagüeyanos are used to baffled travelers asking the way. The train station is on the northern side of town, and several inexpensive hotels are nearby. The city's north–south axis is República, which meets Av Agramonte at the historic La Soledad church. Most of the other hotels, churches and museums are just southwest of the church, in the city center. The Río Hatibonico crosses the southern side of the city center, and the main bus station is on the Carretera Central, about 3km southeast of the river.

Information

AIRLINE OFFICES

Cubana República (☎ 29 21 56; República No 400 btwn El Solitario & San Martín; ☼ 8:15am-4pm Mon-Fri); Aeropuerto Ignacio Agramonte (☎ 26 10 00)

BOOKSTORES

Librería Antonio Suárez (Maceo btwn General Gómez & Plaza Maceo) Large selection of books in Spanish.
Librería Ateneo (República No 418 btwn El Solitario & San Martín)

EMERGENCY

Asistur (☎ 28 63 17, 28 65 17; Agramonte No 449 btwn Independencia & República)

IMMIGRATION

Inmigración (Calle 3 No 156, btwn Nos 8 & 10, Reparto Vista Hermosa; ☼ 8am-11:30am, 1-3pm Mon-Fri, except Wed)

INTERNET ACCESS

Cybercafe Trova Latina (Ramón Guerrero No 121)
Etecsa (Avellaneda No 308 near Oscar Primelles; ☼ 24hr) Least crowded of the options.
InfoTur (Av Agramonte behind Iglesia de la Merced)

LIBRARIES

Biblioteca Provincial Julio A Mella (Parque Ignacio Agramonte; ☼ closed Sun)

MEDIA

Adelante Local newspaper published Saturday.
Radio Cadena Agramonte Broadcasting over frequency 910AM & 93.5FM; it's located south of the city by turning to 1340AM, and to the north, tune your radio to 1380AM.

MEDICAL SERVICES

Policlínico Integral Rodolfo Ramirez Esquival (☎ 28 14 81; Ignacio Sánchez & Joaquín de Agüero) North of the level crossing from the Hotel Plaza.
Farmacia Álvarez Fuentes (Avellaneda No 249 at Oscar Primelles; ☼ 24hr)
Farmacia Turno Especial (República No 269; ☼ 8am-10pm Mon-Sat)

MONEY

Banco de Crédito y Comercio (Av Agramonte & Cisneros)
Banco Financiero Internacional (☎ 29 48 46; Independencia btwn Hermanos Agüero & Martí)
Cadeca (República No 353 btwn Oscar Primelles & El Solitario; ☼ 8:30am-6pm Mon-Sat, 8:30am-1pm Sun)

PHOTOGRAPHY

Photo Service (Av Agramonte 430 btwn República & San Ramón)

POST

DHL (☎ 25 31 47; Bartolomé Masó cnr of Oscar Primelles)
Post Office (Av Agramonte No 461, btwn Independencia & Cisneros; ☼ 8am-6pm)

TOURIST INFORMATION

InfoTur (Av Agramonte behind Iglesia de la Merced)

CAMAGÜEY STREET NAMES

To make things even more confusing, locals doggedly stick to using the old names of streets, even though signs and maps (including those in this book) carry the new names. Here's a cheat sheet:

old name	new name
San Estéban	Oscar Primelles
Estrada Palma	Agramonte
Santa Rita	El Solitario
Francisquito	Quiñones
San José	José Ramón Silva
San Fernando	Bartolomé Masó
Pobre	Padre Olallo
Rosario	Enrique Villuendas

CAMAGÜEY

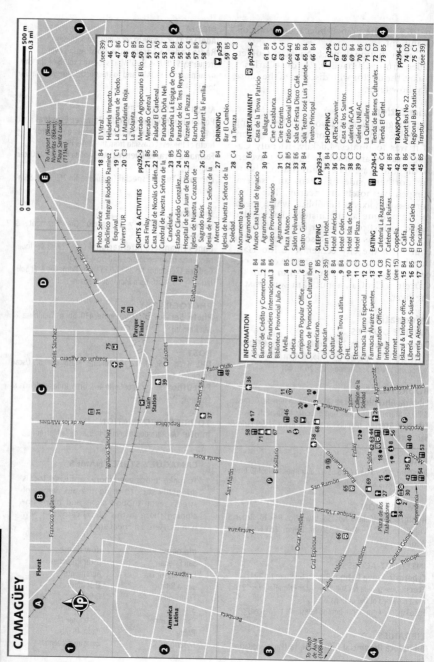

CAMAGÜEY

0   500 m
0   0.3 mi

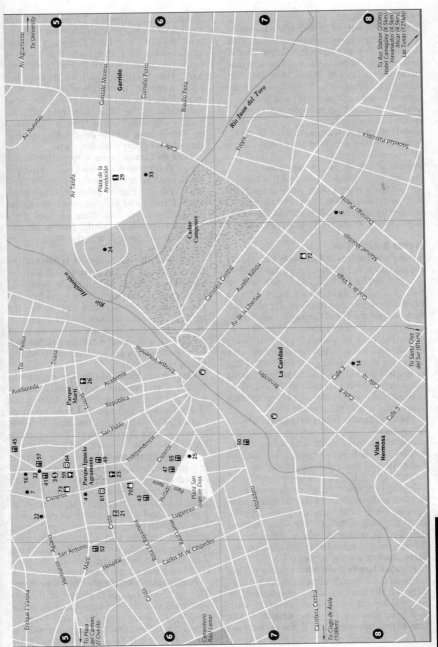

TRAVEL AGENCIES

Campismo Popular (☎ 29 68 55; Av de la Libertad No 208 btwn Pancha & Agramonte, Reparto La Caridad) Of the five camping resorts in Camagüey, you'll likely only need advance reservations for Punta Ganado near Playa Santa Lucía.

Cubanacán Gran Hotel (☎ 29 49 05; Maceo No 67 btwn Agramonte & General Gómez; El Colonial Galería (Av Agramonte near República) Organized tours to Santa Lucía.

Cubatur (☎ 25 47 85; Av Agramonte No 421 btwn República & Independencia)

Islazul (☎ 29 25 50; Av Agramonte behind Iglesia de la Merced; ☾ 8am-noon, 1-5pm Mon-Fri, 8:30-11:30am Sat) Reserve Islazul rooms here.

UniversiTUR (☎ 29 25 61; omarihe@yahoo.com; Avellaneda No 281 btwn Oscar Primelles & El Solitario; ☾ 9am-5pm Mon-Sat) Arranges Spanish & other classes at Camagüey University, with flexible options studying elsewhere (eg Santa Lucía, Holguín); US$260-300/week includes housing; Americans must register in Havana.

Sights & Activities

Museo Provincial Ignacio Agramonte (☎ 28 24 25; Av de los Mártires No 2 at Ignacio Sánchez; admission US$2; ☾ 10am-6pm Tue-Thu & Sat, 2:30-10pm Fri, 9am-1pm Sun). Erected in 1848, this former Spanish cavalry barracks just north of the train station became the Hotel Camagüey after independence in 1902 and a museum in 1948. Its collection (one of Cuba's biggest) is heavy on history, natural history and fine arts. There are three paintings by local late-19th-century artist Fidelio Ponce. Notice the big tinajones in the courtyard and the 2nd-floor caryatid columns on the crumbling building diagonally across the street.

Iglesia de Nuestra Señora de la Merced (Plaza de los Trabajadores) This is Camgüey's most impressive colonial church and it has a long history. According to legend, a miraculous figure floated from the watery depths here in 1601 and it has been a spot worth worshipping ever since. This structure was built in 1748 and rebuilt in 1848. The active convent in the cloister attached to the church is distinguished by it's two-level arched interior, the **catacombs** (where church faithful were buried until 1814) and the dazzling **Santo Sepulcro**, a solid silver coffin.

Plaza San Juan de Dios (Hurtado & Paco Recio) This is one of Camagüey's most picturesque corners and the town's only plaza retaining its original layout and buildings; make sure you have film for this one. **Hospital de San Juan de Dios** (admission US$1; ☾ 8am- 4:30pm Mon-Sat) is a national monument with a front cloister dating from 1728 and a unique triangular rear patio with Moorish touches, built in 1840. Until 1902, this was a hospital administered by Father José Olallo, who is being considered for sainthood for his work here. The sprawling San Juan de Dios has filled many functions in year's past, serving as a military hospital, teacher's college and refuge during the 1932 cyclone. In 1991 the building reverted to the Centro Provincial de Patrimonio, which directs the restoration of Camagüey's monuments.

Plaza del Carmen (Hermanos Agüero btwn Honda & Carmen) This plaza, 600m west of the bustle of Av República, is Camagüey's prettiest (and least visited). Potted palms contrast with pastel facades and big tinajones laze around like Rubens' models. Benches and little incandescent street lamps, plus sculptures dotted about make it a romantic corner at sunset.

Iglesia de Nuestra Señora de la Soledad (Avs República & Agramonte) This massive brick structure from 1775 has a picturesque tower and formidable facade, which is good because you probably won't gain access to see the baroque frescoes within as this church is usually shut tight as a drum. Just north of the church is the quaint **Callejón de la Soledad**, a little alley with an outdoor café and live music most nights.

Casa Natal de Nicolás Guillén (Hermanos Agüero No 58) The great mulatto poet Nicolás Guillén was born here on July 10, 1902. During the 1930s Guillén founded a school of Afro-Cuban poetry and, until his death in 1989, he was Cuba's poet laureate. The museum here documents his work and life.

Mercado Agropecuario El Río This market, one of Cuba's liveliest, sprawls along Calle Matadero just above the Río Hatibonico. Here pregones (singsong offering of wares, often comic) ring through stalls heavy with pineapple and sides of pork. An entire section is given over to herberos, purveyors of herbs, potions and secret elixirs; most of their products are labeled, describing their uses and treatment. See Self-Catering (p295) for more information.

Parque Ignacio Agramonte (Martí & Agramonte) This spotless plaza in the heart of the city welcomes visitors with an equestrian statue (1950) of Camagüey's hero and rings of marble benches. On the southern side of the square is the **Catedral de Nuestra Señora**

de la Candelaria (Cisneros No 168), rebuilt in the 19th century on the site of an earlier church dating from 1530. This cathedral, like many of Camagüey's churches, was restored with funds that flooded in after the 1998 visit of Pope John Paul II.

Museo Casa Natal de Ignacio Agramonte (☎ 29 71 16; Av Agramonte No 459 at Independencia; admission US$2; ☑ 10am-5:45pm Tue-Thu & 8am-noon Sun) Opposite La Merced is the birthplace of the independence hero Ignacio Agramonte (1841–73), the cattle rancher who led the revolt against Spain in this area in 1868. In July 1869, rebel forces under Agramonte bombarded Camagüey, and four years later he was killed in action fighting against the Spanish. Nicknamed 'El Mayor' (The Major), you can hear Silvio Rodríguez's anthem to this hero on his disc *Días y Flores*.

Casa Finlay (☎ 29 67 45; Cristo btwn Cisneros & Lugareño; ☑ 10am-6pm Tue-Thu & Sat) With no shortage of heroes, Camagüey was also where Carlos J Finlay was born. This small museum documents the doctor's life and his medical breakthrough that discovered how mosquitoes transmit yellow fever. There's a splendid indoor patio and cafeteria.

Parque Martí (República & Luaces) Camagüey is full of surprising plazas just off center, like this one a few blocks west of Parque Agramonte. It is fronted by the Cuban-gothic **Nuestra Corazón de Sagrado Jesús**. With its ornate stained glass, iron work and triple spire facade, this church will be a dazzler once it emerges from its scaffold cocoon.

Across the bridge over the Río Hatibonico is the **Casino Campestre**, a large, enjoyable park with lots of shaded benches, the ballpark, concerts and activities.

Festivals & Events

The **Jornadas de la Cultura Camagüeyana**, commemorating the founding of the city, take place during the first two weeks of February. Rocking **Carnaval** is from June 24 to 29. The 10 days beginning on October 10 are also days celebrating culture, during which many musical events take place.

Sleeping

Camagüey has a varied selection of places to stay, all reasonably priced. Look for something with a roof terrace, as Camagüey's city views, dotted with steeples and towers, domes and terracotta, are a highlight.

IN TOWN

Gran Hotel (Islazul; ☎ 29 20 93; Maceo No 67, btwn Agramonte & General Gómez; s/d incl breakfast low season US$29/42, high season US$38/48; [P] [X] [□] [R]) For amenities and charm in the heart of the city, this hotel from 1939 is the place. The 72 clean rooms are reached by worn marble staircase or ancient lift replete with endearing attendants and antique gate. There are terrific citywide views from the 5th-floor restaurant and rooftop mirador. An atmospheric piano bar is accessed through the lobby.

Hotel Plaza (Islazul; ☎ 28 24 13; Van Horne No 1; s/d/tr incl breakfast low season US$17/22/30, high season US$22/28/36; [P] [X]) No two rooms are alike in this gracious colonial-style hotel built at the turn of the 20th century, so look at a few for variety. All have sitting areas, televisions and big fridges – a good value. The lobby is a place to relax, with especially nice staff; despite its queasy color, the lobby bar is the logical chill spot while waiting for nearby train departures.

Hotel Colón (Islazul; ☎ 28 33 46; República No 472 btwn San José & San Martín; s/d incl breakfast low season US$24/30, high season US$28/36) This recently updated, two-story hotel has colorful tile-flanked walls and a stained-glass portrait of Christopher Columbus over the lobby door. There are rocking chairs upstairs and a colonial patio out back, adding atmosphere.

Hotel América (UniversiTUR; ☎ 28 21 13; Avellaneda btwn Oscar Primelles & San Martín; s/d US$10/15; [X]) Designed as student housing for foreign students enrolled at the university, but open to anyone, this older two-story hotel is an incredibly fair deal. The 14 rooms have private bath, TV and phone. Room 9 is probably the best.

Hotel Isla de Cuba (Islazul; ☎ 29 15 15; Oscar Primelles No 453 near República; s/d/tr US$13/18/25) A well-located budget option, this hotel is the simplest of all the choices. It doesn't aspire to something it isn't, which is a winning strategy for a Cuban hotel.

OUTSIDE TOWN

Hotel Camagüey (Horizontes; ☎ 28 72 67; Carretera Central Este Km 4.5; s/d incl buffet breakfast low season US$34/43, high season US$36/47; [P] [X] [R]) About 5km southeast of the center, this four-story hotel is a reliable option if you're driving and don't want to confront Camagüey's crazy streets. The rooms here are simple and clean, with small balconies; there are also six cabañas with fridges and TV for a little more money. For fun, there are four bars, the open air **Disco Tradicuba** (🕐 Thu-Sun) and a **cabaret** (🕐 11pm Fri & Sat).

Eating
RESTAURANTS
Camagüey has a good mix of places to eat and budget travelers will love the selection of peso restaurants. Many eateries here are in colonial buildings, adding ambiance.

Paladar El Cardenal (Martí No 309; dishes US$7-8; 🕐 11am-11pm) This old Camagüey standby is popular for a reason: seriously good *comida criolla* and lots of it. Try the yummy pork steak, salad, *tostones* and *congrí*.

La Volanta (☎ 29 19 74; Independencia & Luaces; dishes 15 pesos; 🕐 seatings at 6pm, 8pm & 10pm) An upscale peso restaurant on the southeastern corner of Parque Agramonte, locals reserve their tables early here to dine on overflowing plates of Cuban food. Jump into line early and you'll likely be able to 'buy' into someone's table for 10 pesos.

El Ovejito (☎ 29 25 24; Hermanos Agüero btwn Honda & Carmen; meals US$6-7; 🕐 noon-9:40pm, closed Tue) With a seriously stunning location on the Plaza del Carmen, this 'little lamb' restaurant serves just that in a colonial setting: lamb chops, lamb fricassee and the odd steak.

La Mandarina Roja (☎ 29 02 67; Padre Olalla No 731 btwn San Martín & José Ramón Silva; dishes 15-22 pesos; 🕐 noon-3pm & 7-10pm, closed Wed) For a real peso paladar experience, head to this Chinese-inspired place serving large portions of chop suey, soup or fried rice. The food is good in that greasy kind of way. Vegetarians should steer clear.

Pizzeria La Piazza (Av Agramonte cnr of Independencia) serves pizza and spaghetti at a peso counter. Upstairs, **La Piazza** (☎ 29 39 73; 🕐 seatings at 6pm, 8pm & 10pm, closed Mon) is the dollar counterpart. The views of Iglesia de Nuestra Señora de la Soledad are terrific from the dining terrace. Call between 10am and 4pm to reserve your space to eat the pizza, pasta and salads.

La Campana de Toledo (Plaza San Juan de Dios No 18; meals US$7; 🕐 10am-10pm) This classic Camagüey

---

CASAS PARTICULARES – CAMAGÜEY

Alba Ferraz (☎ 28 30 30; misleydis2000@yahoo.com; Ramón Guerrero No 106 btwn General Espinosa & Oscar Primelles; r US$15-20; 🗷) Two rooms sharing bath open onto pretty colonial courtyard, roof terrace. Ask about dance & music lessons.

Manolo Banegas Misa (☎ 29 46 06; Independencia No 251 Altos, Plaza Maceo; r US$15-20; 🗷) Big rooms in colonial house, some with balcony, shared bath, roof terrace, meals, street noise; neighbor also rents.

Iliana and Leticia Martínez (☎ 29 67 54; El Solitario No 16A Bajos btwn República & Santa Rosa; r US$12) Simple room sleeps three, friendly family, value; neighbor also rents.

Casa de Caridad – Caridad García Valera (☎ 29 15 54; sracaridad@cubasi.cu; Oscar Primelles No 310A, btwn Bartolomé Masó & Padre Olallo; r US$15; 🗷) Friendly home, safe, huge garden/patio, meals, next to elementary school (read: early morning kid noise).

Leydi Ramirez Gonález & Julio Martínez Rodríguez (☎ 29 13 53; Cisneros No 66 btwn Padre Olallo & San Rafael; r US$15; 🗷) Clean, secure, private, meals.

Los Vitrales – Emma Barreto y Requejo (☎ 29 58 66; Calle Avellaneda No 3 btwn General Gómez y Martí; r US$20; 🅿 🗷) Painstakingly restored colonial house, each (darkish) room different, meals.

Casa Monolo – Manuel Rodríguez Jaén (☎ 29 44 03; El Solitario No 18 btwn República & Santa Rosa; r US$15; 🗷) Rooms with private or shared bath, laundry, roof terrace.

Gladys Alfonso & Yulios Tabares (☎ 29 52 69; Independencia No 211, just off Parque Agramonte; r US$15) Phone, TV & fridge; also rents to Cubans.

Also recommended:
El Hostal de Elsa – Elsa Espinosa (☎ 29 81 04; Bartolomé Masó btwn Triana & Tío Perico; r US$15-20; 🗷) Shared bath, meals, quiet.

Casa Blanca – Blanca Navarro Castro (☎ 29 35 42; San Ramón Apto 201 Altos btwn Heredia & Solitario; r US$15; 🗷) Sleeps three, friendly.

Leydiana Navarro Cardoso (☎ 29 69 69; Calle Astillero No 22 Altos; r US$15-20; 🗷) Roof terrace, fridge, meals.

Migdalia and Manolo (☎ 9-4403, El Solitario No 18; r US$15)

eatery has colonial digs, shady patio and a serenading quartet. **Parador de los Tres Reyes** (grilled shrimp US$4), adjacent, is similar.

The restaurant in the **Gran Hotel** (Maceo No 67, btwn Agramonte & General Gómez; breakfast/dinner buffet US$4/8) has superb city views; get there early.

Also recommended:

Restaurant la Familia (República No 393) Takeaway food in pesos; best selection early, bring your own containers.

Coppelia (Independencia btwn Agramonte & General Gómez) Peso ice cream.

El Califa (Raúl Lamar No 49a btwn Cisneros & Lugareño; meals US$8; noon-midnight)

El Colonial Galería (Av Agramonte at República) Ice cream.

Heladería Impacto (Av República No 358; 10am-midnight) Dollar ice cream.

CAFETERIAS

The lively Gran Hotel **snack bar** (Maceo No 67, btwn Agramonte & General Gómez; 9am-11pm), accessible off Maceo, has coffee, sandwiches, chicken and ice cream. Though kind of stinky, it's the best of its kind in Camagüey. The **El Vitral** (Hotel Plaza; 24hr) is a 'round the clock' option.

The quiet, quaint patio cafeteria in the **Casa Finlay** (29 67 45; Cristo btwn Cisneros & Lugareño; 10am-6pm Tue-Thu & Sat) is a superb place to tuck away to read, write or flirt. There are sandwiches and cocktails, but no beer.

Camagüey has several atmospheric colonial patios for taking drinks and snacks including:

Cafetería La Ragazza (Maceo opposite the Gran Hotel) Peso place.

Cafetería Las Ruinas (Plaza Maceo) Dollar drinks.

SELF-CATERING

Mercado Agropecuario El Río (Calle Matadero above the Río Hatibonico; 7am-6pm) Eat heartily on peso sandwiches, fresh orange juice and guarapo (sugarcane juice) in the fun chaos of this local market.

A large selection of groceries is available at **El Encanto** (Maceo near General Gómez).

For bread in dollars, there's **Panadería Doña Neli** (Maceo opp Gran Hotel; 7am-7pm) and **Panadería La Espiga de Oro** (Independencia No 304; 7am-7pm Mon-Sat, 7am-noon Sun).

Drinking

Bar El Cambio (Independencia & Martí on Parque Agramonte; 7am until you drop) A popular hang-out with rough hewn tables and graffiti-covered walls, you can always get a cocktail here.

La Terraza (Av República No 352 cnr Oscar Primelles; 8am-midnight) Teetotalers need not apply: this open-air peso place is a favorite party spot for getting smashed on peso beer and rum. There's great people watching from the vine-covered patio.

The **piano bar** (Gran Hotel; 1pm-2am) has a long wooden bar, vintage jukebox and grand piano; live music happens nightly after 9pm.

Entertainment

Every Saturday night, the raucous **Noche Camagüeyana** spreads up República from La Soledad to the train station with food and alcohol stalls, music and crowds. A rock concert takes place in the square next to La Soledad. The Galería ACAA has a bulletin board with the week's cultural events posted.

FOLK MUSIC

Casa de la Trova Patricio Ballagas (29 13 57, Cisneros No 171 btwn Martí & Cristo; closed Mon) Folk singers jam here, at one of the Cuba's best trova clubs. Unfortunately, whatever authentic atmosphere is squelched when buses of package tourists roll in from Playa Santa Lucía.

Folk singing and Afro-Cuban dancing happen at **Galería UNEAC** (Cisneros No 159; 5pm & 9pm Sat), south of the cathedral and similar events are held at **Cybercafe Trova Latina** (Ramón Guerrero No 121; admission free; 10pm Thu-Sat). Also check out what's happening at the **Centro de Promoción Cultural Ibero Americano** (Cisneros btwn General Gómez & Hermanos Agüero) a cultural center housed in the former Spanish Club, which hosts tango nights and the like.

DANCE CLUBS

The hottest, new dance club is the **Patio Colonial Disco** (Av Agramonte at República; open bar US$4; 10pm-2am Sun-Fri, 10pm-3am Sat). Saturday is the best night, when the cover charge rises to US$7. Another popular local nightspot is **Sala de Fiesta Disco Café** (Independencia No 208; 10pm-3am nightly).

THEATER

Teatro Principal (29 30 48, Padre Valencia No 64; admission US$4-10; 8:30pm Fri, Sat & 5pm Sun) Home of Ballet de Camagüey, Cuba's second most important ballet company (founded in 1971 by Fernando Alonso, ex-husband of famous dancer Alicia Alonso), see these talented, athletic dancers if you can. The theater building, erected in 1850, has impressive chandeliers and stained glass.

For serious live theater, it's the **Sala Teatro José Luis Tasende** (☎ 29 21 64; Ramón Guerrero No 51; ☽ 8:30pm Sat & Sun), with quality Spanish-language performances.

CINEMAS

For big screen showings, head to **Teatro Guer-rero** (Plaza de los Trabajadores opp Iglesia de la Merced) or **Cine Casablanca** (Ignacio Agramonte No 428). Next door, **Cine Encanto** shows videos.

SPORT

From October to April, baseball games are held at **Estadio Cándido González** on Av Tarafa alongside Casino Campestre. The nearby **Salón Polivalente**, behind the huge Monumento a Ignacio Agramonte on Plaza de la Revolución, hosts other athletic matches.

Shopping

Calle Maceo is Camagüey's top shopping street, with a number of souvenir shops, bookstores and department stores. Look here for **consignment shops** selling all kinds of peso treasure.

Casa de los Santos (Oscar Primelles No 407 btwn Av República & Avellaneda) Hand painted San Lázaro or Virgin Mary statuettes, plus protections against the *mal de ojo* (evil eye): stock up on sacred iconography here.

Galería ACAA (Ramón Guerrero at Padre Valencia; ☽ 9am-4pm Mon-Fri) Original Cuban handicrafts, photography and pottery are the strengths of this store on Plaza de los Trabajadores. For a more personal experience, you can arrange studio visits with local artists (see the boxed text).

For compact discs, check **Tienda El Cartel** (Cisneros No 208) north of Parque Agramonte. **Video Center Imágenes**, (República No 282) just north of La Soledad, and nearby **ARTex Souvenir** (República No 381) also have good selections of compact discs.

Getting There & Away

AIR

Ignacio Agramonte International Airport (airport code CBG) is 9km northeast of town on the road to Nuevitas and Playa Santa Lucía.

Cubana (☎ 26 10 00) flies on Thursday from Havana (US$88 one way, 35 minutes). Air Transat and Skyservice have weekly flights from Toronto in winter.

BUS & TRUCK

The regional **bus station** (Av Carlos J Finlay near the train station) has trucks to Nuevitas (20 pesos, 87km, twice daily) and Santa Cruz del Sur (20 pesos, 82km, three daily). Trucks to Playa Santa Lucía (10 pesos, 109km, three daily) leave from here as well: ask for the último inside the station and you'll be given a paper with a number; line up at door No 2 and wait for your number to come up. Technically tourists are not permitted on these trucks, a rule often bent.

Long-distance Astro buses depart **Álvaro Barba Bus Station** (☎ 27 24 80; Carretera Central), 3km southeast of the center. The following services are offered:

destination	cost (one way)	distance	departure time
Baracoa	US$26	459km	8:05 pm, alt days
Bayamo	US$8	210km	10:30am, alt days
Ciego de Ávila	US$4	108km	7:40am, 10:30am, 1:55pm, 7:20pm
Cienfuegos	US$13	330km	4:40pm, alt days
Havana	US$22	534km	10am, 9:40pm
Manzanillo	US$10	217km	10:30am alt days
Matanzas	US$18	474km	9pm alt days
Sancti Spíritus	US$7	184km	1pm, alt days
Santiago de Cuba	US$13	327km	9am alt days

Tickets are sold for dollars at the regular ticket windows.

STUDIO VISITS IN CAMAGÜEY

You might not know it, but behind that beautiful grille work and those colonial facades, Camagüey's artists are busy capturing their inspiration in great works of art. One couple welcoming visitors and collectors into their magnificent home/studio is Joel Jover and Ileana Sánchez. With something for everyone, Joel is an accomplished painter and poet and Ileana is a folk artist. You must call (☎ 29 23 05) to arrange a visit, but they live a short walk from the heart of Camagüey. Joel and Ileana are well connected with the art scene here and can direct you to other artists' studios as well.

Víazul has daily services to the following:

destination	cost (one way)	distance	departure time
Ciego de Ávila	US$6	108km	12:40am, 2:10am, 4:40am, 6pm
Havana	US$33	534km	6pm, 12:40am, 4:40am
Sancti Spíritus	US$10	184km	12:40am, 2:10am, 4:40am, 6pm
Santiago de Cuba	US$18	435km	4:40pm, 10:05pm, 2:20am
Trinidad	US$15	254km	2:10am

The Santiago de Cuba departure also stops at Las Tunas (US$10), Holguín (US$11) and Bayamo (US$12). The Havana bus stops at Santa Clara (US$15). For Víazul tickets, see the *jefe de turno*.

Passenger trucks to Las Tunas and Ciego de Ávila also leave from this station. Arriving before 9am will greatly increase your chances of getting on one of these trucks.

Private taxis can be hired on Calle Perú outside the bus station, but not to Playa Santa Lucía or Cayo Coco, where they face heavy police controls. Expect to pay considerably more than the bus fare for long hauls, (US$120 to Havana); shorter trips are more reasonable (eg US$5 to Ciego de Ávila or Las Tunas).

TRAIN

The **train station** (☎ 28 32 14; Avellaneda & Finlay) is more conveniently located than the bus station. Foreigners buy tickets for dollars from an unmarked office across the street from the entrance to Hotel Plaza. The trains may leave from another terminal nearby, so check on this and arrive early. See the boxed text below for more information on train routes.

Getting Around
TO/FROM THE AIRPORT

Bus No 22 'Albaisa' (40 centavos) runs to Ignacio Agramonte International Airport every 30 minutes weekdays, hourly on weekends from the stop facing Parque Finlay, opposite the regional bus station. Colectivos from here charge two pesos to the airport. A taxi to the airport should cost US$5 from town or US$8 from Hotel Camagüey.

CAR

Havanautos Hotel Camagüey (☎ 27 22 39; Carretera Central Este Km 4.5); Aeropuerto Ignacio Agramonte (☎ 28 70 67)

Micar (☎ 8-7267/8; Carretera Centro Este Km 4.5 btwn bus station & Hotel Camagüey)

Transtur (☎ 27 10 15; Hotel Plaza, Van Horne No 1) Rents mopeds for US$20/day (not including gas).

El Sereno Parqueo (República No 212 south of Agramonte; ⏰ 24hr) offers 24 hours of guarded parking for US$2. Another guarded **parking lot** (El Solitario No 22 west of República) is convenient for those renting private rooms in the area.

Two 24-hour Servi-Cupet gas stations are on the Carretera Central near Av de la Libertad. An Oro Negro gas station is just outside Camagüey on the road to Nuevitas, 2km before the airport.

BICI-TAXIS

Bicycle taxis are found on the square beside La Soledad or in Plaza Maceo. Technically, bici-taxis aren't permitted to carry tourists, but they do; they usually cost five pesos.

TRAIN INFORMATION FOR CAMAGÜEY

destination	cost (one way) regular/rápido	distance	travel time	departure time
Bayamo	US$7	210km	5 hours	5:40am, alt days
Guantánamo	US$13	371km	7 hours	12:05am
Havana	US$19/32	534km	7-10 hours	12:25 am, 2:15am, 3:55am, 4:34pm, 9:55pm, 11pm
Holguín	US$8	209km	4 hours	5:11am, alt days
Las Tunas	US$4/10	128km	2½ hours	1:23pm, 3:27pm
Manzanillo	US$9	217km	6 hours	5:40am, alt days
Matanzas	US$16/22	474km	8 hours	4:30am, alt days
Santa Clara	US$9/13	263km	5½ hours	11:30am
Santiago de Cuba	US$11/16	327km	5-7hours	12:05am, 1:23pm, 1:22am, 3:27pm

HORSE CARTS

Horse carts shuttle along a fixed route between the bus station and the 'ferro' (train station), though you may have to change carts at Casino Campestre, near the river. Southbound, look for horse carts on the street that runs east from Hotel Plaza, along the southern side of the train tracks. From the train station, it's two pesos to the bus station or one peso to Casino Campestre.

FLORIDA

pop 53,441

The buzzing sugar-mill town of Florida, 46km northwest of Camagüey on the way to Ciego de Ávila, is a fine place to spend the night if you're driving around central Cuba. There's a working **rodeo**, a **hospital** and **Etecsa telephone office**.

Two-story **Hotel Florida** (Islazul; ☎ 5-3011; s/d low season US$17/22, high season US$21/28; ⏚), on the Carretera Central, 2km west of the center of town, has 74 adequate rooms. Next to the hotel is **Cafetería Caney**, a thatched restaurant that's better value than the hotel restaurant. Don't confuse this place with the **Motel Florida** (☎ 5-4623), a 15-cabin peso motel 4km east, by the highway at the eastern entrance to Florida.

A Servi-Cupet gas station is on the Carretera Central in the center of town. Passenger trucks run from Florida to Camagüey.

GUÁIMARO

pop 35,813

Guáimaro, between Camagüey and Las Tunas, earned its place in Cuban history as the site of the constituent assembly of April 1869, which approved the first Cuban constitution and called for emancipation. The same assembly elected Carlos Manuel de Céspedes as president. These events are commemorated by a large monument erected in 1940 on Parque Constitución in the center of town. Around the base of the monument are bronze plaques bearing the likenesses of José Martí, Máximo Gómez, Carlos Manuel de Céspedes, Ignacio Agramonte, Calixto García and Antonio Maceo, the stars of Cuban independence. There's an Islazul **hotel** here.

If you have your own transport, you could head for the campismo at **Monte Oscuro** (☎ 8036) 20km north of Guáimaro via Palo Seco. There are 27 cabins, horseback riding, luxuriant vegetation and swimming in the reservoir. It's advisable to get reservations from the office of **Campismo Popular** (☎ 29 68 55, Av de la Libertad No 208) in Camagüey.

Guáimaro has a Servi-Cupet gas station with a snack bar.

MINAS

pop 21,708

Minas, 60km northeast of Camagüey en route to Nuevitas, is notable only for the musical-instrument factory that opened here in 1976. The **Fábrica de Violines** (admission US$2; ⏰ closed Sun) on Camilo Cienfuegos at the eastern entrance to town, might interest musicians.

A fun place to get wet in this area is **Campismo Las Clavellinas** (☎ 28 58 00) between Cromo and Altagracia on the road from Camagüey to Minas. Coming from Camagüey, the turn-off is near Cromo, about 4km northeast of the airport. From the other direction, the turn-off is 5km southwest of Altagracia, then it's 4km inland to the campismo. The grounds run along the Río Saramaguacán, where there's good swimming. You might get accommodation in one of the 26 concrete units if you turn up, but you should book beforehand at **Reservaciones Campismo Popular** (☎ 29 68 55; Av de la Libertad No 208, Camagüey). Self-sufficient travelers can pitch camp on the opposite shores of the river – turn right on the dirt road 50m before the campismo entrance and follow the rutted road for 2km to the riverbank.

NUEVITAS

pop 40,607

Nuevitas, 87km northeast of Camagüey, is a 27km jaunt north off the Camagüey–Playa Santa Lucía road. It's an industrial town and sugar exporting port with friendly locals and shore access, but not worth a major detour.

Sights

Nuevitas' only specific sight is the **Museo Histórico Municipal** (Máximo Gómez No 66; admission US$1; ⏰ closed Mon) near Parque del Cañón in the center of town. It's got the usual stuffed animal collection, and you can hike up the steps in the center of town for terrific **views**.

Below the Hotel Caonaba is a shaggy amusement park/playground combination kids will like. A bit further along the coast is **Playa Cuatro Vientos**, a local beach, from where you can see two of the three small islands, called Los Tres Ballenatos, in the Bahía de Nuevitas. If you snake along the coast for 2km, you'll come to **Santa Rita** at the end of the road, a friendly place with a pier jutting into the bay.

Sleeping & Eating
The friendly **Hotel Caonaba** (Islazul; ☎ 4-4803; s/d low season US$14/19, high season US$18/24) is a three-story hotel on a rise overlooking the sea. It's at the entrance to town as you arrive from Camagüey. The rooms have fridges and some have views; don't expect the Ritz. In summer, you can also eat at the **restaurant**, 200km along the coast from the amusement park. This is a favorite local swimming spot. The **Bar Terraza** in the hotel is open daily from noon to the wee hours.

Getting There & Away
Nuevitas is the terminus of railway lines from Camagüey via Minas and Santa Clara via Chambas and Morón. The station is near the waterfront on the northern side of town. There should be a daily train to Camagüey (5:15am), and service on alternate days to Santa Clara (6:35am), but they are often canceled. Trucks are more reliable than buses, which often meet the same fate as trains. Trucks to Camagüey leave around 4:30am and 9am; to Santa Lucía there are trucks at 4am and 1pm.

A Servi-Cupet gas station is at the entrance to town, a block from Hotel Caonaba. There's a Transtur taxi office nearby.

AROUND NUEVITAS
Cayo Sabinal, 22km to the north of Nuevitas, is a 30km-long coral key with marshes favored by mosquitoes and birds, including flamingos who nest here. The dirt road to Cayo Sabinal begins 6km south of Nuevitas, off the road to Camagüey. You must show your passport at the bridge to the Cayo and pay US$5. The 2km causeway linking the key to the mainland was the first of its kind constructed in Cuba and the most environmentally destructive. Rumbos operates **Restaurante Los Pinos** (Cayo Sabinal) and a few **cabins** (US$25, half-board). Camping is possible – prepare

for swarms of tiny, early-morning mosquitoes. **Faro Colón**, at Punta Maternillo on Cayo Sabinal, was erected in 1850. The beach here is quite beautiful and you'll feel as though you've reached the end of the world.

En route to Playa Santa Lucía, 4km beyond the crossroads where you join the main highway from Camagüey, is the **King Ranch**, 1.5km off the main highway (signposted) with a restaurant, rodeo and horses for rent. Tour groups are often brought here for a country-style experience.

PLAYA SANTA LUCÍA
The province's main tourist draw is Playa Santa Lucía, 112km northeast of Camagüey. The 20km-long beach is one of Cuba's longest and most people come here to scuba dive and feed sharks on the nearby Atlantic reefs. The swimming, snorkeling, and diving are terrific, and the large hotels lay on plenty of activities. There's also a decent budget hotel. Packages to Playa Santa Lucía are usually cheaper than those to Cayo Coco and you're within easy reach of Camagüey from here, which is infinitely more interesting than Morón, Cayo Coco's gateway city.

Santa Lucía is changing and sprouting new resorts like all the best Cuban beachfronts, so don't be surprised if things have changed once you get there.

Information
Bandec is in the Cuban residential area between the Servi-Cupet at the southeastern entrance to Playa Santa Lucía and the hotel strip. Nearby is **MediClub** a health tourism complex with all manner of medical facilities and services. **Etecsa**, 1.5km further along near the entrance to the hotel zone, has Internet access and international phone capabilities.

Sights & Activities
MAR VERDE CENTRO CULTURAL
Just before the Club Amigo Mayanabo, the Mar Verde Centro Cultural has a pleasant patio **bar** and a **cabaret** (admission US$1; ☽ midnight) with live music nightly. There's also an **ARTex** store here with compact discs and **Librería Tengo** with high quality art books and photographs for sale.

PLAYA LOS COCOS
At the far northwestern end of Playa Santa Lucía, 7km from the hotels, is another white

PLAYA SANTA LUCÍA

INFORMATION	
Bandec	1 C2
Etecsa	2 C2
Internet	(see 2)
Mediclub	3 C2

SIGHTS & ACTIVITIES	pp299-300
Mar Verde Centro Cultural	4 C2
Marlin Dive Center	5 C2
Shark's Friends Dive Center	6 C2

SLEEPING	pp300-1
Brisas Santa Lucía	7 C2
Club Amigo Mayanabo	8 C2
Gran Club Santa Lucía	9 C2
Hotel Escuela Santa Lucía	10 C2
Vita Club Caracol	11 C2

EATING	p301
Bon Sai	12 C2
Doña Yulla	13 D3
El Rápido	14 C2
Las Brisas	15 C2

TRANSPORT	p301
Havanautos	16 C2
Transtur	17 C2

beach with crystal-clear waters facing the mouth of the Bahía de Nuevitas. Sometimes flocks of pink flamingos are visible in Laguna El Real, behind this beach. A horse and carriage from the Santa Lucía hotels to Playa Los Cocos is US$6 each way for one or two persons, US$2 per person for three or more. Several restaurants serve seafood, including **Casa El Pescador** (Playa Los Cocos) and the **Lobster House** (La Boca or Bucanero), on the beach further along. This is a stellar swimming spot, but mind the tidal currents further out. The **lighthouse** on Cayo Sabinal is visible from here. The hotels sell boat excursions to Nuevitas.

You can access a pristine part of the **beach** by turning at the sign for Shark's Friends.

SCUBA DIVING & SNORKELING

The 35 scuba sites in the warm waters off Santa Lucía take in the six Poseidon ridges, the Cueva Honda, shipwrecks, several types of rays and the abundant marine life at the entrance to the Bahía de Nuevitas (see p407 for more information). A highlight is the hand-feeding of bull sharks between 3m and 4m long (June to January).

Shark's Friends Dive Center (Cubanacán Náutica; ☎ 36 51 82; marlin@sunnet.sti.cyt.cu; on the beach btwn Brisas Santa Lucía & Gran Club Santa Lucía) This is a professional outfit with dive masters who speak English, Italian and French. These folk offer dives for US$30, plus night dives (US$40) and shark feeds (US$50). They have boats going out every two hours between 9am and 3pm daily, though the last dive is contingent on demand. Their open-water course costs US$310, and a resort course US$60. They also have snorkelling excursions.

Marlin Dive Center (Cubanacán Náutica; ☎ 33 64 04; beside Hotel Escuela Santa Lucía) Friendly boating and dive outfit with snorkeling trips in catamarans (US$20); an all day boat tour (adult/child US$59/30, includes lunch) and a sunset cruise (US$20, includes cocktail; ☾ 5:30pm). It does fishing trips for US$204 (maximum four people), including gear, guide and drinks.

Sleeping

The hotel strip begins 6km west of the roundabout at the entrance to Santa Lucía.

Valle del Yumurí (p192), Matanzas Province

Windsurfers, **Varadero** (p197), Matanzas Province

Che Guevara (p242) billboard

RICK GERHARTER

Palacio de Valle (p228), Cienfuegos

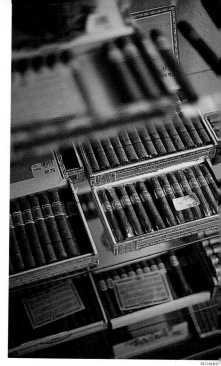

RICHARD

Cigars (p171)

Che Guevara and Fidel Castro on roadside billboard, **Cienfuegos** (p225)

RICHARD

It's prohibited to rent private rooms in Santa Lucía. All of the following are right on the beach.

Hotel Escuela Santa Lucía (Cubanacán; ☎ 33 63 10; per person with breakfast/dinner US$30/35) This is a sweet, one-story motel with 30 nicely furnished rooms (lots of rattan), at the northwestern end of the hotel strip beside a public beach. Every room has a TV and little patio; those in the 200 and 300 block are closest to the beach. It's comfortable for you and your wallet.

Campismo Popular Punta de Ganado (☎ 33 62 89) On the beach about 3km east of the round-about at the entrance to Santa Lucía. To stay in one of the cabins, foreigners should obtain advance reservations from **Campismo Popular** (☎ 29 68 55; Av de la Libertad No 208, Camagüey).

Brisas Santa Lucía (Cubanacán; ☎ 36 51 20; fax 36 51 42; s/d low season US$60/100, high season US$85/120; P ⊠ 🖥 🐂) This all-inclusive resort has 400 rooms in several three-story buildings, tennis courts, a gym etc. Rooms in the 200-800 range are closest to the beach, while those in the 100 block kiss up against the Laberinto Disco. There is special kids programming.

Gran Club Santa Lucía (Cubanacán; ☎ 33 61 09; fax 36 51 47; s/d low season US$65/100, high season US$75/120; P ⊠ 🖥 🐂) Recently renovated, the 249 rooms with minifridges and balconies or patios are in a series of tile-roofed two-story blocks. Prices quoted are for the cheap rooms farthest from the beach with parking lot views. Discoteca La Jungla is here.

Club Amigo Mayanabo and **Vita Club Caracol**, both run by Cubanacán (www.cubanacan .cu),were closed for renovations in 2003. There will likely be good deals and sparkling facil-ities when they reopen in 2004.

Eating

Several upmarket restaurants, including **Las Brisas** and **Bon Sai**, are on the shore road in the residential area between the round-about at the entrance to Santa Lucía and the Brisas Santa Lucía. **El Rápido** opposite Hotel Escuela Santa Lucía, serves inexpensive fast food on its terrace. **Doña Yulla** right before the roundabout entrance to Santa Lucía serves simple, filling meals in pesos.

Getting There & Around

There's one morning and one afternoon bus to and from Nuevitas (70km). Buses to Camagüey (109km) cost US$10 for foreigners. At Santa Lucía, ask about buses and passenger trucks at El Rápido opposite Hotel Escuela Santa Lucía.

You can rent cars or mopeds (US$24/day, including a tank of gas) at the following agencies:

Havanautos (☎ 36 53 55; at the Brisas Santa Lucía)
Transtur (☎ 36 52 60; btwn Gran Club Santa Lucía & the Brisas Santa Lucía)

Servi-Cupet (Playa Santa Lucía strip) is at the south-eastern end of the strip, near the access road from Camagüey. Another large Servi-Cupet station, with a Servi-Soda snack bar, is just east of Brisas Santa Lucía.

Las Tunas Province

Bordered by Camagüey Province to the west, Holguín Province to the east and Granma Province to the south, Las Tunas is not a place people go so much as end up; it's in the middle of nowhere and feels like it. Puerto Padre, Playa La Herradura and Playa Las Bocas on the northern coast see little foreign traffic, but are hospitable places to chill, while the remote, 4km-long windswept beach at Punta Covarrubias on the Atlantic coast is perfect for a romantic holiday. The provincial capital of Las Tunas is the logical stopover if you're stuck between Holguín and Camagüey.

This territory belonged to Bayamo until 1847, and only in 1976 was Las Tunas Province carved out of Oriente. Beef-cattle ranching is the main activity in the center of the province, while sugar cane is grown in the north and west.

HIGHLIGHTS

■ **Moving Memorial**
  See how victims of 1976 terrorist bombing are touchingly remembered in Las Tunas (p304)

■ **Hidden Hamlets**
  Tuck away where Cubans do: in the typical beach towns on the northern coast (p309)

■ **Get Lost!**
  Check out the splendid, unspoiled beach at way-out Punta Covarrubias (p309)

| ■ TELEPHONE CODE: 31 | ■ POPULATION: 532,550 | ■ AREA: 6589 SQ KM |

LAS TUNAS

☎ 31 / pop 139,637

The city of Victoria de Las Tunas was founded in 1752. During the Second War of Independence it was burned to the ground (1895), and until 1975 Las Tunas was just a small market town for the surrounding cattle-ranching area. Today it's a provincial capital with an exuberant populace who will be pleased to see you.

Orientation

The train station is on the northeastern side of town and the bus station is east of the center. Most of the things to see are in the center. A *circunvalación* (bypass road) runs around the south side of the city if you want to avoid Las Tunas altogether.

Information

AIRLINE OFFICES

Cubana Lucas Ortiz No 211 (☎ 4-2702; ☯ 7am–noon Mon, Wed, Fri, 9:30am–3pm Tue & Thu); Aeropuerto Hermanos Ameijeras (☎ 4-2484)

BOOKSHOPS & LIBRARIES

Biblioteca Provincial José Martí (Vicente García No 4; ☯ closed Sun)

Librería Fulgencio Oroz (Colón No 151)

IMMIGRATION

Inmigración (Av Camilo Cienfuegos, Reparto Buenavista) Northeast of the train station.

INTERNET ACCESS

Etecsa (Angel Guardia off Parque Vicente García; ☯ 7am–11pm)

MEDICAL SERVICES

Hospital Che Guevara (☎ 4-5012; Av C J Finlay & 2 de Diciembre) 1km from the highway exit toward Holguín.

MONEY

Banco de Crédito y Comercio (Vicente García No 69; ☯ 8am–2pm Mon–Fri, 8–10:20am Sat)

Banco Financiero Internacional (☎ 4-6202; Vicente García & 24 de Febrero)

Cadeca (Colón No 141; ☯ 8:30am–6pm Mon–Sat, 8:30am–1pm Sun)

POST

Post Office (☎ 4-2738; Vicente García No 6; ☯ 8am–8pm)

TELEPHONE

Etecsa (Angel Guardia off Parque Vicente García; ☯ 7am–11pm)

TRAVEL AGENCIES

Reservaciones Campismo Popular (☎ 4-7001; A Villamar, cnr Angel Guardia)

Sights

Las Tunas' most important site, **Memorial a los Mártires de Barbados** (Lucas Ortíz 344; admission free; ☯ 10am–6pm Mon–Sat), relocated along the

---

EL CUCALAMBÉ

Las Tunas is best known for the poet Juan Cristóbal Nápoles Fajardo (1829–62), nicknamed El Cucalambé. He had a farm at El Cornito, where the motel of that name is today. El Cucalambé was Cuba's leading 19th-century composer of *décimas*, the rhyming, eight-syllable verses that provide the lyrics for Cuban *son*.

In 1855 José Fornaris created a stir with his *Cantos del Siboney* (Songs of the Siboney), which associated the Cuban *guajiro* or country person with the pre-Hispanic Siboney and Taino Indians rather than the Spanish conquerors. The Indians were presented as generous lovers of the earth, family and freedom, stereotypical characteristics of the Cuban *campesino*. A year later, El Cucalambé brought out a book of verses in which blacks, Indians, and creoles all appear without a Spaniard in sight. By formulating the Cuban character in comic situations, Nápoles Fajardo's *décimas* expressed a latent nationalism that was soon to burst forth in the First War of Independence. His poems were enthusiastically recited at country fairs, cockfights and rural family reunions, and thousands of Cubans still flock to Las Tunas every June for the Cucalambé Folklore Festival (Jornada Cucalambeana).

Cuba, delicioso edén	Cuba, delicious Eden
perfumado por tus flores	Perfumed by your flowers,
quién no ha visto tus primores	He who hasn't seen your beauties
ni vió luz ni gozó bien.	Has neither seen light nor enjoyed goodness.

LAS TUNAS PROVINCE

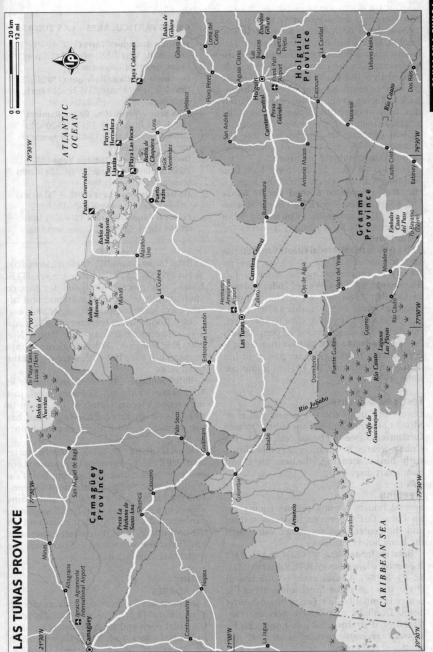

Río Hormigo, belonged to victims in the 1976 Cubana de Aviación terrorist attack. Flight CU-455 had just taken off from Barbados when a bomb exploded underneath a seat, sending the plane and all 73 people aboard into the sea. The bomber left the package beneath his seat when he disembarked during a routine stopover on Barbados. Individual photos of the victims of the attack – including the entire 24-member Cuban Olympic fencing team – line the museum walls in a poignant condemnation of indiscriminate terrorism.

Housed in the 1920s town hall (the building with the clock above the façade), the **Museo Provincial General Vicente García** (☎ 4-8201; Francisco Varona & Angel Guardia; admission US$1; ☺ 11am-7pm Tue-Thu, 2-10pm Fri & Sat, 3-7pm Sun) documents local history; it makes for a short visit.

Nearby is the **Memorial Vicente García** (Vicente García No 7; admission US$1; ☺ 3-7pm Mon, 11am-7pm Tue-Sat), commemorating the entry of Las Tunas into the First War of Independence in October 1868 under the command of Vicente García. In September 1876, he captured the town. If you've time to kill, check out the quirky King Kong-sized pencil which is the **Monumento a Alfabetización** (Lucas Ortiz at Av 2 de Diciembre), marking the act passed in Las Tunas on November 16, 1961 to stamp out illiteracy.

Festivals & Events
Lovers of Cuban country music gather at Motel El Cornito in late June for the **Jornada Cucalambeana** (see the boxed text, p304). It's Cuba's greatest celebration of rural culture, with music, dancing, theater, food and handicraft displays.

Sleeping
Several houses renting private rooms are on Lucas Ortíz, between the train station and the center, and are better value than the basic hotels available.

Hotel Las Tunas (Islazul; ☎ 4-5014; fax 4-5169; Av 2 de Diciembre; s/d low season US$18/24, high season US$23/30; P ☺ ☺) A black stain on the Islazul chain, this 128-room hotel southeast of the center is, pitiably, Las Tunas' main tourist hotel. Don't be surprised if you encounter clogged drains, leaky ceilings, cranky service, aggressive parking attendants and shuttered restaurants.

CASAS PARTICULARES – LAS TUNAS

Yolanda Rodríguez Torres (☎ 4-3641; Lucas Ortíz No 101; r US$20) Independent digs with kitchen, dining and hang-out area.
Marianela Santiago Rodríguez (☎ 4-3259; Lucas Ortíz No 101 Altos; r US$15-20; ☺) Run by a single woman, terrace overlooks the street.
Villa Yany – Yacqueline Reyna Ramírez (☎ 4-2574; Frank País No 37; r US$15-20; ☺) Outfitted room with fridge, friendly, convenient to train; also rents at No 17.
Doña Nelly – Nelly Tamayo Vega (☎ 4-2526; Lucas Ortíz No 111; r US$15-20; ☺) Colonial house, front porch with rockers.
Javier de la Rosa Leyva (☎ 4-2657; Lucas Ortíz No 109 Altos; r with fan/air-con US$20/25)
Carlos A Patiño Alvarez (☎ 4-2288; Lucas Ortíz No 120; r US$15-20; ☺) Comes with fridge.

Hotel Caribe (UniversiTUR; ☎ 4-4262; Lorenzo Ortíz No 64; r US$10-25; ☺) Like other UniversiTUR hotels, this place is designed for foreign students but is open to everyone and offers good value (despite the saggy beds and noise). Room prices increase once you add TV, refrigerator and air-con. Room Nos 200, 213, 300 and 309 have balconies onto the street. A nice bar with a view is on the third floor.

Hotel Santiago (☎ 4-3396; Ángel Guardia No 112; r 28 pesos) This old 32-room hotel, just off Parque Vicente García in the center of town, is rough around the edges but has the nice price. You might use your own bedding.

Motel El Cornito (☎ 4-5015; 7km northwest of Las Tunas; s/d US$15/20) At present El Cornito is not really set up for foreign tourism, but it's a beautiful spot and plans are afoot to renovate the place. Basic bungalows and rooms are set in a large park with bamboo groves, gardens and trails. There's a restaurant on the grounds. A local train shuttles between Las Tunas and an amusement park near the motel three times a day.

Eating
PALADARES
Las Tunas has a few good paladares serving big portions. Don't expect anything beyond the usual pork and chicken dishes at:

Paladar La Roca (Lucas Ortíz No 108; meals US$7-8; ☺ noon-midnight) Tasty food, attentive service.

LAS TUNAS

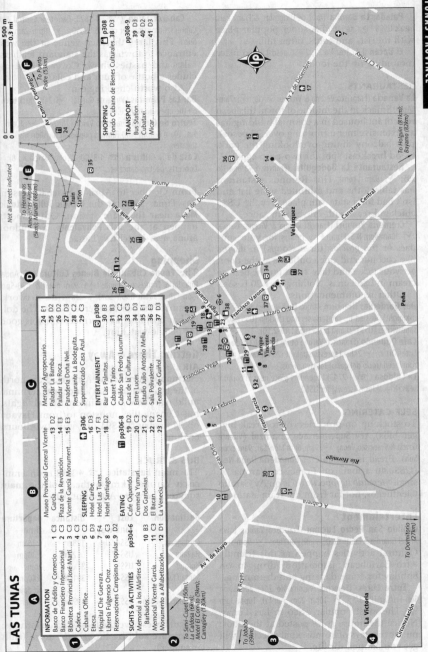

INFORMATION
Banco de Crédito y Comercio **1** C3
Banco Financiero Internacional .. **2** C3
Biblioteca Provincial José Martí .. **3** C3
Cadeca **4** C3
Cubana Office **5** C2
Etecsa **6** D3
Hospital Che Guevara **7** F4
Librería Fulgencio Oroz **8** C3
Reservaciones Campismo Popular .. **9** D2

SIGHTS & ACTIVITIES   pp304-6
Memorial a los Mártires de
  Barbados **10** B3
Memorial Vicente García **11** C3
Monumento a Alfabetización ... **12** D1

Museo Provincial General Vicente
  García **13** D2
Plaza de la Revolución **14** E3
Vicente García Monument **15** E3

SLEEPING   p306
Hotel Caribe **16** D3
Hotel Las Tunas **17** F3
Hotel Santiago **18** D2

EATING   pp306-8
Café Oquendo **19** D2
Cremería Yumurí **20** B3
Dos Gardenias **21** E2
El Bacán **22** E2
La Venecia **23** D2

Mercado Agropecuario **24** E1
Paladar La Bamba **25** D2
Paladar La Roca **26** D2
Panadería Doña Neli **27** D3
Restaurante La Bodeguita **28** C2
Supermercado Casa Azul **29** C3

ENTERTAINMENT   p308
Bar Las Palmitas **30** B3
Cabaret Taíno **31** B3
Cabildo San Pedro Lucumí **32** C2
Casa de la Cultura **33** C3
Entre Luces **34** D3
Estadio Julio Antonio Mella **35** E1
Sala Polivalente **36** E3
Teatro de Guiñol **37** D3

SHOPPING   pp308-9
Fondo Cubano de Bienes Culturales .. **38** D3

TRANSPORT
Bus Station **39** D3
Cubataxi **40** D2
Micar **41** D3

0 _____ 500 m
0 _____ 0.3 mi

Not all streets indicated

To Hermanos
Ameijeiras Airport
(5km); Manatí (48km)

To Puerto
Padre (53km)

To Holguín (81km);
Bayamo (82km)

To Servi-Cupet (150m);
La Caldosa (6km);
Motel El Cornito (9km);
Camagüey (f 30km)

To Jobabo
(39km)

To Dormitorio
(27km)

Paladar La Bamba (Av 2 de Diciembre & Frank País; meals US$8; ☺ 6-11pm) A super-popular place with tourists and touts, often full.

El Bacan (F Suárez No 12; 25-50 pesos) Peso place mounding on the food.

RESTAURANTS

La Venecia (Francisco Verona & Vicente García; ☺ 7am-11pm) Smack in the middle of town, this peso restaurant housed in a colonial building has an extensive menu (nothing over 23 pesos), plus balcony dining overlooking the park. Good breakfast spot for two-peso eggs.

Restaurante La Bodeguita (Francisco Varona No 295; ☺ 9am-11pm) This Rumbos restaurant has tablecloths and a limited wine list and isn't bad for a state-run place. Try the US$5 chicken breast with mushroom sauce.

Cremería Yumuri (Francisco Vega & Vicente García; ☺ 10am-4pm & 5-11pm) Pay pesos for your sundaes or *tres gracias* (three scoops) in flavors like coconut and cafe con leche at the door, get your ticket and take a seat for the best ice cream in Las Tunas. Nothing over 20 pesos.

Other recommendations:

Dos Gardenias (Francisco Varona No 326; ☺ 9am-midnight) Gussied-up cafeteria serving chicken (US$1.80), sandwiches (US$1-2) and pizza (US$1.10-2.50).

Cafe Oquendo (Francisco Varona btwn Vicente García & Lucas Ortíz; ☺ 24hr) Espresso straight (20 centavos) or rum laced (rocío del gallo) for two pesos.

La Caldosa (☎ 4-2743) Legendary place near El Cornito sells rich caldosas (stews) for US$2.

SELF-CATERING

To stock up on groceries (or to break bigger bills), try **Supermercado Casa Azul** (Vicente García & Francisco Vega; ☺ 9am-6pm Mon-Sat, 9am-noon Sun). Bread is available at **Panadería Doña Neli** (US$0.40 a loaf) on Francisco Varona. A small *mercado agropecuario* is on Av Camilo Cienfuegos, not far from the train station.

Entertainment

Cabildo San Pedro Lucumí (Francisco Varona btwn Angel Guardia & Lucas Ortíz; admission free; ☺ 9pm Sun) Cultural activities happen at this friendly Afro-Caribbean association; drop in on Sunday for some dancing and drumming.

Entre Luces (Francisco Varona No 256; admission Sun-Fri/Sat US$3/5; ☺ 10pm-2am Sun-Fri, 10pm-3am Sat) The most popular disco in Las Tunas. Notice the house rules posted at the door: public displays of homosexual affection will get you banned for life.

Cabaret Taino (☎ 4-3823; Carretera Central & A Cabrera; admission per couple US$10; ☺ 9pm-2am Tue-Sun) This large thatched venue at the west entrance to town has the standard feathers, salsa and pasties show. Cover charge includes a bottle of rum and cola.

Also worth checking out:

Bar Las Palmitas (Vincente García; ☺ 24hr) Kick back on the open-air terrace.

Teatro de Guiñol (Francisco Varona No 267; ☺ 10am Sat, 10am & 3pm Sun) Famous puppet and children's theater.

Casa de la Cultura (☎ 4-3500; Vicente García No 8) Concerts, poetry, dance etc.

From October to April is baseball season. Las Tunas plays at the **Estadio Julio Antonio Mella** near the train station. Other sports happen at the **Sala Polivalente**, an indoor arena near Hotel Las Tunas.

Shopping

The **Fondo Cubano de Bienes Culturales** (Angel Guardia & Francisco Varona; ☺ 9am-noon & 1:30-5pm Mon-Fri, 8:30am-noon Sat) sells fine artwork, ceramics and embroidered items. The dollar bar upstairs has a terrace, which is good for people-watching.

Getting There & Away

AIR

Hermanos Ameijeiras Airport, 3km north of the train station, has a nice new terminal building. There are no international flights, but Cubana flies nonstop to/from Havana on Thursday (US$94 one way, two hours, 662km).

BUS & TRUCK

The main **bus station** (☎ 4-3060) is on Francisco Varona, 1km southeast of the main square. There are Astro buses to:

destination	cost (one way)	distance	departure time
Camagüey	US$4.50	128km	6:15am
Havana	US$27	662km	7:30pm
Holguín	US$3	81km	1pm
Santa Clara	US$15	391km	8:40pm, alt days
Santiago de Cuba	US$7.50	199km	5:15am

Víazul buses have the following departures; tickets are sold by the *jefe de turno* (shift manager):

destination	cost (one way)	distance	departure time
Ciego de Ávila	US$13	236km	12:30am, 12:40am, 1:30pm, 8pm
Havana	US$39	662km	12:40am, 1:30pm, 8pm
Sancti Spíritus	US$17	312km	12:30am, 12:40am, 1:30pm, 8pm
Santiago de Cuba	US$6	199km	2am, 7am, 3:35pm, 9pm
Trinidad	US$22	382km	12:30am

All Santiago de Cuba buses also stop at Holguín (US$6) and Bayamo (US$6). To get to Guantánamo or Baracoa, you have to connect through Santiago de Cuba (onward bus departs at 7:30am).

Passenger trucks to Camagüey, Holguín, Bayamo and Puerto Padre pick up passengers on the main street near the train station, with the last departure before 2pm. Buy your tickets at the window. It's easier to reach Playa La Herradura from Holguín, but you can take a truck to Puerto Padre and hitch or connect with ongoing trucks there (for information on the risks associated with hitching see p433). If you have problems getting onto the Camagüey truck, take a bus to Guáimaro from the regional bus station attached to the end of the train station and try again there.

TRAIN
The **train station** (☎ 4-8140) is near Estadio Julio A Mella on the northeast side of town. See the *jefe de turno* for tickets. There are trains to the following destinations:

destination	cost (one way)	distance	hours	departure time
Camagüey	US$4	128km	3	12:30am
Havana	US$23	662km	10	12:30am
Holguín	US$3	81km	2	7:20am, alt days
Matanzas	US$20	602km	10	12:30am
Santiago de Cuba	US$7	199km	3½	1:50am, alt days

Getting Around
A taxi from the airport to Hotel Las Tunas should cost US$2. **Cubataxi** (☎ 4-2036; Villamar No 34) rents taxis and provides secure overnight parking for US$1. Horse carts run along Frank País near the baseball stadium to the town center; a charter trip costs 10 pesos.

Havanautos (☎ 5-5242) is at Hotel Las Tunas. An Oro Negro gas station is on Francisco Varona and Lorca, a block west of the bus station, where there is also a **Micar** (☎ 4-6263) outlet. Servi-Cupet, on the Carretera Central at the exit from Las Tunas toward Camagüey, is open 24 hours.

PUNTA COVARRUBIAS
It seems like the rutted road bumps on forever before you reach Punta Covarrubias, 49km northwest of Puerto Padre. But after 90 minutes you arrive and it's sublime: 4km of spotless sandy beach, the blue-green Atlantic and the **Villa Covarrubias** (Gran Caribe; ☎ 4-6230; fax 36 53 05; s/d from US$85/128; P ✗ ✕). This resort has 122 comfortable rooms in cabinesque blocks (one room is designed for disabled guests). Scuba diving the nearby coral reef is the highlight. Packages including two dives a day and certification courses are offered by **Marsub** (☎ 33-3481) in Havana. Almost all guests arrive on all-inclusive tours and are bussed in from Frank País Airport in Holguín, 115km to the southeast. It's very secluded.

Self-sufficient travelers can turn in to the beach at the **mirador** (a tower with fantastic panoramic views) 200m before the hotel and pitch camp. Old barbecue pits from parties past allow campfire cooking.

PLAYAS LA HERRADURA, LA LLANITA & LAS BOCAS
This string of northern beaches hugging the Atlantic coast begins 30km north of Puerto Padre and 55km from Holguín. Head here to get lost in the fabric of Cuban life. Intrepid travelers who make it up here are certain to discover unknown corners and meet lots of friendly locals.

From Puerto Padre, it's 30km around the eastern shore of Bahía de Chaparra to **Playa La Herradura**. The beach is a scoop of golden sand and the water is clean. There are a couple of houses legally renting rooms (look for the blue triangle). A good choice is **Villa Papachongo** (☎ in Holguín 42 41 74; Casa No 137; r US$15; ✗), right on the beach with a great porch for catching the sunset. If you don't like what you see here, push on to Playa Las Bocas where there are several more houses for rent. There is a dollar store for snacks and an open-air bar at the entrance to town.

Continue west on this road crawling with irascible crabs for 11km to **Playa Llanita**. The sand here is softer and whiter than in Las Herradura, but the beach lies on an unprotected bend and there's sometimes a vicious chop. If you're caught without a roof, check out one of the 112 basic cabins at **Campismo Playa Corella** (☎ 5-5447; per person US$5), 5km before Playa Llanita.

Just a kilometer beyond, you come to the end of the road at **Playa Las Bocas**. Wedged between the coast and Bahía de Chaparra, you can catch a ferry (one peso) to El Socucho and continue to Puerto Padre or rent a room in a casa particular.

There are trucks as far as Puerto Padre from Las Tunas, from where you'll have to connect with another ride to the junction at Lora before heading north to the beaches. It's much easier to get up this way from Holguín, but even this way there are only regular trucks to the junction at Velasco, from where you'll have to connect with another ride north.

If you're driving, it's an easy shot out of Las Tunas 52km north to Puerto Padre (gas up at the Servi-Cupet here), east to the junction at Lora and then north to Playa Herradura. For directions from Holguín, see p322.

Holguín
Province

HOLGUÍN PROVINCE

Holguín
Province

If you could visit only one province after the City of Havana, it would have to be Holguín. Oh, Santiago de Cuba fans can cry foul, but Holguín Province, Cuba's third most populous and fourth largest in overall area, has a blend of beach, history and culture rolled into one, with classic Cuban hospitality sealing the deal.

The entire knot of north coast, from unsung Gibara to the famous beach resort of Guardalavaca beckons travelers with intriguing attractions. Since it's all within striking distance of Holguín city, this makes a good city-beach vacation combination. Undiscovered Holguín includes the dense pine slopes at Pinares del Mayarí in the Altiplanicie de Nipe and the area east of Moa. For history buffs there's Fidel's childhood home in Birán and Columbus' landing site.

In addition to the usual sugarcane and cows, Holguín Province produces most of Cuba's beans and corn, and coffee grows in the eastern hills between the Altiplanicie de Nipe and the Sierra del Cristal. In this range, the highest point is Pico Cristal (1213m); further east are the Cuchillas de Moa, which attain 1175m at Pico del Toldo. Holguín is run through with important hard currency-producing minerals including iron in the Altiplanicie de Nipe, nickel and iron in Nicaro, and nickel and cobalt in Moa.

HIGHLIGHTS

- **Urban Delights**
  Taking in the theater, *trova* (traditional poetic singing/songwriting) and parks of Holguín (p313)

- **Beach Baby**
  Chilling and scuba diving at Guardalavaca (p327)

- **Town to Get Hooked On**
  Colonial homes, views, beaches, history and art of Gibara (p322)

- **Historical Highpoint**
  Former Castro family estate at low-key Finca Las Manacas (p330)

- **Remote Digs**
  Cabins on paradisiacal Cayo Saetía (p331)

■ TELEPHONE CODE: 24　　　■ POPULATION: 1,035,825　　　■ AREA: 9300 SQ KM

HISTORY

Most historians and experts agree that Columbus first made landfall on October 28, 1492 at Cayo Bariay near Playa Blanca, just west of Playa Don Lino. Columbus commented in his journal that this was the most beautiful land he had ever seen. The Spaniards first encountered Seboruco Indians, whose ancestors had lived in Cuba for several thousand years and they captured 13 of them to take back to Europe as specimens. Spanish explorer Diego Velázquez de Cuéllar gifted this most beautiful land of theirs to Bartolomé de Bastidas first, and later to Captain García Holguín.

HOLGUÍN

☎ 24 / pop 264,927

Known as 'the city of parks,' (there are six in the city center alone), Holguín is Cuba's fourth largest city and is laidback and friendly. Though you won't find clusters of colonial architecture like those in Trinidad, Camagüey and Santiago de Cuba, Holguín is undergoing a revitalization, including restoration of picturesque plazas and important buildings.

Founded around 1523, San Isidoro de Holguín became a municipal seat in 1752. The city was the setting of much fighting during the two wars of independence in the late 19th century. With the division of Oriente into five separate provinces in 1975, the city of Holguín became a provincial capital.

Orientation

Parque Calixto García is Holguín's most important central square; just to its north and south are Parque Céspedes and Parque Peralta, either of which would do any city proud. Manduley (aka Libertad) and Maceo are the main north–south thoroughfares, running between the train station and the hills bordering the city on the north. The main bus station is to the west of town, the main tourist hotels to the far east.

Information

AIRLINE OFFICES

Cubana Calle Martí & Manduley (Map p318; ☎ 46 81 11/48; ☯ 8am-4pm Mon-Fri; in Edificio Pico Cristal, 2nd fl); Aeropuerto Frank País (☎ 46 25 12/46 25 34) Also sells Aerocaribbean tickets.

Air Transat (☎ /fax 3-0290; Villa Cabañas Guardalavaca)

BOOKSHOPS

Librería Internacional Pedro Rojena (Map p318; Manduley No 193 on Parque Calixto García) Sells compact discs and 'shiterature' in English.

Librería Villena Botev (Map p318; ☎ 42 76 81; Frexes No 151 at Máximo Gómez) Books in Spanish only.

IMMIGRATION

Inmigración (Map p316; General Marrero & General Vázquez; ☯ 8am-noon & 2-4pm Mon-Fri)

INTERNET ACCESS

Hotel Pernik (Map p316; US$6/hr) was the only place with Internet at the time of writing, but check **Etecsa** under Telephone, below.

LIBRARIES

Biblioteca Alex Urquiola (Map p318; ☎ 42 13 66; Maceo No 178 on Parque Calixto García; ☯ 8:30am-9pm Mon-Fri, 8:30am-4:30pm Sat)

MEDIA

Ahora Local newspaper published on Saturday.
Radio Ángulo CMKO (1110AM & 97.9FM)

MEDICAL SERVICES

Hospital Lenin (Map p316; ☎ 42 53 02; Av VI Lenin) Both Hotel Pernik and Motel El Bosque have infirmaries.
Farmacia Turno Especial (Map p318; Maceo No 170 on Parque Calixto García; ☯ 8am-10pm Mon-Sat)

MONEY

Banco Financiero Internacional (Map p318; ☎ 46 85 02; Manduley No 167 btwn Frexes & Aguilera)
Banco de Crédito y Comercio (Map p318; ☎ 42 25 12; Arias on Parque Céspedes)
Cadeca (Map p318; ☎ 46 81 09; Manduley No 205 btwn Martí & Luz Caballero; ☯ 8:30am-6pm Mon-Sat, 8am-1pm Sun)

PHOTOGRAPHY

Photo Service Frexes No 214 (Map p318; near Parque Calixto García); Manduley No 132 (Map p318)

POST

DHL (Map p318; ☎ 46 82 54; Manduley No 183 on Parque Calixto García; ☯ 10am-noon & 1-6pm Mon-Fri) Stamps sold.
Post Office (Map p318; Maceo No 114 on Parque Céspedes; ☯ 8am-6pm Mon-Sat)

TELEPHONE

Etecsa (Map p318; ☎ 46 11 02; Martí No 122 btwn M Gómez & Mártires)
Servicio Telefónico (Map p316; ☎ 46-26-26; Frexes at Rastro; ☯ 7am-9pm)

HOLGUÍN PROVINCE

TRAVEL AGENCIES

Havanatur (Map p318; ☎ 46 80 91; Frexes No 172 btwn Morales Lemus & Narciso López) Tours to aquarium at Bahía de Naranjo.

Reservaciones de Campismo (Map p318; ☎ 42 28 81; Mártires No 87 at Frexes; ☺ 8am-6pm Mon-Fri, 8am-noon Sat) Reserves cabins at Campismo Silla de Gibara and Campismo Río Cabonico.

UniversiTUR (Map p316; ☎ 46 28 23; fax 48 18 43; universiturhlg@esihl.colombus.cu; Manduley btwn Calle 10 & 12)

Sights

An afternoon exploring the city's parks, plazas and surrounding sights is a great way to discover Holguín. The following descriptions run from Parque Céspedes in the north

to the Plaza de la Marqueta in the south, with some further afield places wrapping up.

PARQUE CÉSPEDES

Founded in the late 18th century, this shady square hosting hot stick ball action is the youngest of Holguín's parks. On its eastern edge is the **Iglesia de San José**, (Map p318; Manduley No 116) with its distinctive bell tower (1842) and dome (visible from La Loma de la Cruz; p317). Locals calls this park Parque San José.

In a colonial building facing the church is the **Galería Holguín** (Map p318; ☎ 42 23 92; Manduley No 137; admission free; ☺ 8am-6pm Tue-Wed, 8am-10pm Thu-Sun). Duck into the high-ceilinged rooms to check out some (good) local art.

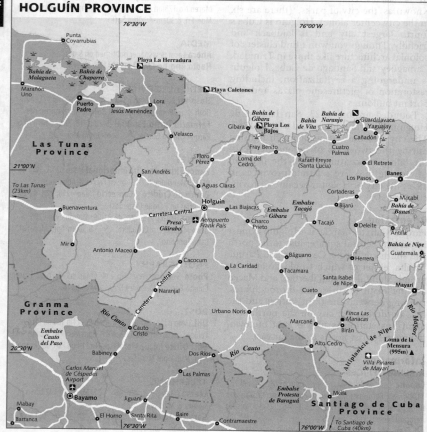

HOLGUÍN PROVINCE

PARQUE CALIXTO GARCÍA

The centerpiece of this park is a 1912 statue of – who else? – General Calixto García, who captured Holguín from the Spaniards in December 1872. In 1898 he was about to repeat his feat when US intervention forced him to rush to Santiago de Cuba. There, his support enabled the quick US military victory over the Spanish. US forces prohibited García and his troops from attending surrender proceedings as the gringos were frightened by the black skin of the legendary *mambises*. Thusly snubbed, the Cubans were slow to aid the Americans when they started dropping at the rate of 200 a day from yellow fever, malaria and dysentery. García then marched westward and re-occupied Holguín.

To learn more about this dynamic hero, head to **Casa Natal de Calixto García** (Map p318; ☎ 42 56 10; Miró No 147; admission US$1; 9am-9pm Tue-Sat) two blocks east of the park. García was born here in 1839.

On the park's northern side is the **Museo de Historia Provincial** (Map p318; ☎ 46 33 95; Frexes No 198; admission US$1; 8am-5pm). Now a national monument, the building was constructed between 1860 and 1868 and used as a Spanish army barracks during the independence wars. It's nicknamed La Periquera ('the parrot cage') for the red, yellow and green uniforms of the Spanish soldiers who stood guard outside. The prize exhibit is an old axe head carved in the likeness of a man, known as the Hacha de Holguín

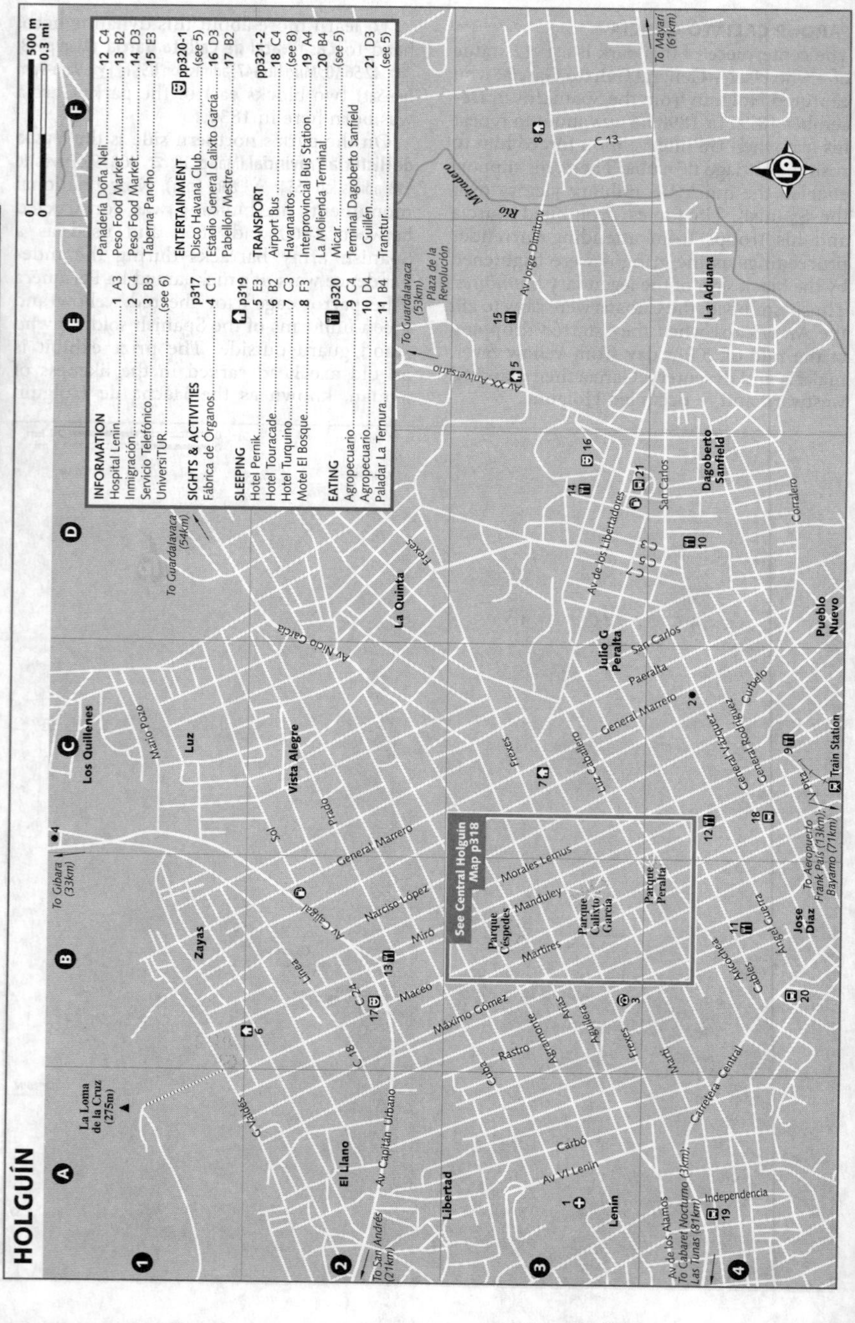

HOLGUÍN
0 500 m
0 0.3 mi
INFORMATION
Hospital Lenin 1 A3
Inmigración 2 C4
Servicio Telefónico 3 B3
UniversiTUR (see 6)
SIGHTS & ACTIVITIES p317
Fábrica de Órganos 4 C1
SLEEPING p319
Hotel Pernik 5 E3
Hotel Turacade 6 B2
Hotel Turquino 7 C3
Motel El Bosque 8 F3
EATING p320
Agropecuario 9 C4
Agropecuario 10 D4
Paladar La Ternura 11 B4
Panadería Doña Neli 12 C4
Peso Food Market 13 B2
Peso Food Market 14 D3
Taberna Pancho 15 E3
ENTERTAINMENT pp320-1
Disco Havana Club (see 5)
Estadio General Calixto García 16 D3
Pabellón Mestre 17 B2
TRANSPORT pp321-2
Airport Bus 18 C4
Havanautos (see 8)
Interprovincial Bus Station 19 A4
La Molienda Terminal 20 B4
Micar (see 5)
Terminal Dagoberto Sanfield Guillén 21 D3
Transtur (see 5)
See Central Holguín Map p318
La Loma de la Cruz (275m)
To Gibara (33km)
To Guardalavaca (54km)
To Guardalavaca (53km)
To Mayarí (61km)
To San Andrés (21km)
Av de los Álamos To Cabaret Nocturno (3km); Las Tunas (81km)
To Aeropuerto Frank País (13km); Bayamo (71km)
Train Station
Plaza de la Revolución
Río Miradero
El Llano
Libertad
Lenin
Zayas
Los Quillenes
Luz
Vista Alegre
La Quinta
Julio G Peralta
Dagoberto Sanfield
La Aduana
Pueblo Nuevo
Jose Díaz
Parque Céspedes
Parque Calixto García
Parque Peralta
Av de los Libertadores
Av XX Aniversario
Av Jorge Dimitrov
Av Nicio García
Av Cajigal
Av Capitán Urbano
Av VI Lenin
Carretera Central

(Holguín axe), discovered in 1860. There's a pretty patio here.

In the southwestern corner of Parque Calixto García is the **Centro Provincial de Artes Plásticas Moncada** (Map p318; ☎ 42 20 84; Maceo No 180 at Martí; admission free; ☺ 9am-4pm Mon-Sat). This bright gallery is Holguín's best and shares space with the **Biblioteca Alex Urquiola** (☎ 46 25 62), housing Hogluín's biggest book collection. Music and theater events are often hosted here.

The **Museo de Historia Natural** (Map p318; ☎ 42 39 35; Maceo No 129 btwn Parques Calixto García & Peralta; admission/camera US$1/1; ☺ 9am-10pm Tue-Sat, 9am-9pm Sun) has scores of stuffed animals behind glass, including the world's smallest frog and world's smallest hummingbird star.

PARQUE PERALTA

This square (called Parque de las Flores locally) is named for General Julio Grave de Peralta (1834–72), who led the uprising against Spain in Holguín in October 1868. His marble statue (1916) faces the cathedral. Big and beige, the **Catedral de San Isidoro** (Map p318; Maceo No 122) dates from 1720 but is heavily restored.

PLAZA DE LA MARQUETA

This exquisitely restored plaza and work-in-progress west of Parque Peralta is fast becoming Hoguín's cultural hub. From the telephone poles turned totems that anchor the plaza's corners to the **mural** by celebrated artist Nelson Dominguez, this is one of Holguín's top spots.

The **Imprenta Lugones** (Map p318; ☎ 42 28 74; Callejón de Mercado 2) on the southern side, is a working press and gallery where you can watch books being handset and printed. Just east is the arty **Galería Estampa** (Map p318; Callejón Mercado 2 s/n) and **Centro Cultural Mona Lisa** (Map p318; ☎ 42 10 58; Callejón Mercado 2s/n) where cultural events are always on the menu (*son* septets, bolero nights, folkloric dancing etc).

The ruins in the plaza's center are undergoing massive restoration as they are transformed into one of Cuba's most atmospheric concert halls. The shopping in this plaza is quality (p321).

BEYOND THE CENTER

At the northern end of Maceo is a stairway built in 1950, with 460 steps ascending **La Loma de la Cruz** (Map p316), a 275m-high hill with panoramic views. A cross was raised here in 1790 in hope of relieving a drought, and every May 3 the Romerías de Mayo brings hundreds of pilgrims. It's a 20-minute walk from town or you can drive up the western side (accessible via G Valdés); a bici-taxi to the foot of the hill should cost 10 pesos.

Holguín is a city most *fiel* (faithful) and the **Plaza de la Revolución** (Map p316) east of the center is a huge monument to the heroes of Cuban independence, bearing quotations from José Martí and Fidel Castro. Massive rallies are held here every May 1. The tomb of Calixto García is also here, as is a smaller monument to García's mother.

Fábrica de Órganos (Map p316; Carretera de Gibara No 301; ☺ 8am-4pm Mon-Fri) is the only mechanical music organ factory in Cuba. This small factory produces about six organs a year, as well as guitars and other instruments. A good organ costs between US$10,000 and US$25,000. Eight professional organ groups exist in Holguín (including the Familia Cuayo, based at the factory), and you may be able to hear one playing on Parque Céspedes at 4pm on Thursday and 10am on Sunday.

Festivals & Events

The **Romerías de Mayo**, in the first week of May, is a week-long art party with exhibitions, music, poetry and festivities, the

---

SMOKING THE LOCAL WAY

This is real cigar culture: blue smoke curls to sports stadium rafters, old men dangle cheroots from toothless grins and the aroma (or stink) drifts through winking louvers. But the average Cuban isn't smoking export-quality Cohibas: they're smoking *tabaco del bodega*, one peso cigars sold at bodegas. While not the stuff of gold medals, bodega cigars are still a good, solid smoke.

Several tobacco factories throughout the country produce machine-rolled cigars for domestic consumption. If you're a poor addict like me, you can buy 25 of these cigars for 25 pesos (US$1) at the local bodega. The best are Selectos from Holguín, followed by El Crédito. El Cacique from Guantánamo is a tolerable smoke, but steer clear of the Bauza from Sancti Spíritus, which doesn't warrant the name of Cuban cigar. Of course, the best domestic cigars are in Pinar del Río.

HOLGUÍN PROVINCE

CENTRAL HOLGUÍN

0 ____ 200 m
0 ____ 0.1 mi

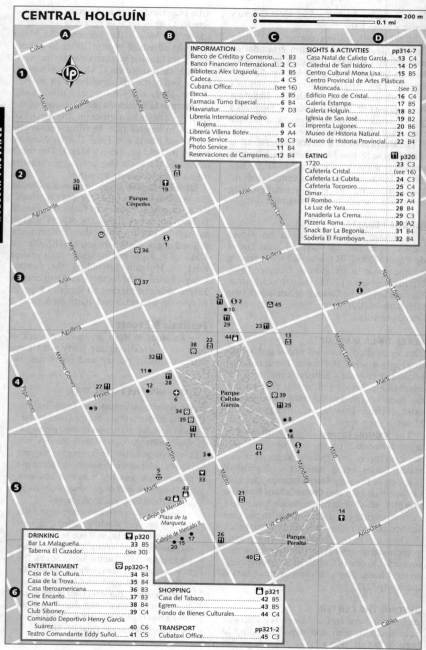

INFORMATION
Banco de Crédito y Comercio.....1 B3
Banco Financiero Internacional..2 C3
Biblioteca Alex Urquiola............3 B5
Cadeca......................................4 C5
Cubana Office....................(see 16)
Etecsa......................................5 B5
Farmacia Turno Especial..........6 B4
Havanatur................................7 D3
Librería Internacional Pedro
  Rojena..................................8 C4
Librería Villena Botev...............9 A4
Photo Service..........................10 C3
Photo Service..........................11 B4
Reservaciones de Campismo....12 B4

SIGHTS & ACTIVITIES   pp314-7
Casa Natal de Calixto García......13 C4
Catedral de San Isidoro.............14 D5
Centro Cultural Mona Lisa.........15 B5
Centro Provincial de Artes Plásticas
  Moncada...........................(see 3)
Edificio Pico de Cristal...............16 C4
Galería Estampa........................17 B5
Galería Holguín.........................18 B2
Iglesia de San José....................19 B2
Imprenta Lugones.....................20 B6
Museo de Historia Natural........21 C5
Museo de Historia Provincial.....22 B4

EATING   p320
1720..23 C3
Cafetería Cristal...................(see 16)
Cafetería La Cubita...................24 C3
Cafetería Tocororo....................25 C4
Dimar......................................26 C5
El Rombo..................................27 A4
La Luz de Yara..........................28 B4
Panadería La Crema..................29 C3
Pizzería Roma...........................30 A2
Snack Bar La Begonia................31 B4
Sodería El Framboyan...............32 B4

DRINKING   p320
Bar La Malagueña......................33 B5
Taberna El Cazador................(see 30)

ENTERTAINMENT   pp320-1
Casa de la Cultura.....................34 B4
Casa de la Trova........................35 B4
Casa Iberoamericana.................36 B3
Cine Encanto.............................37 B3
Cine Martí.................................38 B4
Club Siboney.............................39 C4
Cominado Deportivo Henry García
  Suárez..................................40 C6
Teatro Comandante Eddy Suñol......41 C5

SHOPPING   p321
Casa del Tabaco........................42 B5
Egrem.......................................43 B5
Fondo de Bienes Culturales.......44 C4

TRANSPORT   pp321-2
Cubataxi Office.........................45 C3

national rap competition and the La Loma de la Cruz pilgrimage among the highlights. Holguín's **Carnaval** happens in the third week of August and it's a blowout, with outdoor concerts and copious amounts of dancing, roast pork and potent potables.

Sleeping

IN TOWN

Holguín has several Cuban-only hotels, limiting tourist options to two or three places.

Hotel Pernik (Map p316; Islazul; ☎ 48 10 11; fax 48 16 67; Av Jorge Dimitrov & Av XX Aniversario; s/d incl breakfast low season US$29/38, high US$36/48; P 🗶 🖳 🖭) Holguín's most comfortable and popular tourist hotel, this well-designed place 3km east of town sometimes gets overwhelmed by its own popularity. The big rooms have balconies and the pool is a sprawler (nonguest use is US$2). Ask about the rooms with unlimited Internet access (US$10 extra) and the special 'art' rooms with works-in-progress by local artists. There's public Internet access here (US$6 per hour; 🕑 noon to midnight) and a disco (admission US$2 to US$4, depending on season).

Hotel Touracade (Map p316; UniversiTUR; ☎ 46 28 23; fax 48 18 43; Manduley No 26 btwn Calles 10 & 12; r US$10; 🗶) Small and good value, this place near La Loma de la Cruz has four rooms with fridge often occupied by foreigners studying Spanish (see Travel Agencies p314). You can take just a room or add on meals for extra (breakfast/full board US$2/11).

The hotel restaurant is good. Call ahead for availability.

Hotel Turquino (Map p316; ☎ 46 21 12; Martí No 40 at General Marrero; s/d US$15/17). Neither terribly conveniently located nor attractive, this 40-room hotel is in the 'only if desperate' category.

OUTSIDE TOWN

Motel Mirador de Mayabe (Map p325; Islazul; ☎ 42 21 60; s/d low season US$29/38, high US$36/48; P 🗶 🖭) This motel high up on the Loma de Mayabe, 10km southeast of Holguín, has 24 rooms tucked into lush grounds. The views, taking in vast mango plantations, are especially good from the pool. The Mirador de Mayabe's claim to fame is a beer-drinking donkey named Pancho, who hangs out near the bar. Typical Cuban lunches are served at the Finca Mayabe, just above the motel, where there's also a cockfighting ring. The Casa Campesina nearby is a replica of a traditional farmer's dwelling, and a host of domestic plants and animals are on hand; kids love it. A bus runs to Holguín from the bottom of the hill, 1.5km from the motel, three times a day.

Motel El Bosque (Map p316; Islazul; ☎ /fax 48 11 40; Av Jorge Dimitrov; s/d/tr incl breakfast low season US$29/38/55 high US$36/48/65; P 🗶 🖭). One kilometer beyond Hotel Pernik, the 69 duplex bungalows here are set among extensive green grounds, making it feel more removed than it is. There's a nice bar beside the swimming pool (nonguest use US$5, includes US$3 in drinks).

CASAS PARTICULARES – HOLGUÍN

Haydée Torres Marrero (☎ 42 47 21; Narcisco López No 151 btwn Frexes & Martí; r US$15; P 🗶) Spacious upstairs with fridge, terrace and living room.

Isabel Sera Galves (☎ 42 25 29; Narciso López No 142 btwn Aguilera & Frexes; r with fan/air-con US$15/20; 🗶) Friendly home with great back patio; prices drop by US$5 in slow season.

Georgia Sánchez Oduardo (☎ 42 20 29; Aguilera No 163 btwn Narciso López & General Feria; r US$20; 🗶) Cute, safe and quiet, independent entrance.

Villa Liba Hostal – Jorge A Mezerene (☎ 42 38 23; villaliba@yahoo.es; Maceo No 46 at Calle 18; r US$25; P 🗶) Near the Loma de la Cruz stairway, nicely furnished rooms sleep three to four, patio, professional.

Germán González Rojas (☎ 42 40 75; Ángel Guerra No 178 btwn Camilo Cienfuegos & Carretera Central; r US$20) Festive place near Terminal La Molienda with several rooms; including independent apt with two rooms, bath and patio.

Roberto Polanco Vega (☎ 46 13 77; Calle 7 No 29, apt 4; r US$20) Reparto Julio G Peralta near Terminal Dagoberto Sanfield Guillén, self-catering, good meals served.

Aurora Ferriol Arencibia (☎ 46 11 91; Martí No 102, btwn Morales Lemus & Narciso López; r US$15; 🗶) Central, signposted.

Eddy G Osorio (☎ 42 22 18; Frexes No 166 Altos btwn Morales Lemus & Narciso López; r US$15) Spacious, central.

Sonía Cacer Bejerano (☎ 42 32 96; Miro No 181 btwn Martí & Luz Caballero; r US$15-20; 🗶) Back room facing courtyard best; heavily trafficked by people walking in and out.

Eating

RESTAURANTS

Restaurant 1720 (Map p318; ☎ 46 81 50; Calle Frexes btwn Manduley & Miró; ⏱ 12:30-10:30pm) Holguín's finest dining is in this painstakingly restored cake icing colonial mansion where you can dine on paella (US6$) or shrimp flambé (US$13); try the onion soup (US$2) on a rainy day. No T-shirts or shorts allowed; check out the bar upstairs (see Bar Terraza this page).

Dimar (Map p318; Mártires cnr Luz Caballero; ⏱ 11am-10pm) An intimate, new seafood restaurant specializing in shrimp cocktail (US$2) and grilled fish (US$4.50). Simple, but good.

Taberna Pancho (Map p316; ☎ 48 18 68; Av Jorge Dimitrov btwn Hotel Pernik & Motel El Bosque; ⏱ noon-10pm). Nothing on the menu, including hamburgers and draft Mayabe beer, costs more than US$2.50. Try the sausage special.

Many of Holguín's privately operated paladares have gone under or been closed down. One survivor is **Paladar La Ternura** (Map p316; Jose A Cardet No 293 at Cables) (upstairs), which serves large portions of chicken, pork and beef dishes in its elegant dining room. Prices here hover around US$6 to US$7 for a full meal.

CAFETERIAS

Peso stalls are crowded near the Interprovincial Bus Station on the Carretera Central.

Cafetería Cristal (Map p318; ☎ 42 58 55; Manduley cnr of Martí, ground fl Edificio Pico de Cristal; ⏱ 24hr) Reliable, affordable meals (US$3 for fried chicken and a salad) are served at this popular place with cranking air-con. A more upscale restaurant is upstairs (⏱ noon to 10pm).

El Rombo (Map p318; Frexes btwn Mártires & Máximo Gómez; ⏱ 9am-11pm) Don't be put off by the odd smell: this friendly branch of Cafeterías Cubanitas does a big, tasty ham and cheese sandwich (US$1.50) and other items similar to Cafetería Tocororo, but without the wait.

Cafetería Tocororo (Map p318; Manduley No 189 on Parque Calixto García; ⏱ 24hr) Centrally located and serving reasonable spaghetti, pizza, chicken and sandwiches, this place is often packed with locals and guidebook-toting tourists. Nothing under US$3.50.

Snack Bar La Begonia (Map p318; ☎ 46 85 86; Maceo No 176, on Parque Calixto García; ⏱ 9am-10pm) With ice cream (US$1), sandwiches (US$1.90 to US$2.50) and drinks served beneath flowering trellises, this is a relaxed place to meet other travelers.

Also recommended:

Galería Estampa (Map p318; Callejón Mercado 2 s/n on Plaza de la Marqueta) Pretty patio hidden in the back has a simple cafetería. Prices are from US$1 for pizza to US$1.75 to US$3 for sandwiches.

Sodería El Framboyan (Map p318; Maceo near Frexes; ⏱ 10am-11pm) Ice cream galore (cones US$1, sundaes up to US$2.50).

Cafetería La Cubita (Map p318; Manduley btwn Frexes & Aguilera; ⏱ 24hr) Coffee shots for 20 centavos.

Pizzería Roma (Map p318; Maceo at Agramonte) Get your street pizza here (six pesos).

SELF-CATERING

La Luz de Yara (Map p318; Frexes cnr Maceo on Parque Calixto García; ⏱ 8:30am-7pm Mon-Sat, 8:30am-noon Sun) Bustling department store-supermarket with a bakery section.

Panadería La Crema (Map p318; Manduley No 140; ⏱ 7am-10pm) Good selection of breads and cakes here means long lines. If you can't wait, try the similar **Panadería Doña Neli** (Map p316; Manduley No 285; ⏱ 6am-11pm).

Agropecuarios are off Calle 19, the continuation of Calle Morales Lemus near the train station, and on Calle 3 in Dagoberto Sanfield. Prepared food is sold at open-air peso food markets off Av de los Libertadores, next to the Estadio General Calixto García, and along Manduley at Prado.

Drinking

Bar Terraza (Map p318; ☎ 46 81 50; Calle Frexes btwn Manduley & Miró, above Restaurant 1720; ⏱ 9pm-2am) Spiffy place to sip a *mojito*, with views over Parque Calixto García.

Bar La Malagueña (Map p318; Martí No 129) Popular spot near Parque Calixto García attracts a mixed local/traveler crowd.

Taberna El Cazador (Map p318; Maceo at Agramonte) Terrace (peso) bar with park views.

Entertainment

Teatro Comandante Eddy Suñol (Map p318; ☎ 46 31 61; Martí No 111 on Parque Calixto García) Holguín's premier theater was closed for renovations at the time of writing, but this 1939 theater hosts the Rodrigo Prats Theater Company and the Ballet Nacional de Cuba. Check here for performances by renowned children's theater **Alas Buenas**.

Also recommended:

Casa de la Trova (Map p318; Maceo No 174 on Parque Calixto García; ⏱ closed Mon) Traditional folk singing and music.

Casa de la Cultura (Map p318; Maceo No 172; 🕑 closed Mon) Exhibitions and classical music.

Casa Iberoamericana (Map p318; ☎ 42 25 33; Arias No 161 on Parque Céspedes) Frequently hosts peñas.

Pabellón Mestre (Map p316; Maceo at Capitán Urbano; 🕑 9pm-late) Open-air dancing and cultural activities.

DANCE CLUBS

Disco Cristal (Map p318; ☎ 42 58 55; Manduley No 199, at Martí, 3rd fl of Edificio Pico de Cristal; admission US$2; 🕑 9pm-2am Tue-Thu) Holguín's preferred city center club, locals with dollars get down here; good views from dance floor. You must eat or drink US$3 worth in addition to paying the cost of admission.

Club Siboney (Map p318; ☎ 42 57 15; Manduley No 185 Altos, on Parque Calixto García; admission US$1; 🕑 8pm-midnight Mon-Fri, Sun & 8pm-1am Sat) It's a good sign when there's a line at this local peso disco.

Disco Havana Club (Map p316; ☎ 48 11 40; at the Hotel Pernik; guests/nonguests US$2/4; 🕑 10pm-2am Tue-Sun) Holguín's premier disco, it's a good time if there's a crowd.

Cabaret Nocturno (☎ 42 51 85; admission US$10; 🕑 10pm-2am) Tropicana-style club beyond Servi-Cupet 3km out on the road to Las Tunas. No show when it's raining.

CINEMAS

For big screen movies, head to **Cine Martí** (Map p318; Frexes No 204; one to two pesos cubanos) on Parque Calixto García. Otherwise it's **Cine Encanto** (Map p318; Maceo No 101) for videos.

SPORT

Baseball games are held from October to April at the **Estadio General Calixto García** (one peso), just off Av de los Libertadores, not far from Hotel Pernik. Holguín's Perros won the national championship in 2002 for the first time in history, so they're pretty excited about their ball these days. The stadium also houses a **sports museum**.

You can catch boxing matches at the intimate **Cominado Deportivo Henry García Suárez** (Map p318; Maceo, western side of Parque Peralta; admission one peso; 🕑 8pm Wed, 2pm Sat), a gym where three Olympic medalists trained, including the female judo medalist.

Shopping

Holguín has some decent shopping. If you're in a rush, head directly to the **Plaza de la Marqueta** where there are clusters of shops.

Egrem (Map p318; ☎ 42 61 01; cnr Callejón de Mercado 1 & Mártires in Plaza de la Marqueta) You'll find a phenomenal number of CDs and some musical instruments at this outpost of the famous recording studio; this place also hosts occasional live performances.

Casa del Tabaco (Map p318; Callejón de Mercado 1 in Plaza de la Marqueta) Cool dark place to buy, smoke and talk cigars.

Fondo de Bienes Culturales (Map p318; ☎ 42 37 82; Frexes No 196 on Parque Calixto García) One of the best selections of Cuban handicrafts.

For finer art, check the **Galería Estampa** on Callejón Mercado 2 on the southern side of Plaza de la Marqueta.

Getting There & Away

AIR

There are 11 international flights a week into **Aeropuerto Frank País** (☎ 46 25 12; airport code HOG), 13km south of central Holguín. Martinair arrives from Amsterdam weekly and LTU International Airways arrives from Düsseldorf with connections to other German cities. Condor flies here weekly in winter. Cubana runs flights from London. Air Transat and Skyservice have charter flights from Montreal, Toronto and other Canadian cities. See the Transport chapter for more.

Domestic destinations are served by **Cubana** (☎ 46 25 12/46 25 34), which flies daily to Havana (US$98 one way, 743km, two hours), and Aerocaribbean.

A tourist taxi to the airport costs US$7 to US$10. It's also possible to spend your last night in Bayamo, then catch a taxi (US$17) or a truck (three pesos) to Holguín Airport. The public bus to the airport leaves daily around 2pm from General Rodríguez at No 84 on Parque Martí near the train station.

BUS

The **Interprovincial Bus Station** (Map p316; ☎ 46 10 36; Carretera Central at Independencia), west of the center near Hospital Lenin, has Astro buses going to:

destination	cost (one way)	distance	departure time
Guantánamo	US$11	182km	5am, alt days
Havana	US$30	743km	8pm daily, 9am alt days
Santiago de Cuba	US$7.50	138km	7am, alt days

On the Havana-bound bus you can hop off at Camagüey (US$9), Ciego de Ávila (US$13) or Santa Clara (US$15.50).

Air-con Víazul buses leave daily from here to:

destination	cost (one way)	distance	departure time
Havana	US$44	743km	12:30am, 6:45pm, 11:25pm
Santiago de Cuba	US$11	138km	3:20am, 8:05am, 5pm, 10:05pm
Trinidad	US$26	463km	10:55pm

You can take the Havana bus as far as Las Tunas (US$6), Camagüey (US$11), Ciego de Ávila (US$17), Sancti Spíritus (US$21) or Santa Clara (US$26). The Santiago departure also stops in Bayamo (US$6), but to reach Guantánamo or Baracoa, you have to change in Santiago de Cuba.

TRAIN

The **train station** (Map p316; ☎ 42 23 11) is on Calle V Pita, on the southern side of town. Foreigners must purchase dollar tickets at the special Ladis ticket office (☉ 7:30am to 3pm daily). The ticket office is marked 'U/B Ferrocuba Provincial Holguín' on the corner of Manduley opposite the train station.

Theoretically, there's one daily morning train to Las Tunas (US$3, 81km, two hours), a daily afternoon train to Santiago de Cuba (143km, 3½ hours, US$5), and the daily 6:15pm train to Havana (US$27, 743km, 15 hours). This train stops in Camagüey (US$8, 209km), Ciego de Ávila (US$11, 317km), Guayos (US$17, 393km), Santa Clara (US$17, 472km) and Matanzas (US$26, 683km). You may have to change trains at the Santiago–Havana mainline junction in Cacocum, 17km south of Holguín.

The only service that operates with any regularity is the train to Havana. The Santiago de Cuba service is rather irregular; ask before planning your trip around it.

TRUCK

Trucks to points south and west operate from **La Molienda Terminal** (Map p316; ☎ 46 20 11; Carretera Central No 46), between the bus and train stations. Trucks leave when full for Las Tunas and Bayamo (four pesos each), with the last departure around 2pm. You can also get colectivo taxis from here to either destination for 20 pesos. No trucks go directly to Santiago de Cuba or Camagüey, so you must travel in stages.

The **Terminal Dagoberto Sanfield Guillén** (Map p316; Av de los Libertadores opposite Estadio General Calixto García) has at least two daily trucks to Gibara (two pesos; window 6), Banes (four pesos, window 5) and Moa (nine pesos, window 5). To reach Guardalavaca, take a truck to Rafael Freyre (aka Santa Lucía, two pesos, window 3) and look for something else there. Otherwise, take the Banes truck to Los Pasos and hitch, but the first option is better (for information on the risks associated with hitching see p433).

If you haven't traveled by truck before, Holguín is a good place to try.

Getting Around

BICI-TAXI

Holguín's bici-taxis are ubiquitous. They charge five pesos for a short trip, 10 pesos for a long one.

CAR

You can rent or return a car at:
Havanautos Motel El Bosque (Map p316; ☎ 48 81 57); Aeropuerto Frank País (☎ 46 8412)
Micar Cafetería Cristal (Map p318; ☎ 46 85 59; Manduley cnr Martí); Hotel Pernik (Map p316; ☎ 48 16 52)
Transtur Hotel Pernik (Map p316; ☎ 48 10 11); Aeropuerto Frank País (☎ 46 84 14) Also rents mopeds.

A 24-hour Servi-Cupet station is 3km out on the Carretera Central toward Las Tunas; another is just outside town on the road to Gibara. An Oro Negro service station is on the Carretera Central on the southern edge of town. The road to Gibara is north on Av Cajígal; also take this road and fork left after 5km to reach Playa La Herradura.

TAXI

Cubataxi (Map p318; ☎ 42 32 90; Miró No 133) to Guardalavaca costs US$20 to US$25. To Gibara, negotiate a US$25 round-trip deal.

GIBARA

pop 28,826

Leaving Holguín behind, the road north grows curves, passing through friendly villages until you're dropped into the beautiful bayside town of Gibara, 33km on. Perched along the Bahía de Gibara, this little town packs a punch, with colonial architecture fanning out from pretty plazas, crumbling Spanish ruins boasting panoramic vistas, untouristed beaches and inimitable eastern Cuba hospitality.

Christopher Columbus arrived in 1492 and called it 'Río de Mares' (River of Oceans) for the Rios Cacoyugüín and Yabazón that drain into the Bahía de Gibara. The current name comes from *jiba*, the indigenous word for a bush that still grows along the shore.

Refounded in 1817, Gibara prospered as the main port for northern Cuba in the 19th century. To protect the trade from pirates, barracks were built and a 2km wall constructed around the town in the early 1800s, making Gibara Cuba's second walled city after Havana. The sparkling white facades earned Gibara its nickname: *la villa blanca*.

In 2003, Gibara hosted the first Festival de Internacional de Cine Pobre (International Low Budget Film Festival), which drew 80 films from 70 countries. As a result, the theaters and restaurants are in tip-top shape.

Information

Most services line Calle Independencia. Gibara has a **Banco Popular de Ahorro** (Calles Independencia & Cuba) and further along, a **Bandec** (Calles Independencia & J Peralta). Either should change traveler's checks. Also along here is the **post office** (Independencia No 15). There are few public phones here.

Sights & Activities

At the top of Calle Cabada is **El Cuartelón**, a crumbling brick Spanish fort with graceful arches that provides stunning town and bay views. Continue on this street for 200m to Restaurant El Mirador for an even better vantage point. You'll see remnants of the old fortresses here and at the **Fuerte Fernando VII**, on the point beyond Parque de las Madres, a block over from Parque Calixto García.

The centerpiece of **Parque Calixto García** (lined with weird *robles africanos* – african oaks with large penis-shaped pods) is **Iglesia de San Fulgencio** (1850). The Statue of Liberty in front commemorates the Second War of Independence. On the western side of the square, in a beautiful colonial palace (more interesting than the stuffed stuff it collects), is the **Museo de Historia Natural** (Luz Caballero No 23; admission US$1). Through barred windows

you can watch women rolling cheroots in the cigar factory across the square.

Two museums share the colonial mansion (1872) at Independencia No 19: the **Museo de Historia Municipal** (admission US$1) downstairs and the **Museo de Artes Decorativas** (☎ 3-4407; admission US$2) upstairs. The latter is more interesting, with nearly 800 pieces collected from Gibara's colonial heyday. All of these museums are open from 8am to noon and from 1pm to 5pm daily, with additional Thursday to Sunday hours from 8pm to 10pm. Across the street is the **Galería Cosme Proenza** (Calle Independencia No 32), with wall-to-wall works by one of Cuba's foremost painters (think Hieronymus Bosch).

There are two decent beaches within striking distance of Gibara. **Playa Los Bajos** is accessible by local ferry (two pesos) or skiff (US$3 round trip) from the fishing pier on La Enramada, the waterfront road leading out of town. These boats cross the Bahía de Gibara to Playa Blanca, from where it's 3km east to Playa Los Bajos.

You'll need some sort of transport to get to lovely, little **Playa Caletones**, 17km to the west of Gibara. The apostrophe of white sand and azure sea here is a favorite of vacationers from Holguín. The town here is ramshackle, with no services except the thatched place guarded by a palm tree that serves as a bar in summer; locals will offer to cook you lunch.

Sleeping

The **Hotel Bella Mar** (☎ 3-4206; General Sartorio No 25), near the center, was the only hotel in town but was closed at the time of writing. There are (loose) plans to fix it up.

Eating & Drinking

Restaurante El Faro (La Concha; on Parque de las Madres), run by Rumbos, serves chicken and fish meals overlooking the bay. It's a simple, romantic spot. **Bar El Coral**, just beside, has the same seaside atmosphere and is open 24 hours.

Patio Colonial, wedged between the Museo de Historia Natural and Casino Español, is an atmospheric outdoor cafeteria. Nearby, **El Caribe**, on Parque Calixto García, is a dollar pizza place.

Restaurant El Mirador, high above town near El Cuartelón, was getting ready to open at the time of writing.

CASAS PARTICULARES – GIBARA

Hostal Vitral – Nancy Pérez (☎ 3-4469; Independencia No 36 btwn J Peralta & Calixto García; r US$20; ✗) Gorgeous restored colonial with roof terrace and hammocks, meals provided. Pick from four lovely rooms.

Odalys & Luis (☎ 3-4542; Céspedes No 13 btwn Luz Caballero & J Peralta; r with fan/air-con US$15/ 20) Big rooms in a colonial house with patio a block and a half from Parque Calixto García; good meals.

Villa Miguel – Angelina Avita (☎ 3-4514; J Peralta No 61 btwn J Mora & M Grajales; r US$20; P) Catch the sea spray in one of the three rooms here right on the waterfront.

Leoncia Milagros (☎ 3-4493; J Agüero; r US$20) Behind the bus terminal, with a helpful family, nice rooms and big meals served on the terrace.

Rolando Cajigal (☎ 3-4383; Calle Independencia No 20; r US$20) Facing the Museo de Historia Municipal, this place is basic – try bargaining; meals provided.

Entertainment

For big screen films in recently refurbished digs, check out **Cine Jiba** on Parque Calixto García. For theater and dance, it's the historic **Casino Español** (1889) around the corner.

Getting There & Away

Competition for public transport out of Gibara is fierce, so be early for the one scheduled truck at 5:10am (one peso). Colectivos are more frequent (20 pesos). The bus station is a kilometer out on the road to Holguín.

The road from the junction at Floro Pérez is hell at first, but improves just outside Rafael Freyre. There's an Oro Negro gas station at the entrance to town.

RAFAEL FREYRE TO GUARDALAVACA

The stretch between Rafael Freyre (Santa Lucía on some maps) and Guardalavaca is developing fast. **Campismo Silla de Gibara** (Map p325; ☎ 42 15 86; per person US$7.50; ✗) sits on the hillside between Floro Pérez and Rafael Freyre, 35km southeast of Gibara via a rough road. It's 1.5km off the main road. There are 42 rooms sleeping two, four or six people, but come for the views, not the comfort. A cave is a 1.5km hike up the hill and horses are for rent. Reservations are available from the **Reservaciones de Campismo** (Map p318; ☎ 42 28 81; Mártires No 87 at Frexes) in Holguín.

Villa Don Lino (Map p325; Cubanacán; ☎ 2-0443; per person US$50; ✗) is 8.5km north of Rafael Freyre off a spur road. Mostly couples stay in the 36 single-story *cabañas* – with the small white beach, it makes a romantic retreat. This is a good option for people who want to play, but not stay, at Guardalavaca.

Three kilometers west of Don Lino is Playa Blanca; Columbus landed somewhere near here in 1492, as a monument on adjacent Cayo Bariay proclaims.

Resorts have started colonizing **Playa Pesquero**, a small but sweet 1km beach accessible via a spur road just before the Cuatro Palmas junction. The sand is golden, the water shallow and the crowds rolling in. Travel and hotel brochures call this beach 'Costa Verde.' At the time of writing, you could choose from the lovely **LTI Costa Verde Resort** (Map p325; ☎ 3-0510/11/12; www.lti.de; s/d low season US$130/180, high season US$170/240) and the hyperenthusiastic **SuperClubs Breezes Costa Verde** (Map p325; ☎ 3-0520/1/2; www.superclubscuba.net; s/d from US$121). Both places have the usual all-inclusive amenities. Nonguests can rent horses at LTI.

GUARDALAVACA

Guardalavaca is a string of mega-resorts draped along a 3km-long beach 54km northeast of Holguín. The powdery sand, warm water, colorful scuba sites and relaxing all-inclusive treatment have visitors flocking to this bit of coast. Along with all the usual water sports, whizzing along on a moped or peddling a bicycle to interesting places nearby are other possibilities here.

That's the good part. The bad part is that Guardalavaca is a tourist-resort ghetto: there's no town (workers live in microbrigade housing (dwellings, usually large apartment blocks, built by small armies of workers following the triumph of the revolution) on the outskirts or are bused in from elsewhere) and no local color except for the wristband identifying the resort in which you're staying. If this turns you off, but you still want some beach time, consider staying in a casa particular in Banes (p329) or at one of the 'alternative' places on Bahía de Naranjo (p327).Guardalavaca *is* beautiful and absorbs crowds well, so don't reject it out of hand. Access to a nice part of the public beach is via the steps alongside Disco Club la Roca.

No-one is entirely sure where the name Guardalavaca ('guard the cow') comes from but it sounds like what some resort lifeguards do.

Information

EMERGENCY
Asistur (Map p326; ☎ 3-0148; in Centro Comercial Guardalavaca; ☾ 8:30am-5pm Mon-Fri, 8:30am-noon Sat)

IMMIGRATION
Cubanacán (Map p326; ☎ 3-0226/7; behind Club Amigo Atlántico y Bungalows) Head here for visa extensions; there's also an immigration office in Banes (p329).

MEDICAL SERVICES
Clínica Internacional (Map p326; ☎ 3-0291; opposite Club Amigo Atlántico y Bungalows) A 24-hour pharmacy is here.

MONEY
Euros are accepted in all the Guardalavaca, Playa Esmeralda and Pesquero resorts.
Banco Financiero Internacional (Map p326; ☎ 3-0272; Centro Comercial Guardalavaca) Just west of Club Amigo Atlántico y Bungalows.

Banco de Crédito y Comercio (Map p326; ☎ 3-0223; behind Hotel Guardalavaca near the beach; ☾ 8am-noon, 1:30-3pm Mon-Fri)

PHOTOGRAPHY
Photo Service (Map p326; Centro Comercial Los Flamboyanes on the inland road)

TRAVEL AGENCIES
Cubatur (Map p326; ☎ 3-0171; fax 3-0170, in bungalow complex opposite the Centro Comercial Guardalavaca; ☾ 8am-4pm)
Ecotur (Map p326; ☎ 3-0155; Villa Cabañas No 8) Land/sea adventure tours.
Havanatur (Map p326; ☎ 3-0260; in Centro Comercial Los Flamboyanes)
Sol y Son Travel Agency (Map p326; ☎ 3-0417; at Club Amigo Atlántico y Bungalows; ☾ 8am-noon Mon-Tue & Thu-Fri) Books Cubana de Aviación flights out of Holguín.

Sights & Activities
You can arrange **horseback riding** at Rancho Naranjo next to the helicopter landing area near Meliá Rio de Mares and at the horseback riding center opposite Hotel Guardalavaca. It costs US$4 an hour, or US$10.50

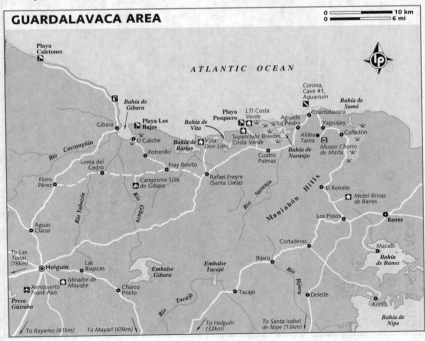

GUARDALAVACA AREA

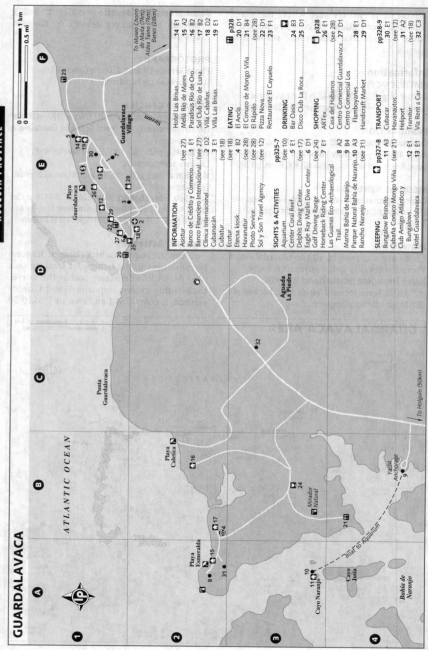

GUARDALAVACA

ATLANTIC OCEAN

Playa Esmeralda

Playa Caletica

Ponta Guardalavaca

Mirador Natural

Playa Guardalavaca

Guardalavaca Village

Stream

To Museo Chorro de Maíta (7km); Aldea Taíno (7km); Banes (28km)

Aguada La Piedra

To Holguín (50km)

boat to Aquarium

Yacht Anchorage

Cayo Naranjo

Cayo JuJía

Bahía de Naranjo

0   1 km
0   0.5 mi

for three hours (including guide), which is enough time to visit the Museo Chorro de Maita (see below). You can rent **mopeds** at all the hotels for US$8/18/24/30 for one/three/five hours/one day. Most all-inclusive packages include bicycle use.

Paracaidismo Guardalavaca (☎ 3-0780, 3-0695; cubasol@guard.gvc.cyt.cu) offers tandem **skydiving** for US$150 per person, including hotel transfer (video of your jump is US$45 extra). You can also soar with them in zodiac-hang glider rigs called ultralights for US$45. Jumps can be arranged at all the hotels.

BAHÍA DE NARANJO

The **Parque Natural Bahía de Naranjo** (Map p326), 4km southwest of Playa Esmeralda and about 8km from the main Guardalavaca strip, is an island complex designed to keep the resort crowds entertained. The **aquarium** (Map p326; ☎ 3-0132; adult/child US$26/13; ☼ 9am-9pm) is on a tiny island in the bay and your entry fee includes a zippy boat tour of the islands included in the complex, and a sea lion and dolphin show (noon daily). For an extra US$26/52, you can swim with the dolphins for 20 minutes. All of Guardalavaca's (and Playa Esmeralda's) hotel tour desks sell aquarium excursions. Boats to the aquarium leave from the Marina Bahía de Naranjo.

On the spur road to the Playa Esmeralda resorts is a **driving range** (Map p326; 60/100 balls US$4/6; ☼ 8am-7pm) and the small thatched **Bar Oasis** (Map p326; ☼ 7am-11pm) where moped-riding swarms descend for icy Cristales. At the end of the road you come to the self-guided **Las Guanas Eco-Archaeological Trail** (Map p326; admission US$6; ☼ 8am-4:30pm). This 1km marked trail (with several more kilometers of bushwhacking on fire trails leading to a picturesque bluff with a lighthouse) boasts 14 endemic plant species and makes a good detour if you're willing to pay the whopping US$6 fee.

MUSEO CHORRO DE MAITA

This archaeological site-based **museum** (Map p325; ☎ 3-0421; admission US$1; ☼ 9am-5pm Tue-Sat, 9am-1pm Sun) protects the remains of an excavated Indian village, including entire human skeletons and the bones of the barkless dog (our favorite kind). Across from the museum is a reconstructed **Aldea**

Taína (Taíno village; admission US$2), which is well done for something as cheesy as a replicated indigenous village.

SCUBA DIVING

The reef is 200m out and there are 32 dive sites, most accessed by boat. There are caves, wrecks, walls and healthy coral and giant sponges, plus lots of colorful fish. The following outfits offer open water certification courses for US$350, resort courses for US$50 and dives for US$35, with discounts for multiple dives.

Center Coral Reef (Map p326; ☎ 3-0774; beside Hotel Las Brisas) Ninety-minute snorkeling tours in glass-bottomed boat (adult/child US$34/24) at 9am and 2:30pm. Also has deep-sea fishing for US$270 for up to six passengers, and 'challenge tour' jeep-zodiac combo including lunch and horseback riding (adult/child US$74/63).

Eagle Ray Marlin Dive Center (Map p326; Cubanacán Náutica; ☎ 3-0316; on the beach behind Disco Club La Roca) Identical programme and prices to Center Coral Reef.

Delphis Diving Center (Map p326; at Sol Club Río de Luna) Offers scuba diving and certification courses for guests of the three Grupo Sol Meliá resorts at Playa Esmeralda.

Sleeping

There are no casas particulares here, as renting rooms is banned. Banes, 33km to the southeast, is the closest town with private rooms.

GUARDALAVACA

Villa Cabañas (Map p326; ☎ 3-0144; behind the Clínica Internacional; cabin US$25; ☒) As the least expensive place in Guardalavaca, the 20 cabins here are booked solid. They're good value, sleeping three comfortably and with a kitchen to boot. Some of the adjacent units have been converted into offices, and the reception desk is a bit hard to find. Ask for the *carpeta* in the middle of the cluster of buildings.

Club Amigo Atlántico y Bungalows (Map p326; Cubanacán; ☎ 3-0121; www.cubanacan.cu; s/d high season US$92/144; P ☒ ▢ ▨) This sprawler of a resort has 370 rooms with 'Miami retirement home' decor, but don't let it fool you: this place caters to activity-oriented tourists. The walk-in prices are high, but you can get reasonable package deals here. The children's programme makes this a good choice for families. Bungalows are some 300m from the beach. Most guests here are on packages from UK and Canada.

Brisas Guardalavaca Hotel (Map p326; Cubanacán; ☎ 3-0218; fax 3-0162; s/d/tr all-inclusive from US$95/134/195; ⓟ ⌧ ▣ ▨) This über-resort comprised of the Villa las Brisas and Hotel las Brisas at the eastern end of the beach is package-tour paradise. Though the beach is smallish, together these are probably Guardalavaca's finest hotels, with big, clean rooms, good service and removed location. Facilities include Disco La Dolce Vita, floodlit tennis courts, and water sports, including scuba diving. This is a good choice for families, as a free Kids Kamp, for children ages two to 11, is available daily.

PLAYA ESMERALDA

Spain's Grupo Sol Meliá hotel chain manages three adjacent resorts on Playa Esmeralda, 6km southwest of Guardalavaca and 2km off the main highway. With its iridescent jade waters, craggy coves and sheltered setting, this beach has a private paradise feel missing at Guardalavaca. You can drool over these resorts at www.solmeliacuba.com (look for online deals). Reserve these resorts through Havanatur or San Cristóbal Agencia de Viajes in Havana (p85) for cheaper rates than the rack rates shown here.

Paradisus Río de Oro (Map p326; Gaviota; ☎ 3-0090; fax 3-0095; s/d low season US$240/300, high season US$270/340; ⓟ ⌧ ▣ ▨) The five stars are glowing at this 292-room resort that seems much smaller thanks to a clever layout, sterling service and landscape screening. Swing in a hammock overlooking the beach or get a massage in a cliffside hut. There's even a Japanese restaurant floating on a koi pond. Garden villas with private pools cost US$900.

Sol Río Luna Mares Resort (Gaviota; s/d low season US$150/200, high season US$165/240; ⓟ ⌧ ▣ ▨) is made up of the **Sol Club Río de Luna** (Map p326; ☎ 3-0030; fax 3-0035), with 222 rooms in a series of two- and three-story buildings and the **Meliá Río de Mares** (Map p326; ☎ 3-0060; fax 3-0065), which is closer to the beach and has a better overall layout. Nonguests are allowed in to the restaurants, bars, shops and activity centers here.

Marina Bahía de Naranjo (Map p326; ☎ 3-0132), 4km southwest of Playa Esmeralda, rents the whimsical Bungalow Birancito, a little two-bedroom cabin on stilts in the middle of the bay for US$75 per room; meals can

be bundled with the room. Access is by boat. These folks also rent a more rustic cabin called Cabaña Conuco Mongo Viña for US$20 that sleeps three. It has a kitchen, bath and dining/living area.

Eating

Pizza Nova (Map p326; ☎ 3-0137; beside Centro Comercial Guardalavaca; ☯ 10am-11pm) Good pizzas, fresh salads and lasagna: this is just what Guardalavaca needed. Dinner with wine won't cost you more than US$15 and budget types can get away for US$6 or so.

Restaurante El Cayuelo (Map p326; ☎ 3-0736; on the beach 800m east of Hotel Las Brisas; ☯ 10am-11pm) Seafood is the house specialty here and a full lobster meal is less than US$16. A nice break from the resorts.

Other recommendations:
El Ancla (Map p326; ☎ 3-0381; ☯ 11am-11pm) Seafood and beautiful coastal setting. Will set you back US$8 for a fish filet.
El Conuco de Mongo Viña (Map p326; ☯ 9am-4pm; 3-course meals US$8) On the Bahía de Naranjo, a 2km walk from the Sol Meliá trio.
El Rápido (Map p326; in the Centro Comercial Los Flamboyanes; ☯ 24hr) The usual pizzas (US$1) and chicken (US$2) or sandwiches.

Entertainment

Disco Club La Roca (Map p326; ☎ 3-0167; admission US$1; ☯ 9:30pm-3am) This disco just west of the Centro Comercial Guardalavaca has a nice open-air locale overlooking the beach. It also opens from 1pm to 5pm with video games, karaoke and other free entertainment.

There's a pool table (US$1) and video games at **El Rápido** (see above).

Shopping

There's a small **handicraft market** next to Club Amigo Atlántico y Bungalows. **ARTex**, behind Hotel Guardalavaca, has a good selection of compact discs. The **Casa del Habanos** in the Centro Comercial Los Flamboyanes has all the smoke you could want.

Getting There & Away

Viajes Fantásticos, at Club Amigo Atlántico y Bungalows and tour desks at most of the other hotels, sell one-way transfers (US$10) to Holguín when space is available. A taxi from Guardalavaca to Holguín will cost around US$36 one way for the car; the older Cuba Taxi vehicles, parked near the

Centro Comercial Guardalavaca, charge US$25 for the same. For radio taxis, call **TaxiOK** (☎ 3-0243) or **Transgaviota** (☎ 3-0966).

Getting Around

Drivers of the various hotel employee buses have strict orders not to carry tourists, and trying to use public transportation is hopeless. Private taxis are banned, but you might hitch a ride with other tourists (for information on the risks associated with hitching see p433). Horse carriages (coches de caballo) run between Playas Esmeralda and Guardalavaca (US$5) and Playa Esmeralda and Bahía de Naranjo (US$3). You can also charter them for US$5 per hour.

All the rental agencies have offices in Guardalavaca and rent mopeds for US$30 per day:

Cubacar btwn Hotel Guardalavaca & Villa Las Brisas (Map p326; ☎ 3-0389); at the Club Amigo Atlántico y Bungalows (Map p326; ☎ 3-0180)

Havanautos (Map p326; ☎ 3-0120; at Club Amigo Atlántico y Bungalows)

Transtur (Map p326; ☎ 3-0134; Villas Cabañas No 6)

Vía Rent a Car Aguada La Piedra (Map p326; ☎ 3-0996); Melía Rio de Mares (Map p326)

A 24-hour Servi-Cupet station is between Guardalavaca and Playa Esmeralda.

BANES

pop 44,983

The sugar town of Banes, just north of the Bahía de Banes, makes a perfect day trip from the Guardalavaca or Playa Esmeralda resorts. Founded in 1887, this effervescent town has cigar-smoking cronies slamming dominoes and moms carrying meter-long loaves of bread. In short, everything Cuban missing from the resorts. The 33km road southeast from Guardalavaca to Banes winds between bohíos and royal palms through the Maniabón Hills – a really beautiful trip. Come on a Sunday when the Cafe Cantante is hopping with live music (p330). Independent travelers wishing to romp or dive at Guardalavaca can find private rooms here.

Information

There's an **immigration** office on Av de Cárdenas No 314A if you need a visa extension. Banes is one of those towns with no street signs and locals who don't know street names, so prepare to lose yourself.

Sights & Activities

If you're coming from the resorts, Banes' biggest attraction may be the street life a stroll through town provides.

On October 12, 1948, Fidel Castro Ruz and Birta Díaz Balart were married in the **Iglesia de Nuestra Señora de la Caridad** on Parque Martí in the center of Banes. (After their divorce in 1954, Birta remarried and moved to Spain, but through their only child, Fidelito, Fidel has several grandchildren.)

Banes is better known for the **Museo Indocubano Bani** (☎ 8-2487; General Marrero No 305 at Av José Martí; admission without/with guide US$1/2; ⏰ 9am-5pm Tue-Sat, 8am-noon & 7-9pm Sun). The museum's small but rich collection of Indian artifacts is one of the best in Cuba. Don't miss the tiny golden fertility idol unearthed near Banes (one of only 20 gold artifacts ever found in Cuba).

Railway junkies shouldn't miss **steam locomotive** No 964 (nicknamed 'El Panchito'), built at the HK Porter Locomotive Works in Pittsburgh, Pennsylvania, in 1888, now on display on Calle Tráfico, 400m east of the bus station. **Playa de Morales**, 13km east of Banes along the paved continuation of Tráfico, is a fishing village where you can while away an afternoon dining with locals and watching the men mend their nets. It's a nice excursion if you have transport.

Sleeping

OUTSIDE TOWN

Motel Oasis (☎ 8-3425; s/d US$10/13), 2km west of town on the main road to Guardalavaca and Holguín, has 28 rooms catering to Cubans, though foreigners are welcome. There's a cabaret, restaurant and bar here. Better located on a pretty patch of beach is **Campismo Puerto Rico Libre**, (☎ 9-6918; per

---

CASAS PARTICULARES – BANES

There are no hotels in town proper, but Banes has some private rooms.

El Castillito (☎ 8-3425; Carretera de Veguita No 3718; r US$20; ✗) Signposted, friendly place, meals.

Julio Dante (☎ 8-3243/8-3643; Robles No 85A btwn Calles 7 & 8; r US$20; ✗) Spotless rooms and linen, good meals.

Sergio Aguilera (☎ 8-2412; Calle Iglesias No 4089, Reparto Nicaragua; r US$20; ✗) Family atmosphere, meals.

person US$3.50) north of Playa de Morales, 13km from Banes. The basic cabins line the rocky shore, there's a restaurant, and people in the nearby fishing villages will happily cook seafood meals for you. Ask about the caves (about 1km from the Campismo), and bring insect repellent.

Motel Brisas de Banes (Map p325; cabin US$30) on a hill overlooking a reservoir 10km northwest of Banes, off the road to Guardalavaca, has eight cabins, each sleeping two people. There are nice views – a pleasant out of the way place for a beer.

Eating & Drinking
Readers like **Restaurant Roberto** (General Marero No 710; ⏰ 11am-11pm) for its attentive service and well-prepared food. Across the street is yet another reliable **La Vicaria** (⏰ 24hr), with pasta, burgers and señor Gordon Bleu, plus eggs and coffee for breakfast (everything is less than US$4). **Paladar Las Delicias** (☎ 8-2638; Augusto Blanca No 1107), off Parque Céspedes, has a printed menu and good reputation.

Several peso bars around town are jumping with atmosphere and cheap hooch, including **Coctelera** (General Marrero No 327A) and the super popular **Doña Yulla** next door.

Or head down the street to **Las 400 Rosas**, an outdoor dollar place selling sodas, beer and snacks next to the Museo Indocubano Bani.

Entertainment
The gregarious, music-filled patio of **Cafe Cantante** (General Marrero No 320) is the top spot in Banes. During the day, you'll hear the municipal band honking through rehearsal; nights brings disco or *son* septets. Sundays afternoons feature traditional *trova* (⏰ 2pm to 7pm) while Sunday nights are when the really special stuff happens like concerts by visiting jazz musicians (who often gig at Guardalavaca, but jam in Banes). Next door the **Casa de Cultura** (☎ 8-2111; General Marrero No 320), housed in the former Casino Español (1926), has a regular Sunday *trova* matinee at 3pm and Saturday *peña del Rap* (rap music session) at 9pm.

On weekends, the **Discoteca Río Azul** on Parque Martí is where Banes comes to party.

Getting There & Away
From the bus station at the corner of Tráfico and Los Ángeles, one daily morning bus goes to Holguín (72km), supposedly.

An afternoon bus connects with the train to Havana. Trucks leave Banes for Holguín more frequently.

BIRÁN
Fidel Castro Ruz was born on August 13, 1926, at **Finca Las Manacas** (aka 'Casa de Fidel') near the village of Birán, south of Cueto. The compound has been closed to visitors in the past, but there are plans to open it as a museum.

To get to there, take the southern turn-off 7km west of Cueto, and drive 7km south to the Central Loynaz Hechevarría sugar mill at Marcané. From there a road runs 8km east to Birán, from which it's another 3km northeast to Las Manacas. You'll first see the thatched huts of the Haitian laborers, the cockfighting ring, and the several large red-roofed wooden houses where the Castro family lived. The graves of Fidel's parents, Ángel Castro and Lina Ruz, are to the right of the entrance gate, where you'll be met by a guard.

MAYARÍ
pop 80,200
Not much more than a pit and potty stop between Holguín and Moa, Mayarí has little to offer the average tourist, although **Parque Natural La Mensura**, 30km south, has waterfalls and forests for green diversion. Cueto is 30km west and Cayo Saetía 37km northeast. There's a Servi-Cupet gas station in Mayarí.

Motel Bitiri (☎ 5-2589; r US$8-25; 🅿️), in the center of Mayarí, a block from the Servi-Cupet gas station, is a basic motel with 21 rooms. Most of the guests are Cuban, but foreigners are accepted and it's a viable option if you can't push on to Holguín.

The **Villa Pinares del Mayarí** (Map pp314-15; Gaviota; ☎ 5-3308; fax 3-0926; s/d rooms US$25/36, cabins US$30/40; 🅿️) stands at 600m elevation between the Altiplanicie de Nipe and Sierra del Cristal, 30km south of Mayarí on a rough dirt road. This mountain hideaway is in one of Cuba's largest pine forests and the two- and three-bedroom cabins (worth the extra US$5 over the rooms), with hot showers and comfortable beds, make a nice retreat.

There's also a large restaurant, bar, tennis court and horses for hire. The villa is within the Parque Natural La Mensura and offers hikes to El Guayabo waterfall and Loma de la Mensura (995m). You can arrange tours to Cayo Saetía (see below) from here. From Santiago de Cuba and Bayamo, the easiest access is via Mella.

EAST OF MAYARÍ

Villa Cayo Saetía (Gaviota; ☎ 9-6900; vsaetia@ip .etecsa.cu; s/d incl breakfast US$60/90; ✖) This is a wonderfully rustic but comfortable resort on a 42-sq-km island at the entrance to the Bahía de Nipe. The control post at the entrance to Cayo Saetía is 15km off the main highway, where a small bridge crosses to the island; then it's another 8km to the resort. Day-trippers are charged US$10 per person admission, which includes a welcome drink and the use of snorkeling gear. The buffet lunch costs another US$15. The *cayo* is remote and lovely, with beaches and coves to make you feel primal. In addition to the regular cabañas, there are other simpler cabins (s/d low season US$25/30, high season US$30/35). The big turn off is that many of the villa's clients come to shoot local birds or to hunt the wild boar, bulls, deer and antelopes that have been introduced on the island's plains. The beach is still terrific, if you can ignore the shots ringing out.

Campismo Río Cabonico (☎ 59 41 18; per person US$5) is at Pueblo Nuevo, 9km east of Levisa and 73km west of Moa, about 900m south of the main road. The 23 cabins with baths and fans on a low terrace beside the Río Cabonico (decent swimming) have four or six beds. Reservations can be made through the Reservaciones de Campismo in Holguín (p314).

MOA

pop 57, 484

Important economically and horrendous ecologically, this is a big, ugly mine at the foot of the verdant scarps of the Cuchillas de Moa. The dirty Ernesto Guevara nickel smelter dominates the eastern side of town, and a few kilometers down the road to

Baracoa are the three huge towers of the newer and cleaner Planta de Niquel Las Camariocas. Since 1990 Sherritt International Corporation of Toronto has invested tens of millions of dollars rehabilitating and expanding the Moa refining facilities, and the nickel is shipped to Alberta for further processing. Unless you're a Canadian mining technician, there's absolutely no reason to come here. It's one of the most desolate, polluted towns in Cuba. As the signs say: No pictures please, this is a strategic industry.

Sleeping

If you must, the **Hotel Miraflores** (Islazul; ☎ 6-6125; s/d low season US$20/29, high season US$23/35; Ⓟ ✖) is a modern four-story hotel on a hillside on the western side of Moa, 5km west of the airport. The local Havanautos office is at this hotel, and there's a tourist taxi stand.

Getting There & Around

Moa's Orestes Acosta Airport is conveniently located beside the highway to Baracoa, just 3km east of downtown Moa. **Cubana** (☎ 6-7916) has flights to/from Havana on Thursday (US$118 one way, 816km, three hours).

The bus station is near the center of town, 3km east of the Hotel Miraflores. A daily bus leaves for Holguín (US$7, 172km) and another goes to Santiago de Cuba (US$7.50, 187km), but there's no bus to Baracoa (70km). You may be prevented from using the regular passenger trucks that leave the bus station for Holguín and Baracoa, as foreigners are officially prohibited. This means that there's no legal public transport except for hitching and tourist taxis between Moa and Baracoa. Taxi drivers will ask US$25 to Baracoa.

Havanautos (☎ 6-6683) has an office at the Hotel Miraflores. The Servi-Cupet gas station is at the entrance to Moa from Mayarí, not far from the Hotel Miraflores.

Granma Province

'How can I talk about the history of Cuba without talking about the history of Granma?' Fidel Castro once queried. The fact is he can't, because history-altering events always seem to spark here: in October 1868 Carlos Manuel de Céspedes launched the revolt that culminated in Cuban independence, and José Martí was shot here fighting for that independence. In December 1956 Castro and 81 rebels disembarked from the yacht *Granma* at Playa Las Coloradas, signaling the beginning of the armed insurgency against the Batista dictatorship, and shortly thereafter set up rebel headquarters at the Comandancia de la Plata, high in the Sierra Maestra of present-day Granma.

Today, 'La Plata' is open to visitors and is the jumping-off point for challenging hikes into the Gran Parque Nacional Sierra Maestra, one of Cuba's finest national parks. Where the Sierra Maestra slopes into the Caribbean near Cabo Cruz there's another park, called Parque Nacional Desembarco del Granma, which commemorates the 1956 rebel landing.

Granma boasts Río Cauto, Cuba's longest river, which stretches 343km from the Embalse Protesta de Baraguá in northern Santiago de Cuba Province to the Golfo de Guacanayabo. It's a monster, draining some 8969 sq km of eastern Cuba. The Cauto delta is mostly mangroves, but paddies on the fertile Cauto Plain produce a third of Cuba's rice. Granma also has extensive beef-cattle ranches around Bayamo and sugar fields south of Manzanillo. Coffee is grown in the Sierra Maestra foothills. Pico Bayamesa (1730m), due south of Bayamo, is Granma's highest peak (and Cuba's third highest).

GRANMA PROVINCE

HIGHLIGHTS

- **Historic Snapshot**

  Visit Parque Céspedes in Bayamo, the cradle of Cuban history (p338)

- **Trekking the Revolution**

  Set off from guerilla headquarters into Gran Parque Nacional Sierra Maestra (p341)

- **The Long View**

  From the valley to the ocean, admire the vista from historic La Demajagua (p344)

- **Go to the Light**

  See the lighthouse at Cabo Cruz in Parque Nacional Desembarco del Granma (p348)

- **Swim with the Fishes**

  Scuba dive the colorful reefs off Marea del Portillo (p349)

- TELEPHONE CODE: 23
- POPULATION: 835,218
- AREA: 8372 SQ KM

History

On October 10, 1868, in La Demajagua near Manzanillo, sugar-plantation owner Carlos Manuel de Céspedes called for the abolition of slavery and freed his own slaves by example, inciting planters in Oriente to take action against Spanish rule. Céspedes made the first move, leading troops against the Spanish at Yara (p341), 23km east of Manzanillo. After a bold beginning during which the rebels captured most of the eastern part of the island, their forces were neutralized by martial law and a defensive ditch the Spanish built that cut the country in half from Júcaro in the south to Morón in the north.

When a reactionary militia was formed in the west to support continued Spanish rule, the rebels met at Guáimaro in present-day Camagüey in April 1869. They passed a constitution emancipating the slaves and elected Céspedes as Cuba's first president. General Máximo Gómez advocated a more proactive strategy of pushing west, but it was rejected by the conservative council (a mistake rebels were careful not to repeat in the Second War of Independence, pushing ever west; a strategy successfully replicated in 1959). Céspedes was subsequently removed from office and killed in a Spanish ambush in October 1873. This First War of Independence dragged on for a decade (and is also known as the Ten Years War) until a peace treaty was signed at Zanjón.

In 1895, forces determined to win Cuba's independence again went to war, under the leadership of José Martí, Antonio Maceo and Máximo Gómez. This time they would be successful, but Martí, who had marshaled the determination and forces for war through his writing, organizing and fundraising, was killed just a month and a half after launching this Second War of Independence. Sniped off his horse at Dos Ríos on May 19, 1895, on the northwestern provincial border, Martí died, but his dream didn't. He's now Cuba's greatest martyr and hero; some believe his was a destined death.

Flash forward some 61 years to December 2, 1956, and Fidel Castro and 81 companions are disembarking from the *Granma* on the coast of Granma Province at Playa las Coloradas. Incidentally, the province was named after the boat (not the other way around), when Oriente Province was split into five provinces in 1975. The rebels were initially routed by Batista's troops, but escaped into the Sierra Maestra mountains, establishing headquarters at Comandancia de la Plata. From there they fought and coordinated the armed struggle, broadcasting their progress from Radio Rebelde, consolidating their support among sympathizers nationwide. After two years of harsh conditions, including tooth extractions without anesthesia and eating raw horse meat (only once, but that's enough we figure), the forces of the M-26-7 triumphed in 1959.

BAYAMO

☎ 23 / pop 143,844

In 1975 the city of Bayamo became the capital of Granma Province. It remains a surprisingly untourist place, though it's right on the Carretera Central between Holguín and Santiago de Cuba. The town's pleasant, relaxed atmosphere is refreshing, especially if you've been worn down by unsolicited attention elsewhere.

History

In November 1513, San Salvador de Bayamo became the second Cuban town (after Baracoa) to be founded by Diego Velázquez, and during the colonial era Bayamo was the

---

HIMNO NACIONAL	**NATIONAL ANTHEM**
Al combate corred, bayameses,	Run to battle, people of Bayamo,
que la Patria os contempla orgullosa.	For our country looks over you with pride.
No temáis una muerte gloriosa,	Fear not a glorious death,
que morir por la patria es vivir.	For to die for your country is to live.
En cadenas vivir es vivir,	To live in chains is to live
en afrenta y oprobio sumi do.	In insult and drowning shame.
Del clarín escuchad el sonido,	Listen to the bugle calling you
a las armas, valientes, corred.	To arms, courageous ones, run.
Perucho Figueredo, 1868	

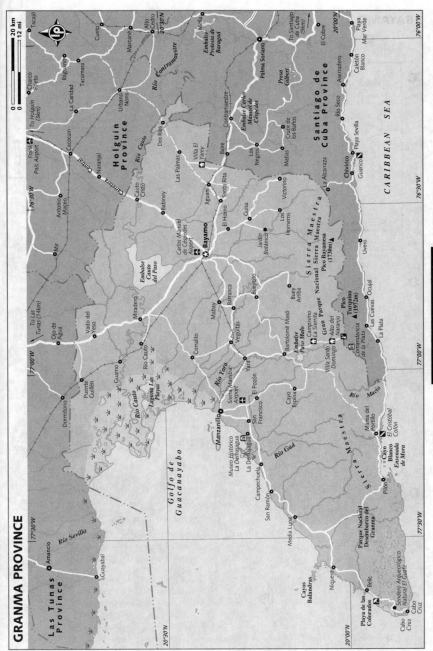

GRANMA PROVINCE

BAYAMO

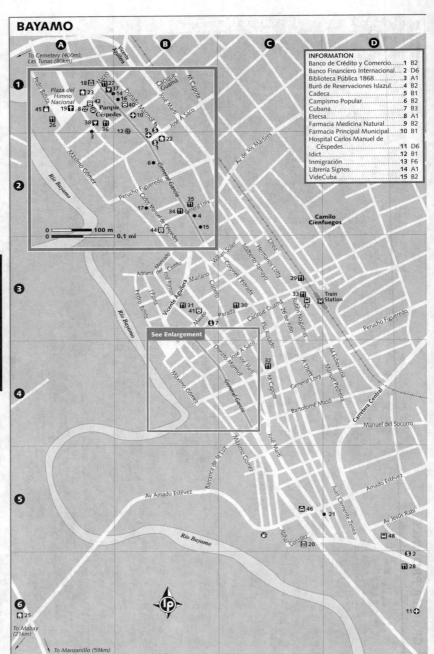

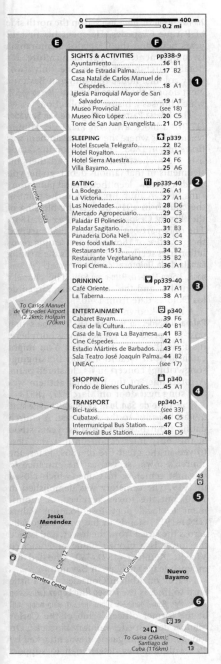

center of a rich ranching and cane-growing region. Bayamo has always been slightly ahead of its time: on October 20, 1868, the 10th day of the First War of Independence struggle, rebels under the command of Céspedes captured the city. The Cuban national anthem, composed in 1868 by Perucho Figueredo, begins with the words *Al combate corred, bayameses* ('Run to battle, people of Bayamo'; for the complete anthem, see p332). After the defeat of an ill-prepared rebel force by 3000 regular Spanish troops near the Río Cauto on January 12, 1869, the townspeople set their town on fire rather than see it fall intact to the enemy. The town was also badly damaged in 1895, during the Second War of Independence, though you wouldn't know it from the sparkling Bayamo you see today.

Orientation

Bayamo turns on Parque Céspedes, which is also known as Plaza de la Revolución for its many impressive monuments to the wars of independence. The train station is located to the east and the bus station to the southeast, about 2km apart. General García (also known as El Bulevar), a bustling pedestrian shopping mall, leads from Parque Céspedes to Bartolomé Masó. Don't miss the squished paint tubes in front of the art school at General Lora. Many of the facilities for tourists (including the bus station, Servi-Cupet gas station and main hotel) are along the Carretera Central, southeast of town.

Information

AIRLINE OFFICES

Cubana (☎ 42 39 16; Martí No 58 at Parada; ❧ 8am-noon & 2-4pm Mon, Wed & Fri, 2-4pm Tue & Thu)

BOOKSHOPS

Librería Signos (General García No 9) On the east side of Parque Céspedes.

IMMIGRATION

Inmigración (Carretera Central Km 2; ❧ 9am-noon & 1:30-4pm Tue & Thu-Fri) In a big complex 200m south of the Hotel Sierra Maestra.

INTERNET ACCESS

Etecsa (Céspedes & Maceo; ❧ 9am-10pm) There's one machine available.
Idict (General García; US$0.10/min; ❧ 8am-8pm Mon-Fri, 8am-noon Sat) Two machines are available.

LIBRARIES

Biblioteca Pública 1868 (Céspedes No 52; ☿ 9am-6pm Mon-Sat)

MEDICAL SERVICES

Farmacia Medicina Natural (General García & Saco)

Farmacia Principal Municipal (General García No 53; ☿ 24hr)

Hospital Carlos Manuel de Céspedes (☎ 42 50 12; Carretera Central Km1)

MONEY

Banco de Crédito y Comercio (General García & Saco; ☿ 8am-3pm Mon-Fri, 8-10am Sat)

Banco Financiero Internacional (☎ 42 73 60; Carretera Central Km 1) In a big white building near the bus terminal.

Cadeca (Saco No 101; ☿ 8:30am-noon, 12:30-5:30pm Mon-Sat, 8am-noon Sun)

PHOTOGRAPHY

VideCuba (General García No 225; ☿ 8am-10pm)

POST

Post Office (Maceo & Parque Céspedes; 8am-8pm Mon-Sat)

TELEPHONE

Etecsa (Céspedes & Maceo; ☿ 9am-10pm)

TRAVEL AGENCIES

Buró de Reservaciones Islazul (☎ 42 32 73; General García No 207; ☿ 8:30am-5pm Mon-Fri, 8am-noon Sat)

Campismo Popular (☎ 42 42 00; General García No 112) Books tours to La Sierrita and Las Coloradas; ask about transport to La Sierrita and tours into the Sierra Maestra.

Cubanacán (☎ 42 79 70; Hotel Sierra Maestra) Arranges hikes to Sierra Maestra (per person two/three days US$40/59), El Saltón waterfall near Marea del Portillo (per person US$35) and the Tropicana in Santiago de Cuba (per person US$40).

Sights

Parque Céspedes is all grand monuments and big, shady trees. There's a bronze statue of Carlos Manuel de Céspedes, hero of the First War of Independence, and a marble bust of Perucho Figueredo, with the words of the Cuban national anthem. Marble benches and friendly *bayameses* make this a nice place to linger. In 1868 Céspedes proclaimed Cuba's independence in front of the **Ayuntamiento** on the east side of the square.

On April 18, 1819, Céspedes was born in the **Casa Natal de Carlos Manuel de Céspedes** (Maceo No 57; admission US$1; ☿ 9am-5pm Tue-Fri, 9am-

2pm & 8-10pm Sat, 10am-1pm Sun) on the north side of Parque Céspedes. He spent his first 12 years here, and the Céspedes memorabilia is complemented by period furniture. It's notable architecturally as the only two-story colonial house remaining in Bayamo. Next door is the **Museo Provincial** (Maceo No 55), which houses a historical collection.

The **Iglesia Parroquial Mayor de San Salvador** (1740), a block away on Plaza del Himno Nacional, is where the national anthem was first sung, in 1868. The plaque on the façade lists the orchestra members and their instruments in that famous debut, giving you an idea of how deep the cultural patrimony runs here. A mural painted at the front of the church in 1919 depicts the blessing of the flag by Céspedes on October 20, 1868. The only part of the building that survived the great fire of 1869, when retreating revolutionaries set fire to the town, is the striking **Capilla de la Dolorosa** (donations accepted; ☿ 9am-noon, 3-5pm Mon-Fri, 9am-noon Sat). The chapel's main altar and the statue of the Virgen de los Dolores date from 1740.

A lesser-known sight is the **Casa de Estrada Palma** (Céspedes No 158). In 1835 Cuba's first post-independence president was born here; it's now the seat of UNEAC. You might catch a *trova* (traditional poetic singing/ songwriting) concert in its cloistered patio. A forerunner of the national anthem was first sung next door on March 27, 1851.

The **Torre de San Juan Evangelista** (José Martí & Amado Estévez) is to the southeast. A church dating from Bayamo's earliest years stood at this busy intersection until it was destroyed in the great fire of 1869. Later, the church's tower served as the entrance to the first cemetery in Cuba, which closed in 1919. The cemetery was demolished in 1940, but the tower survived. A monument to local poet José Joaquín Palma (1844–1911) stands in the park diagonally across the street from the tower, and beside the tower is a bronze statue of Francisco Vicente Aguilera (1821–77), who led the independence struggle in Bayamo.

Nearby on Abihail González, but a little hard to find, is the **Museo Ñico López** (admission US$1; ☿ 8am-noon, 2-5:30pm Tue-Sat, 9am-noon Sun) in the former officers' club of the Carlos Manuel de Céspedes military barracks. On July 26, 1953, this garrison was attacked by 25 revolutionaries determined to support the assault on the Moncada Barracks in Santiago de Cuba by preventing reinforcements from being sent. Ñico López, who led the Bayamo attack, escaped to Guatemala, where he met Ernesto 'Che' Guevara. It was López who introduced Guevara to Fidel Castro; López was killed shortly after the *Granma* landed in 1956.

Sleeping

Hotel Escuela Telégrafo (☎ 42 55 10; Saco No 108, cnr Donato Marmol; s/d US$15/20; 🔀) Glistening after a major renovation, this simple 14-room hotel is clean and comfortable. Rooms have TV, phone and little balconies overlooking the street; the restaurant is efficient and reasonable. There's no hot water, but the friendly staff will heat a bucketful for you, authentic Cuban-style.

Hotel Royalton (Islazul; ☎ 42 22 90, 42 22 24; Maceo No 53; s/d low season US$18/24, high US$28/30; 🔀) Blending in with the colonial buildings on Parque Céspedes, this hotel is a solid choice in the city center. It doesn't see much traffic and a recent renovation ensures things are in good working order. You can people-watch over cocktails on the attractive sidewalk terrace, and there's a broad, breezy lobby and a rooftop terrace.

Hotel Sierra Maestra (Islazul; ☎ 42 79 70; s/d low season US$30/35, high US$36/44; 🅿 🔀 🕮) Inconveniently situated 3km southeast on the Carretera Central toward Santiago de Cuba, this 204-room hotel is not as inviting as the previous two options. Still, there are helpful services, including a post office, infirmary and Cubanacán tourism desk; big groups undoubtedly stay here.

Villa Bayamo (Islazul; ☎ 42 31 02; r US$14; 🅿 🔀 🕮) A bargain place 3km southwest of the town center on the road to Manzanillo, this motel is a good choice if you want to lie around a pool while going easy on your wallet. Locals know this place as 'Casa Central' and 'Hotel XXX Aniversario.'

Casas particulares are starting to pop up in Bayamo; see the boxed text above.

Eating & Drinking

Paladar Sagitario (Marmol No 107 btwn Maceo & Vincente Aguilera; 🕒 noon-11:45pm) is super popular for the filling meals (US$5 to US$7) served in its open courtyard. A better and more affordable bet is **Paladar El Polinesio** (Parada No 125, btwn Pio Rosado & Cisnero). Unlike at Sagitario,

---

here you won't be pestered by *jineteros* (male touts who hustle tourists).

The **restaurant** at the Hotel Royalton (Maceo No 53; 🕒 7:30am-10pm) is Bayamo's 'upmarket' spot, serving *comina Cubana* (traditional Cuban food) on its patio.

Despite the sign, you won't find shrimp at **La Victoria** (☎ 42 25 31; General García & Maceo), on the northeastern corner of Parque Céspedes. However, there are pork, chicken and even beef dishes at this atmospheric state-run place, where US$4 will get you a feed. **Restaurante 1513** (General García No 176 at General Lora; 🕒 sittings at noon, 6pm & 8pm Tue-Sun) is a cheap local favorite.

If staff arrive punctually, a good breakfast option is **Restaurante Vegetariano** (General García No 173; 🕒 7-9am, noon-2:30pm & 6-9pm) in *moneda nacional* (Cuban pesos).

La Bodega (Plaza del Himno Nacional No 34), opposite the Iglesia Parroquial Mayor, has a rear terrace with river views. **Tropi Crema** (southwest cnr of Parque Céspedes; 🕒 10am-10pm) is the place for peso ice cream. **Café Oriente** (General García) is a coffee and rum-shot counter on the northeastern side of Parque Céspedes.

The **mercado agropecuario** (Línea) is in front of the train station. There are many peso food stalls along here also. The giant **Las Novedades** (Carretera Central Km 1; 🕒 9am-6pm Mon-Sat, 9am-noon Sun), between Servi-Cupet and the bus station, has a decent selection of groceries (stock up here before hiking in the Sierra Maestra). For bread, it's **Panadería Doña Neli** (Capote & Perucho Figueredo; 🕒 8am-9pm).

Drinks on the rooftop or sidewalk terraces of the Hotel Royalton are always a good bet. For something grittier, try **La Taberna** (Céspedes No 65), a dark, second-floor saloon with faux stained-glass; it's tucked away behind Tropi Crema.

Entertainment

You can while away a Saturday afternoon at the *tarde de bolero* (Bolero afternoon) on the flowery patio of **UNEAC** (Céspedes No 158; admission free; ◷ from 4pm) before making your way to Máximo Gomez for the 'noche Cubana' **street fair** (◷ Saturday 8pm).

The **Casa de la Trova La Bayamesa** (Maceo at Martí; admission US$1; ◷ from 9pm) is Bayamo's *trova* hot-spot, and concerts sometimes also take place at the **Casa de la Cultura** (☎ 42 59 17; General García No 15), on the east side of Parque Céspedes.

In a stylish old church, the **Sala Teatro José Joaquín Palma** (Céspedes No 164) presents theater on Friday, Saturday and Sunday nights, while the Teatro Guiñol, also here, hosts children's theater on Saturday and Sunday mornings.

Cabaret Bayam (☎ 42 51 11; Carretera Central Km 2; ◷ from 9pm Fri-Sun), opposite the Hotel Sierra Maestra, has shows and dancing. **Disco Bayamesa** (Carretera Central), in the Hotel Sierra Maestra, is Bayamo's dollar disco.

Cine Céspedes (☎ 42 42 67; admission one peso) is on the western side of Parque Céspedes, next to the post office. It could be screening anything – from Cuban animated or dramatic features to the latest flick from Brazil or a Hollywood blockbuster.

From October to April, ask about baseball games at the **Estadio Mártires de Barbados** (Av Grandma), about 2km northwest of Hotel Sierra Maestra.

Shopping

Fondo de Bienes Culturales (Plaza del Himno Nacional No 20) isn't bad for handicrafts.

Getting There & Away

AIR

Bayamo's **Carlos Manuel de Céspedes Airport** (airport code BYM; ☎ 42 75 06) is 4km northeast of town, on the road to Holguín. **Cubana** (☎ 42 36 95) flies to Bayamo from Havana twice a week (US$98 one way, 744km, two hours). There are no international flights to or from Bayamo.

BUS & TRUCK

The **provincial bus station** (Carretera Central at Av Jesús Rabí) has Astro buses three times daily to Santiago de Cuba (US$5; 117km; 9:20am, 6:20pm, 11:20pm), but only one bus a day goes to Holguín (US$2.50, 71km) and Havana (US$30, 744km, 12 hours), leaving at 8pm.

Víazul has two daily buses to Santiago de Cuba (US$7; 117km; 4:45am, 9:25am), and there's a daily bus to Trinidad (US$26, 464km, 7:45pm). The service to Havana (US$44; 744km; 10:50am, 5:20pm, 9:35pm) also stops at Holguín (US$5, 71km), Las Tunas (US$6, 82km), Camagüey (US$12, 210km), Ciego de Ávila (US$17, 318km), Sancti Spíritus (US$21, 394km) and Santa Clara (US$26, 473km).

Passenger trucks leave from an adjacent terminal for Santiago de Cuba (seven pesos), Holguín (three pesos), Manzanillo (three pesos) and Pilón (five pesos). You may be able to get a truck from here to Bartolomé Masó, as close as you can get on public transport to the Sierra Maestra trailhead. Ask which line of people inside the terminal is waiting for the truck you want, then get in line. The trucks leave when full and you pay as you board.

The **intermunicipal bus station** (Saco & Línea) opposite the train station receives mostly local buses of little use to travelers. However, trucks to Las Tunas (four pesos) and Guisa (one peso) leave from here. You might also wrangle space in a collective taxi to Manzanillo (16 pesos), Pilón (41 pesos), Niquero (37 pesos), Holguín (20 pesos), Santiago de Cuba (35 pesos) or Las Tunas (21 pesos) from here.

TRAIN

The **train station** (☎ 42 49 55; Saco & Línea), 1km east of the center, has trains to the following destinations.

destination	cost (one way)	distance	departure time
Camagüey	US$5.75	210km	5:20am, alternate days
Havana	US$26	744km	7:40pm, alternate days
Manzanillo	US$1.75	50km	6:07am, 4:12pm, daily
Santiago de Cuba	US$4	117km	4pm, alternate days

Getting Around

Cubataxi (☎ 42 43 13) can supply a taxi to Bayamo airport for US$3, or to Aeropuerto Frank País in Holguín for US$22. A taxi to Villa Santo Domingo (setting-off point for the Alto del Naranjo trailhead for Sierra Maestra hikes) or Comandancia de la Plata will cost US$45 round trip. Tighter control on private taxis in Bayamo mean they're difficult to arrange. Even if you're successful, you can expect them to drop you some kilometers from Villa Santo Domingo to avoid detection.

The **Havanautos** office (☎ 42 73 75) is adjacent to Servi-Cupet, while **Transtur** (☎ 42 41 87) is at the Hotel Sierra Maestra.

The **Servi-Cupet** (Carretera Central) is between Hotel Sierra Maestra and the bus terminal as you arrive from Santiago de Cuba.

The main horse-cart route (one peso) runs between the train station and the hospital, via the bus station. The carts turn around on the corner behind Servi-Cupet.

Bici-taxis (5 to 10 pesos a ride) are useful for getting around town; negotiate a price before hopping on.

AROUND BAYAMO

For peace, quiet, butterflies and flowers, head to the **jardín botánico** (Carretera de Guisa Km 10; admission without/with guide US$1/2), about 16km outside Bayamo on the Guisa road. It's on very few itineraries, so you can have the 104 hectares of this tranquil garden to yourself. There are 74 types of palms, scores of cacti, blooming orchids and sections for endangered and medicinal plants. The guided tour (Spanish only) gains you access to greenhouses, notable for the showy ornamentals.

To get here, take the road to Santiago de Cuba for 6km and turn left at the signposted junction for Guisa. After 10km you'll see the botanical garden sign on the right. Trucks leave from the intermunicipal bus station in front of the train station (trips are one peso).

DOS RÍOS

At Dos Ríos, 52km northeast of Bayamo, almost in Holguín, a white obelisk overlooking the Río Cauto marks the spot where José Martí was shot and killed on May 19, 1895. It's 22km northeast of Jiguaní on the road to San Germán: take the unmarked road to the right after crossing the Cauto.

Back toward Jiguaní, 23km southwest of Dos Ríos, is **Villa El Yarey** (Cubanacán; ☎ 42 72 56; s/d/tr US$20/25/31), a relaxed, attractive hotel with 16 rooms on a ridge with an excellent view of the Sierra Maestra. To get here, go 4km west of Baire on the Carretera Central and then 6km north on a side road. It makes an ideal stop for anyone caught between Bayamo and Santiago de Cuba, or those taking the backdoor Bayamo–Holguín route.

YARA

pop 29,237

Yara is a bustling town in the middle of nowhere, 46km west of Bayamo and 23km east of Manzanillo. Large banana plantations and vast fields of sugarcane surround the town, and rice fields line the road to Manzanillo. After freeing his slaves at La Demajagua, near Manzanillo, Carlos Manuel de Céspedes and his followers arrived here on October 11, 1868 and fought their first battle against the Spanish, as recalled by a monument in Yara's main square. The town is famous for the *Grito de Yara* (Yara Declaration), in which Céspedes proclaimed Cuba's independence.

Just off the square is the **Museo Municipal** (Grito de Yara No 107; admission US$1; ☸ 8am-noon & 2-6pm Mon-Sat, 9am-noon Sun), which shows a local historical collection.

There's a Servi-Cupet here if you need a gas top-off.

GRAN PARQUE NACIONAL SIERRA MAESTRA

This spectacular national park begins 40km south of Yara, up a very steep 24km concrete road from Bartolomé Masó. The region was made famous as Fidel Castro's base of operations during the revolution, and there's a museum documenting those historic events. The mountainous park also has the country's highest peak, Pico Turquino, in neighboring Santiago de Cuba Province (for hikes starting there, see p386).

Sights & Activities

All trips into the park begin at the end of the near-vertical, corrugated concrete access road at **Alto del Naranjo**, 5km beyond the tourist accommodation at Villa Santo Domingo (an arduous two-hour walk, or you can hire a jeep for US$35 round trip).

There's a good view of the plains of Granma from this 950m-high lookout.

The **Comandancia de la Plata**, 3km west of Alto del Naranjo along a jungle trail, includes a museum, field hospital, command post, the original site of Radio Rebelde, and Castro's residence during the revolution. It's a challenging one-hour hike (though less exhausting than the blister-inducing trek up to Alto del Naranjo). There's only one junction in the trail: go right, uphill. Before heading for Alto del Naranjo, however, you must buy a permit (per person US$11) at the park office, 300m beyond Villa Santo Domingo. The fee includes a mandatory escort.

The mountain closes at 4pm and rangers won't let you pass after 1pm, so go in the early morning to maximize your visit. You must leave your bags and cameras at the ranger's hut, 2km before the Comandancia, as photography is prohibited.

The cloud forest here is quite beautiful. You can cobble together a decent day trip by visiting the Comandancia and hiking to La Platica, 1.5km from Alto del Naranjo (an additional fee may be required).

TREKKING

Certainly Cuba's most popular through-trek (as opposed to the round trip summit hike up Pico Turquino; see p386) is the rugged, three-day grind from Alto del Naranjo across the Sierra Maestra to Las Cuevas, or vice versa. The terrain goes from montane to rain forest, with terrific views, and ends on the inviting shores of the Caribbean.

Guides are mandatory and must be arranged through Flora and Fauna employees at Villa Santo Domingo (US$25 Alto del Naranjo–Pico Turquino; US$8 Pico Cuba–Las Cuevas). Stock up in Bayamo, carrying everything you'll need, including food, warm clothing, candles and some kind of bed roll or sheet arrangement. Even in August it gets cold at the shelters, so be prepared. Sufficient water is available along the trail.

The trail through the mountains from Alto del Naranjo passes the village of La Platica, Palma Mocha (campsite), Lima (campsite), Pico Joachín (shelter), El Cojo (shelter), Pico Joachín, Regino, Paso de los Monos, Loma Redonda, Pico Turquino

TREKKING GRAN PARQUE NACIONAL SIERRA MAESTRA

(1972m), Pico Cuba (1872m, with a shelter at 1650m), Pico Cardero (1265m) and La Esmajagua (600m, shelter) before dropping down to Las Cuevas on the Caribbean coast. The first two days are spent on the 13km section to Pico Turquino (overnighting at the Pico Joachín and Pico Cuba shelters), where a prearranged guide takes over and leads you down to Las Cuevas. As with all guide service, tips are in order. Prearranging the second leg from Pico Cuba to Las Cuevas is straightforward and handled by park staff.

These hikes are well coordinated and the guides efficient (to a fault: don't let them rush you). The sanest way to begin this hike is by spending the night at Campismo La Sierrita or Villa Santo Domingo and setting out in the morning. Transport from Las Cuevas along the coast is sparse, to say the least, with one scheduled truck on alternate days. For this reason, it might be easier to start in Las Cuevas and hike to Alto del Naranjo.

See p386 for a description of the Las Cuevas–Pico Turquino leg.

Sleeping & Eating

At Bartolomé Masó, 16km south of Yara on the road to Santo Domingo, is **Motel Balcón de la Sierra** (Islazul; ☎ 59 51 80; s/d low season US$26/36, incl breakfast US$29/41; P ✗ ◳). Snuggled below the mountains, this has to be one of Islazul's best-located hotels. Go for one of the cabanas with terrace and mountain views, and prepare for chilly nights.

Before heading into the mountains, backpacker types and Cubans usually bunk down at **Campismo La Sierrita** (☎ 5-3326; cabins US$16), 8km south of Bartolomé Masó. It's 1km off the main highway on a very rough road. The 27 cabins have bunks, baths and electricity, and sleep up to four people. There's a restaurant, and a river for swimming. If you have a sturdy rental car, the staff will supply a guide (per person US$8) to take you to the Comandancia de la Plata. Otherwise, ask if any tours are planned. La Sierrita is often full on weekends, so reservations from the Campismo Popular office in Bayamo (☎ 42 42 00) are essential.

The main base for visitors to Gran Parque Nacional Sierra Maestra is **Villa Santo Domingo** (Islazul; s/d incl breakfast US$23/30), 24km south of Bartolomé Masó. There are 20 separate cabins next to the Río Yara, at a 200m altitude. It's not a bad jumping-off point for the hike, and for river swimming. From here a very steep concrete road gains 750m elevation during its 5km climb to Alto del Naranjo. Pitching a tent is a possibility, while renting a private room in Santo Domingo, technically, is not.

Getting There & Away

There's no public transport from Bartolomé Masó to Alto del Naranjo. A taxi from Bayamo to Villa Santo Domingo should cost between US$20 and US$25 one way. Don't pay the driver until you arrive; otherwise you may be dropped off 7km before Villa Santo Domingo, citing steep roads (private taxis, if you can find them, routinely do this). Returning, the hotel should be able to arrange onward transport for you to Bartolomé Masó, Bayamo or Manzanillo.

A 4WD vehicle with good brakes is necessary to drive up to Alto del Naranjo; a compact car might not have the power to make it (although one reader reported driving a Subaru Vivio up there). It may be possible to hire a truck to drop you off at the trailhead.

MANZANILLO
pop 110,952

Not many people make it to Manzanillo (founded in 1784), about 65km west of Bayamo. There's simply little reason, save for the nearby La Demajagua historical site. The one hotel and one casa particular limit your sleeping options as well. On the up side, Manzanillo has Cuba's most elaborate gazebo in its pretty central park, a recently restored theater, and almost everything here is in pesos.

Manzanillo has a place in Cuban musical history as the point of entry of the first mechanical organs. During the late 19th century some 200 French street organs were imported to Manzanillo, and from 1920 to 1950 Francisco and Carlos Borbolla built about a dozen full-size organs here. The tradition lives on, and an organ grinder is often the central player in Cuban rumba bands. Unlike European mechanical organs, Cuban street organs have a second crank that the operator uses to control the speed – another unique feature of Cuban music.

Manzanillo is a port town, so the waterfront isn't so much inviting as industrial. A large shipyard, rice mill and much of Cuba's commercial fishing fleet is based here. Several long coral keys are visible offshore.

Information

There is no tourist information here; **Transtur** (☎ 5-3800) shares offices with Cubana and can help with transfers, taxis and rental cars.

AIRLINE OFFICES

Cubana Maceo (☎ 5-3800; Maceo No 70, off Parque Céspedes; ☼ 8am-noon & 1-5pm Mon-Wed & Fri, 1-5pm Thu); Sierra Maestra Airport (☎ 5-4984)

BOOKSHOPS

Librería Pulso y Onda (Martí, west side of Parque Céspedes) Dollar sales only.

IMMIGRATION

Inmigración (B Masó btwn Martí & Máximo Gómez; ☼ 9am-noon & 1:30-4:30pm Tue, Wed & Fri, 1:30- 4pm Thu)

MEDICAL SERVICES

Farmacia de Turno Permanente (Martí & Masó)
Hospital Celia Sánchez Manduley (☎ 5-4011; near intersection of Circunvalación Camilo Cienfuegos & Av de Céspedes)
Policlínico Principal de Urgencia (☎ 5-7538; Martí & Aguilera) In the center of town.

MONEY

Banco de Crédito y Comercio (Merchán & Saco; ☼ 8:30am-3:30pm Mon-Fri, 8am-noon Sat)
Cadeca (Martí No 184; ☼ 8:30am-6pm Mon-Sat, 8am-1pm Sun)

POST

Post Office (Martí & Doctor Codina)

TELEPHONE

Etecsa (Martí & General Benítez; ☼ 7:30am-11pm) Kiosk outpost while office is relocated.

TOILETS

Public toilets (Maceo No 71) Almost opposite the Cubana office.

Sights

Manzanillo is really spread out and shadeless – not a great town for walking around, though the wooden houses, abandoned towers and chipped cupolas provide quirky visuals. Check out the old **City Bank of NY**

building (1913; Merchán & Doctor Codina) or the old wooden houses around Perucho Figueredo between Merchán and JM Gómez.

The central square of Manzanillo, **Parque Céspedes**, is striking for its precious **glorieta** (gazebo/bandstand), with its Moorish mosaics, scalloped cupola and arabesque-covered columns. Completely restored in 1999, it fairly glows in the dusk's slanting light. Surrounding the park are buildings echoing this Andalusian-Moorish style, particularly the grandiose shopping arcade on the park's western side.

On the eastern side of Parque Céspedes is the **Museo Histórico Municipal** (Martí No 226; admission free; ☼ 8am-noon & 2-6pm Tue-Fri, 8am-noon & 6-10pm Sat & Sun). There's an art gallery next door. The **Iglesia de la Purísima Concepción**, across the square, has a gilded main altar.

Manzanillo's most evocative sight is the **Celia Sánchez Monument**, built in 1990 along Caridad. Colorful ceramic murals decorate the stairway between Martí and Luz Caballero. The birds and flowers on the reliefs represent Sánchez, one of the leaders of the M-26-7 movement and long-time aid to Castro, whose visage appears on the central mural near the top of the stairs. A small **visitors center** (☼ 8am-noon & 2-6pm Mon-Fri, 8am-noon Sat) is adjacent; there are excellent views from here.

The **Museo Histórico La Demajagua** (admission US$1; ☼ 8am-6pm Mon-Fri, 8am-noon Sun), 10km south of Manzanillo, is the site of the sugarfields estate of Carlos Manuel de Céspedes. It was here on October 10, 1868 that Céspedes freed his slaves, setting in motion the process that led to Cuba's independence from Spain 30 years later. Remains of Céspedes' *ingenio* (sugar mill) are behind the museum. The views from the estate are fine and the long, grassy expanses a novelty.

From here, a broad walkway leads to a monument bearing a quotation from Castro: *'Nosotros entonces habriamos sido como ellos, ellos hoy habrían sido como nosotros'* ('We would then have been as they were, they today would be as we are'). Below two huge trees next to the monument are the remains of a steam engine that formerly powered the mill, and hanging nearby is the famous Demajagua bell, once used to call the slaves to work. On October 10, 1868, it tolled announcing Cuba's independence. To get to La Demajagua, travel south

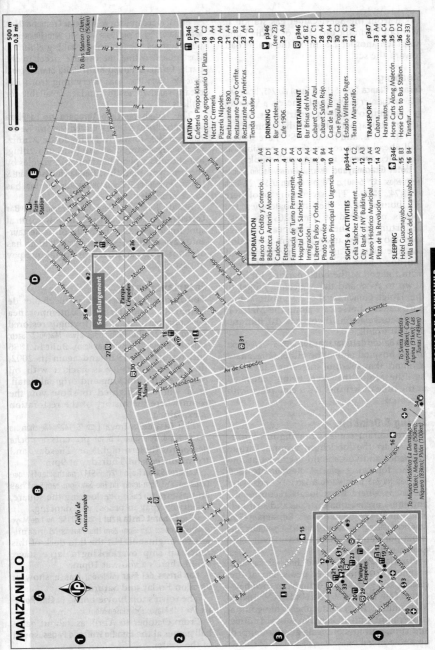

MANZANILLO

INFORMATION
Banco de Crédito y Comercio......1 A4
Biblioteca Antonio Maceo.........2 D1
Cadeca...........................3 A4
Etecsa...........................4 C2
Farmacia de Turno Permanente.....5 A4
Hospital Celia Sánchez Manduley..6 C4
Inmigración......................7 A4
Librería Pulso y Onda............8 A4
Photo Service....................9 B4
Policlínico Principal de Urgencia...10 A4

SIGHTS & ACTIVITIES   pp344-6
Celia Sánchez Monument..........11 C2
City Bank of NY Building.........12 A3
Museo Histórico Municipal........13 A4
Plaza de la Revolución...........14 A3

SLEEPING   p346
Hotel Guacanayabo...............15 B3
Villa Balcón del Guacanayabo....16 D2

EATING   p346
Cafetería Piropo Kikiri..........17 A4
Mercado Agropecuario La Plaza....18 C2
Nectar Cremería..................19 A4
Pizzería Nápoles.................20 A4
Restaurante 1800.................21 A4
Restaurante Cayo Confite.........22 B2
Restaurante Las Américas.........23 A4
Tienda Cubalse...................24 D1

DRINKING   p346
Bar Coctelera................(see 23)
Cafe 1906........................25 A4

ENTERTAINMENT   p346
Bar Brisas del Mar...............26 B2
Cabaret Costa Azul...............27 C1
Cabaret Salón Rojo...............28 A4
Casa de la Trova.................29 A4
Cine Popular.....................30 C2
Estadio Wilfredo Pagés...........31 C3
Teatro Manzanillo................32 A4

TRANSPORT   p347
Cubana...........................33 A4
Havanautos.......................34 C4
Horse Carts Along Malecón........35 D1
Horse Carts to Bus Station.......36 D2
Transtur.....................(see 33)

GRANMA PROVINCE

10km from the Servi-Cupet gas station in Manzanillo, in the direction of Media Luna, and then another 2.5km off the main road, toward the sea.

Sleeping

César & Blanca (☎ 5-3131; Sariol No 245, btwn Saco & Doctor Codina; r US$20; ✗) If there's a vacancy at Manzanillo's only casa particular, take it. It's an atmospheric house, the rooms have private baths, and meals (US$7) are served. Call ahead for a reservation if possible, as this place appears in every guidebook.

Hotel Guacanayabo (Islazul; Circunvalación Camilo Cienfuegos; ☎ 5-4012; s/d low season US$17/22, high US$18/24; ✗ ☒) The swimming pool here is a bonus, as are the little balconies; the rooms numbered in the 320s are best. Unfortunately, the beds appear to have seen too much Cuban honeymoon action and the location is really inconvenient if you don't have a car. A concrete stairway from the end of the hotel parking lot leads down to Av 8 and the Malecón. To get to the Hotel Guacanayabo by public transport, catch a horse cart along the Malecón to Circunvalación, then walk 10 minutes straight uphill.

Villa Balcón del Guacanayabo (☎ 5-5217) Next to the hospital above the Hotel Guacanayabo and 3km south of the center, there are 14 little cabins that were being renovated at the time of writing. It's a cute place with potential.

Eating & Drinking

The restaurant scene is hurting in Manzanillo. Start the food hunt around Parque Céspedes and you should get lucky at one of the following places. **Restaurante 1800** (Merchán No 245 btwn Maceo & Saco; ✗ noon-10pm Tue-Sun) is where most locals recommend, and there are adequate steaks and seafood. Your menu will be in dollars. **Restaurante Las Américas** (Maceo; ✗ noon-2:30pm & 7-10pm) has the usual pork and chicken that you will have grown to tolerate.

Pizzería Nápoles (Merchán) has pizza and spaghetti for under three pesos. Pay at the cashier and grab a seat; bring your own beverage. **Café 1906** (cnr Maceo & Merchán; ✗ 24hr) is Manzanillo's most atmospheric hangout, a corner joint with 20 centavo shots of coffee and rum, and lots of locals getting hopped up and zonked out.

For ice cream, there's **Nectar Cremería** (Martí near Maceo; ✗ noon-10pm Mon-Sat, 9am-10pm Sun); pay in pesos. Get in line by taking el último (last place in line) across the street in the park. **Cafetería Piropo Kikiri** (Martí btwn Maceo & Saco; ✗ 10am-10pm) has everything from ice-cream sandwiches to sundaes, available for dollars.

The lavish **Mercado Agropecuario La Plaza** (Martí btwn Batería & General Benitez; 7am-5pm Tue-Sat, 7am-noon Sun), formerly Mercado de Muñiz, was being restored at the time of writing, but should be peddling fruit and veggies by the time you read this. **Tienda Cubalse** (Martí & Loynaz; ✗ 8:30am-5:30pm Mon-Sat, 9am-noon Sun) has some groceries.

Beside Restaurante Las Américas is **Bar Coctelera** (Maceo), which is a mellow, central spot for a beer. On the Malecón is **Restaurante Cayo Confite** (✗ noon-8pm), which has outdoor tables and hardcore drinking; pay in pesos.

Entertainment

Touring companies such as the Ballet de Camagüey and Danza Contemporánea de Cuba perform at the lovingly restored **Teatro Manzanillo** (Villuendas btwn Maceo & Saco; admission 8 pesos; ✗ shows at 8pm). Built in 1856 and restored in 1926 and again in 2002, this 430-seat beauty is packed with oil paintings, red flocking and original detail. Staff will be delighted to show you the room where the history of the restoration is explained.

The **Casa de la Trova** (☎ 5-5423; Merchán No 213 at Masó; admission 1 peso) presents a noche de boleros (bolero night) on Tuesday, and trova concerts on Thursday at 9pm.

Cabaret Salón Rojo (☎ 5-5117; north side of Parque Céspedes; ✗ 8pm-midnight Tue-Sat, 8pm-1am Sun) has an upstairs terrace overlooking the square, for drinks (pay in pesos) and dancing.

The **Cabaret Costa Azul** (☎ 5-3158; Av 1 de Mayo & Narciso Lopez; ✗ 8pm-2am Thu-Sun) is Manzanillo's top nightspot. Hit the lido deck of this mock-up ship overlooking a large stage, where there's a show at 10pm.

Bar Brisas del Mar (Malecón) has a show at 9pm on Friday and Saturday.

The town's top movie house is **Cine Popular** (Av 1 de Mayo; ✗ closed Mon).

From October to April, ask about baseball games at the **Estadio Wilfredo Pages**, south of the center.

Getting There & Away

AIR

Manzanillo's **Sierra Maestra Airport** (☎ 5-3019; airport code MZO) is on the road to Cayo Espino, 8km south of the Servi-Cupet gas station in Manzanillo. **Cubana** (☎ 5-4984) has a nonstop flight from Havana twice a week (US$98, 623km, two hours). Skyservice flies directly from Toronto in winter.

A taxi between the airport and the center of town should cost US$6 to US$7.

BUS & TRUCK

The bus station, 2km east of town on the road to Bayamo, has **Astro** (☎ 5-2727) buses to the following destinations.

destination	cost (one way)	distance	frequency
Bayamo	US$1.80	50km	twice daily
Camagüey	US$12	217km	daily
Havana	US$29	775km	daily
Pilón	US$3	83km	daily
Yara	US$1.60	23km	daily

Buses and passenger trucks run fairly frequently to Yara and Bayamo. To Pilón, there are two or three morning buses. There is one daily bus to both Holguín and Havana, but to reach Santiago de Cuba you must transfer in Bayamo.

Passenger trucks to Media Luna and Pilón depart from the bus station and stop to pick up passengers at the crossroads near Servi-Cupet and the hospital (which is the local hitching stop).

TRAIN

All services from the train station on the north side of town are via Yara and Bayamo. Trains go to the following destinations.

destination	cost (one way)	distance	frequency
Bayamo	US$1.75	50km	twice daily
Havana	US$28	775km	daily
Jiguaní	US$2.35	79km	twice daily
Matanzas	US$25	696km	daily
Santiago de Cuba	US$5.50	167km	daily

Getting Around

The **Havanautos** office (☎ 5-7204) is adjacent to the Servi-Cupet gas station, opposite the hospital, 3km south of the city center on the road to Media Luna. There's a brilliant new road running through Corralito

up into Holguín, making this the quickest exit from Manzanillo towards points north and east.

Horse carts (1 peso) to the bus station leave from Doctor Codina between Plácido and Luz Caballero. Horse carts along the Malecón to the shipyard leave from the bottom of Saco.

MEDIA LUNA

pop 15,493

The sugar-producing town of Media Luna, about 50km southwest of Manzanillo, is most well known as the hometown of Celia Sánchez (1920–80). Sánchez is famous for having sent essential supplies to Castro's rebels in the mountains, and later becoming one of Castro's closest associates. The **Celia Sánchez Museum** (Paúl Podio No 111; admission US$1; ☺ 9am-noon & 2-5pm Tue-Sat, 9am-1pm Sun) is a grand old clapboard affair on the main road; it's not far from Media Luna's sugar mill.

Media Luna's **glorieta**, while not as outlandish as the one in Manzanillo, is still a charmer. Grab a three-peso ice cream or fruitshake from one of the stalls in the park, and take a look around.

NIQUERO

pop 20,273

One of Cuba's most charming small towns just got more attractive for visitors with the addition of the swell **Hotel Niquero** (Islazul; ☎ 59 24 98; s/d/tr high season $US22/26/34; Ⓟ Ⓧ). Right in the middle of town, this friendly place has clean, comfortable rooms with great beds, and little balconies that overlook the street. The affordable restaurant is surprisingly good. There isn't much to do here but explore the park, where there's a **cinema**, and next door you'll find the best *pru* and *polverones* (butter cookies) in Cuba.

Saturday nights are noches de Cubanilla, when the streets are closed off and dining is at sidewalk tables. Live bands replete with organ grinder are a bonus.

The town makes a good base from which to visit the Parque Nacional Desembarco del Granma. There's a Servi-Cupet in the center of town and another at the edge of town towards Cabo Cruz, where you can get terrific *lechón asado* (smoked pork sandwiches) and fruitshakes.

PARQUE NACIONAL DESEMBARCO DEL GRANMA

Ten kilometers southwest of Media Luna the road divides, with Pilón 30km to the southeast and Niquero 10km to the southwest. Belic is 16km southwest of Niquero. It's another 6km from Belic to the national park entry gate (entrance per person US$3).

Parque Nacional Desembarco del Granma protects 27,545 hectares of forests, cliffs and reefs along the southern coast, from Cabo Cruz almost to Pilón. In 1999 it was named a Unesco World Heritage site. Some of Cuba's last untouched rain forests are here, as well as cacti more than 400 years old. Of the 512 plant species identified thus far, about 60% are endemic, 12 of those are found only here and several are threatened with extinction. The fauna is rich, with 25 species of mollusk, seven species of amphibian, 44 types of reptile, 110 bird species and 13 types of mammal.

The area is famous as the landing place of the yacht *Granma*, which brought Fidel and revolution to Cuba in 1956 (see the boxed text below). A large monument and the **Museo Las Coloradas** (admission US$1; 8am-6pm Tue-Sat, 8am-noon Sun) just beyond the park gate mark the actual spot. The museum outlines the routes taken by Castro, Guevara and the others from here to the Sierra Maestra, and there's a full-scale replica of the *Granma*.

Eight kilometers southwest of the park gate toward Cabo Cruz is the **Sendero Arqueológico Natural El Guafe**, a tame nature trail. An underground river here has created 20 large caverns, one of which contains the famous Ídolo del Agua, carved from stalagmites by pre-Columbian Indians. It is a two-hour stroll, during which you could see butterflies, 170 different species of birds (including the tiny *colibrí*), giant cacti and orchids. A park guard is available to accompany you and point out interesting features.

Three kilometers beyond El Guafe trailhead is **Cabo Cruz**, a classic fishing port with skiffs bobbing offshore and sinewy men gutting their catch on the golden beach. There's not much to see here except a 33m-tall lighthouse, which was erected in 1871. An olive-oil wick provided the light for the lighthouse until gas was installed in 1928. In 1952 the device was electrified. An

---

THE YACHT GRANMA

Granma Province is named for the 12m cabin cruiser *Granma*, which carried Fidel Castro and 81 others from Mexico to Oriente in 1956. After his release from prison in 1955, Castro fled to Mexico, where he organized a revolutionary band for an invasion of Cuba. The group sailed hastily from Tuxpan at 1am on November 25, 1956, just one step ahead of the Mexican authorities.

Their wooden craft was designed to carry 25 persons maximum, and with 82 seasick revolutionaries and their gear crammed aboard, the journey soon became a nightmare. The *Granma's* fuel tanks weren't sufficiently large to reach eastern Cuba and extra drums of diesel competed for deck space. The ship's worn-out engine limited its speed, unexpectedly adding several days to the journey. After five days at sea, the food and water supplies were exhausted and there was a further delay when a man fell overboard at night and had to be rescued.

The *Granma's* radio could only receive and not broadcast; thus, Castro was unable to advise his allies in Cuba of the late arrival, and on November 30 there was a premature uprising in Santiago de Cuba, which tipped off Batista that something was happening. Celia Sánchez was waiting at Niquero, southwest of Manzanillo, with reinforcements and supplies, but on December 2, the group believed they had been spotted and the *Granma* was run aground in a muddy mangrove swamp near Playa de los Coloradas, 23km south of Niquero.

Castro's men were unable to carry most of their weapons through the swamp and were strafed by Batista aircraft soon after the landing. They trudged through the bush for three days until, at Alegría de Pío, 20km east of their landing place, they were betrayed by their guide and ambushed by Batista troops. Only 12 of the original 82 managed to reach the Sierra Maestra, where they regrouped on December 18. Ever confident of eventual success, Castro declared: 'We will win this war... we are only beginning to fight!'

The original *Granma* is now on display at the Museo de la Revolución in Havana, but a replica can be viewed at Playa de los Coloradas.

exhibition room (🕙 8am-noon & 1-5pm Mon-Sat) labeled *Historia del Faro*, which has lighthouse memorabilia, is inside the adjacent building; the attendant at the lighthouse shop has the key .

There's good swimming east of the lighthouse and you can walk out to a stretch of reef that has decent snorkeling; watch the strong currents sweeping from west to east here. If you like to fish, Cabo Cruz is the place for you.

Sleeping & Eating

Campismo Las Coloradas (per person US$5; 🟫) stands on 500m of murky beach 5km southwest of Belic, just outside the park. The 28 duplex cabins fill fast on weekends and in summer, when locals flock to the beach to party. This is an equipped Campertour facility. Nonguests are charged US$1 per person to enter the campismo and use the beach or visit the restaurant. Three buses a day from Niquero and more-frequent trucks from Belic come this far.

Campers with gear can pitch on the beach at Cabo Cruz without a problem. Frequently used fire rings are good for cooking up all the fresh fish available.

Getting There & Away

If you don't have your own transport, you can still get over here, you'll just have to be very patient. During the summer you should be able to hitch out of Las Coloradas, otherwise it's a tough lift (for information on the risks associated with hitching, see p433). The closest gas stations are in Niquero.

PILÓN

pop 11,904

Life was hard in Pilón, a scratch of a sugar town, before they shut the mill in 2002. Now life is *really* hard. There's a small museum dedicated to Celia Sánchez, but the real reason to stop here is to talk and share with the friendly townspeople, who are facing an uncertain future. The town is in the elbow of the Ensenada de Mora on the Caribbean Sea.

From Pilón, the paved road continues 17km east to Marea del Portillo, and all the way to Santiago de Cuba, which is another 90km further on. This is one of Cuba's five-star scenic drives, with high mountains on one side and the sea on the other. The

sugar fields west of Pilón open into cattle country east of the town, and east of Marea del Portillo there's only sparsely inhabited forest and scrubland.

Sleeping & Eating

Motel Mirador (☎ 59 43 65; s/d US$10/15) Six kilometers east of Pilón, this motel is high up on a hillside at a spot with an excellent view. The four cabins, with red-tiled roofs, are simple and there's a restaurant in a thatched building. It's often full.

Villa Turística Punta Piedra (☎ 59 44 21; s/d US$20/25) On a small brown beach 11km east of Pilón and 5km west of Marea del Portillo. Thirteen rooms in two single-story blocks, a restaurant and an intermittant disco.

Getting There & Around

There's a bus between Pilón and Santiago de Cuba via Manzanillo on alternate days. Buses also run along the south coast between Pilón and Chivirico on alternate days.

Servi-Cupet is by the highway at the entrance to Pilón. Be sure to fill up here, as the next gas station is in Santiago de Cuba.

MAREA DEL PORTILLO

This 2km black-sand beach, 108km south of Manzanillo's airport, is on the drier southern side of the Sierra Maestra, and in winter it's the warmest spot in Cuba. There are two resorts, with every creature comfort and outdoor activity available, but not much else. Inexpensive package tours are available, and this area makes a nice stop if you've been crammed into a rental car for too long. Cuba isn't known for its black-sand beaches and there's a reason. If you're looking for a beach holiday, Marea del Portillo is not postcard quality, and the resorts, though cheap, are nothing to write home about either.

Activities

Both hotels operate an all-day hiking and horseback-riding tour to **El Salto**, a waterfall, for US$35 per person including lunch and four drinks (six-person minimum). Other horseback riding costs US$7 per hour.

The **Marlin Dive Center** (☎ 59 70 34, fax 59 70 35), adjacent to Hotel Marea del Portillo, offers **scuba diving** for US$30 a tank, plus US$5 for gear. Deep-sea fishing costs US$45 per hour for four anglers fishing two at a time.

Sleeping & Eating

Club Amigo Marea del Portillo (Cubanacán; ☎ 59 70 81; s/d/tr low season US$60/95/135; P ✗ 🖭 ⊠)
This all-inclusive resort is right on a dark sandy beach. The 74 rooms are comfortable, but not fancy. The prices shown are for the humblest rooms with no view; the pool is small. Day trips to Cayo Blanco and its secluded white sandy beach cost US$15. Marea del Portillo caters to an older crowd compared with Farallón del Caribe.

Hotel Farallón del Caribe (Cubanacán; ☎ 59 40 03; fax 59 70 80; s/d/tr US$48/72/105; P ✗ 🖭 ⊠)
What a great setting for an all-inclusive resort: perched on a low hill overlooking the Sierra Maestra, the views across the mountains from the beach bar are magical. They must have captured it well in the tourist brochures because this place is packed with travelers determined to get good and shnookered while on holiday. The beach

leaves something to be desired. The resorts at Baconao (p381), 160km east, offer more variety and better value.

Getting There & Away

The only scheduled transport along this route is one truck on alternate days from Santiago de Cuba. By the time it arrives at this part of the coast it is overflowing dangerously with folks making their way to Pilón.

Getting Around

The hotels rent scooters for US$8 for the first hour, US$3 for each additional hour (including gas). A rough dirt road crosses the mountains directly from Marea del Portillo to Bartolomé Masó, but a 4WD vehicle, dry weather and considerable driving expertise are required to use it. Be prepared for several steep rocky sections and many fords.

Santiago de Cuba Province

Wedged between the sparkling Caribbean Sea and pine-clad slopes of the Sierra Maestra and Sierra del Cristal, the province of Santiago de Cuba offers an unrivaled combination of beach escape and alpine adventure. The scenery is stunning, especially the 250km Sierra Maestra range that culminates at Pico Turquino (1972m), Cuba's highest peak. Attainable in a day, summiting Turquino is a Cuban rite of passage: like a *quinciñera* for the outdoor set.

Along with adjacent Granma Province, Santiago de Cuba is where the seeds of the Cuban Revolution were sown, and both are a must for history-heavy itineraries. Indeed, the city of Santiago de Cuba is known as the cradle of the revolution. Not only was revolution born here; traditional Cuban music called *son* also traces its roots to this province and music fans will be in heaven here. Santiago de Cuba is the second most populous province and city after the City of Havana and this has created a rivalry akin to the New York/Los Angeles or Rio de Janeiro/São Paulo split.

Just southeast of the city lies Parque Baconao, so big it can contain one of Cuba's largest concentrations of resorts and still be a Unesco Biosphere Reserve. La Gran Piedra is, as the name says, a great big rock (1214m) and beatific La Virgen del Cobre, Cuba's most important shrine, is also in this province.

As in most places in Cuba, tourism is an increasingly important part of the economy, with sugar, oranges, coffee and commercial fishing also figuring in.

HIGHLIGHTS

■ **Revolution Must-Sees**

See the mammoth Moncada Barracks (p363) and quaint Granjita Siboney (p378)

■ **Chan Chan This**

Break out of the Buena Vista box at the Casa de las Tradiciones or International Trova Festival (p373)

■ **Cuba Monumental**

Check out Castillo de San Pedro del Morro, Unesco World Heritage site with kicking views (p365)

■ **Pilgrimage**

Make your way to the sacred shrine of La Virgen de la Caridad in El Cobre (p383)

■ **Get High**

Get sweaty climbing up Pico Turquino, Cuba's highest mountain (p386)

Moncada Barracks
Casa de las Tradiciones
International Trova Festival
Castillo de San Pedro de Morro
Pico Turquino
La Virgen de la Caridad
Granjita Siboney

■ TELEPHONE CODE: 22   ■ POPULATION: 1,041,373   ■ AREA: 6170 SQ KM

HISTORY

The city of Santiago de Cuba was founded in 1514 several kilometers from its present site by Diego Velázquez de Cuellar. Its first mayor was the future conqueror of Mexico, Hernán Cortés. In 1522 the town moved to its current location, on a sharp horseshoe of harbor, one of only three natural harbors on Cuba's south coast (Cienfuegos and Guantánamo are the others). From 1515 until 1607, Santiago de Cuba was the capital, although the Spanish captains-general left for Havana in 1556. The Seminario de San Basilio Magno was founded in 1722, several years before the Universidad de Havana. The Bishop of Santiago remained Cuba's leading cleric until 1788, when Havana also received a bishop, but in 1804 the city's ecclesiastical dominance was re-established when its bishop was promoted to archbishop. All of which goes a long way to explaining the Santiago de Cuba–Havana rift.

Santiago de Cuba's decline in other areas began early, however. As the region's meager gold reserves gave out and the Indian laborers died off due to the cruel treatment they received from Spanish *encomenderos*, the colony's population began shifting toward Havana. Santiago de Cuba was plundered in 1554 by the French privateer Jacques de Sores, sacked by the pirate Henry Morgan in 1662 and hit by an earthquake in 1675, then again in 1852 and 1932.

In 1607 Santiago de Cuba became the capital of the island's Departamento Oriental, comprising the areas of modern Santiago de Cuba, Granma, Guantánamo, Holguín and Las Tunas Provinces, and a chain of forts was built to strengthen the city's defenses. By this time, black slaves from Africa had replaced Indians as the workforce at the region's copper mines and cattle ranches. After a slave uprising in nearby Haiti in 1791, Oriente received an influx of French refugees who developed coffee, cotton and sugarcane plantations throughout the region. Increasing numbers of slaves were imported, and today Oriente has the country's highest percentage of black inhabitants. It's estimated that Santiago de Cuba is half mulatto and another quarter black.

Oriente's isolation from Havana has given it a distinct history and culture. Much of the fighting in both wars of independence took place in Oriente, and in 1845 the great mulatto general Antonio Maceo was born in Santiago de Cuba. In 1898, just as Cuba's long struggle for independence seemed about to triumph, the US intervened in the Second War of Independence, cheating the Cubans of hard-won victory. In Cuba they call this *cogiendo el mango bajito* (picking the low-hanging mango), when help materializes just when the hard work is over. At Santiago de Cuba, the Spanish fleet was sacrificed to save face for Spain, and future US president Theodore Roosevelt managed to cloak himself in glory by leading the charge of the 'Rough Riders' up San Juan Hill, in a battle the Spanish were happy enough to lose. The triumphant Americans graciously accepted the surrender of the gallant Spanish, but the Cuban general Calixto García and his largely black army were not allowed to attend the ceremony.

The US victory ushered in six decades of neocolonial rule by a succession of corrupt politicians and brutal dictators. Despite the resulting poverty, the city's musical and literary life flourished. Batista's 1952 military coup inspired resistance among the Cuban people, and it was at Santiago de Cuba on July 26, 1953, that Fidel Castro and his companions launched an assault on the Moncada Barracks. This was the start of a number of events that changed the course of Cuban history. At his trial here Castro made his famous 'History Will Absolve Me' speech, which became the basic platform of the Cuban Revolution.

On November 30, 1956, the people of Santiago de Cuba rose in rebellion against Batista's troops to distract attention from the landing of Castro's guerrillas aboard the *Granma* on the western shores of Oriente. An underground movement led by Frank and Josue País continued to support the fighters in Oriente's Sierra Maestra. Despite the murder of the País brothers and many others, the struggle continued, and it was in Santiago de Cuba, on the evening of January 1, 1959, that Fidel Castro first appeared publicly to declare the success of the revolution. All these events have earned Santiago the title 'Hero City of the Republic of Cuba.'

In 1975 Oriente Province was split into five provinces, and the amount of territory administered from Santiago de Cuba was much reduced.

ARTS

Santiago de Cuba has a rich cultural history that goes back to the construction of the Catedral de Nuestra Señora de la Asunción in the 1520s and the formation of a church choir. The French planters from Haiti brought opera with them, and regular performances were staged at various theaters from 1800 onward. The first philharmonic society was created in 1832, and in 1851 the Teatro de la Reina opened with a series of French operas. In 1871 *La Hija de Jefté*, by Laureano Fuentes Matons, became the first *zarzuela* (operetta) by a Cuban composer to be staged in Cuba.

Aside from this academic musical culture, Oriente has a distinctive folk culture that has resulted from 19th-century French–Haitian immigration. This is the original home of *son*, the forerunner of salsa. The genres of Cuban popular music, from Afro-Cuban drumming to rumba, are all alive and well in Santiago de Cuba and it's a good place to deepen your knowledge of these traditions.

Two of the country's foremost 19th-century romantic poets, José María Heredia

(1803–39) and his cousin José María de Heredia y Giralt (1842–1905), were born here, although both spent most of their adult lives abroad.

SANTIAGO DE CUBA

☎ 226 / pop 443,926

Santiago de Cuba is Cuba's second-largest city and a strong rival to Havana in literature, music and politics. During the 19th century, French settlers arrived and contributed to the Haitian, African and Spanish mosaic that makes this Cuba's most Caribbean city, and there are many festivals celebrating this heritage (see p368). The Universidad de Oriente (founded 1947) is one of Cuba's leading educational institutions. This is the birthplace of the Cuban revolution and numerous 'political' museums tell the tale.

In an effort to move into the new millennium and properly outfit Santiago de Cuba for tourism, a flurry of monumental buildings were thrown up in the 1990s including the Legoland Hotel Santiago de Cuba, the hangar-esque Teatro José María Heredia, the dramatic Antonio Maceo Monument,

SANTIAGO DE CUBA PROVINCE

the modern train station on the north-western side of the city and the flashy new terminal building at Antonio Maceo International Airport.

Yet nothing has dulled Santiago de Cuba's desperate edge and travelers will sense it right away with the constant come-ons and hustle from *jineteros/as*. Arriving from the quieter provinces of Holguín, Granma or Guantánamo, it can be a shock, as can the congested streets of the city center, thick with auto exhaust. For more, see Dangers & Annoyances (p359).

Santiago de Cuba lies in a partly submerged valley of the Sierra Maestra, and the city's large natural harbor has made it an important port for almost five centuries. The Cuban Central Railway from Havana terminates here and the Carretera Central passes through on its way to Guantánamo. Local plants process coffee and sugar, distill rum, construct furniture, make cement, refine petroleum, generate electricity, build ships and manufacture garments. Yet this industry is well away from the historic center and seldom imposes on the visitor.

Orientation

The city's main monuments, museums, *trova* clubs and restaurants are in a narrow corridor running east from Parque Céspedes to Plaza de Dolores and Plaza de Marte along Calle José A Saco, the city's most important shopping street (which becomes a pedestrian mall and street fair on Saturday night). The old residential neighborhoods north and south of this strip also contain interesting things. Taken together, this is the city's *casco histórico* or historic core. The main monuments to the revolution are along Av de los Libertadores.

The big tourist hotels are in Vista Alegre, 3.5km east of the train station, 2.5km east of Parque Céspedes (via Aguilera and Av Victoriano Garzón), 2km southeast of the Nacionales Bus Station (via Av de las Américas) and 1.5km southeast of the Inter-municipales Bus Station (via Av Céspedes). Antonio Maceo International Airport is 7km to the south.

Santiago de Cuba is spread out and if you don't have a car, learning the public-transport ropes can save you bunches of taxi fares.

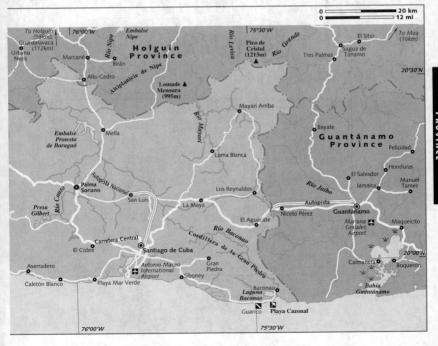

Information

AIRLINE OFFICES

AeroCaribbean (Map p360; ☎ 68 72 55; Gral Lacret & Heredia; ☽ 9am-noon & 1-4:30pm Mon-Fri, 9am-noon Sat)

Cubana Saco & Gral Lacret (Map p360; ☎ 65 15 77; ☽ 8:15am-1:30pm Mon-Fri); Aeropuerto Antonio Maceo (☎ 69 10 14)

BOOKSHOPS

José A Saco between Hartmann and Porfirio Valiente near Plaza de Dolores has no fewer than eight bookstores, selling books mostly in Spanish.

Librería Internacional (Map p360; Parque Céspedes south side) Decent selection of political titles in English, sells postcards and stamps.

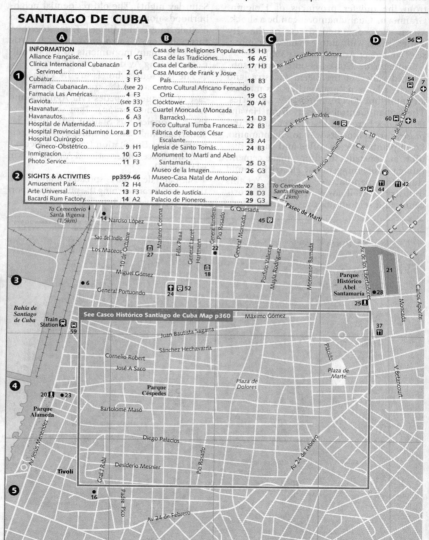

SANTIAGO DE CUBA

A

INFORMATION
Alliance Française...................... 1 G3
Clínica Internacional Cubanacán
Servimed.............................. 2 G4
Cubatur.................................. 3 F3
Farmacia Cubanacán.............(see 2)
Farmacia Las Américas............ 4 F3
Gaviota.............................(see 33)
Havanautos........................... 5 G3
Havanautos........................... 6 A3
Hospital de Maternidad............ 7 D1
Hospital Provincial Saturnino Lora. 8 D1
Hospital Quirúrgico
Gineco-Obstétrico................ 9 H1
Inmigración........................... 10 G3
Photo Service........................ 11 F3

SIGHTS & ACTIVITIES   pp359–66
Amusement Park.................... 12 H4
Arte Universal....................... 13 F3
Bacardí Rum Factory.............. 14 A2

B

Casa de las Religiones Populares.. 15 H3
Casa de las Tradiciones........... 16 A5
Casa del Caribe..................... 17 H3
Casa Museo de Frank y Josue
País................................... 18 B3
Centro Cultural Africano Fernando
Ortiz................................. 19 G3
Clocktower........................... 20 A4
Cuartel Moncada (Moncada
Barracks)........................... 21 D3
Foco Cultural Tumba Francesa.. 22 B3
Fábrica de Tabacos César
Escalante........................... 23 A4
Iglesia de Santo Tomás........... 24 B3
Monument to Martí and Abel
Santamaría......................... 25 D3
Museo de la Imagen............... 26 G3
Museo-Casa Natal de Antonio
Maceo............................... 27 B3
Palacio de Justicia.................. 28 D3
Palacio de Pioneros................ 29 G3

C

D

Librería La Escalera (Map p360; Calle Heredia No 265; ⌚ 10am-11pm) Used and rare books, trova ephemera, old 78s, movie posters, the works.

Librería Manolito del Toro (Map p360; Saco No 411; ⌚ 8am-4:30pm Mon-Fri, 8am-4pm Sat) Good for political literature.

Librería Viet Nam (Map p360; Aguilera No 567; ⌚ 9am-5pm Mon-Fri & alt Sat) A top bookstore.

CULTURAL CENTERS

Alliance Française (Map pp356-7; ☎ 64 15 03; Calle 6 No 253, at Calle 11 in Vista Alegre; ⌚ 9am-7pm Mon-Fri, 9am-noon Sat) French cultural center with photo exhibitions and a French library. Free films are shown here weekly. Native French speakers are in short supply and are encouraged to pursue cross-cultural exchanges with the Alliance.

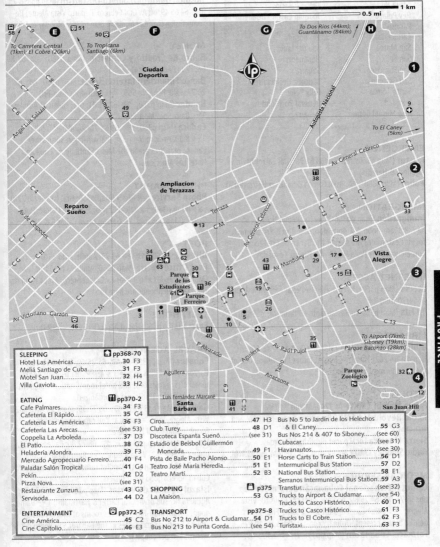

SLEEPING	🏠 pp368-70
Hotel Las Américas	**30** F3
Meliá Santiago de Cuba	**31** F3
Motel San Juan	**32** H4
Villa Gaviota	**33** H2

EATING	🍴 pp370-2
Cafe Palmares	**34** F3
Cafetería El Rápido	**35** G4
Cafetería Las Américas	**36** F3
Cafetería Las Arecas	(see 53)
Coppelia La Arboleda	**37** D3
El Patio	**38** G2
Heladería Alondra	**39** F3
Mercado Agropecuario Ferreiro	**40** F4
Paladar Salón Tropical	**41** G4
Pekín	**42** D2
Pizza Nova	(see 31)
Restaurante Zunzun	**43** G3
Servisoda	**44** D2

ENTERTAINMENT	🎭 pp372-5
Cine América	**45** C2
Cine Capitolio	**46** E3

Ciroa	**47** H3
Club Turey	**48** D1
Discoteca Espanta Suenó	(see 31)
Estadio de Beisbol Guillermón Moncada	**49** F1
Pista de Baile Pacho Alonso	**50** E1
Teatro José María Heredia	**51** E1
Teatro Martí	**52** B3

SHOPPING	🛍 p375
La Maison	**53** G3

TRANSPORT	pp375-8
Bus No 212 to Airport & Ciudamar	**54** D1
Bus No 213 to Punta Gorda	(see 54)

Bus No 5 to Jardín de los Helechos & El Caney	**55** G3
Bus Nos 214 & 407 to Siboney	(see 60)
Cubacar	(see 31)
Havanautos	(see 30)
Horse Carts to Train Station	**56** D1
Intermunicipal Bus Station	**57** D2
National Bus Station	**58** E1
Serranos Intermunicipal Bus Station	**59** A3
Transtur	(see 32)
Trucks to Airport & Ciudamar	(see 54)
Trucks to Casco Histórico	**60** D1
Trucks to Casco Histórico	**61** F3
Trucks to El Cobre	**62** F3
Turistaxi	**63** F3

SANTIAGO DE CUBA PROVINCE

SANTIAGO DE CUBA STREET NAMES

Welcome to another city where the streets have two names:

old name	new name
Enramada	José A Saco
Calvario	Porfirio Valiente
Reloj	Mayía Rodríguez
Santa Rita	Diego Palacios
Rey Pelayo	Joaquín Castillo Duany
Paraíso	Plácido
Carniceria	Pio Rosado
San Mateo	Sao del Indio
San Félix	Hartmann
San Francisco	Sagarra
San Gerónimo	Sánchez Hechavarría
Santo Tómas	Felix Peña
Trinidad	General Portuondo
José Miguel Gómez	Habana

EMERGENCY
Asistur (Map p360; ☎ /fax 68 61 28; Gral Lacret btwn Aguilera & Heredia)
Police (Map p360; ☎ 106; Corona & Sánchez Hechevarría)

IMMIGRATION
Inmigración (Map pp356-7; Av Raúl Pujol No 10; ☽ 8:30am-noon & 2-4pm Mon, Tue, Thu & Fri) Stamps for visa extensions are sold at the Banco de Crédito y Comercio at Felix Peña No 614 on Parque Céspedes.

INTERNET ACCESS
Etecsa (Map p360; Heredia at Félix Peña; ☽ 9am-11pm; US$4/30 min)
Tu Isla (Map p360; in Restaurante Matamoros; US$6/hr)

LIBRARIES
Biblioteca Elvira Cape (Map p360; ☎ 62 46 69; Heredia No 262) The city's largest public library and one of the nation's most prestigious.

MEDIA
Radio Mambí CMKW At 1240AM and 93.7FM.
Radio Revolución CMKC Broadcasting over 840AM and 101.4FM.
Sierra Maestra Local paper published Saturday.
Radio Siboney CMDV Broadcasting at 1180AM and 95.1FM.

MEDICAL SERVICES
Clínica Internacional Cubanacán Servimed (Map pp356-7; ☎ 64 25 89; Av Raúl Pujol cnr Calle 10, Vista Alegre; ☽ 24hr) Capable staff speak some English. A dentist is also present. Ordinary consultations are US$25.
Farmacia Cubanacán (Map pp356-7; ☎ 64 25 89;

Av Raúl Pujol cnr Calle 10; ☽ 24hr) City's best dollar pharmacy. Another dollar pharmacy is in the lobby of the Meliá Santiago de Cuba (☽ 8am-6pm).
Farmacia Las Américas (Map pp356-7; Av Victoriano Garzón No 422; ☽ 24hr)
Hospital Provincial Saturnino Lora (Map pp356-7; ☎ 64 56 51; Av de los Libertadores) Recompression chamber.
Hospital Quirúrgico Gineco-Obstétrico (Map pp356-7; ☎ 64 66 49; off Av Gral Cebreco, Reparto Vista Alegre) Re-compression chamber available 8am to 3pm Monday to Friday.

MONEY
Banco de Crédito y Comercio (Map p360; ☎ 62 80 06; Felix Peña No 614)
Banco Financiero Internacional (Map p360; ☎ 62 20 73; Felix Peña No 565; ☽ 8am-4pm Mon-Fri)
Bandec (Map p360; ☎ 62 75 81; Gral Lacret at Aguilera; ☽ 8am-5pm Mon-Fri)
Cadeca (Map p360; ☎ 68 61 76; Aguilera No 508; ☽ 8:30am-6pm Mon-Sat, 8:30am-noon Sun) Other Cadeca branches are in the Meliá Santiago de Cuba and Hotel Las Américas.

PHOTOGRAPHY
Photo Service Gral Lacret (Map p360; Gral Lacret No 728); Saco (Map p360; Saco No 422 near Plaza de Dolores); Av Garzón (Map pp356-7; Av Garzón btwn Calles 6 & 7)

POST
DHL (Map p360; ☎ 68 63 23; Aguilera No 310)
Post Office Aguilera (Map p360; Aguilera No 519); Calle 9 (Map pp356-7; Calle 9 near Av Gral Cebreco, Ampliación de Terazzas) Telephones are here too.

TELEPHONE
Etecsa (Map p360; Heredia at Félix Peña; ☽ 24hr)

TRAVEL AGENCIES
Cubatur (Map pp356-7; ☎ 65 25 60; fax 68 61 06; Av Garzón No 364, btwn Calle 3 & 4; ☽ 8am-8pm) Books rental cars, excursions, and hotel rooms nationwide; sells entrance to the Tropicana; disorganized.
Gaviota (Map pp356-7; ☎ 68 71 35; Manduley No 502, Vista Alegre, in Villa Gaviota) You can arrange visits to Guantánamo naval base here.
Havanatur (Map pp356-7; ☎ 68 72 80; Calle 8 No 54, btwn Calles 1 & 3, Vista Alegre; ☽ 8am-noon, 1-5pm Mon-Fri, 8am-noon Sat) Handles reservations at most large Cuban hotels, good for transfers.
Islazul Agencia de Ventas (Map p360; ☎ 62 31 24; Aguilera No 308 btwn Gral Lacret & Hartmann; ☽ 9am-noon, 2-4pm Mon-Fri) Reserves rooms at Islazul hotels around Santiago and tables at the Cabaret San Pedro del Mar (US$10 per couple).

Reservaciones de Campismo (Map p360; ☎ 62 90 00; Cornelio Robert No 163; ☿ 8:30am-noon, 1-4:30pm Mon-Fri, 8am-1pm Sat) Reserve cabin accommodation at La Mula, Loma Blanca, and Playa Larga in Parque Baconao.

Rumbos (Map p360; ☎ 68 60 33, 62 48 23; Gral Lacret at Heredia; ☿ 7:30am-8pm) Bus or air tickets booked here involve a US$5 commission. Helpful, English spoken.

Dangers & Annoyances

The historical center of Santiago de Cuba is rife with *jineteros*, all working their particular angle. Solo female travelers will feel it especially, as one guy after another fishes for conversation, trinkets, beer or *besitos* (little kisses). See the boxed text for some ideas on how to shake that dollar-with-legs feeling.

It always seems like it's rush hour here thanks to traffic in the congested city center. Making things worse are all the motorcyclists bobbing and weaving for position, becoming a real hazard at the rotaries, of which Santiago de Cuba has many. Narrow, nonexistent sidewalks and crowded streets are a pain for pedestrians.

Sights

CASCO HISTÓRICO   Map p360

Parque Céspedes & Around

Most visits begin on **Parque Céspedes**, where a bronze bust memorializes Carlos Manuel de Céspedes, the man who issued *El Grito de Yara* declaring Cuban independence

---

HINTS ON JINETERISMO

From Times Square to Red Square, every corner of the world has its hustlers. But there are touts and there are *jineteros/as*. In reality, Cuban 'jockies' are not nearly as persistent as touts in Moroccan medinas or as desperate as Rio de Janeiro orphans. They don't have to be: their housing, education, health care and food is provided by the government. OK, so soy protein isn't a steak and the coffee sucks; the point is Cubans aren't hustling to survive, and that allows them to charm you doing what they do best: being friendly, funny and yes, helpful.

But if readers' letters and personal experience are any indication, *jineteros* are the number-one travel bummer in Cuba. Here are some tips:

▪ Be aware of who's around you as you approach casas particulares or paladares: one scam involves someone sneaking alongside of you to ring the doorbell or knock so it looks like they've brought you there and will therefore get their commission.

▪ If you need directions, ask a matron, kid or shopworker.

▪ If approached while having a beer with a friend, say kindly that you're in the middle of a conversation and would prefer to continue with it. Implicitly saying 'hey, you're interrupting' will often do the trick.

▪ Helpful phrases include: 'no gracias, no necesito nada' (no thanks, I don't need anything); 'por favor, no me moleste' (please don't bother me); and 'No me ineterés. Tengo habitación/paladar ya' (I'm not interested. I already have a place to stay/eat).

▪ More aggressive types might have to hear something more direct like 'dejame coño,' which is unequivocal in Cuban terms.

▪ 'Where you from' is the most common opener and you'll hear it everywhere. Develop some conversation-stopping rejoiners like: Iceland, Iraq, the CIA or Marianao (a tough, respected Havana neighborhood).

▪ The other common opener is 'what's your name?' Women can repond 'casada felizmente' (happily married) to good effect, but use your imagination.

▪ If it's really getting to you, consider staying in a more residential neighborhood (eg Vista Alegre in Santiago de Cuba or Playa Miramar in Havana).

▪ If it's really, really getting to you, consider visiting Matanzas, Remedios, Sancti Spíritus, Holguín or Guantánamo, all refreshingly hustler free.

▪ Learn some Spanish so you can talk to real people, not just those who want to get into your wallet or pants.

▪ Of course, the easiest way to quit being hassled by hustlers is to hook up with one!

CASCO HISTÓRICO SANTIAGO DE CUBA

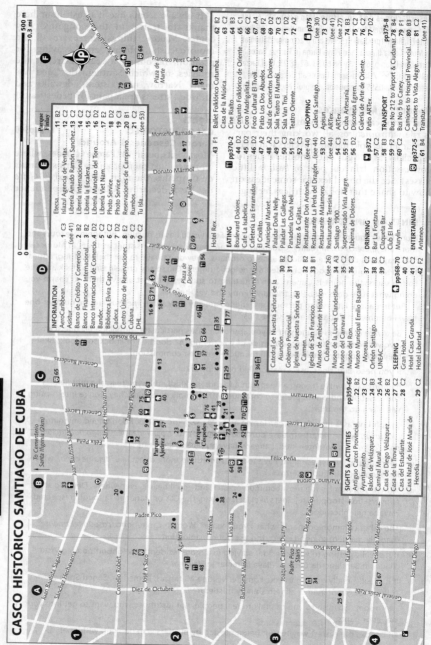

in 1868. In daylight it's a hot and glaring square, but in the evenings it's cool, with music from the nearby Hotel Casa Granda drifting across the park. Some of Santiago de Cuba's most impressive buildings ring this former Plaza de Armas. The **Casa de la Cultura Miguel Matamoros** (Gral Lacret 651), on the eastern side of the square, is the former San Carlos Club, a social center for wealthy residents until the revolution. The neoclassical **Ayuntamiento** (Gral Lacret & Aguilera), on the northern side of the square, was erected in the 1950s using a design from 1783. Fidel Castro appeared on the balcony of this building on the night of January 1, 1959, trumpeting the revolution's triumph.

Facing the northwestern corner of Parque Céspedes is the **Casa de Diego Velázquez** (Felix Peña No 602). Dating from 1522, it's the oldest house still standing in Cuba. Restored in the late 1960s, this Andalusian-style building (you'll know it by its enclosed balcony with the fine, Moorish-style woodwork) was restored in the late 1960s, and opened in 1970 as the **Museo de Ambiente Histórico Cubano** (☎ 65 26 52; unguided/guided US$2/5; 🕑 9am-1pm, 2-4:45pm Mon-Thu, 2-4:45pm Fri, 9am-9pm Sat & Sun). The ground floor was originally a trading house and gold foundry, while the upstairs was the personal residence of Diego Velázquez. Today, rooms display period furnishings and decoration from the 16th to 19th centuries. Visitors are also taken through an adjacent neoclassical house dating from the 19th century.

You can't miss the imposing, five-nave **Catedral de Nuestra Señora de la Asunción** on the southern side of the park. This cathedral is only the latest in a series of churches on this spot that have been ravaged by pirates, earthquakes and architects. Cuba's first cathedral was built here in the 1520s, originally positioned with its façade facing the bay. The present cathedral with its coffered ceiling, dome and graceful archangel was completed in 1922, while the choir stalls date from 1910. It's believed that Diego Velázquez is buried beneath the cathedral, though this has never been proven and there's no marker. Unfortunately the cathedral is usually closed outside of mass hours (🕑 6:30pm Mon, Wed, Thu & Fri, 5pm Sat, 9am & 6:30pm Sun). The **Museo Arquidiocesano** (☎ 62 21 43; 🕑 9am-5pm Mon-Fri, 9am-2pm Sat, 9am-noon Sun), on the southern side of the cathedral

through an independent doorway, houses a collection of furniture, liturgical objects, and paintings including the *Ecce Homo*, believed to be Cuba's oldest painting. Behind the cathedral and two blocks downhill from the park is the **Balcón de Velázquez** (Bartolomé Masó & Mariano Corona), the site of an old Spanish fort with lovely harbor views.

Other interesting nearby churches include **Iglesia de Nuestra Señora del Carmen** (Félix Peña No 505), an 18th-century hall church that is the final resting place of Christmas-carol composer Esteban Salas (1725–1803), *maestro de capilla* (choir master) of Santiago de Cuba's cathedral from 1764 until his death; and the 18th-century three-nave **Iglesia de San Francisco** (Juan Bautista Sagarra No 121).

On Heredia, east of the Hotel Casa Granda, is a strip of culturally significant buildings, including the **Casa del Estudiante** (☎ 62 78 04; Heredia No 204) and the one-time home of composer Rafael Salcedo (1844–1917), **Casa de la Trova** (☎ 65 26 89; Heredia No 208). In the next block is national monument **Casa Natal de José María de Heredia** (Heredia No 260; without/with guide US$1/2; 🕑 9am-6pm Tue-Sat, 9am-9pm Sun), containing a small museum illustrating the life of the romantic poet born here on December 31, 1803. Heredia is known for his lyrical poetry, most notably *Ode to Niagara* and other romantic poems extolling the natural beauty of the Americas. As an independence advocate, Heredia was forced into exile in the US and Mexico, where he died in 1839.

Nearby on Heredia are the **Biblioteca Elvira Cape** (founded 1899; Heredia No 259) and the **Unión Nacional de Escritores y Artistas de Cuba** (UNEAC; Heredia No 266). The colorful **Museo del Carnaval** (☎ 62 69 55; Heredia No 303; admission US$1; 🕑 9am-5pm Tue-Sun) displays the history of Santiago's carnaval tradition, the oldest in Cuba. Drop in for the talented folkloric dance group performing in the patio (admission US$1; 🕑 4pm Tue-Sat & 11am Sun, provided a small audience is present). One block south and a bit west of here is the fun and informative **Museo del Ron** (Bartolomé Masó 358; admission US$2; 🕑 9am-5pm Mon-Sat), outlining the history of Cuban rum; entrance includes a taster of añejo.

Pío Rosado, the narrow alley running alongside the Museo del Carnaval, leads to the fabulous neoclassical buidling of the **Museo Municipal Emilio Bacardí Moreau** (☎ 62 84 02; admission US$2; 🕑 10am-6pm). This is one of Cuba's oldest functioning museums, founded in 1899 by the famous rum distiller and first mayor of Santiago de Cuba, Emilio Bacardí y Moreau (1844–1922). Downstairs are exhibits relating to the 19th-century independence struggles (including an interesting weapons collection), upstairs are European and Cuban paintings. There are a dozen paintings by the Tejada brothers, including *La confronta de billetes* by José Joaquín Tejada Revilla (1867–1943), a typical work of the Spanish *costumbrismo* school, which sought to portray the customs and life of the common people. Dating from the 1920s, the **Gobierno Provincial** or 'Poder Popular,' at Pío Rosado and Aguilera opposite the Museo Bacardí, is the seat of the provincial assembly.

If you're on a magical history tour, you'll want to visit the **Antiguo Carcel Provincial** (1906; Aguilera No 131), two blocks west of Parque Céspedes. Fidel Castro and other rebels were incarcerated here immediately after the 1953 Moncada attack. A half-block west on Aguilera is the **municipal market**, and south on Padre Pico are a series of picturesque **steps** (almost 100 years old and still hosting rousing games of dominoes) leading to the **Tivolí** neighborhood.

Up the slope to the right at the top of the Padre Pico steps was where revolutionaries attacked a police station on November 30, 1956 to divert attention from the arrival of the yacht *Granma*, carrying the M-26-7 guerrillas. The colonial-style station now houses the **Museo de la Lucha Clandestina** (☎ 62 46 89; admission US$1; Gral Jesús Rabí No 1; ☽ 9am-5pm Tue-Sun), detailing the underground struggle against Batista. The view from the balcony is excellent. Across the street is the house where Fidel Castro lived (Gral J Rabí No 6) from 1931 to 1933 while a student in Santiago de Cuba. On the next corner of Rabí and Rafael Salcedo is a series of **carnival murals** facing a small park.

Plaza de Dolores

East of Parque Céspedes is the pleasant and shady Plaza de Dolores at Aguilera and Porfirio Valiente, a former marketplace now dominated by the 18th-century **Iglesia de Nuestra Señora de los Dolores**. After a fire in the 1970s, the church was rebuilt as a concert hall (Sala de Conciertos Dolores). Many restaurants and cafés flank

this square. If there's a cruising corner in Santiago de Cuba, it's here on the benches once the sun goes down.

Plaza de Marte

Three busy blocks east of Plaza de Dolores is this 19th-century Spanish parade ground where prisoners were executed by firing squad during the colonial era. Today, Plaza de Marte is the site of Santiago de Cuba's *esquina caliente*, where baseball fans debate the sport with wild abandon among monuments to various heroes of Cuban independence. Baseball is the most democratic space we have, Cubans will tell you, and it shows here. A block west is the **Museo Tomás Romay** (☎ 65 35 39; Jose A Saco s/n cnr Monseñor Barnada; admission US$1; ☽ 8:30am-4pm Tue-Sat, 9am-noon Sun). This is the city's natural sciences museum, collecting natural history and archaeology artifacts, with some modern art thrown in.

SANTIAGO DE CUBA   Map pp356–7
Tivolí

Downhill from the Padre Pico steps on the edge of the Casco Histórico on General Jesús Rabí is the **Casa de Las Tradiciones** (Gral J Rabí No 154) with a free art gallery and a bar; at night some of Santiago's best *trova* happens here. One block west via José de Diego, the street just before the Casa de Las Tradiciones, you'll get a superb viewpoint over Santiago Bay.

Rounding the next corner north of this viewpoint, Desiderio Mesnier descends to **Parque Alameda**, a popular bayside promenade that opened in 1840 and was redesigned in 1893. Opposite the old **clock tower** and *aduana* (customs house) at the north end of Parque Alameda is the **Fábrica de Tabacos César Escalante** (☎ 62 23 66; Av Jesús Menéndez No 703; admission US$5; ☽ 9-11am & 1-3pm), a working cigar factory open for visits. The factory shop sells the finished product.

North of Casco Histórico

North of the historic center, Santiago de Cuba turns residential. Even bustling Felix Peña quiets down as you come upon the 18th-century bell tower of **Iglesia de Santo Tomás** (Félix Peña No 308), five blocks north of Parque Céspedes.

Two long blocks northwest of the church is the important **Museo-Casa Natal de Antonio**

Maceo (☎ 62 37 50; Los Maceos No 207; admission US$1; ☼ 9am-5pm Mon-Sat). The famous general who fought in both wars of independence was born in this early 19th-century house on June 14, 1845. In his 1878 *Protest of Baraguá*, Maceo rejected any compromise with the colonial authorities and went into exile after further combat. During the 1895 war he was second in command, after Máximo Gómez, and died fighting in western Cuba in 1896. This simple museum exhibits highlights of Maceo's life, including the tattered flag flown in battle.

Another home-turned-museum is the **Casa Museo de Frank y Josue País** (Gral Banderas No 226; admission US$1; ☼ 9am-5pm Mon-Sat), about five blocks southeast. Integral to the success of the revolution, the young País brothers organized the underground section of the M-26-7 in Santiago de Cuba until Frank's murder by the police on July 30, 1957. The exhibits tell the story.

You can behold a different side of Cuban history at the original **Bacardí Rum Factory** (Fábrica de Ron; Av Jesús Menéndez near Narciso López), opposite the train station on the northwestern side of town. The factory was founded by the Bacardí family in 1838, but after the revolution the company moved to Puerto Rico taking the Bacardí patent with them (they're now suing the Cuban government under the US's extraterritorial Helms-Burton law). The Santiago de Cuba product was renamed Ron Caney. Also produced here are quality rums such as Matusalem, Ron Santiago and Ron Varadero. The factory consists of three sections: the production room, the aging storehouse (with 42,000 barrels of rum) and the bottling section. In total the distillery produces nine million liters a year, 70% of it exported. The **Barrita Ron Havana Club** (☼ 9am-6pm), a tourist bar attached to the factory, offers rum sales and tastings. There are no factory tours.

Cuartel Moncada (Moncada Barracks)

The **Parque Histórico Abel Santamaría** (Gral Portuondo & Av de los Libertadores) is the site of the former Saturnino Lora Civil Hospital. On July 26, 1953, a group of revolutionaries (including female fighters Haydee Santamaría and Melba Hernández) led by second-in-command Abel Santamaría occupied this hospital during the attack on the adjacent Moncada Barracks. Most of those involved

were later killed (and some tortured) by Batista's troops. On October 16, 1953, Fidel Castro was tried in the Escuela de Enfermeras here for leading the Moncada attack; this is where he made his famous 'History Will Absolve Me' speech. A site **museum** (admission US$1; ☼ 9am-4:30pm Mon-Fri) opened in 1976 with a photo exhibit on socioeconomic conditions in Cuba during the 1950s.

The **Cuartel Moncada** (Moncada Barracks), with a trapezoid footprint from General Portuondo to Paseo de Martí and Av de los Libertadores to Av Moncada, is named for Guillermón Moncada, a prisoner here in 1874 who later fought for independence from Spain during the 'Little War' of 1879. The first barracks on this site were constructed by the Spanish in 1859, and in 1938 the present buildings were completed. On the morning of July 26, 1953, more than 100 revolutionaries led by Fidel Castro attacked Batista's troops here at what was at the time Cuba's second-most important military garrison. The revolutionaries had hoped the assault would spark a general uprising throughout Cuba, but things went awry and the armed struggle against the dictator was put on hold for another 3½ years. The **monument** depicting Martí and Abel Santamaría on General Portuondo marks the spot from where the first shots were fired.

In 1960, after the triumph of the revolution, these barracks, like all barracks in Cuba, were converted into a school called Cuidad Escolar 26 de Julio, and in 1967 a **museum** (☎ 62 01 57; admission US$2, guide/camera/video extra US$1/1/5; ☼ 9am-5pm Mon-Sat, 9am-1pm Sun) was installed near gate No 3, where the main attack took place. The outer walls are still bullet-pocked. The museum outlines the history of Cuba from the Spanish conquest to the present, with heavy emphasis on the revolution. A scale model of Moncada illustrates the 1953 assault.

The **Palacio de Justicia** (Av de los Libertadores & Calle H) also figured prominently in the assault on Moncada, as fighters led by Raúl Castro provided covering fire from the rooftop. Most Moncada defendants were tried here in September 1953.

Vista Alegre

Broad, dappled avenues lined with bowed trees mark the entrance to Santiago de

Cuba's old upper-class neighborhood **Vista Alegre**, on the east side of town. From near Hotel Las Américas, Av Manduley runs east through Vista Alegre, past a number of stately neocolonial mansions, some of which were converted into schools, clinics, cultural centers, government offices and restaurants after the former owners went into exile in the US. The side streets here are peppered with beautiful casas particulares (p369). The **Centro Cultural Africano Fernando Ortiz** (Av Manduley No 106; admission free; ☺ 9am-5pm Mon-Fri, alt Sat) contains African artifacts, handicrafts and fine art collected by Cuba's most important ethnologist. A block away is the **Museo de Imagen** (☎ 64 22 34; Calle 8 No 106; admission US$1; ☺ 9am-5pm Mon-Sat) which is one dollar well spent. From Kodak to Korda, little CIA spy cameras and lots of historical and contemporary photos, the history of Cuban photography is housed here.

Nearby, there's a large eclectic palace now used as the **Palacio de Pioneros** (Av Manduley & Calle 11). Parked in a corner patch of grass, there's an old MiG fighter plane on which the younger pioneers play. The traffic circle at Av Manduley and Calle 13 contains an impressive marble statue of poet José María Heredia y Heredia.

Around the corner is the **Casa del Caribe** (☎ 64 22 85; fax 64 23 87; Calle 13 No 154; admission free; ☺ 9am-5pm Mon-Fri & concert nights), founded in 1982 to study Caribbean life. It organizes the Festival of Caribbean Culture every July (see Festivals & Events, p368). The Promotor Cultural can arrange mini-courses with tutors experienced in most aspects of Cuban culture, including Afro-Cuban religions and popular music and dance.

A block south is the affiliated **Casa de las Religiones Populares** (Calle 13 No 206; admission without/with guide US$1/2; ☺ 9am-6pm Mon-Sat), with a large, bright collection of all things Santería.

Santiago de Cuba's **Parque Zoológico** (Av Raúl Pujol; admission US$1; ☺ 10am-5pm Tue-Sun) is 1km east of Hotel Santiago de Cuba.

Next to the zoo entrance is a fenced-in expanse surrounded by cannons. On this spot, Santiago de Cuba's Spanish garrison surrendered two weeks after the battle of San Juan Hill in 1898. Continue through the grounds of the adjacent Motel San Juan to **San Juan Hill** proper, where US, Cuban and Spanish troops faced off on July 1, 1898.

Some of the original cannons and trenches can still be seen, and there are numerous monuments (free admission), including a bronze figure of a 'Rough Rider' in the center of the park. There's a whopping view of La Gran Piedra from this hill. A large **amusement park** is down the stairway from the Ferris wheel on San Juan Hill. Built in 1985 by Japanese investors, most of the rides are dormant, but the shaded benches are alluring.

Cementerio Santa Ifigenia

A visit to **Cementerio Santa Ifigenia** (Av Crombet; admission US$1, plus camera US$1; ☺ 8am-6pm), 1km northwest of the distillery, is a stroll through history. The cemetery was created in 1868 to accommodate the victims of the War of Independence and a simultaneous yellow-fever outbreak. Among the 8000 tombs here are the graves of many great Cuban historical figures, including national hero, José Martí (1853–95). Erected in 1951, the Martí mausoleum is flanked by the muses and has a side for each of Cuba's former six provinces. There's an impressive changing of the honor guard every half hour here.

The mausoleum of those who died during the 1953 attack on the Moncada Barracks is nearby, as is the grave of Tomás Estrada Palma (1835–1908), Cuba's first president. To the right of the cemetery's main entrance is Emilio Bacardí y Moreau (1844–1922), the son of Facundo Bacardí, founder of the famous rum distillery. María Grajales, the widow of independence hero Antonio Maceo, and Mariana Grajales, Maceo's mother, are to the right of the main avenue. Eleven of the 31 generals of the independence struggles are buried in this cemetery, marked by a tower nearby. Across the avenue again is a monument (1906) to the Spanish soldiers who died in the battles of San Juan Hill and Caney. The father of Cuban independence, Carlos Manuel de Céspedes (1819–74), is further along on the left.

The tombs of revolutionaries Frank and Josue País are in the middle of the cemetery, back from the Martí mausoleum. Like all persons buried here who died during the struggle against Batista, the País' graves are marked by two flags: the black, white, and red flag of Fidel's M-26-7, and the Cuban

RICHARD I'ANSON

Schoolchildren, **Remedios** (p246), Villa Clara Province

Youth **baseball** team (p38), Santa Clara, Villa
Clara Province

RICK GERHARTER

RICHARD I'ANSON

Video theater program,
Remedios (p246), Villa Clara
Province

Che memorial (p240), Santa Clara, Villa Clara Province

RICK GERHARTER

MARTIN LLADO

Slave watchtower, **Manaca Iznaga** (p270), Valle de los Ingenios, Sancti Spíritus Province

MARTIN

Cuban girls, **Trinidad** (p259), Sancti Spíritus Province

Saddling the burro, **Trinidad** (p259), Sancti Spíritus Province

RICHARD I'A

flag. A tip is in order if one of the staff gives you a guided tour.

Horse carts travel up Av Jesús Menéndez, from Parque Alameda to Parque Barca de Oro via Cementerio Santa Ifigenia (one peso).

SANTIAGO DE CUBA AREA   Map below
Castillo de San Pedro del Morro

A Unesco World Heritage site since 1997, the **Castillo de San Pedro del Morro** (☎ 69 15 69; admission US$3, plus camera US$1; ☒ 9am-5pm Mon-Fri, 8am-4pm Sat & Sun) stands dramatically on a 60m-high promontory on the eastern side of the harbor entrance, 10km southwest of town via Carretera del Morro (which passes the airport access road). El Morro was de-

signed in 1587 by the Italian military engineer Giovanni Bautista Antonelli to protect the town from pirates, but building didn't actually start until 1633 (it was finished in 1693). El Morro's massive batteries, bastions, magazines and walls are considered the best-preserved 17th-century Spanish military complex in the Caribbean. Inside the castle is a museum tracing the naval battle here in 1898. The stupendous views from here take in the western ribbon of coast backed by the Sierra Maestra. Paul McCartney dined in Restaurante El Morro here, and Beatlemaniacs can ogle the chair he sat in, now wall mounted and autographed.

From El Morro you also get a good look at the hamlets of La Socapa and Cayo

SANTIAGO DE CUBA AREA

0	4 km
0	2 mi

INFORMATION
Universidad de Oriente............	**1** C1
UniversiTUR........................	(see 1)

SIGHTS & ACTIVITIES   pp359-66
Caleta La Estrella....................	**2** A4
Castillo de San Pedro del Morro................	**3** A4
Ciudamar...........................	**4** A4
Jardín de los Helechos............	**5** D2
La Socapa..........................	**6** A4
Marina Marlin......................	**7** A4

SLEEPING   🛏 pp368-70
Hotel Balcón del Caribe...........	**8** A4
Hotel Rancho Club..................	**9** C1

EATING   🍴 pp370-2
Restaurante El Cayo................	**10** A4
Restaurante El Morro..............	**11** A4
Restaurante El Paradíso...........	**12** A4

ENTERTAINMENT   🎭 pp372-5
Cabaret San Pedro del Mar......	**13** A4
Tropicana Santiago................	**14** C1

Granma across the bay, both accessible by ferry from Punta Gorda or Ciudamar. In La Socapa you can hike uphill to the ruins of an old Spanish battery where five cannons, designed to create crossfire with the castle, still stand guard. The only shooting nowadays is by photographers taking in the excellent castle views; for some private beach time, you can explore west along the deserted coast. Cayo Granma is a little fantasy island of red-roofed dwellings tucked in a crook of the Bahía de Santiago de Cuba. A short uphill hike to its highest point brings you to the Iglesia de San Rafael. Alternatively, you can circumvent the island in 15 minutes.

To get to El Morro from the city center, take bus No 212 to Ciudamar on the Carretera Turística and wend south along the coast, following the road up to the castle. A more scenic option is to cut across the sandy beach at **Caleta La Estrella** and connect with a broad trail on the opposite hillside. It's a 20-minute, steepish walk with a dicey bridge crossing and wall scaling once you leave the beach. Buses (20 centavos) and trucks (two pesos) to Ciudamar leave regularly from Av de los Libertadores, opposite the Hospital Maternidad. This bus also stops on Felix Peña, five blocks south of Parque Céspedes, where it will be nearly impossible to squeeze on. Public transport thins considerably after 5pm, so go early. A round trip by taxi from Parque Céspedes to El Morro with a 30-minute wait will cost US$10.

Theoretically **ferries** (10 centavos; ☼ hourly) travel a fixed route from Punta Gorda to Cayo Granma via Ciudamar and La Socapa, but the Ciudamar leg is sometimes chopped off, in which case you can cross the bay from Punta Gorda (Bus No 213 from Santiago de Cuba terminates here).

Jardín de los Helechos

Just minutes from downtown Santiago de Cuba, the lush, peaceful **Jardín de los Helechos** (☎ 64 83 35; Carretera de El Caney No 129; admission US$1; ☼ 9am-5pm Mon-Fri) is a wonderland of 350 types of ferns, 90 types of orchids and lots of tender loving care. The entrance fee gets you a detailed tour (in Spanish) by one of the Centro Oriental de Bioversidad y Ecosistemas staff working on this project. Even in May there will be a dozen types of orchids in psychedelic bloom (best time

for orchids is November to January) and the center of the garden has a dense copse-cum-sanctuary dotted with benches. There are unique, handmade artworks and cards (US$3 to US$25) on sale.

The garden is about 2km from Santiago de Cuba on the road to El Caney. Bus No 15 (20 centavos) leaves from Plaza de Marte in central Santiago or you can hire a taxi for US$3 (one way).

Puerto Boniato

For a sweeping panorama of the Santiago de Cuba basin and a bird's-eye view of the provincial penitentiary, you can't beat Puerto Boniato. It's on the ridge that separates the Santiago de Cuba basin from the province's Valle Central. To get there, go through the underpass near the Oro Negro gas station on the Carretera Central at the northern edge of Santiago de Cuba, and wind around and up for 8km. Over the pass, this road continues on to the Autopista Nacional and Dos Caminos.

Walking Tour

A short walking tour taking in some Casco Histórico highlights will give you a taste of the colonial vibe and rich art scene here. We've included ideas for where to duck in for a cold drink en route.

There's no better place to start than on the corner of Bartolomé Masó and the tumbledown bay views from **Balcón de Velázquez (1)**, site of an ancient fort. This corner of Santiago de Cuba is jammed with history and if you walk north up Mariano Corona for two blocks and turn right on Aguilera and right again when you hit **Parque Céspedes (3)**, you come to the mother lode of architectural sites. The **Casa de Diego Velázquez (2)**, with its Moorish fringes and intricate wooden arcades, is believed to be the oldest house still standing in Cuba. It's certainly one of the most striking.

Continue along the park's western side (need to check email? Etecsa is right there on the southwestern corner), and you're drawn to the mighty, mustard façade of the **Catedral de Nuestra Señora de la Asunción (4)**. This building has been ransacked, burned, rocked by earthquakes and rebuilt, remodeled and restored many times. Statues of Christopher Columbus and Fray Bartolomé de las Casas flank the entrance in ironic

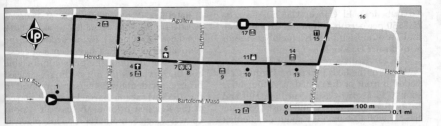

juxtaposition. If you're into religious art, the **Museo Arquidiocesano (5)** (say that three times fast!) is here.

Even if there isn't music drifting from the terrace bar at the **Hotel Casa Granda (6)** on the southeastern corner of the park, it's still a good place to sip a *mojito* and watch the action in Parque Céspedes. Graham Greene used this hotel as literary landscape in his novel *Our Man in Havana*. Head east on Heredia and it's three blocks of wall-to-wall art, music and historic sites. Prick up your ears for what's happening at the **Casa del Estudiante (7)** and **Casa de la Trova (8)** on the right, as there are often rehearsals here, or check the schedule for tonight's concerts.

Keep walking east for a block and you're upon **Casa Natal de José María de Heredia (9)**, birthplace of one of Cuba's greatest poets. You might even run into some writers at **UNEAC (10)** a few doors down or pop into the funky **Librería La Escalera (11)** across the street to hunt for chapbooks. At this corner (Pio Rosado) you can abandon the tour and head to the **Museo del Ron (12)** one parallel block south for a shot of something fiery or continue one block further east to **Patio ARTex (13)** where there's always something fun happening, including good browsing for CDs and souvenirs. Across the street is the **Museo del Carnaval (14)**, which shows how Santiago de Cuba lets loose when it lets its hair down every July in the country's most fabulous, far-out carnaval celebration.

At the next corner (Porfirio Valiente), turn right and grab a 20 centavo coffee in the atmospheric (in a Cuban kind of way) **Cafe La Isabelica (15)**. It's amazing how tranquil **Plaza de Dolores (16)** is considering the traffic zooming around and you might grab an ice cream at any of the places around the plaza and settle into a shaded bench. Otherwise, turn back towards Parque Céspedes and take Aguilera for a bit over a block

to finish up the tour at the **Museo Municipal Emilio Bacardí Moreau (17)** – where Santiago's prize possessions (including a couple of mummies!) are housed in the country's oldest functioning museum.

Courses
LANGUAGE
UniversiTUR (Map p365; ☎ 64 22 10; fax 64 31 86; Universidad de Oriente, Av Patricio Lumumba s/n), 2km north of the city center, arranges Spanish courses. It's also possible to combine instruction in music, literature, and history with language studies; see Courses in the Directory (p411) for details. Note that Americans must enroll through Havanatur in Havana.

MUSIC & DANCE
Instruction in guitar, drum, piano and more are offered at the **Escuela de Música Lauro Fuente** (☎ 65 23 73; Sánchez Hechavarria No 505). Lessons are US$10 for 90 minutes and you can use the practice rooms and instruments Monday to Friday, depending on availability.

For instruction in *son, salsa, mambó, danzón, mozambique, chachachá, pilón* or *conga santiaguera*, get in touch with **Rafael Navarro Gómez** (☎ 62 77 12; José A Saco No 824). A member of the Compañia Teatro Danza del Caribe, based at Teatro Heredia, Rafael offers beginning dance lessons at US$15 for two hours, and advanced classes at US$35 for three hours. Reader feedback on these classes has been mixed.

For Afro-Cuban dancing, see Casa del Caribe (p364).

Tours
Rumbos and Cubatur (see Travel Agencies p358) have essentially the same menu, selling excursions to La Gran Piedra (US$40, includes the Jardín Botánico and Cafetal

SANTIAGO DE CUBA PROVINCE

La Isabelica), El Cobre (US$25), Baracoa (US$50 per person, minimum four people), and Tropicana Santiago Nightclub (without/with dinner US$35/45).

You can easily arrange a tour on the spot with one of the taxis parked on Parque Céspedes in front of the cathedral. A four-hour tour to El Morro Castle, San Juan Hill and Santa Ifigenia Cemetery could cost US$20 for the car with Cubataxi (or about double that in a newer tourist taxi). A similar tour taking in Plaza de la Revolución, El Cobre and the Monumento Al Cimarrón goes for US$12.

Festivals & Events

Summer is an exciting time in Santiago de Cuba, with events coming one after the other. The season begins with the Fiesta de San Juan (June 24), celebrated with processions and conga dancing by cultural associations called *focos culturales*. Mid to late June is also when the Boleros de Oro extravaganza happens. It's followed by the Festival del Caribe, Fiesta del Fuego (Fire Celebration Festival of Caribbean Culture) in early July with exhibitions, music, song and dance from all around the Caribbean. Santiago de Cuba's Carnaval, held during the last week of July, is the hottest in Cuba, with open-air grandstands erected along Av Garzón. The International Chorus Festival is in late November and the Festival Internacional de Trova is in mid-March.

Sleeping

BUDGET

Many families rent rooms to visitors, and they're easy to find, either from the listings in this book (see the boxed text opposite), recommendations from other travelers or casa owners, or by looking for the blue triangles on front doors. Avoid having a *jinetero* lead you to a room, as their commission will jack up the price. There's a good selection of hotels in all price ranges here.

City Center

Hotel Libertad (Map p360; Islazul; ☎ 62 83 60; Calle Aguilera No 658; s/d low season US$26/34, high season US$34/38; ☒ ▣) The 18 rooms at this hotel right on Plaza de Marte were recently renovated and everything is spiffy and new (though the air-con sometimes goes wacky). Good value, but some rooms are windowless – blech. The restaurant is a fair deal, too.

Hotel Rex (Map p360; Islazul; ☎ 65 35 07/8/9; Av Victoriano Garzón No 10; s/d low season US$19/24, high season US$24/28; ☒) By all accounts, the renovation of the Rex has been a success: the air-con is good, the beds comfortable and the service, while not sterling, is at least bronze. Incidentally 20 persons involved in the 1953 Moncada Barracks attack stayed at the Rex just prior to the assault (Room 25 was Abel Santamaría's). This place is often full.

Gran Hotel (Map p360; ☎ 65 30 20; Saco No 310, at Hartmann; s/d US$26/32; ☒) This old four-story hotel with an impressive lobby and great location has big rooms with fridge and TV. Upstairs units have balconies overlooking the street. A bit rougher around the edges than the Libertad (but still a good choice), this place has a mostly Cuban clientele.

Outside the Center

Hotel Rancho Club (Map p365; Islazul; ☎ 63 32 80/63 39 40; Altos de Quintero; s/d incl breakfast low season US$26/34, high season US$32/38; ☒ ☒) If you have a car and don't mind being a bit out of the center, this place 4km north of Santiago de Cuba off the Carretera Central is a winner. The 30 rooms are well kept, the restaurant is good (with city views to boot!) and the staff are friendly and helpful. There are big cabaret shows here Friday to Sunday (guests/nonguests US$1/2; ☒ 10pm to 2am) when US$10 gets you two portions of fried chicken, a bottle of rum and four cokes – a cheap, fun party.

Hotel Balcón del Caribe (Map p365; Islazul; ☎ 69 10 11; on Carretera del Morro Km 7.5; s/d US$34/42, cabañas incl breakfast s/d US$36/48; ☒ ☒) This complex near the Castillo del Morro, 10km south of town, has 72 rooms, but spring for a cliffside cabaña – only a few dollars extra, but worth it for the privacy and views. The pool is saltwater and the hotel has a sailing yacht that does dinner and dancing tours. Right next door is Cabaret San Pedro del Mar, with a gala floorshow. Ask for a room away from the cabaret and swimming pool, if you want some shut eye.

MID-RANGE

Hotel Las Américas (Map pp356-7; Horizontes; ☎ 64 20 11; Av de las Américas & Av Gral Cebreco; s/d/tr low season incl breakfast US$42/56/75, high US$57/67/91; ▣ ☒ ▣ ☒) By far the most popular hotel for groups, this good medium-priced choice

CASAS PARTICULARES – SANTIAGO DE CUBA

Marlon Romaguera Cala (☎ 65 40 52; Aguilera No 612, Apt No 2; r US$15) Small room, great bed, friendly, others in same building.

Ramona and Manuel Tur (☎ 65 26 24; Corona No 555; r US$15-20)

Magda Avalo and Ángel Martínez (☎ 65 20 31; Rafael Salcedo No 163; r US$20) Large garden, ideal for long stays; ask for Isabel or Angel.

Santiago M Vallina García (☎ 62 51 62; Aguilera No 563, Apt No 2; r US$15-20) Central, ring bell marked 'Carmen.'

Nardys Aguilera Rodríguez (☎ 62 24 09; Aguilera No 565; r US$15)

Carmen F Valls Rodríguez (☎ 62 40 84; Gral Lacret No 256; r US$15) Nice couple.

Doña Mery Escalona (☎ 64 14 11; Anacaona No 111, Reparto Terrazas; r US$20) Friendly, near zoo, English spoken.

Ada Tornés Ortíz (☎ 64 13 67; Calle 11 No 323, Reparto Santa Bárbara; r US$20-25) New rooms, can rent individually or take the whole three-bedroom, three-bath apartment.

Gisela Fuste Duharte (☎ 62 51 76; Pío Rosado No 409; r US$15-20) Rooms off upstairs terrace, one with direct access and fridge.

Casa Schmidt – Tania & Sorangel (☎ 62 31 82; Corona No 656; r US$15-20) Colonial house, basic bathroom, private.

Armando Carballo Fernández (☎ 62 86 43; Hartmann No 306; r US$15-20) Nice house out of center, private, dog/child here.

Mujeres de Arena – Yadira and Clivia Rodríguez (☎ 62 00 76; Félix Peña No 554; r US$15) Central, meals served, owned by two sisters.

Lourdes de la Caridad Gómez Beaton (☎ 65 44 68; Félix Peña No 454; r US$15-20) Friendly.

Gloria Bové Alonso (☎ 62 38 37; Calle J No 212, Reparto Sueño; r US$20)

Gardenia de la Peña (☎ 65 29 85; Calle J No 213, Reparto Sueño; r US$20) Fridge.

Frank Martínez (☎ 62 45 14; Calle J No 264, Reparto Sueño; r US$20)

Edgardo Gutierrez Cobas (☎ 64 25 36; Terraza No 106, Ampliación de Terraza; r US$20)

Jorge Soulary (☎ 64 39 94; jsoulary@hotmail .com; Calle 13 No 309, Reparto Vista Alegre; r US$20) Mod house, big, plush rooms, especially one with bathtub.

René Miranda Leyva (☎ 64 29 55; Calle 13 No 352, Reparto Vista Alegre; r US$20) Big house, ask for Caridad.

Juan L Martínez and Evis Noa (☎ 64 29 42; Calle 13 No 354, Reparto Vista Alegre; r US$20) Spacious, private, quiet, parking.

Natacha Alvarez Pérez (☎ 65 31 07; Aguilera No 509B; r US$15-20) Central, clean; sweet owner.

María de la Cruz Figueroa (☎ 62 87 78; Joaquín Castillo Duany No 83; r US$15-20) Upstairs room with terrace sleeps three, private; skip the meals; also renting at No 82 Altos.

Luisa Gómez Villamil (☎ 64 34 58; Calle 6 No 353, Reparto Vista Alegre; r US$15-20) Two big, airy rooms share bath, friendly.

Doña Elena Ponce Favero (☎ 65 12 97; pepin@sierra.scu.sld.cu; Hatmann No 213; r US$20-25) Clean, safe colonial house perfect for groups.

Magalis Palencia Domínguez (☎ 64 10 87; Calle 4 No 204, Reparto Vista Alegre; r US$15-20) Independent.

Xiomara Lozada Menés (☎ 62 08 44; Aguilera No 602; r US$15-20) Two spiffy rooms open onto rooftop terrace, views.

Villa Doña Isabella – Isabel González Díaz (☎ 64 41 24; Calle 6 No 309, Reparto Vista Alegre; r US$15-20) Comfortable, near Alliance Française, others nearby.

Antonio Abad Valle (☎ 62 46 34; Calle K No 100, Reparto Sueño; r US$15-20) Warm hosts.

Ana María Echezarreta Noa (☎ 64 56 89; irainae@hotmail.com; Calle I No 160, Reparto Sueño; r US$15-20) Fridge, private, helpful.

Gloria Boué Alonso (☎ 64 49 69; Calle J No 212, Reparto Sueño; r US$15-20) Spotless, others nearby.

Yolanda Elena Pérez Silva (☎ 64 17 76; Calle 4 No 206, Reparto Vista Alegre; r US$15-20) Colonial house, fridge, safe, nice hostess.

Ricardo & Nidia (☎ 64 16 63; Calle 10 No 257, Reparto Santa Bárbara; r US$20-25) Two nicely equipped apartments open onto terrace, kitchen, independent.

Eduardo Halley (☎ 62 48 78; Heredia No 251 at Hartmann; r US$15-20) Right on top of the action, hostel feel, three rooms share one bath.

Arelis González (☎ 65 29 88; Aguilera No 615; r US$15-20) Central, independent room with TV, fridge, can cook, big house lots of traffic.

Omar & Yasmari (☎ 62 53 30; José A Saco No 607; r US$20) Street noise, meals.

Adelaida & Paco (☎ 62 53 28; paco@frm.uo.edu .cu; Calle N No 4, Reparto Sueño; r US$20) Comfortable, English and German spoken.

has a convenient location (near Vista Alegre and attractions in the center) and lots of facilities (restaurant, 24-hour cafeteria, pool, nightly entertainment, car rental etc). Watch for overcharging in the restaurant.

Motel San Juan (Map pp356-7; Horizontes; ☎ 68 72 00; on San Juan Hill; s/d low season incl breakfast US$42/56, high US$51/67; P X ☎) On historical San Juan Hill, with lots of lawn and a kiddie pool, this place is great for history buffs and families. Rooms are spread on expansive grounds and have terraces and lots of extras (including radios – rare in Cuban hotels). Drive 1km east of Hotel Las Américas via Av Raúl Pujol to get here.

Villa Gaviota (Map pp356-7; Gaviota; Av Manduley No 502, Vista Alegre; P X ☎) Undergoing renovations at the time of writing, this pleasant little motel in a nice residential neighborhood will be a good choice, with doubles in the US$50 to US$60 range, after the facelift.

TOP END
City Center
Hotel Casa Granda (Map p360; Gran Caribe; ☎ 65 30 21/22; fax 68 60 35; Heredia No 201; s/d incl breakfast low season US$73/96, high season US$83/112; ☐ X) This elegant old hotel (1914) has 58 rooms and makes a good splurge. One room is arranged for disabled persons. The hotel's fifth-floor Roof Garden Bar (☼ 11am to 1pm) is well worth the US$2 minimum consumption for its excellent view of the casco histórico and beyond. There's music most nights at the terrace bar; check your bill carefully.

Meliá Santiago de Cuba (Map pp356-7; Cubanacán; ☎ 68 70 70; www.solmeliacuba.com; Av de las Américas & Calle M; s/d from US$60/85; P X ☐ X) A mirrored monster in red, white and blue by respected Cuban architect José A Choy, this Meliá property is the lux choice in town, with real bathtubs in every room, city views, three pools, shopping, you name it. The views from the Pico Real bar on the 15th floor are tops, and there are four good restaurants on site. Rooms are priced to move.

Eating
Santiago has an inordinate amount of cheap, crappy state-run restaurants (as opposed to other cities like Camagüey that has stylish, tasty ones). We've tried to separate the wheat from the chaff here, but keep expectations low as mediocre food and sluggish service are hallmarks. If a place is empty at

mealtime, there's a reason (of course, being Cuba, the reason could be that they ran out of food). Also, beware of places with long lines of peso-paying Cubans and a parallel dollar menu – you'll spend ages waiting to be served a small, second-rate meal. Better to fill up on street food or eat in a dollar cafetería and save for a splurge.

CAFÉS
Cafe La Isabelica (Map p360; Aguilera & Porfirio Valiente; ☼ 9am-9pm) Strong coffee in smoky cantina-type atmosphere. You might get away paying pesos, but foreigners typically pay in dollars.

ICE-CREAM PARLORS
Coppelia La Arboleda (Map pp356-7; ☎ 62 04 35; Av de los Libertadores & Av Victoriano Garzón; ☼ 10am-11: 40pm Tue-Sun or until ice cream runs out) As good as Havana's Coppelia and, as always, in pesos. But you have to get in line: ask for *el úlitmo* from the folks grouped on the Av de los Libertadores side of the parlor. Milkshakes are sometimes sold from the outside window.

Heladería Alondra (Map pp356-7; ☎ 68 60 78; Av Garzón & Calle 7; ☼ 9am-10pm) Alondra is a good dollar ice-cream parlor, but we wouldn't know about this outpost: it never seems to open. Maybe you'll get lucky.

PALADARES
With all the tourist traffic, you would think there would be more paladares here, but they come and go (high taxes, owners leaving for foreign shores and law breakers mean places shut down often). As a result, the following paladars are well established and will still be around when you show up.

Paladar Las Gallegas (Map p360; Bartolomé Maso No 305; ☼ 1pm-11pm) Around the corner from the cathedral, this place packs them in with US$8 meals of pork, chicken and sometimes even *carnero* (lamb). Try for an intimate table on the plant-filled balcony.

Paladar Salón Tropical (Map pp356-7; ☎ 64 11 61; Fernández Marcané No 310, Reparto Santa Barbara; ☼ 5pm-midnight Mon-Sat, noon-midnight Sun) A few blocks south of the Hotel las Américas, this rooftop paladar serves tremendous portions of succulent smoked pork (US$8), with the *congrí*, salad and plantains piled on. The *yuca con mojo* is especially delicious (US$0.50). There are good views too.

RESTAURANTS

Santiago 1900 (Map p360; ☎ 62 35 07; Bartolomé Masó No 354; ☼ noon-midnight) Housed in the former residence of the Bacardí clan, you can dine on the standard chicken, fish or pork in a lush dining room replete with piano-bass-bongo trio. Nothing is over 35 pesos, the service is sufficient and the *mojitos* ace (six pesos). There are two good bars here (p372).

Hotel Casa Granda (Map p360; in Casa Granda, Parque Céspedes; ☼ 9am-midnight) One of Santiago's top spots for food, service and location, it's hard to go wrong here for US$3 to US$5 for burgers, sandwiches, even the odd salad. The hotel restaurant proper is a little disappointing considering.

Pizza Nova (Map pp356-7; Av de las Américas & Calle M, Meliá Santiago de Cuba; ☼ 11am-11pm) Yummy pizza (US$4.95 and up) and lasagna (US$7), ravioli and garlic bread (US$1), this is the number-one option for breaking away from all that chicken and pork. Save room for ice cream or coconut flan. The Meliá has two other fine dining restaurants you might try for a splash out.

Cafe Palmares (Map pp356-7; Calle M across from Meliá Santiago de Cuba; ☼ 24hr) Cool courtyard setting under flowering trees is complemented by extensive menu with many egg, pizza, sandwich and chicken options. Nothing is over US$3. Fresh juice and strong espresso make this a good breakfast or post-bar choice.

El Patio (Map pp356-7; ☎ 64 32 42; Av Gral Cebreco; ☼ 9am-11pm) Don't let the name fool you: this is a basement restaurant with little atmosphere, but the food is consistently good and dirt cheap. A pork filet with *congrí* and a little salad costs US$3 and there's a full bar. Come early because they sometimes run out of things.

Cafetería Las Américas (Map pp356-7; ☎ 64 59 23; on traffic circle near Hotel Las Américas; ☼ 24hr) A local hang-out of sorts, this cafeteria terrace does good basics: chicken, spaghetti and pork for under US$2. Inside is the affiliated restaurant with decent full meals of *comida criolla* for US$4.95.

Taberna de Dolores (Map p360; ☎ 62 3913; Aguilera No 468) An inexpensive, colorful place on Plaza de Dolores, its drinks are better than its *comida criolla*. But the patio tables are a bonus and it's a good hang-out spot if you can get a table.

Cafetería Las Enramadas (Map p360; northwest cnr of Plaza de Dolores; ☼ 24hr) It's the usual fried chicken, ice cream and fries here (nothing over US$2.25). The terrace is shady, the beers affordable and the hours long: perfect *jinetero* turf. Good place for hair of the dog or drowning a hangover in grease.

Pekín (Map pp356-7; ☎ 62 91 19; Av de Céspedes & Calle A; ☼ noon-3pm, 6-9:30pm) Chop suey Cuban-style or fried chicken cost under US$1 at this state-run joint four long blocks north of the Moncada Barracks. Peso pizza is on the corner; join the line.

Cafetería Las Arecas (Map pp356-7; Av Manduley No 52; ☼ 10am-1am) Nestled in the garden patio of this mansion turned mod shopping center, this cafeteria has an inexpensive menu with spaghetti, pizzas and chicken dishes for under US$3. Fish filets start at US$5.50. The fancier dining-room restaurant in the rear part of the main building is open until 10pm.

Restaurante Zunzun (Map pp356-7; Tocororo; ☎ 64 15 28; Av Manduley No 159; ☼ noon-10pm Mon-Sat, noon-3pm Sun) Dine in bygone bourgeois style in this palace turned restaurant. This is a good place for something different (chicken curry US$7), rich (paella or lobster for US$15 to US$25) or outrageous (cheese plate US$6 and cognac US$5). Expect professional, attentive service.

Balcón del Puerto (☎ 62 13 43; Carretera Puerto Boniato; ☼ noon-9pm Mon-Sat) A local favorite for finer dining, this place is 8km from Santiago on the Carretera Puerto Boniato via the Carretera Central and has terrific views.

Restaurante El Morro (Map p365; ☎ 69 15 76; Castillo del Morro; ☼ noon-9pm) You can't beat the views and sea breezes that come with your meal here on the terrace perched over the sea. The complete 'servicio a la Criolla' lunch is US$12 including a drink, but you can also order à la carte for US$6 to US$23.

Boulevard Dolores (Map p365; north side of Plaza de Dolores) is a cluster of Rumbos-operated dollar restaurants with variable food and service in a prestige location. The best of the lot may be **Restaurante Don Antonio**, next to Los Enramados, which offers everything from mixed grill (US$2.50) to lobster (US$20). Next door is **Restaurante La Perla del Dragón**, offering chop suey and chow mein. Beyond that is **Restaurante Teresina**, with inexpensive pizza and spaghetti. These places never seem to have customers. Hmmmm.

On the eastern side of Cayo Granma, out by the Castillo de San Pedro, you'll find state-run **Restaurante El Cayo**, charging US$6 to US$20 for a seafood lunch. **Restaurante El Paraíso**, on the western side of the island, has much cheaper chicken dishes.

Other recommendations:

Pizzas & Cajitas (Map p360; B Masó No 260 at Gral Lacret) Coffee and cheese sandwiches in the morning, pizzas in the afternoon, cajitas at night (one to 20 pesos).

Cafetería El Rápido (Map pp356-7; Av Raúl Pujol & Calle 7) Great shady courtyard for snacks and drinks near the zoo. Pizzas are US$1 and ice-cream and sandwiches are under US$2.

Restaurante Matamoros (Map p360; ☎ 62 26 75; west side of Plaza de Dolores) OK cheap set menu (US$3.95), otherwise skip it.

El Criollito (Map p360; Aguilera & Padre Pico; ☺ noon-9pm Tue-Sun) Super budget saver (everything under 20 pesos), basic.

SELF-CATERING

Supermercado Vista Alegre (Map p360; Av Garzón, northeastern cnr Plaza de Marte; ☺ 9am-6pm Mon-Sat, 9am-noon Sun) One of the better-stocked supermarkets in town, with a great ice-cream selection and cheap bottled water.

Panadería Doña Neli (Map p360; Aguilera & Plácido on Plaza de Marte; ☺ 7:30am-8pm) Reliable hardcurrency bakery is good for bread.

Servisoda (Map pp356-7; Av de los Libertadores; ☺ 11am-10:30pm) Fill up on bread and snacks here.

The main **municipal market** (Map p360; Aguilera & Padre Pico) is two blocks west of Parque Céspedes, while the **Mercado Agropecuario Ferreiro** (Map pp356-7; Nuñez de Balboa) is across the traffic circle from Hotel Las Américas and up the side street beside the gas station. The selection at both is surprisingly poor.

Drinking

Claqueta Bar (Map p360; Felix Peña No 654) A hopping local scene marks this open-terrace bar just off Parque Céspedes. There's sometimes live music and salsa dancing in the evening.

Santiago 1900 (Map p360; ☎ 62 35 07; Bartolomé Masó No 354; ☺ noon-midnight) You can choose from two equally atmospheric drinking spots in this old Bacardí palace. Out back is a vine-covered patio buzzing with locals while upstairs is a quieter balcony bar serving food. Tourists pay in dollars, meaning they can glide past the red velvet rope at the door.

Bar La Fontana (Map p360; Gral Lacret, off José A Saco; ☺ noon-2am) Could it be the lounge trend has hit Santiago de Cuba? You might think so walking into this cocoon with low stools grouped around individual tables lining the wall. Just don't order any apple martinis; it's strictly peso beer and rum at this cool saloon.

Club 300 (Map p360; ☎ 65 35 32; Aguilera No 302; ☺ 10am-5pm & 10pm-5am) Santiago's plush club bar off Parque Céspedes attracts well-heeled patrons who sip whiskey behind the curtained windows.

The **Bar del Marqués**, inside Restaurante Don Antonio on Plaza de Dolores, is one of the few tourist bars not connected to a hotel. The terrace at Casa Granda, while fully connected to a hotel, has live music and excellent voyeur opportunities. Also try its roof garden.

Marylin (Map p360; ☎ 65 45 75; Gral Lacret & Saco; ☺ 24hr) is a local favorite serving shots of rum to standing patrons: more a dive counter than a dive bar. If you'd like to touch base with the city's underworld, try the gloomy **Kon Tiki Club** (Map p360; Gral Lacret & Saco) behind Marylin.

Entertainment

For what's happening, look for the bi-weekly *Cartelera Cultural*. The reception desk at the Hotel Granda usually has copies. Or go straight to the paper's office (Felix Peña at Diego Palacios). Every Saturday night Calle José A Saco becomes a happening place called Noche Santiagüera where street food, music and crowds make an all-night outdoor party; beware of pickpockets.

FOLK & TRADITIONAL MUSIC

The sounds of *tambores* (drums) and *trova* waft all up and down Calle Heredia where a cluster of live-music places can be found. You might head there first for easy-access music, but don't discount the further-flung places, all of which showcase quality players.

Casa de la Trova (Map p360; ☎ 65 26 89; Heredia No 208; admission US$2; ☺ 11am-3pm & 8:30-11pm Tue-Sun) The most famous of all the city's traditional clubs (and therefore the most commercial), this is where the *nueva trova* originated. The atmosphere varies from inspiring to canned. On a good night, head to the back patio after the official sets finish.

Casa del Estudiante (Map p360; ☎ 62 78 04; Heredia No 204; admission US$1; ⏰ 9pm Wed, Fri & Sat, 1pm Sun) Grab a seat (or listen from the street) and settle in for the folksy house orchestra and *trovadores*.

Patio ARTex (Map p360; ☎ 65 48 14; Heredia No 304; admission free; ⏰ 11am-11pm) Art lines the walls of this shop-and-club combo that hosts live music most nights; check the posted cartelera.

Patio Los Dos Abuelos (Map p360; ☎ 62 33 02; Francisco Pérez Carbo No 5; admission US$2; ⏰ 10pm-1am Mon-Sat) Intimate club on the east side of Plaza de Marte features traditional Cuban music in a mixed local-tourist atmosphere. Its monthly schedule is posted at the door.

Casa de la Cultura Miguel Matamoros (☎ 62 57 10; Gral Lacret No 651 at Aguilera; admission US$1) This culture club in historic digs on Parque Céspedes hosts many musical events, including a 'Sábado de la Rumba' at 11am Saturday; check the cartelera posted at the door for the week's happenings.

Casa de las Tradiciones (Map pp356-7; Rabí No 154; admission US$1; ⏰ 8:30pm sets) This hip spot in the Tivolí district hosts some of Santiago de Cuba's most exciting ensembles, singers and soloists taking turns improvising. Friday nights are reserved for straight-up, classic *trova*, so all you Ñico Saquito and Trio Matamoros fans should head over then.

Casa de la Música (Map p360; José A Saco cnr Hartmann; admission US$5; ⏰ 10pm-2am) Similar to those in Havana, this Casa del Música features a mix of live salsa and taped disco. Come ready to shake that thang.

TRADITIONAL DANCE

Ballet Folklórico Cutumba (Map p360; Saco No 115; admission US$3) This internationally known Afro-Cuban folkloric dance group founded in 1960 currently appears at Teatro Oriente. If you're in Santiago de Cuba on a weekend, don't miss Cutumba's exciting café teatro, at 9:30pm every Saturday or at 10:30am for their Sunday morning dance show where

---

CUBAN MUSICAL INSTRUMENTS

During slavery in the US, drumming was prohibited, but in Cuba the opposite was true. When Cuban popular music began to diversify and spread in the early 20th century, Cuban musicians had a whole range of instruments at their disposal.

The strong rhythms in Cuban music are usually provided by the *tumbadora* (conga), a tall barrel-like drum held together by metal hoops. The *bongó* is a pair of small round drums joined by a piece of wood. The *batá* is a conical two-head drum of varying size used in Afro-Cuban religious dances and rituals. Folk dances are often accompanied by a single-skinned drum of Congolese origin called a *joca*.

The gourd-shaped rattle called the maraca is one of the only Cuban musical instruments of pre-Hispanic origin. *Chequeré* rattles (a gourd covered with beads) are used in all sorts of Cuban music, from religious rituals to rap. The *maruga* is a metal shaker. The *güiro* is an elongated gourd rasped with a stick, although there are also tin *güiros*. The *cata* or *guagua*, is a wooden tube beaten with sticks. No band would be complete without claves, two wooden sticks tapped together to set the beat. The *cajón* is a simple wooden box used to thump out the rhythm.

The *tres* is a small folk guitar with three sets of steel double strings. The similar *cuatro* has four sets of double strings. Cuban folk groups often include a West African hand piano or *marímbula*, a wooden box with five metal keys. The only wind instrument in Cuban folk music is the *botija*, a clay jug with a short narrow neck bearing an opening on the side for blowing. Musicians vary the pitch of the tones by moving a hand along the neck of the jug. During Carnaval a small five-note horn called a *corneta china* produces a sharp sound like the bagpipe. Modern instruments commonly used in Cuba include the bass, clarinet, guitar, saxophone, trombone and trumpet.

Cuba is the only country outside Europe with a tradition of street organs. During the 19th century refugees from Haiti brought the French mechanical organ to Oriente, where Hispano-Cuban *sones*, boleros and *danzones* soon replaced waltzes and mazurkas in the repertoire. The Cubans made the European organ dynamic by adding a second crank that the operator uses to vary the speed at which the boards pass through the machine. Five or six percussionists join an organ-grinder to form an orchestra playing popular Cuban dance music under the control of the organ-grinder, who can innovate stops or breaks.

they perform such dances as the *tumba francesa*, *columbia*, *gagá*, *guaguancó*, *yagüetó*, *tajona* and *conga oriental*. It's one of the finest programmes of its kind in Cuba.

Foco Cultural El Tivolí (Map p360; Desiderio Mesnier No 208; ☼ 8pm Mon-Fri) Carnaval practice for the Sarabanda Mayoubé happens weekly at this Tivolí Foco. Saturdays at 5pm they perform a *mágica religiosa* rogramme of *orishas*, *bembé* and *palo monte* at the nearby **Casa de las Tradiciones** (Map pp356-7; Rabí No 154).

Also ask about practice sessions at the studios of the **Conjunto Folklórico de Oriente** (Map p360; Hartmann No 407) at Sagarra and the **Foco Cultural Tumba Francesa** (Map p360; Los Maceos No 501) at General Banderas. Traditional dancing also takes place at other *focos culturales* around town most evenings.

DANCE CLUBS

Club El Iris (Map p360; ☎ 65 35 00; Aguilera No 617; admission US$3; ☼ 10pm-2am) Just off Plaza Marte, this is Santiago de Cuba's hottest disco, still after all these years. The cover includes one drink, but at night it's couples only. Stags can check out the matinee (five pesos) daily from 10am to 4pm, but don't expect much.

Discoteca Espanta Sueño (Map pp356-7; Av de las Américas & Calle M; ☼ 10:30pm-3am Fri-Sun) This is the Meliá Santiago de Cuba's house disco; entry is through the hotel lobby to keep out *jineteras*.

Other recommendations:

Ciroa (Map pp356-7; Av Manduley at Calle 13) Local night spot with a band Thursday to Sunday and a 10pm floorshow.

Pista de Baile Pacho Alonso (Map pp356-7; behind Teatro Heredia; admission US$5; ☼ 8:30pm Sat, 5pm Sun) Check out the charanga orchestra playing en plein air here.

Anteneo (Map p360; Felix Peña No 755; admission US$3; ☼ 9pm Sat, Sun) Disco dancing for the young 'uns.

Club Turey (Map pp356-7; Patricio Lumumba No 213; admission 20 pesos; ☼ 10am-11pm) Very local, very caliente.

NIGHTCLUBS

Tropicana Santiago (Map p365; ☎ 68 70 90; ☼ 10pm Wed-Sun) Styled after the original Tropicana in Havana, these Las Vegas-style floorshows feature plenty of babes with strategically placed baubles. After the show, you can dance at a disco in the same complex. Rumbos, Cubatur and most hotels have package tours to Tropicana Santiago for US$35 per person, including admission, one drink and transportation. Saturday night is the best time to go. To get here,

take Circunvalación, northeast of Hotel Las Américas for 4km.

Cabaret San Pedro del Mar (Map p365; ☎ 69 23 73; Carretera del Morro; admission per couple US$10; ☼ 9pm-3am) This cabaret next to the Hotel Balcón del Caribe, 7km southwest of the center, presents a droopier version of the Tropicana show. Dancers are on at 10:30pm.

THEATERS

Teatro José María Heredia (Map pp356-7; ☎ 64 31 34; Av de las Américas & Av de los Desfiles; ☼ box office 9am-noon & 1-4:30pm) Santiago's huge, modern theater and convention center faces the Plaza de la Revolución on the northeastern side of town. Rock and folk concerts often take place in the 2459-seat Sala Principal, while the 120-seat Café Cantante Niagara hosts varied events. Ask about performances by the Compañia Teatro Danza del Caribe.

Sala Teatro El Mambí (Map p360; Bartolomé Masó No 303), near the cathedral, and **Sala Van Troi** (Map p360; ☎ 62 68 88; Saco No 415) present Spanish-language plays in the evening and puppet/clown theater for children on weekends (☼ 5pm Saturday, 10am and 5pm Sunday). Another children's show is staged at 5pm Saturday and Sunday at **Teatro Martí** (Map pp356-7; ☎ 2-0507; Félix Peña No 313), General Portuondo opposite Iglesia de Santo Tomás.

CLASSICAL MUSIC

Sala de Conciertos Dolores (Map p360; ☎ 65 38 57; Aguilera & Mayía Rodríguez; ☼ 8:30pm) Housed in a former church on Plaza de Dolores, you can catch the Sinfónica del Oriente Oriental here, plus the impressive children's choir (☼ 5pm). Bigger *trova* concerts are also held here by up-and-coming acts like William Vivanco and Ariel Díaz. The *cartelera* is posted on the Aguilera side of the street.

A classical choir, the **Orfeón Santiago** (Map p360; Heredia No 68), allows visitors to attend its practice sessions at 9am to 11:30am Monday to Friday. The **Coro Madrigalista** (Map p360; Pío Rosado No 555 at Aguilera), across from the Museo Bacardí, is similar.

CINEMAS

Cine Rialto (Map p360; ☎ 62 30 35; Félix Peña No 654), next to the cathedral, is Santiago de Cuba's favorite cinema, showing large-screen films and video. Videos are also the usual fare at **Cine Capitolio** (Map pp356-7; ☎ 62 71 64; Av Victoriano Garzón No 256).

Cine América (Map pp356-7; ☎ 65 11 84; Porfirio Valiente No 64; ☺ noon-10pm except Thu) shows movies, plus has a weekly *peña de rap*.

SPORT

The **Estadio de Béisbol Guillermón Moncada** (Map pp356-7; ☎ 64 26 40; Av de las Américas) is on the northeastern side of town within walking distance of the main hotels. During the baseball season, from October to April, there are games at 7:30pm Tuesday, Wednesday, Thursday and Saturday, 1:30pm Sunday (one peso).

Shopping
ART GALLERIES

A number of galleries in the center sell original paintings and prints. By international standards the prices are reasonable, but always get an official sales receipt to show Cuban customs (see p107). Also ask about obtaining an export permit. For studio visits, see the boxed text.

Galería de Arte de Oriente (Map p360; Gral Lacret No 656) Probably the best gallery in Santiago de Cuba, the art here is consistently good.

Galería Santiago, below the cathedral on the southern side of Parque Céspedes, is another gallery with quality art and there are several more galleries along Heredia east of here. **Arte Universal** (Map pp356-7; Calle 1, btwn Calle M & Terraza, Ampliación de Terrazas; ☺ 9am-5pm Tue-Sun), behind the Monument to the Martyrs of Bolivia, has shows and sells the work.

SHOPS

Discoteca Egrem (Map p360; Saco No 309; ☺ 9am-6pm Mon-Sat, 9am-2pm Sun) If you're into buying music, look no further than this retail outlet of Egrem Studios; especially good selection of local musicians.

ARTex (Map p360; Gral Lacret btwn Aguilera & Heredia) From mouse pads to mumus, this shop collects any type of Cuban souvenir imaginable. Other ARTex branches (Patio ARTex Map p360; Heredia No 208; ☺ 11am-7pm Tue-Sun; ARTex Map p360; Heredia No 304; ☺ 11am-11pm) focus more on music, with a respectable selection of CDs and cassettes.

Cuba Artesanía (Map p360; Felix Peña No 673 at Bartolomé Masó; ☺ 9am-9pm) Cuban handicrafts and ice-cold drinks go well together here.

Apisun (Map p360; Casa de la Miel; ☎ 62 44 33; Gral Lacret btwn Heredia & Bartolomé Masó; ☺ 9am-9pm) Cuba has a huge bee industry and you can

---

STUDIO VISITS IN SANTIAGO DE CUBA

Collectors and art hounds are in for something special at the home of art critic Luisa Ramirez and her husband Luis Rodríguez, where the works of El Grupo Bayate are exhibited. This community of self-taught artists from the nearby town of Mella creates unique, inspired art that's properly appreciated in this cozy home setting in Santiago de Cuba's Casco Histórico. Here you'll see works by Luis Rodríguez (father of your host), Ricardo Bruff Bruff, Daniel Alvarez and more. Call ☎ 65 64 01 to arrange a visit.

Local painter Efraín Nadereau (☎ 65 23 84; Aguilera No 170; ☺ 9am-noon & 3-6pm), two blocks west of Parque Céspedes, welcomes foreign visitors in his studio. Nadereau is also a noted poet with 16 books in print.

---

get your quality products here, including *apiron*, a tasty drink made from rum and honey and *propólio*, an amazing bee product that has almost all the vitamins and minerals the body needs.

La Maison (Map pp356-7; Av Manduley No 52; ☺ 10am-6pm Mon-Sat) Headed for a resort and lack the proper attire? Head here.

Getting There & Away
AIR

Antonio Maceo International Airport (☎ 69 10 14; airport code SCU) is 7km south of Santiago de Cuba, off the Carretera del Morro. International flights arrive from Paris-Orly, Madrid, Milan and Rome on Cubana and from Toronto on Air Transat and Skyservice. AeroCaribbean flies weekly between here and Port Au Prince, Haiti and twice weekly to Santo Domingo.

Cubana flies nonstop from Havana to Santiago de Cuba two or three times a day (US$108 one way, 1½ hours). At the time of writing, there were no flights between Santiago de Cuba and Baracoa.

AeroCaribbean flies to Havana (US$105) and Holguín daily.

BUS

The **National Bus Station** (Map pp356-7; Av de los Libertadores at Calle 9), opposite the Heredia Monument, is 3km northeast of Parque Céspedes. See the boxed text (p376) for **Astro** (☎ 62 60 91) departure information.

Passage on Astro buses to Baracoa and Guantánamo are only sold the day of departure (read: if a bus materializes) at the ticket window in the back of the bus station. Competition is heavy for seats; you're better off traveling with Víazul or taking a truck. Tickets to all other destinations on Astro are sold in dollars at the Víazul window beside the station.

Víazul (☎ 62 84 84) buses leave from the same station; see the boxed text below for departures.

The Havana bus stops at Bayamo (US$7), Holguín (US$11), Las Tunas (US$11), Camagüey (US$18), Ciego de Ávila (US$24), Sancti Spíritus (US$28) and Santa Clara (US$33). The Trinidad bus can drop you at Bayamo, Las Tunas, Camagüey, Ciego de Á'vila and Sancti Spíritus.

TRUCK

Passenger trucks leave **Serrano Intermunicipal Bus Station** (Map pp356-7; ☎ 62 43 25; Av Jesús Menéndez & Sánchez Hechavarría) near the train station to Guantánamo (five pesos, two hours) and Bayamo (seven pesos, two hours) throughout the day, but early morning is always better for public transport. For these destinations, don't fuss with the ticket window, just find the truck parked out front going

your way. Trucks for Caletón Blanco (three pesos, 45 minutes) and Chivirico (five pesos, 1½ hours) also leave from here; get a boarding pass from the person at the counter and pay as you board.

The **Intermunicipal Bus Station** (Map p356-7; ☎ 62 43 29; Av de los Libertadores & Calle 4), also know as 'Terminal Cuatro', 2km northeast of Parque Céspedes, has two buses a day to El Cobre. Trucks to El Cobre leave from Anden No 1 at this station throughout the day. Two daily buses also leave for Bacanao from here (6am, 6:30pm).

TRAIN

The new French-style **train station** (Map pp356-7; ☎ 62 28 36; Av Jesús Menéndez), near the rum factory northwest of the center, has trains to the following destinations:

destination	cost (one way)	distance	duration
Bayamo	US$4	117km	3 hours
Camagüey	US$11	327km	5½ hours
Ciego de Ávila	US$14.50	435km	8 hours
Guayos	US$17.50	526km	9½ hours
Havana	US$30	861km	14½ hours
Holguín	US$5	138km	3½ hours
Manzanillo	US$5.50	167km	5 hours
Matanzas	US$27	764km	13 hours
Santa Clara	US$20	590 km	10 hours

BUS TIMETABLE

Astro

destination	cost(one way)	distance	duration	departure time
Baracoa	US$9	234km	5 hours	8am
Bayamo	US$5	117km	2½ hours	9:40am, 10:40am
Camagüey	US$12.50	327km	6½ hours	6pm alt days
Ciego de Ávila	US$16.50	435km	9 hours	4:30pm alt days
Cienfuegos	US$25.50	657km	14 hours	4pm alt days
Guantánamo	US$3	84km	2 hours	9am, 10:20am, 3pm
Havana	US$42	861km	16 hours	2:30pm, 7:30pm
Holguín	US$7.50	138km	4½ hours	12:20pm alt days
Matanzas	US$30.50	801km	17 hours	3:20pm alt days
Niquero	US$10	175km	7 hours	7am alt days
Pilón	US$10.50	213km	7½ hours	7:20am alt days
Santa Clara	US$22.50	590km	12 hours	4pm alt days

Víazul

destination	cost (one way)	distance	duration	departure time
Baracoa	US$15	234km	5 hours	7:30am
Guantánamo	US$6	84km	2 hours	7:30am
Havana	US$51	861km	16 hours	7:05am, 11:30am, 3:15pm, 8pm
Trinidad	US$33	581km	11½ hours	7:30pm

The Santiago de Cuba–Havana route listed in the table is for train No 12, the slowest option, which departs Santiago at 10:30am. Other trains serving this route are Train No 2 (aka *locura verde*) leaving at 6:25am daily (US$19 to Camagüey, US$33 to Santa Clara, US$50 to Havana) and a coche motor railcar called the *locura azul* to Havana (US$62), which is scheduled to leave Santiago de Cuba at 11pm on Monday and Thursday. Another service from Santiago de Cuba terminating in Santa Clara leaves at 4:35am, but is often cancelled.

Cuban train schedules are fickle, so you should always verify beforehand what train leaves when and get your ticket as soon as possible thereafter. The easiest, most efficient way to do this is at **Centro Único de Reservaciones** (Map p360; ☎ 65 21 43, 65 1097; Aguilera No 565; ◷ 8:30am-3:30pm Mon-Fri) near Plaza de Marte. You can buy your tickets here and current schedules are posted in the window. You can also go to the train station where dollar tickets are sold at window No 3; go early and prepare for crowds.

Getting Around

TO/FROM THE AIRPORT

A taxi to or from the airport should cost around US$5. The airport is 7km south of the city and up a long access road, so it's hard, though not impossible, to find private taxis. From the center, a private taxi will leave you about 1km from the terminal to avoid police contact (it is illegal for private taxis to transport tourists).

You can also get to the airport on bus No 212, which leaves from Av de los Libertadores opposite the Hospital de Maternidad. Bus No 213 also goes to the airport from the same stop, but visits Punta Gorda first. If boarding at the airport, bus No 213 is better as it goes straight to town, while No 212 goes first to Ciudamar. Both buses (20 centavos) turn around at the top of the grade, just beyond the west end of the airport parking lot to the left of the entrances, not in front of the terminal.

TO/FROM THE TRAIN STATION

To get into town from the train station, catch a southbound horse cart (one peso) to the clock tower at the north end of Alameda Park, from which Aguilera (to the left) climbs straight up to Parque Cés-pedes. Horse carts between the National Bus Station (they'll shout 'Alameda') and train station (one peso) run along Av Juan Gualberto Gómez and Av Jesús Menéndez respectively.

BUS & TRUCK

Useful city buses include bus No 212 to the airport and Ciudamar, bus No 213 to Punta Gorda (both of these start from Av de los Libertadores, opposite the Hospital de Maternidad and head south on Felix Peña in the casco histórico), and bus No 214 or 407 to Siboney (from near Av de los Libertadores No 425, opposite Empresa Universal, with a second stop at Av de Céspedes No 110 near Restaurante Pekín). Bus No 401 from here goes to Siboney and Bacanao. Bus No 5 to Caney stops on the northwestern corner of Plaza de Marte and at Gral Cebreco and Calle 3 in Vista Alegre. You pay the conductor. These buses (20 centavos) run every hour or so; more frequent trucks (one peso) serve the same routes.

Trucks ('camiones') run along fixed routes. From the center to the Moncada Barracks and the Hospital Provincial (near the National Bus Station), hop on along Mariano Corona one block west of Parque Céspedes or on Aguilera. Trucks for Vista Alegre also run along Aguilera; there's a stop in front of the Etecsa building. From the Hotel Las Américas to the casco histórico, hop on a truck at the Parque de los Estudiantes on the roundabout. Trucks to El Cobre and points north leave from Av de las Américas near Calle M. On trucks and buses you should be aware of pickpockets and wear your backpack in front; bigger packs will not be accommodated on local buses and trucks.

CAR & MOPED

Santiago de Cuba suffers from a chronic shortage of cars (Transtur in particular) and you might find there are none available; reservations are only accepted 15 days in advance, making things more difficult. The airport offices usually have better availability than those in town. If you're completely stuck for a car, you can usually rent one at the Hotel Guantánamo, two hours away (p393). With so many cool sites near Santiago de Cuba, demand way outstrips supply for mopeds; a pity. Try the following places:

Cubacar (Map pp356-7; ☎ 65 45 68; in Melía Santiago de Cuba)

Havanautos Hotel Las Américas (Map pp356-7; ☎ 68 71 60; ⏰ 8am-10pm); Jesús Menéndez (Map pp356-7; ☎ 62 26 66; cnr Av Jesús Menéndez & Gral Portuondo); Aeropuerto (Map p365; ☎ 68 61 61; Aeropuerto Antonio Maceo). The Hotel Las Américas office rents mopeds for US$24 per day.

Transtur Parque Céspedes (Map p360; ☎ 68 61 07; below Hotel Casa Granda on Parque Céspedes; ⏰ 9am-8:30pm); Motel San Juan (Map pp356-7; ☎ 68 72 06). The Casa Granda office has eight mopeds for rent; availability is a joke.

Micar, Cubacar and Vía Rent a Car all have desks in **Rumbos** (Map p360; Gral Lacret at Heredia); you might get lucky renting a moped here.

Guarded parking is available on the street in front of the Transtur office, directly below the Hotel Casa Granda. Official attendants, complete with small badges, charge US$1 a day, US$1 a night and US$2 for 24 hours.

The **Servi-Cupet** gas station (Map pp356-7; Av de los Libertadores & Av de Céspedes) is open 24 hours. One **Oro Negro** gas station is at Av 24 de Febrero and Carretera del Morro, and another is on the Carretera Central at the northern entrance to Santiago de Cuba, not far from the Hotel Rancho Club.

TAXI

There's a Turistaxi stand in front of Melía Santiago de Cuba. Taxis also wait on Parque Céspedes in front of the cathedral, including Transgaviota taxis and older Cubataxi vehicles. Always insist the driver use the meter (*taxímetro*) or hammer out a price beforehand. To the airport, it will be just over US$3 by Cubataxi or US$5 by tourist taxi.

Bicitaxis charge about five pesos per person per ride, but it's illegal to carry tourists, so they'll drop you a couple of blocks from Parque Céspedes.

PLAYA SIBONEY

Playa Siboney, 19km southeast of Santiago de Cuba, is the closest Caribbean beach to the city; it's fair to middling as far as beaches go, but still fun. Overlooking the stony shoreline is an American war memorial dated 1907, which recalls the US landing here on June 24, 1898. This local village has

regular bus and truck services from Santiago de Cuba, making it a good choice for anyone interested in a couple of days in seaside private accommodation. Playa Siboney has a refreshing mix of Cubans and foreigners (despite the overweight, balding tourists with their nubile mulattas).

Sights

Granjita Siboney (admission US$1; ⏰ 9am-5pm) The energy fairly bounces off this simple red-and-white farmhouse 2km inland from Playa Siboney and 2km south of the Gran Piedra turn-off on the road to Santiago de Cuba. It was from here, at 5:15am on July 26, 1953, that 26 cars under the command of Fidel Castro left to attack the Moncada Barracks in Santiago de Cuba. Of the 119 persons involved in the action, six died in combat and 55 were executed after their capture by Batista's troops (19 Batista soldiers were also killed); and so the Cuban Revolution was born. The house retains many of its original details, including the dainty room used by the two compañeras who saw action, Haydee Santamaría and Melba Hernández. There are also displays of weapons, interesting documents, photos and personal effects related to the attack. Notice the well beside the building, where weapons were hidden prior to the attack. In 1973, 26 monuments were erected along the highway between the Granjita Siboney and Santiago de Cuba to commemorate the assault.

The **Museo de la Guerra Hispano Cubano Norteamericano**, adjacent to the Granjita Siboney, displays several objects related to the 1898 American military intervention at Santiago de Cuba. Several scale models of both the land and sea battles are provided. It was closed for renovations at the time of writing.

You can arrange horse rides in this area; ask around.

Sleeping & Eating

Villa Siboney (☎ 3-9321; bungalow US$23) Five heavily booked bungalows facing the main beach sleep up to four persons. Ask at the *carpeta* (reception desk), below the apartment building beside the commercial center. For good private rooms here, see the boxed text Casas Particulares – Playa Siboney, opposite.

**CASAS PARTICUALRES –
PLAYA SIBONEY**

Evaristo 'Chicho' Caballero Cabrera (☎ 3-9248; Av Serrano No 1; r US$10-15) Colonial clapboard at entrance to town, simple, friendly, great porch.

Ovidio González Salgado (☎ 3-9340; Av Serrano above the pharmacy; r US$10 -15) Meals, whole house US$35, warmly recommended by a reader.

Ángel Figuredo Zolórzano (☎ 3-9181; Av Serrano No 63; dgarrido1961@yahoo.es; r US$15) Seaside location, patio, nicely outfitted room, at end of street.

Marlene Pérez (☎ 3-9219; on coast a block south of the post office; r US$15-20) Seaside apt with balcony, fridge, parking.

Javier Francisco Hernánedez Rotger (☎ 3-9121; Obelisco No 1; r US$15-20) Near beach.

Marina Ginarte Díaz (☎ 3-9515; Av Serrano No 50; r US$15) OK room with fridge sleeps three.

A number of cheap peso food stalls overlook the beach. They're multiservice, providing information, breaking large bills etc. There is also an open-air dollar bar on the beach. Rumbos operates **Restaurante La Rueda** (☎ 3-9325), signposted just up the road from the beach. It's nice, but casas particulares serve better meals at lower prices.

Getting There & Away

Bus No 214 runs to Siboney from near Av de los Libertadores No 425 opposite Empresa Universal, with a second stop at Av de Céspedes No 110 near Restaurante Pekín in Santiago de Cuba. It leaves about once an hour, and bus No 407 carries on to Juraguá three times a day. Passenger trucks also shuttle between Santiago de Cuba and Siboney. If you're driving, slow down for the police checkpoint 2km south of Sevilla village on the road to Playa Siboney.

A taxi to Playa Siboney will cost US$22 to US$25 with a state taxi, US$15 with a private taxi.

LA GRAN PIEDRA

The Cordillera de la Gran Piedra, a branch of the Sierra Maestra, is a 30km-long barrier separating the Caribbean coast from the Valle Central. It culminates in a gigantic rock 1234m above sea level. The range has a cool microclimate, and it's wise to come in the morning as the peak is often shrouded in

clouds by early afternoon. The tourist hotel near the summit, 28km east of Santiago de Cuba, makes a good base for hikes through the surrounding pine and fern forest.

Sights & Activities

Near the beginning of the access road to the Gran Piedra, 16km southeast of Santiago de Cuba, is the **Prado de las Esculturas** (admission US$1; ☉ 8am-4pm). Strewn along a 1km loop road here are 20 monumental sculptures of metal, wood, concrete, brick and stone by the artists of 10 countries. Inspired sculpture or cheesy lawn art? You be the judge.

The steep, 12km road up the mountain range itself is beautiful, as the trees close in and the valley opens up below. Between May and August, feast on as many mangoes as you can stomach. One kilometer before Villa La Gran Piedra and 800m down a muddy road is the **Jardín Botánico** (admission US$3; ☉ 8am-4:30pm Tue-Sun) with orchids (best November to January) and other flowers. Look for the showy yellow, orange and violet *ave de paraíso* (bird of paradise).

Almost anyone can climb the 459 stone steps to the summit of **La Gran Piedra** (1234m; admission US$1). The huge rock on top measures 51m long and 25m high and weighs an estimated 63,000 tons. On a clear day there are excellent views and on a dark night you can see the lights of Jamaica.

Cafetal La Isabelica (admission US$1; ☉ 8am-4pm) is part of the Unesco World Heritage site bestowed upon the First Coffee Plantations in the Southeast of Cuba (2000). Two kilometers beyond La Gran Piedra on a rough road, there's a museum describing the coffee-processing technology of a century ago. The impressive two-story stone mansion, with its three large coffee-drying platforms, was built in the early 19th century by French émigrés from Haiti. Stroll around the pine-covered plantation grounds if you feel like it.

Sleeping & Eating

Villa La Gran Piedra (Horizontes; ☎ 65 12 05; s/d low season US$29/38, high US$31/42), near the mountain's summit, has 22 one- and two-bedroom cottages. Villa No 1 has the best view, and sleeps four (US$60). There's a restaurant with decent pizza (US$2) and bar 1km down the road in the reception building.

LA GRAN PIEDRA & PARQUE BACONAO

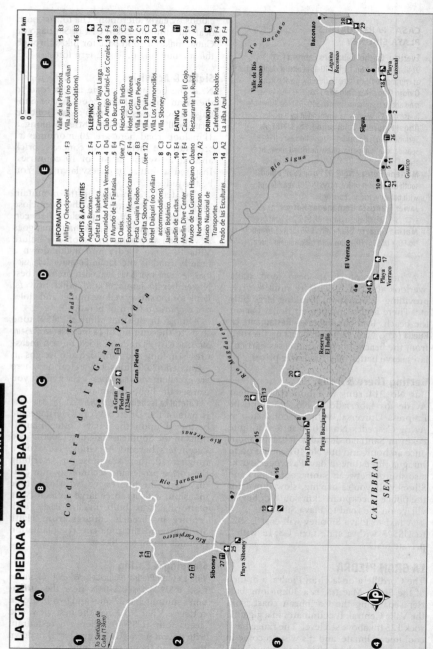

| 0 | 2 mi |
| 0 | 4 km |

INFORMATION
Military Checkpoint...............1 F3

SIGHTS & ACTIVITIES
Aquario Baconao.....................2 F4
Cafetal La Isabelica................3 C1
Comunidad Artística Verraco....4 D4
El Mundo de la Fantasia..........5 E4
El Oasis..............................(see 7)
Exposición Mesamericana........6 F4
Fiesta Guajira Rodeo..............7 B3
Granjita Siboney...................(see 12)
Hotel Daiquirí (no civilian
   accommodations)..................8 C3
Jardín Botánico.....................9 C1
Jardín de Cactus..................10 E4
Marlin Dive Center................11 E4
Museo de la Guerra Hispano Cubano
   Norteamericano.................12 A2
Museo Nacional de
   Transportes......................13 C3
Prado de las Esculturas..........14 A2

Valle de la Prehistoria............15 B3
Villa Juraguá (no civilian
   accommodations)................16 B3

SLEEPING
Campismo Playa Larga............17 D4
Club Amigo Carisol-Los Corales..18 F4
Club Bucanero.....................19 B3
Hacienda El Indio..................20 C3
Hotel Costa Morena...............21 E4
Villa La Gran Piedra...............22 C1
Villa La Punta......................23 C3
Villa Los Mamoncillos............24 D4
Villa Siboney......................25 A2

EATING
Casa del Pedro El Cojo...........26 E4
Restaurante La Rueda............27 A2

DRINKING
Cafetería Los Robalos............28 F4
La Jaiba Azul......................29 F4

Getting There & Away

A steep, winding paved road climbs 12km up the mountain's spine. It's not possible to visit by public transport, as the bus arrives only once a week. A taxi from Santiago de Cuba will cost around US$35 round trip. Otherwise, have a taxi drop you at the top for about US$25 and walk back down (take water).

PARQUE BACONAO

Parque Baconao covers 800 sq km between Santiago de Cuba and the Río Baconao, an area declared a biosphere reserve by Unesco in 1987. Of interest to travelers is the 30km-long coastal plain squeezed between the Gran Piedra Range and the Caribbean. The beaches are smaller than those on the northern coast and golden (as opposed to white); if you want a beach vacation, this shouldn't be your first choice, but it's a good place to wet your toes and catch some rays between hiking the Sierra Maestra and soaking up Santiago de Cuba's culture. Most of the shore is rocky; inhospitable for sunbathing, but terrific for fishing. There are several oddly fascinating tourist attractions here and numerous hotels. Several of the well-spaced hotels close from September to April.

The northern slopes of the Sierra Maestra catch the northeastern trade winds and are moist, but over here it's hot and dry. This is cactus country and you'll see it growing along the coastal cliffs. From mid-March to mid-May, tens of thousands of large land crabs congregate along the coast from Playa Verraco to Baconao, getting smooshed under passing tires and sending up a stench as they bake in the sun.

There's a motel-restaurant combo called Complejo la Punta and a Servi-Cupet, 28km from Santiago de Cuba.

Sights

A dozen painters have studios where their works are displayed and sold in the small artistic community of **El Oasis** at the turn-off to Club Bucanero, 3km east of the Playa Siboney road.

One of the quirkiest attractions we've ever seen is **Valle de la Prehistoria** (admission US$1; ☺ 8am-4:45pm), another 3km along the main road to Baconao. Here giant brontosauri nibble at trees, wooly mammoths graze on grassy expanses and cavemen slay sabre-toothed tigers. Fun for kids of all ages, there are 200 life-size concrete dinosaurs and cavepeople scattered over 11 hectares – even the bathrooms are in little caves. The dinosaurs were built by inmates from the nearby prison. The **Museo de Historia Natural** (☎ 3-9329; admission US$1; ☺ 8am-4pm Tue-Sun) is also here, but kind of a yawn after the prehistoric beasts.

Another must-see in Parque Baconao is the **Museo Nacional de Transportes** (☎ 3-9197; admission US$1, plus camera/video US$1/2; ☺ 8am-5pm), adjacent to the Servi-Cupet gas station 2km east of the Valle de la Prehistoria. The museum has dozens of classic cars, including singer Benny Moré's 1958 Cadillac and a collection of 2500 automotive miniatures. The main US landings during the US intervention in Cuba's Second War of Independence took place on June 22, 1898, at **Playa Daiquirí**, 2km down a side road from the museum. This area is now a holiday camp for military personnel and entry is prohibited.

Ten kilometers southeast of La Punta is the **Comunidad Artística Verraco** (admission free; ☺ 9am-6pm), a village of painters, ceramicists and sculptors who maintain open studios. Here you can visit the artists and buy original works of art.

After a couple of bends in the road you burst onto the coast, where the hotels begin. **Jardín de Cactus** (admission US$5; ☺ 8am-3pm), 800m east of Hotel Costa Morena, has 200 kinds of cactus beautifully arrayed along the rocky hillside, with a large cave at the rear of the garden. Keep your eyes peeled for tiny green hummingbirds (*colibrí*) suckling nectar from flowering cacti.

Compulsory for travelers with children is **El Mundo de la Fantasia** (adult/child US$0.50/0.10), a miniature, Disneyland-style park 1km east of the Hotel Costa Morena, populated with Cuban cartoon characters like Elpidio Váldes. A small amusement park called Sigua Central is just beyond.

Aquario Baconao (☎ 63 51 45; adult/child US$5/3; ☺ 9am-5pm), between the Costa Morena and Hotel Carisol, has dolphin shows (with sultry narration) at 10:30am and 3pm. The aquarium has a good collection of sharks, sea lions, fish and lobsters, though the fish tunnel and shark tank were closed at the time of writing. For an additional US$35/17 you can swim with the dolphins.

Every Cuban resort area seems to have an attraction replicating indigenous scenes. Here it's the **Exposición Mesoamericana** (admission US$1), just east of Club Amigo Carisol-Los Corales. Indigenous cave art from Central and South American is arranged in caves along the coastal cliffs.

At the **Laguna Baconao** (admission US$1; ☻ 8am-5pm), a couple of kilometers northeast of Los Corales, there are a dozen crocodiles kept in pens below a restaurant, plus other caged animals like lizards and *jutías* (rodents of unusual size). Horses are (supposedly) for hire here.

From Playa Baconao, 5km northeast of Los Corales, the paved road continues 3.5km up beautiful **Valle de Río Baconao** before turning into a dirt track. A dam up the Río Baconao burst in 1994, inundating Baconao village. Soldiers at a checkpoint at the village turn back folk trying to use the direct coastal road to Guantánamo because it passes alongside the US naval base. To continue east you must backtrack to Santiago de Cuba and take the inland road. Someday this will change.

Activities

The **Fiesta Guajira Rodeo** (admission US$5; ☻ 9am & 2pm Wed, Sun) at El Oasis, opposite the turn-off to Club Bucanero, stages rodeos with *vaqueros* (Cuban cowboys). Horseback rid-ing is available for US$5 for the first hour, US$3 for each additional hour. The rodeo's restaurant serves typical Cuban food from noon to 2pm daily.

Marlin Dive Center (Cubanacán Naútica; ☎ 68 63 14) at Sigua, a 10-minute walk along the beach from Hotel Costa Morena, picks divers up at the hotels at 8:30am daily. Scuba diving costs US$30 with gear. Marlin's open-water certification course is US$365. They'll also take you deep-sea fishing for grouper, barracuda and red snapper at US$180/360 for three/six hours for up to six anglers (lunch and drinks not included). There's another **Marlin Dive Center** (☎ 68 60 70) offering similar services at Club Bucanero. The water off this bit of coast is some of Cuba's warmest (25°C to 28°C); best visibility is between February and June.

Hands down the best public beach here is **Playa Cazonal**, with lots of tawny sand, natural shade and a big sandy swimming hole (much of the coast here is clogged with seaweed forests). Turn into the Club Amigo Carisol – Los Corales and then it's a quick left to the beach access road.

Sleeping

BUDGET

If you get the urge to explore those side roads, you should note that several resorts used as holiday camps for the Cuban military are off limits to civvies, including Villa Juraguá and Hotel Daiquirí.

Campismo Playa Larga (☎ 35 62 80; per person US$7.50; ☻ open Fri-Sun Sep-Jun only; ☒) Five new cabins are available for foreigners at this spot 1km east of Playa Verraco. It's right on the beach and the best budget option in Bacanao. Check for availability at **Reservaciones de Campismo** (Map p360; ☎ 62 90 00; Cornelio Robert No 163) in Santiago de Cuba.

Villa Los Mamoncillos (☎ 3-9233; r/ste US$14/30; ☒ ☒) This motel has a good location at Playa Verraco, 37km southeast of Santiago de Cuba, but is designed as a holiday resort for Cubans and foreigners may or may not be accepted; it closes September to April.

MID-RANGE

The former El Indio Hunting Reserve, between Complejo la Punta and Playa Verraco, was converted into an 'ecotourism park,' called **Reserva El Indio** (Horizontes; ☎ 68 62 13; www.horizontes.cu; s/d incl breakfast low season US$30/40,

THE CRABS OF BACONAO

From mid-March to early May, the coastal highway between Playa Verraco and Baconao swarms with red and yellow crabs (*cangrejos colorados*), which descend en masse from the adjacent hills to lay their eggs in the sea. Many pop beneath the tires of passing vehicles, while others are harvested by Cubans, who consume the eggs as an aphrodisiac. The females are distinguished from the males by a wider breastplate and pinchers of equal size (the male has one claw larger than the other). From May to July the blue crab (*cangrejo azul*) emerges from its holes in humid areas and scrambles toward the ocean as part of a reproductive cycle that exposes the animal to hunters who value its meat. Year-round, the Cubans pursue the green cangrejo moro in the sea, using a mask and hook. It's another great delicacy.

high US$36/47) after the boundary fence collapsed during heavy rains and most of the deer, antelope, and other hoofed beasts escaped into the nearby hills. These days it's the turf for outdoor types who snorkel, horseback ride and hike in the surrounding area. Individuals stay at Hacienda El Indio, one of two lodges here. If you want to chill unmolested, this is a good spot.

Hotel Costa Morena (Horizontes; ☎ 35-6126; ⓅⓍ Ⓑ) is at Sigua, 44km southeast of Santiago de Cuba and 17km east of the Complejo La Punta Servi-Cupet gas station. It has attractive architecture, a large terrace right on the cliffs and a brown sandy beach with good snorkeling 200m away. The 115 rooms were being renovated at the time of writing.

TOP END

Club Bucanero (Gran Caribe; ☎ 68 63 63; fax 68 60 70; s/d/tr low season US$70/100/145, high US$80/110/160; ⓅⓍ Ⓑ) Tucked up against low limestone cliffs with a small scratch of beach, this resort at Arroyo La Costa, 25km southeast of Santiago de Cuba, has 200 rooms in eight rustic buildings. The price includes all food (we've received complaints), drinks and activities. Take care in rough weather as the underwater rocks are sharp. A shuttle bus goes to Santiago de Cuba four times a day at US$5 round trip. Car rentals available.

Club Amigo Carisol – Los Corales (Cubanacán; ☎ 35 61 21; www.cubanacan.cu; s/d low season US$45/90, high US$50/100; Ⓟ Ⓧ Ⓑ) This massive all-inclusive resort is a five-minute walk from the area's best beach, Playa Cazonal, near the east end of the coastal road through Parque Baconao. A tennis court and a disco are available. Nonguests can purchase a US$15 day pass, which includes lunch and the use of all facilities. This place is frequented mostly by French tour groups.

Eating

The most reliable year-round restaurant out this way is **Casa del Pedro El Cojo** (☎ 35 62 10) just beyond Sigua on the coast. A simple fish meal in this thatched *ranchón* costs US$5. **Restaurante El Mirador**, above the Marlin Dive Center at Sigua, serves dollar meals and drinks on an open terrace with excellent mountain and sea views. **Cafetería Arenas Blancas**, inside Sigua Central near El Mundo de la Fantasía, sells spaghetti and other light meals plus drinks for pesos.

Entertainment

One of the few nonhotel discos in the area is **Dancing Light** (☉ 9pm Sat) at Sigua near El Mundo de la Fantasía.

La Jaïba Azul (☎ 35 00 01) on Playa Baconao, 1km east of the laguna turn-off, is a local drinking place. **Cafetería Los Robalos** (☎ 35 00 02), just across the bridge from La Jaïba Azul, has a variety of drinks for pesos or dollars.

Getting There & Away

Bus service runs only twice a day along the 40km coastal road from Playa Siboney to Playa Baconao. Bus No 407 from Santiago de Cuba goes as far as Complejo La Punta (Villa Juraguá) three times a day; it's a hard hitch from there to points east. Bus No 401 to Baconao departs the **Intermunicipales Bus Station** (Map pp356-7; Av de los Libertadores and Calle 4) in Santiago de Cuba, at 6am and 6:30pm. About two hours later it departs Baconao for the return trip. Arrive at the Santiago de Cuba terminal around 4:30pm to get a pass that will allow you to board the 6:30pm bus. Otherwise just ask for *el último* and wait.

When planning your visit to this area, remember that the coastal road from Baconao to Guantánamo is closed to non-residents.

Getting Around

Havanautos (☎ 68 63 63; in Hotel Bucanero) has cars and mopeds. Cubacar has offices in Hotel Carisol and Club Amigo Carisol – Los Corales.

Servi-Cupet at the Complejo La Punta, 28km southeast of Santiago de Cuba, is open 24 hours.

EL COBRE

The **Basílica de Nuestra Señora del Cobre**, high on a hill 20km northwest of Santiago de Cuba on the old road to Bayamo, is Cuba's most sacred pilgrimage site. It all began in 1606 when three fisherman found a wooden image of the Virgin floating on the Bahía de Nipe in northeastern Cuba. It carried a label reading 'I am the Virgen de la Caridad.' The statue was brought to the copper mine at El Cobre and in 1608 the first hermitage was erected. A century later a larger sanctuary was built, and the present shrine opened in 1927. In 1977 the church was proclaimed a 'basilica menor.'

On May 10, 1916, Pope Benedict XV declared the modest image the patron saint of Cuba, and in 1936 it was solemnly crowned during an elaborate ceremony in Santiago de Cuba. Pope John Paul II recrowned the image during his celebrated 1998 visit to Santiago de Cuba. Many pilgrims come here on September 8, when 'Cachita' (as the image is popularly called) is carried at the head of a procession around the village. In Santería, the Virgen de la Caridad is associated with the beautiful *orisha* Ochún, the Yoruba goddess of love and dancing, who is represented by the color yellow. In the minds of many worshipers, devotion to the two religious figures is intertwined.

The copper mine at El Cobre, active since pre-Columbian times and once the oldest European-operated mine in the western hemisphere (by 1530 the Spanish had a mine here), was shut in 2000. Many young fellows who previously worked in the mine, now work over tourists in the parking lot of the basilica, offering to 'give' you shiny but worthless chalcopyrite stones from the mine. The road to the basilica is lined with sellers of elaborate flower wreaths (20 pesos), intended as offerings to La Virgen, and hawkers of miniature 'Cachitas.'

Sights

Stunning as it materializes above the village of El Cobre, the **basilica** (⏰ 6:30am-6pm, mass at 8am except Wed, with additional Sun services 10am & 4:30pm) shimmers against the verdant hills behind. Except during mass, La Virgen lives in a small chapel above the visitors center on the side of the basilica. To see her, ignore the gory pro-life propaganda at the desk as you enter and take the stairs on either side. For such a powerful entity, she's amazingly diminutive, some 40cm from crown to the hem of her golden robe. An amazing work of embroidery, check out the fine Cuban coat of arms in the center. During mass, Nuestra Señora de la Caridad faces the congregation from atop the altar inside the basilica.

The 'room of miracles' downstairs in the visitors center contains thousands of offerings giving thanks for favors bestowed by the Virgin. Clumps of hair, a TV, a thesis, a tangle of stethoscopes, a balsa raft and inner-tube sculpture (suggesting they made it across the Florida Straits safely) and floor-to-ceiling clusters of teeny metal body parts

crowd the room. The most notable is a small golden guerrilla fighter donated by Lina Ruz, Fidel Castro's mother, to protect her son during his Sierra Maestra campaign against Batista. Ask one of the nuns to point it out to you. Until 1986, the 1954 Nobel Prize won by Ernest Hemingway for his novel *The Old Man and the Sea* was also on display, but in that year a visitor smashed the showcase's glass and carried the medal off. The police recovered the medal two days later, but it has since been kept in a vault, out of sight and reach. The nuns will fill small bottles with holy water if you ask (bring your own).

Follow the signs through the town of El Cobre to the **Monumento al Cimarrón.** A quick 10-minute hike up a stone staircase brings you to this anthropomorphic sculpture commemorating the 17th-century copper-mine slave revolt. The views are superb from up here; walk to the far side of the sculpture for a vista of copper-colored cliffs hanging over the aqua-green reservoir.

Sleeping & Eating

The **Hospedaría El Cobre**, a large two-story building behind the basilica, has 16 basic rooms with one, two, or three beds, all with private bath, at eight pesos per person, plus two 40-bed dormitories at five pesos per person. Meals are served punctually at 7am, 11am and 6pm, and there's a pleasant large sitting room with comfortable chairs. The nuns here are very sweet. House rules include no drinking and no unmarried couples. A hard-currency donation to the sanctuary equivalent to what you pay to stay in pesos is the classy thing to do. Parking here costs US$1.

There are several peso stalls in town where you can get *batidos* (fruit shakes), pizza and smoked-pork sandwiches.

Getting There & Away

Bus No 202 goes to El Cobre twice a day from the Intermunicipal Bus Station, Av de los Libertadores and Calle 4, in Santiago de Cuba. Trucks are more frequent on this route.

A Cubataxi from Santiago de Cuba costs around US$20 round trip. A private taxi will be US$12.

If you're driving toward Santiago de Cuba from the west, you can join the Autopista Nacional near Palma Soriano, but unless you're in a big hurry, it's better to continue on the Carretera Central via El Cobre, which winds through picturesque hilly countryside.

EL SALTÓN

If you're ready for some full-time relaxing, escape to **Villa El Saltón** (Cubanacán; ☎ 5-6495; s/d incl breakfast US$36/47; P ⊠ ☎), a beautiful mountain hotel in Tercer Frente municipality, 75km west of Santiago de Cuba and just west of Cruce de los Baños. It's almost lodge-like, with just 22 rooms in wooden buildings nestled into the landscape, and no-one will blame you if you kick back on your balcony while deciding between a sauna, hot tub, massage or dip in the 30m waterfall. Or a horseback ride or hike to nearby cocoa plantations at Delicias del Saltón. The food is passable and the bar has a pool table.

To get to El Saltón, continue west from El Cobre to Cruce de los Baños, 4km east of Filé village. El Saltón is 3km south of Filé. With some tough negotiating in Santiago de Cuba, you can get a taxi to take you here for US$40 to US$50. Make sure the car is sturdy.

You may hear about a road over the Sierra Maestra from Cruce de los Baños to Río Seco on the south coast. Southbound from Cruce de los Baños, the first 10km are OK, passing through hamlets in coffee-growing country. Then the road goes south, becoming a very rough jeep track with 'oh shit!' slippery, steep sections that can only be covered by a 4WD vehicle in dry weather. In a regular car or in rainy weather, the last 20km to Río Seco would be impossible, although ecotour jeeps regularly use this road. Good luck.

WEST OF SANTIAGO DE CUBA

The coastal road west from Santiago de Cuba is magnificent as the mountains and the sea meet in rugged, aqueous harmony reminiscent of Highway 1 near Big Sur, California. Playa Mar Verde, 19km west of Santiago de Cuba, is the first beach on the road to Chivirico. At Ensenada Juan González, 8km further west, is the wreck of the Spanish cruiser *Almirante Oquendo*, two of its cannons clearly visible above the waterline. It's only 50m offshore and you can snorkel out from the beach when the water isn't too choppy. A waterfall with a swimming hole at its foot is less than 1km inland from this beach. **Caletón Blanco**, another 7km west, has a protected public swimming area by the sea. Many trucks from Santiago de Cuba end their runs here.

The gun turret of another Spanish cruiser wrecked in 1898, the *Vizcaya*, is visible on the reef half a kilometer offshore at Aserradero, 10km west of Caletón Blanco. Nine kilometers west again, you'll pass a vacation camp for the Cuban military called **Villa Turquino**. Río Seco and the beginning of the previously mentioned rough road to Cruce de los Baños are 3km west of this camp, and the Sierra Mar Resort is about 8km east of there. There are no gas stations between Santiago de Cuba and Pilón (175km).

The isolated **Brisas Sierra Mar** (Cubanacán; ☎ 2-9110; www.cubanacan.cu; s/d low season US$68/116, high US$80/136; P ⊠ ☐ ☎) is at Playa Sevilla, 63km west of Santiago de Cuba and a two-hour drive from the airport. This big, pyramid-shaped hotel is built into a terraced hillside with an elevator down to a brown-sand beach famous for its sand fleas. Get into the water quick and discover a remarkable coral wall great for snorkeling just 50m offshore (dolphins sometimes frequent these waters too). Horseback riding is available and a Marlin Dive Center is on the premises. Families with children will appreciate the special kids programming daily and guests under 13 stay free with their parents. Nonguests can buy a US$35 day pass that includes lunch, drinks and sports until 5pm. You might be able to find a ride into Santiago de Cuba from here.

Motel Guamá (☎ 2-6124; s/d US$15/20; ⊠), on a hill with great sea and mountain views, is 7km east of Chivirico and 68km southwest of Santiago de Cuba. There are eight basic rooms (best are Nos C3 and C4, with terrace) and a restaurant. The Guamá is nothing fancy, but its gorgeous perch over the ocean is unbeatable (especially at the nice price).

CHIVIRICO

Chivirico is a big village of around 4000 inhabitants on the south-coast highway, 75km southwest of Santiago de Cuba and 106km east of Marea del Portillo. The deep, clear waters of the Cayman Trench just offshore wash the many beaches along this portion of the south coast.

There's a challenging trek that begins at Calentura 4km west of Chivirico and passes through La Alcarraza (12km), crossing the Sierra Maestra to Los Horneros (20km), from where truck transport to Guisa is usually available. At last report, however, skittish local authorities were turning people back as they attempted this hike. This may have changed by the time you show up.

Sleeping

Brisas Sierra Mar Los Galeones (Cubanacán; ☎ 2-6160; s/d/tr US$75/115/160; P 🅿 🔲) This is a small hotel with big surprises like the funky, forward décor, the good food, nice views and great diving. All rooms have balconies, there's a sauna and a small, unspectacular beach 100m below the hotel via a steep 296-step stairway. Children under 16 are not accommodated here. All in all, a nice place to relax.

Getting There & Away

Trucks run to Chivirico throughout the day from the Serrano Intermunicipal Bus Station opposite the train station in Santiago de Cuba. There are also three buses a day.

Theoretically, buses operate along the south coast from Chivirico to Campismo La Mula on alternate days, but don't count on it. The bus to Río Macío leaves at 5pm daily, and to Pilón at 11am on Tuesday, Thursday and Saturday. Chivirico's bus and truck station is 700m up off the coastal road from Cine Guamá.

UVERO

The first major battle won by Fidel Castro's guerrilla army took place at Uvero, 23km west of Chivirico, on May 28, 1957, when a government position guarded by 53 Batista soldiers was overwhelmed and much-needed supplies were captured. By the main road are two red trucks taken by the rebels. A double row of royal palms leads to a large monument commemorating these events. It makes a good goal for a day trip on horseback from the Sierra Mar Resort.

PICO TURQUINO AREA
Trekking

The Pico Turquino section of Gran Parque Nacional Sierra Maestra contains 17,450 hectares, including a spectacular trail across the Sierra Maestra, through a cloud forest where daily fogs rolls in, soaking the wild orchids, giant ferns, mosses and pines that grace Cuba's highest peaks. This ambient fog combines with great uninterrupted stands of primary forest to obscure views through much of the hikes here, but when the veil parts, the vista imbues that top-of-the-world feeling.

There are several options for this trek, though doing it independently is not one of them: all hikers must be accompanied by a guide. If your main interest is summiting Cuba's highest peak, you'll want to set out from Las Cuevas in Santiago de Cuba Province. If you're hooked on history and want to hike from Fidel and company's headquarters through and/or across the Sierra Maestra, you should set out from Alto de Naranjo in adjacent Granma Province (p341). If you want a little of both (or want a good, long hike), you can combine the two, starting from either end. The hiking is strenuous either way and onward transport is better from Alto del Naranjo, which may influence your planning. See p342 for the map of this hike.

The **Pico Turquino Trail**, up Cuba's highest mountain (1972m), begins at Las Cuevas on the south-coast highway, 7km west of Ocujal and 51km east of Marea del Portillo. This trek also passes Cuba's second highest peak, Pico Cuba (1872m). Allow at least six hours to go up and another four hours to come down, more if it has been raining as the trail floods in parts, becoming a mud slick in others. Most climbers set out at 4am (but if you're on the trail by 6:30am, you'll be OK), having slept at Base de Campismo La Mula, 12km east; self-sufficient hikers also have the option of pitching camp at Las Cuevas information center. The US$15 per person fee (camera US$3 extra) that you pay at the information center/trailhead includes a compulsory Cuban guide. You can overnight at the shelter on Pico Cuba if you don't want to descend the same day. Alternatively, you can do the entire Las Cuevas to Alto Naranjo three-day hike by arranging to be met by a new team of guides at Pico Turquino.

This hike is grueling because you're gaining almost two kilometers in elevation across only 9.6km of trail – it's hard and hot, but not a killer. Even in August, when Santiago de Cuba province routinely registers the nation's highest temperatures, the wooded slopes provide plenty of coverage from the glaring sun. Fill up on water before setting out. The well-marked route leads from Las Cuevas to La Esmajagua (600m, 3km; there's water here and a hospitable campesino family), Pico Cardero (1265m, quickly followed by a series of nearly vertical steps called 'Saca La Lengua,' or 'flops your tongue out'), Pico Cuba (1650m, 2km, water and shelter here) and Pico Real del Turquino (1972m, 1.7km). When the fog parts and you catch your breath, you'll behold a bronze bust of José Martí that stands on the summit of Cuba's highest mountain. You can overnight at either Pico Cuba on the ascent or La Esmajagua on the descent. The Pico Cuba shelter has a rudimentary kitchen and a wood fire stove, plank beds (no mattresses) or, if those are taken, floor space. It's possible to continue across the mountains to Alto del Naranjo and Santo Domingo (see p342).

Trekkers should bring sufficient food, warm clothing and a poncho – precipitation is common up here (some 2200mm annually), from a soft drizzle to pelting hail. Except for water, you'll have to carry everything you'll need, including extra food to share if you can carry it and a little something for the *compañeros* who take 15 day shifts up on Pico Cuba.

A note on guides: it's probable your guide will only speak Spanish, if he talks at all. Little is pointed out on the trail and the vibe may be one of 'been there, done that. Let's get this over with.' Still, these guys are earning the usual US$10 or so dollars a month, so tips will be appreciated (US$3 to US$5 per hiker is appropriate). By the way, the (unofficial) summit record by a guide is two hours, 45 minutes.

Museo de La Plata

Five kilometers west of Las Cuevas is the **Museo de la Plata** (admission US$1; ☼ Tue-Sat) at La Plata, next to the river just below the highway. The access road is very rough, and you should leave your vehicle at the store near the east side of the river and cover the last 800m to the museum on foot. The first successful skirmish of the Cuban Revolution took place here on January 17, 1957. The museum has three rooms with photos and artifacts from the campaign, and on a clear day you can see Pico Turquino. Marea del Portillo is 46km to the east (see p349). Don't confuse this La Plata with the Comandancia de La Plata, Fidel Castro's revolutionary headquarters high up in the Sierra Maestra (p342).

The well-preserved wreck of the Spanish cruiser *Cristóbol Colón* lies where it sank in 1898, about 15m down and only 30m offshore near La Mula. No scuba gear is available here but you can see the wreck with a mask and snorkel. (Divers from the Sierra Mar Resort are brought here by bus for a shore dive on the wreck.) If you have the time, hike up the Río Turquino to Las Posas de los Morones where there are a few nice pools where you can swim (allow four hours round trip). You must wade across the river at least three times unless it's dry.

Sleeping & Eating

The **Base de Campismo La Mula** (Cubamar), on a clean pebble beach at the mouth of Río La Mula, 12km east of the Pico Turquino trailhead, has 50 small cabins (US$5 per person) used mostly by Cuban vacationers and hikers on the eve of the Pico Turquino ascent. Electricity is only available for a few hours in the evening. The Oficina de Reservaciones de Campismo (see p359) in Santiago de Cuba handles bookings here or you can just show up. One of the international cabins is usually available. They won't let you pitch your tent.

Locals with a big catch may be able to arrange fresh-fish meals; ask around.

A bus connects La Mula to Chivirico on alternate days. This is a very hard stretch to hitch a ride.

Guantánamo Province

CONTENTS

Guantánamo Province occupies the strategically important eastern end of Cuba, and the US occupies Guantánamo – continuously since 1902 and in perpetuity since 1934. By now, Guantánamo is nearly synonymous with the US naval base located here; some tourists come to this province just to get a distant glimpse of it. But the colonial charm of Baracoa, the scenic hikes along the northern coast and long stretches of untrodden beaches on the southern coast give Guantánamo new meaning.

Entering the province from the north, it's incredibly tropical and you might think 'Wow, Guantánamo is green.' All that exuberant vegetation is thanks to prevailing trade winds which make this one of the wettest parts of Cuba. If you approach from Santiago de Cuba, where the vegetation wouldn't hold the attention of a goat, you'll think 'Dang! Guantánamo is desert.' That's because the south coast is in the shadow of the Macizo de Sagua-Baracoa range. At the southwest gateway to the province is the Cuenca de Guantánamo, a huge basin that tilts toward the 85-sq-km Bahía de Guantánamo, site of the famous base. Remote Punta de Maisí is Cuba's easternmost point.

HIGHLIGHTS

- **Historic Infamy**
  Espying the US naval base at the mouth of the Bahía de Guantánamo (p395)
- **Colonial Kickback**
  Chilling out and slowing down in seaside Baracoa (p397)
- **Great Outdoors**
  Hiking El Yunque, hitting the beach or swimming in a cave – all from Baracoa (p397)
- **Green Party**
  Keeping vigil for manatees and exploring in Parque Nacional Alejandro de Humboldt (p404)
- **Alone Time**
  Getting a room at Villa Maguana and beaching yourself (p403)

| ■ TELEPHONE CODE: 21 | ■ POPULATION: 516,311 | ■ AREA: 6186 SQ KM |

GUANTÁNAMO PROVINCE

GUANTÁNAMO PROVINCE

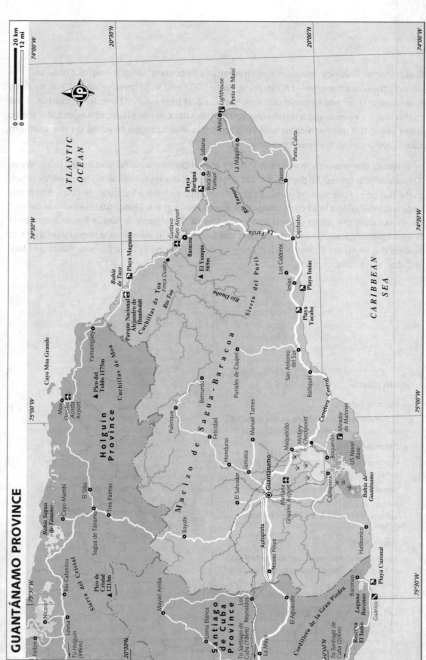

HISTORY

In the 16th century, this mountainous region was the first in Cuba to be colonized by the Spanish. The US followed in the Spaniards' footsteps, swooping in at the end of Cuba's Second War of Independence, negotiating the Spanish surrender and presenting Cuba with a choice: indefinite occupation by American troops or the establishment of a US naval base at Guantánamo. After Haiti's 1791 slave rebellion, French immigrants arrived in this area, cultivating coffee, cotton and sugarcane. The main agricultural activities today are sugarcane and beef-cattle ranching in the Cuenca de Guantánamo, and coffee in the mountains of the north and east.

Before all these foreign folks came on the scene, there were Taino-speaking Arawaks hunting, fishing and gathering in these parts. Some of Cuba's most treasured archaeological finds were unearthed in Guantánamo and Cuba's premier rebel, Hatuey, hailed from here.

GUANTÁNAMO

☎ 21 / pop 210,408

The city of Guantánamo ('Gitmo') was founded in 1819 between the Jaibo, Bano, and Guaso rivers, and until 1843 it was called Santa Catalina del Saltadero del Guaso. It's a big, bustling city without any special attractions, but makes a decent stopover between Santiago de Cuba and Baracoa. It's particularly attractive on Noches Guantanameras (Saturday nights) when Pedro A Peréz becomes a pedestrian mall crowded with outdoor restaurants, live music and plenty of peso rum.

Orientation

Mariana Grajales Airport (airport code GAO) is 16km southeast of Guantánamo, 4km off the road to Baracoa. A one-peso bus will take you into town from the airport (see Getting Around p395). Parque Martí, Guantánamo's central square, is several blocks south of the train station and 5km east of the Terminal de Omnibus (bus station). The main tourist hotel is 2km northwest of the train station.

Information

AIRLINE OFFICES

Cubana (☎ 3-4533; Calle Calixto García No 817 btwn Prado & Aguilera; ☾ 7-11am & 2-4pm Mon-Fri)

BOOKSHOPS

Librería Asdrubal López (Calixto García No 951 at Emilio Giro; ☾ 9am-noon & 2-5pm Mon-Fri, 9am-noon Sat)

IMMIGRATION

Inmigración (Calle 1 Oeste btwn 14 & 15 Norte; ☾ 8:30am-noon & 2-4pm Mon-Thu) Directly behind Hotel Guantánamo.

INTERNET ACCESS

Etecsa (Calle 15 Norte & Ahogados; US$0.10/min; ☾ 7am-10:30pm) Near Hotel Guantánamo.

LIBRARIES

Biblioteca Policarpo Pineda Rustán (Los Maceo & Emilio Giro; ☾ 8am-9pm Mon-Fri, 8am-5pm Sat, 9am-noon Sun) An architectural landmark.

MEDIA

Venceremos & Lomería Two local newspapers published on Saturday.
Radio Trinchera Antimperialista CMKS Trumpets the word over 1070AM.

MEDICAL SERVICES

Farmacia Principal Municipal (Calixto García & Aguilera; ☾ 24hr) On the northeast cnr of Parque Martí.
Hospital Agostinho Neto (☎ 35 54 50; Carretera de El Salvador Km 1; 24hr) West end of Plaza Mariana Grajales in front of Hotel Guantánamo.

MONEY

Banco de Crédito y Comercio (Calixto García btwn Emilio Giro & Bartolomé Masó) Two branches on this block.
Bandec (Ahogados cnr of Calle 4) Big new branch near Hotel Guantánamo.
Cadeca (Calixto García & Prado; ☾ 8:30am-6pm Mon-Sat, 8am-1pm Sun) Sells Cuban pesos and cashes traveler's checks.

PHOTOGRAPHY

Photo Service (Calixto García btwn Flor Crombet & Emilio Giro)

POST

Post Office (Pedro A Pérez; ☾ 8am-1pm & 2-6pm Mon-Sat) On the west side of Parque Martí. DHL also has an office here.

TELEPHONE

Etecsa (Aguilera btwn Los Maceos & Calixto García; ☾ 7am-10:30pm) There's also a branch at Calle 5 Norte & Ahogados, near Hotel Guantánamo.

TRAVEL AGENCIES

Reservaciones de Campismo (Flor Crombet No 410; ☾ 9am-noon & 1-4pm Mon-Fri) Reserves two coastal campismos en route to Baracoa and another at El Yunque.

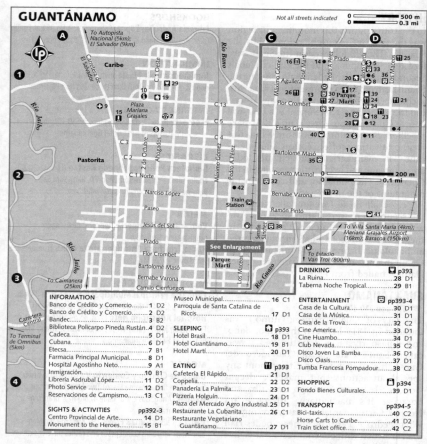

GUANTÁNAMO

Not all streets indicated

0 .... 500 m
0 .... 0.3 mi

Dangers & Annoyances

Guantánamo is a big city with a mellow town feel that pickpockets exploit. Stay alert especially on public transport and during Noches Guantanameras.

Sights

Museo Municipal (José Martí & Prado; admission free; ☺ 2-6pm Mon, 8am-noon & 3-7pm Tue-Sat) The quirky collection here includes pre-revolution day passes to the naval base and the antique Harley-Davidson used to shuttle secret messages during the revolution. Don't miss the cigar bands in the back gallery.

The **Parroquia de Santa Catalina de Riccis**, in Parque Martí, dates from 1863. In front of the church is a statue of Major General Pedro A Pérez, erected in 1928. The seated Martí statue here is particularly striking, as are the tulip fountain and provençal-colored bandstand.

Local architect Leticio Salcines (1888–1973) left a number of impressive works around Guantánamo, including the market building **Plaza del Mercado Agro Industrial** (Los Maceos & Prado), the **train station**, and his personal residence, the eclectic Palacio Salcines (1918). The last is now the **Centro Provincial de Arte** (Pedro A Peréz & Prado; admission free; ☺ 8am-noon & 2-6pm Mon-Fri). On the palace's turret is *La Fama*, a symbol of Guantánamo, her trumpet announcing good and evil. Salcines also designed the beautiful provincial library **Biblioteca Policarpo Pineda Rustán**

(Los Maceo & Emilio Giro), which was once the city hall (1934–51). Trials of Fulgencio Batista's thugs were held here in 1959, and a number were killed when they snatched a rifle and tried to escape.

A huge **Monument to the Heroes**, glorifying the Brigada Fronteriza 'that defends the forward trench of socialism on this continent,' dominates Plaza Mariana Grajales, the gigantic square opposite Hotel Guantánamo. Electrifying mass rallies occur here on May Day.

Sleeping

Hotel Guantánamo (Islazul; ☎ 38 10 15, 38 10 25; Calle 13 Norte btwn Ahogados & 2 de Octubre; s/d US$20/25 low season, US$30/36 high season; P ⊠ ⊠) The few tourists who visit this city usually stay 2.5km northwest of the center at this modern, four-story hotel on Plaza Mariana Grajales in Reparto Caribe. Clientele is mostly Cubans and their foreign husbands back to visit the family. The service is exemplary, but unless you have a car, it's inconveniently located.

Villa Santa María (☎ 38 11 13, 38 11 35; s/d US$18/20; ⊠) In Reparto Santa María, 4km north of the Servi-Cupet gas station, this place is also inconveniently located, but a group of four can bunk down in a US$25 suite. A sweet deal.

The two-story **Hotel Martí** (☎ 32 24 56; Calixto García No 820; r 11 pesos), at the northeast corner of Parque Martí, has 26 rooms. Nearby, a block south of Parque Martí, is the **Hotel Brasil** (☎ 32 20 97; Calixto García; r 7-10 pesos), a green, four-story building with 35 rooms. These old peso hotels fill up fast on Saturdays when people pour into town for Noches Guantanameras; they sometimes rent to foreigners.

Eating

Restaurante La Cubanita (José Martí No 864, cnr Flor Crombet; meals 50 pesos; ⊗ 6-10am, noon-2pm, 5pm-midnight) If you eat but one meal in Guantánamo, it should be here. You'll waddle out of this peso paladar the way they load on the pork, salad, *congrí* and *mariquitas*.

Restaurante Vegetariano Guantánamo (Pedro A Pérez; ⊗ noon-2:30pm & 5-10:30pm) Vegetarians will be delighted with the newest place in town, next to the Casa de la Cultura – the menu is in *moneda nacional*.

> ### CASAS PARTICULARES – GUANTÁNAMO
>
> The few private rooms for rent are good value and centrally located:
>
> **Cira Alberti Otero** (☎ 32 65 46; José Martí No 819 btwn Prado & Aguilera; r US$15; ⊠) Rents out two rooms each with private bath. There's a roof terrace and cooking facilities here.
>
> **Lissett Foster Lara** (☎ 32 59 70; Pedro A Pérez No 761 btwn Prado & Jesús del Sol; r US$15; ⊠) There's terrific hot water and a little porch overlooking the street action at the home of Lissett Foster Lara. Lissett speaks English.
>
> **Elyse Castillo Osoria** (☎ 32 37 87; Calixto García No 766 btwn Prado & Jesús del Sol; r US$15-20; ⊠) Nearby, this place has rooms with refrigerators and is licensed to rent to both Cubans and foreigners.

Plaza del Mercado Agro Industrial (Cnr Los Maceos & Prado; ⊗ 7am-7pm Mon-Sat, 7am-2pm Sun) Guantánamo's public vegetable market has a red dome in each corner of the building. It is another of Leticio Salcines' many works.

Other places to get a cheap meal in town:

Pizzería Holguín (Calixto García, west side of Parque Martí) Next to Cine Huambo. Sells peso pizzas to those with the patience of a saint.

Panadería La Palmita (Flor Crombet No 305 btwn Calixto García & Los Maceos; ⊗ 7:30am-5pm Mon-Sat) For fresh bread.

Cafetería El Rápido (Flor Crombet & Los Maceos; ⊗ 10am-10pm) Pizza, fried chicken and ice cream.

Coppelia (General Pérez & Bernabe Varona) Several blocks south of the park.

Drinking

La Ruina (Calixto García cnr Emilio Giro; ⊗ 10am-1am) This hulk of a ruined colonial building has 30ft ceilings. It's a dollar bar with log tables and benches for propping you up after many beers. Thursday is karaoke night.

Taberna Noche Tropical (☎ 38 16 01; Calle 15 Norte at Ahogados) If you're staying at the Hotel Guantánamo you might grab a Bucanero upstairs at this place, two blocks from La Ruina.

Entertainment

Guantánamo was the home town of Elio Revé (1930–97), former leader of the Orquesta Revé, who popularized *son-changüí*.

Today you can still hear groups playing this combination of urban dance music and rural Afro-Cuban drumming.

Casa de la Trova (Máximo Gómez No 1062, btwn Donato Marmol & Bernabe Varona; admission US$1; ☽ 8pm-1am) Guantánamo's folk music scene centers on the Casa de la Trova. House policy is couples only, but they'll probably let you slide.

Casa de la Música (Calixto García btwn Flor Crombet & Emilio Giro) Thursdays there's a *peña de Rap* and Sunday there's a *trova* matinee at the Casa de la Música.

Tumba Francesa Pompadour (Serafín Sánchez No 715) Four blocks east of the train station, this place presents Haitian-style dancing on certain evenings.

Casa de la Cultura (☎ 32 63 91; admission free) Classical concerts frequently take place here, in the former Casino Español, on the west side of Parque Martí. This place also puts on Afro-Cuban concerts and dance performances.

The fun, new disco in town is **Club Nevada** (Pedro A Pérez cnr of Bartolomé Masó; admission US$1), a rooftop, tiled terrace affair blasting all the salsa and disco standards you've tolerated thus far. Similar is **Disco Joven La Bamba** (Aguilera btwn Calixto García & Los Maceos) above Etecsa. Both of these places heat up after 10pm on weekends.

Cine Huambo (Calixto García & Flor Crombet) and **Cine America** (Calixto García), a block north, next to the Cubana office, are both near Parque Martí.

Baseball games are played from October to April at the **Estadio Van Troi** in Reparto San Justo, 1.5km south of the Servi-Cupet.

Shopping
Fondo de Bienes Culturales (Calixto García No 855, upstairs) Next to Pizzería Holguín, on the east side of Parque Martí, sells handicrafts.

Getting There & Away
AIR
Cubana flies daily from Havana (2½ hours, US$118 one way). There are no international flights to this airport.

BUS & TRUCK
The Terminal de Omnibus, 5km west of the center on the old road to Santiago de Cuba (a continuation of Av Camilo Cienfuegos), has **Astro** buses to these destinations:

destination	cost (one way)	distance	departure time
Baracoa	US$7.50	50km	7:30am
Camagüey	US$13	371km	7:30pm
Havana	US$46	905km	7:30pm
Holguín	US$11	182km	noon
Santiago de Cuba	US$3	84km	8am, 1:20pm

On some of the Baracoa services, you change buses at Imías.

There are Víazul buses daily to Baracoa (US$10, 150km, 8:30am) and Santiago de Cuba (US$6, 84km, 5:15pm).

Collectivos to Santiago de Cuba (20 pesos) leave from Calle 9 Oeste and the old Carretera Central, midway between the Terminal de Omnibus and the city center. Foreigners are often prevented from using them. Trucks to Santiago de Cuba (five pesos) and Baracoa also leave from the Terminal de Omnibus; foreigners may also be banned from them. One reader reported taking a 20-centavo city bus marked 'Paraguay' to 'El Punto,' where he was able to catch a truck to Baracoa.

Trucks for Moa (seven pesos) park on the road to El Salvador north of town near the entrance to the Autopista Nacional.

CAR
The Autopista Nacional to Santiago de Cuba ends near Embalse La Yaya, 25km west of Guantánamo, where the road joins the Carretera Central. At El Cristo, 12km outside Santiago de Cuba, you rejoin the Autopista. To drive to Guantánamo from Santiago de Cuba, follow the Autopista Nacional north about 12km to the top of the grade, then take the first turn to the right. Eastbound, be aware of a police checkpoint near the end of the Autopista Nacional, a few kilometers short of Guantánamo. Any local will know the route and speed traps well (another benefit to sharing extra space in your car with a rideless Cuban).

TRAIN
The **train station** (☎ 32 55 18; Pedro A Pérez), several blocks north of Parque Martí, has one departure for Havana (US$32, 905km, 6:50pm) on alternate days. This train also stops at Camagüey (US$13), Ciego de Ávila (US$16), Guayos (US$20, closest you can get to Sancti Spíritus on this line), Santa Clara (US$22) and Matanzas (US$29). There was no Santiago de Cuba service at the time

of writing. Purchase tickets the morning of the day the train departs at the office on Pedro A Pérez.

Getting Around

A one-peso bus departs for the airport from the **Cubana office** (Calixto García No 817), two hours before Cubana flights. From the airport, follow Cuban passengers onto this bus.

Transtur (☎ 35 59 00; Calle 13 Norte btwn Ahogados & 2 de Octubre) on Plaza Mariana Grajales in Reparto Caribe is in the Hotel Guantánamo. They usually have plenty of cars for hire, and mopeds too.

A Servi-Cupet gas station is at the beginning of the road to Baracoa, just east of the center. **Oro Negro** (Los Maceos cnr of Jesús del Sol) is more central, two blocks north of Parque Martí.

You can catch a one-peso horse cart to Hotel Guantánamo from Ramón Pintó next to the zoo, five blocks south of Parque Martí. Ask for the one to 'Caribe.' A bici-taxi from the center to the bus terminal costs 20 pesos and takes around 30 minutes, depending on the peddler.

Taxis hang out around Parque Martí or you can call **CubaTaxi** (☎ 32 36 36). The No 48 bus (20 centavos) runs between the center and the Hotel Guantánamo every 40 minutes or so. You can catch it at the park on your way to the hotel and at the junction of Calle 9 Norte and Ahogados returning.

GUANTÁNAMO US NAVAL BASE

Guantánamo is most famous for its US naval base near Caimanera, 21km south of the city of Guantánamo. In 1903 the US government used the Platt Amendment, imposed on Cuba as a condition of independence, to slice off 116 sq km of Cuban territory at the mouth of the Bahía de Guantánamo. In 1934 US President Roosevelt amended the terms (but not the substance) of the treaty, whereby both sides must agree before the lease can be terminated.

The base was intended to protect the eastern approach to the Panama Canal and during WWII the base was greatly expanded. Although its original mission is long over, the oldest US military base on foreign soil remains useful as a thorn in the side of Cuba. Immediately after the 1959 revolution, the Castro government asked the US to return the base to Cuba, but the US refused. As relations between the countries deteriorated, Cuba cut off water and electricity to the base, and the US troops on duty were denied permission to leave their camp.

The recent history of the facility is infamous. In January 1992, 11,000 Haitian migrants were held here, and in August 1994 the base was used as a dumping ground for 32,000 Cubans picked up by the US Coast Guard on their way to Florida. Of these, some 8000 of the old, young, and sick were later allowed into the US on humanitarian grounds, and another 2000 returned voluntarily to Cuba. In May 1995 the Cuban and US governments signed an agreement under which most of the remaining 22,000 Cuban refugees at Guantánamo (18,000 of them young men between 18 and 21) were allowed into the US. Since then, illegal Cuban immigrants picked up by the US Coast Guard at sea have been returned to Cuba. If they actually touch US soil, they're allowed to stay, which creates dangerous high seas standoffs between Cubans trying to get to shore and the US Coast Guard. In July 2003 several armed hijackers attacked Coast Guard officers as they tried to board the US-bound vessel.

Since the September 11, 2001 attacks, the US has held over 600 prisoners at Guantánamo Bay without charging them with crimes. Denied legal counsel and family contact while facing rigorous interrogations, the detainees (some as young as 13 and one as old as 98) have mounted hunger strikes and there have been dozens of suicide attempts. Following protests from Amnesty International, the UN High Commissioner for Human Rights and allies, who considered the detentions in violation of international law, the US released a small group of prisoners. At the same time, the US indicated it would establish military tribunals able to mete out death penalties for when the detainees finally come to trial.

Across the fence, the 7000 US military personnel and their dependents living on the base have a golf course, yacht club, sporting facilities, hospitals, cinemas and supermarkets. The whole facility is surrounded by trenches, security fences, watch towers, and a 'no-man's-land,' where US troops have laid 75,000 mines in 22 areas, the largest minefield in the western hemisphere. Each year about US$30 million in US tax money is spent here.

AROUND GUANTÁNAMO US NAVAL BASE

A distant view of the base can be obtained from the **Mirador de Malones** (admission US$5, drink included; 🕑 8am-3pm) on a 320m-high hill just west of the complex. Opened in 1992, the *mirador* (viewpoint) is operated by the Cuban tourism organization Gaviota. The entrance is at a Cuban military checkpoint off the main highway, 27km southeast of Guantánamo. You then drive another 15km south toward the sugar exporting port of Boquerón, and on up to the viewpoint. Just before the final climb to the *mirador*, there's a large bunker containing a huge scale model of the base, which guides use to highlight points of interest. Using a telescope made in Kentucky, you can observe the US flag fluttering at Northeast Gate and pick out American vehicles driving along the road. You can't just arrive unannounced at the checkpoint, but have to arrange bookings beforehand either at the Gaviota office in Santiago de Cuba (p358) or the Hotel Guantánamo (US$10 includes entrance and guide). If you don't have your own transport, a round-trip taxi with wait will cost US$30/38 for older/newer car.

Sleeping

Hotel Caimanera (Islazul; ☎ 9-9414; s/d/tr incl breakfast US$23/30/36; 🅿 🍴 🍷) This hotel is on a hilltop at Caimanera, near the perimeter of the US naval base, 21km south of Guantánamo. It's not at all convenient for regular travelers; only groups of seven or more on prearranged tours with an official Cuban guide are accepted. Besides, the view is much better from the Mirador de Malones.

SOUTH COAST

Leaving Guantánamo in the rearview, you come onto the sere, rugged coast with cacti-studded expanses on one side and the lapis lazuli Caribbean on the other. Several little stone beaches between Playa Yacabo and Cajobabo make refreshing pit stops. You can follow this road all the way east to Punta de Maisí.

Campismo Yacabo (☎ 8-0289; per person US$4), by the highway 10km west of Imías, has 18 new cabins overlooking the sea near the mouth of the river. The cabins sleep four to six people and make a great beach getaway for groups on a budget.

There are two places to stay at Imías, midway between Guantánamo and Baracoa. **Cabañas El Bosque**, a few hundred meters down the road to Los Calderos from Imías, has seven cabins near a river. A better choice is **Cabañas Playa Imías** (1-2 people US$9; 🍴), near a long dark beach that drops off quickly into deep water, 2km east of the center of Imías. The 15 cement cabins have baths, fridges and TVs.

More accommodation is available at **Campismo Cajobabo** (per person US$3.50), about a kilometer off the main highway near the point where the main road turns north toward Baracoa. There are 73 basic cabins right on the beach.

At the far end of deserted Playita de Cajobabo, 2km east of the Campismo, is a **monument** commemorating José Martí's 1895 landing here to launch the Second War of Independence. It's a good snorkeling spot, flanked by dramatic cliffs. The famous La Farola road turns north toward Baracoa at Cajobabo.

PUNTA DE MAISÍ

From Cajobabo, the coastal road continues 51km northeast to La Máquina. As far as Jauco, the road is good; thereafter it's not so good. Coming from Baracoa to La Máquina (55km), it's a good road as far as Sabana, then rough in places from Sabana to La Máquina. Either way, La Máquina is the starting point of the very rough 13km track down to Punta de Maisí, best covered in a 4WD vehicle.

This is Cuba's easternmost point and there's a **lighthouse** (1862) here. Otherwise there's not much to Punta de Maisí. The light was restored in 1975, and you can climb the 144 wooden steps to the top for an outstanding view of the area (all the way to Haiti on a cloudless day). Directly below the lighthouse is a fine white beach. Self-sufficient travelers should be able to camp at the lighthouse.

BOCA DE YUMURÍ

From Sabana, a very steep concrete road zigzags down the hillside to Boca de Yumurí at the mouth of the Río Yumurí. Just before the bridge over the river is the Túnel de los Alemanes (German's Tunnel), an amazing natural arch of trees and foliage. Though lovely, this dark beach has become *the* day trip from Baracoa. Hustlers hard sell fried fish meals (US$5), while other fellows

Street scene, **Trinidad** (p259), Sancti Spíritus Province

Making **cigars** (p171)

Salto del Caburní (p272), Topes de Collantes, Sancti Spíritus Province

Castillo de San Pedro del Morro (p365), Santiago de Cuba

Traditional guitar making, **Fábrica de Órganos** (p317), Holguín

Students of **dance** (p44), Santiago de Cuba

Basílica de Nuestra Señora del Cobre (p383), Santiago de Cuba Province

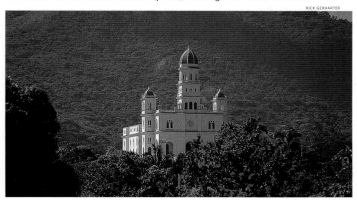

peddle colorful land snails called *polimitas,* which have become rare as a result of being harvested wholesale for tourists.

West of Boca de Yumurí, a good road runs 28km along the coast toward Baracoa, passing many inviting black beaches and countless excellent vistas. This makes a superb bike jaunt from Baracoa (56km round trip): hot, but smooth and flat and you can stop at any beach that catches your fancy (try Playa Bariguá at Km 24.8). You can arrange bikes in Baracoa – ask at your casa particular. Alternatively, taxis will take you there from Baracoa for US$5 one way.

BARACOA
☎ 21 / pop 42,285

A mellow, colonial town on a tropical headland between two bays, Baracoa is one of Cuba's best destinations. Beaches, hiking and one of Cuba's top national parks are all in the vicinity. History permeates the narrow streets, which are liberally sprinkled with charming casas particulares, and getting there is easy with the twice-weekly flights from Havana.

Christopher Columbus called the area Porto Santo, and left a journal description of El Yunque, the anvil-shaped mountain that shimmers due west across the Bahía de Baracoa, today a popular day hike. This corner of the country is thick with forests, coconut palms and citrus groves, creating a tropical atmosphere unmatched elsewhere in Cuba. Along with coconuts, cocoa is an important crop, used to make a distinctive body cream and as the raw material used at the Peters Baracoa chocolate factory (no visitors), 4km out on the road to Moa.

Baracoa was the first Spanish settlement in Cuba, founded in December 1512 by Diego Velázquez and 300 fellow Spaniards who had to battle fierce indigenous forces led by Hatuey to take over the land. Baracoa served as the colony's capital until 1515, when Velázquez moved to Santiago de Cuba. A bishopric subservient to the one in Santo Domingo in the Dominican Republic was established in Baracoa in 1518, and the town remained an important Spanish outpost. Between 1739 and 1742, work began here on three forts to protect Baracoa from pirates, smugglers and the English.

Baracoa was accessible only by sea and remained cut off from the rest of Cuba until the famous highway 'La Farola,' was built across the Sierra del Purial from Cajobabo in the 1960s. This project was much celebrated as one of the revolution's first great achievements. You can putter along La Farola with its majestic vistas at every steep curve. Along the way campesinos sell balls of cocoa, *cucurucho* (a sweet, addictive coconut concoction) and *plátanos manzanos* (small, red bananas).

With only four decades of regular outside contact, Baracoa feels suspended in time (but you can still check your email!). The road northwest from the Río Toa to the border of Holguín Province is still very rough, though passable by any car – a worthy, picturesque trip.

Orientation

Gustavo Rizo Airport (airport code BCA) is 1km off the road to Moa beside Hotel Puerto Santo, 4km from central Baracoa. The best way to get there is by taxi (US$2)

A REBEL'S REBEL

Cuba has had its share of forward-thinking revolutionaries. Carlos Manuel de Céspedes freed his slaves and called on Cubans to fight for their independence; José Martí was one of the greatest, most underrated political theorists of the modern era; and Fidel Castro is one of history's most masterful strategists, and has defied global vilification for his pursuit of the ideal society. Who will be next in this impressive tradition no-one knows, but it all began with Taino *cacique* (chief) Hatuey, who, interestingly, hailed from Hispaniola, not Cuba.

In 1512 the Spanish occupied Baracoa to establish their first colonial settlement on the island. Unwilling to take the conquest lying down, Hatuey organized and led indigenous troops in a doomed battle against the better equipped, avaricious Spaniards. After holding out for some months, Hatuey was caught, the resistance fizzled and he was burned at the stake.

Hatuey's regal visage and strapping body captured in wood, bronze and stone sculptures will surprise you throughout Baracoa. Cuba's first dissident also lives on through his namesake beer.

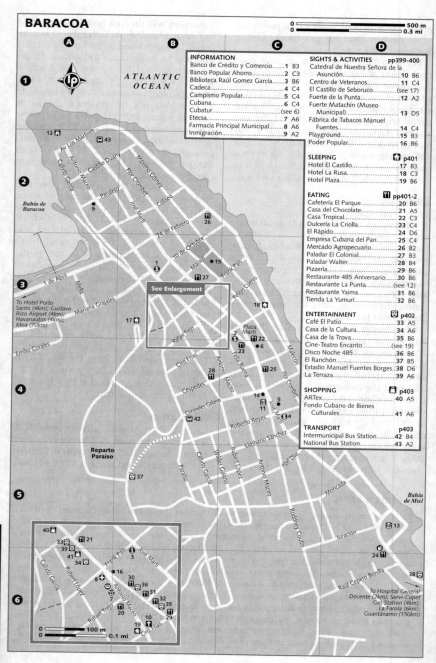

BARACOA

0 — 500 m
0 — 0.3 mi

ATLANTIC OCEAN

Bahía de Baracoa

Bahía de Miel

Reparto Paraíso

To Hotel Porto Santo (4km); Gustavo Rizo Airport (4km); Havanautos (4km); Moa (70km)

To Hospital General Docente (2km); Servi-Cupet Gas Station (4km); La Farola (6km); Guantánamo (150km)

See Enlargement

INFORMATION
Banco de Crédito y Comercio......1 B3
Banco Popular Ahorro.................2 C3
Biblioteca Raúl Gomez García......3 B6
Cadeca.....................................4 C4
Campismo Popular.....................5 C4
Cubana....................................6 C4
Cubatur...............................(see 6)
Etecsa......................................7 A6
Farmacia Principal Municipal........8 A6
Inmigración...............................9 A2

SIGHTS & ACTIVITIES   pp399-400
Catedral de Nuestra Señora de la
  Asunción..............................10 B6
Centro de Veteranos.................11 C4
El Castillo de Seboruco.........(see 17)
Fuerte de la Punta....................12 A2
Fuerte Matachín (Museo
  Municipal).............................13 D5
Fábrica de Tabacos Manuel
  Fuentes.................................14 C4
Playground..............................15 B3
Poder Popular..........................16 B6

SLEEPING   p401
Hotel El Castillo........................17 B3
Hotel La Rusa...........................18 C3
Hotel Plaza..............................19 B6

EATING   pp401-2
Cafetería El Parque....................20 B6
Casa del Chocolate....................21 A5
Casa Tropical............................22 C3
Dulcería La Criolla.....................23 C4
El Rápido.................................24 D6
Empresa Cubana del Pan...........25 C4
Mercado Agropecuario..............26 B2
Paladar El Colonial....................27 B3
Paladar Walter.........................28 B4
Pizzería...................................29 B6
Restaurante 485 Aniversario.......30 B6
Restaurante La Punta............(see 12)
Restaurante Yaima.....................31 B6
Tienda La Yumurí......................32 B6

ENTERTAINMENT   p402
Café El Patio............................33 A5
Casa de la Cultura.....................34 A6
Casa de la Trova........................35 B6
Cine-Teatro Encanto.............(see 19)
Disco Noche 485.......................36 B6
El Ranchón..............................37 B5
Estadio Manuel Fuentes Borges...38 D6
La Terraza...............................39 A6

SHOPPING   p403
ARTex....................................40 A5
Fondo Cubano de Bienes
  Culturales.............................41 A6

TRANSPORT   p403
Intermunicipal Bus Station..........42 B4
National Bus Station..................43 A2

0 — 100 m
0 — 0.1 mi

or bici-taxi (US$0.75), but the latter will likely leave you 500m or so from the airport, as it sits atop a largish hill. Baracoa's two bus stations are on opposite sides of town. The closest train station is in Guantánamo, 150km southwest. There are two good hotels in or near the old town and another next to the airport. Most of Baracoa can be explored on foot, but a bicycle is useful for visiting nearby beaches and rural pockets.

Information

Upholding the tropical standard, Baracoa closes down for a siesta from noon to 2pm; Sundays are equally quiet. Touts will offer you private rooms, meals, *jineteras*, taxis, tours and the like. Don't rely on plastic money here as Baracoa sometimes experiences problems with phone lines and credit card machines. Cash advances are difficult in Baracoa.

AIRLINE OFFICES
Cubana (☎ 4-2171; Calle Martí No 181) Has a bus connection from its office to the airport (US$1). Ask when booking.

IMMIGRATION
Inmigración (Antonio Maceo No 48 at Peralejo; ☙ 8am-noon & 2-4pm Mon-Fri)

INTERNET & TELEPHONE
Etecsa (Antonio Maceo cnr Rafael Trejo on Parque Central; ☙ 7am-10:20pm) Internet (US$0.10/hr) and international calls.

LIBRARIES
Biblioteca Raúl Gómez García (José Martí No 130 at Frank País; ☙ 8am-noon & 2-9pm Mon-Fri, 8am-4pm Sat)

MEDIA
Granma is a commodity here and sells out fast; get your copy at the post office around 3pm daily except Sunday.

Radio CMDX '*La Voz del Toa*', broadcasts over 650AM.

MEDICAL SERVICES
Farmacia Principal Municipal (Antonio Maceo No 132; ☙ 24hr)
Hospital General Docente (☎ 4-3014) Two kilometers from town, on the road to Guantánamo.

MONEY
Banco de Crédito y Comercio (☎ 4-2771; Antonio Maceo No 99; ☙ 8am-2:30pm Mon-Fri)

Banco Popular de Ahorro (José Martí No 166; ☙ 8-11:30am & 2-4:30pm Mon-Fri) Cashes traveler's checks.
Cadeca (José Martí No 241)

POST
Post Office (Antonio Maceo No 136; ☙ 8am-8pm)

TRAVEL AGENCIES
Campismo Popular (☎ 4-2776/4-5263; José Martí No 225; ☙ 8am-noon & 2-6pm Tue & Wed) Make essential reservations for cabins at Yacabo or El Yunque here.
Cubatur (Calle Martí No 181) Tours to El Yunque and Parque Nacional Alejandro de Humboldt.
Havanatur (Antonio Maceo No 120)
Rumbos (☎ 4-5225; Antonio Maceo & Rafael Trajo) In Cafetería El Parque.

Sights & Activities
IN TOWN
The **Catedral de Nuestra Señora de la Asunción** (1833; Antonio Maceo No 152; ☙ mass 6pm daily & 9am Sun) on Parque Central houses the Cruz de La Parra, said to have been erected by Columbus near Baracoa. Though carbon dating disproves the legend that Columbus brought the cross from Europe, an exhaustive investigation by Cuban and foreign scholars indicates that this is indeed the last remaining cross of the two dozen or so the Spaniards erected throughout Latin America (the one in Santo Domingo is a replica). Knock on the last door on Calle Maceo to gain access outside of mass hours. Donations are accepted.

Facing the cathedral is a bust of Indian chief Hatuey, who was burned at the stake near Baracoa by the Spanish in 1512. Also on Parque Central is the neoclassical **Poder Popular** (Antonio Maceo No 137; no visitors).

To see a couple of dozen *torcedores* rolling cigars, visit the **Fábrica de Tabacos Manuel Fuente** (José Martí No 214; ☙ 7am-noon & 2-5pm Mon-Fri, 7am-noon Sat). The **Centro de Veteranos** (José Martí No 216; admission free) displays photos of those who perished in the 1959 revolution and in Angola.

Baracoa's **Museo Municipal** (José Martí at Malecón; admission US$1; ☙ 8am-noon & 2-6pm) in the **Fuerte Matachín** (1802) at the southern entrance to town has pretty bay vistas outside and a powerful sculpture of Hatuey at the stake inside. There's a good overview of local history, including the guitar of local *trovador* Cayamba ('the singer with the ugliest voice in the world') and ephemera relating to pouty Magdalena Menasse (nee Rovieskuya, 'La Rusa').

Another Spanish fort, the **Fuerte de la Punta**, has watched over the harbor entrance at the other end of town since 1803. Today it's a restaurant serving ice-cold beers and killer views.

Baracoa's third fort, **El Castillo de Seboruco**, begun by the Spanish in 1739 and finished by the Americans in 1900, is now Hotel El Castillo (see p401). There's an excellent view of El Yunque's flat top from the swimming pool. A stairway at the southwest end of Frank País climbs directly to the castle.

Two blocks north of Parque Central is a big **playground** (Frank País & Flor Crombet) that kids will love; rock, pop and rap concerts are sometimes held here.

OUTSIDE TOWN

Southeast of town are two natural wonders that together make a nice day trip. From beyond the Fuerte Matachín, hike southeast past the stadium and along the beach for about 20 minutes to a rickety wooden bridge over the Río Miel. From April to June, you'll have to take a skiff across the flooded river mouth before reaching the bridge (admission one peso; ☾ sunrise-sunset). After the bridge, turn left until you come to a Gaviota hut, where you have to pay US$2 to continue. If you continue left for 15 minutes you come to **Playa Blanca**, an idyllic spot for a picnic or sunset cocktails.

If you go to the right at the Gaviota hut and follow the dirt road through coconut groves and past clapboard houses for 45 minutes, you'll come to the blue and yellow **homestead of Raudeli Delgado**. For a donation (US$3 to US$5 per person), he'll lead you on a 30-minute hike, through coconut and citrus groves to a *mirador* that takes in the lush coconut plantations below and the blue sea beyond. After a short, steep descent into a lush canyon, you come to **Cueva del Aguas**, a cave with a sparkling, freshwater swimming hole inside. Ask about the coconut oil Raudeli's family makes, the cure for sun-cracked skin.

Heading west out of town toward Moa, take the one lane road for 2km beyond the airport where a break in the low-lying scrub leads to **Playa Duaba**. This is where Antonio Maceo and Flor Crombet landed and it's a beautiful band of dark beach backed by mountains. The water gets better further from the river mouth. The *jejenes* (sand fleas) are ferocious in the late afternoon. Fifty meters further along the road is the tranquil monument to the rebel landing.

Tours

One of Baracoa's most challenging day trips is summiting **El Yunque** (569m). It's not a high hike, but the views are stupendous. Cubatur offers this tour daily (US$18 per person, minimum two people). The fee covers admission, guide, transport and a sandwich. The hike is hot (bring sufficient water). If you have a car or bike you can arrange your own guide at the campismo (US$13). Take the road toward Moa for 6km and then turn left into the spur to the campismo. Four kilometers on is the trailhead and the campground. Bring a swimsuit for a dip in the Río Duaba.

The most interesting trips offered by Baracoa agencies are to **Parque Nacional de Humboldt** (US$28 per person, minimum five people) lunch, transport and guide included in the price. The Balcón de Iberia trail is 5km, with significant elevation gains, *mirador* and river swimming. The Bahía de Taco circuit has a short hike followed by a boat tour around the bay, with the possibility of seeing manatees. You can get yourself to the park with a car or on the Moa-bound passenger truck and arrange a guide on-site.

Excursions are also available to **Boca de Yumurí** (US$15 per person, minimum three people) and **Playa Maguana** (US$18 per person, minimum three people), two trips that you can do independently. A minibus shuttles tourists from Parque Central to Playa Maguana daily (US$4 round trip). It leaves at 11am.

Entrepreneurs all over town will customize tours to any of these destinations except Parque Nacional de Humboldt which is too far afield. Readers have reported positive experiences; expect to pay US$7 to US$10 per person for the El Yunque hike.

Festivals & Events

During the first week of April, Baracoa commemorates the landing of Antonio Maceo at Duaba on April 1, 1895, with a raucous carnival along the Malecón. Check the **Casa de la Cultura** (☎ 4-2349; Antonio Maceo No

124 btwn Frank País & Maraví) during Carnaval, as it presents a concurrent Semana de la Cultura that week. Every Saturday night, Calle Maceo is closed off for Noche Baracuensa, when food, drink and music take over.

Sleeping

Renting out private rooms is a booming industry in Baracoa. Rules are strict around here, so take care that you're staying in a legal casa; see the Casas Particulares boxed text.

Hotel La Rusa (Islazul; ☎ 4-3011; Máximo Gómez No 161; s/d US$16/18 low season, US$20/26 high season; ✷) You can't miss this three-story yellow beauty right on the Malecón. The 12 simple rooms have little balconies, some over-looking the sea. The hotel was built by Magdalena Rovieskuya, a Russian woman who inspired Alejo Carpentier's *La Consagración de la Primavera*. Former guests include Errol Flynn, Che Guevara and Fidel Castro. It's a popular place, still.

Hotel Plaza (☎ 4-2283; Antonio Maceo No 148a; r US$15; ✷) This super cheapie is above Cine-Teatro Encanto next to the cathedral. Only four of the nine rooms with bath and TV are available for foreigners; for the few extra bucks, you're better off at La Rusa.

Hotel El Castillo (Gaviota; ☎ 4-5165; Loma del Paraíso; s/d US$30/44 low season, US$34/48 high season; ✷ ✷) Another famous Baracoa hotel is this historic castle, once part of the Spanish fort. It's a relaxed, friendly place, with only 34 rooms (some dark and dampish) and there's a good view of the bay and El Yunque from the pool (open to nonguests for a small fee). The hotel also organizes day trips to El Yunque and Río Toa among other places. It is a 10-minute walk from town up the steps on Frank Pais or Calixto García.

Hotel Porto Santo (Gaviota; ☎ 4-5106; Carretera del Aeropuerto; s/d/tr US$30/44/51 low season, US$34/48/55 high season; P ✷ ✷) This modern, airy hotel with exposed-beam ceilings is 200m from the airport and 4km from the town center. There are 36 rooms, mostly given over to bus tour groups because the access road to El Castillo is too steep for big tour buses. It's rather inconvenient unless you have wheels. A stairway leads down to the beach.

Eating
PALADARES

Baracoa has several paladares, and though they're more expensive than state places,

---

CASAS PARTICULARES – BARACOA

Villa Haydee – Elio Frómeta (☎ 4-3750; Av Malecón No 43A; r US$15) Two rooms with terraces facing sea; one with kitchen and shared dining room.

Nelsy Borges Teran (☎ 4-3569; Antonio Maceo No 171 btwn Ciro Frias & Céspedes; r US$15-20; ✷) Several outfitted rooms, great roof terrace, views.

Isabel Castro Vilato (☎ 4-2267; Mariana Grajales No 35; r US$15; ✷ P) Colonial house, terrific garden, porch, meals.

Casa Colonial – Gustavo & Yalina (☎ 4-2536; Flor Crombet No 125 btwn Frank País & Pelayo Cuervo; r US$12-15; ✷) Big rooms sleep three.

Idania de la Cruz Blanco (☎ 4-3885; Antonio Maceo No 80 btwn 24 de Febrero & Coliseo; r US$12-15; ✷) Colonial house, roof terrace, friendly.

Elsa Figueroa Toirac (☎ 4-2460; José Martí No 152; r US$15; ✷) Central, two rooms.

Miriams Zoila Montoya (☎ 4-3529; José Martí No 301; r US$15-20)

Andrés Abella (☎ 4-3298; Antonio Maceo No 56 btwn Peralejo & Coliseo; r US$15) Large room, friendly; also rent at No 53.

Lidia Cobas (☎ 4-3464; 10 de Octubre No 21C; r US$15)

Manuel Rubio Ramírez (☎ 4-2760; Edificio 30, Apt C, btwn Frank País & Pelayo Cuervo; r US$12-15) On Malecón, apartment, English spoken.

Lourdes Balga (☎ 4-3218; Av Malecón No 72 near Coroneles Galano; r US$10) Room can sleep three, friendly.

Williams Montoya Sánchez (☎ 4-2798; José Martí No 287; r US$15; ✷ P) Serves meals.

Isabel Artola Rosell (☎ 4-5236; Rubert López No 39, btwn Céspedes & Ciro Frías; r US$12-15; ✷) English spoken.

Josefina Guilarte (☎ 4-3532; Flor Crombet No 269; r US$12-15) Meals served, quiet, out of center; also rent at 265A.

Eugenio Ona Abella (☎ 4-3310; Moncada No 18B btwn José Martí & República; r US$15) Private, good meals.

Denny Rodríguez (☎ 4-2431; Rupert López No 86 btwn Limbano Sánchez & Lope Pena; r US$25; ✷) Big, private, TV and fridge.

Alina Oliveros (☎ 4-2652; Emilio Corrales No 11, off Mariana Grajales; r US$12-15; ✷ P) Friendly, parking.

Nelia Y Yaquelin (☎ 4-3625, 4-3353; Mariana Grajales No 11 btwn Calixto García & Julio Mella; r US$10; ✷) Two rooms.

you're almost guaranteed to eat well. You'll always pay a few dollars more if you arrive with a tout.

Paladar El Colonial (José Martí No 123; meals US$6) This place has an impressive patio dining set-up and a varied menu to match (skip the turtle); meals come with rice and salad.

Paladar Walter (Rubert López No 47; meals US$7-8; ☯ 5-11pm) Has chicken and fish meals.

Casa Tropical (☎ 4-3437; José Martí No 175; meals US$7) With its efficient service and good portions, Casa Tropical shows what men can do in the kitchen; try the fish in coconut milk.

Many cheap peso food stalls selling pork sandwiches are along Antonio Maceo between Nos 102 and 110.

RESTAURANTS
The local specialty is *cucurucho* – grated coconut mixed with sugar, chocolate, guava, orange, or papaya. It's sold in cones along La Farola (three/six pesos for small/large cone) and makes a terrific hiking snack. Coconut is also pulped into a rich, yummy milk used to stew seafood. Hot chocolate is another Baracoa delicacy.

Cafetería El Parque (Antonio Maceo No 142; ☯ 24hr) Flowering terrace, occasional live bands, pool table, fried chicken (US$2), ice cream (US$1) and cold drinks means this place is Baracoa's main hangout. It's right across from Parque Central and a good spot to connect with people.

Restaurante La Punta (Fuerte de la Punta; mains US$1.50-7; ☯ 10am-11pm) In an old fort overlooking the water, this is a great place for an afternoon lemonade or sunset *mojito*. It's a Rumbos restaurant, so the menu is chicken (US$1.50 to US$2) or fish (US$5.50 to US$7) once again.

Casa del Chocolate (Antonio Maceo No 123; ☯ 7:20am-11pm) Steaming cups of super-sweet hot chocolate (40 centavos) is the house specialty here, but they also have desserts. Grab a table with the toothless old dudes.

Two other decent places right on the park include friendly **Restaurante Yaima** (Antonio Maceo No 143), with basic peso meals served in an agreeable atmosphere (read: napkins) and **Restaurante 485 Aniversario** (Antonio Maceo No 139; mains US$1.50-3.50; ☯ 11:30am-2pm & 6-9pm), with good fried chicken (US$1.50) and fish (US$3.50). You can hear live *trova* here after 9pm most nights.

The **pizzería** (Antonio Maceo No 155; at Ciro Frías) sells acceptable three-peso pizza; skip the 'bacon' (*tocino*) variety. **El Rápido**, at the Servi-Cupet at the southeast entrance to town, serves drinks (US$0.50 to US$1), ice cream (US$1) and pizza (US$1).

SELF-CATERING
Tienda La Yumurí (Antonio Maceo No 149; ☯ 8:30am-noon & 1:30-5pm Mon-Sat, 9am-noon Sun) Get in line for the good selection of groceries here.

Mercado Agropecuario (24 de Febrero & Malecón) The selection at Baracoa's market makes it abundantly clear how remote you really are: if it isn't growing right here, right now, you won't find it.

Dulcería La Criolla (José Martí No 178) sells bread. **Empresa Cubana del Pan** (José Martí btwn Céspedes & Coroneles Galano) has regular 10 peso short loaves, and also fruit bread.

Entertainment
For such a small town, Baracoa is rocking.

Casa de la Trova Victorino Rodríguez (Antonio Maceo No 149a) For *trova* and *son*, this venue, next to the cathedral, presents talented amateur musicians relying heavily on the *Buena Vista Social Club* set.

El Ranchón (admission US$1; ☯ after 9pm) Atop a long flight of stairs at the western end of Coroneles Galano, El Ranchón has an enchanting hilltop setting with a bird's eye view of Baracoa. Check out studly Hatuey up here. There's sometimes good live music and, other times, the usual taped disco and salsa. Watch for overcharging at the bar and watch your step on the way down – it's a scary 146-step drunken tumble.

Also drop in at:

Casa de la Cultura (☎ 4-2349; Antonio Maceo No 124 btwn Frank País & Maraví) Check here for musical events.

La Terraza (Antonio Maceo btwn Maraví & Frank Pais; admission US$1; ☯ 9pm-2am Mon-Thu, 9pm-4am Fri-Sun) Rooftop disco with occasional hot salsa septets.

Disco Noche 485 (Antonio Maceo No 141; ☯ from 9pm nightly) Another rooftop disco, on the park.

Café El Patio (Antonio Maceo No 120) Nice courtyard for a drink; one of the only night spots without a cover charge.

Cine-Teatro Encanto (Antonio Maceo No 148) Cinema in front of the cathedral.

From October to April, baseball games are held at the **Estadio Manuel Fuentes Borges**, southeast along the beach from Fuerte Matachín.

Shopping

The **Fondo Cubano de Bienes Culturales** (Antonio Maceo No 120; 🕙 9am-5pm Mon-Fri, 9am-noon Sat & Sun) sells Hatuey woodcarvings and T-shirts with indigenous designs. For the usual tourist fare (postcards, shotglasses and mainstream music), check out **ARTex** (Antonio Maceo No 108).

Getting There & Away

AIR

Cubana has two weekly flights from Havana to Baracoa (3½ hours, US$128 one-way). Arriving international flights are continuations from Havana or Santiago de Cuba.

Be aware that the planes and buses out of Baracoa are sometimes fully booked, so don't come here on a tight schedule without outbound reservations.

BUS

The **National Bus Station** (☎ 4-3670; Av Los Mártires & José Martí) has Astro buses to Santiago de Cuba (US$9, 234km, five hours, 1:50pm) on alternate days and Havana (US$44/53 regular/air-con, 993km, 19 hours, 7:30pm), also on alternate days. For some odd reason, the bus to Guantánamo (US$7.50, 150km, three hours, 11am) is only for people connecting there with trains. Dollar tickets are sold from 8am to 4pm.

Víazul leaves for Guantánamo (US$10, 150km, three hours), continuing to Santiago de Cuba (US$15, 234km, five hours) daily at 2:15pm. If you intend to connect in Santiago de Cuba to points east with Víazul or if you're making a flight out of Santiago de Cuba and must depart on a certain day, consider reserving your bus ticket through Cubatur (US$5 commission) as Víazul is flaky with reservations and advance sales.

The Intermunicipal Bus Station, Galano and Calixto García, has two or three trucks a day to Moa (five pesos, 78km, 90 minutes, departures from 6am) and Guantánamo (10 pesos, four hours, 150km, departures from 2am). If you can't find a truck right to Guantánamo, take anything as far as San Antonio del Sur, where you'll find onward trucks.

Getting Around

There's a helpful **Havanautos** car-rental office (☎ 4-5344) at the airport. Cheaper **Vía Rent a Car** (☎ 4-5135) is inside the Hotel Porto Santo. **Servi-Cupet** (🕙 24hr) is right at the entrance to town on José Martí and 4km from the center, on the road to Guantánamo. Drivers hightailing it to Havana should note that the northern route through Moa and Holguín is fastest.

Bici-taxis around Baracoa should charge five pesos a ride, but they often ask 10 to 15 pesos from foreigners.

One-peso horse carts from the beginning of Mariana Grajales opposite the Banco de Crédito y Comercio go as far as the roundabout at El Turey, about a kilometer from Hotel Porto Santo and the airport.

Locals will approach travelers with bike rental offers; expect to pay around US$3 a day.

NORTHWEST OF BARACOA

The **Finca Duaba** (🕙 noon-4pm Tue-Sun), 6km out of Baracoa on the road to Moa and then 1km inland, is designed to give visitors a taste of country life. On this verdant farm you'll see profuse tropical plants, swim in the Río Duaba, and be served a massive Creole lunch (US$12 per person).

The **Río Toa**, 10km northwest of Baracoa, is the third longest river on the north coast of Cuba. It carries more water than any other river in the country and is an important bird and plant habitat. Cocoa trees and the ubiquitous coconut palm are grown in the Valle de Toa. A vast hydroelectric project on the Toa was abandoned after a persuasive campaign led by the Fundación de la Naturaleza y El Hombre convinced authorities it would do irreparable ecological damage; engineering and economic reasons also played a part. This is great news because the Reserva Cuchillas de Toa, the largest of Cuba's four Unesco-sanctioned biosphere reserves, is here.

Rustic **Campismo El Yunque** is beautifully located at the foot of El Yunque, 6km north of Baracoa on the road to Moa, then another 4km inland on a rough road through a cocoa plantation. There are 14 wooden cabins, sleeping four or six people. The setting is lush and it only takes about four hours round-trip to climb the mountain from here. Reservations from the Campismo Popular office in Baracoa are essential.

One of the nicest little hideaways in Cuba is **Villa Maguana** (Gaviota; no phone; s/d US$37/51 low season, US$42/57 high season, incl breakfast), facing an idyllic, palm-fringed, white-sand beach, 54km southeast of Moa and 22km north-west of Baracoa. It's about 11km beyond Río Toa via a rough gravel road. The four rooms with fridges are in a quaint guesthouse with porch rockers fronting a little lawn. The restaurant adjacent has a decent wine selection. Advance reservations are essential, and can be had through Hotel El Castillo in Baracoa (p401). Rumbos has a snack bar on Maguana Beach nearby, just 500m off the Moa highway, a super picnic spot.

PARQUE NACIONAL ALEJANDRO DE HUMBOLDT

Designated a Unesco World Heritage site in 2001, this beautiful national park perched above the Bahía de Taco should serve as a paradigm for Cuba's protection efforts. Forty kilometers northwest of Baracoa, it contains some of Cuba's most pristine forest, protecting 60,000 hectares of land and 2641 hectares of lagoon and mangroves. With 1000 flowering plant species and 145 types of fern, it is the most diverse plant habitat in the entire Caribbean. Almost 70% of the plants found here are endemic. According to Unesco, this park 'is one of the most biologically diverse terrestrial tropical ecosystems in an island setting anywhere on earth.' Several endangered species can be found here including the Cuban Amazon parrot and the hook-billed kite. The last ivory-billed woodpecker ever sighted was spotted here in the late 80s and has been heard (but not seen) since then. It's also home to the endangered manatee.

There's a **visitors center** (☎ 38 14 31) staffed with biologists here. An extensive network of trails lead to waterfalls, a *mirador* and a massive karst system with caves around the Farallones de Moa. The three trails that are currently open include Balcón de Iberia, a 5km challenging loop; El Recrea, a 2km stroll around the bay; and the Bahía de Taco circuit, which incorporates a boat tour (with a manatee-friendly motor developed by scientists here) through the mangroves and the bay, plus the 2km hike. Each option

is accompanied by a professional guide who will teach you more about Cuban flora and fauna than you'll ever need to know! Prices range from US$8 to US$13 depending on the hike. There's a great camping spot right on the shore and several more intended for scientific research throughout the park; smooth talkers with *mucho* solidarity might be able to wriggle into one of these.

You can arrange a tour through an agency in Baracoa or get here independently.

MERMAID OR MANATEE?

The slow-moving Caribbean manatee (*manatí*) is descended from a land mammal that returned to life in the water. The Atlantic manatee can grow up to 4.5m long and weigh as much as 600kg. (A smaller 'sea cow' called a dugong plows the Indian Ocean.) It's a graceful but ugly animal, with a small head, a thick neck and a wide bristly snout. Its poorly developed eyes have glands that secrete an oily substance for protection against salt water.

An adult manatee has a thick tapered body ending in a wide horizontal tail flipper. It uses two front flippers to swim and to bring food to its mouth. The manatee's ribs aren't attached to a rib cage, so its lungs are crushed if the animal lies on its belly on dry land. To avoid suffocating, a manatee caught by low tide will flip over onto its back and wait for the water to return. Manatees live from 30 to 60 years.

Unlike whales and seals, this marine mammal never takes to the open ocean. It prefers to linger around thick plant growth and grazes on seaweed in brackish coastal waters, estuaries, and rivers, where it consumes up to 50kg of plant-life a day. While grazing in the shallows with its head and shoulders above the water, it resembles a human figure, which perhaps gave rise to mermaid legends. Although the manatee has no natural enemies except man, it has become endangered due to hunting, injury from boat propellers and habitat destruction.

Directory

CONTENTS

ACCOMMODATION

Cuban accommodation runs the gamut from little US$5 beach cabins to luxury five-star resorts. Solo travelers are penalized as far as prices go, paying 75% of the price of a double room.

In this book, budget means anything under US$40 for two people. In this range, casas particulares are almost always better value than a hotel. In cheaper casas particulares (US$10), you may have to share a bath and will have a fan instead of air-con. In the rock bottom places (campismos, mostly), you'll be lucky if there are sheets and running water, though there are usually private baths. If you're staying in a place intended

> ### PRACTICALITIES
>
> **Electricity** The most common voltage is 110 volts, 60 cycles, but you'll also find 220 volts. Side by side sockets with different voltage are usually labeled, but always ask. The sockets are suited to North American–style plugs with two flat prongs.
>
> **Laundry** Commercial laundries are rare. Most casas particulares have a machine you can use or there's always hand washing.
>
> **Newspapers and Magazines** *Granma*, *Juventud Rebelde* and *Trabajadores* are the three national papers. *Bohemia* and *Temas* are two of the best general interest magazines (in Spanish).
>
> **Radio & TV** There are 69 radio stations and three TV channels. Radio Habana (www.radiohc.cu) is broadcast worldwide on the shortwave band; most hotels have satellite.
>
> **Telephone** Phone numbers in this and the Transport chapter include area codes.
>
> **Video Systems** Like electricity, the common system is NTSC, but videos are sold in various formats.
>
> **Weights & Measures** Cuba uses the metric system, except in some fruit and vegetable markets where the imperial system takes over.

for Cubans, you'll compromise materially, but the memories are guaranteed platinum.

The mid-range category is a crapshoot, with some stylish accommodation for US$40 to US$70 a double and some awful places. Only the most deluxe casas particulares in Havana get this expensive, where you're assured quality amenities and attention. In mid-range hotels, you can expect air-con, private hot water bath, clean linens, satellite TV, restaurant and swimming pool. Many of the loveliest hotels near mountains, valleys or hot springs fall into this range.

Unsurprisingly, the most comfortable hotels cost US$70 and up for two people. These are usually partly foreign-owned and maintain international standards (more or less). Rooms have everything that a mid-range hotel has, plus big quality beds and linens, a minibar, international phone service and perhaps a terrace or view.

Factors influencing rates are time of year, location and hotel chain. Low season is generally mid-September to early December and February to May (except for Easter week). Christmas and New Year is what's called extreme high season, when rates are 25% more than high-season rates. Bargaining is only possible in casas particulares – the more Spanish you speak, the better. Prearranging Cuban accommodation is difficult, but not impossible.

The following chains and Internet agencies offer online booking:

Casa Particular Organization (www.casaparticularcuba .org) Reader recommended for prebooking private rooms.

Cuba Connection (☎ 800-645-1179, toll free in the US and Canada; www.cuba.tc)

Cubalinda.com (www.cubalinda.com) Havana-based, so they know their business.

Gran Caribe (www.grancaribe.cu)

Horizontes (www.horizontes.cu)

Islazul (www.islazul.cu)

Sol Meliá (www.solmeliacuba.com) Also offers discounts.

Vacacionar (www.dtcuba.com) Official site of Directorio Turístico de Cuba.

Campismos

Over 80 of these holiday camps are sprinkled throughout the country and are wildly popular (an estimated 1,000,000 Cubans used campismos in 2003). Hardly 'camping', these installations are simple concrete cabins with bunk beds, foam mattresses and cold showers. Campismos are the best place to meet Cubans, make friends and party in a natural setting.

Campismos are either *nacional* or *internacional*. The first are (technically) only for Cubans, while the latter host both Cubans and foreigners, with cabins for tourists being more upscale, including air-con and/or linens. In practice, campismo staff may rent a *nacional* cabin (or tent space) to a foreigner pending availability, but it depends on the installation, your attitude (positive always works wonders!) and your Spanish abilities. Campismos are usually booked solid in July and August and on weekend nights year-round, possibly closing outside of these peak periods. Because Cuban rules are often flexible, this book includes information on both types of campismos.

Cubamar (☎ 7-66-25-23/4; fax 7-33-31-11; www.cu bamarviajes.cu; Calle 3 & Malecón, Vedado) in Havana handles reservations for *internacional* campismos, but doesn't reserve cabins intended for Cubans. Try the provincial Campismo Popular office to make a reservation closer to the installation proper (the details of these offices can be found in the relevant regional chapters). Dropping in occasionally works at *nacional* campismos. Cabin accommodation costs US$3 to US$7 per bed and you might be asked to pay for all the beds in one cabin. Prices at the plush Villas Aguas Claras (Pinar del Río Province; p167) and Guajimico (Cienfuegos Province; p235) cabins are higher.

Cubamar also rents mobile homes (campervans) called Campertours, which sleep four adults and two children. These cost US$165 per day including insurance (plus US$400 refundable deposit). You can park these campers wherever it's legal to park a regular car. A handful of campismos have Campertour facilities giving you access to electricity and water. These are a great alternative for families.

Renegade cyclists aside, few tourists are tent camping in Cuba. The abundance of beaches, plus the helpfulness and generosity of Cubans make camping surprisingly easy and rewarding. Beach camping means insanely aggressive sand fleas and mosquitoes. The repellant sold locally just acts as a marinade for your flesh, so bring something strong – DEET-based if you're down with chemicals. Camping supplies per se don't exist; bring your own or improvise.

Casas Particulares

Private rooms are the best option for independent travelers. You'll know houses renting rooms by the blue triangle on the door marked 'Arrendador Inscripto.' From penthouses to historical homes, all manner of rooms are available from US$10 to US$25. It must be emphasized that these are not homestays, but businesses more like hostels. Whereas some hosts will welcome you like family, others will treat you as a paycheck.

Government regulation of casas is intense and it's illegal to rent private rooms in resort areas. Owners pay US$100 to US$250 per room per month depending on location, plus extra for off-street parking, to post a sign advertising their rooms and to serve meals. These taxes must be paid whether the rooms are rented or not. Owners must keep a register of all guests and report each within 24 hours of their arrival. For these reasons, you will find it hard to bargain for rooms, will be requested to produce your passport immediately and will have difficulty finding private rooms off the beaten track. Penalties are high for infractions, and new regulations (eg only two adults to a room or prohibition of renting independent apartments) are being introduced all the time. Without a marriage license, travelers with Cuban spouses or partners will have a hard time finding accommodation.

In this book, we list email addresses of the owners who provided them, but don't be surprised if your email gets lost in the cyber swirl.

Hotels

Hotels in Cuba fall into three categories: peso, tourist and mixed. Peso hotels are payable in *moneda nacional* (Cuban pesos) and are intended for Cubans only. While foreigners sometimes manage to pay in pesos, this is the exception and most pay dollars. Since these places are generally dirty, noisy, in bad repair with light and water failures, and have cold-water showers and questionable linens, there's only value in them if you get the peso price.

All tourist hotels and resorts are at least 51% owned by the Cuban government and are administered by Islazul (cheapest option, rents to foreigners and Cubans), Cubanacán (mid-range resorts and city properties), Gaviota (high-end resorts and spas), Gran Caribe (mid-range to top-end beach resorts), Horizontes (mid-range hotels, many in natural settings) and Habaguanex (historic hotels in Habana Vieja; profits go toward restoring this Unesco site). Because each chain has its niche, throughout this book we mention the chain to which a hotel belongs to give you some idea of what to expect at that particular installation. Except for Islazul properties, tourist hotels are for dollar-paying foreigners only. Cubans who are not legally married to foreigners (and have the papers to prove it) are technically not allowed to stay in dollar hotels. Among the many legitimate reasons for this, controlling prostitution (which resurfaced with a vengeance once dollars were legalized in 1993) is high on the list and foreigners cannot take Cubans up to their room. However, mixed Cuban-foreign couples may find some flexibility with the rules in Islazul or Horizontes hotels. The latter

generally offers rock-solid mid-range accommodation (see www.horizontes.cu).

Mixed hotels have a peso price for Cubans and a dollar price for tourists. Most of these are run by the Islazul chain, where you can usually expect clean, decent-value rooms, but quality varies so buyer beware. When Islazul is the only game in town, you might find ineffective air-con, terrible food, saggy beds, leaky ceilings, disinterested service, cold showers or boisterous crowds of partying Cubans.

ACTIVITIES

As the biggest (and best!) Caribbean country, with 5746km of coastline, Cuba is known for all things aquatic: scuba diving, snorkeling and deep-sea fishing especially. On land, erosion over the ages has created more than 20,000 caves and a 6km valley blanketed with weird pincushion hills – prime spelunking and rock climbing turf. Lots of unexplored corners mean cyclists, horseback riders, backpackers and other independent traveler types will find kilometers of wide open road beckoning exploration.

Any gear you can donate at the end of your trip to individuals you meet along the way (headlamps, snorkel masks, fins, carabiners etc) will be greatly appreciated.

Diving

Cuba has superb scuba diving suitable for all levels and interests. There are more than 30 dive centers throughout Cuba managed by either **Marinas Puertosol** (www.puertosol.net), **Cubanacán Naútica** (www.cubanacan.cu) or **Cubamar** (www.cubamarviajes.cu). Though equipment does vary between installations, you can expect safe, professional and often multilingual service with these operators. Environmentally sensitive diving is where things can get wobbly, and individuals should educate themselves about responsible diving (see p408).

Dives and courses are comparably priced islandwide at US$25 to US$35 per dive, with a discount after four or five dives. Full certification courses are US$310 to US$365 and 'resort' or introductory courses cost US$50 to US$60. Because of those nasty US embargo laws, PADI certification is generally not offered in Cuba; instead, you'll likely receive ACUC (American Canadian Underwater Certification) credentials.

The most popular diving areas are María la Gorda (Pinar del Río; p172), Playa Girón (on the famous Bay of Pigs; p221), Playa Rancho Luna and Guajimico (both in Cienfuegos; p233 and p235 respectively), Cayo Coco (Ciego de Ávila; p283), Playa Santa Lucía (Camagüey; p300) and Guardalavaca (Holguín; p327). Varadero (p202) has over 30 dive sites, but only one with shore access. The quality sites around Playa Girón and Cienfuegos are good areas for first timers. Dedicated and advanced divers will want to check out the stellar underwater conditions around Isla de la Juventud (p157) and the pristine area of Jardines de la Reina (p258).

Marsub SA (☎ 7-96-13-49; Calle 3ra No 34004, Tarará, Havana) specializes in scuba tours. It has packages based at Havana, María La Gorda, Varadero, Playa Larga (Bay of Pigs), Cienfuegos, and Villa Covarrubias (Las Tunas). Cubamar offers similar trips.

For the complete skinny on scuba in Cuba, pick up Lonely Planet's *Diving & Snorkeling Cuba*.

Snorkeling

You don't have to go very deep to enjoy Cuba's tropical aquarium: snorkelers will be thrilled with treasures along the south coast from Playa Larga (p220) to Caleta Buena (Matanzas; p221) and around Cienfuegos (p233), Playa Jibacoa (Havana Province; p142) and along the Guardalavaca reef (Holguín; p327). In Varadero, daily snorkeling tours sailing to Cayo Blanco (p204) promise abundant tropical fish and good visibility. If you're not into the group thing, you can don a mask at Playa Coral (p193), 20km away.

Good boat dives for snorkeling happen around Isla de la Juventud (p157) and Cayo Largo (p158) especially, but also in Varadero (for sunken wrecks and reef; p202) and in the Cienfuegos (p233) and Guajimico (p235) areas. If you anticipate spending a lot of time snorkeling, bring your own gear as the rental stuff can be tattered.

Rock Climbing

The Viñales valley (p176) has been described as having the best sport rock climbing in the western hemisphere. There are over 150 routes now open (at all levels of difficulty, with several 5.14s) and the word is out among the international climbing crowd, who are creating their own scene in one of Cuba's prettiest settings. Independent

---

RESPONSIBLE DIVING

Please consider the following tips when diving and help preserve the ecology and beauty of reefs:

■ Never use anchors on the reef, and take care not to ground boats on coral.

■ Avoid touching or standing on living marine organisms or dragging equipment across the reef. Polyps can be damaged by even the gentlest contact. If you must hold on to the reef, only touch exposed rock or dead coral.

■ Be conscious of your fins. Even without contact, the surge from fin strokes near the reef can damage delicate organisms. Take care not to kick up clouds of sand, which can smother organisms.

■ Practice and maintain proper buoyancy control. Major damage can be done by divers descending too fast and colliding with the reef.

■ Take great care in underwater caves. Spend as little time within them as possible as your air bubbles may be caught within the roof and thereby leave organisms high and dry. Take turns inspecting the interior of a small cave.

■ Resist the temptation to collect or buy corals or shells or to loot marine archaeological sites (mainly shipwrecks).

■ Ensure that you take home all your rubbish and any litter you may find as well. Plastics in particular are a serious threat to marine life.

■ Do not feed fish.

■ Minimize your disturbance of marine animals. *Never* ride on the backs of turtles.

travelers will appreciate the free reign that climbers enjoy here.

Though you can climb here year-round, the heat can be oppressive, and locals stick to an October to April season, with December to January being the optimum months. For more information, visit the **Cuba Climbing** site (www.cubaclimbing.com) or contact **Aníbal Fernández** (anibalpiaz@yahoo.com), president of the national climbing club.

Caving

Cuba is riddled with caves – over 20,000 and counting – and cave exploration is available to both casual tourists and professional speleologists. The Gran Caverna de Santo Tomás (p179), near Viñales, is Cuba's largest cavern with over 46km of galleries; Cueva de los Peces (p220), near Playa Girón, is a flooded cenote with colorful snorkeling; and the Cueva de Ambrosio (p202) and Bellamar (p192), both in Matanzas, have tours daily.

Specialists have virtually unlimited caves from which to choose. With advance arrangements, you can explore deep into the Gran Caverna de Santo Tomás (p179) or visit the Cueva Martín Infierno (p234), with the world's largest stalagmite. Also ask about San Catalina near Varadero, which has unique mushroom formations. Speleodiving is also possible, but only for those already highly trained. Interested experts should contact Angel Graña, secretary of the **Sociedad Espeleológica de Cuba in Havana** (☎ 7-209-2885; angel@fanj.cult.cu). The **Escuela Nacional de Espeleología** (☎ 8-77-10-14), in Moncada just at the entrance to the Caverna de Santo Tomás, is another good resource for professionals.

Fishing

Cuba's finest deep-sea fishing for sailfish, swordfish, tuna, mackerel, barracuda and shark is along the northwest coast where the fast-moving Gulf Stream supports prime game fishing. Facilities for sport anglers exist at Cayo Levisa (p180), Havana (p117), Playas del Este (p133), Varadero (p203), Cayo Guillermo (p285), Bahía de Naranjo (p327), Isla de la Juventud (p157) and Cayo Largo del Sur (p158). Shore casting for bonefish and tarpon is practiced off the south coast at Jardines de la Reina (p285) and Cayo Largo del Sur.

Fly fishing is superb in the vast Ciénega de Zapata (p217) in Matanzas, where enthusiasts can arrange multiday catch-and-release trips. You can cast for largemouth bass (*trucha*) at Laguna Grande (p170), Lago del Tesoro (Guamá; p218) and Laguna La Redonda (p281). The main season is November to May.

Cycling

Biking in Cuba is big time. The decent roads, wonderful scenery, and opportunity to get off the beaten track and meet Cubans eye to eye, make this a popular way to vacation here. It surely has more than a little to do with Lonely Planet's highly readable *Cycling Cuba*, an indispensable guide for anyone interested in getting around on two wheels.

If you're not into the bugs-in-your-teeth zoom around and just want some mellow peddling, you can rent a bike from individuals (going rates are around US$3 per day) or ask at your resort: most places have bikes on their all-inclusive perks list.

Hiking & Trekking

Top hikes here include the three-day Pico Turquino summit (p386); the Cuevas las Perlas stroll in Península de Guanahacabibes (p170); hoofing to flat-topped El Yunque (p400) and exploring Parque Nacional Alejandro de Humboldt (p404), both in Guantánamo; and the various hikes around Las Terrazas (p182) in Pinar del Río. All these hikes are completely different, but share one thing in common: they all require a guide.

If you want to hike independently, check out the Salto del Caburní trail (one of the few unguided trails in Topes de Collantes; p272), the various hikes around Viñales (p175) and the Las Guanas trail in the Bahía de Naranjo (p327). This last is a one-kilometer yawner, but with lots of exploration potential.

BUSINESS HOURS

Cuban business hours are hardly etched in stone, but offices are generally open 9am to 5pm Monday to Friday. Cubans don't take a siesta like in other Latin American countries, so places normally don't close midday. The exception is provincial museums (which also keep late night hours – an interesting time for an art crawl). Museums and vegetable markets are usually closed Monday.

Post offices are open 8am to 6pm Monday to Saturday, with some main post offices keeping later hours. Banks are usually open from 9am to 3pm weekdays, closing at noon on the last working day of each month. Cadeca exchange offices are generally open 9am to 6pm Monday to Saturday, and 9am to noon Sunday.

Pharmacies are generally open 8am to 8pm, but those marked *turno permanente* or *pilotos* are open 24 hours.

In retail outlets everything grinds to a halt during the *cambio de turno* (shift change) and you won't be able to order a beer or buy cigarettes until they're done doing inventory. Shops are usually closed after noon on Sunday. The earlier in the morning you attend to whatever tasks you have (banking, car rental, immigration, flight confirmations etc), the better.

CHILDREN

Children are encouraged to talk, sing, dance, think, dream and play, and are integrated into all parts of society: you'll see them at concerts, restaurants, church, political rallies (giving speeches even!) and parties. Travelers with children will find this embracing attitude heaped upon them, too.

In Cuba there are many travelers with kids, especially Cuban Americans visiting family with their children; these will be your best sources for on the ground information. One aspect of the culture here parents may find foreign (aside from the material shortages) is the physical contact and human warmth that is so typically Cuban: strangers ruffle kids' hair, give them kisses or take their hands with regularity, which may be odd for you and/or your child. For more general advice, see Lonely Planet's *Travel with Children*.

Practicalities

A lot of simple things aren't available in Cuba or are hard to find, including baby formula, diaper wipes, disposable diapers, crayons, any medicine, clothing, sun block etc. On the upside, Cubans are very resourceful and will happily whip up some squash and bean baby food or fashion a cloth diaper. In restaurants,

there are no high chairs because Cubans cleverly turn one chair around and stack it on another, providing a balanced chair at the right height. Cribs are available in the fancier hotels and resorts, and in casas particulares one will be found. Quality baby-sitting abounds: your hotel concierge or casa owner can connect you with good childcare. What you won't find are car seats (or even seat belts in some cases), so bring your own from home.

The key to traveling in Cuba is simply to ask for what you need and some kind person will help you out.

Sights & Activities

Like any great city, Havana is terrific for kids (see p85). It has kids' theater and dance, two aquariums, two zoos, a couple of great parks and some massive playgrounds. Resorts are packed with kids' programs, from special outings to designated kiddy pools. Guardalavaca (p324) has the added advantage of being near many other interesting sights such as the aquarium at Bahía de Naranjo (p327). Parque Baconao in Santiago de Cuba (p381) has everything from old cars to dinosaurs and is a fantasy land for kids of all ages.

Other activities kids will groove on include horseback riding, baseball games, cigar factory tours, snorkeling, miniature golf, and exploring caves, the waterfalls at El Nicho (p234) and Topes de Collantes (p271).

CLIMATE CHARTS

Cuba is hot, hot, hot, with humidity ranging from 81% in summer to 79% in winter. Luckily the heat is nicely moderated by the gentle Northeast Tradewinds. Cuba's hurricane season (June to November) should be considered when planning; see When to Go (p13) for more.

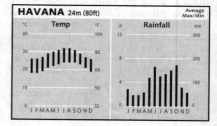

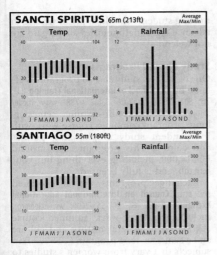

SANCTI SPIRITUS 65m (213ft)

Temp / Rainfall

SANTIAGO 55m (180ft)

Temp / Rainfall

COURSES

Cuba's rich cultural tradition and the abundance of highly talented, trained professionals make it a great place to study. Officially matriculating students are afforded longer visas and issued a *carnet* – the identification document that allows foreigners to pay for museums, transport (including colectivos) and theater performances in pesos. Technological and linguistic glitches, plus general unresponsiveness, make it hard to set up courses before arriving, but don't worry: you'll be able to arrange everything once you arrive. In Cuba, things are always better done face-to-face.

Private one-on-one lessons are available in everything from *bata* drumming to advanced Spanish grammar, but work of this type is officially restricted. Still, classes are easily arranged, typically for US$5 to US$10 an hour at the institutions specializing in your interest. Other travelers are a great source of up-to-date information in this regard.

While US citizens can still study in Cuba, their options shrank dramatically when George W Bush discontinued people-to-people (educational) travel licenses in 2003.

Language

The largest organization offering study visits for foreigners is **UniversiTUR SA** (☎ 7-55-56-83, 7-55-57-94, 7-55-55-77; agencia@universitur.com; Calle 30 No 768-1, btwn 41 & Kohly, Nuevo Vedado). UniversiTUR arranges regular study and working holidays at any of Cuba's universities and at many higher education or research institutes. Its most popular programs are intensive courses in Spanish and Cuban culture at **Universidad de la Habana** (San Lazaro & Calle L, Vedado, Havana). They vary from two weeks to six months, with three levels of participation; placement tests are given at the university at 9am on the first Monday of every month. Classes of three to 10 students receive four hours of instruction daily from Monday to Friday. Courses cost US$250/400 for two/four weeks, or US$800/1280 for four/six months. You can sign up in person at the UniversiTUR office on the 2nd floor of the Edificio Varona at the university, or contact them in advance (☎ 7-870-4667; eventos@rect.uh.cu; ☺ 8am-5pm Mon-Fri). UniversiTUR has 17 branch offices at various universities throughout Cuba, all providing the same services, though prices vary. While US students can study anywhere, they must arrange study programs for the provinces (except Havana or Matanzas) through Havanatur (p435).

Students heading to Cuba should bring a good bilingual dictionary and a basic 'learn Spanish' textbook, as such books are scarce or expensive in Cuba. You might sign up for a two-week course at a university to get your feet wet and then jump into private classes once you've made some contacts.

Culture & Dance

The Promotor Cultural at the **Casa del Caribe** (☎ 226-64-22-85; fax 226-64-23-87; Calle 13 No 154, Vista Alegre, 90100 Santiago de Cuba) organizes courses on culture, Afro-Cuban religions, history, music, and dance, lasting from two weeks to one month. You can probably set something up with a private tutor on the spot here. During the Festival del Caribe, Fiesta del Fuego in early July (of which they are the organizing body), there are workshops on Caribbean culture costing anywhere from US$20 to US$80 tuition for the week.

The **Conjunto Folklórico Nacional** (☎ 7-830-3060; Calle 4 No 103, btwn Calzada & Calle 5, Vedado, Havana) teaches highly recommended classes in *son*, salsa, rumba, mambo and more. Classes start on the first Mondays in January and July and cost US$400 to US$500 for a 15-day course. An admission test places students in classes of four different levels.

Tango lessons are available at the **Centro Andaluz** (☎ 7-863-6745; fax 7-66-69-01; Prado No 104, Centro Habana) from Monday to Friday at 5: 30pm. Price depends on class and skill level. You can arrange private lessons at **El Caserón del Tango** (Jústiz No 21, off Oficios, Habana Vieja).

Salsa Alegre (☎ 7-863-2800; Prado 212, Casa del Scientífico), at Aventour in Havana, has recommended salsa classes for US$120 for 10 hours. Maybe start here and then spin into private lessons, which will work out cheaper.

Art & Film

Courses for foreigners can be arranged throughout the year by the Oficina de Relaciones Internacionales of the **Instituto Superior de Arte** (☎ 7-208-8075; isa@cubarte.cult.cu; Calle 120 No 1110, Cubanacán, Playa, Havana 11600). Courses in percussion and dance are available almost anytime, but other subjects, such as the visual arts, music, theater and aesthetics, are offered when professors are available.

Courses usually involve four hours of classes a week at US$10 an hour (US$15 an hour for postgraduate studies). Prospective students must apply in the last week of August for the fall semester or the last three weeks of January for spring. The school is closed for holidays throughout July and until the third week in August. The institute also accepts graduate students for its regular winter courses, and an entire year of study here (beginning in September) as part of their regular five-year program costs US$2500. Accommodation in student dormitories can be arranged.

The **Taller Experimental de Gráfica de La Habana** (☎ 7-862-0979; fax 7-824-0391; Callejón del Chorro No 6; Plaza de la Catedral, Havana) offers classes in the art of engraving. Individualized instruction lasts one month (US$250), during which the student creates an engraving with 15 copies; longer classes can be arranged.

The **Escuela Internacional de Cine, Televisión y Video** (☎ 650-3152; fax 650-33-53-41/51-96; Apartado Aereo 4041, San Antonio de los Baños, Provincia de La Habana) trains broadcasting professionals from all over the world (especially developing countries). Under the patronage of novelist Gabriel García Márquez, it's run by the foundation that also organizes the annual film festival in Havana. The campus is at Finca San Tranquilino, Carretera de Vereda Nueva, 5km northwest of San Antonio de los Baños. Prospective film-making students should apply in writing in advance (personal inquiries at the gate are not welcome).

Study Abroad Programs

One of the best study abroad programs is offered by the **School of International Training** (SIT; ☎ 802-257-7751; toll free 888-272-7881; www.sit.edu/ studyabroad). This credit-earning, semester-long program combines course work with independent study emphasizing politics and culture. This program costs around US$14,000, including everything but your bar tab, and is fully licensed.

Exchange programs are also offered by the **Council on International Educational Exchange** (CIEE; ☎ 207-553-7600; www.ciee.org), including a three-week summer course (US$2100) in general history and culture and a semester-long program (US$8900) in subjects that vary from women's studies to philosophy. Requirements include Spanish proficiency and a minimum Grade Point Average (GPA).

CUSTOMS

Cuban customs regulations are complicated. For the full scoop see www.aduana.islagran de.cu. Travelers are allowed to bring in personal belongings (including photography equipment, binoculars, musical instrument, tape recorder, radio, personal computer, tent, fishing rod, bicycle, canoe and other sporting gear), gifts up to a value of US$250, and 10kg of medicine in its original packaging. Those over the age of 18 may import 2L of liquor and one carton of cigarettes.

Items that do not fit into the categories mentioned above are subject to a 100% customs duty to a maximum of US$1000.

Items prohibited entry into Cuba include narcotics, explosives, pornography ('any items attempting against good manners'), electrical appliances broadly defined, global positioning systems, prerecorded video cassettes and 'any item attempting against the security and internal order of the country,' including some books. Canned, processed and dried food are no problem, nor are pets.

Exporting art and items of cultural patrimony is restricted and involves fees, paperwork and forethought. See Exporting Artwork (p107) for details. You are allowed to export 50 cigars duty-free.

DANGERS & ANNOYANCES

Cuba is generally safer than most countries, and violent attacks are extremely rare. Petty theft (eg rifled luggage in hotel rooms, or unattended shoes disappearing from the beach) is common, but preventative measures work wonders. Pickpocketing is also preventable: wear your bag in front of you on crowded buses and at busy markets, and only take what money you'll need to the disco.

Begging is more widespread than other crimes and is exacerbated by tourists who amuse themselves by handing out money, soap, pens, chewing gum and other things to people on the street. Sadly, many Cubans have dropped out of productive jobs because they've found it's more lucrative to hustle tourists or beg than to work. It's painful for everyone when beggars earn more money than doctors. If you truly want to help, pharmacies and hospitals accept medicine donations, schools happily take pens, paper, crayons etc, and libraries take books. Hustlers are called *jinetero/as* (male/female jockeys), and can be a real nuisance. See the boxed text on p359.

Annoyances include travel agents promising services they can't deliver and masturbators *(tiradores)* who frequent dark places, especially movie theaters. If you're sensitive to smoke, you'll choke in Cuba, where even in hospitals surgeons are lighting up.

Despite the many strides the Cuban Revolution has made in stamping out racial discrimination, traces still linger and visitors of non-European origin are more likely to attract the attention of the police than whites might. Latin or black visitors may have to show passports to enter hotels and other places from which ordinary Cubans are barred. Likewise, racially mixed pairs (especially black-white couples) will usually encounter more questions, demanding of papers and hassle than other travelers.

Scams

Most common scams are petty: selling tourists three-peso Che coins for a dollar (they're worth less than US$0.10 and are available at any Cadeca), or padding a bar bill.

Other scams are more serious. A common one is to sell Cuban pesos on the street at a one-to-one exchange. Hustlers convince you this is a straight-up deal by showing you the official exchange rate in the paper, which says one peso equals one dollar. What that rate refers to is *convertible pesos,* which are pegged to the dollar. What they're selling you is *Cuban pesos (moneda nacional),* which were selling at 26 to the dollar at the time of writing. There's a simple way to avoid this: don't change money in the street. There's absolutely no advantage in it anyway and it's a highly punishable offense.

Also, you wouldn't be the first foreigner to fall madly in love only to find your money belt fleeced on the eve of your departure.

DISABLED TRAVELERS

Cuba's inclusive culture translates to disabled travelers, and while facilities may be lacking, the generous nature of Cubans generally compensates. Sight-impaired travelers will be helped across streets and given priority in lines. The same holds true for travelers in wheelchairs, who will find the few ramps ridiculously steep and will have trouble in colonial parts of town where sidewalks are narrow and streets are cobblestone. Elevators are often out of order. Etecsa phone centers have telephone equipment for the hearing impaired and television programs are broadcast with closed captioning.

EMBASSIES & CONSULATES
Cuban Embassies & Consulates

Australia Consulate-General (☎ 61-2-9311-4611; fax 61-2-9311-1255; PO Box 1412, Maroubra, NSW 2035)

Belgium Embassy (☎ 32-2-343-0020; fax 32-2-344-9691; Robert Jonesstraat 77, 1180 Brussels)

Canada Embassy (☎ 613-563-0141; fax 613-563-0068; 338 Main St, Ottawa, Ontario K1S 1E3); Consulate-General (☎ 416-234-8181; fax 416-234-2754; Suite 401, 5353 Dundas St W, Etobicoke, Ontario M9B 6H8); Consulate-General and Trade Commission (☎ 514-843-8897; fax 514-982-9034; 1415 Av des Pins Ouest, Montréal, Québec H3B 1B2)

France Embassy (☎ 33-1-45-67-55-35; fax 33-1-45-66-80-92; 16 rue de Presles, 75015 Paris)

Germany Embassy (☎ 49-30-9161-1811; Stavanger Strasse 20, 10439 Berlin); Consulate (☎ 49-228-3090; Kennedy Allee 22, 53175 Bonn)

Italy Embassy (☎ 39-06-571-7241; fax 39-06-574-5445; Via Licina No 7, 00153 Rome)

Mexico Embassy (☎ 52-5-280-8039; fax 52-5-280-0839; Presidente Masarik 554, Colonia Polanco, 11560 Mexico, DF)

Netherlands Embassy (☎ 31-70-360-6061; fax 31-70-364-7586; Scheveningseweg 9, 2517 KS, La Haya); Consulate (☎ 31-10-206-7333; fax 31-10-206-7335; Stationsplein 45, 3013 AK Rotterdam)

DIRECTORY

Spain Embassy (☎ 341-359-2500; fax 341-359-6145; Paseo de la Habana No 194, Pinilla 28036 Madrid)
UK Embassy (☎ 44-020-7240-2488; fax 44-020-7836-2602; 167 High Holburn, London WC1 6PA) Closest embassy to Ireland.
USA Cuban Interests Section (☎ 202-797-8609/10; fax 202-986-7283; 2630 16th St NW, Washington, DC 20009)

Embassies in Cuba

Most embassies are open from 8am to noon on weekdays.
Australia see Canada.
Austria (☎ 7-204-2825; fax 7-204-1235; Calle 4 No 101 at Av 1, Miramar)
Belgium (☎ 7-204-2410; fax 7-204-1318; Av 5 No 7406 at Av 76, Miramar)
Canada (☎ 7-204-2516; fax 7-204-2044; Calle 30 No 518 at Av 7, Playa) Also represents Australia.
Denmark (☎ 7-33-81-28; fax 7-33-81-27; 4th fl, Paseo de Martí No 20, Centro Habana)
France (☎ 7-204-2308; fax 7-204-0335; Calle 14 No 312 btwn Avs 3 & 5, Miramar)
Germany (☎ 7-33-25-69; fax 7-33-15-86; Calle 13 No 652, at Calle B, Vedado)
Italy (☎ 7-204-5615; fax 7-204-5661; Av 5 No 402, Miramar)
Japan (☎ 7-204-8904; fax 7-204-8902; cnr Av 3 & Calle 80, Playa)
Mexico (☎ 7-204-2498; fax 7-204-2666; Calle 12 No 518 at Av 7, Miramar)
Netherlands (☎ 7-204-2511; fax 7-204-2059; Calle 8 No 307, btwn Avs 3 & 5, Miramar)
New Zealand see UK.
Spain (☎ 7-33-80-29; Capdevila No 51 at Agramonte, Centro Habana)
Sweden (☎ 7-204-2831; fax 7-204-1194; Calle 34 No 510 at Av 5, Miramar)
Switzerland (☎ 7-204-2611; fax 7-204-2729; Av 5 No 2005, btwn Avs 20 & 22, Miramar)
UK (☎ 7-204-1771; fax 7-204-8104; Calle 34 No 708 at Av 7, Miramar) Also represents New Zealand.
USA (☎ 7- 33-35-51; Interests Section, Calzada, btwn Calles L & M, Vedado)

FESTIVALS & EVENTS

For more information on these and other festivals and events, visit www.afrocubaweb .com/festivals.htm.

JANUARY
Liberation & New Year's Day (Jan 1) Big street parties countrywide and dozens of outdoor concerts in Havana.
Birthday of José Martí (Jan 28) Prideful observances include book launchings and cultural performances.

Fería Internacional del Libro (Last week of Jan) Impressive two-week book fair with concerts, readings, book launches and sales; moves from Havana across the country in February.

APRIL
PerCuba (Festival Internacional de Percusión; third week of Apr) Bang your drum at Havana's annual thump-fest.
Baseball playoffs (Location varies) Two weeks of top ball playing excites fans of all ages.

MAY
Día de los Trabajadores (May 1) May Day means massive rallies held in Plazas de la Revolución countrywide.
Romerías de Mayo (First week of May) Rap, rock, poetry and dance take over Holguín in one of Cuba's most popular events.
Festival Internacional de Guitarra (Second week of May) Axe masters flock to Havana for loads of concerts; 2004 & 2006.
Fería Internacional Cubadisco (Second week of May in Havana) Like the Cuban Grammy's, with so many stellar concerts you won't be able to choose.

JUNE
Festival Internacional Boleros de Oro (Third week of June) International bolero stars move crowds to tears in Havana, Santiago de Cuba and elsewhere.

JULY
Festival del Caribe, Fiesta del Fuego (First week of July) Raucous week-long festival celebrating Caribbean dance, music and religion in Santiago de Cuba.
Day of the National Rebellion (July 26) Celebrates the July 26, 1953 attack on the Moncada Barracks in a different province each year.
Carnaval, Santiago de Cuba (Last week of July) The country's biggest and best.

AUGUST
Festival de Rap Cubano Habana Hip Hop (Mid-month) Everyone's bustin' rhymes in this wildly successful international event.

OCTOBER
Festival Internacional de Ballet (Mid-month) Tremendous event packed with performances morning, noon and night; 2004 & 2006.

NOVEMBER
Bienal de la Habana (Mid-month) Havana's art extravaganza showcases Cuba's best contemporary art for three months; 2005 & 2007.

DECEMBER

Festival Internacional del Nuevo Cine Latino-americano (First week of December) This prestigious film festival features hundreds of screenings.

Festival Internacional de Jazz (First week of December) Straight ahead, be-bop, Latin, far out or funkified: whatever type of jazz, it happens here; 2004 & 2006.

Las Parrandas (December 24 in Remedios) Extravagant fireworks and floats make this one of Cuba's most outrageous festivals.

FOOD

It will be the very rare meal in Cuba that costs over US$25. In this book, we present restaurant listings in the following order: budget (meals for under US$10, which includes almost all paladares), mid-range (meals for US$10 to US$20) and top end (meals for over US$20). Before you dig in, check out the detailed information in the Food & Drink chapter (p50).

GAY & LESBIAN TRAVELERS

While Cuba can't be called a queer destination (yet), it's more tolerant than many other Latin American countries. The hit movie *Fresa y Chocolate* (Strawberry and Chocolate) sparked a national dialogue about homosexuality, and Cuba is pretty tolerant, all things considered. Folks from more accepting societies may find this tolerance too 'don't ask, don't tell' or tokenesque (everyone has a gay friend/relative/co-worker, whom they'll mention when the topic arises), but hey, you have to start somewhere and Cuba is moving in the right direction.

In Havana the cruising scene revolves around the Cine Yara (p105). Head there on Friday and Saturday and it's easy to find the private fiestas (US$2 cover), moving shindigs that are mostly gay, with a healthy dose of fag hags, bi-folks and friends. They're renowned for their talented drag shows (no pictures please). Entrepreneurial folks have even organized taxi services to shuttle between Vedado and wherever the party is, so don't worry about finding that random address in Marianao. There are no gay bars per se, but try classic cruise spots such as the theater, ballet or parks. Santiago de Cuba has a subtle scene happening in Plaza de Dolores (p362) and a reader reported meeting some folks in the central park in Baracoa (p397).

Machismo shows an ugly face when it comes to lesbians (the idea that a women can't be satisfied by a man just doesn't jive with most Cuban males' world view) and female homosexuality has not enjoyed the aperture of male homosexuality. For this reason, female lovers can share rooms and otherwise 'pass' with facility. However Jurassic you might find that, it's a workable solution to a sticky problem. There are occasional *fiestas para chicas* (not necessarily all-girl parties, but close); ask around at the Cine Yara.

Cubans are physical with each other and you'll see men hugging, women holding hands and lots of friendly caressing. This type of casual touching shouldn't be a problem, but take care when that hug among friends turns overtly sensual in public.

HOLIDAYS

The Cuban calendar is loaded with holidays, but there are only a few that might affect your travel plans; among them are December 25 (not declared an official holiday until after the Pope visited in 1998), January 1, May 1 and July 26. On these days, stores will be closed and transport (except for planes) erratic. On May 1, especially, buses are dedicated to shuttling people to the Plazas de la Revolución in every major city and town and you can just forget about getting inner-city transport.

July and August mean crowded beaches and sold out campismos and hotels.

INSURANCE

Insurance pays off only if something serious happens, but that's what insurance is for, so you might consider it. Outpatient treatment at international clinics designed for foreigners is reasonably priced, but emergency and prolonged hospitalization get expensive (the free medical system for Cubans should only be used when there is no other option).

If you're really concerned about your health, consider purchasing travel insurance once you arrive at **Asistur** (☎ 7-33-85-27, 7-867-1315; fax 7-33-80-87; Paseo de Martí No 212). They have two types of coverage. For non-Americans the policy costs US$2 per day and covers up to US$400 in lost luggage, US$7000 in medical coverage and US$5000 each for repatriation of remains or jail bail. For Americans, similar coverage costs US$8 per day and provides up to US$25,000 in health care costs, plus US$7000 to repatriate remains or evacuate you.

It's recommended that you take car insurance for a variety of reasons; see p432 for details.

INTERNET ACCESS

Most travelers make constant use of Internet cafés and free Web-based email such as **Yahoo** (www.yahoo.com) or **Hotmail** (www.hotmail.com). If you need to access a specific account of your own, you'll need to carry three pieces of information with you: your incoming (POP or IMAP) mail server name, your account name and your password. Your Internet service provider (ISP) or network supervisor will be able to give you these. With this information, you should be able to access your Internet mail account from any Net-connected machine in the world, provided it runs some kind of email software (remember that Netscape and Internet Explorer both have mail modules).

Cuba has leapt into the 21st century but the bugs are still being worked out, so don't expect the access you're used to. You can get on the Internet in almost every big city and town, but forget about connecting via a laptop anywhere. Havana has a variety of places to connect (p64), but outside of the capital the most reliable access is at Etecsa (Empresa de Telecomunicaciones de Cuba, SA). Full Internet access costs US$6 per hour, you must show your passport when connecting and they usually keep long hours (eg 7am to 11pm). Scanners, printers and other peripherals are typically not available. If you're in need of a web-based account, check out www.ekno.com, which has a variety of services, including free email, that are useful to travelers.

IN CUBA YOU HAVE TO BE...

- 18 years old to vote
- 14 years old to have heterosexual sex if you're female
- 18 years old to drive
- 16 years old to buy cigarettes or liquor

LEGAL MATTERS

Cuban police are everywhere and they're usually very friendly – more likely to ask you for a date than a bribe. Corruption is a serious offense in Cuba and typically no one wants to get messed up in it. Getting caught out without identification is never good; carry some around just in case (a driver's license, a copy of your passport or student ID card should be sufficient).

Drugs are prohibited in Cuba and though people indulge, it is always very quietly and privately. Penalties for buying, selling, holding or taking drugs are serious, and Cuba is making a concerted effort to treat demand and curtail supply; it is only the foolish traveler who partakes while on a Cuban vacation.

MAPS

Signage is improving in Cuba, but is still awful: drivers will want a good map. The comprehensive *Guía de Carreteras* (US$6), published in Italy, has the best maps available in Cuba. It has a complete index, a detailed Havana map and useful information in English, Spanish, Italian and French. Handier is the all-purpose *Automapa Nacional*, available at hotel shops and car rental offices.

The Instituto Cubano de Geodesia y Cartografía (aka Ediciones GEO) publishes several excellent maps including the *Mapa Turístico La Habana* (1:25,000, US$2, 2002) and the *Mapa Turístico Cuba*. You can buy these maps at www.cubamapa.com.

The best map published outside of Cuba is the Freytag & Berndt 1:1,250,000 *Cuba* map. The island map is good, and it has indexed town plans of Havana, Playas del Este, Varadero, Cienfuegos, Camagüey and Santiago de Cuba.

MONEY

This is a tricky part of any Cuba trip and the double economy takes some getting used to. Three currencies circulate in Cuba: US dollars, convertible pesos and Cuban pesos (also called *moneda nacional*). Most things tourists buy are in US dollars (eg accommodation, rental cars, bus tickets, museum admission and Internet access). Convertible pesos are interchangeable with US dollars and you'll receive them as change, in banks and from ATM machines. At the time of writing, Cuban pesos were selling at 26 to the dollar, and while there are many things you can't buy with *moneda nacional*, once you've been in Cuba a while, you'll learn that a lot *can* be bought with Cuban pesos; with pesos you'll see a bigger slice of authentic Cuba. Making things a little more confusing, euros are accepted at the Varadero, Guardalavaca, Cayo Largo del Sur, and Cayos Coco and Guillermo resorts, but once you leave the resort grounds, you'll still need dollars. For information on costs, see p13.

The best currency to carry is US dollars. At the time of writing, traveler's checks issued by US banks could be exchanged at branches of Banco Financiero Internacional, but credit cards issued by US banks could not be used at all.

Cadeca branches in every city and town sell Cuban pesos. You won't need more than US$10 worth of pesos a week. In addition to the offices located on the maps in this book, there is almost always a branch at the local agropecuario (vegetable market). If you get caught without Cuban pesos and are drooling for that ice cream cone, you can always use dollars; in street transactions such as these, US$1 is equal to 25 pesos and you'll receive change in pesos. There is no black market in Cuba, only hustlers trying to fleece you with money changing scams (see p413).

ATM & Credit Cards

When the banks are open, the machines are working and the phone lines are live, credit cards can be great – if the cards are not issued by US banks. Non-Americans planning on using plastic should always carry a stash of cash, as even the fanciest hotels sometimes experience difficulties processing credit card requests. You'll be taking cash advances rather than using ATMs, of which there were only a handful in the entire country in mid-2003. If you do find a working ATM, it will accept only six-digit PIN codes. In banks, cash advances are free; in Cadecas that give cash advances, the commission is 1%.

Credit cards accepted in Cuba are Master-Card, Visa and Cabal.

Cash

It is best to carry cash, as you can use US dollars brought with you (non-Americans can change before they leave home, which is

> ### DOLLARS ON THE OUTS?
>
> Beginning in July 2003, companies doing business in Cuba were no longer able to use US dollars; all transactions between the state and joint enterprises had to be in convertible pesos. Although individuals could use both US dollars and convertible pesos at the time of writing, restricting the use of dollars by companies is seen as a 'step toward a single currency, though it's still a ways away,' according to a Cuban executive. Still, there's an outside chance that US dollars could stop circulating entirely before the next update of this guide. For up-to-date information in five languages, see www.havanajournal.com/business.php.

faster and less hassle than doing it in Cuba). It's riskier than the traditional cash/credit card/traveler's check mix that you may be used to, but it's damn convenient. If you use a money belt and keep the cash on you or in your hotel's safe deposit box, you should be OK.

You'll have to show your passport and sign a paper when using US$50 or US$100 bills. You can always break big bills at hotels and many restaurants, including paladares, but it's good to bring plenty of US$20 notes.

Denominations & Lingo

One of the most confusing parts of a double economy is terminology. Cuban pesos are called *moneda nacional* (abbreviated MN) or pesos Cubanos or simply pesos. Dollars are called *fula*, *divisa* or simply…pesos. Sometimes you'll be negotiating in pesos (Cubanos) and your counterpart will be negotiating in pesos (dollars). You must always clarify whenever 'peso' figures are being bandied about. Worse, the symbol for both dollars and pesos Cubanos is $. You can imagine the potential scams just working these combinations.

The Cuban peso comes in notes of one, five, 10, 20, 50 and 100 pesos, and coins of one (rare), five and 20 centavos, and one and three pesos. The five-centavo coin is called a *medio*, the 20-centavo coin a *peseta*. Centavos are also called *kilos*.

The convertible peso comes in multi-colored notes of one, three, five, 10, 20, 50 and 100 pesos. Special convertible coins the same size and value as US coins (five, 10, 25 and 50 cents and one peso) circulate as change for both dollars and convertible pesos. You can tell them from the Cuban peso coins because the face has a subtle octagonal edge.

Tipping

If you're not in the habit of tipping, you'll learn fast in Cuba. Wandering *son* septets, parking guards, ladies at bathroom entrances, restaurant wait staff, tour guides – they're all working for hard currency tips. Musicians who besiege tourists while they dine, converse or flirt will want a dollar, but only give what you feel the music is worth. Washroom attendants expect five or ten cents, while parking attendants (*parquea-dores*) should get US$0.25 for a short watch and US$1 for each 12 hours. For a day tour, US$2 per person is appropriate for a tour guide. Taxi drivers will appreciate 10% of the meter fare, but if you've negotiated a ride without the meter, don't tip as the whole fare is going straight into their wallets.

Tipping can quickly *resuelvan las cosas* (fix things up). If you want to stay beyond the hotel check-out time or enter a site after hours, for instance, small tips (US$1 to US$5) bend rules, open doors and send people looking the other way. For tipping in restaurants and other advice, see the Food & Drink chapter (p50).

Traveler's Checks

While they add security and it makes sense to carry a few for that purpose, traveler's checks are a hassle in Cuba. You'll pay commission at both the buying and selling ends (3% to 4%), cashing them takes time, and smaller hotels don't accept them. Furthermore, some banks in the provinces won't cash traveler's checks (American Express checks are particularly troublesome). Readers have reported that Thomas Cook checks work well and Banco Financiero Internacional is by far the most efficient bank in which to cash them.

PHOTOGRAPHY

Clouds filter sensuous sunbeams, old men puff half-chewed cigars and palm fronds brush against faded stucco in an irresistible combination of light, subject and moment. But while the composition is thrust in your lap, the means to make memorable pictures aren't. Good film is expensive (US$7 for a roll of 24 Kodak Gold prints) and developing is terrible and costly (US$0.35 a shot). Photo Service is the biggest chain in Cuba and they develop film and sell supplies, but anyone serious about photography should bring their own. Cuba is so photogenic, you may want to bone up on some techniques. Take it from the fuzzy snapshot queen: Lonely Planet's *Travel Photography* can help you make some great photos.

Most Cubans love to have their pictures taken and will happily pose if you ask '*¿puedo tirar una foto?*' (can I take a photo?). Photos are treasured, so you might offer to send along copies.

POST

Letters and postcards sent to Europe and the US take about a month to arrive. While stamps (*sellos*) are sold in pesos and dollars, correspondence bearing the latter has a better chance of arriving. Postcards cost US$0.65 to all countries. Letters cost US$0.65 to the Americas, US$0.75 to Europe and US$0.85 to all other countries. Prepaid postcards, including international postage, are available at most hotel shops and post offices and are the surest bet for successful delivery. For important mail, you're better off using DHL, located in all the major cities; it costs US$55 for a two-pound letter pack to Australia, or US$50 to Europe.

The Cuban post has a well-organized telegram (*telegrama*) system whereby messages can be sent from any post office to any address in the country. A nostalgic, economical way to communicate (it costs about US$1.15 for 100 words), this is also how to contact people who don't have phones. Every post office has a telegram window.

SHOPPING

Cigars, rum, music and anything with Che on it are quintessentially Cuban souvenirs. The *guayabera*, a snappy, pleated men's shirt that's Cuban for formalwear, is all the rage from Prague to Vancouver. All of these items (and more) can be purchased in hotel and souvenir shops, but if you want the best selection and price, go to specialist stores.

Egrem is the state recording company and its studio shops in Havana (p121), Holguín (p321) and Santiago de Cuba (p375) have fantastic CD selections. ARTex, a more general souvenir store, also sells CDs.

As an icon, Che is on everything from shot glasses to watch faces (look for the limited-edition Swatch at the Havana airport), and artisan fairs (ferías) in Varadero (p201) and Havana (p105) have a wide selection of all things Che. You can also buy coral and tortoise-shell treasures at these fairs, some quite lovely, but it's best if you don't: these items, plus shells, many plants and reptiles are protected under CITES (Convention on International Trade in Endangered Species). These environmental protection rules prohibit individuals from importing or exporting such items.

You can also buy 'artwork' at these fairs, most of it tourist kitsch, but sometimes you'll find something that strikes you. You shouldn't have a problem exporting this type of art under Cuban patrimony rules, but you might. To avoid disappointment at the airport, you should assume that any artwork that cannot fit in your luggage will be confiscated if you don't have the correct documentation. If you've bought an original painting or sculpture from an official store, the only documentation you'll need is the receipt. If you've purchased a piece of art on the street or directly from the artist, you'll need an export certificate (see p107). Antiquities are also subject to patrimony restrictions.

Cuba has some fabulous antiques and every town has a *casa de comisiones*, literally 'commission house', where people put up their heirlooms for sale. These shops sell everything in Cuban pesos. Good vintage clothing is also available.

Cigars

The best Cuban cigars are completely hand-rolled and packed in sealed, stamped cedar boxes. There are 42 different types and sizes of Havana cigars, classified as fine, medium or thick. A single brand can come in several different sizes, and the same size category can refer to various types of cigars of other brands. The most common types are Mareva (129mm), Corona (142mm) and Julieta (178mm). Choosing the right cigar requires a degree of knowledge, and connoisseurs will be very familiar with the varying tastes and styles.

Cuba's flagship brand is the spicy Cohiba, created in 1966 for diplomatic use (it's still

gifted in the highest political circles) and only available to the general public since 1982. Named for the original Taino word for tobacco, it comes in 11 medium to strong types. The five numbered varieties of Montecristo are among Cuba's most popular cigars. Before he quit smoking in 1989, President Castro's favorites were Corona Grande Montecristo and Cohiba Espléndidos. Medium-flavored Punch cigars were designed for export to the United Kingdom as far back as 1840. Another classic is the stronger Partagás, rolled in Havana since 1845. The milder Romeo y Julieta was invented in 1903 by a globetrotting Cuban. Other mild brands include Quintero and Rafael González.

The five main tobacco-growing areas are Vuelta Abajo and Semi Vuelta (around San Cristóbal; both in Pinar del Río), Partido (around San Antonio de los Baños), Remedios (west of Sancti Spíritus), and Oriente (north of Ciego de Ávila, south of Bayamo and south of Mayarí). Most export quality cigars are made from Vuelta Abajo or Partido tobacco.

Black-market cigars sold on the street are mostly scams (sealed boxes filled with sand or the lowest grade one-peso cheroots), but if you act like you know what you're doing, you might at least get quality fakes. Examine the individual cigars to make sure they're tightly rolled without any tiny air pockets or protuberances. The cigar should be soft when squeezed gently between your fingers. The covering should be smooth as silk, and all cigars in the box should have a uniform shape, though color can vary slightly. The cigars should be pungent. The litmus test is to put the lighting end in your mouth and puff in and out with care: the outer leaf should 'breathe.' If not, it's probably a counterfeit made from waste tobacco swept from factory floors, which have no draw and are impossible to smoke. Occasionally, stolen genuine cigars are available on the black market for a quarter what they'd cost in the shops, but this is the exception.

Unless you know cigars well, it's advisable to pay more to be sure of what you're getting. Also, an official sales receipt from a shop eliminates the possibility of problems with Cuban customs. Some marketeers offer fake receipts but customs officers spot them easily. Visitors are allowed to export US$2000 worth of documented cigars per person. Amounts in excess of this, or black-market cigars without receipts, will be confiscated (Cuban customs is serious about this, with ongoing investigation into cigar rings and over a half million seizures of undocumented cigars annually). Of course, you can buy additional cigars in the airport departure lounge after you've passed Cuban customs, but the 50 cigar tax-free limit applies in most countries. Mexican customs in Cancún conducts rigorous cigar searches. If you traveled without a license to Cuba, US customs will seize any tobacco you have upon entering; licensed travelers are permitted to bring US$100 worth of cigars into the US. (Imitation Cuban cigars sold in the US contain no Cuban tobacco.)

La Casa del Habano (www.habanos.net) is the national cigar store chain, where the staff is well-informed, there's a wide selection and sometimes a smoking lounge.

Smokers on a budget can buy smokable Selectos cigars in bodegas for a peso each.

TELEPHONE

At the time of writing, Cuba was still digitizing its phone system, so that eventually all phone numbers will have six digits (some in Havana have seven). You'll usually just need to add one or two digits to existing numbers, and taped advisories in Spanish will play before your call is connected during the changeover period. Be aware of this especially in Trinidad and Sancti Spíritus Province during 2004 and 2005. If you have any problems, the friendly Etecsa people can help (see Phone Cards).

Mobile Phones

Cuba's two mobile-phone companies are c.com and **Cubacel** (www.cubacel.com). While you may be able to use your own equipment, you have to prebuy their services. Cubacel has over 15 offices around the country (including at the Havana airport) where you can do this. Their plan costs US$3 per day (plus US$7 per day if you use their equipment, though most Nokia phones will work) and each local call costs from US$0.52 to US$0.70. Note that you pay for incoming as well as outgoing calls. International rates are US$2.70 per minute to the US and US$5.85 per minute to Europe.

Phone Cards

Etecsa is where you buy phone cards, send and receive faxes, use the Internet and make international calls. Blue public Etecsa phones accepting magnetized or computer chip cards are everywhere. The cards are sold in dollar denominations of US$5, US$10 and US$20 and peso denominations of three, five and seven pesos. You can call nationally with either, but you can call internationally only with dollar cards. If you are mostly going to be making national and local calls, buy a peso card as it's much more economical.

The best cards for calls from Havana are called Propia. They come in pesos (five and 10 denominations) and dollars (10 and 25 denominations) and allow you to call from any phone – even ones permitting only emergency calls – using a personal code. The rates are the cheapest as well.

Phone Codes

To call Cuba from abroad, dial your international access code, Cuba's country code (☎ 53), the city or area code, and the local number. In this book, area codes are indicated under city headings. To call internationally from Cuba, dial Cuba's international access code (☎ 119), the country code, the area code and the number. To the US, you just dial ☎ 119, then 1, the area code and the number.

To place a call through an international operator, dial ☎ 09, except to the United States, which can be reached with an operator on ☎ 66-12-12. Not all private phones in Cuba have international service, in which case you'll want to call collect (reverse charges or *cobro revertido*). This service is available only to Argentina, Brazil, Canada, Chile, Colombia, Costa Rica, Dominican Republic, France, Italy, Mexico, Panama, Spain, UK, US and Venezuela. International operators are available 24 hours and speak English. You cannot call collect from public phones.

Phone Rates

Local calls cost five centavos per minute, while interprovincial calls cost from 35 centavos to one peso per minute (note that only the peso coins with the star work in pay phones). Since most coin phones don't return change, common courtesy asks that you push the 'R' button so that the next person in line can make their call with your remaining money.

International calls made with a card cost US$2.45 per minute to the US and Canada and US$5.85 to Europe and Oceania. Calls placed through an operator cost US$3.71 and US$8.78 respectively.

TIME
Cuba is five hours behind GMT/UTC, the equivalent of Eastern Standard Time in the US and Canada. When it's noon in Havana it's 6pm in continental Western Europe, 5pm in Britain, 11am in Mexico City, 9am in California, 5am in New Zealand and 2am in Melbourne, Australia.

Cuba is on daylight saving time from April to September, during which Cuba is only four hours behind GMT/UTC. In other words, clocks are turned an hour back at the beginning of October and an hour forward in late March.

TOILETS
Look for public toilets in bus stations, tourist hotels or restaurants, and gas stations. We have yet to meet a Cuban who would deny a needy traveler the use of their bathroom. In public restrooms there often won't be water or toilet paper and never a toilet seat. The faster you learn to squat and carry your own supply of paper, the happier you'll be. Frequently there will be an attendant outside bathrooms supplying toilet paper and you're expected to leave five or ten cents in the plate provided. If the bathrooms are dirty or the person doesn't supply paper, you shouldn't feel compelled to leave money.

Cuban sewer systems are not designed to take toilet paper or tampons and every bathroom has a small waste basket beside the toilet for this purpose. Aside from at top-end hotels and resorts, you should discard your paper in this basket or risk an embarrassing backup.

TOURIST INFORMATION
At the time of writing, **Infotur** (www.infotur.cu), Cuba's official tourist information bureau, had offices only in Havana, Playas del Este and Camagüey. Travel agencies can usually supply some general information; try Rumbos.

VISAS & TOURIST CARDS
Regular tourists who plan to spend up to two months in Cuba do not need visas. Instead, you get a tourist card *(tarjeta de turista)* valid for four weeks, which can be easily extended for another four weeks once you're in Cuba. Those going 'air only' usually buy the tourist card from the travel agency or airline office that sells them their plane ticket (US$15 extra). Package tourists receive their card with their other travel documents.

Unlicensed tourists originating in the US buy their tourist card at the airline desk in the country through which they're traveling en route to Cuba (US$25). You are usually not allowed to board a plane to Cuba without this card, but if by some chance you are, you should be able to buy one in Aeropuerto Internacional José Martí in Havana. Once in Havana, tourist card extensions or replacements cost another US$25. You cannot leave Cuba without presenting your tourist card, so don't lose it. You are not permitted entry to Cuba without an onward ticket.

The 'address in Cuba' line should be filled in, if only to avoid unnecessary questioning. In the old days, travelers entering the address of a casa particular or the cheapest hotel risked facing a hassle and/or compulsory on-the-spot reservations in a state-run hotel. This has largely been relaxed and as long as you are staying in a legal casa particular or hotel, you shouldn't have problems. Staying at a lover's or friend's house (which you can do, but it requires special paperwork at immigration) does not qualify.

Business travelers and journalists need visas. Applications should be made through a consulate at least three weeks in advance (longer if you apply through a consulate in a country other than your own).

Visitors with visas or anyone who has stayed in Cuba longer than 90 days must apply for an exit permit from an immigration office. The Cuban Consulate in London issues official visas (£32 plus two photos). They take two weeks to process, and the name of an official contact in Cuba is necessary.

Extensions
For most travelers, obtaining an extension once in Cuba is easy: you just go to an immigration office and present your documents and US$25 in stamps (obtainable only at Bandec or Banco Financiero Internacional).

You'll only receive an additional four weeks after your original four weeks, but you can exit and re-enter the country for 24 hours and start over again (some travel agencies in Havana have special deals for this type of trip; see p66). Attend to extensions at least a few business days before your visa is due to expire. See individual chapters for details of immigration offices.

Entry Permits for Cubans & Naturalized Citizens

Naturalized citizens of other countries who were born in Cuba require an entry permit (autorización de entrada) issued by a Cuban embassy or consulate. Called a Vigencia de Viaje, it allows Cubans resident abroad to visit Cuba as many times as they like over a two-year period. Persons hostile to the revolution or with a criminal record are not eligible.

The Cuban government does not recognize dual citizenship. All persons born in Cuba are considered Cuban citizens unless they have formally renounced their citizenship at a Cuban diplomatic mission and the renunciation has been accepted. Cuban Americans with questions about dual nationality can contact the Office of Overseas Citizens Services, Department of State, Washington, DC 20520.

Licenses for US Visitors

In 1961 the US government imposed an order limiting the freedom of its citizens to visit Cuba, and airline offices and travel agencies in the US are forbidden to book tourist travel to Cuba via third countries. However, the Cuban government has never banned Americans from visiting Cuba, and it continues to welcome US passport holders under exactly the same terms as any other visitor.

Americans traditionally go to Cuba via Canada, Mexico, the Bahamas, Jamaica or any other third country. American travel agents are prohibited from handling tourism arrangements, so most Americans go though a foreign travel agency. Travel agents in those countries (see p426) routinely arrange Cuban tourist cards, flight reservations and accommodation packages.

The immigration officials in Cuba know very well that a Cuban stamp in a US passport can create problems. However, many Americans request that immigration officers not stamp their passport before they hand it over. The officer will instead stamp their tourist card, which is collected upon departure from Cuba. Those who don't ask usually get a tiny stamp on page 16 or the last page in the shape of a plane, barn, moon or some other random symbol that doesn't mention Cuba.

The US government has an 'Interests Section' in Havana, but American visitors are advised to go there only if something goes terribly wrong. Therefore, unofficial US visitors are especially careful not to lose their passports while in Cuba, as this would put them in a very difficult position. Many Cuban hotels rent security boxes (US$2 per day) to guests and nonguests alike, and you can carry a photocopy of your passport for identification on the street.

There are two types of licenses issued by the US government to visit Cuba: general licenses (typically for family members, artists and academics) and special licenses (for journalists on assignment, for foreign officials based in the US, and occasionally on humanitarian grounds). In 1995 the list of permissible travel was expanded to include educational and cultural exchanges, but George W Bush discontinued this license category in 2003, cutting off 70% of the travel that had been deemed 'legal.' Cuban Americans may visit relatives in Cuba once a year with a general license. Such permits are never issued for the purpose of business travel or tourism.

For more information, contact the **Licensing Division** (☎ 202-622-2480; www.treas.gov/ofac), Office of Foreign Assets Control, US Department of the Treasury, 2nd floor, Annex Building, 1500 Pennsylvania Ave NW, Washington, DC 20220. Travel arrangements for those eligible for a license can be made by specialized US companies such as Marazul or ABC Charters (see p429). License holders are only allowed to spend US$100 per person per day for land arrangements.

Under the Trading with the Enemy Act, goods originating in Cuba are prohibited from being brought into the US by anyone but licensed travelers. Cuban cigars, rum, coffee etc will be confiscated by US customs, and officials can create additional problems if they feel so inclined. Possession of Cuban goods inside the US or bringing them in from a third country is also banned.

American travelers who choose to go to Cuba (and wish to avoid unnecessary hassles with the US border guards) get rid of anything related to their trip to Cuba, including used airline tickets, baggage tags, travel documents, receipts and souvenirs, before returning to the US. If Cuban officials don't stamp their passport, there will be no official record of their trip. They also use a prepaid Cuban telephone card to make calls to the US in order to avoid there being records of collect or operator-assisted telephone calls.

Since September 11, 2001, all international travel issues have taken on new import, and there has been a crackdown on 'illegal' travel to Cuba. Though it has nothing to do with terrorism, some Americans returning from Cuba have had 'transit to Cuba' written in their passports by Jamaican customs officials. Customs officials at major US entry points (eg New York, Houston, Miami) are onto backpacker types coming off Cancún and Montego Bay flights with throngs of honeymoon couples, or tanned gentlemen arriving from Toronto in January. They're starting to ask questions, reminding travelers that it's a felony to lie to a customs agent as they do so.

The maximum penalty for 'unauthorized' Americans traveling to Cuba is US$250,000 and 10 years in prison. In practice, people are usually fined US$7500. Since George W Bush came into the White House, the number of people threatened with legal action has more than tripled and it's likely to go higher still. Over 100,000 US citizens a year travel to Cuba with no consequences. However, as long as these regulations remain in place, visiting Cuba certainly qualifies as soft adventure travel for Americans. There are many organizations, including a group of congress people on Capitol Hill, working to lift the travel ban (see www.cubacentral.com for more information).

VOLUNTEER WORK

One of the most rewarding ways to experience Cuba is by volunteering. International labor brigades have a rich history in Cuba and each year teams of between 50 and 200 workers from around the world (*brigadistas*) arrive to work in solidarity with Cuba. The US's Venceremos and Antonio Maceo Brigades, the Juan Rius Rivera Brigade (Puerto Rico), the Ernesto Che Guevara Brigade (Canada), the José Martí Brigade (Western Europe), the Nordic Brigade (Scandinavia) and the Southern Cross Brigade (Australia and New Zealand) are among them.

Volunteering involves three challenging weeks doing agricultural or construction work alongside Cubans. There's also a full program of activities, including educational and political events and visits to factories, hospitals, trade unions and schools. Entertainment is provided at the camp and excursions to the beach and places of interest are organized.

Participants pay their own airfare to Cuba, plus food, accommodation and excursion fares. For more information, contact the following:

Amigos de Cuba (☎ /fax 604-327-6844; www.nscuba .org/amigos) In Vancouver, BC.

Brigade Québec-Cuba (☎ 514-201-8434; www.bqc .qc.ca)

International Work Brigade (☎ 020-7263-6452; fax 020-7561-0191; www.cuba-solidarity.org.uk/ brigades.htm)

Southern Cross Brigade (☎ 03-9470-5300; www.geocities.com/australiacubafriendship/brigades.htm) Organized by branches of the Australia-Cuba Friendship society throughout Australia and New Zealand.

Every July since 1992 the **Pastors for Peace** (PFP; ☎ 212-926-5757; www.ifconews.org) has led US/Cuba Friendshipments that collect donations in three-week long caravans across the US and Canada, which then travel to Cuba with the goods. PFP is a faith-based organization open to everyone and has donated over 2,250 tons of humanitarian aid. PFP refuses to ask permission from the US government to travel to Cuba on moral and religious grounds and *caravanistas* travel without a license.

Spanish-speakers looking for longer-term commitments in Cuba should investigate **Witness for Peace** (WFP; ☎ 202-588-1471; www.witnessforpeace.org), a respected solidarity organization with teams throughout Latin America, including Cuba. After the initial training, a two-year commitment is required. While stipends, housing and airfare are provided, the salary is extremely low. WFP also brings delegations to Cuba (see p429).

DIRECTORY

WOMEN TRAVELERS

In terms of personal safety, Cuba is a dream destination for women travelers. Most streets can be walked alone at night, violent crime is rare and the chivalrous part of machismo means you'll never step into oncoming traffic. But machismo cuts both ways, with protecting on one side and pursuing – relentlessly – on the other. Cuban women are used to *piropos*, the whistles, kissing sounds and compliments constantly ringing in their ears, and might even reply with their own if they're feeling frisky. For foreign women, however, it can feel like an invasion. Like any cross-cultural situation, if you want to travel in Cuba, you'll have to come to terms with it somehow.

Ignoring *piropos* is the first step. But sometimes ignoring them isn't enough. Learn some rejoinders in Spanish so you can shut men up who can't seem to themselves. *'No me moleste'* (don't bother me), *'esta bueno yá* (all right already) or *'que falta respeto'* (how disrespectful) are good ones, as is the withering 'don't you dare' stare that is also part of the Cuban woman's arsenal. Wearing plain, modest clothes might help lessen unwanted attention; topless sunbathing is out. An absent husband, invented or not, seldom has any effect. If you go to a disco, be very clear with Cuban dance partners what you are and are not interested in. Dancing is a kind of foreplay in Cuba and may be viewed as an invitation for something more. Cubans appreciate directness and as long as you set the boundaries, you'll have a fabulous time. Being in the company of a Cuban man is the best way to prevent *piropos*, and if all else fails, retire to the pool for a day out of the line of fire and re-energize.

Traveling alone can be seen as an invitation for all kinds of come-ons, and solo women travelers will not have an easy time of it. Hooking up with a male traveler (or another woman, at least to deflect the barrage) can do wonders. Marriage proposals will come fast and from all corners, as matrimony is an easy way to immigrate for Cubans who want out.

Transport

CONTENTS

THINGS CHANGE...

The information in this chapter is particularly vulnerable to change. Check directly with the airline or a travel agent to make sure you understand how a fare (and ticket you may buy) works and be aware of the security requirements for international travel. Shop carefully. The details given in this chapter should be regarded as pointers and are not a substitute for your own careful, up-to-date research.

GETTING THERE & AWAY

ENTERING CUBA

Whether it's your first time or fiftieth, it's exciting waiting to pass beyond the locked doors of immigration to enter Cuba. The procedure is straightforward as long as you have a passport valid for six months, an onward ticket and your tourist card filled out (be sure to put something in the 'Address in Cuba' space; see Visas p421).

Outside Cuba, the capital city is called Havana, and this is how travel agents, airlines and other professionals will refer to it. Within Cuba, it's almost always called Habana or La Habana by everyone.

AIR
Airports & Airlines

Cuba has 11 international airports and over 60 carriers serving the island. Most travelers fly into Aeropuerto Internacional José Martí in **Havana** (HAV; ☎ 7-33 56 66), Aeropuerto Juan Gualberto Gómez in **Varadero** (VRA; ☎ 045-24 70 15) or Aeropuerto Antonio Maceo in **Santiago de Cuba** (SCU; ☎ 022-69 10 14). Travelers on package tours might fly into **Holguín** (HOG; ☎ 024-46 25 12), **Ciego de Ávila** (AVI; ☎ 033-26 66 26), **Cayo Largo del Sur** (CYO; ☎ 046-34 82 07) or **Aeropuerto Cayo Coco** (CCC; ☎ 033-30 11 65).

Cuba's national airline is **Cubana de Aviación** (www.cubana.cu). Its modern fleet flies major routes and its fares are usually among the cheapest. Still, overbooking and delays are nagging problems and it has zero tolerance for overweight luggage, charging stiffly for every kilogram above the 20kg allowance. In terms of safety, Cubana's reputation precedes it (it had back-to-back crashes in December 1999, with 39 fatalities), but it hasn't had any incidents since. Still, you might want to check the latest at www.airsafe.com.

AIRLINES FLYING TO & FROM CUBA

Aerocaribbean (☎ 7-33 36 21; Airline Bldg, Calle 23 No 64 & Maelcón)

Aeroflot-Russian International Airlines (AFL; www.aeroflot.com; ☎ 7-33 32 00; hub Moscow; Airline Bldg, Calle 23 No 64 & Malecón)

Aeropostal (LAV; ☎ 7-55 40 00; www.aeropostal.com; hub Caracas; Hotel Habana Libre)

Air Canada (www.aircanada.com)

Air Europa (AEA; ☎ 7-204 6905/6/7/8; www.air-europa .com; hub Madrid; Av 5 cnr Calle 76, Miramar)

Air Europe (AEL; ☎ 7-33 01 15; www.easyspain.com; hub Madrid; Hotel Habana Libre)

Air France (AFR; ☎ 7-66 26 42; www.airfrance.com; hub Paris; Airline Bldg, Calle 23 No 64 & Malecón)

DEPARTURE TAX

Everyone must pay a US$25 departure tax at the airport. It's payable in cash only.

Air Jamaica (AJM; ☎ 7-66 24 47; www.airjamaica.com; hub Montego Bay)

Air Transat (TSC; www.airtransat.com)

British Airways (BAW; www.britishairways.com; hub London–Heathrow)

Condor (CFG; ☎ 7-33 35 24; www.condoramericas.com; hub Frankfurt; Calle 23 No 64) Represented by LTU.

Copa Airlines (CMP; ☎ 7-33 15 03; www.copaair.com; hub Panama City; Airline Bldg, Calle 23 No 64)

Cubana (www.cubana.cu; hub La Habana) Airline Bldg (☎ 33 49 49; Calle 23 No 64); Habana Libre (☎ 55 46 00); Lonja del Comercio (☎ 33 60 69); Playa (☎ 202-9367; Av 5 btwn Calles 98 & 100)

Iberia (IBE; ☎ 7-204-3444; www.iberia.com; hub Madrid; Calle 74, Miramar)

Lacsa (LRC; ☎ 7-33 31 14; www.grupotaca.com; Hotel Habana Libre) Also represents Taca.

LanChile (☎ 7-831-6186; www.lanchile.com; hub Santiago de Chile)

LTU International Airways (☎ 7-33 35 24; www.ltu .com; hub Düsseldorf; Airline Bldg, Calle 23 No 64)

Martinair (MPH; ☎ 7- 33 43 64; www.martinair.com; hub Amsterdam; Calles E &23, Vedado)

Mexicana de Aviación (www.mexicana.com.mx; MXA; ☎ 7-33 35 33; Mexico City; Airline Bldg, Calle 23 No 64) Also the regional carrier Aerocaribe.

Skyservice (www.skyserviceairlines.com; hub Toronto)

Tickets

Since Americans can't buy tickets to Cuba and can't use US-based travel agents, a host of businesses in Mexico (p427), Canada (this page) and the Caribbean (p428) specialize in air-only deals. They sometimes won't sell you the first leg of your trip to the third ('gateway') country for fear of embargo-related repercussions. When booking online or if an agency requires financial acrobatics to steer clear of US embargo laws (which sometimes happens), be sure to confirm details, take contact names and clarify the procedure. You need a Cuban tourist card and these agencies should arrange that. Except during peak holiday seasons, you can usually just arrive in Mexico, Jamaica or whatever third country and buy your roundtrip ticket to Cuba there.

The choice for non-Americans is varied, straightforward, cheap and accessible. Oftentimes, an air-hotel package deal to one of the beach resorts works out cheaper than just airfare alone.

From Canada

Cubana flies to Havana from Montréal four times weekly (via Cayo Coco, Varadero or Cayo Largo). From Toronto, Cubana flies to Havana three times weekly, with a Varadero stopover once a week. Lacsa (the good Costa Rican carrier) also has several weekly flights from Toronto and Montreal to Havana. Mexicana flies from Vancouver to Havana five times weekly.

You might find a cheaper fare, though, with the reliable charter lines Air Transat and Skyservice, flying weekly from Toronto and Montréal to almost all international airports in Cuba. Some of these flights operate

---

US CITIZENS & CUBA

In conjunction with the US embargo against Cuba, the US government currently enforces a 'travel ban', preventing its citizens from visiting Cuba. Technically a treasury law prohibiting Americans from spending money in Cuba, it has largely squelched leisure travel for over forty years.

The 1996 Helms-Burton Bill, which was signed into law by President Clinton on March 12, 1996, imposes *without judicial review* fines of up to US$50,000 on US citizens who visit Cuba without US government permission. It also allows for confiscation of their property. In addition, under the Trading with the Enemy Act, violators may also face up to US$250,000 in fines and up to 10 years in prison. Although fines were only occasionally levied when Clinton was in the White House, the number of individuals fined since Bush came into office has more than tripled. The author and publisher of this guide accept no responsibility for repercussions suffered by US citizens who decide to circumvent these restrictions. You are strongly encouraged to visit www.cubacentral.com to inform yourself of the latest legislation on Capitol Hill.

Supporters of the embargo argue that travel to Cuba supports a 'communist dictatorship.' Lonely Planet believes that travel promotes positive, humanistic, cross-cultural exchanges and where and how you travel is an individual decision. Many Cubans depend on the tourist trade to survive, and by using the information in this book, travelers can spend their money in ways that most benefits ordinary Cubans.

only from mid-December to April, when Canadian flights go directly to Cuba from as far afield as Vancouver and Halifax.

Unfortunately, 'open jaw' ticket arrangements allowing you to fly into one airport and out of another are usually not available. The maximum stay on most Canadian charters is 28 days. If you wish to stay longer than that, the price soars. Flight dates cannot be changed and there are heavy cancellation penalties. Always compare the price of a tour package as it may be only a few hundred dollars more and airport transfers, accommodation, and often meals will be included.

The following are reliable agencies selling packages and air-only tickets:

Alba Tours (www.albatours.com)

A Nash Travel (☎ 905-755 0647, toll free 800-818 2004; www.anashtravel.com)

Cuban Connection (☎ toll free 800-645 1179; www.cuba.tc) An informative website.

Go Cuba Plus (www.gocubaplus.com)

Hola Sun Holidays (☎ 905-882 0136/7/8/9; www.holasunholidays.com)

Netssa (☎ toll free in Canada 866-504 9988; www.netssa.com) Last-minute flight specials, plus multilingual staff.

From Europe

Continental Europe is a good gateway to Cuba. Air Europa flies daily to Havana from Barcelona, Bilbao, Las Palmas, London, Madrid, Milan, Paris and Rome. Air Europe has flights to Havana from Madrid, Milan and Rome four times weekly, and it often offers cheap specials to fill seats. Iberia flies to Havana from Madrid four times weekly and connects through most European capitals; check out their reasonable fares with a maximum three-month stay. Air France arrives from Paris–Charles De Gaulle five times a week.

From Amsterdam, Martinair has twice weekly flights to Havana and one flight weekly to both Varadero and Holguín. It's possible to book Martinair flights into one Cuban airport and out of the other: convenient if you want to travel overland without backtracking. Also look into Air France and Iberia flights from Amsterdam, connecting through Paris or Madrid.

From Germany, Düsseldorf-based LTU International Airways flies weekly from Düsseldorf to Holguín and Varadero, with connections in Düsseldorf to/from Berlin–Tegel, Frankfurt and Munich. Condor has weekly flights from Frankfurt to Cayo Largo, Ciego de Ávila, Havana and Holguín in winter.

From Russia, Aeroflot flies from Moscow–Sheremetyevo to Havana.

Cubana flies to Havana from Las Palmas, London, Madrid, Milan, Moscow, Paris–Orly and Rome. Other Cubana flights go from Paris–Orly, Madrid, Milan and Rome to Santiago de Cuba. London to Holguín and Milan to Cayo Largo are also served. Most operate only once or twice a week, except Havana–Paris, which runs three times weekly. Cubana sometimes offers reduced last-minute fares. There are Cubana offices all over Europe, including **Rome** (☎ 06 700 0714; fax 06 700 0688), **Paris** (☎ 01 53 63 23 23; fax 01 63 53 23 29) and **Madrid** (☎ 91 758 9750; fax 91 541 6642).

The following European-based agencies can help arrange your details:

Amber Reisbureau (☎ 20 685 1155; fax 20 689 0406; Amsterdam) Excellent selection of maps of Cuba.

Guamá SA (☎ 91 782 3780; www.havantur.cu) In Madrid.

Havanatour Benelux (☎ 10 411 2444; www.havana tour.nl) In Rotterdam.

Havanatour Italia (☎ 02-676 0691; www.havanatur.cu)

Havanatour Paris (☎ 01 48 01 44 64; fax 01 48 01 44 66)

Journey Latin America (☎ 020 8747 3108; www.journeylatinamerica) Professional and usually has good deals.

Sol y Son Moscú (☎ 095 931 9964; sol-y-son@mtu net.ru) Sells Cubana flights from Moscow.

Sol y Son Roma (☎ 06-4470 2320; www.sol-y-son .com) Handles Cubana flights from Italy.

Travel Ways Swiss (☎ 908 3838; travelway@span.ch)

Tropicana Turistik (Frankfurt ☎ 69 943 3970, in Berlin ☎ 4930 853 7041/2; www.tropicana.turistik.de)

From Mexico

Mexico is a direct and convenient gateway to Cuba, with many flights to choose from. Both Cubana and Aerocaribe (the regional airline of Mexicana de Aviación) fly from Cancún to Havana daily. Cancún itself is easily accessible on cheap charter flights, and Aerocaribe connects with Mexicana flights from many US cities. If space is available, you can buy same-day tickets to Havana at the Cubana and Aerocaribe offices in the Cancún airport.

Mexicana also has frequent flights from another dozen cities to Havana including Mexico City, Mérida and Tijuana. Cubana flies to Havana from Mexico City daily.

From Mexico City to Havana, a round-trip fare will cost around US$450, from Cancún about US$275. Mexicana has a reservations office in **Mexico City** (☎ 5-448-0990; 1-800-502-2000; www.mexicana.com) or **Cancún** (☎ 98-87-4444). Mexicana offices in the US are prohibited from booking these flights.

Cubana (www.cubana.cu) has offices in **Mexico City** (☎ 5-250 6355; fax 5-255 0835) and **Cancún** (☎ /fax 98-86 0192). Also check these agencies:

Acuario Tours (Acapulco ☎ 74-85 6100, in Mexico City ☎ 5-575-5922; www.acuario.com.mx)

Divermex (☎ 99-887 5487; www.divermex.com)

Sol y Son México (☎ 5-250 6355; www.sol-y-son.com)

Taino Tours (☎ 5-259 3907; www.tainotours.com.mx)

From the Caribbean

Cubana has flights to Havana from Curaçao, Fort de France, Kingston, Montego Bay, Pointe-a-Pitre and Santo Domingo. The Cuban regional carrier Aerocaribbean flies between Puerto Príncipe, Haiti and Santo Domingo and Santiago de Cuba weekly, and Grand Cayman and Havana weekly.

Air Jamaica (www.airjamaica.com) flies from Montego Bay and Kingston to Havana daily, with numerous convenient connections from the US. Air Jamaica also has a liberal baggage policy, often allowing you to bring oversized and overweight luggage without problems. These agencies are worth consulting:

CubaLinda.com (www.cubalinda.com) Havana-based online agency selling gateway tickets from Mexico and the Caribbean

Eddy Tours (☎ 345-945 0871; www.eddystours.com) Located in Grand Cayman.

BRINGING YOUR BICYCLE

Cuba has no problem with travelers bringing in bikes, though customs may ask you to open the box just to check what's inside. If they ask you if you intend to leave the bike in Cuba, just say no. Policies vary wildly across airlines and even within the same carrier as to how you should pack your bike and how much it will cost. Your best bet is to call your carrier two weeks before you travel and arrive extra early for your flight.

From the Bahamas, Cubana flies daily between Nassau and Havana; the Cuban tourist card and the US$15 Nassau airport departure tax should be included in the ticket price, but ask. Due to US embargo laws, these agencies may not accept online payment or credit card guarantees with cards issued by US banks or their subsidiaries. The financial rigmarole for Americans (mailing certified checks, paying in cash or wiring funds through Western Union for example) may not be worth the time and energy if that's the case. Check on the payment system before settling on the Bahamas as a gateway. Nassau bookings can be made through the following companies:

Havanatur Bahamas (☎ 393 5281/2/3/4; fax 393 5280)

Majestic Holidays (☎ 328 0908; www.majesticholidays.com)

San Cristóbal Travel (☎ toll free in US & Canada 866-510 7756; http://sancristobaltravel.com) Offices in Canada and Havana.

From South & Central America

From Caracas, Venezuela, Aeropostal flies to Havana five times weekly. Cubana also flies from Caracas to Havana six times weekly. Book in Caracas, through **Ideal Tours** (☎ 2-793 0037/1822; idealtours@cantv.net) or go straight to **Cubana** (☎ 2-12 286 8639; cubana@intercon.net.ve).

Cubana flies to Havana from Bogotá, Buenos Aires, São Paulo, Santiago de Chile, Quito and Guayaquil. Aeroflot also has weekly flights between Havana and Lima. Cubana also has a weekly flight from Buenos Aires to Cayo Coco and Varadero. Cubana has offices in **Buenos Aires** (☎ 1-326 5291; cubana@tournet.com.ar); **Quito** (☎ 2-54 49 30; cubana@hoy.net); and **Bogota** (☎ 1-610 5800; solyson@colomsat.net.co).

Cubana flies to Havana from San José, Costa Rica and Guatemala City twice weekly and Panama City three times a week. Lacsa (Líneas Aéreas de Costa Rica) operates flights to Havana from San José, Guatemala City and San Salvador several times a week. Copa also has frequent flights between Central America and Cuba.

The Cuban regional airline Aerocaribbean flies from Managua to Havana weekly.

SEA

Thanks to the US embargo, which prohibits vessels calling at Cuban ports from visiting the US for six months, few cruise ships include Cuba on their itineraries. Many companies also canceled Cuba cruises after September 11, 2001, which is odd, because there really is no place safer. European lines however, tired of being locked out, are starting to trickle in. A specialist travel agent will be able to tell you what cruise ships currently call at Cuban ports.

Access by private yacht or cruiser is easy, and there are numerous harbors around Cuba. This book is not intended to replace a comprehensive cruising guide. We recommend Simon Charles' *The Cruising Guide to Cuba*. Good charts (US$16 per sheet, or kits for US$35 to US$45) are sold at **Tienda El Navegante** (☎ 861 3625; fax 66 67 63; VHF Canal 16; Mercaderes No 115, btwn Obispo & Obrapía, Habana Vieja). For more information see p421.

There are no scheduled ferry services to Cuba.

TOURS

A quick Internet search delivers scads of tours focusing on the beach, culture, the environment or adventure. Note that many outfitters anxious to sell packages to Americans, aren't always providing 'legal' travel; Americans are still subject to Treasury laws (see www.treas.gov/ for all the details). Persons holding US passports will find agencies handling 'air only' packages on p426 and tours for US-license holders following.

The US

US citizens eligible for a US government 'license' to visit Cuba should contact **Marazul Charters Inc** (☎ 201-861-9950, 305-461-1317, toll free 800-223-5334; www.marazulcharters.com), which books charter flights direct from Los Angeles, New York and Miami to Havana.

ABC Charters (☎ 305-871 1260, toll free 866-422 2247; www.abc-charters.com), with flights most days from Miami to Havana, Santiago de Cuba or Holguín, has been recommended for its user-friendliness.

Since the people-to-people educational exchange license was revoked in 2003, some of the most rewarding tours from the US have been scuttled – for now. Contact the following for their current tour status:

Center for Cuban Studies (☎ 212-242 0559; fax 212-242 1937; www.cubaupdate.org) Arranges trips through universities.

Global Exchange (☎ 415-255 7296, 800-497 1994; fax 415-255 7498; www.globalexchange.org)

One organization still licensed is **Witness for Peace** (☎ 202-588 1471; www.witnessforpeace.org), a grassroots solidarity organization that brings about 20 delegations from the US to Cuba each year. Trips of 10 to 14 days are spent visiting hospitals, schools and community organizations, with an emphasis on the effects of the US embargo on Cubans and what US individuals can do to change the policy.

GETTING AROUND

AIR

Cubana de Aviación (www.cubana.cu) and its regional carrier Aerocaribbean have flights to La Habana, Baracoa, Bayamo, Camagüey, Cayo Coco, Cayo Largo del Sur, Ciego de Ávila, Gunatánamo, Holguín, Isla de la Juventud, Las Tunas, Manzanillo, Moa and Santiago de Cuba. One way flights are half the price of round-trip flights and weight restrictions are strict (especially on Aerocaribbean's smaller planes). You can purchase tickets at most hotel tour desks and travel agencies for the same price as at the airline offices, which are often chaotic. Sol y Son is Cubana's own travel agency and is known for its customer service and efficiency. (☎ 53 53 48; fax 33 40 64, Calle 27 & M, Vedado)

Aerotaxi (☎ 53 53 48; fax 33 40 64, Calle 27 & M, Vedado) flies charters to smaller airports around the country. You have to rent the entire plane; their smallest aircraft seats four and costs US$680 from Havana to Trinidad.

BICYCLE

Cuba is bike country, with bike lanes, bike workshops and drivers accustomed to sharing the road countrywide. Spare parts are difficult to find in Cuba and you should bring important spares with you. Still, Cubans are grand masters at improvised repair and though specific parts may not be available, something can surely be juryrigged. *Poncheros* fix flat tires and provide air; every small town has one.

Helmets are unheard of in Cuba except at upscale resorts, so you should bring your own. A lock is imperative as bicycle theft is rampant. *Parqueos* are bicycle parking lots located wherever crowds congregate (eg markets, bus terminals, downtown etc) and cost one peso.

Throughout the country, the 1m-wide strip of road to the extreme right is reserved for bicycles, even on highways. It's illegal to ride on sidewalks and against traffic on one-way streets and you'll be ticketed if caught. Road lighting is deplorable and it's not recommended to ride after dark (over one third of vehicular accidents in Cuba involve bicycles); carry lights with you just in case.

Trains with baggage carriages *(coches de equipaje* or *bagones)* should take bikes for around US$10 per trip. These compartments are guarded, but take your panniers with you and check over the bike when you arrive at your destination. Víazul buses also take bikes.

Purchase

Limited selection and high prices make buying a bike in Cuba through official channels unattractive. Better to ask around and strike a deal with an individual to buy their *chivo* (Cuban slang for bike) and trade it or resell it when you leave. With some earnest bargaining, you can get one for around US$30. If you're determined to cycle around

Cuba, you're better off bringing your own and donating or trading it when you leave.

Rental

At present, official bike rental agencies exist only at beach resorts (US$2 per hour or US$15 per day) and in Viñales (US$6 to $8 per day). Bikes are usually included as a perk in all-inclusive resort packages.

Don't worry if there are no official bike rental outlets; no matter where you are, you'll find someone willing to arrange a private rental. The going rate is US$3 to $7 per day.

FERRY

The most important ferry services for travelers are from Surgidero de Batabanó to Nueva Gerona, **Isla de la Juventud** (☎ 62-8-5355) and from Havana to **Regla** and **Casablanca** (☎ 7-867-3726). These ferries are generally safe, though in 1997 two hydrofoils crashed en route to Isla de la Juventud. In both 1994 and 2003, the Regla/Casablanca ferry was hijacked by Cubans trying to make their way to Florida. The 2003 incident involved tourists, so you can expect tight security.

CUBAN AIR ROUTES

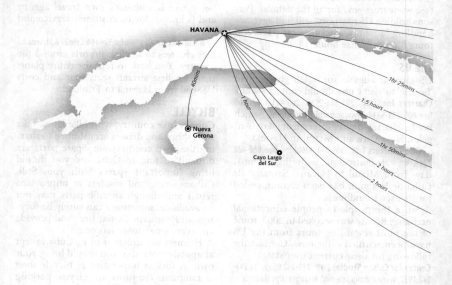

BUS

Bus travel is a viable, dependable option. Víazul runs punctual, air-conditioned coaches to destinations of interest to travelers, while Astro has buses of negligible comfort and varying reliability to Cuba's every corner. Víazul is a dollar service for tourists and well-heeled Cubans, and you can be confident you'll get where you're going on these buses. They cost more, but have daily departures and it's a good place to meet other foreigners.

Astro sells passage to Cubans in pesos and tourists in dollars, so the journey is more interesting and you'll meet lots of locals this way (trucks are another great way to make friends; see p434). If you plan on taking Astro buses, check ahead of the scheduled departure time as things often change and only a few tickets are available for dollars on most departures. There are theoretically different classes of buses, but really, whatever shows up is what you take. Foreigners with a carnet pay for Astro tickets in pesos. Many services only run on alternate days.

Going from east to west, the bus departures are very inconvenient, with buses leaving in the middle of the night.

Astro (Havana ☎ 7-879 2456) Serves every major and minor town in the country; useful for getting off the beaten track and between towns not served by Víazul, including Manzanillo and anything west of Bayamo and the north coast east of Varadero to Baracoa.

Víazul (☎ 7-881 1413, 7-881 5652, 7-881 1108; www.viazul.cu) Routes are Havana–Viñales, Havana–Varadero, Havana–Trinidad, Varadero–Trinidad, Habana–Santiago de Cuba, Trinidad–Santiago de Cuba and Santiago de Cuba–Baracoa. Depending on the route, these buses also stop in Pinar del Río, Santa Clara, Cienfuegos, Ciego de Ávila, Sancti Spíritus, Camagüey, Las Tunas, Holguín, Bayamo or Gunatánamo. They take on-line reservations, but take those with a grain of salt.

Costs

Víazul always costs more than Astro, but is more reliable and has shorter travel times (especially on long hauls). On short trips, the price difference can be a whopping 20% to 25%. From Havana to Viñales for example, you'll pay just US$8 on Astro, but US$12 on Víazul. The value of Víazul over

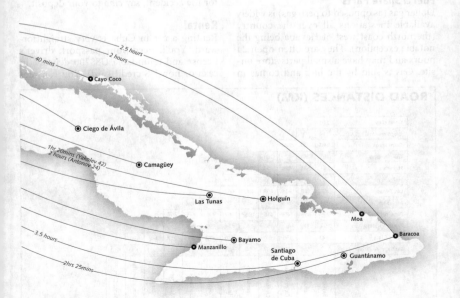

Astro skyrockets over longer trips when the price difference is less drastic and travel times, service and comfort are superior. From Havana to Santiago de Cuba, passage costs US$42/51 with Astro/Víazul.

Reservations

Reservations with Víazul are advisable during peak travel periods (June to August, Christmas and Easter) and on popular routes (Havana–Trinidad, Trinidad–Santa Clara and Santiago de Cuba–Baracoa). Víazul out of Baracoa is almost always booked, so reserve an advance seat on this service and arrange through-reservations if you intend to connect in Santiago de Cuba to points north and west.

Since it's advisable to double check on Astro services before you intend to travel, and only a few seats are reserved for dollar passengers, you might as well make a reservation while you're at it.

CAR
Driving License

Your home license is sufficient to rent and drive a car in Cuba.

Fuel & Spare Parts

Dollar gas (as opposed to peso gas) is widely available in stations all over the country (the north coast west of Havana being the notable exception). They are often open 24 hours and may have a small parts store on-site. Gas is sold by the liter and comes in regular (US$0.75/L) and especial (US$0.90/L) varieties. Either works equally well. Steer clear of black market gas which is usually more water than anything else and could seriously screw up the car.

While you cannot count on spare parts per se to be available, Cubans have decades of experience keeping cars running without factory parts and you'll see them do amazing things with cardboard, string and rubber to keep a car mobile.

If you need air in your tires or you've got a puncture, visit the local *ponchera*. Air costs one peso; flats up to 10 pesos.

Insurance

Rental cars come with an optional US$10 per day insurance which covers everything but theft of the radio. You can decline the insurance, but then the refundable deposit you must leave upon renting the car (in cash if you don't have a credit card issued by a non-US bank) soars from US$200 to US$500. If you have an accident, you must get a copy of the police report (*denuncia*) to be eligible for the insurance coverage, a process which can take all day. If the police determine that you are the party responsible for the accident, say *ciao* to your deposit.

Rental

Renting a car in Cuba is very straightforward. You'll need your passport, driver's license and refundable US$200 deposit (in cash or non-US credit card). You can rent

ROAD DISTANCES (KM)

	Bayamo	Camagüey	Ciego de Ávila	Cienfuegos	Guantánamo	Havana	Holguín	Las Tunas	Matanzas	Pinar del Río	Sancti Spíritus	Santa Clara
Camagüey	210											
Ciego de Ávila	318	108										
Cienfuegos	540	330	222									
Guantánamo	161	371	479	701								
Havana	744	534	426	254	905							
Holguín	71	209	317	539	182	743						
Las Tunas	82	128	236	458	243	662	81					
Matanzas	684	474	366	194	845	105	683	602				
Pinar del Río	906	696	588	416	1067	162	905	824	267			
Sancti Spíritus	394	184	76	151	555	354	393	312	294	516		
Santa Clara	473	263	155	67	634	276	472	391	217	438	590	
Santiago de Cuba	117	550	435	657	84	861	138	199	801	1023	511	590

TRANSPORT

a car in one city and drop it off in another for a reasonable fee, which is handy. If you're on a tight budget, ask about diesel cars – some agencies stock a few and you'll save bundles in gas money considering a liter of regular gas is US$0.75 while a liter of diesel (petroleo) is US$0.45. Note that there are very few rental cars with automatic transmission.

If you want to rent a car for three days or fewer, it will come with limited kilometers, while contracts for three days or more come with unlimited kilometers. In Cuba, you pay for the first tank of gas when you rent the car (US$0.90/L) and return it empty. You will not be refunded for any gas left in the tank. Petty theft of mirrors, antennas, taillights etc is common, so it's worth it to pay someone a dollar or two to watch your car for the night. If you lose your rental contract you'll pay a US$50 penalty. Drivers under 25 pay a US$5 fee, while additional drivers on the same contract pay a US$15 surcharge.

Check over the car carefully with the rental agent before driving into the sunset as you'll be responsible for any damage or missing parts. Make sure there is a spare tire of the correct size, a jack and lug wrench. Check that there are seatbelts and that all the doors lock properly.

We have received many letters about poor/nonexistent customer service, bogus spare tires, forgotten reservations and other car hire problems. Reservations are only accepted 15 days in advance and are still not guaranteed. While agents are usually accommodating, you might end up paying more than you planned or have to wait hours until someone returns a car. The more Spanish you speak and the friendlier you are, the more likely problems will be resolved to everyone's satisfaction (tips to the agent might help). As with most Cuban travel, always be ready to go to Plan B.

Road Conditions

The Autopista, Vía Blanca and Carretera Central are generally in good repair, but be prepared for roads suddenly deteriorating into chunks of asphalt and unexpected railroad crossings. While motorized traffic is refreshingly light, bicycles, pedestrians, ox carts, horse carriages and livestock can test your driving skills. Many old cars and trucks lack rearview mirrors. Stay alert, drive with caution and use your horn when passing or on blind curves.

Driving at night is not recommended due to variable roads, drunk drivers, crossing cows and poor lighting. Drunk driving remains a troublesome problem despite a government educational campaign. Late night in Havana is particularly dangerous, when it seems there's a passing lane, cruising lane and drunk lane.

Signage in Cuba is improving, but still pathetic. Traffic lights are often busted and right of way rules thrown to the wind.

Road Rules

Cubans drive how they want, where they want. It seems chaotic at first, but has its rhythm. Seatbelts are supposedly required and maximum speed limits are technically 50km per hour in the city, 90km per hour on highways and 100km per hour on the Autopista, but some cars can't even go that fast and those that can go faster still.

With so few cars on the road, it's hard not to put the peddle to the floor and just fly. Unexpected potholes are a hazard, as are police. There are some clever speed traps along the Autopista especially. Speeding tickets start at US$30 and are noted on your car contract; the fine is deducted from your deposit when you return the car. When pulled over by the cops, you're expected to get out of the car and walk over to them with your paperwork. An oncoming car flashing its lights means a hazard up ahead (usually the police).

The Cuban transport crisis means there are a lot of people waiting for rides by the side of the road. Giving a botella (a lift) to local hitchhikers has advantages aside from altruism. With a Cuban passenger you'll never get lost, you'll learn about secret spots not in any guidebook and you'll meet some great people. There are always risks associated with picking up hitchhikers; giving lifts to older folks or families may reduce the risk factor. In the provinces, people waiting for rides are systematically queued by los amarillos (yellow-jacketed workers) and they'll hustle the most needy folks into your car, usually an elderly couple or pregnant women.

HITCHHIKING

The transport crisis, culture of solidarity and low crime levels make Cuba a popular hitchhiking destination. Here, hitchhiking is more like ride-sharing. Traffic lights, railroad crossings and country crossroads are regular stops for people seeking rides. In the provinces and on the outskirts of Havana, *los amarillos* organize and prioritize ride seekers and you're welcome to jump in line. Rides cost five to 20 pesos depending on distance. Travelers hitching rides will want a good map and some Spanish skills. Expect to wait two or three hours for rides in some cases. Hitching is never entirely safe in any country in the world. Travelers who decide to hitch should understand that they are taking a small but potentially serious risk. People who do choose to hitch will be safer if they travel in pairs and let someone know where they are planning to go.

TRUCK

Camiones (trucks) are a cheap, fast way to travel within or between provinces. Every city has a provincial and municipal bus stop with *camiones* departures. They run on a (loose) schedule and you usually have to take your place in line by asking for 'el último' to your destination; you pay as you board. A truck from Santiago de Cuba and Guantánamo costs five pesos (US$0.20), while the same trip on Astro/Víazul buses costs US$3/6. A reader traveling by truck enthused: 'Camion traveling was the best way to meet regular people and usually fairly fast. There is a camaraderie between *camion* travelers that I didn't find on buses. One hundred sweaty people locking arms, swerving through the mountains in an open air truck…ah, I'll take that any day over a crowded (and more expensive) bus.'

Sometimes terminal staff tell foreigners they're prohibited from traveling on trucks. Crying poor, striking up conversation with the driver, appealing to other passengers for aid or being persistent usually helps.

LOCAL TRANSPORT
Bici-Taxi

Bici-taxis are big tricycles with a double seat behind the driver and are common in Havana, Camagüey, Holguín and a few other cities. In Havana they'll insist on a US$1 minimum fare (Cubans pay five or 10 pesos). Some bici-taxistas ask ridiculous amounts. The fare should be clearly understood before you hop aboard. By law, bici-taxis are not allowed to take tourists (who are expected to take regular taxis) and they're taking a risk by carrying foreigners. Bici-taxi rules are more lax in the provinces and you should be able to get one for five pesos.

Colectivos & Maquinas

Colectivos are taxis running on fixed, long-distance routes, leaving when full. State-owned dollar taxis hanging about bus stations are faster and usually cheaper than the bus. State-owned peso taxis and private peso taxis (*maquinas*), are prohibited from taking foreigners (except the carnet-carrying kind).

Boat

Some towns such as Havana, Cienfuegos, Gibara and Santiago de Cuba have local ferry services. Details of these are provided in the respective chapters.

Bus

Very crowded, very steamy, very challenging, very Cuban – local buses (*guaguas*) are useful in bigger cities. Buses work fixed routes, stopping at bus stops (*paradas*) that always have a line, even if it doesn't look like it. You have to shout out '¿el último?' to find out who was last in line before you showed up. You give this call when the next person arrives and then you know exactly where you fall in line, allowing you to go have a beer until the bus shows up.

Buses cost from 40 centavos to one peso (the *camello* costs 20 centavos). You must always walk as far back in the bus as you can and exit through the rear. Make room to pass by saying 'permiso,' always wear your pack in front and watch your wallet.

Horse Carriage

Many provincial cities have horse carriages (*coches de caballo*) that trot on fixed routes and cost one peso.

Taxi

Tourists are only supposed to take taxis that charge in dollars, including the little yellow coco-taxis. Car taxis are metered and cost US$1 to start and US$0.75 per kilometer. Taxi drivers are in the habit of offering foreigners a flat, off-meter rate that usually works out very close to what you'll pay with the meter. The difference is that with the meter, the money goes to the state to be divided up; without the meter it goes into the driver's pocket. Coco-taxis are not metered, can hold three people and cost US$0.50 per kilometer.

TOURS

Of the many tourist agencies in Cuba, the following are the most useful:

Cubamar Viajes (☎ 7-66 25 23/24; www.cubamar viajes.cu) Rents campismo cabins and mobile homes (caravans).

Cubanacán (☎ 7-208 9479; www.cubanacan.cu) General tour agency that also has divisions called Cubanacán Naútica (scuba diving, boating and fishing) and Turismo Y Salud (surgery, spas and rehabilitation).

Cubatur (☎ 7-33 41 55; fax 7-33 40 37)

Havanatur (☎ 7-204 0993; www.havanatur.cu) Works with Marazul Tours in the US.

Marsub (☎ 7-96 13 49, 7-96 13 69; fax 7-96 12 85) Runs diving trips.

Paradiso (☎ 7-832 9538/9; paradis@paradiso.artex.co m.cu) Multiday cultural and art tours.

Rumbos (☎ 204-6229) General travel agency with countrywide day tours and multiday tours.

TRAIN

Public railways operated by Ferrocarriles de Cuba serve all of the provincial capitals and are a great way to experience Cuba if you have time and patience. As a Cuban traveler said '80% of the trains are late and the other 20% are cancelled.' While train travel is safe, the departure information provided in this book is purely theoretical. Getting a ticket is usually no problem as there's a quota for dollar tourists. The most useful routes for travelers are Havana–Santiago de Cuba and Havana–Santa Clara.

Foreigners must pay for their tickets in cash, but prices are reasonable and the carriages, though old and worn, are fairly comfortable, offering lots of local color. The bathrooms are foul. Watch your luggage on overnight trips and bring some of your own food. Vendors come through the train selling coffee (you supply the cup).

The Hershey Train is the only electric railway in Cuba and was built by the Hershey Chocolate Company; it's a fun way to get between Havana and Matanzas (see p131).

Classes

Trains are either *especial* (air-con, faster trains with fewer departures); *regular* (slowish trains with daily departures); or *lecheros* (milk trains that stop at every dinky town on the line). Trains on major routes such as Havana–Santiago de Cuba will be *especial* or *regular* trains.

Costs

Regular trains costs under US$3 per 100km, while *especial* trains cost closer to US$5.50 per 100km. The Hershey Train is priced like the *regular* trains.

Reservations

In most train stations, you just go to the ticket window and buy a ticket. In Havana, there's a separate waiting room and ticket window for dollar passengers. In La Coubre train station and in Santiago de Cuba there's the handy Centro Único de Reservaciones in the center of town. Be prepared to show your passport when purchasing tickets. It's always wise to check beforehand at the station for current departures because things change.

Services

There are overnight *especial* trains between Havana and Santiago de Cuba at alternate days (861km, 14½ hours, US$30). Train No 1 leaves Havana daily at 6:05pm, passing Matanzas (7:45pm), Santa Clara (10pm), Guayos (11:20pm), Ciego de Ávila (12:20pm), Camagüey (2:25am) and Las Tunas (4:35am), before reaching Santiago de Cuba at 8:35am. Train No 2 leaves Santiago de Cuba daily at 6:25am, passing Las Tunas (8:15am), Camagüey (10am), Ciego de Ávila (noon), Guayos (1:25pm), Santa Clara (2:30pm), and Matanzas (5:24pm) before reaching Havana at 7:05pm. Train No 11 serves this same route and leaves Havana on alternate days at 2:55am.

The above schedules are only an approximation of what should happen.

Other routes of interest to travelers include Pinar del Río–Sábalo, Havana–Matanzas, Havana–Cienfuegos, Havana–Sancti Spíritus, Havana–Holguín, Havana–Manzanillo, Santa Clara–Morón–Nuevitas, Cienfuegos–Santa Clara–Sancti Spíritus, Camagüey–Nuevitas, Camagüey–Bayamo, Bayamo–Manzanillo, Manzanillo–Bayamo–Santiago de Cuba, and Santiago de Cuba–Holguín. Many additional local trains operate at least daily and some more frequently. Additional information is provided in the regional chapters of this book.

TRANSPORT

Health by Dr David Goldberg

From a medical standpoint, the Caribbean islands are generally safe as long as you're reasonably careful about what you eat and drink. The most common travel-related diseases, such as dysentery and hepatitis, are acquired by consumption of contaminated food and water. Mosquito-borne illnesses are not a significant concern in most of the islands.

Prevention is the key to staying healthy while traveling in Cuba. Travelers who receive the recommended vaccines and follow commonsense precautions usually come away with nothing more than a little diarrhea.

BEFORE YOU GO

Since most vaccines don't produce immunity until at least two weeks after they're given, visit a physician four to eight weeks before departure. Ask your doctor for an International Certificate of Vaccination (otherwise known as the 'yellow booklet'), which will list all the vaccinations you've received. This is mandatory for countries that require proof of yellow fever vaccination upon entry, but it's a good idea to carry it wherever you travel.

Bring medications in their original, clearly labeled containers. A signed and dated letter from your physician describing your medical conditions and medications, including generic names, is also a good idea. If carrying syringes or needles, be sure to have a physician's letter documenting their medical necessity.

INSURANCE

If your health insurance doesn't cover you for medical expenses abroad, consider getting extra insurance; check Subwwway on www.lonelyplanet.com for more

---

RECOMMENDED VACCINATIONS

No vaccines are required for Cuba, but a number are recommended:

Vaccine	Recommended for	Dosage	Side effects
Typhoid	All travelers	Four capsules orally, one taken every other day	Abdominal pain; nausea; rash
Hepatitis B	Long-term travelers in close contact with the local population	Three doses over a six-month period	Soreness at injection site; low-grade fever
Rabies	Travelers who may have contact with animals and may not have access to medical care	Three doses over a three- to four-week period	Soreness at injection site; headaches; body aches
Tetanus-diphtheria	All travelers who haven't had a booster within 10 years	One dose lasts 10 years	Soreness at injection site
Chickenpox	Travelers who've never had chickenpox	Two doses one month apart	Fever; mild case of chickenpox
Hepatitis A	All travelers	One dose before trip; booster 6 to 12 months later	Soreness at injection site; headaches; body aches

information. Find out in advance if your insurance plan will make payments directly to providers or reimburse you later for overseas health expenditures. (In many countries doctors expect payment in cash.)

MEDICAL CHECKLIST

- acetaminophen (Tylenol) or aspirin
- adhesive or paper tape
- antibacterial ointment (eg Bactroban; for cuts and abrasions)
- antibiotics
- antidiarrheal drugs (eg loperamide)
- anti-inflammatory drugs (eg ibuprofen)
- antihistamines (for hay fever and allergic reactions)
- bandages, gauze, gauze rolls
- DEET-containing insect repellent for the skin
- iodine tablets (for water purification)
- oral rehydration salts
- permethrin-containing insect spray for clothing, tents and bed nets
- pocketknife
- scissors, safety pins, tweezers
- steroid cream or cortisone (for poison ivy and other allergic rashes)
- sun block
- syringes and sterile needles
- thermometer

ONLINE RESOURCES

There is a wealth of travel health advice on the Internet. For further information, the **Lonely Planet website** (www.lonelyplanet.com) is a good place to start. The World Health Organization publishes a superb book called *International Travel and Health*, which is revised annually and is available online at no cost (www.who.int/ith). Another website of general interest is the **MD Travel**

THE MAN SAYS...

It's usually a good idea to consult your government's travel health website before departure, if one is available:

- **Australia** (www.dfat.gov.au/travel)
- **Canada** (www.travelhealth.gc.ca)
- **United Kingdom** (www.doh.gov.uk/traveladvice)
- **United States** (www.cdc.gov/travel)

Health website (www.mdtravelhealth.com), which provides complete travel health recommendations for every country and is updated daily.

FURTHER READING

If you're traveling with children, Lonely Planet's *Travel with Children* may be useful. The *ABC of Healthy Travel*, by Eric Walker et al, is another valuable resource.

IN TRANSIT

DEEP VEIN THROMBOSIS (DVT)

Blood clots may form in the legs (deep vein thrombosis) during plane flights, chiefly because of prolonged immobility. The longer the flight, the greater the risk. Though most blood clots are reabsorbed uneventfully, some may break off and travel through the blood vessels to the lungs, where they could cause life-threatening complications.

The chief symptom of deep vein thrombosis is swelling or pain of the foot, ankle or calf, usually – but not always – on just one side. When a blood clot travels to the lungs, it may cause chest pain and difficulty breathing. Travelers with any of these symptoms should immediately seek medical attention.

To prevent the development of deep vein thrombosis on long flights, you should walk about the cabin, perform isometric compressions of the leg muscles (ie flex the leg muscles while sitting), drink plenty of fluids and avoid alcohol and tobacco.

JET LAG & MOTION SICKNESS

Jet lag is common when crossing more than five time zones, resulting in insomnia, fatigue, malaise or nausea. To avoid jet lag try and drink plenty of (non-alcoholic) fluids and eating light meals. Upon arrival, get exposure to natural sunlight and readjust your schedule (for meals, sleep etc) as soon as possible.

Antihistamines such as dimenhydrinate (Dramamine) and meclizine (Antivert, Bonine) are usually the first choice for treating motion sickness. Their main side effect is drowsiness. A herbal alternative is ginger, which works like a charm for some people.

HEALTH

IN CUBA

AVAILABILITY & COST OF HEALTH CARE

The Cuban government has established a for-profit health system for foreigners called **Servimed** (☎ 07-24-01-41), which is entirely separate from the free, not-for-profit system that takes care of Cuban citizens. There are more than 40 Servimed health centers across the island, offering primary care as well as a variety of specialty and high-tech services. If you're staying in a hotel, the usual way to access the system is to ask the manager for a physician referral. Servimeds accept walk-ins.

Almost all doctors and hospitals expect payment in cash, regardless of whether you have travel health insurance. If you develop a life-threatening medical problem, you'll probably want to be evacuated to a country with state-of-the-art medical care. Since this may cost tens of thousands of dollars, be sure you have insurance to cover this before you depart. See the Directory (p415) for insurance options.

There are special pharmacies for foreigners and those with dollars, also run by the Servimed system, but all Cuban pharmacies are notoriously short on supplies, including pharmaceuticals. Be sure to bring along adequate quantities of all medications you might need, both prescription and over-the-counter. Also, be sure to bring along a fully-stocked medical kit.

INFECTIOUS DISEASES

Dengue (Break-bone Fever)

Dengue fever is a viral infection found throughout the Caribbean. A major outbreak of dengue fever, centering on Havana and resulting in more than 3000 cases, was reported from November 2001 through March 2002. Since then, an aggressive governmental program has all but eradicated dengue from the island.

Hepatitis A

Hepatitis A is the second most common travel-related infection (after traveler's diarrhea). It occurs throughout the Caribbean, particularly in the northern islands. Hepatitis A is a viral infection of the liver that is usually acquired by ingestion of contaminated water, food or ice, though it may also be acquired by direct contact with infected persons. The illness occurs throughout the world, but the incidence is higher in developing nations. Symptoms may include fever, malaise, jaundice, nausea, vomiting and abdominal pain. Most cases resolve without complications, though hepatitis A occasionally causes severe liver damage. There is no treatment.

The vaccine for hepatitis A is extremely safe and highly effective. If you get a booster six to 12 months after the first vaccine, it lasts for at least 10 years. You really should get this vaccine before you go to Cuba or any other developing nation. Because the safety of the hepatitis A vaccine has not been established for pregnant women or children under the age of two, they should instead be given a gamma globulin injection.

Hepatitis B

Like hepatitis A, hepatitis B is a liver infection that occurs worldwide but is more common in developing nations. Unlike hepatitis A, the disease is usually acquired by sexual contact or by exposure to infected blood, generally through blood transfusions or contaminated needles. The vaccine is recommended only for long-term travelers (on the road more than six months) who expect to live in rural areas or have close physical contact with the local population. Additionally, the vaccine is recommended for anyone who anticipates sexual contact with the local inhabitants or a possible need for medical, dental or other treatments while abroad, especially if a need for transfusions or injections is expected.

The hepatitis B vaccine is safe and highly effective. However, a total of three injections are necessary to establish full immunity. Several countries added hepatitis B vaccine to the list of routine childhood immunizations in the 1980s, so many young adults are already protected.

Malaria

In the Caribbean, malaria occurs only in Haiti and certain parts of the Dominican Republic. Malaria pills aren't necessary for Cuba.

Rabies

Rabies is a viral infection of the brain and spinal cord that is almost always fatal. The rabies virus is carried in the saliva of infected animals and is typically transmitted through an animal bite, though contamination of any break in the skin with infected saliva may result in rabies. Rabies occurs in several of the Caribbean islands, including Cuba. Most cases in Cuba are related to bites from dogs, bats and wild animals, especially the small Indian mongoose.

Rabies vaccine is safe, but a full series requires three injections and is quite expensive. Those at high risk for rabies, such as animal handlers and spelunkers (cave explorers), should certainly get the vaccine. In addition, those at lower risk of animal bites should consider asking for the vaccine if they are traveling to remote areas and might not have access to appropriate medical care if needed. The treatment for a possibly rabid bite consists of rabies vaccine with rabies immune globulin. It's effective, but must be given promptly. Most travelers don't need rabies vaccine.

All animal bites and scratches must be promptly and thoroughly cleansed with large amounts of soap and water, and local health authorities must be contacted to determine whether or not further treatment is necessary (see Animal Bites p440).

Typhoid

Typhoid fever is caused by ingestion of food or water contaminated by a species of *Salmonella* known as *Salmonella typhi*. Fever occurs in virtually all cases. Other symptoms may include headache, malaise, muscle aches, dizziness, loss of appetite, nausea and abdominal pain. Either diarrhea or constipation may occur. Possible complications include intestinal perforation, intestinal bleeding, confusion, delirium or (rarely) coma.

This vaccine is usually given orally, but is also available as an injection. Neither vaccine is approved for use in children under age two. If you get typhoid fever, the drug of choice is usually a quinolone antibiotic such as ciprofloxacin (Cipro) or levofloxacin (Levaquin), which many travelers carry for treatment of diarrhea.

Other infections

BRUCELLOSIS

Brucellosis is an infection of domestic and wild animals that may be transmitted to humans through direct animal contact or by consumption of unpasteurized dairy products from infected animals. In Cuba, most human cases are related to infected pigs. Symptoms may include fever, malaise, depression, loss of appetite, headache, muscle aches and back pain. Complications may include arthritis, hepatitis, meningitis and endocarditis (heart valve infection).

FASCIOLIASIS

This is a parasitic infection that is typically acquired by eating contaminated watercress grown in sheep-raising areas. Early symptoms may include fever, nausea, vomiting and painful enlargement of the liver.

HIV/AIDS

HIV/AIDS has been reported in all Caribbean countries. Be sure to use condoms for all sexual encounters.

LEPTOSPIROSIS

Acquired by exposure to water contaminated by the urine of infected animals. Outbreaks often occur at times of flooding, when sewage overflow may contaminate water sources. The initial symptoms, which resemble a mild flu, usually subside uneventfully in a few days, with or without treatment, but a minority of cases are complicated by jaundice or meningitis. There is no vaccine. You can minimize your risk by staying out of bodies of fresh water that may be contaminated by animal urine. If you're visiting an area where an outbreak is in progress, as occurred in Cuba in 1994, you can take 200mg of doxycycline once weekly as a preventative measure. If you actually develop leptospirosis, the treatment is 100mg of doxycycline twice daily.

TRAVELER'S DIARRHEA

To prevent diarrhea, avoid tap water unless it has been boiled, filtered or chemically disinfected (with iodine tablets); only eat fresh fruits or vegetables if cooked or peeled; be wary of dairy products that may contain unpasteurized milk; and be highly selective when eating food from street vendors.

If you develop diarrhea, be sure to drink plenty of fluids, preferably an oral rehydration solution containing lots of salt and sugar. A few loose stools don't require treatment, but if you start having more than four or five stools a day, you should start taking an antibiotic (usually a quinolone drug) and an antidiarrheal agent (such as loperamide). If diarrhea is bloody, persists for more than 72 hours or is accompanied by fever, shaking chills or severe abdominal pain, you should seek medical attention.

ENVIRONMENTAL HAZARDS
Animal Bites

Do not attempt to pet, handle or feed any animal, with the exception of domestic animals known to be free of any infectious disease. Most animal injuries are directly related to a person's attempt to touch or feed the animal.

Any bite or scratch by a mammal, including bats, should be promptly and thoroughly cleansed with large amounts of soap and water, followed by application of an antiseptic such as iodine or alcohol. The local health authorities should be contacted immediately for possible post-exposure rabies treatment, whether or not you've been immunized against rabies. It may also be advisable to start an antibiotic, since wounds caused by animal bites and scratches frequently become infected. One of the newer quinolones, such as levofloxacin (Levaquin), which many travelers carry in case of diarrhea, would be an appropriate choice.

Spiny sea urchins and coelenterates (coral and jellyfish) are a hazard in some areas.

Heatstroke

To protect yourself from excessive sun exposure, you should stay out of the midday sun, wear sunglasses and a wide-brimmed sun hat, and apply sunscreen with SPF 15 or higher, with both UVA and UVB protection. Sunscreen should be generously applied to all exposed parts of the body approximately 30 minutes before sun exposure and should be reapplied after swimming or vigorous activity. Travelers should also drink plenty of fluids and avoid strenuous exercise when the temperature is high.

Insect Bites & Stings

Because of an aggressive program of mosquito control, mosquito-borne illnesses are usually not a concern in Cuba. However, outbreaks of dengue fever have occurred in the recent past, so you should be aware of the means of preventing mosquito bites, if necessary. If dengue or other mosquito-borne illnesses are being reported, you should keep yourself covered (wear long sleeves, long pants, a hat, and shoes rather than sandals) and apply a good insect repellent, preferably one containing DEET, to exposed skin and clothing. Do not apply DEET to eyes, mouth, cuts, wounds or irritated skin. Products containing lower concentrations of DEET are as effective, but for shorter periods of time. In general, adults and children over 12 should use preparations containing 25% to 35% DEET, which usually lasts about six hours. Children between two and 12 years of age should use preparations containing no more than 10% DEET, applied sparingly, which will usually last about three hours. Neurologic toxicity has been reported from DEET, especially in children, but appears to be extremely uncommon and generally related to overuse. DEET-containing compounds should not be used on children under age two.

Insect repellents containing certain botanical products, including oil of eucalyptus and soybean oil, are effective but last only 1½ to 2 hours. Products based on citronella are not effective.

For additional protection, you can apply permethrin to clothing, shoes, tents and bed nets. Permethrin treatments are safe and remain effective for at least two weeks, even when items are laundered. Permethrin should not be applied directly to skin.

Water

Tap water in Cuba is not reliably safe to drink. Vigorous boiling for one minute is the most effective means of water purification.

Another option is to disinfect water with iodine pills. Instructions are usually enclosed and should be carefully followed. Alternatively, you can add 2% tincture of iodine to one quart or liter of water (5 drops to clear water, 10 drops to cloudy water) and let stand for 30 minutes. If the water is cold, longer times may be required. The taste of iodinated water may be improved by adding vitamin C (ascorbic acid). Iodinated water should not be consumed for more than a few weeks. Pregnant women, those with a history of thyroid disease, and those allergic to iodine should not drink iodinated water. See Food & Drink (p51) for more treatment options.

A number of water filters are on the market. Those with smaller pores (reverse osmosis filters) provide the broadest protection, but they are relatively large and are readily plugged by debris. Those with somewhat larger pores (microstrainer filters) are ineffective against viruses, although they remove other organisms. Manufacturers' instructions must be carefully followed.

TRAVELING WITH CHILDREN

In general, it's safe for children to go to Cuba. However, because some of the vaccines listed previously are not approved for use in children (or during pregnancy), these travelers should be particularly careful not to drink tap water or consume any questionable food or beverage. Also, when traveling with children, make sure they're up-to-date on all routine immunizations. It's sometimes appropriate to give children some of their vaccines a little early before visiting a developing nation. You should discuss this with your pediatrician.

TRADITIONAL MEDICINE

The following table lists some traditional remedies for common travel-related issues:

Problem	Treatment
Jet lag	Melatonin
Motion sickness	Ginger
Mosquito bite prevention	Oil of eucalyptus and soybean oil

HEALTH

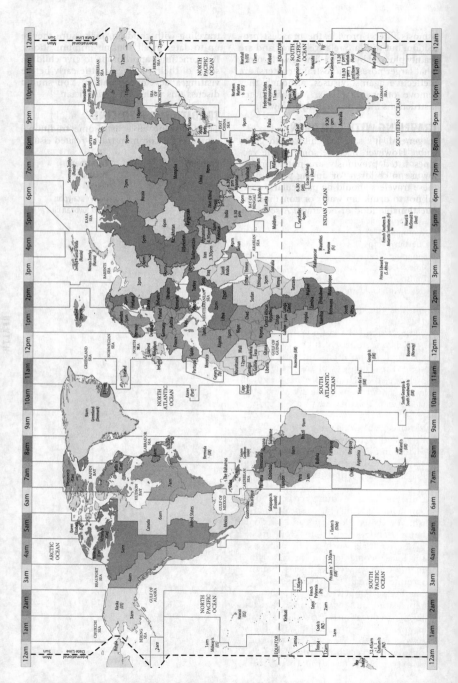

Language

CONTENTS

Spanish is the official language of Cuba, and a knowledge of it is a great help in traveling around the country. Away from the hotels and tourist centers, few people speak English and then only very poorly. Despite this, many Cubans have some knowledge of English, since it's taught in primary school from grade six. Almost all museum captions in Cuba are in Spanish only.

If you speak no Spanish at all, you can always ask directions simply by pointing to the name in this guidebook. Never hesitate to try out your broken Spanish on Cubans! A Belgian reader sent us this:

Cuba really is a country where you gain a lot by being able to speak Spanish. We visited Honduras and Mexico before, and especially in Honduras, it doesn't make such a difference, as the local people are not interested in telling their views and stories (which is quite normal, I guess, when there has been so much state and military repression and when the average level of education is low). In Cuba, people are highly skilled and they have a point of view and an opinion on almost everything, which makes it extremely interesting to be able

to talk to them (and we experienced that most of them were quite willing to talk to us). I think the effort to learn Hindi before going to India might be too great, but I would recommend everybody to learn some Spanish before going to Cuba – otherwise you miss the best of the country's culture and complex reality.'

Words of Arawak Indian origin that have passed into Spanish and other European languages include *barbacoa* (barbecue), *canoa* (canoe), *cigarro* (cigarette), *hamaca* (hammock), *huracán* (hurricane), *maíz* (maize), *patata* (potato) and *tabaco* (tobacco, cigar). The only commonly used words that are of African origin are generally associated with the Afro-Cuban religions, but Afro-Cuban speakers have given Cuban Spanish its rhythmical intonation and soft accent.

LEARNING SPANISH

If you don't speak Spanish, don't despair. It's easy enough to pick up the basics, and courses are available in Havana (p84) and Santiago de Cuba (p367). Alternatively, you can study books, records and tapes while you're still at home and planning your trip. These study aids are often available free at public libraries – or you might consider taking an evening or college course. For words and phrases for use when ordering at a restaurant, see Eat Your Words on p54.

Lonely Planet's *Latin American Spanish phrasebook* is a compact guide to the Spanish of the region. Another useful resource is the *University of Chicago Spanish-English, English-Spanish Dictionary*. It'll also make a nice gift for some friendly Cuban when you're about to leave the country.

PRONUNCIATION

Spanish spelling is phonetically consistent, meaning that there's a clear and consistent relationship between what you see in writing and how it's pronounced. In addition, most Spanish sounds have English equivalents, so English speakers shouldn't have

CUBAN SPANISH

Cuban Spanish is rich, varied and astoundingly distinct. Slang and *dichos* (sayings) so dominate daily conversation, even native Spanish speakers sometimes get lost in the mix. Borrowing words from African languages, bastardizing English terms ('Spanglish') and adopting language from movies, marketing and sports, Cuban Spanish is constantly evolving, with new, invented words surfacing all the time. Indeed, the origins of some relatively new slang words seem to have been lost entirely. Ask a Cuban where *rickenbili* comes from for instance (the word for those motorized bicycles you see around town), and they'll laugh and shrug. Here are some of the most common slang and colloquialisms travelers are likely to hear; see also the Glossary (p450):

asere – man, brother
bárbaro – cool, 'killer'
barro – money (dollars or pesos)
brother – as in the English word: brother
compay – brother, friend (frequently used in Oriente)
¡Coño! – frequently used exclamation akin to 'damn!'; used for good or bad things/situations
cubalse – plastic bag (in Oriente); also see nylon
dame un chance – let me pass, excuse me; literally 'give me a chance'
está en llama – it's screwed/messed up
fiana – police cruiser
fula – dollars
güiro – party
jama – food, also *jamaliche* which loosely translates as food junkie
kilo(s) – centavo(s)
la lucha – daily struggle
loca – homosexual, queen

mami – mommy/mum, used as term of endearment for females
nylon – plastic bag
papaya – vagina; the fruit itself is called *fruta bomba* everywhere except in Oriente, where it's called *papaya*
papi – daddy, used as term of endearment for males
pepe – someone from Spain
pincha – job
pollito – pretty girl
por la izquierda – attained through the informal/black market
prieto/a – dark skinned
puto/a – gigolo/prostitute
¿Qué bolá asere? – What's happening man/brother?
¿Qué es la mecánica? – What's the process here; how does this work? (eg when buying bus tickets, entering a crowded club or renting a catamaran)
tortillera – lesbian, dyke
yuma – someone from the US

too much trouble being understood if the rules listed below are adhered to.

Spanish language soap operas are probably the best vehicle for getting a grip on pronunciation – the actors tend to speak overdramatically and a lot slower than the Spanish speakers you're likely to meet on the street – it's also easy to follow the plot. Just be careful you don't get hooked!

Vowels

a	as in 'father'
e	as in 'met'
i	as in 'marine'
o	as in 'or', without the 'r' sound
u	as in 'rule'; the 'u' is not pronounced after **q** and in the letter combinations **gue** and **gui**, unless it's marked with a diaeresis (eg *argüir*), in which case it's pronounced as English 'w'
y	at the end of a word or when it stands alone, it's pronounced as the Spanish **i** (eg *ley*). Between vowels within a word it's as the 'y' in 'yonder'.

Consonants

While the consonants **ch**, **ll** and **ñ** are generally considered distinct letters, **ch** and **ll** are now often listed alphabetically under **c** and **l** respectively. The letter **ñ** is still treated as a separate letter and comes after **n** in dictionaries.

b	similar to English 'b,' but softer; referred to as 'b larga'
c	as in 'celery' before **e** and **i**; otherwise as English 'k'
ch	as in 'church'
d	as in 'dog'; between vowels and after **l** or **n**, it's closer to the 'th' in 'this'
g	as the 'ch' in the Scottish *loch* before **e** and **i** ('kh' in our guides to pronunciation); elsewhere, as in 'go'
h	invariably silent; worth noting if your name begins with 'h' and you're waiting for public officials to call you
j	as the 'ch' in the Scottish *loch* (written as 'kh' in our guides to pronunciation)

ll	as the 'y' in 'yellow'	
ñ	as the 'ni' in 'onion'	
r	a short **r** except at the beginning of a word, and after **l**, **n** or **s**, when it's often rolled	
rr	very strongly rolled	
v	similar to English 'b', but softer; referred to as 'b corta'	
x	as in 'taxi' except for a very few words, when it's pronounced as **j**	
z	as the 's' in 'sun'	

Word Stress

In general, words ending in vowels or the letters **n** or **s** have stress on the next-to-last syllable, while those with other endings have stress on the last syllable. Thus *vaca* (cow) and *caballos* (horses) both carry stress on the next-to-last syllable, while *ciudad* (city) and *infeliz* (unhappy) are both stressed on the last syllable.

Written accents will almost always appear in words that don't follow the rules above, eg *sótano* (basement), *América* and *porción* (portion). When counting syllables, be sure to remember that diphthongs (vowel combinations, such as the 'ue' in *puede*) constitute only one. When a word with a written accent appears in capital letters, the accent is often not written, but is still pronounced.

GENDER & PLURALS

In Spanish, nouns are either masculine or feminine, and there are rules to help determine gender (there are of course some exceptions). Feminine nouns generally end with **-a** or with the groups **-ción**, **-sión** or **-dad**. Other endings typically signify a masculine noun. Endings for adjectives also change to agree with the gender of the noun they modify (masculine/feminine **-o/-a**). Where both masculine and feminine forms are included in this language guide, they are separated by a slash, with the masculine form first, eg *perdido/a*.

If a noun or adjective ends in a vowel, the plural is formed by adding **s** to the end. If it ends in a consonant, the plural is formed by adding **es** to the end.

ACCOMMODATION

I'm looking for ...	*Estoy buscando ...*	e·stoy boos·kan·do ...
Where is ...?	*¿Dónde hay ...?*	don·de ai ...
a hotel	*un hotel/*	oon o·tel/
	una villa	oo·na vee·lya
a boarding house	*una pensión/ residencial/ un hospedaje*	oo·na pen·syon/ re·see·den·syal/ oon os·pe·da·khe
a youth hostel	*un albergue juvenil*	oon al·ber·ge khoo·ve·neel

I'd like a ... room.	*Quisiera una habitación ...*	kee·sye·ra oo·na a·bee·ta·syon ...
double	*doble*	do·ble
single	*individual/ para una persona*	een·dee·vee·dwal/ pa·ra oo·na per·so·na
twin	*con dos camas*	kon dos ka·mas

How much is it per ...?	*¿Cuánto cuesta por ...?*	kwan·to kwes·ta por ...
night	*noche*	no·che
person	*persona*	per·so·na
week	*semana*	se·ma·na

MAKING A RESERVATION

(for phone or written requests)

To ...	*A ...*
From ...	*De ...*
Date	*Fecha*
I'd like to book ...	*Quisiera reservar ...* (see the list under 'Accommodation' for bed/ room options)
in the name of ...	*en nombre de ...*
for the nights of ...	*para las noches del ...*
credit card ...	*tarjeta de crédito ...*
number	*número*
expiry date	*fecha de vencimiento*
Please confirm ...	*Puede confirmar ...*
availability	*la disponibilidad*
price	*el precio*

Does it include breakfast?

¿Incluye el desayuno?	een·kloo·ye el de·sa·yoo·no

May I see the room?

¿Puedo ver la habitación?	pwe·do ver la a·bee·ta·syon

I don't like it.

No me gusta.	no me goos·ta

It's fine. I'll take it.

OK. La alquilo.	o·kay la al·kee·lo

I'm leaving now.

Me voy ahora.	me voy a·o·ra

full board	*pensión completa*	pen·syon kom·ple·ta

private/shared bathroom	baño privado/ compartido	ba·nyo pree·va·do/ kom·par·tee·do
all-inclusive	todo incluído	to·do een·klwee·do
too expensive	demasiado caro	de·ma·sya·do ka·ro
cheaper	más económico	mas e·ko·no·mee·ko
discount	descuento	des·kwen·to

CONVERSATION & ESSENTIALS

In their public behavior, Cubans are very informal, but if you approach a stranger for information, you should always preface your question with a greeting like *buenos días* or *buenas tardes*. Cubans routinely address one another as *compañero* or *compañera* (comrade), but the traditional *señor* and *señora* are always used with foreigners. In addition, you should use only the polite form of address, especially with the police and public officials. Young people may be less likely to expect this, but it's best to stick to the polite form unless you're quite sure you won't offend by using the informal mode. The polite form is used in all cases in this language guide; where options are given, the form is indicated by the abbreviations 'pol' and 'inf'.

Hello.	Hola.	o·la
Good morning.	Buenos días.	bwe·nos dee·as
Good afternoon.	Buenas tardes.	bwe·nas tar·des
Good evening/ night.	Buenas noches.	bwe·nas no·ches
Goodbye.	Adiós.	a·dyos
See you soon.	Hasta luego.	as·ta lwe·go
Bye.	Chau.	chow (inf)
Yes.	Sí.	see
No.	No.	no
Please.	Por favor.	por fa·vor
Thank you.	Gracias.	gra·syas
Many thanks.	Muchas gracias.	moo·chas gra·syas
You're welcome.	De nada.	de na·da
Pardon me.	Perdón.	per·don
Excuse me.	Permiso.	per·mee·so

(used when asking permission)

Forgive me.	Disculpe.	dees·kool·pe

(used when apologizing)

How are things?
¿Qué tal?   ke tal
What's your name?
¿Cómo se llama?   ko·mo se ya·ma (pol)
¿Cómo te llamas?   ko·mo te ya·mas (inf)
My name is ...
Me llamo ...   me ya·mo ...
It's a pleasure to meet you.
Mucho gusto.   moo·cho goos·to

The pleasure is mine.
El gusto es mío.   el goos·to es mee·o
Where are you from?
¿De dónde es/eres?   de don·de es/e·res (pol/inf)
I'm from ...
Soy de ...   soy de ...
Where are you staying?
¿Dónde está alojado?   don·de es·ta a·lo·kha·do (pol)
¿Dónde estás alojado?   don·de es·tas a·lo·kha·do (inf)
May I take a photo?
¿Puedo sacar una foto?   pwe·do sa·kar oo·na fo·to

DIRECTIONS

How do I get to ...?
¿Cómo puedo llegar a ...?   ko·mo pwe·do lye·gar a ...
Is it far?
¿Está lejos?   es·ta le·khos
Go straight ahead.
Siga/Vaya derecho.   see·ga/va·ya de·re·cho
Turn left.
Voltée a la izquierda.   vol·te·e a la ees·kyer·da
Turn right.
Voltée a la derecha.   vol·te·e a la de·re·cha
I'm lost.
Estoy perdido/a.   es·toy per·dee·do/a
Can you show me (on the map)?
¿Me lo podría indicar (en el mapa)?   me lo po·dree·a een·dee·kar (en el ma·pa)

north	norte	nor·te
south	sur	soor
east	este/oriente	es·te/o·ryen·te
west	oeste/occidente	o·es·te/ok·see·den·te
here	aquí	a·kee
there	allí	a·yee
on foot	a pie	a pye
avenue	avenida	a·ve·nee·da
block	cuadra	kwa·dra
street	calle/paseo	ka·lye/pa·se·o
beach	playa	pla·ya
bathing resort	balneario	bal·ne·a·ryo

EMERGENCIES

Help!	¡Socorro!	so·ko·ro
Fire!	¡Incendio!	een·sen·dyo
I've been robbed.	Me robaron.	me ro·ba·ron
Go away!	¡Déjeme!	de·khe·me
Get lost!	¡Váyase!	va·ya·se

Call ...!	¡Llame a ...!	ya·me a
the police	la policía	la po·lee·see·a
a doctor	un médico	oon me·dee·ko
an ambulance	una ambulancia	oo·na am·boo·lan·sya

It's an emergency.
Es una emergencia.   es oo·na e·mer·khen·sya
Could you help me, please?
¿Me puede ayudar,   me pwe·de a·yoo·dar
por favor?   por fa·vor
I'm lost.
Estoy perdido/a.   es·toy per·dee·do/a
Where are the toilets?
¿Dónde están los baños?   don·de es·tan los ba·nyos

HEALTH

I'm sick.
Estoy enfermo/a.   es·toy en·fer·mo/a
I need a doctor.
Necesito un médico.   ne·se·see·to oon me·dee·ko
Where's the hospital?
¿Dónde está el hospital?   don·de es·ta el os·pee·tal
I'm pregnant.
Estoy embarazada.   es·toy em·ba·ra·sa·da
I've been vaccinated.
Estoy vacunado/a.   es·toy va·koo·na·do/a

I'm allergic to ...	Soy alérgico/a a ...	soy a·ler·khee·ko/a a ...
antibiotics	los antibióticos	los an·tee·byo·tee·kos
penicillin	la penicilina	la pe·nee·see·lee·na
nuts	las fruta secas	las froo·tas se·kas

I'm ...	Soy ...	soy ...
asthmatic	asmático/a	as·ma·tee·ko/a
diabetic	diabético/a	dya·be·tee·ko/a
epileptic	epiléptico/a	e·pee·lep·tee·ko/a

I have ...	Tengo ...	ten·go ...
altitude sickness	soroche	so·ro·che
diarrhea	diarrea	dya·re·a
nausea	náusea	now·se·a

a headache	un dolor de cabeza	oon do·lor de ka·be·sa
a cough	tos	tos

LANGUAGE DIFFICULTIES

Do you speak (English)?
¿Habla/Hablas (inglés)?   a·bla/a·blas (een·gles) (pol/inf)
Does anyone here speak English?
¿Hay alguien que hable   ai al·gyen ke a·ble
inglés?   een·gles
I (don't) understand.
Yo (no) entiendo.   yo (no) en·tyen·do
How do you say ...?
¿Cómo se dice ...?   ko·mo se dee·se ...
What does ...mean?
¿Qué quiere decir ...?   ke kye·re de·seer ...

Could you please ...?	¿Puede ..., por favor?	pwe·de ... por fa·vor
repeat that	repetirlo	re·pe·teer·lo
speak more slowly	hablar más despacio	a·blar mas des·pa·syo
write it down	escribirlo	es·kree·beer·lo

NUMBERS

1	uno	oo·no
2	dos	dos
3	tres	tres
4	cuatro	kwa·tro
5	cinco	seen·ko
6	seis	says
7	siete	sye·te
8	ocho	o·cho
9	nueve	nwe·ve
10	diez	dyes
11	once	on·se
12	doce	do·se
13	trece	tre·se
14	catorce	ka·tor·se
15	quince	keen·se
16	dieciséis	dye·see·says
17	diecisiete	dye·see·sye·te
18	dieciocho	dye·see·o·cho
19	diecinueve	dye·see·nwe·ve
20	veinte	vayn·te
21	veintiuno	vayn·tee·oo·no
30	treinta	trayn·ta
31	treinta y uno	trayn·ta ee oo·no
40	cuarenta	kwa·ren·ta
50	cincuenta	seen·kwen·ta
60	sesenta	se·sen·ta
70	setenta	se·ten·ta
80	ochenta	o·chen·ta
90	noventa	no·ven·ta
100	cien	syen

LANGUAGE

101	ciento uno	syen·to oo·no
200	doscientos	do·syen·tos
1000	mil	meel
5000	cinco mil	seen·ko meel
10,000	diez mil	dyes meel
50,000	cincuenta mil	seen·kwen·ta meel
100,000	cien mil	syen meel
1,000,000	un millón	oon mee·yon

QUESTION WORDS

Who?	¿Quién/es?	kee·en/es (sg/pl)
What?	¿Qué?	ke
Which?	¿Cuál/es?	kwal/es (sg/pl)
When?	¿Cuándo?	kwan·do
Where?	¿Dónde?	don·de
How?	¿Cómo?	ko·mo
How many?	¿Cuántos?	kwan·tos

SHOPPING & SERVICES

I'd like to buy ...
| Quisiera comprar ... | kee·sye·ra kom·prar ... |

I'm just looking.
| Sólo estoy mirando. | so·lo es·toy mee·ran·do |

May I look at it?
| ¿Puedo mirar(lo/la)? | pwe·do mee·rar·(lo/la) |

How much is it?
| ¿Cuánto cuesta? | kwan·to kwes·ta |

That's too expensive for me.
| Es demasiado caro | es de·ma·sya·do ka·ro |
| para mí. | pa·ra mee |

Could you lower the price?
| ¿Podría bajar un poco | po·dree·a ba·khar oon po·ko |
| el precio? | el pre·syo |

I don't like it.
| No me gusta. | no me goos·ta |

I'll take it.
| Lo llevo. | lo ye·vo |

Do you accept ...?	¿Aceptan ...?	a·sep·tan ...
American dollars	dólares americanos	do·la·res a·me·ree·ka·nos
credit cards	tarjetas de crédito	tar·khe·tas de kre·dee·to
traveler's checks	cheques de viajero	che·kes de vya·khe·ro

less	menos	me·nos
more	más	mas
large	grande	gran·de
small	pequeño/a	pe·ke·nyo/a

I'm looking for (the) ...
| Estoy buscando ... | es·toy boos·kan·do |
| **ATM** | el cajero automático | el ka·khe·ro ow·to·ma·tee·ko |

bank	el banco	el ban·ko
bookstore	la librería	la lee·bre·ree·a
embassy	la embajada	la em·ba·kha·da
exchange house	la casa de cambio	la ka·sa de kam·byo
general store	la tienda	la tyen·da
laundry	la lavandería	la la·van·de·ree·a
market	el mercado	el mer·ka·do
pharmacy/ chemist	la farmacia/ la droguería	la far·ma·sya/ la dro·ge·ree·a
post office	el correo	el ko·re·o
supermarket	el supermercado	el soo·per·mer·ka·do
tourist office	la oficina de turismo	la o·fee·see·na de too·rees·mo

What time does it open/close?
| ¿A qué hora abre/cierra? | a ke o·ra a·bre/sye·ra |

I want to change some money/traveler's checks.
| Quiero cambiar dinero/ cheques de viajero. | kye·ro kam·byar dee·ne·ro/ che·kes de vya·khe·ro |

What is the exchange rate?
| ¿Cuál es el tipo de cambio? | kwal es el tee·po de kam·byo |

I want to call ...
| Quiero llamar a ... | kye·ro lya·mar a ... |

airmail	correo aéreo	ko·re·o a·e·re·o
black market	mercado (negro/ paralelo)	mer·ka·do ne·gro/ pa·ra·le·lo
letter	carta	kar·ta
registered mail	certificado	ser·tee·fee·ka·do
stamps	estampillas	es·tam·pee·lyas

TIME & DATES

What time is it?	¿Qué hora es?	ke o·ra es
It's one o'clock.	Es la una.	es la oo·na
It's seven o'clock.	Son las siete.	son las sye·te
midnight	medianoche	me·dya·no·che
noon	mediodía	me·dyo·dee·a
half past two	dos y media	dos ee me·dya

now	ahora	a·o·ra
today	hoy	oy
tonight	esta noche	es·ta no·che
tomorrow	mañana	ma·nya·na
yesterday	ayer	a·yer

Monday	lunes	loo·nes
Tuesday	martes	mar·tes
Wednesday	miércoles	myer·ko·les
Thursday	jueves	khwe·ves
Friday	viernes	vyer·nes
Saturday	sábado	sa·ba·do
Sunday	domingo	do·meen·go

January	enero	e-*ne*-ro
February	febrero	fe-*bre*-ro
March	marzo	*mar*-so
April	abril	a-*breel*
May	mayo	*ma*-yo
June	junio	khoo-nyo
July	julio	khoo-lyo
August	agosto	a-*gos*-to
September	septiembre	sep-*tyem*-bre
October	octubre	ok-*too*-bre
November	noviembre	no-*vyem*-bre
December	diciembre	dee-*syem*-bre

TRANSPORT
Public Transport

What time does	¿A qué hora ...	a ke *o*-ra ...
... leave/arrive?	sale/llega?	*sa*-le/ye-ga
the bus	autobús/	ow-to-*boos*/
	guagua/	*gwa*-gwa/
	ómnibus	*om*-nee-boos
the plane	el avión	el a-*vyon*
the ship	el barco/buque	el *bar*-ko/*boo*-ke
the train	el tren	el tren

airport	el aeropuerto	el a-e-ro-*pwer*-to
train station	la estación de	la es-ta-*syon* de
	ferrocarril	fe-ro-ka-*reel*
bus station	la estación de	la es-ta-*syon* de
	autobuses	ow-to-*boo*-ses
bus stop	la parada de	la pa-*ra*-da de
	autobuses	ow-to-*boo*-ses
luggage check	guardería/	gwar-de-*ree*-a/
room	equipaje	e-kee-*pa*-khe
ticket office	la boletería	la bo-le-te-*ree*-a

I'd like a ticket to ...
Quiero un boleto a ... kye-ro oon bo-*le*-to a ...
What's the fare to ...?
¿Cuánto cuesta hasta ...? kwan-to *kwes*-ta *a*-sta ...

student's	de estudiante	de es-too-*dyan*-te
1st class	primera clase	pree-me-ra *kla*-se
2nd class	segunda clase	se-*goon*-da *kla*-se
single/one-way	ida	*ee*-da
return/round trip	ida y vuelta	*ee*-da ee *vwel*-ta
taxi	taxi	*tak*-see

Private Transport

I'd like to	Quisiera	kee-*sye*-ra
hire a/an ...	alquilar ...	al-kee-*lar* ...
4WD	un todo terreno	oon *to*-do te-*re*-no
car	un auto	oon *ow*-to
motorbike	una moto	*oo*-na mo-to
bicycle	una bicicleta	*oo*-na bee-see-*kle*-ta

ROAD SIGNS	
Acceso	Entrance
Aparcamiento	Parking
Ceda el Paso	Give way
Despacio	Slow
Dirección Única	One-way
Mantenga Su Derecha	Keep to the Right
No Adelantar/	No Passing
No Rebase	
Peaje	Toll
Peligro	Danger
Prohibido Aparcar/	No Parking
No Estacionar	
Prohibido el Paso	No Entry
Pare/Stop	Stop
Salida de Autopista	Exit Freeway

pickup (truck)	camioneta	ka-myo-*ne*-ta
truck	camión	ka-myon
hitchhike	hacer botella	a-ser bo-*te*-lya

Is this the road to (...)?
¿Se va a (...) por se va a (...) por
esta carretera? es-ta ka-re-*te*-ra
Where's a petrol station?
¿Dónde hay una don-de ai oo-na
gasolinera/un grifo? ga-so-lee-*ne*-ra/oon *gree*-fo
Please fill it up.
Lleno, por favor. ye-no por fa-*vor*
I'd like (20) liters.
Quiero (veinte) litros. kye-ro (*vayn*-te) *lee*-tros

diesel	diesel	*dee*-sel
leaded (regular)	gasolina con	ga-so-*lee*-na kon
	plomo	*plo*-mo
petrol (gas)	gasolina	ga-so-*lee*-na
unleaded	gasolina sin	ga-so-*lee*-na seen
	plomo	*plo*-mo

(How long) Can I park here?
¿(Por cuánto tiempo) (por kwan-to *tyem*-po)
Puedo aparcar aquí? pwe-do a-par-*kar* a-*kee*
Where do I pay?
¿Dónde se paga? don-de se *pa*-ga
I need a mechanic.
Necesito un ne-se-*see*-to oon
mecánico. me-*ka*-nee-ko
The car has broken down (in ...).
El carro se ha averiado el *ka*-ro se a a-ve-*rya*-do
(en ...). (en ...)
The motorbike won't start.
No arranca la moto. no a-*ran*-ka la *mo*-to

I have a flat tyre.
Tengo un pinchazo.   ten·go oon peen·cha·so
I've run out of petrol.
Me quedé sin gasolina.   me ke·de seen ga·so·lee·na
I've had an accident.
Tuve un accidente.   too·ve oon ak·see·den·te

TRAVEL WITH CHILDREN

I need ...	*Necesito ...*	ne·se·see·to ...
Do you have ...?	*¿Hay ...?*	ai ...
a car baby seat	*un asiento de seguridad para bebés*	oon a·syen·to de se·goo·ree·da pa·ra be·bes
a child-minding service	*un servicio de cuidado de niños*	oon ser·vee·syo de kwee·da·do de nee·nyos
a children's menu	*una carta infantil*	oona kar·ta een·fan·teel

a creche	*una guardería*	oo·na gwar·de·ree·a
(disposable) diapers/nappies	*pañoles (de usar y tirar)*	pa·nyo·les de oo·sar ee tee·rar
an (English-speaking) babysitter	*una niñera (de habla inglesa)*	oo·na nee·nye·ra (de a·bla een·gle·sa)
formula (milk)	*leche en polvo*	le·che en pol·vo
a highchair	*una trona*	oo·na tro·na
a potty	*una pelela*	oo·na pe·le·la
a stroller	*un cochecito*	oon ko·che·see·to

Do you mind if I breast-feed here?
¿Le molesta que dé de pecho aquí?   le mo·les·ta ke de de pe·cho a·kee
Are children allowed?
¿Se admiten niños?   se ad·mee·ten nee·nyos

Also available from Lonely Planet:
Latin American Spanish phrasebook

Glossary

ache – positive energy and luck

agropecuario – vegetable markets; also sell rice, beans, fruit

aguardiente – fermented cane; literally 'fire water'

altos – upstairs apartment, when following an address

ama de llaves – housekeeper; see *camarera*

americano/a – in Cuba this means a citizen of any Western Hemisphere country (from Canada to Argentina); a citizen of the USA is called a *norteamericano/a* or *estadounidense*; see *gringo/a* and *yuma*

apagón – electricity blackout

Arawak – linguistically related Indian tribes that inhabited most of the Caribbean islands and northern South America

arroba – an antiquated measurement representing about 25 Spanish pounds

audiencia – a court representing the Spanish crown in colonial time

Autopista – the national highway that's four, six or eight lanes depending where you are

babalawo – a *Santería* priest; also babalao

bárbaro – cool, killer

bajos – lower apartment, when following an address

batey – originally an open space in the center of an Indian village; later adopted to refer to a group of service buildings around a sugar mill

bici-taxi – bicycle taxi

bodega – stores distributing ration-card products

bohío – thatched hut

bombo – annual lottery for US visas; also called the white card

botella – hitchhiking; literally 'bottle'

caballería – antiquated Spanish measurement representing about 13.4 hectares

caballito – motorcycle police; literally 'small horse'

cabildo – a town council during the colonial era; also an association of tribes in Cuban religions of African origin

cacique – chief; originally used to describe an Indian chief and today used to designate a petty tyrant

cajita – take-out meal; literally 'small box'

camarera – housekeeper or waitress (the Spanish term criada, which also means 'brought up,' is considered offensive in revolutionary Cuba); see *ama de llaves*

camello – Metro buses in Havana named for their two humps; literally 'camel'

campañero/a – widely used in revolutionary Cuba as a respectful term of address (in place of señor/a); literally 'a female revolutionary'

campesinos – people who live in the campo (country)

campismo – national network of 82 camping installations, not all of which rent to foreigners

candela – literally 'fire,' but used to mean 'hot', as in 'the party/fight/baseball game is en candela'

canoñazo – shooting of the cannons, a nightly ceremony performed at the Fortaleza de la Cabaña across Havana harbor

carpeta – hotel reception desk

cartelera – culture calendar or schedule

casa de la cultura – literally 'culture house' where music, art, theater and dance events happen

casco histórico – historic center of a city (eg Trinidad, Santiago de Cuba)

cayo – a coral key

CDR – Comités de Defensa de la Revolución; neighborhood-watch bodies originally formed in 1960 to consolidate grassroots support for the revolution; they now play a decisive role in health, education, social, recycling and voluntary labor campaigns

central – modern sugar mill; see *ingenio*

chequeré – a gourd covered with beads to form a rattle

cimarrón – a runaway slave

circunvalación – a road that circumvents city centers, allowing you to drive on without plunging into the heart of urban hell

claves – rhythm sticks used by musicians

coco-taxi – egg-shaped taxis that hold two to three people; also called huevitos (literally 'little eggs')

cola – line, queue

colectivo – collective taxi that takes on as many passengers as possible; usually a classic American car

compañero/a – companion or partner, with revolutionary connotations

congrí – rice flecked with black (or sometimes red) beans; called moros y cristianos in *Oriente*

criollo – Creole; Spaniard born in the Americas

c/u – *cada uno*; used in vegetable markets to denote price per unit

Cubanacán – soon after landing in Cuba, Christopher Columbus visited a Taino village the Indians called Cubanacán, meaning 'in the center of the island'; a large Cuban tourism company uses the name

cuenta propista – self-employed worker

cuerpo guardia – area offering emergency services at hospitals

daiquirí – rum cocktail made with crushed ice and other ingredients, named for the Río Daiquirí, near Santiago de Cuba, where it was invented in 1899

diente de perro – jagged rock shelf that lines most of Cuba's southern shore

divisas – dollars, see *fula* and *verdes*

dolarización – literally 'dollarization,' the legalization of US dollars in August 1993

el último – literally 'the last,' this term is key to mastering Cuban queues (you must 'take' the último when joining a line and 'give it up' when someone new arrives)

Elegguá – the god of destiny in Cuban religions of African origin like Santeriá

embalse – reservoir

encomienda – a section of land and an indigenous workforce entrusted to an individual by the Spanish crown during the early colonial era

entronque – crossroads in rural areas

esquina caliente – where baseball fanatics debate stats, teams, history and who's up and who's down; literally 'hot corner'; also called a *peña*

flota – the Spanish treasure fleet

FMC – Federación de Mujeres Cubanas (Federation of Cuban Women); founded in 1960 and active in local and national politics

fula – a bad or fucked-up situation or person; also means 'dollars'; see *divisas* and *verdes*

Granma – the yacht that carried Fidel and his companions from Mexico to Cuba in 1956 to launch the revolution; in 1975 the name was adopted for the province where the *Granma* arrived; also the daily newspaper

gringo/a – any Caucasian; see *americano/a* and *yuma*

guagua – a bus

guajiro/a – a country bumpkin or hick

guaracha – a satirical song for a single voice backed by a chorus

guarapo – fresh sugarcane juice

guayabera – a pleated, buttoned men's shirt; tropical formal-wear

Habanero/a – someone from Havana

herbero – seller of herbs, natural medicines and concocter of remedies; typically a wealth of knowledge on natural cures

imperio, el – 'the empire'; a term used in the official Cuban media to refer to the USA, which is led by imperialistas

ingenio – an antiquated term for a sugar mill; see *central*

jaba – plastic bag; also called a jabita, nylon or (in the *Oriente*) Cubalse

jefe de turno – shift manager

jején(es) – sand flea(s)

jinetera – a woman who attaches herself to male foreigners for monetary or material gain; the exchange may or may not involve sex

jinetero – a male tout who hustles tourists; literally 'jockey'

joder – to mess or fuck up, to spoil

lenguaje chavacán – a type of slang used by young people

libreta – the ration booklet

luchar – literally 'to struggle or fight'; used in all sorts of daily situations

M-26-7 – the '26th of July Movement,' Fidel Castro's revolutionary organization, was named for the abortive assault on the Moncada army barracks in Santiago de Cuba on July 26, 1953

machetero – sugarcane cutter who uses a machete

mambí/ses – 19th-century rebel/s fighting Spain

maqueta – scale model

máquina – an old North American car; also called almendrón (literally 'big almond')

maraca – a rattle used by musicians

microbrigade housing – dwellings (usually large apartment blocks) built by small armies ('microbrigades') of workers following the triumph of the revolution

mirador – lookout or viewpoint

mogote – a limestone monolith found at Viñales

mojito – cocktails made from rum, mint, sugar, seltzer and fresh lime juice

Moncada – a former army barracks in Santiago de Cuba named for General Guillermo Moncada (1848–1895), a hero of the wars of independence

moneda nacional – abbreviated to MN; Cuban pesos

Oriente – the region comprised of Las Tunas, Holguín, Granma, Santiago de Cuba and Guantánamo Provinces

orisha – a *Santería* deity

paladar – a privately owned restaurant

palenque – a hiding place for runaway slaves during the colonial era

parada – bus stop

patria – homeland, country

PCC – Partido Comunista de Cuba; Cuba's only political party, which was formed in October 1965 by merging cadres from the Partido Socialista Popular (the pre-1959 Communist Party) and veterans of the guerrilla campaign

pedraplén – stone causeways connecting offshore islands to mainland Cuba

peña – musical performance or get-together in any genre: *son*, rap, rock, poetry etc; see also *esquina caliente*

peninsular – a Spaniard born in Spain but living in the Americas

piropo – flirtatious remark/commentary

ponchero – a fixer of flat tires

pregón – a singsong manner of selling fruits, vegetables, brooms, whatever; often comic, they are belted out by pregoneros/as

presa – dam

quinciñera – Cuban rite of passage for girls turning 15 (quince), whereby they dress up like brides, have their photos taken in gorgeous natural or architectural settings and then have a big party with lots of food and dancing

quintal – an antiquated measurement representing 100 Spanish pounds

rancheador – one who hunted down fugitive slaves during the colonial period

reconcentración – a tactic of forcibly concentrating rural populations, used by the Spaniards during the Second War of Independence

resolver – to resolve or fix a problematic situation; along with *el último*, this is among the most indispensable words in Cuban vocabulary

rumba – an Afro-Cuban dance form that originated among plantation slaves during the 19th century; during the '20s and '30s, the term *rumba* was adopted in North America and Europe for a ballroom dance in 4/4 time; in Cuba today, to *rumba* simply means to 'party'

salsa – Cuban music based on *son*

salsero – salsa singer

Santería – Afro-Cuban religion resulting from the syncretization of the Yoruba religion of West Africa and Spanish Catholicism

santero – a priest of *Santería*

Santiagüero – someone from Santiago de Cuba

sello – stamp (in a passport or on a letter)

SIDA – síndrome de inmunodeficiencia adquirida; AIDS

s/n – sin número, indicates an address that has no address number

son – Cuba's basic form of popular music that jelled from African and Spanish elements in the late 19th century

Taino – a settled, Arawak-speaking tribe that inhabited much of Cuba prior to the Spanish conquest; the word itself means 'we the good people'

taquilla – ticket window

telenovela – soap opera

temporada alta/baja – high/low season

terminal de omnibus – bus station

trago – an alcoholic drink

trova – traditional poetic singing/songwriting

UJC – Unión de Jóvenes Comunistas; a student group active in politics

UNEAC – Unión Nacional de Escritores y Artistas de Cuba, National Union of Cuban Writers and Artists

verdes – slang for 'dollars', see *divisas* and *fula*

VIH – *virus de inmunodeficiencia humana*; HIV

Yoruba – a pantheistic religion originating in Nigeria

yuma – slang for someone from the US; can be used for any foreigner; see *americano/a* and *gringo/a*

zafra – sugarcane harvest

zarzuela – operetta

Behind the Scenes

THIS BOOK

This 3rd edition of *Cuba* was written by Conner Gorry. The Health chapter was written by Dr David Goldberg. The 1st and 2nd editions of *Cuba* were written by David Stanley.

THANKS FROM THE AUTHOR

In Cuba it's all about teamwork. People I'm proud and thankful to have on my team include Juan Francisco Santos, María de los Angeles, Rosa Pablos, Luis López, Roberto Novo, and Pastor Argudín and the entire El Pesebre congregation (all in Pinar del Río); Pastor Abel Cotelo and Baby Hernández (in Morón); Ñico and Dora (in Holguín); and Asli Pelit, Jenry Álvarez, Sandy Levinson, Teresita and Gisella for their home cooking, and the folks at the Fundación de Naturaleza y El Hombre (all in Havana). The many technical problems were gracefully handled by Gladys Ibarra (again!) and Fidelito Pérez Cabrera. Tanya of Witness for Peace was a great scuba buddy and terrific help after that lost notes fiasco. A very special thanks to everyone at Havana's Centro Memorial Martin Luther King and the entire Gorry & Suárez family. Last but not least, David Stanley's superb work on the previous edition was the best LP text I have ever inherited. Thank you.

This book would not have been possible without the unflagging solidarity, love, home cooking and 'five minutes' of my husband Joel Suárez.

CREDITS

Cuba 3 was commissioned and developed by David Zingarelli. Cartography for this guide was developed by Graham Neale. The book was coordinated by Danielle North (editorial), Celia Wood (cartography) and Sonya Brooke (colour and layout). Editorial assistance was provided by Meaghan Amor, Andrew Bain, Bridget Blair, Carolyn Boicos, Kerryn Burgess, Helen Christinis, Michelle Coxall, Melanie Dankel, Barbara Delissen, Justin Flynn, Jocelyn Harewood, Nancy Ianni, Kate James, Thalia Kalkipsakis, Craig Kilburn, Tegan Murray, Stephanie Pearson, Simon Sellars, Suzannah Shwer, Linda Suttie, Julia Taylor, Katrina Webb, Simon Williamson and Helen Yeates. Cartographic assistance was provided by Tony Fankhauser, Huw Fowles, Cris Gibcus, Anneka Imkamp, Anthony Phelan and Andrew Smith. Layout assistance was provided by Vicki Beale, Pablo Gastar, Indra Kilfoyle, Katharine Marsh, Angela Robinson and Jacqui Saunders. Quentin Frayne prepared the Language chapter. The index was prepared by Kristin Odijk. Yukiyoshi Kamimura designed the cover. Overseeing production were Huw Fowles (Project Manager), Kerryn Burgess (Managing Editor), Alison Lyall (Managing Cartographer) and Adriana Mammarella (Layout Manager). Series Publishing Manager Virginia Maxwell oversaw the redevelopment of the country guides series with help from Maria Donohoe, who was also the Regional Publishing Manager and steered the development of this title. The se-

---

THE LONELY PLANET STORY

The story begins with a classic travel adventure: Tony and Maureen Wheeler's 1972 journey across Europe and Asia to Australia. There was no useful information about the overland trail then, so Tony and Maureen published the first Lonely Planet guidebook to meet a growing need.

From a kitchen table, Lonely Planet has grown to become the largest independent travel publisher in the world, with offices in Melbourne (Australia), Oakland (USA), London (UK) and Paris (France).

Today Lonely Planet guidebooks cover the globe. There is an ever-growing list of books and information in a variety of media. Some things haven't changed. The main aim is still to make it possible for adventurous travellers to get out there – to explore and better understand the world.

At Lonely Planet we believe travelers can make a positive contribution to the countries they visit – if they respect their host communities and spend their money wisely. Since 1986 a percentage of the income from each book has been donated to aid projects and human rights campaigns, and, more recently, to wildlife conservation.

ries was designed by James Hardy, with mapping development by Paul Piaia. The series development team included Shahara Ahmed, Susie Ashworth, Gerilyn Attebery, Jenny Blake, Anna Bolger, Verity Campbell, Erin Corrigan, Nadine Fogale, Dave Mc-Clymont, Leonie Mugavin, Lynne Preston, Rachel Peart and Howard Ralley.

THANKS FROM LONELY PLANET
Many thanks to the hundreds of travelers who used the last edition and wrote to us with helpful hints, useful advice and interesting anecdotes:

A Bruce Abrahams, Vivien Abrahams, Inger Abrahamsen, Juliette Adams, Kevin R Adlard, Frances Adlington, Noel Aflague, Robert Aikman, Nikolaos Aktypis, Z Ali, David Alison, Karen Allacker, Peter Almklov, Bill Almolky, Christine Altenbeck, Claudia Amaya, Christian Ambruster, Ia Ameen, Oliver Ammann, John Amoroso, Elena Anaya, Jon Anders, Jonas Andersson, Rafael Andrade, Mr Andre, Hilberger Andreas, Malcolm Andrews, Louse Angel, Anders Ansar, Gerry Anslow, Miguel Angel Quevedo Apolinario, Lucy Arbuthnott, Charlotte Arconada, Charlotte & Marcelino Arconada, Enrique Arnaiz, Fabio Arnone, Claessens Arnout, Tim Ashley, Janni Aspridis, David Aston, Roland Auferbauer, Daniela Avino, Patrick Awart, Angel Ayala, Ciaran Ayton **B** Roman Baedorf, Vivi Baek Jensen, Robert L Baer, Lawrence Bailey, Maxine Bailey, Robert Bailey, Ryan Bailey, Klaus Bajohr, Dr Klaus Bajohr-Mau, RA Balmanoukian, Andreas Balmer, Rolando Bangerter, Mandy Banton, Gabrielle Bardall, Bilge Barhana, John Barnett, Roger Barr, Manuel Barragan, Anna Barratt, Veronique Barthes, Mary Bash, Alessandra Basilico, Don Bastedo, Christopher Bateman, CR Bateman-Jones, Alexander Baxter, Maureen Beard, Sandra Beardsall, Gerard Beaumont, Tania Beccaceci, M C Beck, Miriam Becki, Moran Beit Halachmi, Kim Belcham, Pamela Bell, Beverly Benmoussa, Brent Bennett, Richard Bentley, Randi Berg, Guillaume Bernardi, Raffaele Bernardo, Andrew Berry, Chrys Berryman, Marie Berteau, Terje Bertelsen, J Bezemer, C Bharadia, Cristina Bianchi, Mark Bickerdike, Charles Bierley, Vera Billen, Jan Billow, Adela Binding, G Birds, John Birdsall, Rob Birkbeck, Claudio Bisani, Mathias Bischer, Liz Bissett, Mike Bissett, Ric Bisson, Rainer Bitschi, Lisa Blaire, Felix Blanco, Melissa Blanco, Karin Blokzile, Uli Bohm, Marianne Bollier, Gary Bonar, Nancy & Hans-Jan Bonsma, Tjeerd Boonman, Kevin Boreham, David Borenstein, Sarah-Jane Borradaile, Mieke Bos, Amarante Bottger, Maryse Bouchard, Adriana Bouchat, Alexandros Bousoulegkas, Claude Bouvy, Tina Bowden, Raymond Bowen, Jay Boynton, Fernand Bradley, Sara Bragg, Fabio Brait, Sarah Bransdon, Barbara Brauchle, Annemarie Breeve, Mireille Bremer, Alex Bremmer, Jo Brennan, Alan Breslauer, Ingo Breuer, Izumi Breuer, Richard Breyer, Timor Britva, Adrian Brock, Gies Broekhuyse, Dorothy Brooks, Alana Brown, Dave Brown, Lance Browne, Kathy Bruppacher, Isabella Bruschi, Alan Buchan, Chiara Buffa, Bruce Burger, J Burgess, Ilonka Burmann, Sally Burnett, Derek Burnside, Carla Burshtein, David Burstyner, Julie Butler, Jonna Byskata **C** Angelique Cachia, Juan Cados, Jon Calder,

David Calderwood, Serena Camedda, Stanley Campbell, Elizabeth Campisi, Seamus Canavan, Andy Cannon, Christopher Cannon, Paola Carpino, Michael Carrigan, Angeles Carriles, Tom Carslake, Lorraine Casey, Aoife Cassidy, Juan Castineira, Todd Cater, Tanguy Ceulemans, Stefano Cevenini, Jean Pierre Chadelaud, Phung Chain, Yvette Chalom, Tom Chatfield, Richard Chauss, Bob Chessey, Tasa Chesterman, Ruth Chiarini, Claire Chick, Artur Chmielewski, Seulki Choi, Rikke Christensen, Jan Cimerman, Mariangeli Cintron, Bart Claeys, Thom Clark, Adam Cleary, Steve Cleary, Ronnie Clifton, Mato Colak, Richard Colbey, Mara Colombo, Timothy Conlin, Carol Connery, Mike Connolly, Jerry Cook, Jonathan Cook, Nelson Cook, Paul Cook, Isabelle Corbasson, Margarita Cordoba, Phil Corlett, Eleanor Cornwall, Adolfo Corsi, Andrea Nathan Costa, Con Costello, Inez Costenoble, Philip Cottrell, Marie-Noelle Coudray, Rafael Coutin, Glenn Cox, Gabrille Cozzolino, Stephanie & Gary Craig, Mark Cramer, Sarah Crawford, Gary Crocker, John Cross, Graham Crouch, Tony Cruz, Tomas Cruz Guerra, Carlos Cuesta, Johnathan Culver, Mike Curtis, Susan Cushnaghan **D** Anne D' Enhgien, Steve Dalton, Steve Daltrey, Geisseler Daniel, Roblin Daniele, Richard Daniels, Zod Dare Hall, Mike Darley, Esben Darling Meng, Matthew Davies, Alex Davis, MJ Davis, Mark Dawson, Inez de Coo, Linda de Jong, Annemarieke de Jonghe, Marma Mercedes de la Peqa, Quirino de Leon Tio, P de Lepper, Marc & Claus De Pauw, Leo de Rooij, Natasja De Winter, Marco de Zwart, Phil Dean, Koenraad DeBacker, Sandra Dedecker, Jeannette Degen, Evert Dekker, Janez Demsar, Laswrence Denger, John Devlin, Melanie Devlin, Monica Devlin, Sebastian R Diaz, Guy Dickerson, Irene Dickman, Phil Dickman, Merete Dideriksen, Emiliano Diego-Franceskides, Al Dieste, Walter Dill, Andrew Dix, Charlie Dobbie, William Dodge, David Dodgson, David Dolberg, Daniel Dolci, Bennett Donahue, Thomas Donegan, Faye Donnaway, Peter Donnelly, Gail Donner, Jochen Doppelhammer, P Dove, Tim Dowley, Jane Downing, Eileen Doyle, Achim Draeger, Gerardo Dragoni, Natasha Dragun, Christopher J Dresser, Mark Driskill, Brian Dudden, Laurien Dudden, Silvia Duerrsperger, Dave Duffy, Laurent-jan Dullaart, Katrina Duncan, Michael Dunphy, Tyler Durden, Simon Dye **E** Ken Earhart, Joan & Dave Easingwood-Wilson, Monika Ebenhoeh, Michle Egger, Taco Ekkel, Nina Ellefsen, Dan Ellis, David Ellis, Gretchen Ellis, Alex Elston, Russ Elwell, Han en Renske, Nikolai Engel, Chris Enting, Evelyn Escobar Alvarez, David Evans, Paige Evans, Inge Van den Eynde, Dan Eynon, Luis Ezra **F** Rebecca Falik, Marisa Falle Lopez, Dorothy Fallows, Helmut Farkasch, Rita Fazio, Marek Feldman, Birte Feldmann, Katja Feldmer, Keith Ferguson, Jennifer Fernandes, Sara Fielder, Sylvia Fiers, Rolando Figueroa, Michael Filliol, Patricia Filliol, Christoph Finger, Dagmar Fischer-Colbrie, Renate Fischer-Nolte, Paul Fisher, Barbara Fishman, Darren Fitzgerald, Paul Fitzsimmons, John Fizell, Trish Flanagan, Juliet Fleming, John Foitzik, Felicity & Matthew Foley, Carmen Folgar, Benoit Fontaine, Emma Forester, Ian Forrester, Jordi Fortia-Huguet, Fabienne Fossez, Kent Foster, Majorie Foster, Shane Foster, Kate Fowkes, Mel Fowler, Paula & Ian Francis, Hans Dam Frandsen, Alex Frankel, Sanne Fredsted, M Freeman, Rene Frei, David Friedrich, Nikolaus Frinke, Claudia Fritz, Mette Frost Bylling, Lut Froyen, Aaron Fuermetz **G** Max Gadney, Sonia Gainza, Israel Galan, Paolo Galantina, Jeanne Gallagher, Nan Gallagher, Chuck Galvin, Claire Gammon,

Bernard Gangloff, Aiming Gao, Lindsay Garbutt, Matthew Gardan, Mike Garner, Sean Garrity, Aggy Gartner, Reinhard Gast, Marco Gatti, Aldo Gatto, Richard Geary, Maud Geerbex, Markus Gehring, Thomas Gennaro, Debra L George, Nicole Gerber, Ludger Gerdes, Danny Gerro, Udo Geske, Roger Geyer, Chris Gibson, Bernard Gillespie, John C Gilroy, Dan Gingold, Fabio Giudici, Sarah Glazebrook, Patrick Glennie-Smith, J Goedhart, Annika Goldenbaum, Brad S Goldman MD, Carmen Gomez Aparicio, Pedro Goncalves, Pilar Gonzalvo Sanzo, Bryn Gooding, Saul Goodwin, Harry Goovarts, Joel Gordon, Leo Gorman, Christopher Goski, Louise Goulding, Sotiris Goulias, John R Graham, Anne-Sophie Grandguillaume, Nicholas Green, Mihal Greener, Gregers Gregersen, Line Gregorie, Anna Greissing, Urs Gretler, Teresa Griffiths, Jens Groth, Grzegorz Grzyb, Alfred Gstottenmayr, Ruth Gualerzi, James Guilbeau, Anna-Karin Gunberg, Christian Gunther, Walter Gusmag, Gerald Guzzwell, Bernard Gygax **H** Caroline Hadrbolec, Daniela Haenni, Alice Haertlein, Edmund Haffmans, Anneliese Hafner, Alf Hageselle, Steve Haines, Meir Hakkak, Martin Halbach, Diallo Hall, RJ Hall, Tom Hall, Rachel Halpern, Philip Halsall, Lorna Hamblin, Lee Hammond, Neil Hammond, Marc Handler, Judith Hanna, Paul Hansen, Paul & Kim Hansen, Horst Harbecke, Andrea Harley, I W Harris, Lee Hartman, Tobias Hauser, Tina Haux, Greg Haverbeke, Colin Hawkins, Dymphna Hawkins, Jeremiah Hayes, Helen Hayward, Lane Haywood, Damien Heary, Bernhard Heck, Ellen Heizman, Clemens Hellenschmidt, Elizabeth Henderson, Claudine Hendrix, Ted Henken, David Herd, Dr Renate Herold, Renate Herold, Friedrich Herrmann, Joachim Hesse, Elaine Hewson, Debbie Heywood, Thom Hiemstra, Michael Hilbinger, Jutta Hillebrand, Michele Hillier, Jacob Himmelrich, Graeme Hind, Ken Hind, Robert Hines, Annabel Hobley, Anne Marie Hofman, Manfred Hohl, G A Hoines, JE Hok, Jan Jo Holden-Peters, Vern & Jaye Holland, Mike Hollar, Sharon Hollowell, Signe Holme Soelvmose, Jenny Holmgren, Jenny & Niklas Holmgren, Gerald Holt, Michael Holtey, Joachim Horn, J Hornbuckle, Chet Hornung, Richard Hough, Anthony Houghton, Janneke Höweler, Robin Howie, Sarah Howling, Viktor Hskansson, Deborah & Mark Huard, Roberta Huber, Marian Hudson, Brian Hughes, Eleanor Hughes, Hugh W Hughes, Lorrain Hughes, Richard Hughes, Sharon Huizinga, Deborah Hull, Hilary Hull, Ingeborg & Gerald Hulsebos, Roos Hunsche, Mark Hunt, Bill Hunter, Jules Huot, Fer Hurk, Annette Hurst, Kris Huyghe, Michel Huyghe, Darinka Hvalec **I** Heidi Ilg, Boris Ilovar, Jerry Inglehart, Miren Iregi, Kealin Ireland, Ewout Irrgang, Ian Irvine **J** Stefan Jackle, Greg Jackson, Helena Jackson, Jasper Jacobs, Anne Jahn, Susanne Jakszus, Doug James, Paul James, Gabriel Coll Janer, Volkmar E Janicke, Ingrid Jedeckova, Dianne Jefferson, Georg Jenichl, Fred Jenkins, Brenda Jerome, Vigi B Jerven, Chris Jiggins, B Jobst, Helena Johansson, Nils Johnsen, Errol Johnson, Grietje Johnson, Cynthia Johnston, David Jones, Georgina Jones, Penny Jones, S H Jones, Francien Jonge Poerink, Christina Joost, Frank Joostens, Sidsel Homann Jorgensen, Arthur Jost, Claudia Jost, Larry A Gordon Jr, Sara Junker, Tim Justice, Lydia Justice Edwards **K** Ilja Kaffanke, Kris Kallmeyer, Ofir Kanter, Vlasta Kappus, Jan Karasek, Tuomas Karkkainen, Stephan Karkowsky, Liz Karman, Elad Katz, Jane Kavanagh, Anke Kayser, Peter Kearns, Tom Keator, George Kechagioglou, Darius Kedros, Aubkey Kee, Hans Keeren,

John Kelleher, Robin Kelley, Jonathan Kelly, Stacey Kelly, Mick Kemp, Corene Kendrick, P Kenton, Chris Kepler, Serge Kervevan, Philip Kestelman, Noa Kfir, Dave Kiely, Glen Kilday, J Kim, John Kim, Angela King, Jeff King, Paul Michael Kirchhof, Jens Kirkegaard, Sandra Kirsch, Wendy Kirton, Ruth Kitching, Peggie Klekotka, Pieter Klompen, Bert Knol, Brendan Knox-Peebles, Kim Knuuti, Susy Koch, Lucia Koerner, Martin Kohler, J Koijenga, Benna Kolinsky, George Komodromou, John Konheim, Rainer Konietzny, Drew Koning, Nadine Koopmann, June Koplewitz, Harrie Kortekaas, Petri Kosonen, Gerhard Kotschenreuther, Fritz Kraemer, Kristof Krahl, Harry Kranick, Mark Kregel, Uta Kreibig, Friedhelm Krey, Mateja Krivec, Felix Krohn, J Kroijenga, Ruth Krugel, Roger Kubler, Mateja Kukovec, Tom Kulinski, Agnes & Hans Kusters, Piotr Kustosz, Haakon Kvidal, Kaisa Kylakoski, Matthew Kyte **L** Marie La Cespedes, Nicole La Valette, Danielle Labbad, Ingrid Lagerberg, Anniina Lahtinen, Lillemor Laidlaw, Tanya Lake, Dr Pierre Lambert, Paul Lamot, F B Lane, Mike Lane, Gwen Lansbury, Laura Larghi, Jana Lasandova, Gregor Lasch, Markus Lauber, Michiel Le Blanc, Alan Leahy, Janelle LeBlanc, Ron Lebuela, Stephane Lecuyer, Caz Lederman, Alfred Lee, Justin Lees, Hans JA van Leeuwen, Alexandre Leger, Eric LeGresley, Stephan Leinert, Marc Lenot, Manfred Lenzen, Emanuela Leonardi, Vanessa & Lucas Leonardi, Connie Lepe, Trevor Letcher, Guy Lether, Gerd Leutner, Amir Levi, Shlomo Levi, John Levings, Dr Jay Levinson, Brian and Maggie Lewis, Remco Liem, Adrian Lim, Louise Lindenmeyr, Duaine Lindstrom, Peter Lipson, Rosa Lisa, Mark Little, Saffron Lodge, Pia Löhlein, Margaret Longrish, Margareta & Anders Loof, Kate Loosley, Luis Lopez, Marie Lord, Ing Omelio Moreno Lorenzo, Herick Louis,

---

SEND US YOUR FEEDBACK

We love to hear from travelers – your comments keep us on our toes and help make our books better. Our well-traveled team reads every word on what you loved or loathed about this book. Although we cannot reply individually to postal submissions, we always guarantee that your feedback goes straight to the appropriate authors, in time for the next edition. Each person who sends us information is thanked in the next edition – and the most useful submissions are rewarded with a free book.

To send us your updates – and find out about LP events, newsletters and travel news – visit our award-winning website: **www.lonelyplanet.com**.

Note: We may edit, reproduce and incorporate your comments in Lonely Planet products such as guidebooks, websites and digital products, so let us know if you don't want your comments reproduced or your name acknowledged. For a copy of our privacy policy, email privacy@lonelyplanet.com.au.

Kiresten Louis, Michael Loungo, Zsuzsa Lovas, Gudmund Love, Mike Love, Tom Love, Christopher Lowry, Roger Lowry, Rick Loy, Terry Lozo, Iris Lubitsh, Matthew Luck, Peter Luescher, Roland Luethi, Pernilla Lundmark, David Luttig, Lieke Luttmer, Alexander Lutz, Patrick Lutz, Kerstin Lynen **M** Steven MacCormack, Alan D Macdonald, Gregor Macek, John Macgregor, Alastair Mackay, Heather Mackay, Alice MacKenzie, Joanne MacKinnon, Ken Macklin, Gordon MacQueen, Robert Maher, Ged Maheran, Heather Maitland, Maryam Majedi, Susana Maldonado, Keith Mallaburn, Boris Maloff, Wolgang Malzahn, Monique Manders, Christiane Manglitz, Jason Mann, Chris Manthorp, Sinead Mac Manus, Jean Marc Dugauquier, Sylvain Marchand, Antonio Margaroli, Yossi Margoninsky, Daniel Margot, Jennifer Lou Markes, Claire Marks, Clara Ferreira Marques, Nada Marrazzo, D Marsden, Allegra Marshall, Peter Marshall, Peter Marti, Ann Martin, Charles Martin, Dario Martin, Paul Martin, Achim Martin Draeger, Claudio Martini, Luciano Martini, Kelly Marvo, Royston Mascarenhas, Petra Masclee, Carol Mason, Peter Mason, Sally Loren Massmann, Uwe Masuch, Cliff Matheson, Fred Mathijsen, Alexander Matskevich, Takao Matsuda, Debiie Mattina, David Mattock, Bodzia Matulaniec, Sibylle Mau, Brent Maupin, Emily May, Ute Mayer, Bob Maysmor, Edward & Pamela McCamley, Doug McDonald, Graham McDonald, Graham & Tracey McDonald, Angela McGee, David McGee, Mrs K McGrath, Sarah McKinney, Catriona McLean, Neil McLeay, E Mcleod, Marc McLeod, Siobhan McMahon, Bron McWhinney, Joseph Mea, Anthony Meagh, Renate Mehr, Sharon Meieran, L Meire, Marc Melanie, Thea Melholt, Wendy Meller, Amos Meltzer, Fred Mendelsohn, Shari Mendelson, Linda Menendez, Armando Menocal, Vicki Metcalfe, Corinna Meyer, Stefan Meyer, Andrea & Bettor Mietta, Juan Miguel, Lynn Mikami, Maria Milis, Daryl Miller, Michael Miller, Perry Miller, Sheila Miller, Tamsin Miller, Claudio Milletti, James Milligan, Brian Mills, Antonella Minelli, Mike Mirecki, Stephanie Misa, Gina Mitchell, John Mitchell, Jordan Mitchell, Sam Mitter, Oystein Moen, Bill Moffett, April Moir, Jan Molgaard, Manual Molina, Inie Moltzer, Gerard Mooney, Mr Moose, Thomas Moran, Gerry Morbin, Omelio Moreno, Willie Moreschi, Evelyne Morin, Peter Mork, Mark Morris, Penny Morris, Susan Morrison, Siobhan Mortell, Richard Mortorff, Dean Moss, Susanne Mossal, Carmen Moya, Christine Mueller, Frank Mueller, Michael Mueller, Roger Muggli, Tom Muirhead, Geoff Murphy, T P Murphy, Terry Murphy, Jon Murray, Shauna Murray, Jennifer Mussett, Ann Myhre **N** Christian Nabe, Benjamin Naef, Yann Navet, Anne Marit Nearby, Barbora Necas, Peter Necas, Alexis Neffe, Pascal Negm, Susanne Negm Johansson, Barbara Ellen Nehring, Nicola Wendy Nelson, Bernarda Nemec, Jenny Nicholls, Norm Nickle, Gitte Nielsen, Klaus Niggl, Marron Nijhuis, Andreas Nilsson, Bruce Nisker, Manfred Noa, R Nogue, Ricardo Nogueira, Hans Noltes, Yen Alexandra Nomikos, Iver Nordentoft, Sylvia Noury, Greg Nuk, Michael Nunner, Melanie Nussbaumer, Niklas Nyberg **O** RY Oates, John O'Brien, Jeffrey F Obser, Marie O'Connor, Nina Ogrin, David O'Keefe, Mette Olaisen, Jo Oliver, Ria Olsen, Vibeke Olsen, Jan O'Malley, Phillip Oppenheim, Dennis Orchard, Nigel Orchard, Gregor Ordon, Bearnard O'Riain, Bearnard & Vere O'Riain, Rimon Orni, Carmen Orosz, Celia Ortega, Alejandro Oses Gil, Joe O'Shaughnessy, Francesca Osnago, Arnaud Otte, Arjan Otten, Joe Overtveld, Don Owens **P** Juan Pablo Cristiano, Tim Pagel, John Palcic, Manoli Pardo, Danic Parenteau, Jim Parish, Aristea Pariss, Ed Parker, Jennifer Parker, Judith Parker, David Parry, Zvi Pasman, Ed Patriquin, Giuseppe Patti, Gordon Patton, Marco Pavia, Steffi Pawlowsky, Amit Paz, Melissa Pearce, Ole Ravn Pedersen, Anna Pedroli, Marc Peeters, Carole Penot, David Pepper, Hiram Perez, Paz Perez, Jesus Perez Alejo, Janez & Tanja Perko, Enrique Pernia, No Peschers, Dorine Peters, Wolfgang Pfaelzner, Christian Pfister, Sue Phares, Peter Phelan, Peter & Marian Phelan, Signe Philip, Allison Phillips, Chantal Phillips, Rachel Phillips, John E Philp, Maria Laura De Piano, Enrico Piccardo, Katy Pickering, Gemma Pilgrim, Kathryn Pimpan, Davide Pino, J del Pino, Maciek Piotrowski, Jean Piret, Martina Pirnat, Judy Pisano, Alessandra Pistani, Luigi Pittalis, Antonio Placido, Willem Plandsoen, Francis Plante, Stefan Portmann, Clifford Power, Julian Powers, Michael Praschma, Brian Preece, Jan Preisler, Heimo Preiss, Hemo & Christine Priess, Ann Priestley, Caroline Priestley, Emma Prinsley, Stephen Privett, Charlotte Pryke, Stephen Psallidas, Patrick Pudduy, Caroline Pugh-Roberts, Elaine Purnell **Q** Stans Quik **R** Inge Raasch, Jose Rabelo, Ella Rachamin, Lynn Ragghianti, Henk Raijer, Fiona Maria Rainsford, Clara Rakestraw, Patricia Ramonet, Henry W Randle, Elise Rasmussen, Nadiu Rathgeber, Arjun Rawla, Nick Read, Ursula Read, William J Read, Phil Reavley, Doug Reese, Gavin Reese, Vincent Reh, S Reher, Jo Reid, Larry Reid, Anne Marie Reinholdt, Marco Reisbock, Christl Reissenberger, Steffen Rennstich, Ernst Reuss, Jill Reynolds, Ramon Acosta Ricardo, Luigi Ricci, Tom Richards, Thomas Richwhite, Paul Rigg, Antonella Rigoni, Mieke Rijs, Sven Ring, Ondine Ripka, Judith Ripoli, Kristina Risberg, Guy Robert, Amanda Roberts, Carol Roberts, Sue Roberts, Ingrid Robeyns, Todd Robin, Daniel B Robinson, Gordon Robinson, Luis Rocha, Craig Rodgers, Fiona Roe, Lewis Roger, Steve Rogowski, Sonja A Rohner, Fred Rohole, Matthias Rohrig Assuncao, Benzi Ronen, Sherry Ronick, Lasse Ronningen, Philippe Roose, Lluis Ros, Susannah Rosenberg, Alistair Ross, Nicola Ross, Josef Rotter, Tim Rout, Luciano Rovesti, Tania Ruddick, Krystyna Rudzki, Andreas Ruefenacht, Joseph Ruiz, Nikki Ruiz, Patricia Ruiz Rincon, Angel Rumbo, Sebastian Ruschak, Tom Ruyten, Helen Ryan **S** Victor Alejandro Sahagun, Carlos Sainz Mata, Fred Salaff, Fred Saliez, Paul & Andrew Salisbury, Russell Salton, Ewa Samborska, Leigh Sampson, Jana Sanchez, Lothar & Rosa Sand, Judy Sanderman, Hugh Sandison, Bea Sandler, Cristi Sane, Ed Sango, Timothy Sanjule, Gillian Sare, Fen Sartorius, Paul and Ina Sauer, Uwe Sauerteig, Arno Sauli, Cyrille Saulnier, Charles Saunders, Javier Saura, Les Savage, Sharon Savage, Jo Scard, Meike Scheerschmidt, Klaus Scheiman-Burkhardt, Roberto Schenone, Markus Scheuermaier, Eric J Schiller, Carola Schlüter, Martin Schmidt, Ute Schmidt, Heinz Schmolz, Jeroen Schols, Hans Scholtz, Joop Schreur MD, Raymond Schrijver, Natascha Schroten, Nancy Schuler, Wolfgang Schuler, Edwin Schultz, Pamela Schwartz, Martin Schwietzke, Jan Scibor-Kaminski, Mary Scott, Clarence Sears, Fiona Seath, Niel Sebag-Montefiore, Odelia Sebba, Diana Seemann, Anneke Seesing, Katharina Seifert-Prenn, Arne Seime, Jacob Seligmann, Maria Serrano, Frederic Servieres, David Shaked, Peter Shanks, Kerry Sharpe, Matt Shattuck, Yana Shechterman, Fran Sheets, Nir N Shemie, Daniel Sher, Billy Shields, Adam Shire, Gail Shutiank, Paul

Sidler, Jody Sie, Helen Siegel, Anouk Siegelaar, Samantha Silk, Natasha Silva, Mark Simmeren, Ian Simmons, Carolina Simon, Rainhard Simon, Andrea Simonette, Andrea Simonetti, Dan K Simpson, Glenn Simpson, Dorothy Sims, Rosanne Sims, Karmel Sims-Eakins, Balwant Singh, Saso Skalic, Oyvind Skarbo, Elisabeth Skatvold, Lars Rune Skaug, Rebecca Skinner, A Slight, Katja Slovenia, Lia Smallegange, Anna Smith, Anthony Smith, Charlotte Smith, Chris Smith, Colin Smith, Katie Smith, Paul Smith, Marcel Smits, Paul Smits, Adie Smitz, Lynn Snel, Dan Snow, Ane Soegaard, Eric Sokolsky, Anna Soloviova, Janne Solpark, Aimee Solway, Vassilis Sourrapas, Scott Sowers, Leon Spaans, Daniel Sparla, James Spears, Silas Spenser, Elke Spiegelenberg, Christian Staeubli, Martin Staines, Res Staudenmann, Inka Steffens, Viviane Steiner, Magnus Stensson, Katie Stewart, Paul Stewart, Dirk C Stienstra, Robert Stoessel, Nancy Stokes, Frank Stone, Colin Stoneley, Martin Strauch, Lawrence & Anne Straus, Robert Strauss, Nele Stroebel, Michael Stuart, Rae Sturtevant, Thomas Stutz, Lars Sundin, Melanie Surry, Marc Süssmeier, G Sutton, Miha Svalj, Patrick Swinnen, Katalin Szilagyi **T** Pia Talja, Peter Tallon, Sally Tankard, Jill Tanner, Kristian Taraldsen, Robin & Janice Tausig, Anna & Chonette Taylor, Eric Taylor, Imogen Taylor, Nick Taylor, Peter Taylor, Suzanne Taylor, Mark Tebbutt, Melanie Temin, Herwig Temmerman, Michiel Ten Raa, Mihoko Teshigawara, Nathan Teske, Nikki Thanos, Sid The Geezer, Tobias Thelen, Ian-Thomas, Marlene Thomas, A Thompson, Hilary J Thompson, Megan Thompson, Nandra Thompson, Klavs B Thomsen, Robin Thomson, Erik Thorbjornsen, Alan Thornhill, Mircea-Ioan Ticudean, Michael Tilden, Han Timmers, Boyan Timotiyevich, Ana Tintocalis, Jasmine Tom, Gideon Tomaschoff, Brigitte Tombers, Diego Tonelli, Cecilia Jardines & Gabriel Tornes, Alfredo Torres Lehmann, Elliot Trester, Clare & Chris Trimbur, Matthew Trump, Penny Trurnit, Katerina Tsiplacis, Devin Tucker, Henning Tuerk, Fielding Turner, Marianne Tveit, L V Twomey, Svend Tychsen, Paul Tzimas **U** Othmar Ulrich, Bruno Uriarte, Urtzi Urrutikoetxea **V** Luc Valade, Nina Valas, Edward Valeau, Jan van Baarle, Jean Pierre van Beers, Isabel van de Kant, Caron van den Brink, Martin van den Broek, Jerry van den Broeke, Kok van der Meer, John van der Woude, Hans van Dommele, Ingrid van Dommele, Jacob van Duijn, Brice Van Dyck, Rob van Herpt, Marja van Loenen,

Hylkia van Meer, Bart Van Steirteghem, Serge van Verseveld, RL van Wagtendonk, Arno van Wouwe, Ilona Vandenberghe, Wim Vandenbussche, Jos Vandendriessche, Birgitte Vartdal, Heidi Veluw, Yvonne ven der Hork, Antony Verbaeys, Arne Verbeke, Anna Verbiesen, Gaynor Vere, Anja Verlaan, Peter en Helene Versnel, Jose Vervaet, Frank Vester, Eduardo Victor Sanchez, Patricia Villar, Antti Virkkunen, Bert Vissers, Marco Vogt, Susanne Vollmer, Johanna Von Boetticher, Bernd Von Richter, Mitja Vrhovnik-Smrekar, Pascal Vugts **W** Dirk Antony Wahl, Lisa Waldburger, Brigette Walenius, Alexander Walford, Debbie Walker, Michael Walker, SR Walker, Markus Wallet, A Walsh, Klaus Walter, Eugene Wang, Barbara Ward, Diana Ward, Roy Ward, Harriet Warnock-Graham, John Washington, Marijew Wassenaar, Siegbert Weber, Tracy Webster, Margit Wehner, Beatrix Weijermars, Kjetil Welle, Judy Wells, Kerie Wells, Thomas Welvaadt, Ann Berit Werner, Peter Werner, Hans Werner Meyer, Erwin Wesenhagen, Patrick Westdorp, Esther Westerhuis, Rob Whadcock, Anna White, Annie White, Maggie White, Nick White, Graham Whittal, Holger Wiechert, Harm Wierenga, Froy Lode Wiig, Johan Wijnen, Charles Wilding-White, Dave Wildman, Bernd Jurgen Wildner, Zack Wiley, Robert Wilkinson, Debbie Williams, Louisa Williams, Lucy Williams, Rick Williams, Tom Williams, Tugomir Williams, Vivienne Williams, Matthew Willner Reid, Mike Wilsher, Diarmuid Wilson, Howard Wilson, JP Wilson, Margaret Winn, Peter Winneke, Michael Witte, Leslie Wolke, Bob Wollam, Alwin Wollinger, Frank Wombacher, John & Betty Wondergem, Chris Wood, Sara Wood, Mark Woodward, Ruth Wragg, Alexandra Wright, Thomas Wurzlbauer **X** Joerdis X **Y** Rob Ye, Lasse Ylinen, Scott York, John Young **Z** Ondrej Zapletal, Raul Ruiz de Zarate, Ales Zerjav, Dr Med Zierer, Oded Zilinsky, Andrea Zobrist, Annie Zumba, Michael Zurbuchen, Craig Zwicky, Wanda Zyla

ACKNOWLEDGMENTS

Many thanks to the following for the use of their content:

Mountain High Maps® Copyright © 1993 Digital Wisdom, Inc.

Index

000 Map pages
000 Location of color photographs

INDEX